MW01199870

PRAISE FOR *CHOSEN PATH*

"The public Michael Quinn combined impeccable academic credentials with prodigious energy to become one of the most prominent Mormon historians of the twentieth century. The private and largely unknown Quinn is the centerpiece of this compelling memoir. With disarming candor, he pulls back the curtain on the two major, unresolved tensions of his life: his sexual orientation, which placed him in continual conflict with his church; and the conflict between his religious orthodoxy and his historical heterodoxy. Quinn's lifelong conviction that Mormonism was strong enough to weather all truths of its past placed him on a collision course with a church not yet mature enough to fully engage with its history. Ultimately, these tensions cost him his marriage, his professorship, and his church membership. By giving us a window into his complex life, Quinn provides us a looking glass into our own lifelong tensions."

—**Gregory A. Prince**, author of *Gay Rights and the Mormon Church: Intended Actions, Unintended Consequences*

"This memoir is double penned, chronologically and retrospectively, as contemporary diary entries and reminiscences decades later, with self and meta-self interacting. Quinn typically inhabited distinctive realms— metaphorical and literal, spiritual and physical, past and present—hoping to synthesize them. *Chosen Path* shares his private self in public, no longer possible in life yet possible beyond life. His identities we knew and didn't know are integrated in a memoir that finally synthesizes himself."

—**Maxine Hanks**, editor of *Women and Authority: Re-emerging Mormon Feminism*

"Born gay and raised in Southern California in a working class family, Mike Quinn suppressed his sexual orientation to marry a woman from a prominent Utah family, yet his marriage ended in divorce. As a Latter-day Saint scholar in the New Mormon History, he believed that he must tell the true history of the church he loved, yet his work led to his excommunication. Like a Shakespearean tragedy, Quinn's memoir engages and torments us, pushing us to grapple with contradictions."

—**Thomas G. Alexander**, Lemuel Hardison Redd Jr. Professor Emeritus of Western American History, Brigham Young University

CHOSEN PATH

D. Michael Quinn

CHOSEN PATH
a memoir

D. MICHAEL QUINN

FOREWORD BY MOSHE QUINN

SIGNATURE BOOKS | 2023 | SALT LAKE CITY

Join our mail list at www.signaturebooks.com for details on events and related titles we think you'll enjoy.

Cover photograph: *Looking West 11*, by Moshe Quinn, 2012.

Design by Jason Francis

FIRST EDITION | 2023

LIBRARY OF CONGRESS CONTROL NUMBER: 2023948380

Hardback ISBN: 978-1-56085-451-7
Ebook ISBN: 978-1-56085-426-5

CONTENTS

FOREWORD

My father's memoirs were an emerging project over several decades.

When I was twelve or thirteen years old and living with my mother in Missoula, Montana, we received an autobiography from him in the mail. It was more than forty pages, and I think I read all of it. This was in 1988 or '89, not long after he left his tenured professorship at BYU under hostile conditions. He shipped it from New Orleans where he was hiding out from church authorities—who, as he believed, had their fingers on the excommunication-button—and where he enjoyed an openly gay life for the first time. A copy of this version may exist with my father's papers at the Yale archives, but I haven't seen it since that time.

Two episodes from that manuscript stayed with me. First was the story of a conscious choice he made at age twelve between "being gay" and being Mormon. Second was the story of his hearing God's voice in a dark cave, saving him from stepping off an unseen ledge and presumably falling to his death. I had heard him tell us this second story before in person. Reading it then, it landed with me because of the absence of any such divine interventions or magical experiences in my own life. (There is a chance that our brother, Adam, later would hear his own kind of voices, too. As I write this I wonder how this story of our father hearing the voice of God landed with *him*.) However, it was the first story, about our father making that momentous decision for his life, that struck me most.

We learned later that this early autobiography wasn't his first go at it. When our father died in 2021, amongst the many offerings of condolences and reminiscence we heard from friends, loved ones, and colleagues were several allusions to "his memoirs." When I received the first inquiry about it my only thought was of the short manuscript I had read in the late 1980s. It soon became apparent that a number of people had more recent knowledge of an updated and expanded version, or versions. Gary Bergera at Signature Books expressed interest in his memoirs days after we learned of Mike's death. At the memorial, his lifelong friend Clifton Jolley mentioned reading his memoirs more than ten years prior. In his message of condolences, Bill Handley of the University of Southern California described the privilege of having read the "fascinating, even epic story" of our father's life in a draft of the memoirs.

Over the next weeks and months we pieced together details of our father's decades-long journey with his autobiography project. He provides a summary of this himself: after drafting his first attempt at age twenty-one, over the next many years he engaged in "repeated revisions, reassessments, reductions, expansions and self-doubts." Significant moments of attention to this project occurred when he was twenty-three, forty-four, forty-nine, fifty-four and in his mid-sixties. What he wrote about "self-doubts" touches on an important strand in the story. How should one write one's own life? What to include or omit? Who to identify by name, or not? What degree of candor? What tone or style? What structure to use for conveying his "memories, emotions, and identities"?

Not only did he struggle with *how* to write his own life, he struggled to publish it in his lifetime. In 1998 he submitted his draft of that time to Signature Books for consideration. Reviewers on its editorial board shared varying reactions. One reader thought it would be better for him to write his autobiography "20 years hence," with the advantages of greater distance and perspective.

He wouldn't wait that long. About twelve years later, he floated around a new version, greatly expanded from the 1998 draft. Clifton Jolley told us about seeing this draft at that time, and that he expressed to Mike with (I imagine) characteristically droll bluntness that it was unpublishable. Mike also shared this version with his eldest child, Mary. As he put it to her, Signature Books wasn't interested, so he submitted it "to other publishers" and, "if they don't want it, well, so be it, it's out of my hands." Mary read a few pages, put it aside and forgot about them in the ensuing years. Neither our sister Lisa nor I recall his ever mentioning the memoirs to us. While his epilogue is dated 2009, timestamps in the digital files show that he made his last edits in 2019 at age seventy-five, two years before his death.

When a writer's life ends it should be no surprise when new interest emerges for what he wrote of that life. We like our stories to be complete. A life means something new when the story gets an ending. But meaning is never so complete or final. The "repeated revisions" and "self-doubts" that occupied his attention for more than half a century suggest the scope, depth and duration of his struggle with meaning. How to make sense of his life. How to account for himself.

I return to the story in the 1988 autobiography that stayed with me most then as it does now: the choice his twelve-year-old self made between being gay and being Mormon. There's a crushing pathos there. It set him up for a life of great hopes and of tremendous anguish—a life of inner struggles and pain, which I could see only from the distance he allowed as a protective, emotionally reticent father. There at the age of twelve myself, *I* knew he didn't have to make this decision. He could have both! He could be both. It seemed tragic—frustratingly tragic—for all its needlessness. But knowing my father as I did, I understood that he did have to make a choice. He was making the best sense of things that he could. He did the best that he could. Standing at the edge of young adulthood, this sensitive boy in Southern California made a choice for his life. In the spirit of Sartre's existentialist philosophy, he affirmed his selfhood in the face of a sometimes painfully baffling world. That was his chosen path. There are many chosen paths for each of us in our lives. This final version of his memoirs offers the stories of many choices, and many paths.

Moshe Quinn
September 30, 2023

PUBLISHER'S INTRODUCTION

D. Michael Quinn submitted a significantly shorter draft of this memoir to Signature Books in 1998, when he was fifty-four years old. Signature's editorial reviewers recommended that he "revise and resubmit," encouraging him to include more introspection and sharing of his feelings about the events he had chronicled in his life. A comparison of that early draft with his final draft reveals that indeed he did so, but for unknown reasons never resubmitted his manuscript. Signature Books is grateful—as undoubtedly thousands of readers will likewise be—that Quinn's children located his memoir in his computer files and entrusted Signature with publishing it.

Readers will notice that Quinn did not write his life story in typical memoir style. Rather, he frequently quotes his daily journals or memoirs he wrote at age twenty-one, twenty-three, twenty-five, and twenty-eight, then expounds on his thoughts surrounding those entries in what he called "a chronologically structured self-biography."

"Admittedly," Quinn acknowledged, "its relentlessly episodic, choppy style violates most people's preference for 'narrative flow.' But, like pointillism in the paintings of a previous era or like Rob Silver's 'photomosaics' in the twenty-first century, even the smoothest narrative is a subtle mosaic of separate events which our minds 'see' as an uninterrupted flow. Throughout most of my life, I've been neither slick nor subtle. Should my self-biography be otherwise?"[1]

Though we at Signature did not engage in the same kind of editing that we do with living authors who are able to participate in the process, we did copy edit the manuscript to standardize spelling, punctuation, capitalization, and other matters of style—with one exception. Following the modern, professional practice used with historical documents, we preserved spelling and style errors within the journals and memoir that Quinn quotes. Quinn occasionally added bracketed material within these quoted paragraphs to provide context. Readers should be aware that these bracketed comments are original to the manuscript and were not added by the publisher.

Readers should also be aware of our content advisory: In writing about his adolescence in chapters three and four, Quinn includes some descriptions of sexual acts and pornography, as well as an incident in which he was physically assaulted.

1. See page 59.

The original manuscript was more than three times the length of a typical memoir. With the approval of Quinn's estate, we trimmed approximately 20,000 words of extraneous detail. The original manuscript in its entirety is available in the archives of Signature Books.

Believing that *Chosen Path* is a source that historians and others will refer to long into the future, we have sought to provide greater context by annotating the text with explanatory notes when Quinn mentions individuals, organizations, places, events, or themes. Historians and editors Barbara Jones Brown, Sue Bergin, Connell O'Donovan, and Calvin Burke provided these annotations.

As readers engage with the "pointillism" or "photomosaic" style of Quinn's telling, a central theme comes into focus: his relentless drive to research, write, and speak about controversial topics of the Mormon past. Toward the end of his life, he reflected that "there were subconscious factors operating in my choices as a Mormon historian." These factors were his relationship with himself as a closeted gay man, his relationship with his oft-absent and secretive father, and his relationship with his church, which was not yet ready to grapple with controversial aspects of its own identity.

"First, I sought out areas of apparent ambiguity or contradiction in the LDS Church's past and tried to resolve them" because "that was something I hadn't been able to do with the ambiguity and contradiction within me," he explained. "Second, I now recognize that I saw my father reflected in the church's official concealment of its controversial past. I was as determined to uncover the secrets of the Mormon past, as I was to discover those of my father's [secreted] Mexican heritage. After all, the leaders of the LDS Church had been an earthly father-substitute for most of my life. Third, I also realize that I saw the LDS Church in my own situation—outwardly happy and prospering, but burdened with unspoken secrets and wounds that needed to be opened for the process of healing and health. Guess I hoped to obtain some vicarious comfort by bringing a resolution for the Mormon experience that I couldn't give to my own life."

Despite what he felt were his own shortcomings, Quinn felt "a greater confidence in the spiritual resiliency of the Latter-day Saints," believing "that if they are gradually given an awareness of the 'truth of all things' in the proper perspective, that they will be the stronger thereby."

When a friend asked him "to what extent I really thought the 'broader' and more open understanding of Church history can be part of general Latter-day Saint awareness," Quinn wrote in his 1974 entry, "I told him that I looked forward to its total accomplishment in 50 years."[2] Those words seem prophetic today, especially upon their publication in this memoir almost exactly fifty years later.

---

2. See pages 308–9.

CHAPTER ONE

EARLY CHILDHOOD

1944–1949

26 March 1944–Identities and Defects

I was conceived amid my Mexican American father's anxieties during the "Zoot Suit Riots" of June 1943 in East Los Angeles. Thousands of Anglo bullies wearing US military uniforms battered every male they could find who looked Mexican, while white civilians and cops cheered or joined them. LA was only seven percent Hispanic at that time.

Dad was a lapsed Catholic, but Mom was a devout sixth-generation Mormon of Anglo-Swiss heritage. Her pioneer ancestor John Workman was mentioned in the journal of latter-day prophet Joseph Smith on 7 June 1843.[1] Was that exactly one hundred years before my conception? If so, it was the first of many Mormon coincidences in my life. Mom and Dad divorced when I was four, and religious differences were part of the problem. Thereafter, Mom and I resided with her parents, the only grandparents I remember. Dad's widowed mother Carmen died the year of his divorce.

My birthdate, March 26, was when the Book of Mormon went on sale in 1830 in western New York state, where Mormonism's founding prophet organized a new church. According to apostle Orson Hyde, exactly one hundred years before my birth, Joseph Smith gave his "last charge" to the Quorum of the Twelve Apostles, led by Brigham Young. Brigham cited "Joseph's Last Charge to the Twelve" as the basis for his claim to be the legitimate leader of the Church of Jesus Christ of Latter-day Saints after this living prophet was martyred by an Illinois mob in June 1844.[2] I was an adult when I learned of those coincidences.

Like one in 700 births, I was born with a cleft palate (a gaping hole in the roof of my mouth). When I was about a year old, US Army surgeons repaired the palate through recently improved methods of plastic surgery. This operation was possible because my father was in the US military. At

1. John Workman (1789–1855) joined the LDS Church in 1839 and moved to the church's headquarters in Nauvoo, Illinois, in 1843. "Workman, John," Joseph Smith Papers, josephsmithpapers.org.

2. This "last charge" was based on a reminiscent account. "Orson Hyde, Statement about Quorum of the Twelve, ca. Late March 1845," Joseph Smith Papers, josephsmithpapers.org.

my birth, he was serving in an Oregon detention camp for German military prisoners during the Second World War. Two years earlier, after the Pearl Harbor attack, when Japanese Americans of Los Angeles were herded into the Santa Anita Racetrack near Pasadena, Dad patrolled the makeshift camp with a rifle and .45 caliber handgun.

A year after my father guarded these fearful citizens, LA's 1943 riots showed how tenuous was the security of *all* peoples of color in the USA. This reinforced a decision Dad had made ten years earlier: to become as White Anglo-Saxon Protestant (WASP) as he could. Marrying my blue-eyed, redheaded, ivory-skinned mother in 1942 was part of his becoming "Americanized," although Dad was born in the USA.

In 1918, the year of the end of America's First World War to "make the world safe for democracy," a racially segregated Arizona town had required his father's body to be buried in a "Mexican cemetery." The so-called "liberal" Far West mimicked for *its* minorities the American South's segregation of Blacks. Jim Crow without a Southern drawl.

Possibly due to my cleft palate and the recovery time from its corrective surgery, I spoke with a bilateral lisp. Because I made sibilant sounds from the sides of my mouth, my S's sounded thick rather than crisp.

Apparently resulting from the cleft palate, there was a more serious problem with the internal structure of my ears. The eustachian tubes didn't function well, which restricted the drainage of fluid. Middle-ear infections almost always ruptured my eardrums—multiple times each year. Antibiotics were unable to prevent ruptures, so the only thing physicians could do was lance my eardrums to prevent the greater damage of rupturing.

My family usually didn't call a doctor when throbbing earaches woke me in the middle of the night. Typically, an hour of excruciating pain ended with the strange relief of hearing my eardrum rupture, after which I fell asleep in exhaustion.

Some of my earliest memories are of my mother's mother ("Nana") sitting beside me those nights, trying to comfort me and praying aloud for my pain to end. During each occasion of agony, I heard her say through tears that she wished she could suffer the earaches instead of me.

I think these ruptured eardrums helped shape my personality. From early childhood, I learned to live with fear (of colds and their resultant earaches), to cope with intense pain (which I did my best to hold in), to recognize that no one else could help me (despite their good intentions), to accept that God did not spare me this problem (despite my faith and love for him), and to thank God daily that things were no worse. I was still able to hear!

Many years later, I learned that there was a philosophy describing my response: Stoicism.

Dennis Michael Quinn at three months. This photo was the only one found in his father's wallet after his father's death. *Courtesy Quinn family.*

2 July 1944–Fledgling Mormon

After my birth in the US military hospital of Pasadena, California, Dad was still away on duty with the army, and Mom moved us to South Central Los Angeles. We resided with her parents on 24th Street, about two miles east of the University of Southern California. We were near the "Mexican district" of East LA, where the Zoot Suit Riots of white brutality had occurred barely a year earlier.

This Sunday, Grampa Workman performed my ordinance of "blessing" in the Adams Ward of the Los Angeles Stake. This enrolls infants on the LDS Church's records as quasi-members until their formal baptism and "confirmation" after turning eight.

In his capacity as Mormonism's first prophet, Joseph Smith uttered many divine pronouncements, or revelations. Most have been published in the Doctrine and Covenants (D&C), whose Utah edition of Section 68, verse 27 specified that "children shall be baptized for the remission of their sins when eight years old." (As an adult historian, I would become famous for extensive footnoting of sources, but have limited that to occasional citations within this self-biography.)

My Workman family's sojourn in the Los Angeles area began in 1928, when they moved from Salt Lake City, where Nana had been a cleaning woman in the Newhouse Hotel. She told me that this Jewish-owned establishment paid better wages than the city's famously elegant Hotel Utah, which was owned and operated by the LDS Church.[3]

My grandparents were not typical of Utah's twentieth-century outmigrants, who left the state for higher education or better paying jobs. During the freezing winter of 1928, their seven-year-old-daughter Joyce (my future mother) started coughing up blood. A physician told them to move to Los Angeles or Phoenix if they wanted her to survive.

They chose the LA area, settling first just east of Redondo Beach in Torrance. Grampa became the first counselor in its small LDS congregation, and the mild climate healed their little girl.

By 1930, they had moved fifteen miles north to the city of Long Beach, which was soon devastated by a coastal earthquake in March 1933.[4] With their four children, my grandparents then abandoned its rubble and tent cities for nearby Los Angeles.

That growing metropolis had sustained little damage. Nonetheless, twenty-one-year-old Daniel (Donald) Peña Quinn (who became my father a decade later) praised "a Negro conductor" for saving his life in the underground terminal of the city's streetcar system. At the first jolt of this earthquake, the uniformed Black man grabbed my future father and pulled him inside a streetcar—just before overhead masonry and steel cables crashed on the platform where Dad had stood.

After leaving Long Beach in 1933, my family moved in with a Mormon friend who resided in LA's upscale Wilshire District. In its LDS ward, the blue-collar Workmans had an otherwise unlikely friendship with a former Assistant Solicitor of the US State Department, Preston D. Richards, his wife, Barbara, and their four children. He was currently a well-connected attorney as a former partner and close friend of J. Reuben Clark Jr., who had recently resigned as US Ambassador to Mexico. Then a counselor to LDS President Heber J. Grant in the First Presidency over the LDS Church, Clark would be the subject of my first, prize-winning book.[5]

For the last half of 1933, my family lived in the Hollywood Stake, whose temporary president was LeGrand Richards, with whom I would have a significant meeting as a teenager. They also attended Sunday services in the Wilshire

---

3. The church built the Hotel Utah in 1911 near the Salt Lake Temple. The church reconfigured the structure as a multipurpose building, reopening it as the Joseph Smith Memorial Building in 1993.

4. The quake measured 6.4 on the Richter scale and killed 120 people.

5. *J. Reuben Clark: The Church Years* (Provo, UT: Brigham Young University Press, 1983) won the Mormon History Association's Best Book Award.

Ward with Antoine R. Ivins, who was on temporary assignment away from LDS headquarters in Salt Lake. Like Counselor Clark, he had the full-time, lifelong calling to be a general authority over Mormons throughout the world.[6]

Ivins had the particular assignment of a Seventy's President over part of the church's missionaries. Then called the First Council of Seventy, his was technically the third echelon of general authorities, just below the Quorum of the Twelve. Nonetheless, most Mormons knew that an adjunct quorum called the Presiding Bishopric wielded far more power than the Seventy's Presidents. Its three Bishops had responsibility for LDS finances, businesses, buildings, welfare, and other temporal matters throughout the world. Five years after my family moved into his stake, LeGrand Richards became the church's Presiding Bishop. Ecclesiastical status was of importance to average Mormons, but it would become my obsession.

In early 1934, my grandparents traded squatter's charity for an apartment on Valencia near 10th Street. Still grinding away at the US economy, the Republican-caused Great Depression then forced them to a succession of ever-cheaper tenements in South Central LA.

Nana often told me that for months she had only a nickel in her purse. She was afraid to buy a hamburger or other treat that cost only five cents, "in case the family might need this nickel for an emergency," she said.

Thus, ten years before the blessing ordinance I received, my grandparents and future mother became downwardly mobile members of the Adams Ward, where college student Sterling M. McMurrin also attended LDS services with his family each summer. Later becoming a professor of philosophy at the University of Utah, this liberal Democrat would eventually serve as US Commissioner of Education by appointment of Democratic President John F. Kennedy.[7]

Two years after my family moved me into the ward of an adjacent city in LA's Southland, Sterling was one of its guest speakers. Decades later I would share conversation, laughter, and ideas with him during many lunches and dinners in Salt Lake City. Ours was a small Mormon world.

While my family was still in the Adams Ward during 1944–45, Nana babysat me while my mother tried to earn money by selling cosmetics and Nutrilite vitamins door-to-door in South Central. For decades, it had been the only district of Los Angeles where African Americans could live. Yet Mom was so tender-hearted that she simply gave away the products to poor Black families whose tenements and houses she entered in their shared

6. LeGrand Richards (1886–1983) served as Presiding Bishop from 1938 until he was ordained an apostle in 1952. Antoine R. Ivins (1881–1967) served as a member of the First Quorum of the Seventy from 1931 until his death in 1967.

7. See Sterling McMurrin and L. Jackson Newell, *Matters of Conscience: Conversations with Sterling M. McMurrin* (Salt Lake City: Signature Books, 1996).

neighborhood. After months of little income, she quit this business of direct sales, subsequently called Amway—The American Way.

Spring 1945–Hometown of Glendale, Los Angeles County

As a mailman for the US Post Office, Grampa had managed to save enough money during World War II's economic boom to make a down payment for purchasing land in an upscale "bedroom community" of Los Angeles. After six days weekly of delivering mail in downtown LA, he was now working side-by-side with Nana late into each night and full days on some weekends and holidays to build from scratch what became a court of apartments in Glendale. The balance of the family's wartime savings paid for the increasingly available building supplies as rationing eased up after the surrender of Nazi Germany this May.

In the fall of 1945, shortly after Imperial Japan's surrender finally ended World War II, Mom moved with me into one of the two apartments of newly white-washed stucco that faced the street in Glendale. Each apartment had one bedroom and a pull-down Murphy bed in a double-door closet of the living room. Her parents resided in the second front apartment. Nana raised me while my parents worked.

Their property was at the south end of Pacific Avenue. It followed a nearly straight line from the elegant foothills of Glendale's 3,126-foot-high Mount Verdugo until the still-residential street ended abruptly at San Fernando Road. This industrial thoroughfare separated the bedroom community from Los Angeles. Though only a block from the railroad tracks and in "the poor part" of Glendale, this new residence at 613 South Pacific was a major step up from my grandparents' tenement in South Central LA.

Social boundaries of geography, occupation, income, and rank were ingrained within my upbringing: my self-identity.

Fall 1945–Brush with Death

When I was an adult, Dad told me that I was "so sickly and accident-prone," that he wondered if I would survive childhood. Mom said this started when I was a toddler and pushed one of her hair pins into a wall socket of our Glendale apartment shortly after we moved there. The electrical jolt knocked me across the room.

Regarding my being "sickly," I still marvel at the report cards that show my absences during elementary school. I averaged twenty-four days of absentee sickness during the nine months of each school year.

24 November 1946–Anti-Catholicism in Mormon Congregations

After my family's move from LA, our congregation was the Glendale West Ward, whose minutes and manuscript history are housed at Salt Lake City's

Church History Library. Mormons are commanded to be record keepers by revelations to Joseph Smith (see D&C 21:1; 128:2–4, 8).

The minutes for tonight's sacrament meeting note that speaker Roland P. Jones "also took occasion to ridicule the 'holy water' of the Catholics, which, of course, furnished amusement to some of those present." This was not unusual. During his sermon three years later, our ward's bishop, Harry V. Brooks, "showed how that the Catholics in Utah were trying to undermine the work of the Mormon Church in Utah."

As part of the effort to distinguish themselves from Catholics, Mormons never use the word Communion for the ceremony of remembering Christ's body and blood. Like some Protestant denominations, Mormons emphasize the symbols of their sacrament as bread and water, instead of wafers and wine. Moreover, because Mormons see the LDS Church as a divine restoration of original Christianity, they don't regard themselves as Protestants.

In sermons and class lessons, Mormons identified Roman Catholicism as "the Church of the Devil" and all Protestant churches as its well-intentioned children. This was explicitly stated in the book *Mormon Doctrine*, which general authority Bruce R. McConkie published in 1958.[8]

Therefore, my mother developed her virulent anti-Catholicism quite naturally. Not her fault.

Nana expressed unabashed love and open adulation for only one LDS leader: Bishop Brooks. After his release from that position in Glendale, none of his successors as our ward's bishop gained my grandmother's affection as he did.

20 June 1948–The Sound of One Boy Clapping

Partway through tonight's sacrament meeting, "Joyce Workman Quinn" sang solos of "I Walked Today Where Jesus Walked" and "Into the Night." The Glendale West Ward's minutes don't describe what happened next.

I clapped as loud as I could—in a meeting that is never supposed to hear applause. Mom often retold this incident with embarrassment, pride, and love. I've heard that applause was not formally banned in LDS meetings until 1954, but Mom instructed me that it was *"verboten"* in Glendale this early. She used this "ugly" German word to emphasize anything that was forbidden.

Despite the ban on clapping, LDS worship services (especially sacrament

---

8. Bruce R. McConkie (1915–1985) was not yet an apostle when he wrote *Mormon Doctrine*. But because of the book's title, many viewed it as representing official doctrine even though it was not endorsed by the church and was strongly criticized by some church leaders. Church President David O. McKay requested the first edition of *Mormon Doctrine* be removed from shelves in large part because of the anti-Catholic views it espoused. The book, which also has racist themes, went through two more editions but has been out of print since 2010. See Gregory L. Prince & Wm. Robert Wright, *David O. McKay and the Rise of Modern Mormonism* (Salt Lake City: University of Utah Press, 2005), 121–23.

meetings) remain the noisiest in solemn Christendom. There are crying babies, indulgent parents, talkative kids, and loudly whispering old people. Organists try to hinder the chatter with prelude and postlude music, but most Latter-day Saints just talk louder. Even that noise pales when compared to the pandemonium in hallways between meetings.

I was one of the worst. My young voice was as penetrating as a siren, then like a foghorn after it deepened.

I know this because people often commented on it. I tried to speak more quietly, but loudness remained the pattern of my discourse. Even now in restaurants, diners ten or fifteen feet away often scowl at me and my booming voice when I'm animatedly conversing.

Fall 1948–Divorce and Mom's Patriarchal Blessing

LDS Stake Patriarch Joseph Reece told my mother on 7 November 1948: "Inasmuch, dear sister, as you have met with disappointment in your marriage relation and have been under the necessity of obtaining a divorcement and you have as a result of that marriage a son, your responsibility is great upon you to rear this son to manhood in the admonition of the Lord that he may, when he comes to a mature age, be baptized into the Church and in due time receive the Priesthood and become a useful instrument in the hands of the Lord to labor in His vineyard."

In a revelation (see D&C 124:92), Joseph Smith provided for patriarchal blessings to members of the church for comfort, instruction, and prediction. LDS headquarters currently keeps a verbatim transcription of the exact words in every such blessing uttered by ordained patriarchs since the mid-1830s.

The patriarch also designates which Tribe of Israel the recipient has descended from.[9] As is true for most Mormons today, Mom's patriarchal blessing stated that she was from the ancient Biblical tribe of Joseph, through his son Ephraim. With this tribal identity as modern Israelites, Mormons feel profound kinship with Jews. Both are "God's Chosen People" (see Robert L. Millet, *Mormon Faith: A New Look at Christianity*, 124–25).

Early 1949–Polio and Priesthood

When my mother's patriarchal blessing referred to me, the Los Angeles area was struggling with an epidemic of paralytic poliomyelitis. Often causing paralysis or death, it continued for almost two years, subsided, then rebounded during 1952 as the worst polio outbreak in US history. Soon

---

9. Latter-day Saint patriarchs are men who have been ordained to give patriarchal blessings to church members. Many Mormons receive their patriarchal blessing when teenagers or young adults. The blessings are considered sacred, and the patriarch is expected to be inspired to include information, reassurance, and life counsel specific to the person being blessed. The blessings are private but are recorded and transcribed for the recipient.

thereafter, Dr. Jonas Salk's vaccine would stop it, and Mom often reminded me that "he is one of God's noble Jews!"

About the time of my fifth birthday, I was among this year's 20,000 cases nationally. At least once a year until Mom died, she shook her head grimly while saying that I was diagnosed as having "bulbar polio."[10]

From the memoir I wrote at age 23: "I remember the day I first contracted the feverish and nauseous symptoms. I remember gradually becoming so weakened and ill that I could not stand and, when taken to the hospital, I had to be carried by my grandfather down the stairs."

My family took me to a physician in Glendale, who told them to drive me immediately to the LA County Hospital. On the way, I asked that they take me to Brother Jackman, a "high priest" in our ward. Grampa and Nana didn't want to stop, but I begged them—and I seem to recall that I wanted him to heal me with a blessing.

Somehow, I knew that he held the Melchizedek Priesthood, which has "the keys of all the spiritual blessings of the church" (see D&C 107:18). I have no idea why I asked for this blessing from Brother Jackman instead of asking Grampa, who had also been ordained to the same priesthood "by laying on of hands" (see Alma 6:1 in the Book of Mormon).

My grandparents and Mom were amazed that I even thought of this at such a young age. After anointing my head with consecrated olive oil, sixty-year-old Wallace A. Jackman promised that I would recover fully from the disease and would leave the hospital shortly.

I always retained a clear memory of my father's arrival in the hospital to be with me that first night. By contrast, I could never remember my grandmother's visits. She often told me that I blamed her for leaving me alone in a strange place, but I have no memory of this dramatic encounter she often described. Nana always expressed irritated disappointment that I didn't, despite her repeated reminders: "Why don't you remember this?!"

I left the LA County Hospital after a few weeks of terrifying spinal taps that I screamed throughout. I merely whimpered and moaned during the misery of having hot pack compresses applied to my back and legs. This "and manipulation of limbs" were part of the regimen advocated by Australian nurse and polio activist Elizabeth Kenny. I had years of physical therapy, but no noticeable disabilities from polio. Mom often spoke of Methodist "Sister Kenny" with gratitude and awe.

I was lucky, or unusually blessed. One of my friends, Clifton Jolley, had atrophied muscles in his leg and foot from polio.[11] When I was an adult,

---

10. A form of polio that affects the brain stem, which controls basic physical functions like breathing. Spinal cord involvement can lead to paralysis.

11. Clifton Jolley (1945–) became one of Mormonism's best-loved poets, essayists, and

Back row, left to right: Michael's parents, Daniel (Donald) Peña Quinn and Joyce Workman Quinn; Michael's uncle, Ysmael (Jimmy) Peña Quinn. Front row, left to right: Dennis Michael Quinn; Ysmael's daughter, Linda Mary Quinn. *Courtesy Quinn family.*

my friend Jim McConkie told me that he also had some atrophy in one leg and had lost his young father to polio. My future in-law, Phil Darley, had a wizened shoulder and arm after nearly dying from polio. All of them also received priesthood blessings and prayers by loved ones. The distribution of suffering and death, health, healing, and survival has been a profound and disturbing mystery to me.

Decades afterward, I had a flashback memory. At four years old, I had thought that somehow I was to blame when my parents separated and divorced. In the polio ward of the hospital, I felt that God was punishing me. When a boy in the bed next to mine died in our large room of bedridden children, I wished it was me. Until this flashback, I was aware of no emotion at his death, or while watching the nurses quietly bundle him up and take his lifeless body away. I didn't cry about him until years later, feeling as if he were a long-lost brother.

I spent the rest of my life trying to be the perfect son, the righteous Mormon, the good student, and the perpetually nice guy in order to earn people's love and respect. I felt there was something wrong deep inside me.

At age twelve, I learned it had a label. Homosexuality.

Deseret News columnists. He received a PhD in English from BYU in 1980 and taught in the Church Education System as a seminary instructor for many years. He later converted to Judaism.

CHAPTER TWO

EMERGING IDENTITIES

1950-1953

January 1950–First Memory of LDS Church

I have one very early memory of the Glendale West Ward. I watched Grampa paint the wall in a hallway that I later walked through every Sunday. Like all Mormons at this period, my family helped build and decorate their new meeting house before its dedication.

LDS Church President and prophet George Albert Smith dedicated our meeting house in February 1950. His predecessor Heber J. Grant had died in May 1945, a month after my family's anguished grief at the death of America's wartime commander-in-chief, Franklin D. Roosevelt. They had revered him since first casting their Democratic votes for FDR in 1932, as did two-thirds of America's Mormons for his three re-elections. This was in open opposition to the living prophet's frequently expressed pro-Republican and anti-FDR views during those years.

"The Democratic Party is for common people," Nana often told me, adding, "Republicans care only for the rich and for big businesses." That has never changed, yet three-fourths of LDS general authorities remained Republican.

Prior to this chapel's completion, our ward's members had met on the fifth floor of Glendale's ten-story Masonic Temple at the corner of Colorado and South Brand Boulevard.

Compared with the millions of residents in adjacent Los Angeles, Glendale was a *town*. Its census population was 95,702 in 1950 and 119,442 in 1960. With a city boy's perceptions and bias, I regarded anything below 50,000 inhabitants as a village or rural area.

Late July 1950–Bobby Driscoll and Mom's New Perception of Me

Shortly after its release, my mother took me to see Walt Disney's movie *Treasure Island*, whose comically benign view of pirates thoroughly entertained me. But, as a six-year-old, I couldn't take my eyes off the cute face and slender form of thirteen-year-old actor Bobby Driscoll—and I might have innocently mentioned that to Mom. In retrospect, I think he was the first male for whom I felt childishly sexual interest.[1]

Although she didn't tell me this until four decades later (after I confided my orientation to her), my mother began to think that I was "homosexually inclined at age six." When I asked what caused her to suspect this, she could remember nothing specific except that she knew I was "different from other boys."

Part of that difference was my precocious enjoyment of high culture. A week after she took me to a theater's re-showing of Disney's decade-earlier animated movie *Fantasia*, Mom was surprised to hear me humming long segments of its classical music soundtrack. She encouraged this by taking me to see *Fantasia* dozens of times throughout my childhood.

Soon we were also going to an art-house cinema in Hollywood that frequently showed films of full-length grand operas. A soloist and member of LDS ward choirs, Mom encouraged me to sing. She took me to those French and Italian operas so I could see how beautifully "the professionals" sang choruses and arias. Unless in English translation, she shunned classic operas by Mozart, Strauss, and Wagner: "German is an ugly language."

For regular movies, Mom often rode with me on the streetcar from Glendale to Los Angeles and Hollywood Boulevard's theater district. Saturdays and vacation days, we spent afternoon and evening there, going to movies in one theatre after another. When showtimes made dinner in a restaurant impossible, we snuck lox-and-cream-cheese sandwiches into the day's last (usually third) theater.

Mom also took me to Hollywood for auditions to appear on children's programs. I made it onto television sometime in the early 1950s. I recall sitting on a wooden horse of a miniature merry-go-round, waving each time I came within view of the TV camera's red light. I wasn't very impressive and got no callback.

13 August 1950–Fledgling Orator

Like all Mormon children, at age four I began attending junior Sunday School in a room separate from the main chapel. As part of the LDS Church's program for teaching its children to be comfortable in public speaking, I was six when I first gave a "two-and-a-half-minute talk" to the assembled children and teachers in our ward's junior Sunday School. Before my talk this morning, Mom wrote the words on a piece of my school paper and rehearsed the talk with me during the week prior. For some reason, I wasn't embarrassed about my bilateral lisp.

1. Robert Driscoll (1937–68) starred in several Disney films, including as the voice and model for Peter Pan for the 1953 animated film of the same name. As he aged out of being a child star, he turned to heroin. Tragically at thirty-one, he died in an abandoned New York building. He was buried in a pauper's grave until his mother was able to locate his body. Donna Larsen, "No Reruns for Bobby," *San Francisco Examiner*, Feb. 13, 1972.

Compared with my speaking once at the small pulpit to our junior Sunday School this year, the minutes show same-aged LaMar Johnson giving four such talks. The following year, I didn't speak even once, while same-aged friends each gave two or three talks. This seems odd to me now in view of my one-time participation.

When I mentioned it nearly sixty years later to my devout LDS friend Betty Ann Marshall, she gave a likely explanation. Sunday School teachers select the upcoming speakers to represent their class, "and don't usually choose the most talkative students." I smiled in agreement, remembering all the times I was scolded for whispering during class—when I wasn't raising my hand to eagerly answer a question or make a comment.

Early 1951–Stop Confiding

Sometime between my polio and the age of ten, shortly after I confided something (which I've long forgotten) to my mother with the earnestness of a child, I overheard her retelling it to a neighbor as a "cute" story about me.

I promised myself: "I'll never tell her any secrets again!" I let my family and others know me only as a spiritual, talented person, and built emotional walls to keep them from knowing my inner reality.

God was the only one I confided in.

Summer 1951–Brush with Blindness

A drunk driver ran a stop sign as my mother was driving through an intersection, and we hit his car broadside. American automobiles were ten years away from seatbelts and safety glass, so I was catapulted from the front passenger seat into the windshield. Shards of glass ripped through my eyebrows and eyelids.

The accident itself remains a blank, but I have a memory of being pulled out of the car by someone. I distinctly remember his strong arms lifting me as blood blocked my sight, streaming down my face and neck.

Even if a Mormon man was around, there wasn't time for anyone to give me a priesthood blessing, which is probably why I never told this as a faith-promoting incident to LDS testimony meetings. Nonetheless, I've always been grateful to God that I wasn't blinded by the shattered windshield.

Fall 1951–Another Mishap

I think this was the year of my unpleasant experience on a thrill ride at The Pike amusement center near Long Beach's boardwalk. My favorite was the giant wooden roller coaster, which extended scarily over the waters of the ocean.

I asked Dad to buy me a ticket for a vertically circular ride with a spinning compartment shaped like a missile at each end of opposing arms of steel that rotated very fast. It looked fun and exciting.

The attendant put me in the compartment, locked its door, and started the ride. However, he hadn't fastened the straps that should have secured me in the seat. Suddenly I was being thrown around inside the compartment as it spun sideways while traveling in a circle from ground level to apex. Dad heard me screaming, but thought I was having fun. By the time the attendant stopped the ride, I was sobbing and shaking with fear. This "ruined" Dad's only day with me this month, and he took me straight back to my grandparents' place.

I later learned that there was no limit to the number of days he could see me since court papers showed that Dad had filed for the divorce. In those documents he maliciously called Mom "unfit as a wife and mother," but paradoxically the judge granted her sole custody of me. Dad told me that Nana had alienated my mother's affections from him. In retrospect, I think that was certainly true.

However, Mom laughed bitterly when I repeated Dad's claim. She described spending Christmas Eves alone with me, while Dad was out "drinking beer with his poker buddies and smelling of it when he came back." There were accusations aplenty and truth on all sides.

5 April 1952–Baptism as Ecstasy

While Uncle Frank Workman and I were putting on the white baptismal clothing side-by-side in the men's changing room of the LDS stake meetinghouse, I was acutely aware of his naked body. My next memory of this Saturday event was happiness as my uncle took me in his arms, baptized me "in the name of the Father, and of the Son, and of the Holy Ghost," and gently lowered me into the warm water of the baptismal font. In his embrace, I felt a burning within me of what I knew was God's presence.

For decades thereafter, my eyes often filled with tears whenever I sang Bernard of Clairvaux's hymn, "Jesus, the very thought of Thee with sweetness fills my breast."

Those words by the medieval mystic and Catholic saint are frequently sung by LDS congregations before the bread and water of the sacrament are blessed and distributed to them. Those sacred duties are performed by youthful members of the Aaronic Priesthood (see D&C 20: 46, 68; 107: 20).

6 April 1952–Church Membership and Service

I was confirmed a member of the LDS Church on the anniversary of its 1830 organization. A month afterward, attorney Reed E. Callister became bishop.[2] He's the bishop I remember whenever I think of the Glendale West Ward.

---

2. Reed E. Callister (1901–89) later served as an LDS mission president in London. His wife, Norinne Richards, was the daughter of Apostle LeGrand Richards. Callister's son, Tad, became a member of the Quorum of the Seventy and the Sunday School general presidency. Greg Hill, "Following the Paths of Righteous Examples," *Church News*, July 26, 2008.

For me, partaking of the sacrament was always a celebration of my relationship with God and Christ. This sacrament became the main reason I wanted to attend LDS services on Sunday. I felt that God wanted me to show my love by serving His Church and people.

Early August 1952–Idaho Cousins

Nana and Grampa took me to southeastern Idaho to visit with her sisters, their children, and grandchildren. Like most Mormons, I didn't pay attention to whether someone was my first cousin-once-removed, second cousin, second-cousin-once-removed, third cousin, or an in-law variation of the above. As a child, I learned to say "Uncle" or "Aunt" when referring to a distant cousin who was an adult. Those who were same-aged or younger were okay to call "Cousin" or by first name.

My favorite boy cousin in Idaho was tow-headed "Coy" Jemmett. Although older than me, he was the only young relative I knew who rode horses. I was thrilled the day he gave me a ride at his farm near Rexburg, one arm across my mid-section, hand grasping my side, as his other hand held the reins. I felt warm and tingly leaning back into him. That night in the basement where he slept, I froze in my tracks at the sight of Coy's naked body as he changed into pajamas. Noticing this, he paused quizzically as I stared at his groin, then slowly shifted my gaze to his tight stomach and chest before locking eyes with him. Expressionless, he silently resumed dressing for bed, as did I. We said "good night" while crawling into separate beds.

In Pocatello, where two of Nana's sisters lived, my same-aged cousin was Linda Whittaker. I know we shared diverse activities in town during my several visits, but all I recall was going with her to Audie Murphy's movies.[3] Always at my urging.

This year, he starred in a western, *Cimarron Kid*, but I fell in love with this war-hero actor when I saw the previous year's *Red Badge of Courage*. I also watched a television re-run of his first starring role in the movie, *Bad Boy*. I felt a childish yearning to know him, to be bodily close to him.

Mid-August 1952–Craters of the Moon and Nuclear War

Among our travels this summer, my grandparents took me to see Idaho's Craters of the Moon. I gaped in astonishment as we drove on compressed-ash roads throughout its vastness, walked along its ancient lava flows, and visited its large cinder cones.

I wondered if this bleak landscape was how Glendale would look if an

---

3. Audie Murphy (1925–71) was a decorated American soldier who served in World War II and later became an actor, appearing primarily in westerns. David A. Smith, *The Price of Valor: The Life of Audie Murphy, America's Most Decorated Hero of World War II* (Washington, DC: Regnery Publishing, 2015).

atomic bomb hit us. One day each month, the city's Civil Defense (CD) sirens wailed and our teacher at Edison Elementary shouted: "Air Raid!"[4] Then us kids did as we were trained. Jumping under our desks, each curled into a ball, our eyes shut tightly and hands clasped behind our heads. We thus rehearsed monthly for the atomic blast wave we had seen demolish entire structures in theater newsreels and CD films during school assemblies. We lived in the shadow of a Cold War that threatened to become blistering hot any day.

Late August 1952–Birds, Bees, and Cops

On the way back to LA from Idaho, we stopped in Salt Lake City. Nana and Grampa took me to the Sunday morning broadcast by the Tabernacle Choir on Temple Square. As a newly baptized Mormon, I was wearing the dark suit and adult-looking formal hat she had bought for me.

While crowds left the performance, I joined many in walking to the Seagull Monument, which memorialized the birds that saved pioneer crops from crickets in 1848.[5] The animal of next importance to Mormons is the honeybee, which represented our hard-working unity, as every Sunday School teacher had informed me.

Looking at the monument's surrounding reflection pool, I noticed a bee struggling to get onto a piece of paper floating in the shallow water. Next to me, an older boy stood on the granite edge of the pool, leaning over and saying he was going to hit that bee with a rock. In a flash of anger, I shoved him toward the water, where he did a belly flop. Amid his screams, flailing limbs, and rush of adults to aid him, I slipped away.

When my grandparents found me, I was sitting in a chair next to the Temple Square museum, hat pulled down over my eyes. Nana lectured me about leaving their side but knew nothing about the drenched boy. I didn't tell her or anyone else. Until now.

As we drove through Utah's small towns this summer and other years, Grampa often complained about the speed traps set up by local police "just so they can get money from tourists who don't stop for food or gasoline." Whenever Nana saw a motorcycle cop concealed behind a ground-level billboard on a road, she exclaimed: "Look at the sneaky cur!"

Such sentiments led to my having a constant suspicion of the police. This

---

4. "Civil defense" is a general term for systems that protect civilians from enemy attack. After the December 1941 air attacks on Pearl Harbor, local West Coast governments began placing air raid sirens to alert civilians in case of further attacks. When World War II ended, the sirens were turned off, then reactivated in 1949 after the Soviet Union successfully tested a nuclear bomb and the Cold War began. Los Angeles County tested its sirens on the last Friday of every month until 1985. "The Region: Air-Raid Sirens Silenced," *Los Angeles Times,* Jan. 30, 1985.

5. Located just south of the tabernacle on Temple Square, the monument was sculpted by Mahonri Young and dedicated in 1913. The California Gull is Utah's state bird.

became gut-level animosity when I saw theater newsreels and televised images of northern cops clubbing white union strikers and southern cops clubbing Black civil rights protestors. I later learned what LA's cops did to peaceful Mexican Americans during the Zoot Suit Riots. Thus, a decade before I heard the phrase "fascist pigs," I regarded cops as brutes with badges.

By the time my law-and-order mother tried to retrain me as a child that "policemen are your friends," it was too late. I saw law enforcement as a necessary evil that could turn from Dr. Jekyll to Mr. Hyde whenever it chose. With no need of personal encounters to be convinced of that, I remained wary and on edge whenever a uniformed cop came within my view. Even now.

Day or night, driving in the deserts from Utah to Los Angeles was an ordeal of heat and exhaustion in the summers before air-conditioned automobiles. I loved warm weather, but there were limits. And I found mine in Nevada's desert.

Across the car's front grille were two canvas bags filled with water. Unpredictable stops were frequent due to boiling radiators. We always stopped in Las Vegas. Grampa and Nana gambled with "one-armed bandits," while I looked on as watchful guards made sure I didn't pull down those slot-machine levers. I loved the place, especially at night, when the street by the Golden Nugget Casino was ablaze with lights.

September 1952–Fledgling Writer

Still impressed by Audie Murphy's *Cimarron Kid*, I wrote what I called a "short story." As an eight-year-old, I had never heard of plagiarism, so innocently listed myself as the author of my childish reworking of his movie. Merely restating its scenes and dialogue, I occasionally added a flourish of my own. My retellings of his many westerns sometimes reached fifty-six hand-written sheets of memo paper.

Fall 1952–Meeting Liberace

It was about this time when I met a flamboyantly homosexual pianist whose new TV program Mom had watched this summer. I don't know how she knew he was at Union Station in LA (or why we were there, if not to see him), but she walked right up to him with me in tow, calling: "Mr. Liberace!" repeatedly in the train depot.

When he turned to me, he was beaming with the kindest expression I had ever seen on a man's face. After asking my name and shaking hands, he made quick movements with a pen on a piece of paper. I expected to see just a scrawl of ink when he handed me his autograph. Instead, "Liberace" was inside his wonderful sketch of a grand piano. I've always thought of him fondly since then.

November 1952–Dad Marries Again and Helps Earn an Oscar

In Las Vegas, Dad married Kathryn ("Kaye") Christensen (Balos), the childless widow of a soldier killed in the Korean War. My sisters Kathy and Patricia were born in August 1953 and August 1954.

During these years, Dad said he was the chief pattern cutter in Los Angeles for elite clothing designer Edith Head. She won an Oscar from the American Academy of Motion Picture Arts and Sciences for costume design three times, but he regarded her as a tyrannical boss.[6]

18 February 1953–Attending Primary

Whereas same-aged LaMar Johnson had been going to the church's midweek Primary classes for young children regularly since 1948, I went to my first today. Nonetheless, the Glendale West Ward's class rolls had not listed me with the "inactive" kids who declined to participate in this "auxiliary program." Instead, I remained unmentioned until the 1951 roll included me with those who had "No Transportation"—despite their willingness to attend.

I've forgotten the name of the ward's sweet sister who made this possible by giving me a ride each Wednesday mid-afternoon. But I remember being picked up and added to the noisy gaggle of kids in her car.

Spring 1953–Praying for Testimony

According to the memoir I wrote at age twenty-one: "The companionship and revelations of the Holy Ghost are one of the most important parts of the Gospel. I cannot remember a time in my life when I have not been filled with the assurances of the Spirit....

"When I was about nine years old, I remember that I felt that I should pray to gain a testimony of the above things I mentioned that I had always known.... And I remember kneeling by my bed one night after my grandmother had tucked me in for the night. After she left, I had knelt down to pray alone, to ask for what I felt the Lord desired me to request. And so I asked for a testimony of those things which I had always known: that God lives, that Jesus was His Son and that Jesus died for me and loved me, that Joseph Smith was a Prophet of God, and that there was a Living Prophet upon the earth.

"The Lord answered my prayers with an onrushing of the Spirit that burned even more fervently in my child breast. The Lord had answered my prayers, but I was too young to ask for more at that time."

That was good enough for me, even though LDS meetings still seemed awfully dull. My boredom led to a noisy embarrassment one Sunday evening.

---

6. Edith Head (1897–1981) won eight Academy Awards for Best Costume Design, including for the films *A Place in the Sun* (1951), *Roman Holiday* (1953), and *Sabrina* (1954).

After partaking of the sacrament while my family sat in the overflow chairs adjacent to the chapel, I lost interest in the speaker. Excusing myself for a restroom break, I instead snuck behind the curtains on the stage at the back of the "recreation hall" (later called "the cultural hall").

I pretended to be sword fighting with an imaginary opponent who kept backing me into corners. Then I careened backward through the stage's front curtains, landing with a loud crash on the hardwood floor below. If attention was what I subconsciously wanted, I certainly got it. From the congregation. From the speaker. And from Nana.

July 1953–Grampa's Tears and Nana's Malice

On a family road trip, I had my first view of Grampa's emotional sensitivity. In one of Northern California's tourist traps, The Trees of Mystery, there was a spot called Cathedral Tree where loudspeakers played a recording of voices singing the words of Albert Joyce Kilmer's poem tribute to trees.[7] It was the only time in my life that I saw my grandfather crying. Years afterward, I learned that his older brother Joseph—like Kilmer—had died as a soldier in the trench warfare of World War I.

This day in the woods, I couldn't comprehend why Nana showed quiet amusement at seeing Grampa in tears. Even though I knew she detested him.

In 1936, Los Angeles Stake Patriarch Joseph A. West had somehow known this about their marriage. He blessed her to eventually become a "happier" person so that "it will not be hard for you to be pleasant, affectionate and kind to all who are around you." Mom later wrote that Nana had sung "sad morbid songs to [her children] as lullabyes." I don't remember what she sang to me in childhood but have a searing recollection of the things Nana said.

Her emphatic statements were hard to forget. During the frequent arguments between my grandparents, Nana often said "bastard" or "sonofabitch." They both shouted "Goddamn!"

Beyond swearing, Grampa never seemed to use personal insults, but their late-night arguments were always about his wanting to have sex with her. If I didn't hear their words at night, Nana summarized their confrontation the next day to me as a very reluctant listener. Because she had insisted for years that they sleep in separate single beds in their bedroom, Grampa couldn't nuzzle against her during the night. "But that doesn't stop the cur," she told me in disgust, describing in detail how he touched her sexually.

With me, Nana had "no boundaries." A psychological term I heard in sessions of counseling decades later. For example, from my grandmother I

---

7. Alfred Joyce Kilmer (1886–1918) was an American poet and writer. Published in 1914, his poem, "Trees," became most popular in the 1940s and '50s and was set to music several times. He was a distant cousin of actor Val Kilmer.

learned the phrase: "Take a flying fuck!" Although the words sounded funny, I didn't repeat them even to my "rough" friends. I couldn't separate this vulgarity's humorous sound from the hatred in Nana's voice as she uttered it. She claimed that Grampa said those words to her, but I never heard him even mutter anything vulgar. Nana swore far more and louder than he did. And with greater diversity.

As the three of us stood in their kitchen one day, she growled at him: "I'd like to plunge a butcher knife in your heart!" Grampa's only reply: "What a thing to say in front of a boy!" And he walked away. To escape from such chaos and drown out the sounds of hatred, I often went to my room, locked the door, and listened to classical music. I played those soothing melodies at full volume on the radio or my record player.

Contrary to what one might think, their arguments, their swearing, and her various vulgarities weren't the reason Nana frequently told me: "We're not good Mormons, but *you* be a good one." It was because they drank coffee every morning, which violated one of the now strict requirements in the LDS Church's nineteenth-century, advice-only Word of Wisdom (see D& C 89: 1–21, "not by commandment or constraint").[8]

In spite of that, Nana and Grampa had served together as "stake missionaries" from 1947–49. I don't know if they converted anyone to Mormonism, but I grew up in a church that treated its members with the long-suffering and undying patience of a family religion. Not the my-way-or-the-highway demands of a corporate religion.

July 1953–God's Voice

In what I recall only as "The Oregon Caves," I became separated from the tour inside.[9] Then the lights went out for a demonstration of total darkness.

From the memoir I wrote at twenty-three: "I suddenly decided to catch up with my family, thinking it an easy thing to walk the few yards to my family. I began to walk slowly in the dark as the guide talked to the group.

"I had slowly proceeded a short distance in the pitch blackness when a quiet voice whispered to me, 'Go no further!' I hesitated, and thinking it either my imagination or an echo of the guide's voice, I started to take a few more steps.

"Suddenly a stern voice, though still a calm whisper within said, 'Stop!' I stopped abruptly and momentarily the lights came on again and the guide continued to lead the tour through the caves. As the lights came on, I found

---

8. Adherence to the Word of Wisdom, the church's code of health, did not become a requirement for temple entrance until 1921. Thomas G. Alexander, "The Word of Wisdom: From Principle to Requirement," *Dialogue: A Journal of Mormon Thought* 14, no. 3 (Fall 1981): 78–88.

9. Located in the Siskiyou Mountains of southwest Oregon, the Oregon Caves National Monument was created in 1909.

that my steps in the dark had actually been leading away from the group and that I had stopped only a few feet from the edge of a chasm."

I frequently told the monthly fast-and-testimony meetings of my LDS ward how God's voice saved me from falling to my death in the Oregon Caves. Also that his priesthood spared me death and disability from polio.

Perhaps because I was such a regular testimony bearer, I grew up hearing older Mormons telling me that I was "special" and that our Heavenly Father was preparing me for "great things" in his church. Nana was more direct: "I wouldn't be surprised if God makes you one of his apostles." She repeated this frequently. From age nine onward, I expected to become an apostle of Mormonism.

August 1953–YMCA Camp

Because Mom's experience was limited to family swim hours at Glendale's YMCA, she didn't know of the Y's national policy for males to swim nude in its pools.[10] I never volunteered this because I expected my prudish mother to stop my participation. When I told her about it decades later, she verified that she would have forbidden me from going there if she had known about the Y's nudity. As a prepubescent, I froze in my tracks the first time I saw teenage boys standing by the YMCA pool in all their dangling, pubescent glory.

After a boat ride this August from San Pedro Harbor to Avalon, Catalina, we and our adult supervisors hiked a few miles across the island's countryside and hills to the Y's secluded Camp Fox in a cove by the Pacific Ocean. While making this trek, we boys watched in drop-jawed astonishment as two mountain goats butted heads atop a ridge. They battled until one lost its footing and tumbled down.

At Camp Fox, we were assigned to large tents that had wooden floors, with prepubescent boys on one side of the camp and teenage boys on the other. Clothing was optional, and I especially remember the camp's naked adult supervisor who was tall, blond, muscled, and hairy chested. I felt jealous of him for being surrounded by the tight-chested, naked teenagers I wanted to embrace as a nine-year-old.

Fall 1953–Fledgling Genius

In the *Los Angeles Examiner* one Sunday, I came across an article about nine-year-old Fred Safier Jr., who was preparing himself to enter Harvard University in three years. He was currently a student at San Francisco's Drew

10. Before about 1960, the Young Men's Christian Association required boys and men to swim nude, partly because early pool filters became clogged by fibers from cotton and wool swimming trunks. Hygiene was also cited as a reason, since those with signs of disease could be prevented from entering pools.

College Preparatory School. I couldn't pronounce "prodigy" correctly, but could say "genius," and was impressed that he was my same age.

I decided that I could prepare myself like Fred Safier was doing. I needed to get busy and read lots of books so I could also become a genius and be in college at age twelve. I told Mom what I wanted to do, and she agreed to go with me to the Glendale Public Library the next day.

That Monday evening, I commenced my lifelong pattern of browsing titles in book stacks as I slowly walked down the library's aisles of nonfiction books for adults, pulling down every title that struck my fancy. The twenty-or-so volumes of this checkout were mainly historical, including biographies of George Washington, Thomas Jefferson, and Abraham Lincoln. I read those three but was disappointed to finish so few of the twenty books during the following week.

"I'm *never* going to become a genius at this rate," I groused. Mom just smiled. I don't remember if the newspaper said that young Safier was reading twenty books weekly, but that's what I thought was necessary to be a prodigy.

I *had* completed my first of several readings of Audie Murphy's European War memoir, *To Hell and Back*. Noticing that I was absorbed in his autobiography, Mom recommended that I also read *Three Came Home* about Agnes Newton Keith's family surviving a Japanese prison camp for civilians. World War II fascinated me, and I likewise devoured military books such as Captain Ted Lawson's *Thirty Seconds Over Tokyo* and Richard Tregaskis's gritty *Guadalcanal Diary*. Those personal memoirs were my first introduction to published history, followed in 1953 by academic biographies of America's leaders.

I was also regularly going through magazines my family received: *Life, Look, Saturday Evening Post* and *Reader's Digest*. I wasn't interested in the salacious *Police Gazette* that was Nana's favorite, but occasionally looked at the women's magazines Mom preferred. Grampa seemed interested only in newspapers. We were working-class readers.

CHAPTER THREE

FATHER FIGURES

1954–1956

Early 1954–Father Figures

By the age of ten I was aware that I used intense prayer with Heavenly Father as a substitute for a father's relationship. I saw my own father only once a month for a few hours, and there was an emotional distance between us. In one of my "sickly" episodes, I vomited at a restaurant where he had taken me. Several months passed before Dad even phoned me again.

Technically, my grandfather helped raise me, but Grampa was emotionally unavailable to me or anyone else due to my grandmother's dominating influence. Nana, Mom, and Aunt Darlene were the only affectionate, emotionally available persons in my life.

I now recognize that Nana created an unhealthy relationship with me. She told me that I was *her* son more than my mother's because I was really the spirit child that Nana had lost in a miscarriage of her fifth pregnancy. I later learned that she said the same to Mom, whom Nana tried to make me regard like a sister or a friend. "I'm your *real* mother," Nana often said. "She's done nothing to deserve the name since your birth."

Nana told me that she hated her father because he brutally beat her and her sisters until they left home. Unlike his frail-looking wife and sons, his daughters were all "big-boned" and husky in the old photographs Nana showed me. "We girls worked like men," she said with triumph.

She also relished telling me about the time an Idaho neighbor, after an argument, had blindsided her father with a shovel, knocking him unconscious. This "thrilled" her because she thought the man had killed him. She felt "disappointed" when her father regained consciousness. Nana acknowledged that George P. Simpson's seething personality and brutal temper might have resulted from being raised in an orphanage after he was abandoned by his Utah Mormon mother and Canadian Anglican father.

Whenever we watched a hero fist fighting with some villain in TV reruns of movie Westerns, Nana always shouted: "Kill the cur!" Which she sometimes uttered in movie theaters during such fights.

Nana often explained that she hated Grampa because of his sexual advances toward her. And she hated most men because they were "lustful animals."

Nana expressed hatred toward her father-in-law, John Alma Workman Jr., for being "a selfish tyrant." She mocked her mother-in-law, Susan Barben Workman, for deferring to him and serving him first at the dinner table. Nana said, "He didn't deserve such groveling," even though John A. Workman had been bishop of the Glines Ward near Vernal, Utah, for five years.

Nana made a point at dinners of serving me first, instead of Grampa. And she did her best to make me hate my father, who was "just a Catholic."

Mom didn't mention it, but my grandmother told me repeatedly that Dad slapped Mom in the face while I was a toddler in a highchair. I have a false memory of witnessing that slap—only because Nana described it to me so often. She sneered about Mom's "weak personality" and cursed Dad: "I would have killed him on the spot!"

I could never force myself as a child or teen to ask Mom about the incident but mentioned it when I was middle-aged. "Nana told you about *that*," Mom exclaimed, adding sadly, "She should never have told you." Another uncomfortable secret.

It seems clear to me now that, as a young boy, I didn't want to be part of this family. When I was eight or nine, I packed a suitcase to run away, but Nana discovered it, after which she kept all suitcases locked up. In 1954 I was stunned to find a 1944 newspaper clipping of my birth announcement, which gave the names of my Dad and Mom. At age ten, I was really disappointed to learn I wasn't adopted.

What might I have inherited from these people? From my passive grandfather? From my hate-filled grandmother? From my secretive father? From my "weak" mother? Very early, I defined myself in the negative: "I refuse to be like *them*."

Whereas tight-chested teens and smooth-chested men filled my thoughts and dreams, most males didn't have a chance with Nana. They were "brutes" or "milk toasts," "tyrants" or "spineless," "rutting pigs" or "sissies," "curs" or "weasels." She reserved her funniest insult for one of Grampa's brothers: "A cabby parked his empty taxi at the curb, and Alley got out of it." John Alma Workman III was one of Grampa's few siblings who were straight-arrow Mormons. The rest Nana dismissed as "weak drunks," one of whom eventually committed suicide in LA.

Nevertheless, she taught me to revere Mormon leaders for their spirituality and goodness. They were the only men I ever heard Nana praise, aside from Democratic president Franklin D. Roosevelt. As I grew up, the LDS Church's leaders were my only role models for assertive males and the only alternative I had against my grandmother's hatred of men.

I consciously rejected Nana's hateful indoctrinations yet wrote gushing love notes to her on her birthday, Mother's Day, Christmas, and other holidays. Decades afterward, I realized that her hatreds and fears stunted my ability to trust and love myself. Or to be intimate with anyone, especially males.

On the other hand, she could be complex in what she said. For example, Nana taught me to pray nightly "for the starving Chinese and for our soldiers who are fighting in Korea." It didn't seem to make any difference to her that the starving Chinese were killing US soldiers in America's Korean War against Communism.

Tender-hearted about poverty, Nana told me that while riding on the bus one cold LA day, she saw "a Mexican boy" shivering without a jacket. She bought one and kept boarding the bus at the same hour on other days until she finally saw him again. Still wearing only a long-sleeve shirt to shield against the chill, the boy began crying as she handed him a leather jacket.

She was also generous to a fault with me. I learned that it took Nana a year on various installment plans to pay for the previous year's Christmas gifts. Just in time to holiday shop again, mostly for me—her own little Mexican.

As a teenager, I often turned down the extra cash she offered me each day for lunch, knowing that she did without something to give me everything I wanted. But she never told me that, nor made the stereotypical whine of doting mothers who think their overly indulged children are ungrateful.

Still, Nana did say that I was "a spoiled boy" who had "no idea what poverty is, or what it was like to live during the Depression." That was her common refrain, which led me to think a lot about people who were really poor.

Because of their own limited resources, I heard her arguing with Grampa in 1954 after she signed a contract to buy the most recent edition of the *Encyclopaedia Britannica* for me. "Now you won't have to go to the library to look up every little thing," Nana told me. Knowing that it was a financial hardship for my grandparents, I wanted to make this purchase worth their sacrifice.

It took me eight years, but by the time I graduated from high school, I had read every one of this encyclopedia's twenty-four volumes, page-by-page. I tried to do the same with the dictionary we had but only made it through the "B" words. Too boring. The British spellings in *Britannica* spellings caused years of mistakes in my American-English compositions.

Retention of what I was reading in the *Britannica*'s volumes was difficult, and I still looked up things in its index. I also used most of the golden stamps given to new owners for requesting the encyclopedia's publishing staff to send special five-to-ten-page reports of additional research on any topic. I really liked those.

Spring 1954–Fledgling Dancer

For some reason, Nana wanted me to learn tap dance and sent me to a dance school. I hated it because I was the only boy in a room full of tap-dancing girls.

I postponed leaving the house as long as possible and one afternoon fell head-over-heels down the flight of stairs in our building as I rushed to Grampa's car. Ended up flat on my back on the ground, very lucky that I didn't break my neck or spine in the tumble. I refused any more lessons soon after this accident.

Thereafter, Nana often called me "stumblebum."

Summer 1954–Bonding with Grampa

As if to verify her assessment, I soon broke my left arm while showing off for my seven-year-old cousin by jumping off things in our backyard. I don't recall if I was playing Superman this time, but I hit the ground so hard that both bones of my left arm snapped near the wrist. Seeing the sudden valley across my arm, I screamed from hysteria more than from pain. Grampa came running and scooped me up from the ground.

There was a clinic-sized emergency hospital about five blocks from our house, but for some reason he didn't drive me there. Instead, at age sixty-two, Grampa carried me while hurriedly walking the full distance, and I was big for my age. Cradled in his arms, my head on his shoulder, this was the closest emotional experience I ever had with the man who helped raise me.

Staying overnight in the hospital to have my arm set in a plaster cast the next morning, I couldn't keep my eyes off the patient in the bed next to me. He was a slender, blond, good-looking man in his thirties. Woozy from medications and too unsteady to walk to the bathroom, he had to be helped by nurses to use a urinal in bed. I gawked at this while feeling a strange sensation in my groin at the sight of his large penis. At the time, I thought this made my accident worthwhile.

August 1954–Visiting Apostles

Glendale West Ward's manuscript history noted for this month: "Elder LeGrand Richards of the Quorum of the Twelve Apostles is visiting in our ward and has spoken several times." Previously the LDS Church's Presiding Bishop, this recently ordained apostle's long visit was understandable. His daughter Norinne was Bishop Callister's wife.

Despite living more than 700 miles from church headquarters in Salt Lake City, regular Mormons in the LA area often saw general authorities. Each stake routinely had one Sunday of stake conference (held quarterly at this time), where at least one general authority spoke. At this time, even local congregations in California got visits from these highest-ranking leaders from Utah.

For example, in three years, First Presidency counselor Stephen L Richards spoke to our ward's priesthood meeting. He was a second-cousin-once-removed of LeGrand Richards. Apostle Hugh B. Brown also spoke at our sacrament meeting six months after President Richards was at the priesthood meeting. I'm sure that's why those three and the prophet David O. McKay are the speakers I most remember watching on black-and-white telecasts of general conference from the Salt Lake Tabernacle each April and October.[1] Its speakers often told us: "You are a chosen generation" before Christ's return (see, for example, *October 1948 Conference Report*, 173; *October 1959 Conference Report*, 67).

September 1954–"Under God"

Signed into law after the start of Edison Elementary's summer recess, the Pledge of Allegiance now had an addition of "under God." Besides this daily reminder of deity, our school also had one hour a week for religion class. Unless officially excused, all students walked to a nearby house for Catholic, Protestant, or Jewish class.

Because I had attended Primary class at our LDS ward each Wednesday after school for the previous eighteen months, Mom tried to get me excused from the school's religion class. She changed her mind after learning I would be spending that hour in an otherwise empty classroom with the children of atheists. Mom regarded them as a worse contagion than "apostate" churches and "heathen" religions.

Thus, for years I listened to Protestant women telling Bible stories in their homes (with flannel-board illustrations) during this weekly school recess.[2]

Fall 1954–Three-Way Shouting Match

I was awakened one night by the curses and shouts of a family argument. My grandparents' voices alternated with high-pitched, tearful screams, including: "I'm thirty-four years old!" It was Mom's voice. Answered more

---

1. Stephen L Richards (1879–1959) was called to the Quorum of the Twelve Apostles in 1917 and served as first counselor in the First Presidency from 1951 until his death. David O. McKay (1873–1970) became an apostle in 1906, a member of the First Presidency in 1935, and the ninth president of the LDS Church in 1951. Hugh B. Brown (1883–1975) became an apostle in 1958 and a member of the First Presidency in 1961, where he served until President McKay's death in 1970. Though McKay's successor, Joseph Fielding Smith, did not choose Brown to be one of his counselors in the First Presidency, Brown continued to serve as an apostle until he died in 1975.

2. Flannel-covered boards were commonly used in Protestant evangelical congregations to teach scriptural stories to children. Teachers placed cut-out figures on the boards to illustrate lessons. Randall Balmer, *Encyclopedia of Evangelicalism* (Louisville: Westminster John Knox Press, 2002). Flannel boards were also commonly used in Latter-day Saint classes for young children.

than once by Nana's loud retorts: "But you're behaving like a two-year-old!" and "Show some common sense!"

Mom had returned from a local movie after 10:00 p.m., just to bathe and change clothes before leaving again. She planned "to meet some girlfriends" for dancing at the Hollywood Palladium.[3] Her parents opposed this. The argument hit a fever pitch when Mom discovered that Grampa had taken her car keys. At that point, I crawled back into my bed.

While trying to fall asleep, I wasn't upset by this confrontation. Instead, I felt proud of Mom. I didn't know whether her plans for the night were sensible or not, but this was the only time I could recall that she stood her ground against Nana.

By contrast, she even submitted to Nana's nagging her to have a dentist perform a full-mouth extraction, when he wanted to pull only one of Mom's front teeth that had abscessed. She got dentures in her thirties! Mainly because Nana had chosen to have all her own teeth pulled out at about the same age, due to the family's lack of money during the Great Depression.

"You've always had bad, ugly teeth," she told Mom, "so dentures will save you from having to have your teeth pulled out one-by-one. And the dentist can make your false teeth look better than the ones you've had to live with." Due to a discolored front tooth from a playground accident in childhood, Mom always covered her mouth when laughing, was embarrassed to grin, and required commercial photographers to remove the darkness of her tooth from every portrait. After getting dentures, she smiled a lot.

Maybe Nana was right to insist on it. Regardless, I felt sorry for Mom and tried to talk her out of having a dentist pull all her healthy teeth.

19 November 1954–Fledgling Actor

Tonight I began a major role in a play at the 100-seat Glendale Center Theater on the city's southern thoroughfare, Colorado Boulevard. Founded by Mormon couple Ruth and Nathan Hale, it was a small theater-in-the-round that performed plays without swear words or risqué situations.[4] Mom acted as a non-professional in several plays there, her favorite role being Princess Tamara in Clare Boothe Luce's *The Women.*

I played a Filipino boy ("Little Noah") at tonight's world premiere of the Hale-written drama *Change of Heart* about American soldiers in World War II. Dressed in a *sarong*, I had pages of dialogue to speak in several scenes. I continued acting in plays at the Center Theater. By age thirteen, I was a

---

3. Opened in 1940, the art deco-style building on Sunset Boulevard has long been a popular spot for dancing, drinking, concerts, and live-performance theater. In 2016 it was listed on the National Register of Historic Places.

4. Ruth and Nathan Hale were prominent LDS dramatists who, following the success of the Glendale Center Theater, opened many other theaters throughout Utah and Arizona.

member of the Glendale Youth Drama Workshop, which performed such plays as *Lily of the Valley* there.

I never forgot the name of one play where I was only a member of the audience. *Lilacs in the Rain* co-starred Nathan Hale himself. He was my first father figure who wasn't a Church leader. Just a devout Mormon of the kindest demeanor.

Like dreams, memory can be erratic, highlighting what seems less important and leaving what seems significant in the shadows. If, as John Keats once observed, truth is beauty and beauty is truth, the latter also seems to be in the eye of the beholder.

Spring 1955–Asking God about The Book of Mormon

According to the memoir I wrote at twenty-one: "I felt prompted to read the Book of Mormon and pray for a testimony of it. Again, I could not understand why I should ask for a testimony of something I seemed to have always known was true, even though I had never read that sacred book. But the principle was the same as it was before when I was 9, and so I tried to read the Book of Mormon at age 11.

"I remember trying several times and not getting past the first page, but I knew that I must read it and pray about it. Finally, I remember reading the first twenty or so pages in Nephi and then reading the last few pages in Moroni. I had a hard time understanding phrases like 'And it came to pass' and 'without the walls of the city.' I just didn't feel that I could read and understand anymore at that time, and I told the Lord so.

"But it was sufficient for that time because I felt prompted that it was enough and that I should pray for a testimony of the Book of Mormon, even though I had not read all of it. I prayed for it, and the Lord gave me the strong assurance of the Spirit that I had expected."

August 1955–Stopping YMCA

A man, who was dating my mother, stayed at the Y and invited me up to his room one Saturday. I felt tingly and out-of-breath when I saw his unmade bed. Nothing happened, but I didn't trust him. Or myself. Especially when he asked me to return another day.

I never went back to Glendale's YMCA.

At eleven I was sexually mature and experiencing desire. I lusted only for men and other boys, about whom I fantasized while masturbating.

I accidentally discovered that very pleasant pastime earlier this year while shimmying up the diagonal metal poles in the playground area of my neighborhood's small Pacific Park. It took me weeks to figure out that I could achieve orgasms in the privacy of my bedroom or bathroom. Without walking to the park several times a day to climb that damned pole! Slow learner.

On this Saturday, I bicycled from the YMCA in tears, praying and cursing—because I wished that something *had* happened between me and Mom's good-looking boyfriend. I had desperately wanted him to caress me and gently touch me sexually because I was too scared to touch him first.

This insecure retreat and passive celibacy became my usual pattern with males from this day onward. I don't know how long afterward Mom stopped dating this man, but I had said nothing about his invitation or my visit. For very different reasons, I adopted Dad's secretiveness.

30 September 1955–James Dean's Death

Audie Murphy was the actor who made my heart skip a beat, but James Dean suddenly burst into my awareness when I saw *East of Eden* a few months previous. I resonated with the painful son-father relationship he portrayed as "Cal," and was deeply affected by news of today's accident. I stared a long time at the front-page photo of his demolished Porsche.

In theaters shortly after his death, *Rebel Without a Cause* affected me even more deeply, due to what I perceived as love in the scenes between James Dean and Sal Mineo. Decades afterward, I learned that both of these young actors were "active homosexuals."[5]

November 1955–Leaving Mom

While my grandparents were away from our shared home, Mom told me that she was driving to Las Vegas. To marry a man she had met the previous evening.

I knew that her second husband wouldn't have the approval of my grandparents or the church. He wasn't LDS, and Mom had met him at the Hollywood Palladium. The cause of last year's blowup, that "den of ravenous men" was now Nana's grim, "I told you so!"

And Wayne Hood didn't have my secret approval because he wasn't physically appealing to me. For months before this, I'd been fantasizing about Audie Murphy. He had written me a nice personal letter in response to my asking him how to become a Hollywood actor. Slender with blue eyes and light-brown hair like smooth-chested Grampa, Audie Murphy was my ideal as a stepfather. Not Mom's husky, hairy husband.

With his black hair, high cheekbones, reddish complexion, and broad face,

---

5. Actors James Dean (1931–55) and Salvatore Mineo Jr. (1939–76) both had male and female lovers. Both men met tragic ends after starring opposite one another in *Rebel Without a Cause*. Dean died in a car accident, and Mineo was later murdered at age thirty-seven. Val Holley, *James Dean: The Biography* (New York: St. Martin's Press, 1995); Michael Gregg Michaud, *Sal: A Biography* (New York: Crown, 2010).

Wayne looked far more Indian than my father. Yet not as appealing to me as Native American actor Jay Silverheels, who played "Tonto" in "The Lone Ranger" series I watched every week on TV.

After eloping, Mom prepared to move with Wayne to Arizona. I told her that I would *not* go with them. I said that I wouldn't leave my grandparents and friends to live with a stepfather I didn't know, didn't like, and couldn't respect. She shed tears but seemed relieved.

At the elegant home of Pearlyne Crowley Goddard's physician father in Glendale's foothills, my Sunday School teacher hosted a going-away party for Mom. Pearlyne was the blonde, slender wife of LDS river-explorer John Goddard.[6] Their marriage lasted about as long as Mom's second.

It was years before Mom told me that my stepfather had served time in prison. I never learned the charge.

Nana was very happy about my decision to stop living with Mom. I don't recall if she encouraged me not to move with my mother. In any event, Nana now had me to herself.

Early 1956–Self-Image

Alone in the boys' restroom of Edison Elementary's modern buildings one day, I leaned toward its mirror and said aloud: "You're ugly!" The anger in those words surprised me. Then my thoughts expressed what I couldn't say aloud, even alone: "No good-looking boy would want you."

Self-image isn't necessarily rational, but my perception of ugliness persisted. When Mom, Nana, or others said that I was good-looking, I was sure that wasn't how sexy boys saw me. That feeling persisted even when good-looking boys seemed to want me sexually. But most didn't.

7 February 1956–Beefy Guys Drag Me to the Bushes

I had an unpleasant experience the first Tuesday evening I attended the LDS Church's Mutual Improvement Association (MIA). Beginning at 7:00 p.m., this weekly meeting was for girls and boys from age 12 to 18 in separate programs, and for co-ed classes of young women and young men to age 25. I was so eager to attend it, that I went uninvited to my first meeting seven weeks before my twelfth birthday.

In the ward's darkened parking lot, I was accosted and dragged into the bushes by three Mormon guys in their twenties whom I barely knew. While one of these tall young men clenched my mouth shut to keep me from screaming, the other two held me down, while one of them undid my belt, yanked the zipper down, and tried to pull my pants off.

---

6. John Goddard (1924–2013) was the first man to kayak the length of the entire Nile and Congo rivers. Tiffany Kelly, "'Real Life Indiana Jones,' Adventurer John Goddard Dies at 88." *Los Angeles Times*, May 20, 2013.

As I struggled, they said it was an MIA initiation to "pant" new attendees, but it felt like attempted rape to me. My hands, which seemed exceptionally strong, were free enough to keep pulling up my pants and underwear, so these young men gave up after a few minutes, calling me a "spoilsport."

After adjusting my clothes and dusting off, I walked into the LDS meetinghouse and acted as if nothing had happened. I told no one. I didn't return to MIA for two months after this first visit—or so say the rolls for our Scout Troop 26, which I commenced attending regularly in April.

I think my experience of this February night is why I've often felt anxiety when standing close to a tall, husky guy since then—no matter how cute and sweet he might seem. Even if they seemed like rough "bad boys," short, slinky "studlees" have felt safe to be around.

26 March 1956–Mixing Social Classes

My twelfth birthday party was the first time I had a social event with some of my separate groups of friends. The four attendees included one non-LDS boy from my working-class neighborhood near the railroad tracks of Los Angeles and three of my Mormon friends from the foothills of Glendale. Among them was our wealthy bishop's daughter.

As far as I was aware, there were no Mormons in my elementary school. And no active LDS kids in my neighborhood, which included a trailer park.

During these years I saw my Mormon friends only on Sunday and at the mid-week Primary class in our ward, two miles north of where I lived. Four days later, I graduated from Primary and was voted by the congregation to be ordained a deacon.

Early April 1956–Sex and the Aaronic Priesthood

While I was sitting with the twelve- and thirteen-year-old deacons on the front row of the chapel during sacrament meeting, a wiry "tough guy" (whom I'll call "Bart") leaned across with his hand on my groin and whispered a sexual invitation. He was my age and sexually mature like me. This excited and frightened me.

Despite my determination not to confide secrets to my family, I inexplicably told my grandmother what Bart did. She said, "This boy must be a pervert," and told me to stay away from him. Difficult to do since we were both active Mormons in the same deacons' quorum, Sunday School class, and Scout troop.

By June, I had observed Bart engaging in sex acts with a somewhat older deacon in various areas of the LDS meetinghouse, usually during MIA when our Scout troop met. Barely beyond the observation of adult advisers, the two youths mutually masturbated at Boy Scout camps and even groped each other at a deacons' quorum bowling game. Our friends looked away, but I gaped and yearned.

15 April 1956—Preaching to Adults

This morning I gave a two-and-a-half-minute talk to the adult congregation of our Glendale West Ward. This occurred during the opening exercises of senior Sunday School, held in the chapel.

As usual, Mom (who had moved back to Glendale with her new husband) rehearsed this talk with me for days. I read my remarks word-for-word, rather than saying them from memory, but don't recall being nervous. Afterward it seemed like a dozen adults walked up to congratulate me. I was thrilled and gave another talk in seven months.

In sacrament meeting, youths spoke to the entire congregation for what was then called a "five-minute talk" or "inspirational talk." My first was at age thirteen, and then about yearly thereafter. This was the advanced part of the LDS Church's method for training children to be confident as public speakers.

April-June 1956—Confronting My Sexuality

I was reading about "the forbidden" in Glendale's library. In its card catalog, I started with my grandmother's word "pervert," which led to "perversion," to "abnormal psychology" and to "homosexuality."

Now I knew the name for what was wrong with me, what had warmed my senses toward men and boys for *years* before now. I was a "homo." And now I knew what that insult meant.

Everything I read about homosexuality in the library was negative. Even then-available novels about male lovers: *The City and the Pillar*, *Finisterre*, *Giovanni's Room*, and *Never the Same Again*.

The last affected me deeply. Although a cautionary tale, the boy-hero's seduction by a man was exactly what I wanted for myself. When the teen was left alone, crying at a bus stop, I sobbed. I've always remembered that scene and that book.

Unfortunately, I wouldn't know about Mary Renault's 1956 *The Last of the Wine* until decades after this summer. Her novels portrayed ancient Greece's happy, loving, and enduring relationships of male-male sexuality. This perception would have been a very healthy influence on my adolescent self-image.

By June graduation from elementary school, I had engaged in sex play with male classmates. Though nothing more than fondling while fully clothed, I knew that I was already becoming known among the neighborhood's boys for this kind of mutual masturbation. I wanted sex with guys but didn't want the label nor the rejection I expected from my family and "normal" Mormons.

At twelve, I wanted to die and sometimes thought of jumping in front of speeding cars as I walked along the street. I struggled against suicidal feelings and homosexual attractions during the next four decades.

August 1956–Trying to Reside with Mom Again

After touring eight western states with me this summer, my grandparents took an extra vacation due to Mom's request to move back temporarily so that I could get better acquainted with her husband, Wayne Hood. This became a disaster because of our mutual dislike.

Once he claimed he had been a circus knife-thrower, put me against one of the wooden garage doors, and from fifteen or twenty feet away repeatedly threw what he called "a balanced knife" at my head.[7] Sometimes the blade embedded a couple of inches from my head and once two feet away. He said that the wild throw was "on purpose."

I learned afterward that he never worked in a circus, but I didn't tell Mom why I asked. Had no idea where my stepfather got the balanced knife, but I never stood against the garage door for him again. I was suicidal, not crazy.

The final blowup of their stay occurred when my stepfather tied me up with ropes. "Playing Indian," he tightened the ropes until they were cutting into me. When he refused to loosen them, I called Wayne a "bastard." He dropped the rope like he'd been hit.

The look on his face scared me, and I ran inside, locking the front door. When he started crawling through a window, I locked myself in the bathroom and refused to come out until I heard Mom's voice more than an hour later.

She had me go into my grandparents' bedroom to explain what happened. When I admitted what I called Wayne, she said it deeply hurt him because he was taunted with that word as a child, since his mother wasn't married when he was born. I said, "That doesn't give him any right to tie me up and hurt me," whereupon my stepfather slapped me across the face so hard it nearly knocked me off my feet.

I straightened up and stared at him with feelings of pure hatred. I don't know whether I actually said it, but my thought was: "Hit me again, you bastard!" Whether for those words or the expression on my face, he lunged at me in fury.

Mom grabbed his arms and screamed for me to leave the house. I didn't come back for hours and tentatively approached the door when I did. The rest of the night is a blank.

When my grandparents returned from vacation, I felt that Nana was rescuing me. She said "I told you so," and there was no more talk about me living

---

7. Professional knife throwers use specially made knives weighted or "balanced" toward the center, which makes hitting a target easier.

with Mom. For the time being, Nana didn't have to persuade me to hate my stepfather.

He and Mom had made Glendale their new residence, but I didn't move in with them. Still, I adored Mom as a pure and innocent person whom everyone seemed to love.

September 1956–Abandoning Sexuality and Friends

During the summer, I decided not to touch a guy sexually ever again. I stopped groin-grabbing games and abandoned my non-Mormon friends who knew about this. I decided to associate only with Mormons. Planned to live the rest of my life without fulfilling the homosexual needs I knew were repulsive to my family and to "normal" friends.

I also *knew* that Heavenly Father accepted me, despite my homosexuality, but I thought he didn't want me to "behave that way." I wasn't afraid of God but didn't want to offend him. Or hurt him. Mormons believe that our Heavenly Father is as vulnerable as most parents are. [see Lowell L. Bennion, An *Introduction to the Gospel* (Salt Lake City, UT: Deseret Sunday School Union Board, 1955), 296; and Eugene England, "The Weeping God of Mormonism," *Dialogue: A Journal of Mormon Thought,* 35, No. 1 (Spring 2002), 63–80].

Now I had the ultimate reason for trusting no one and withdrew still further into myself. I began using intense concentration on academic study as a way of shutting out people and forgetting my inner pain.

I didn't want to attend the junior high in my neighborhood and told my family that I preferred Eleanor J. Toll Junior High School in the north part of Glendale. The rich part. Nana allowed this when I said I wanted to get away from my grade school friends who were "bad boys" and instead go to school with LDS friends. She wanted that for me, too. It was settled.

I told school officials the lie that I was living with Uncle Frank, whose house was in the right school district. He and his wife, Darlene, agreed to this arrangement, taking messages whenever the school phoned about me. I had a far closer association with Aunt Darlene than with Mom's own sisters. My grandmother may have regarded her daughter-in-law as a rival for my affections (as well as for her only son's) because Nana never mentioned Darlene to me without being critical, demeaning, or sarcastic.

For two years, I bicycled two-and-a-half miles uphill each morning to school so that I could be with LDS friends daily. Downhill return trips were fun.

Whenever it seemed necessary, I maintained the pretense that I resided in the school district. And I stopped associating with non-LDS friends in my neighborhood.

Young Quinn with his father. A girl—probably Michael's younger sister, Tricia—is peeking from behind their legs. *Courtesy Quinn family.*

September 1956–Fun and Games in Junior High

During the first month of junior high, a non-Mormon student handed me a pornographic photo he said was from Tijuana, Mexico. The black-and-white image showed in crisp detail a naked man from the waist up and a fully naked woman sprawled on a bed.

Aside from the gross-out factor, I wasn't interested in the image. It didn't show me enough of the man's body.

Still, I asked where the boy got the photo as I returned it. He pointed out a somewhat older student in the schoolyard and said that he was the go-between for buying "dirty pictures."

"He can get you marijuana weed, too," the first one told me with a grin. I wasn't interested in experimenting with cigarettes, let alone marijuana.

Not until the ninth or tenth grade did Glendale's schools give a lecture against recreational drugs at one of our general assemblies. That was years too late for many students in Southern California, especially at this stage of America's expanding drug culture.

In seventh-grade gym class at Toll, I was the constant companion of a fellow I often fantasized about. Surnamed Quinn, Richard was like my Irish blood-brother with blue eyes, pale skin, black hair, smooth chest, and lanky body. Calling us "the Quinns," Coach Ballenger sometimes praised our athleticism to the entire P.E. class.

We did well in football, I on the line and he as quarterback. One day, I bent over to hike the ball as my friend hunched behind me with his hands between my knees. Instead of clapping for the hike, Richard grabbed my hips, and rubbed against me.

I jumped, exclaiming, "What the Hell?!" He laughed and announced, "We'll do the hike for real this time." The other boys also laughed and seemed to think it was just a joke. I thought it was more, but Richard and I never mentioned it again.

We were inseparable in gym class throughout the year, but I turned down several offers to go to his house after school. Eventually, we hardly talked outside gym class. If he had been LDS, I think we would have ended up in love or in bed for sex. Probably both.

My yearning to have a "real" brother might have been part of my homosexuality. Not the cause, but mixed up with that other kind of desire. God knows.

One day in this first semester of junior high, I watched two naked teenagers wrestling in the locker area of the boys' gym. One blond and the other dark-haired, their faces filled with lust.

In a few days, the blond-with-a-beautiful-face told me he wanted to meet after school and "have some fun where no one can see us." For the rest of the day, I had sexual fantasies about him but didn't go to the appointed meeting place. He never spoke to me again.

However, most of the sexually active boys in Toll Junior High were "doing it" with girls. This semester, one non-Mormon showed me "the rubber" he kept in his wallet, a protection he used occasionally and replaced. Another avoided that kind of contraceptive and described how his girlfriend used carbonated drinks as a post-coital douche. The sex-education film we saw in the ninth grade was years too late for many of us. Glendale's White Anglo-Saxon teenagers were at the forefront of America's "Sexual Revolution."

But school friends told me that I seemed "pure" or "innocent." Whether that was a compliment or a put-down, I didn't want to dispute it by revealing my non-naif self. That was part of my survival mechanism as a hidden homosexual.

I embarrassed some of my Mormon friends with the wide-eyed innocence of asking them to explain their dirty jokes. This was my private joke and defense. Because of this faux-naivete, few tried telling dirty jokes to me a second time.

I was an academic workhorse, but had realistically given up trying to turn myself into a "child prodigy." *Genius* was a label that some other kids deserved. But not me. I was already beginning to see my limitations, even though Nana often told me: "You can be *anything* you want in this life! You have it in you."

October 1956–Stepfather Tries to Out Me

While my mother and Wayne Hood attended back-to-school night, he asked my gym teacher in front of me if the coach thought that I "act effeminate." Mr. Ballenger's middle-aged face went beet red as he angrily answered, "Absolutely not!" I don't recall feeling anything but surprise at the question and happiness at the coach's answer, but I must have felt humiliated.

Nevertheless, within months, my stepfather and I were on good terms that I regarded as non-sexual love. I even shrugged off Wayne's calling me "snaggle tooth" due to the braces I had after the early descent of my adult teeth.

Was this an example of Stockholm Syndrome (bonding with your abuser)? Dunno.

With my grandmother, both the bonding and my humiliation were explicit. Nana didn't like the fact that my hair and eyelashes are straight (due to my Mexican father), and she often complained that I "look like an Indian." To correct this, Nana encouraged me to use an eyelash curler every morning. She also put my hair in pink rubber curlers.

One Sunday this year, she refused to comb out my hair before Grampa drove us to evening church services. She said it wasn't dry enough. I remember feeling humiliated as I watched people walking through the ward's parking lot while I sat in our car as Nana slowly removed the curlers and combed my hair to her satisfaction. Then I passed the sacrament to people who surely thought of me as the boy in pink curlers.

Decades later, I watched the charming French movie *Ma Vie En Rose* but felt no self-identification with its gender-ambiguous boy. I was happy being a male, but not so happy about wanting sex with other males.

Another humiliation involved the long arms I had at an early age. Thus, full-sleeve shirts that fit my shoulders wouldn't even reach my wrists. For years, Nana had to buy me shirts that were too large in the shoulders, and she often told me: "You have the arms of an ape!"

I internalized that image. While shopping alone during my mid-teens, I apologized for having "ape-like arms" when the salesman discovered that I needed a larger-sized shirt. It made me feel wonderful when he looked me in the eyes and said sternly: "*Never* say that about yourself, or even think it! You're a growing boy with a man's arms. That's something to be proud of."

As a teenager, I spent a lot of time visiting Mom and my stepfather Wayne, who eventually converted to Mormonism. I was often with them a couple of times a week. Still, we all accepted the fact that my home was with Nana, who now had another man she tried to make me hate.

18 November 1956–Bishop's Daughter

This mid-morning, Paula Callister and I sat together in one of the rows of seats on the stand behind the speaker's rostrum of our ward's chapel. She gave a two-and-a-half-minute talk to the adult Sunday School's opening services. My talk followed.

From a reminiscence I wrote at eighteen: "I had had a 'puppy love' for Paula since I was seven. After I was thirteen it had matured into a firm conviction that one day we would be married in the temple together."

Three years from today, we again sat side-by-side to give such talks. It would be her last.

Late November 1956–Family Comments about Homosexuality

Nana told me that a woman in our ward said, "It's terrible that dirty books are available to boys" in our city. She said that this LDS woman "even saw a deacon from our ward looking at a dirty picture book called *Vim*" in a certain store.[8] I'd been caught.

Two of my same-aged friends in the ward also liked this magazine's photos of slender young men wearing only g-strings. I was stunned when one of these nearly naked guys was identified underneath his photo as a "graduate of Brigham Young University." God's college!

We three boys gave *Vim* the code name *Children's Friend*, the title of the church's magazine for Primary kids. That way, we could talk about it in the chapel without others realizing.

Nana said nothing more about it, and I just switched to a store next to the Alex Theater for my heavy-breathing magazine. Then she began repeating two new warnings: boys who "play with themselves can be locked up like monkeys in a zoo," and "perverts" castrate and kill boys after "abusing their privates." Neither warning scared me nor changed my behavior.

Some time afterward, my mother directly confronted me about these muscle magazines that stood for pornography in my young life. As a precaution against discovery, I threw away each issue of *Vim* magazine in sidewalk wastebaskets as soon as I clipped my favorite photos. I hid those in a game box inside my room. Mom discovered them while she and my stepfather were visiting my grandparents during my absence when they wanted to play that game. At least that's what she told me.

This led to Mom's only effort to indoctrinate me about homosexuality. While working on the assembly line of an aircraft factory during World War II, a lesbian coworker "tried to get too friendly" with her before I was born. She then told me that a young man can be treated terribly by others if they

8. *Vim* was a magazine that focused on scantily clad photos of young men. Many "male physique" publications were launched mid-century to appeal to gay men without explicitly stating their purpose. Most ceased publication by the end of the 1960s, when the gay rights movement began enabling more openness about homosexuality. David K. Johnson, "Physique Pioneers: The Politics of 1960s Gay Consumer Culture," *Journal of Social History* 43, no. 4 (Summer 2010): 867–92.

think he likes to look at men's bodies. She said that my stepfather Wayne was in the Navy and that as a punishment, such young men are called "queers" and are "forced to suck the penis of sailors." I knew that Mom expected me to react with the same disgust her face showed as she said these things. I don't know how my reaction looked, but my only thought was, "Why would they think that's punishment for a queer?!"

Not long afterward, I was in the balcony of Glendale's cheap Temple Theater, where for fifteen cents on Saturdays I watched three old movies in a row of a particular genre. Two other boys were sitting next to me this Saturday afternoon when an usher in his late teens sidled up to us and whispered, "Wanna have some fun?"

While recalling my commitment to be homosexually celibate, I whispered, "No, but I'd like to watch." As he fumbled in the flickering dark with a boy's zipper, the young usher snarled toward me, "Go downstairs, cuz I don't want an audience."

I went alone to this Art Deco cinema most Saturdays and was disappointed not to see any of those boys again. But I watched a lot of old movies. Three at a time.

CHAPTER FOUR

SECRETS AND REVELATIONS

1957–1959

Early 1957—Harsh Honesty, Concealment, and White Lies

I was about thirteen when I recognized the stark contrast between my grandmother's honesty and my father's dishonesty. "Lying is the worst thing you can do," she had often told me since early childhood. Nana had severe problems, many of which she imposed on me, but she always told the truth as she saw it—about herself and others.

Yet even then I recognized that Nana's truth-telling was often insensitive, even cruel. I argued a lot with my grandmother but did my best to tell the truth gently and diplomatically with her and with everyone else.

On the other hand, from age thirteen onward, I struggled to get my father to tell me *any* truth about himself. Mom told me that when they first met, Dad said both his parents were dead. After I was born, he suddenly took Mom to East LA's *barrio* to meet his mother, Carmen. She was Mexican and couldn't speak much English.

To the end of their marriage, Mom thought (as I did for many years) that Dad had only one brother, also named Quinn. However, at Carmen's funeral in 1948, my mother met a "very Mexican-looking man" who introduced himself as one of my father's brothers. This "unknown brother" told her that he was "Michael Peña" and that Peña was Dad's "real name."

I knew him as Donald Peña Quinn, and this year he denied everything Mom had recently told me. Dad said that his mother "was Spanish, not Mexican," that his father was "an Irishman named Ishmael Quinn," and that Dad's only brother was the one I knew. He explained their brown skin by saying that my grandfather was "Dark Irish," Ireland's descendants of sailors who survived the Spanish Armada's sinking in the sixteenth century.[1] This seemed reasonable.

However, Mom also told me that he once claimed he was related to

---

1. In 1588, a fleet of ships known as the Spanish Armada attempted to invade England. Some of these ships wrecked on or off the coast of Ireland. The later idea that the surviving Spanish sailors are the ancestors of brown-skinned Irish people ("Black Irish" or "Dark Irish") has no foundation in known fact. Keith Muckelroy, *Maritime Archaeology* (Cambridge: Cambridge University Press, 1978).

Hollywood actor Anthony Quinn, whose publicity bios later referred to his Irish-*Mexican* ancestry. When I asked Dad about this, he said, "There are a lot of Quinns in the phone book," and refused to say anything more.

Eventually, Dad acknowledged that he had other brothers. He did this only because I found the obituary for "Carmen Peña Quinn" in Los Angeles newspapers, which listed "Michael P. Quinn" as a son. Then Dad admitted that Michael was one of his older brothers. He said that the other was "Henry," but "they are dead to me." Henry, he informed me, was literally dead—of suicide.

As far as I knew, their real names could have been Enrique and Miguel, but Dad refused to answer any more of my questions about himself or his family. "Never again!" he said, "so don't ask me."

Between the extremes of Nana's and Dad's approach to truth-telling was Mom's justification for "white lies." That was the term she used when I exclaimed in shock at age four or five: "Mommy, you told a *lie*!" I had just heard her say something on the phone that I knew was untrue. She explained that "white lies" were "innocent" ways to avoid hurting other people. Or to avoid embarrassing yourself.

But I could never accept her oft-repeated excuse. I grimaced every time Mom whispered for me to tell someone on the phone that she wasn't home when they asked for her. She also told white lies on my behalf. I knew she did this out of love, so never complained, despite discomfort.

It was such a pattern in her life, that Mom told Nana that we were delayed in traffic while driving home, instead of simply acknowledging that we had stopped for ice cream. It was Mom's way to avoid being nagged about being overweight. If asked for verification of her excuse, I would have told the truth, but remained silent otherwise.

And so I consciously rejected Nana's, Dad's, and Mom's approaches. I either told the truth or held my tongue. I realized that my frequent silence was a form of deception, but it was something I could live with.

Nevertheless, repeatedly lying to stay in the "right school" was the notable exception in my adolescence. I felt guilty about it every day but saw no better alternative.

Early 1957–Fledgling Genealogist

I regarded my father's background as a dark secret which I did my best to uncover through genealogical research. Eventually, I discovered that my grandfather's name was Ysmael Peña, that both of Dad's parents were born in Mexico, and that he had adopted the name Quinn as a teenager—due to his friendship with Anthony Quinn in the East Los Angeles *barrio*.[2] The younger

---

2. Anthony Quinn (1915–2001), born Antonio Rodolfo Quinn Oaxaca in Chihuahua,

uncle I knew as James P. Quinn had been born as Ysmael Peña Jr. I never could find American birth certificates for older brothers Henry/Enrique or Michael/Miguel. They were undoubtedly born in Mexico before Grandfather Ysmael and Grandmother Carmen fled the Mexican Revolution of 1910 by crossing the Rio Grande River to become despised "wetbacks" in Arizona.

Dad had used an alias to marry my Anglo mother and stepmother. Uncle Jim did the same with his Anglo wife. I was the firstborn Quinn in my family. After realizing that, whenever I said "I have the luck of the Irish," it was my private joke.

Dad's secrets coursed through two sides of my family. Uncle Lee and Dad both told me that they were friends before marrying the Workman sisters and that Dad had introduced Lee to my Aunt Norma. Yet neither Uncle Lee nor Dad ever answered my questions about how an Italian American living amid San Bernardino County's vineyards and orchards met his "Spanish-Irish" friend forty miles away in Los Angeles. Strangely, I don't think I ever asked Mom or Aunt Norma.

For twenty years, without Dad's knowledge and against his explicit wishes, I scoured every source I could find that might piece together his family history. Not until the 1970s did I consciously recognize the irony that I was devoting all this energy to uncovering my father's concealed Mexican identity at the same time I was just as resolutely concealing my homosexual identity.[3]

May 1957—Passionate Proxies

This is the month that Mormons commemorate the restoration of the Aaronic Priesthood by the Angel Moroni to Joseph Smith in 1829. The Glendale West Ward organized an excursion for its twelve-to-eighteen-year-old boys to the temple in Mesa, Arizona. We were to be proxies in baptism for the dead (see D&C 128:12–18).

On the overnight bus trip, thirteen-year-old Bart and his deacon-age boyfriend were sitting together across the aisle from my seat. After everyone seemed to be asleep in the darkened bus, they unzipped their pants and whispered for me to reach across and "play with" them. I wanted to but turned toward the sleeping boy at my side and shut my eyes. Bart kept whispering my name until an adult supervisor in the bus yelled sleepily: "Pipe down!"

Mexico, grew up in East Los Angeles. With an acting career that spanned six decades, he won two Academy Awards for Best Actor in a Supporting Role for the films *Viva Zapata!* (1952) and *Lust for Life* (1956). Anita Gates, "Anthony Quinn Dies at 86; Earthy Tough Guy," *New York Times*, June 4, 2001.

3. Michael Quinn's lifelong friend, Clifton Jolley, wrote about eighteen-year-old Quinn's spending much of his free time researching his genealogy when they were college roommates: "I wasn't sure what was going on inside him, what sort of strange obsession controlled his thinking." Clifton H. Jolley, "But ... isn't genealogy just for grandmas?" *Deseret News*, Aug. 9, 1980.

In the men's changing rooms of the Mesa Temple's basement the next morning, the same two boys locked themselves inside a dressing cubicle. Others seemed to ignore their giggles as we followed a temple worker out of that area. I knew why their faces were flushed when Bart and his boyfriend belatedly joined the rest of us, dressed in white clothing, standing next to the baptismal font atop its twelve sculptured oxen.

Still, when it was my turn to be submerged a dozen times on behalf of males who had died ages ago, I forgot about Bart and felt the burning of God's Spirit within me. I was happy to aid the salvation of others.

From that day onward, I always declined Bart's occasional invitations for me to sleepover at his house. Or for the three of us to swim in the pool at his older boyfriend's house. Eventually, he stopped asking.

Though I wasn't the only Mormon kid who knew what Bart was doing, I discussed it with no one. Five months after this temple trip, our ward's annual conference voted by upraised right hand to sustain the three of us boys to various positions of leadership in the ward's two quorums of deacons. To the ward, we were good, clean boys.

July 1957–Fledgling Surfer

Now and during the next several summers, Wayne and Mom took me to the beach for surfing. Usually at Huntington Beach or Laguna Beach in Orange County.

I often had ruptured eardrums in the middle of the night after surfing. A trade-off I was willing to endure for the fun and excitement of hitting the waves.

Mid-Summer 1957–Fledgling Novelist

After seeing Audie Murphy's *Night Passage*, I wrote my longest and last short story based on his Westerns. I titled it "Follow the River" from this movie's theme song, whose lyrics I quoted for my handwritten version of forty-seven pages.

I was emotional about watching the death scene of bad-brother Audie in the arms of his older, good-brother Jimmy Stewart. And wrote it as I saw it. But I wanted the bad brother to live. The bad boy.

Soon I began writing a "novel." In its plot, I consciously symbolized my internal divisions between the actively Mormon boy I was and the actively homosexual boy I longed to be.

First, having recently read Margaret Mitchell's *Gone With the Wind*, my novel was about the Civil War. A nation divided. Second, its main characters were two brothers who would fight on opposite sides. Third, one of them would die.

After a lot of research about pre-1861 plantations, I abandoned the novel because I couldn't decide how I wanted my psycho-drama to proceed. Initially, I thought that the Union brother represented my conformist needs, while the Confederate brother represented my rebellious needs. Because the Union would inevitably win, this seemed to guarantee that my rebellious needs would be defeated. I wasn't sure that's what I wanted, so my second plan was to have the Union brother die and the Rebel brother live. However, after spending three years trying to create two equally likable brothers, I didn't want my novel to kill either of them.

After redrafting the first chapter several times, I gave up the project. But I didn't forget its main question: Which side of me should triumph?

Three years later, I would think about this psycho-drama in a startling way. My mind reeled when I saw MacKinlay Kantor's essay in *Look* magazine: "What If the South Had Won the Civil War?"[4]

My civil war was sexual and spiritual, and I wasn't sure which side of me was going to win. I knew which side *should* win, but was that really what I wanted to happen? God knows.

August 1957–Wrong Social Class

For the first year I was a deacon, my grandfather had taken me as an unofficial junior companion to see LDS members he visited once a month. For years, Grampa supervised this ward teaching (subsequently called home teaching) in the elders quorum, and then in the high priest group.

In August, I was temporarily assigned to twenty-two-year-old Brent Pratley, who had recently left BYU.[5] Ordained an elder this month, he became a full-time missionary in September. Until 1962, it was church policy for males to wait until age twenty-one before going on proselytizing missions.

One hot day, he was driving me from the trailer park near my home where we had just visited some inactive Mormons. My new ward teaching companion stuck his head out the car's window and shouted to a woman in short-shorts: "Wear a dress, you low-class bitch!" I cringed with shame.

I silently agreed with Pratley. She *was* low class. I saw myself as low class and was determined to escape my family's working-class identity. He just gave crude reinforcement to my grandmother's explanation for why she didn't accept the occasional invitations to attend a social at the homes of Mormons

---

4. MacKinlay Kantor (1904–77) was a reporter and Pulitzer Prize-winning author. His article, "What If the South Had Won the Civil War?" was the November 22, 1960, cover story for *Look,* a biweekly magazine published from 1937–71.

5. Brent Pratley (1935–2017) grew up partly in Glendale, California, and later became an orthopedic surgeon in Provo, Utah. In the 1980s he was a part-time team surgeon for BYU's football team. In 1987, BYU forced his resignation, and the Utah State Physicians Board restricted his prescription license after he was accused of prescribing painkillers to several players without keeping records as legally required. Robert Thomas Jr. and Michael Janofsky, "What Did a Doctor Order," *New York Times,* Feb. 6, 1987; UPI, "Former BYU doctor has license restricted," Feb. 19, 1987.

in the foothills of Glendale: "They're cultured, and we'd stick out like a sore thumb." If given the opportunity, I vowed I would go and fit in.

September 1957–Male Mentor

After enrolling in a public-speaking class with junior high school teacher Leonard DiGrassi, he encouraged me to participate in speech contests and drama competitions. I got a first-place award in the Novice Speech Tournament. This school year and the next, I also made it to the drama finals, held at UCLA, with a solo cut from plays by Shakespeare or Arthur Miller. I especially liked playing the father in the climactic scene of Miller's *All My Sons*.

One year, Oscar-winning Anthony Quinn was the keynote speaker in Royce Hall for the competition's finals at UCLA. Sitting less than ten rows from the podium, I agonized about going up to shake his hand. If I couldn't refrain from identifying myself as Donald Peña Quinn's son—and this got back to Dad—I was sure that my father would disown me. I couldn't put myself in such a position, so didn't even try.

I eventually shared a second-place trophy for my portrayal of the William Jennings Bryan character in the climax of *Inherit the Wind*. After school, in his office for hours weekly, Mr. DiGrassi coached my memorization, delivery, blocking (positions on the stage), and gestures for these competitions. One day, he gave me an effusive compliment, and I stammered out a blushing response. He said: "You're going to get a lot of compliments throughout your life, so you'd better learn to accept them with ease and no embarrassment." I did.

While in his public-speaking class, I hadn't yet finished the *Encyclopaedia Britannica*'s "E" entries. Thus, I had no idea what a student was talking about when she commenced a speech about ethical issues involved with "euthanasia." She hadn't defined it when I raised my hand: "What does this have to do with teenagers in Asia?"

Without laughing (bless him!), Mr. DiGrassi immediately spelled the unusual word on the blackboard. Then he stated its definition to the class generally (not to me specifically). In later decades, I tried to always follow his example of considerate diplomacy with my own students.

He was likewise tactful when I gave my big speech. It was an anti-evolutionary diatribe, based on Joseph Fielding Smith's *Man, His Origin and Destiny*.[6] I showed the thick volume to the class—"in case any of you want to read this book by a modern apostle of Jesus Christ."

---

6. Joseph Fielding Smith (1876–1972) became an LDS apostle in 1910. He served as the Church Historian and Recorder from 1921 until 1970, when he became the tenth president of the church. He served in that position until his death in 1972. His *Man, His Origin and Destiny* (Salt Lake City: Deseret Book, 1954) received disapproval from LDS Church President David O. McKay, who made clear that the book was not authorized by the church and was not to be considered church doctrine. But because Smith was the Acting President of the Quorum of the

Without criticizing my presentation, Mr. DiGrassi told me that he had to "physically restrain" Ray Bradley, a very liberal student, "from leaping to his feet to challenge your every sentence." Subsequently, this boy's speech was an equally impassioned condemnation of the role of Greek Orthodox Archbishop Makarios in the politics of Cyprus.[7]

I admired this green-eyed student's knowledge but was standoffish the day Bradley tried to infiltrate our group of Mormon boys who ate together at lunch recess. It was easy to self-righteously grimace when he began a gross-sounding tale to break the ice, but I had to force myself not to laugh at its punchline. Whether or not they also had to suppress themselves, none of the other Mormon boys laughed and some groaned at his dirty joke. Never again stopping by the Mormon group's regular eating place, he maintained only a nodding acquaintance with me during the rest of our school years.

Scientific evidence eventually persuaded me to accept organic evolution, but not until I was in college. Protestant fundamentalist William Jennings Bryan had failed to explain away evolution, but for eight years I retained my unshakable conviction that LDS Apostle Smith did so.

10 December 1957–Leaving LDS Youth Program

The previous Tuesday was the last time the MIA rolls show me in attendance. A "100 Percent Attender" in every other meeting of the Church, tonight I became totally inactive in its youth program ("Mutual"). For one reason.

Bart and some other Boy Scouts were openly engaging in the kind of sex games and horseplay I was struggling to avoid. Our ward's Scoutmaster Vernon Ragsdale seemed oblivious to what was going on, but his teenage assistant Mike Doyle knew and kept trying unsuccessfully to persuade Bart to stop. Still, Mike didn't report him to any of the adults. All of us teens maintained an informal code of silence.

Because Bart was so aggressively sexual and unromantic, I never felt attraction for him, even though he looked like the kind of slender studlee I usually yearned for. On the other hand, his gentle boy-next-door sex partner filled my fantasies for years.

After Grampa drove me to the ward this night, I entered the chapel and saw those two teenagers talking together. For some reason, I immediately turned around and walked the two miles home, vowing not to go back to Mutual. I forget the excuse I gave to my surprised grandfather for not needing

Twelve Apostles when the book was published and later became church president himself, his views shaped the conception of evolution in the minds of many Mormons for generations. Prince and Wright, *David O. McKay*.

7. Makarios III (1913–77) was a Greek Cypriot clergyman and politician who served as the Archbishop of the Church of Cyprus (1950–77) and as the first president of Cyprus (1960–77). In his three terms as president he survived four assassination attempts and a coup d'état.

him to pick me up. Although Nana often nagged me for "going inactive," she didn't force me to return to MIA.

By this time, I was fasting and praying for twenty-four to seventy-two hours every week or so, which I continued throughout my teenage years. I did this to obtain the presence of the Spirit within me for comfort and strength, and to somehow change the homosexual passions of my flesh. I felt the warmth of the Spirit frequently within me but managed only to chain the flesh—not change it.

Exuberant, seemingly uninhibited males have been the Unknown and Mysterious to me, and I've always felt awkward around sexually attractive young men. Flirting with girls was easy because I knew they found me attractive. I didn't understand why and saw nothing in myself that an attractive guy would want. So, beginning this holiday season at age thirteen, I started dating girls. The first date was going to a semi-formal LDS dance with one of my second cousins in LA Until I was sixteen, Grampa drove me on my various dates.

This commenced another phase of my grandmother's indoctrination. Nana said that I shouldn't trust girls: "They might try to seduce you into having dirty sex with them." She demonstrated this by telling me about a "good, sweet boy" she knew in Idaho who had to get married. "A girl took advantage of his weakness and had sex with him."

Nana never said the following words, but I now realize that her real message was: "I'm the only person you can trust, the only person you should be intimate with." That was behind all she told me about Dad, Grampa, my stepfather, Mom, and about all males and females. My grandmother's relationship with me was emotional incest, something I didn't consciously realize until I was middle-aged.

None of the rest of the family seemed to know about the hate-filled arguments between my grandparents or the dark side of Nana's relationship with me, but my aunts and uncles all disliked my stepfather Wayne. One Christmas, Uncle Vaude Nye and his wife, Joy (my Mom's oldest sister), took me aside and said: "If anything ever happens to Nana, we want you to know that you have a home with us." They had no children.

All the while, my secret adoration for young men's bodies competed with my open adulation for the souls of old church leaders. I didn't reach out sexually to any studlee, but dreamed of meeting an attractive young man who would persuade me to share my body with his. The longer it didn't happen, the more I was sure it never would.

As a teenager, I often told Heavenly Father that I wanted to "go home" to him because I was so lonely, so sexually frustrated and miserable. Nonetheless, when the older brother of my LDS friend David Schimmer committed suicide, I was amazed that this brother could let his own misery (whatever it was) make him forget his duty to his family. Seeing their grief decided me against suicide.

I felt that my life's only value was to serve my family and other people, to make them happy and not disappoint them. Otherwise, my life was worthless. My Mormon religion reinforced this in several ways and became the focus of my reason to live.

I didn't fear death or the Final Judgment. I knew that Heavenly Father accepted me unconditionally. It was this life that was hell.

But I would not commit suicide and bring unhappiness to my family. So I struggled against suicidal feelings as successfully as I struggled against my desire to be in the embrace of a naked young man.

12 December 1957–Fledgling *Paparazzo*

LA newspapers had an order form for tickets to attend the Beverly Hills premiere of *Peyton Place*. Although it was based on a scandalous novel, Mom let me order tickets because the movie's stars included Terry Moore and Russ Tamblyn. Mom admired them as LDS celebrities. At least, they had a Mormon background.[8]

Inside the theater, I spoke longest with the Nelson Family of TV's "Ozzie and Harriet Show." Seventeen-year-old Ricky Nelson was as cute as could be. His mother was quick to make comic remarks while we spoke, and I took a picture of the four. Older brother Dave Nelson was in the movie.

I photographed other actors as they left the theatre. This included Jack Lemmon (who had amused me as Ensign Plover in *Mister Roberts*) and the demure Audrey Hepburn (who charmed me with her role in *Roman Holiday*) while walking with her Spanish-Catalan husband, Mel Ferrer (who appeared with her in last year's *War and Peace*). Also outside, I took a photo of Lloyd Nolan, whose portrayal of a compassionate father figure had moved me deeply when I first saw Audie Murphy's *Bad Boy*.

Early 1958–Vietnam and Colonial Wars

I had undoubtedly read about Indo-China, the Viet Minh guerrillas, and the French defeat at Dien Bien Phu in my family's copy of the *Los Angeles*

---

8. Terry Moore (1929–) was nominated for the Academy Award for Best Supporting Actress for her role in the 1953 film *Come Back, Little Sheba*. Russ Tamblyn (1934–) earned an Academy Award nomination for Best Supporting Actor in *Peyton Place*. In 1961 he played Riff, the leader of the Jets gang, in *West Side Story*. In 1990 and again in 2017, he starred as Dr. Lawrence Jacoby in David Lynch's television drama *Twin Peaks*. Both Moore and Tamblyn were raised in LDS families in Los Angeles.

Examiner, and had certainly seen news reports on TV.[9] Yet they remained remote and easily forgotten.

That changed when I saw Audie Murphy's starring role in *The Quiet American*. Because of my emotional connection to him, the movie had a personal impact on my awareness of colonialism, Saigon, the ease of assassinations there, and the guerrilla war that became America's "Vietnam Conflict." From this year onward such headlines got my attention, especially after the renamed Viet Cong guerrillas were killing Americans who served there as "advisors." Newspapers headlined the deaths of two in 1959.

This increased the ambivalence I felt about colonialism and anti-colonial warriors after seeing last year's *Something of Value.* Starring Rock Hudson and Sidney Poitier, it portrayed British colonialism in Kenya and the insurgency against it by Mau Mau natives.

After watching those two movies, I had a different perception of my great-grandfather's letters of complaint to his wife in 1899–1900. Leaving his wife and children in Idaho, George P. Simpson had volunteered in the War of 1898 to free Cuba from vicious Spanish colonialism. Instead, he was sent to the Philippines, where he found himself fighting against Filipinos who wanted independence and rejected American colonialism. Thereafter, he often said that he felt like spitting whenever he heard the word "patriotism."

July 1958–Dare-Devil Photographer

During this summer's trip to Yellowstone Park with my grandparents, I showed how dangerously single-minded I could be. I wanted every one of my photos to be perfect, and took as long as necessary to get each of them "just right." One day, we were stopped with other cars while several people were photographing bears on the road. As Grampa filmed this with his little movie camera, I saw some movement in a tree within the woods and walked off the road toward it.

A bear cub was in the branches about seven feet above the ground, and I prepared to take the best photo of my trip. Suddenly, I saw a large bear charging toward me from deeper in the woods. I knew two things: the mother bear would attack me to protect her cub, and I *had* to get a photo of it. Squinting into the Brownie camera's viewfinder again, I took two flash photos from different angles before I started running.

Looking over my shoulder, I saw that the big bear had passed her cub-in-the-tree and was gaining on me. Without thinking consciously about it, I darted back to the highway.

9. The Viet Minh was a Communist front organization founded by Ho Chi Minh to resist colonial rule. The Viet Minh fought a long and bloody guerrilla war against French colonial forces in Indochina, decisively defeating them at the Battle of Dien Bien Phu in May 1954.

Midway onto the road, I turned around as the charging bear reached its paved edge. She stopped, looked right at me, then at the cars and tourists on each side of me. After a pause, it turned slowly back into the woods.

While catching my breath, I realized that if I had kept running within the woods, the bear would have mauled me. I thanked God I wasn't hurt or killed.

Summer 1958–The Good Part of Town

I couldn't have been happier when my grandparents moved us into a pink duplex apartment of two stories on North Columbus Avenue, a residential neighborhood close to the junior high and high school in Glendale's foothills. They sold their hand-built home and its entire court of apartments so that I didn't need to continue lying to attend school with my LDS friends. I was so grateful to Nana and Grampa!

Now we resided near the chapel, which was the social center for Mormon youths who lived in "good neighborhoods." As far as I knew, I was still the only one in an apartment building, but at least it was in the "good part of town."

Late August 1958–Adventures in High Sierras

Although I was inactive in the ward's scouting program, my friend David Henry persuaded me to go on a weeklong campout in the Sierras. His repeated, friendly invitations worked, and I was one of sixteen boys on this trip.

Halfway up the grueling eight-mile switchback trail, I gave up trying, dropped my heavy backpack, sat down, and refused to go any farther. Dave's best friend, cute Dennis Shanklin, joked and encouraged me, then cajoled and cursed when I wouldn't get up. Finally, out of words and patience, he quietly began taking things out of my overloaded backpack and putting them into his loosely packed one until it was heavier than mine had been. After straining to get his backpack on, Dennis turned to me with a dimpled grin, and extended his hand to pull me up: "Okay, Quinncy, put your pack on and let's make it all the way together." I loved him for that, which I wrote in a letter to him decades later.

I had difficulty sleeping during our first night on the mountain and left David slumbering in our tent while I looked at the stars. Thanks to a crystal-clear view of the midnight sky, I watched the progression of a star-like object across the background of the Milky Way. Mesmerized by its moving slower than an airplane, I was sure that this was my first and only sighting of *Sputnik 3*, Communist Russia's most recently launched earth-orbiting satellite. I yearned to share this wondrous view in the arms of my friend who had cajoled me up the trail, but I was alone.

Fall 1958–Learning of Homosexual Outpost

My stepfather told me about going to a dance club called "Finocchio's" while he was a young sailor on shore leave in San Francisco.[10] He danced with some "good-looking women," then learned that they were actually young men pretending to be women.

Explaining the term "transvestites," Wayne chuckled good-naturedly while reminiscing without ridicule nor negative judgment. He added that this bar "is a fun place to go in San Francisco, where lots of homosexuals live."

I don't recall that Wayne mentioned homosexuality to me again, but I was amazed at the contrast between this anecdote and what Mom had previously told me about "queers" in the Navy. He and I were on very good terms now and had bonded emotionally. In retrospect, I think he was trying to portray that lifestyle positively. For the first time in my young life.

Twelve years later, pop culture reminded me of my stepfather's anecdote. When the Kinks sang "Lola," I thought of Wayne at Finocchio's in his sailor uniform.

I'm sure this is why San Francisco was the location of the only heterosexual romance I ever wrote. I soon penned "Eternal Love" about the intended marriage of a young man and young woman. The earthquake of 1906 interrupted their plans, and the resulting fires trapped them in a deserted chapel, where they burned to death in each other's arms. This united them in "Eternal Love," as I melodramatically wrote at the end of this nineteen-page story.

Freudian overstatements are not needed to see in it the adolescent anxieties of a self-defined homosexual who felt obligated to marry a woman one day. In spite of being located in San Francisco, there was no male competitor for the groom's attentions, but there was also no joyful wedding or sexual consummation with his bride. In my teenage imagination, marital bliss would be in the afterlife only.

Speaking of Sigmund Freud, by age fourteen I had read a couple of his books, including *The Interpretation of Dreams*. I had also carefully examined social scientist Alfred Kinsey's *Sexual Behavior of the Human Male* in the city library.[11] I skimmed only a couple of chapters in his volume about females. Less interesting, I thought.

This Halloween of 1958, my closest friend, Clifton Jolley, and I went trick-or-treating as "the Kinsey Brothers." It was his idea, and he dressed us in white smocks and stethoscopes he got from his dentist father.

10. From 1936 until its closure in 1999, Finocchio's Club featured female impersonators, gay and straight performers, and diverse and ethnic-inspired performances, attracting many celebrity patrons and racially diverse crowds—an unusual occurrence during times of segregation. Claude Summers, *The Queer Encyclopedia of Music, Dance, and Musical Theater* (Hoboken: Cleis Press, 2012).

11. Alfred C. Kinsey (1894–1956) et al., *Sexual Behavior in the Human Male* (Philadelphia: W. B. Saunders, 1948) was a bestselling book that included a scale, later dubbed the Kinsey Scale, to describe sexual orientation as a spectrum of behavior from 0 to 6, with 0 exclusively heterosexual and 6 exclusively homosexual. The authors published *Sexual Behavior in the Human Female* in 1953.

A year younger than me (but in the same school grade due to his intelligence), Clifton was as interested in sex as I was. Regardless, it was clear to me that he was even more straight than I was secretly queer. So he was the perfect Mormon for me, as a determined celibate, to fall in love with and feel sexually frustrated about.

7 November 1958–Overly Zealous Mormons

A member of our ward, Sister Frances A. Welker, died after fourteen days of going without eating anything. She was a thirty-eight-year-old mother of four children. Her husband told the *Glendale News-Press* that two years previously they had both fasted forty days without physical difficulties. When I asked Bishop Callister about this tragedy, he dismissed them as "religious fanatics." I didn't tell him that I sometimes fasted for two-to-three days in a row. That might have led to the question: Why? Also, I didn't want him to think of me as a fanatic.

19 November 1958–Perplexing Promises

In giving me my patriarchal blessing, my stake patriarch said I was an "heir to the blessings of Abraham, Isaac, and Jacob." Also, "many of the choice spirits of the Lord were held in abeyance to come forth in this dispensation [of] great events. You, Dennis, are one of them." These are powerful things for a fourteen-year-old Mormon to hear, and tears streamed down my face.

I was comforted by how this patriarchal blessing reinforced what I already knew about myself. First, that "you have, in part, learned to love the scriptures." Second, that "burning will come into your bosom and understanding will be manifest to you."

Immediately thereafter, Patriarch Wilford G. Edling emphasized the "choices" I would face in life. That "it will be hard for you, yea, even impossible for you in your own wisdom, to know which is of the Lord and which is of the evil one." This was unsettling because it didn't fit what I had always been taught—that there is only *one* righteous path for everyone to follow. My patriarchal blessing instead indicated that what appeared good might be bad for me, and what appeared bad might be good. It wouldn't be obvious.

In view of my previous years of longing for male sexual companionship, those perplexing words were followed by disturbing comments about my "associates." It was no news that some would "fear not the Lord and respect not men." But the patriarchal blessing next referred to male "companions who know the Lord as you know Him." It specified: "Through these companionships, love of your fellowmen, and of these men particularly, will grow to a stage where it will be everlasting, for the privileges that you will experience in their company will be perpetuated into the life to come."

Just as I was trying to comprehend what those words meant, the patriarch next promised that God would give me a wife and that we would raise "children to maturity in this life." I was sure this *proved* (despite my homosexuality) that my struggle would succeed, and that (despite illnesses and accidents) I would live to be at least forty-five or fifty. This section of the written blessing really comforted me.

Nonetheless, there were disappointments. It didn't mention that I would serve a full-time mission. Also, Patriarch Edling referred only generally to "the offices that you hold in the Church," and not specifically (as I had hoped) to my one day becoming a member of its Quorum of Twelve Apostles.

March 1959–Death and Friendship

On the 13th, my friend Clifton's forty-three-year-old father died of a heart attack at their home. Clifton unsuccessfully tried to resuscitate him, and this threw the teenager into an emotional tailspin. He withdrew socially and manifested hostility toward everyone, including me.

Since his family's arrival in Glendale in February of last year, Clifton had often invited me to join his parents and five siblings for meals and movies. Now I couldn't accept his suddenly ending our friendship, especially when I wanted to give him support in his grief. Yet he wanted no one's sympathy or empathy, and for about eight months his antagonism threw me into emotional turmoil.

July 1959–Deep Sea Fishing and Old Boys Club

Dad took me deep-sea fishing once a year since I was ten. There was always at least one other boy among the twenty or so fishermen on board the boat trawler, but it was clearly a grown-up activity of male bonding.

Each man put $1 in the pot for the day's prize to the one who caught the heaviest fish. By the end of today, I had caught the biggest, heaviest fish, a sea bass. As the boat headed back to San Pedro Harbor, I could hardly wait for the usual ceremony in which the boat's captain awarded the prize to "The Best Fisherman of the Day." Amid cheers, handshakes, and backslapping.

I didn't pay much attention when a couple of men took Dad aside for a whispered conversation. I was shocked when he quietly informed me that the captain was going to give the prize to the *man* who caught the biggest fish, not to me. "But that isn't *fair*!" I protested. "You put a dollar into the pot for me this morning, and I caught the biggest fish. The prize belongs to me!" Dad shook his head: "They gave your dollar back to me, Son. You have to understand—the prize is a lot of money. It should go to a man with a family to support."

I protested that some of these fishermen didn't look old enough to have families. "But they're *men*," Dad said. I cried, said nothing more, and felt hatred for the back slappers and the man who got *my* prize. I didn't care about the money. It was the recognition I'd been robbed of.

Dad and I drove back to Glendale in silence. After parking the car in front of my grandparents' place, he told me how proud he was of me. "You were the best fisherman today, and you know it. *That's* what's important."

As I heard those words, I felt overwhelming love for my father. I leaned over and kissed him on the cheek. He seemed stunned, became silent, and looked straight ahead. "I love you, Dad," I said while getting out of his car.

August 1959–Returning to Youth Program

On the 18th, I began attending the Explorer Scouting program of Glendale West Ward. It had been nearly two years since I went inactive in MIA. Nonetheless, by this time, I had completely read the New Testament, Book of Mormon, and two of the LDS Church's other Standard Works: The Doctrine and Covenants and The Pearl of Great Price.

My same age, raven-haired Suzanne Scherer had spent a lot of time during school trying to persuade me to go back to Mutual, which now had co-ed activities for my age group. Thanks to her, the one I most enjoyed was learning various dances for the church's annual dance festivals.

During the next few years in MIA, we teenagers mastered several variations of the waltz, foxtrot, Charleston, jitterbug, swing, square dancing, cha-cha, mambo, rumba, samba, tango, as well as polka, schottische, and other folk dances. Each summer, I joined thousands of Mormon youth from Southern California in performing unison dances on the playing fields of LA's Coliseum or Pasadena's Rose Bowl, where audiences numbered in the tens of thousands. Although taught by someone in each of our wards, the dance routines had been choreographed by the church-wide general MIA leaders in Salt Lake City.[12]

In that regard, non-Mormon academics increasingly echoed Catholic sociologist Thomas F. O'Dea. Two years earlier, he wrote with a kind of awe about the military-style obedience of Mormonism's rank-and-file to a complex hierarchy of volunteer leaders.[13] General authorities were like generals over an army, a top-down organization where every subordinate LDS officer served temporarily.

---

12. The church's youth programs have gone by various names over the years. In 1959, the program was named the Mutual Improvement Association or MIA. General leaders are those at church headquarters in Salt Lake City who manage church organizations and programs worldwide.

13. Thomas O'Dea was a University of California Santa Barbara professor of sociology and religious studies who previously served on the University of Utah's faculty from 1959–64. His interest in Mormonism led to his publishing two books, *The Sociology of Mormonism* (1955) and *The Mormons* (1957). Mormon scholar Sterling M. McMurrin called the latter book, which Quinn refers to above, "the best general statement yet published on the Mormons." *Utah Historical Quarterly* 26, no. 2 (Apr. 1958): 183–85.

Those kids who participated in the summer dance festivals also sparkled on the dance floor of the more formal Gold & Green Ball held each July. It occurred in every ward, and then in the stake center's larger recreation hall.

After major dances, our group of Mormon teens met for late-night dinners at steakhouses in the Valley's Toluca Lake or on La Cienega Boulevard's "restaurant row" in Beverly Hills. On 'regular weekends, we often went to Magoo's Pizza in Hollywood. Standing on the sidewalk, we watched through its large side window as men deftly spun pizza dough in the air. Our Glendale hangout was Bob's Big Boy hamburger restaurant on Colorado Boulevard.[14]

On our own or at Saturday excursions organized by the Mutual, we went as a group to the recently opened Pacific Ocean Park. Its thrill rides and squeaky-clean grounds in Santa Monica were far better than Long Beach's grungy Pike. And, for years, we had gone with our families at least once a year to squeakier-clean Disneyland in Anaheim.

Our MIA leaders provided other very fun activities, from bowling to swimming pool parties, to beach outings to a taffy pull, to Yo-Yo tournament & volleyball, to kayak building.

One autumn, our ward's MIA rented a flatbed truck, put hay in the back, and gave us teenagers a hayride through residential streets while we sang songs spontaneously. I especially remember tall and lanky Larry Noble leading us in "You Are My Sunshine," for which he sang the tenor harmony.

Another evening was a scavenger hunt, during which my partner and I were invited into a Glendale home where some of the interior scenes of the movie *Gone With the Wind* were filmed. Those in the Atlanta house of Aunt Pittypat. Of course, I was spellbound by the current owner's private tour. She showed us autographed cast photos and a large doll of slender Scarlett wearing a dress identical to one of those in the movie. Due to this long visit, we two boys were the last to return from our scavenger hunt.

September 1959–Oddly Homophobic High School

I was an adult before I heard the word homophobia, but Hoover High School openly manifested that anxiety and discomfort. Hatred would be too strong a word to describe the reactions of its generally good-natured students. Nonetheless, I soon learned that they called you "queer," "homo," or "faggot" if you wore green on Thursdays or red on Fridays. Ironically, our school's color was purple, a more popular shade to me and other homosexuals. Moreover,

---

14. Glendale resident Bob Wian opened Bob's Pantry in Glendale in 1936 as a hamburger stand. He later renamed it Bob's Big Boy, and it eventually became a 1,000-outlet worldwide franchise. In 1967 it was purchased by the Marriott Corporation. See John A. Jakle and Keith A. Sculle, *Fast Food: Roadside Restaurants in the Automobile Age* (Baltimore: Johns Hopkins University Press, 2002).

SECRETS AND REVELATIONS, 1957–1959

those nicknames didn't stick to me or anyone else who occasionally violated this informal color ban.

A strange irony, which I learned from a school athlete, was that some of Hoover High's student officers (who were lettermen in various sports) also participated in "jack-off parties." This often occurred at a rich student's home while his parents were away. I never went. Nor disclosed their existence until writing this self-biography in old age.

I was too convinced of my own unattractiveness to ask myself why this popular studlee told me about the jack-off parties. Yet I dreamed of lying on a living room floor next to him, or another lithe athlete, as we stroked each other.

And I still recall one of the very funny, dirty jokes Bob told me for months after his invitation. As usual, I pretended not to understand the joke, but he just grinned and winked. I think this non-Mormon studlee understood me far better than I wanted to be known. He probably wasn't the only perceptive person.

September 1959–Hostile Locker Mate

Before Clifton ended our friendship last spring, I had followed through on the opportunity for my junior high's ninth-graders to select who would be their locker mate for the first year at Hoover High. He was shocked and sullen to discover this on the first day of classes. He continued to be estranged from me for a couple of months, during which he didn't say a word when we happened to be at our hall locker.

One day, his widowed mother invited me to their large house, expressing her hope that I could get Clifton to talk to someone or at least smile a little. I walked into his room while he was playing chords on a guitar, and tried to engage him in casual conversation. He looked at me with malice and walked wordlessly out of the room. I sat there gloomily for a few minutes, then went looking for him. When I found him in another room, he walked out again.

After returning to my nearby apartment home that evening, I started crying. When I told Nana the reason, she said that I should accept the fact that Clifton didn't want to be my friend anymore. "But I *love* him!" I blurted out. "Nonsense," my grandmother scoffed: "boys don't love boys."

With unwavering eye contact I said, "*I* do."

From that day forward, Nana made it clear to me that she despised Clifton. I doubt that she herself knew whether she added him to her hate list of males because of how he was treating me or because he was her new rival. Decades afterward, she sneered whenever I mentioned his name.

September 1959–Fledgling Athlete

I was an aggressive lineman in football during gym class, and my teacher Bill Heil was also a coach for Hoover High's Junior Varsity football team.

He asked me to join it. As I walked home from school, I felt both proud and fearful. This would mean spending more time in the showers and locker room with young men.

When I told my grandmother about the coach's offer, she immediately warned about the likelihood of injuries. "Besides," Nana added, "why would they want someone as clumsy and uncoordinated as you are?" I answered: "Dunno," and tried to shrug off the hurt of what she said.

The next day, I told Coach Heil that playing on the school's football team would take too much time away from my homework. It's good the offer wasn't from the track team's coach. Nana probably would have supported it, and those slender runners were the ideal type of my sex fantasies.

Fall 1959–Opposite-Sex Attraction?

At a party of LDS friends, I got an erection while slow dancing to "You Are My Destiny" with a buxom blonde girl. Known as "an easy lay," she was from another ward.

I was surprised by my reaction to her and bought the record to listen to over and over again, thinking about marriage in the abstract, but not about her or any other girl in the flesh. It didn't occur to me for decades, but I might have been subconsciously focused on the young singer, Paul Anka, instead of the girl in my arms as I heard him saying: "You Are My Destiny" while my groin throbbed.

I felt no sexual attraction toward the one girl I thought of marrying (the bishop's daughter). As a teenager, I felt nothing but a sense of obligation when I kissed my dates—and never asked for dates from the few girls I regarded as sexy, such as the buxom blonde. Instead, I usually dated brunettes I wasn't sexually attracted to. The only blonde was an LDS girl who asked me to our school's Draft Dance, when girls asked the boys.

All through high school, I routinely dated a straight-arrow LDS brunette who lived in a hilltop house with a panoramic view and a pool. Lois Losee was fun to be with, and I thoroughly enjoyed her company.

Her Dad was strong-willed, yet openly affectionate with his wife and children. Her mother Fay was independent, yet devoted to him. They were my first role models for a "normal" family. Her father Ferron C. Losee was a university professor at Cal State LA, politically liberal in California of the 1950s–60s, and became president of Dixie College in Southern Utah. He later served as mission president in Guam and Micronesia.

After years of our teenage dating, Lois told her closest friend Pam Winkelman (Clifton's steady girlfriend) that she was frustrated that I never kissed her, and of course he told me. So, from a sense of duty, I kissed Lois at the end of a date.

Decades later, I was stunned when her late-twenties son introduced himself to me. He said: "I want to shake hands with the man my mother has idolized and praised her entire marriage and my whole life." I had attended Lois's wedding in the St. George Temple, being flown there from Salt Lake City in a four-seat Cessna airplane piloted by her father.

Mid-November 1959–*Candide* and Me

Shortly after Clifton Jolley decided to be my friend again, Nana heard me laughing in my room. I had never before read such a hilarious book as Voltaire's *Candide*. In English translation from the French, of course.

After knocking on my door and listening to my explanation, Nana said sweetly: "It's good to hear you laugh again. It's been months, I think." She was right, and it was good to *feel* happy once more.

Eighteenth-century *Candide's* satire was my first experience with what literary scholars called "a *picaresque* novel." With an erratic plot, such books hop, skip, and jump through a narrative as meandering and disjointed as their likable anti-hero's stunts, adventures, travels, and strange encounters. Cervantes invented the style for his bumblingly errant Don Quixote, who thought he was a Spanish knight errant.

I eventually learned that twentieth-century novelists refined that technique into what literary scholars called "stream-of-consciousness." A meandering, self-interrupting, disjointed, back-and-forth chronology in narratives full of sentence fragments, this portrayed the thought processes of the narrative's speaker/thinker/observer/memoirist. Contrary to the whimsy, satire, and constant humor of *picaresque* novelists, modern writers have used stream-of-consciousness for serious, often somber narratives.

This became my favorite literary style. So much so that I echo it a little here, juxtaposing memories with quotes from my daily journals. Some compartments of this self-biography likewise mix past with present and future.

Accustomed to academic writing since my teenage years, however, I've simplified my self-conscious *stream-of-writing* into the disciplined path of this chronologically structured self-biography. Admittedly, its relentlessly episodic, choppy style violates most people's preference for "narrative flow." But, like pointillism in the paintings of a previous era or like Rob Silver's "photomosaics" in the twenty-first century, even the smoothest narrative is a subtle mosaic of separate events that our minds "see" as an uninterrupted flow.

Throughout most of my life, I've been neither slick nor subtle. Should my self-biography be otherwise?

Late November 1959–*Ben-Hur* and Me

Mormons with connections in the film industry arranged for a free screening of this Biblical epic for the LDS youth of Los Angeles. Tickets were distributed through our wards.

When Judah Ben-Hur (acted by Charlton Heston) had his onscreen reunion with Roman friend Messala (acted by Stephen Boyd), its intensity made me think that they were supposed to have been sexual lovers while teenagers. I took special note that Boyd Messala looked Heston up and down—from head to groin—as they conversed. Despite liking this idea as a fifteen-year-old homosexual, I just assumed at the time that I was reading too much into the scene.

Decades later, I laughed out loud when a documentary, *The Celluloid Closet*, interviewed *Ben-Hur*'s openly gay contributing scriptwriter. Gore Vidal said that Boyd had conspired with him to act the scene as if a homosexual lover. Their joke was on Heston, a right-wing homophobe, who was clueless about the scene's intentional subtext.

Now that Clifton was reconciled with most of those he had abandoned while grieving, he sat next to me during this special screening of *Ben-Hur*. With thousands of us in Hollywood's largest theatre, he cheered while watching the thrilling chariot race. I loved his enthusiasm. I loved him.

There were audible sobs throughout this young Mormon audience during the movie's Crucifixion scene. I was among the others who quietly wept for Jesus. And for myself.

26-27 December 1959–Up Cripple Creek

Our ward's winter Camp of Explorers in the nearby Angeles National Forest was memorable because of the good-natured generosity these teenagers showed me.

A week before our scheduled departure, I had one of my many accidents. This time I dislocated a knee. On crutches, with my right leg in a cast, I told these friends that I'd have to skip the trip for which I had made most of the arrangements. They didn't accept my decision and borrowed a gurney sled from the snow patrol.

Those sweet guys fastened me securely into the sled and pulled me up the snowy trail from the cars to where we camped overnight. Aside from the difficulty of their exertions in dragging me uphill, the weather was so cold, that the breakfast eggs actually froze solid by morning. Although I hobbled on crutches around our tents, everyone knew I couldn't walk down to the cars.

I felt such gratitude and love for those friends who again strapped me into the sled and pulled it down the trail from our snow camp. One of them was Dennis Shanklin, who had rendered similar assistance in the more distant High Sierras two summers ago. Another was rough-and-ready Bart, who had stopped inviting me to caress and be caressed.

Also alongside on that icy path was his sweet boyfriend, whom I could not have turned away if *he* had asked me to sleep over. Luckily—regrettably—he never did.

I often think of him gently falling asleep in the back of a pickup truck leaving this camp. As his sexually active body relaxed against me, I quietly pulled away. Loving him.

Or perhaps loving the *idea* of him next to me. Biblical Pilate asked: "What is truth?" but I asked: "What is love?"

CHAPTER FIVE

BUDDING INTELLECTUAL

1960–1961

Early January 1960–Talks by General Authorities

For the first three months of this year, all of us aged fourteen to eighteen listened each week at MIA to recorded talks by general authorities. As described by Bishop Callister in a speech at BYU later this year, Apostle Spencer W. Kimball spoke to us "on chastity and moral cleanliness and ... how important it was to keep ourselves morally clean." I took this to heart.

February 1960–Running from the Music Industry

Since age twelve, I had taken voice lessons by my mother's arrangement with the husband of one of her friends. Every week Grampa had driven me to Hollywood for the lesson, during which he patiently waited in his car, parked on Western Avenue, just below Los Feliz.

In an elegant section of Los Feliz Boulevard was the mansion of Cecil B. DeMille. He had directed the first, silent version of *Ben-Hur*, as well as the stunning production of *The Ten Commandments* that I had watched at Grauman's Chinese Theatre in 1956. In our frequent drives from Glendale to Hollywood, Mom often pointed to DeMille's house and reminded me that his daughter had married actor Anthony Quinn. I thought that made her dad's friend-in-law.

From the beginning of my lessons, the voice teacher was impressed with my vocal range and said that there was "no break between its lower and upper register." When he told me this year that he had made arrangements for me to audition with a record company, I could think of only one thing: *This would put me into close contact with sexually active homosexuals whom I might find irresistibly attractive.*

One time in the car with my grandparents after my voice lesson a year or two previous, we happened to drive by Coffee Dan's on Hollywood Boulevard, and Nana said: "Well, will you look at those sissies!"[1] I turned to see a sidewalk crowd of slender young men with bleach-blond hair. I couldn't

---

1. Coffee Dan's was a twenty-four-hour diner and a gay hangout that closed in the 1970s. *The Timely Gay Bar Guide* (Timely Books, 1971).

stop staring at these beautiful guys and the bulges in their tight Levi's, even looking through the car's back window until their image was gone. I thought that several returned my stare, grinning.

A week after my voice teacher's proposal to arrange for a recording contract, I told him that I didn't want the audition and wanted to stop our lessons. Boredom was the excuse I gave, but singing professionally could take me into the world of homosexual opportunities I wanted. And feared. That was my last lesson. I soon had a driver's license, but never headed for the Hollywood coffee shop to seek out someone irresistible.

Spring 1960–Active in Dramatics

Despite running away from the music industry for fear of its homosexuals, I paradoxically continued my extensive participation in dramatics, famous for its high proportion of "that kind." I served as vice president, then president, of my high school's acting society, Thespians.

Other students predictably called us lesbians, which some boys in our group co-opted by announcing in hallways: "Yes, I'm a Thespian-lesbian. What of it?" I wasn't that bold.

Notwithstanding all the reasons I could have been teased or bullied in school, that was never my experience. Either the other boys were extraordinarily accepting, or I had a knack for getting along with everyone from rich athletes to juvenile delinquents.

This spring, I played the romantic role of Tony in our school's production of *You Can't Take It With You*. Two years older than me, my co-star in onstage romance was an aggressively overbearing girl I could barely stand to be around.

Robert Baker, Hoover High's cute drama teacher and the play's director, wanted one of our scenes to be a make-out session on stage. I thought this was odd since he was clearly homosexual. At least, obvious to me.

It was so difficult for me to pretend to enjoy kissing this girl, that she and I had to repeatedly rehearse the scene. It became such a joke among members of the cast, that Clifton (playing Mr. DePinna) and other student actors sat on the stage in front of us, gawking in mock solemnity at our make-out rehearsals.

When I complained to Mr. Baker, he gestured with a limp wrist: "If you can't kiss her convincingly in front of the cast, you won't be able to do so in front of an audience." I think he recognized my concealed homosexuality and was doing what he could to help me pass as straight.

Mr. Baker's direction and our perseverance succeeded so well that, when she and I performed this spit swapping, touchy-feely scene on opening night, I heard gasps from the auditorium. Might have been Mom and Nana, but I thought it was girls in my high school.

I also participated in roadshow musicals sponsored every spring and autumn by the Church's MIA program. Unlike the predetermined format of dance festivals, each roadshow was the original idea, dialogue, music, and staging of its sponsoring ward.

This year, *Carnival Time in Schnitzlburg* was the creation of my former ward-teaching companion, Brent Pratley, who returned this spring from his mission in Germany. With his madcap sense of humor and inexhaustible energy as scriptwriter, choreographer, set designer, and director, our roadshow won a prize in the competition among Glendale Stake's various wards.

Aside from the occasional roughness of his language (which was mild compared with Nana's), Brent Pratley impressed me with his devotion to the gospel. I watched him struggle with tears during a summer camp of the ward's Explorer Scouts. At its outdoor Sunday devotional, several of the tough kids he had been fellowshipping expressed a testimony of God and his church for the first time in their lives. Afterward, Brent was nearly sobbing.

2 June 1960–Fledgling Biographer in American Nazi Outpost

My term paper for English was a study of Adolf Hitler. To prepare it, I had read scholarly biographies and his *Mein Kampf*, purchased in English translation from Glendale's Nazi outlet. I had learned about this Fuhrerbunker Antiques store from my regular stamp dealer, who said it was where I could fill the gaps of Germany's Nazi-era stamps in my extensive collection of international postage. The store also provided me with an ink stamp of the Eagle-and-*Swastika* emblem with which I illustrated my term paper's title page. Always a stickler for details.

I showed astonishing insensitivity for a well-informed teenager. After buying an original Iron Cross medal and new *Swastika* armband at the Nazi store, I glued a square mustache on my lip and went as Hitler to this year's Halloween party in my LDS ward. Nana and Grampa thought it was amusing, but Mom was distraught when she found out afterwards: "What if someone with Jewish ancestry saw you?!"

George Lincoln Rockwell even made Glendale the West Coast headquarters of his American Nazi Party.[2] To newspaper reporters, this new *Fuehrer* explained: "It's a white man's town. It's the best town for us." I never understood why there wasn't violence involving Glendale's Jewish synagogue, the

---

2. George Lincoln Rockwell (1918–67) founded the American Nazi Party in 1959. Beginning in 1964, a party member rented a home in Glendale for its West Coast headquarters, though Glendale city officials and the homeowner fought to evict him. The headquarters moved to El Monte, California, in 1967, the same year Rockwell was killed by a disaffected party member. Frederick James Simonelli, *American Fuehrer: George Lincoln Rockwell and the American Nazi Party* (Urbana: University of Illinois Press, 1999).

Fuhrerbunker store, or the city's Nazi Party headquarters. Rockwell was assassinated elsewhere, not in Glendale.

Before her father's murder, Bonnie Rockwell would be attending Brigham Young University at the same time I was. Although I didn't know her personally, the new *Fuehrer's* daughter told BYU's President Ernest L. Wilkinson that its students never made the connection. They thought she was related to Orrin Porter Rockwell, pioneer Utah's tough enforcer and Mormon folk hero on a frontier of us/them conflict. Their perception was a double irony. Or triple.

George Lincoln Rockwell liked BYU. It took years for me to understand this Nazi's affinity for it.

15 July 1960–Death of Bishop's Daughter

During a student bus tour of the South, my bishop's petite daughter Paula Callister developed acute hepatitis. After an emergency flight from New Orleans back to Glendale, she died in the hospital.

I had been at her side among Mormon friends at the previous New Year's Eve dance, throwing confetti at midnight. As a bitter irony in February, she asked me to the Draft Dance of her high school, and (due to my putting the wrong day on my calendar) I stood her up. It's still painful to think of her waiting for me at her house in a formal dress.

Aunt Darlene phoned and told me of Paula's death. As soon as I hung up, I asked God to comfort the Callisters in their grief but thanked Him that Paula had been spared the struggles and unhappiness of mortality. Those were my feelings at that time, but I've often been embarrassed that my teenage view of life was so dark that I felt that a girl of such goodness and purity would welcome death.

LeGrand Richards spoke at his granddaughter's funeral on the 18th. Looking down at our openly sobbing bishop on the front row, this apostle said that he didn't understand why our Heavenly Father allowed young people to die. Apostle Richards said that he himself had doubted God when his own son drowned during a family party at the beach. This was shortly before the son was to begin a mission for the church. Mortal life is filled with tragedies and losses, this apostle told us, but our Heavenly Father loves us and will help us to accept the unexplainable. One day, we will be reunited in His presence, where our understanding will be complete, our doubts resolved, and our happiness eternal.

Contrary to my usual emotionalism, I don't remember crying at Paula's funeral. But Clifton and I were hypercritical of LaMar Johnson for sobbing. I barely understand any of my reactions during this week of loss and grieving. But everyone noticed how grief seemed to drain Reed Callister's health and happiness. He was released as our bishop in nine months.

September 1960–Fledgling Existentialist and Failed Peacemaker

In high school, my junior and senior honors English classes with Mr. Lee Roloff emphasized philosophical existentialism. I merged existentialism with my intense Mormon religious experience. Life was futile, except where God intervened.

Since I knew Heavenly Father was directing my life toward specific purposes, I kept the conviction that my life and its choices were significant to God and humanity. And would be fulfilling to me. As long as I served other people, my life was not futile.

One of my LDS friends was critical of the insights I occasionally shared from this perspective. When I enthusiastically repeated Mr. Roloff's definition of God as "the ultimate expression of our best hopes and highest virtues," Brent Frost said that was "a terrible way to define God."

By modern revelation, Mormons know that our Heavenly Father has an exalted "body of flesh and bones as tangible as man's; the Son also" (D&C 130: 22). I knew this too, but still regarded my teacher's definition as beautifully expressed. For a Gentile. Or perhaps a Jew. I didn't know about his religion, although I made sure he knew what mine was.

I subsequently learned that Mr. Roloff was paraphrasing Paul Tillich. His classroom comment might even have attributed his definition to that Existentialist theologian. But in my mind, the words were my teacher's.

Some of the existentialist works I was reading were among the extra books for my non-graded tutorial with Mr. Roloff. After class, he asked me to write a several-page analysis of novels and poetry in addition to those he assigned to the entire class. His critiques of my extra work were both incisive and encouraging. For the third semester of these honors English courses, he gave me an A+ as my grade. I was thrilled.

More than any of my other teachers, Mr. Roloff introduced me to "The Life of Mind."[3] Which he always encouraged me to "embrace in a headlong rush."

Increasingly, I did.

On my own initiative, I also began reading pamphlets and books about other churches and religions. This included the Watchtower Society (Jehovah's Witnesses), Seventh Day Adventism, Christian Science, Unitarianism, Catholicism, Judaism, Buddhism, Shinto, Hinduism, Islam, and Baha'i. For some reason, my very Mormon grandparents liked watching televangelists Billy Graham and Oral Roberts, who provided my introduction to Evangelical Protestantism. Despite emphasizing non-polemical and academic publications, I always compared the diverse religions and doctrines with Mormonism, which I regarded as superior to all competitors.

---

3. Colloquially in the United States, "the life of the mind" refers to taking pleasure in cultural and intellectual stimulation.

Mr. Roloff said in class once that I was constantly trying to find a middle ground between opposing sides. I just shrugged, but it occurred to me that this was a result of being raised by my grandparents who hated each other and yet loved me. Nana often said that I was a peacemaker.

Rather than being a peacemaker in my family, I felt like a performing pet, with Nana and Dad demanding that I give each the attention she/he deserved and deny it to the other. This was especially a problem at Thanksgiving and Christmas. Nana complained every year I spent one of those holidays with Dad and his family, while Dad complained that I was with him only on alternate Christmas Eves and Thanksgivings.

On a few occasions, I stayed with Dad's family until mid-Christmas morning before going back to Nana's and Grampa's apartment. Dad complained that I remained only a couple of hours with him, but on my return, Nana said something sarcastic: "Did you have a nice time while I sat here alone on Christmas morning?" Somehow Grampa didn't exist to Nana, except to earn money, drive us around, cook for, and argue with (usually about his sexual advances, which she continued telling me about in detail until I walked out of the room).

After those few Christmas mornings that I shared with Dad and my half-sisters, Nana either continued complaining in the car or barely spoke to me after we left her apartment for the forty-five-minute drive to her daughter's house in San Bernardino County. Mom and my stepfather, Wayne, never put that kind of pressure on me, and they always spent the holidays with her parents.

Every holiday season, I argued with Nana and refused to give in to her demands that I stay away from my father. Likewise at each monthly visit with Dad. Nana often said: "You like arguing so much, you should become a lawyer." It wasn't a compliment.

Aside from such moments of conflict, I usually felt happy on Thanksgiving, Christmas Eve, Christmas Day, and regular weekends. No matter which family I chose to be with.

Fall 1960–Right-Wing Conflict

Tuesday evening erupted in controversy this fall. A member of the recently organized John Birch Society arranged to show the politically conservative film *Operation Abolition* to all the teenagers and young adults in our ward's recreation hall.[4]

---

4. The John Birch Society is a right-wing political advocacy group that has been criticized for its promotion of radical anti-communism, ultraconservatism, and conspiracy theories. Founded in 1958 by businessman Robert W. Welch Jr., the society developed an infrastructure of chapters throughout the United States, quickly growing its influence and membership.

Previous to this movie's release last July, a member of the ward (Kay Christensen) had given lectures on Communism to the MIA's special interest class every Tuesday evening in June. Whereas the surviving class rolls show that no more than sixteen adults had attended those lectures, nearly a hundred of us now watched this presentation.

Splicing together newsreel footage, the film presented the protests of mid-May 1960 in San Francisco against the House Un-American Activities Committee (HUAC). The narrator claimed this "documentary" showed that such protests were actually led by Communists and had "nothing to do with freedom of speech."

The forty-five-minute film's editing also indicated a not-so-subtle bias of its producers against Negroes. In an uninterrupted loop, it repeatedly replayed one scene of a Black woman falling on granite stairs that the cops had hosed with water to disperse demonstrators. Race ridicule was the obvious intent of this repeated scene in the Birch Society's film. I initially laughed at the accidental pratfall but didn't laugh at its repetitions.

Afterward, two devout members of the ward stood up in the audience and criticized the film's host for showing this "right-wing propaganda to our youth in a church meeting." One was Charles M. Brown Sr., a professor at the University of Southern California and son of First Presidency counselor Hugh B. Brown. The other was my Sunday school teacher, Alvin W. Barlow, who taught in Glendale High School—Hoover's crosstown rival.[5]

These two well-known liberals of our ward became livid when the young man who had introduced the film then replied that it was "a completely unbiased documentary." Upon their repeated inquiries, he admitted that he was a member of the John Birch Society, which he affirmed was for American patriots. This was an unpleasant meeting, but memorable. It foreshadowed a political conflict that would divide faithful Mormons and cause rifts among general authorities.[6]

24 November 1960—New Perceptions of Family

As was traditional on Mom's side of the family, this Thanksgiving dinner was at the elegant home of her younger sister's husband, millionaire real estate developer Lee Lucas. Unlike Dad, he was a devout Catholic, so his children Steve and Sue attended parochial schools.

---

5. Alvin W. Barlow (1918–2002) was born in Ogden, Utah, and held degrees from the University of Utah and Cal State Los Angeles.

6. Latter-day Saint apostle Ezra Taft Benson was a prominent member and supporter of the John Birch Society throughout the 1960s and '70s, often against the wishes of his fellow church leaders. Gregory A. Prince, "The Red Peril, the Candy Maker, and the Apostle: David O. McKay's Confrontation with Communism," *Dialogue: A Journal of Mormon Thought* 37, no. 2 (Summer 2004): 37–94.

Uncle Lee had married blonde, statuesque Norma when she was a singer and dancer in a professional group that was touring nationally. Now they traveled widely and spoke with sophistication.

By their teenage years, the three sisters in the Workman Family had been stereotyped. The oldest, Mary Orlena "Joy," was the smart one; Joyce, my mother, was the spiritual one; and Norma was the beautiful one. All three married non-Mormons, but only Mom continued following the LDS lifestyle, while her two sisters joined their husbands in smoking cigarettes and drinking alcohol.

Though Joy and Norma barely got along with their mother, they had Nana's sharp tongue and harsh honesty. At one point, I was playing cards with my two aunts at the kitchen table, while the rest of the family was scattered from the living room to the backyard. During our game, Joy and Norma openly referred to Mom as "scatter-brained" and lacking "common sense."

She sometimes described herself to me as being "flighty" or "of an artistic mind." Nonetheless, it would have hurt Mom deeply to hear what her sisters said today. Yet I didn't object or try to defend her. Then both of them said that they "can't stand" listening to Mom speak baby talk to my stepfather Wayne. He was six years her junior and often spoke baby talk to her. I had always regarded that as Mom's romantic departure from the hateful-to-indifferent ways Nana and Grampa spoke to each other, but Norma winced as she said, "After five years of marriage, it seems unnatural." I silently disagreed, but my aunt had suggested an uneasy perception that would be verified decades later. Mom would tell me that she eventually realized that, underlying all the romance in their marriage, Wayne was using her as a substitute mother and she was using him as a substitute son.

But it was a socio-political comment from my aunt that stunned me this holiday. John F. Kennedy's recent election as America's first Roman Catholic President was an obvious topic in the only Catholic household of Nana's family. Because he promised a liberally Democratic departure from eight years of Republican rule, the family's dinner talk shifted to questions about what effect Kennedy would have on the civil rights movement after his inauguration next January.

At this point, Aunt Norma said she had a relevant story to tell. Decades ago, one of her married friends was rich enough to hire a maid but was surprised that the family's electric bill jumped dramatically in the summer. This was years before air conditioning was available. Arriving home early one hot day, this white woman found her Black servant ironing the family's clothes in front of the open refrigerator door. I joined in the laughter. Because I was amused at the cleverness of a servant in coping with oppressive heat.

I stopped laughing when Norma ended the anecdote by saying: "And yet some people think Negroes have the intelligence to vote!" I said nothing but was shocked at hearing my aunt express such a view. For years, I had felt embarrassed that I recalled the anti-Black jokes I had heard since elementary school. Yet here was unabashed racism in my own family. And expressed by its most sophisticated member!

While pondering Aunt Norma's story, I considered other things. She hadn't attended the LDS Church for twenty years, but apparently remembered its teachings about the curse of Cain on Blacks and the second-class status of people with even brown-red-yellow skin. I had recently read John J. Stewart's faithful explanation in *Mormonism and the Negro*, so didn't question that view doctrinally. Still, it seemed wrong to apply it to civil rights.[7]

Then I thought of Mom's months-earlier comment to me about "troublemakers" when we saw a sit-in at the soda fountain of Woolworth's in Los Angeles. The city's activist Blacks (and some whites) were supporting the boycotts against segregated seating in Woolworth's stores of the South. Throughout her life, Mom claimed to have no prejudice against Blacks ("who have been some of my dearest friends at work"), yet every time she saw a news report about Black people asserting that there was civil discrimination or police brutality, she complained about *their* prejudice against whites.

Early 1961—Unintended Impact of Faith-Promoting Stories

This school year, our early morning seminary was taught by Reed Richards Callister, our bishop's oldest son, who preferred to be known as Dick. One morning, he told a story that he said demonstrated the compassion of our church's prophet, David O. McKay.

While visiting the Utah State Hospital for the mentally ill, he came across a sixteen-year-old boy in deep depression. President McKay took his hand and said to the young man: "I love you." The teenager looked up and said, "Nobody can love me as I am."

My stomach knotted as I listened to this story. I vowed I would never let any family member, any Mormon friend, or *anyone* become close enough to discover in me the homosexual reality I knew they could not love or respect.

Shortly afterward, in sacrament meeting on February 19, Dr. Edmund Crowley (representing the stake high council) told about a man who had lived a rough and sinful life as a non-Mormon, then converted to the LDS Church in old age. This high councilman said that the old man was happy to

---

7. John J. Stewart (1925–2014) was a professor of English and journalism at Utah State University for more than thirty years. With assistance from BYU and Church Educational System vice president William E. Berrett, Stewart authored "an explanation and defense of" the LDS Church's refusal to ordain Black church members to the priesthood or allow them to receive temple ordinances. John J. Stewart, *Mormonism and the Negro* (Salt Lake City: Bookcraft, 1960).

find the gospel but had "wasted" almost his whole life in self-indulgence and had lost the joy of a lifetime in service to others.

On the edge of turning seventeen, I asked myself: "Would it be better to leave the church now, so I can live as I want to live? Then when I'm too old to have those homosexual needs anymore, I can come back to the church and serve people." I decided again—as I had at age twelve—that I would do my best to serve others ·in the LDS Church. Now and for the rest of my life. I couldn't think of any other reason for me to stay alive.

19 March 1961–Faithful Dissenters

At the Glendale Stake's regular conference, its president announced the boundaries of the city's new Third Ward. I was saddened to recognize from to-day's announcement that several longtime friends and families I knew would be transferred out of our ward. Nonetheless, when the change was put to a "vote for all in favor," I raised my right arm as automatically as everyone always did.

When the conducting officer asked for "all opposed," I was stunned to see about fifty adults voting against the announced boundaries. To be sure he saw their negative votes, some even stood while raising their right arms in opposition.

More surprising was that I recognized most of these naysayers as stalwart members of the stake. They included one high councilman and also my Sunday School teacher, Alvin Barlow.

The stake presidency said that they would "confer with those who voted in the negative." The dissenters didn't suffer for their publicly expressed opposition. Brother Barlow was even chosen as a counselor to the new ward's bishop five weeks afterward. The dissenting high councilman during this public vote of common consent (see D&C 26:2) remained in that position until after I left Glendale for college.

Decades later, such dissent would seem impossible. And official tolerance of it would be a long-lost ideal.

Spring 1961–Researching Non-Traditional Mormonism

During 1960, I had read the main sources about LDS Church history in my ward's library. I started with Joseph Fielding Smith's one-volume *Essentials in Church History*, then read Brigham H. Roberts' six-volume *Comprehensive History of the Church* (1930). I finished his often-candid history last fall. Since then, I had been reading shorter works—including two by BYU religion professor Hyrum L. Andrus: *Joseph Smith and World Government* (1958) and *Joseph Smith: The Man and the Seer* (1960). Since September, my seminary class had also been studying William E. Berrett's history, *The Restored Church* (1944). He contributed a section in Stewart's *Mormonism and the Negro* that I had avidly read.

In 1961, I commenced researching non-traditional topics. First, I stumbled on a copy of *The Mormon Conflict* (1960) in Hoover High's library. I read with fascination its engaging narrative by non-LDS historian Norman Furniss about the US Army's invasion of Utah Territory in 1857. This footnoted book was published by Yale University Press. Its title had immediately triggered my defensive expectation to mock an anti-Mormon diatribe. To the contrary, I found myself in awe of the even-handedness with which Furniss approached this controversy in the Mormon experience.

Second, Pam Winkelman (Clifton Jolley's girlfriend) gave me a copy of Samuel W. Taylor's *Family Kingdom* (New York: McGraw-Hill, 1951). This family memoir emphasized his apostle-father's experience with plural marriage after the church's 1890 Manifesto supposedly ended it.[8]

Third, during a visit with my LDS friends to a nearby chapel of the Reorganized Church of Jesus Christ of Latter Day Saints this spring, I had an argument with its pastor. As members of the Church of Jesus Christ of Latter-day Saints, we had been trained to regard the Reorganized Church as an apostate sect. This pastor claimed that Brigham Young taught that the Garden of Eden's Adam is actually God the Father. I challenged the pastor's honesty and denied ("in the name of Jesus Christ!") what he said about President Young. Without rancor, he patiently countered that I could read it myself—in the first volume of something called *The Journal of Discourses*.[9] Of course, I didn't believe the man!

However, shortly afterward I noticed that set of twenty-six volumes in the library of the Jolley family's home. I looked in its index (prepared at BYU), and sure enough there was a page listed for Adam-God. So I read that sermon.

I soon concluded that Brigham Young had preached the Adam-God doctrine in August 1852 and, after reading *Family Kingdom*, that polygamous apostle John W. Taylor had been sacrificed by the church in April 1906 to

8. The full text of Church President Wilford Woodruff's "Manifesto" is found in "Official Declaration 1" of the LDS Church's Doctrine and Covenants.

9. Transcribed and published in England between 1854 and 1886, *The Journal of Discourses* is a multi-volume collection of public sermons by early leaders of the church, including Brigham Young, John Taylor, Orson Pratt, Heber C. Kimball, and George Q. Cannon. Though it is a rich source of early Latter-day Saint theology. Brigham Young said that Joseph Smith taught him the Adam-God theory, which held that the biblical Adam is "our Father and our God, and the only God with whom we have to do." Young, "Self-Government," *Journal of Discourses*, vol. 1 (London: Latter-day Saints' Book Depot, 1854), 50–51. According to this theology, Adam was a mortal on another planet whose righteousness earned him exaltation into godhood, who then as "Michael" helped form Earth. He then took another physical body and, with wife Eve, became mortal by eating the forbidden fruit in the Garden of Eden. After Young's death, the theology fell out of favor and was formally denounced in the 1890s. See David John Buerger, "The Adam-God Doctrine," *Dialogue* 15, no. 1 (Spring 1982): 14–58; and J. Chase Kirkham, "'Tempered for Glory': Brigham Young's Cosmological Theodicy," *Journal of Mormon History* 42, no. 1 (Jan. 2016): 128–65.

protect Apostle-Senator Reed Smoot (a Republican).[10] Neither was a happy conclusion for me to reach.

28 May 1961–Seminary Graduation and Future General Authorities

As the seminary president in our ward, I was one of four speakers in the Glendale Stake's newly built center. My assigned topic was preparing for my mission in life.

One of the students in my seminary class was Tad R. Callister, nearly two years younger than me. He would become a general authority in 2008 but wasn't the first to emerge from the youths I grew up with. When I was ordained a deacon, Lance Wickman was a priest in the Aaronic Priesthood of our ward. He would become our ward's first general authority in 1994.

Moreover, Tad's next older brother, Douglas L. Callister, would also become a general authority in April 2000, just weeks after he successfully coordinated the LDS Church's political campaign in California to prohibit the legalization of same-sex marriage. I would write about this and quote Doug in an article that would be published in *Dialogue: A Journal of Mormon Thought*, a liberal outlet established in 1966.[11]

Lance Wickman would also eventually become LDS headquarters' lawyer spokesman against legalizing same-sex marriage. Decades—and a cultural revolution—after 1961.

July 1961–Dinkey Creek and Anti-Feminist Sisterhood

Clifton Jolley invited me to join his family's campout with longtime friends in Northern California. Since their graduation from BYU, these families had made an annual reunion in the cabins of this small campground. Among these friends, now with teenage children, was Helen B. Andelin, who gave me a haircut this weekend.

In four years, this very gracious and sweet lady would publish *Fascinating Womanhood*. Intended as a Mormon rebuttal to Betty Friedan's feminist classic, *The Feminine Mystique*, Sister Andelin's book advised young women how to flatter, simper, sweet talk, wheedle, and white lie their way into the heart of any man so that they could become ever-beloved and ever-successful as his domestic goddess.[12] Notwithstanding my fond memories of Sister Andelin, I

---

10. For more on this historic episode, see Kathleen Flake, *The Politics of American Religious Identity: The Seating of Senator Reed Smoot, Mormon Apostle* (Chapel Hill, NC: University of North Carolina Press, 2004); and Michael Harold Paulos, ed., *The Mormon Church on Trial: Transcript of the Reed Smoot Hearings* (Salt Lake City: Signature Books, 2008).

11. Quinn, "Prelude to the National 'Defense of Marriage' Campaign: Civil Discrimination Against Feared or Despised Minorities," *Dialogue: A Journal of Mormon Thought* 33, no. 3 (Fall 2007), 1–52.

12. Friedan's *The Feminine Mystique* (New York: W. W. Norton, 1963) challenged the then-widely held belief that fulfillment as a woman only comes through being a housewife and mother.

would laugh out loud upon reading her book's recommendations during my college years. None of the women in my extended family would be caught dead behaving that way, except perhaps great-grandmother Susan Barben Workman. No girl, nor young woman, nor older woman should ever do so. Anywhere, anytime, with any male of any age or any position.

If that was the price of a happy marriage (which few of the women in my family ever experienced for very long), too bad. Such a life of deception and self-negation was too great a price for women to pay. Even as a teenager, I didn't enjoy being around simpering wives, nor did I feel comfortable with harridans like Nana. I liked women who were as kind, as gracious, as honest, as genuine, and as independent as I expected men to be. Those were qualities I wanted in a wife. Or boyfriend.

Nonetheless, as a celibate homosexual, I always recognized the contradiction and irony of concealing my orientation so that I could become a domestic god for an LDS wife. Who was *I* to mock Helen Andelin's advice?

8 August 1961–Doubting the Devil

From my writings this day at seventeen: "I was reading in the *History of the Church* about the first miracle of the Latter-day Church, when an evil spirit which had possessed Newel Knight was cast out by Joseph Smith. Although I accepted evil spirits being cast out in biblical times, for some reason I doubted this miracle.

"After reading this account, I immediately went to my room to pray for a testimony of this miracle. I had been engaged in a period of fasting and prayer, to cleanse my sins and come closer to the Lord, for the past forty hours.

"As I knelt down to pray, I realized that the Spirit of the Lord was no longer upon me as it had been. I began to ask the Lord that His Spirit might be upon me before I asked for this testimony of the miracle.

"However, my words seemed to no avail. The Spirit of the Lord had withdrawn from me and I felt farther from Him than ever before in my life.

"Soon I became aware of a strange feeling filling my body; I had never experienced anything like it before. I had never felt so oppressed. I began to beg the Lord to free me from it, but it still persisted. I was experiencing mental and emotional anguish.

"I seemed to be losing control of my body—I swayed back and forth, was extremely restless, and my arms and legs felt so tense and strange that I could

---

The bestselling book is credited with sparking second-wave feminism in the United States. Andelin derived her bestselling *Fascinating Womanhood* (New York: Random House, 1963) from a set of booklets published by the Psychological Press in the 1920s and 30s. The book aims to help women make their marriages "a lifelong love affair." Feminist writers regard the book as detrimental to women in many ways.

no longer kneel and had to lay on the bed. My speech became sluggish. I had never felt so alone.

"This terrible feeling persisted for what must have been more than fifteen minutes, during which I constantly begged the Lord to be freed of this oppression. I was now convinced that some evil force was assailing me and that the Lord had forsaken me because of my sins [i.e., my homosexuality].

"Finally, I prayed that I might overcome this influence by the power of the Holy Ghost and of the Priesthood which I held as a [Latter-day Saint] Priest. I commanded the malevolent force to leave and continued to pray until it did.

"Though thrilled that through the love of the Lord and through the power and strength He had given me, I had been able to overcome this evil, I was still a little depressed because I felt myself unworthy of the Lord's influence. I felt that it was my unworthiness before God which had enabled this satanic force to come upon me.

"However, in a few minutes the realization that my original prayer had been answered came to me. My bosom burned as I realized that the Lord had given me a testimony of that 1830 miracle by allowing an evil force to come upon me, then giving me the faith to cast it out by the power of my Priesthood and His love. Immediately the influence of the Holy Ghost returned to me and my joy was complete."

I would copy the above narrative within the chronological entries of episodic memoirs I wrote at twenty-three. At that time, they served as my introduction to the daily journal I began shortly after my eighteenth birthday.

Mid-September 1961–The Jewel City

Despite the existence of a neo-Nazi Fuhrerbunker store in Glendale, I was surprised when my teacher for American government commented that our city had long been attractive to fascists. As a boy before World War II, Mr. John Gaines had watched members of the German-American Bund drilling in Nazi uniforms on Hoover High School's athletic field.[13] He told us that "those of that ilk" still lived here because they were attracted by the race code of Glendale's nickname, The Jewel City.

My hometown of 119,442 maintained its ninety-eight percent of white Anglo Saxons through homeowner's covenants (now called CCRs). These prohibited selling residential property to Blacks, Asians, and Hispanics. Apartment owners likewise cooperated by excluding the forbidden groups as renters. Many members of the excluded had menial jobs in Glendale but were on the first bus out of town after work.

---

13. The German American Bund, or the German American Federation, was a Nazi organization established in 1936 as a successor to the Friends of New Germany, another domestic Nazi organization. Its main task was to promote a favorable view of Nazi Germany in the United States.

As a white man's town, it was a racial and ethnic outpost of exclusivity. Glendale was bounded by the more ethnically diverse La Crescenta Montrose community on the north, Pasadena on the east, Burbank on the west, and Los Angeles on the south. Such housing discrimination wouldn't even begin to change until a Democratically controlled Congress outlawed it in 1968.

Glendale's racial exclusivity was evident to me as a teenager. My large LDS ward—whose southern boundary extended to the intersection of San Fernando Road and Los Feliz Boulevard in Los Angeles—had more than a thousand members, but only one Hispanic-named family.

Of the 684 seniors in my high school's graduating class, our yearbook showed that six had Hispanic surnames. Only one senior (a boy) was Asian American, and there were no Black students among us.

I think Dad tried to compensate sometimes for the lily whiteness of my Glendale associations. In our monthly visits during the summers of my pre-adolescence, he often drove me to a Los Angeles swimming pool where the bathers seemed to be equally Black, Asian, and Hispanic.

Meanwhile, shielded in the Jewel City by my Chicano father's fake name, I felt like a concealed spic. As a teenager, I read *The Diary of Anne Frank* with empathy, even though I was hiding in plain sight.

8 December 1961–Queen for a Day

Mom went on television's *Queen for a Day* series and won. The audience voted her story as the saddest one of the day's contestants who were desperately asking for the show's gifts (none of which was monetary). Hosted by Jack Bailey, this TV program was the worst kind of commercial exploitation. It let the audience gawk at unfortunate women and see the products which were donated by the show's otherwise indifferent sponsors.

Featured in local newspapers, this was one day of Mom's public humiliation during her years of private struggle with a lazy husband whose spendthrift ways forced them into bankruptcy. I didn't feel bitter toward Wayne Hood, but this was the truth of their marriage.

Due to her love for him and the romance this younger man brought into her life, Mom put up with a lot. He worked a total of about ten months during their nine years of marriage, yet always ran up debts with extravagant purchases for himself and token ones for her. She told me once that she tried to pretend her tears were from the joy of seeing those surprises, rather than from fear about their finances.

"Wayne was more of a child," Mom said, "than the newborn daughter I learned he had abandoned in Oregon a few months before he moved to California and married me."

31 December 1961—Chatting with an Apostle

LeGrand Richards came to our ward this December to visit his daughter Norinne Callister and her surviving children. New Year's Eve was on Sunday this year, so we had a youth fireside with him at our former bishop's home.

The apostle spoke to our small group of teenagers for an hour about his faith-promoting experiences as a young missionary in Holland. Also about his service as mission president there and in the Southern States.

Then he told our group to "ask any questions you want." A risky invitation when I was around.

Waiting until there was a long pause after the other kids had made their devotional-type inquiries, I then asked Apostle Richards about Brigham Young's teaching in 1852 that Adam is "our God." My second question was about Apostle John W. Taylor's being punished for marrying plural wives after the 1890 Manifesto.

As noted in the memoir I wrote at twenty-three: "He replied that he finds it necessary to place many of the statements of Brigham Young and other early Church leaders on the shelf until the Lord reveals more." At age seventeen, that seemed like an honest and sensible approach to me.

Regarding my second question, Apostle Richards said that pride was the basic problem with those who continued to practice polygamy after the church officially abandoned it in 1890. I knew enough of my own pride that I could accept this as a reason for what he described as "spiritual error."

I deeply appreciated this apostle's patience with my teenage inquiries and valued his forthright answers. Satisfied with his explanations, I no longer felt concern about Mormon polygamy after the 1890 Manifesto or about the "one statement" about Adam-God in 1852. Both had bothered me for months.

At the conclusion of this gathering, I got the autograph of Apostle Richards in the front pages of the leather-bound Standard Works I had received at Christmas.[14] I decided to get the signature of every member of the First Presidency and Quorum of the Twelve currently living. During the upcoming year, I would make special trips on Sundays to the LA area's stake conferences, whose visiting apostle speakers were traditionally pre-announced in the weekly *Church News,* published by Salt Lake City's church-owned newspaper, the *Deseret News.*

This section of twelve to sixteen pages was mailed to Mormons throughout the world who subscribed to it for a nominal fee. This helped unite Mormonism's family of latter-day Israelites.[15] Local, statewide, regional, national, and international.

14. The "Standard Works" refers to Latter-day Saint scripture, including the Book of Mormon, the Doctrine and Covenants, and the Pearl of Great Price.

15. Influenced by British Israelism, Latter-day Saints consider themselves descendants of the

I ignored the listing of stake conferences whose speakers were lower-ranking leaders. It would take me several years, but I eventually got the autographs of all the leading general authorities.

1961-62—Priest Quorum's Group Leader, Glendale West Ward

Technically, the ward's bishop is president of the priests quorum, although a designated boy officially conducts all its meetings. While serving in this position, I began my own card indexes of Mormon-oriented topics that I could find references to in the New Testament, plus important LDS references in the Book of Mormon, Doctrine and Covenants, and Pearl of Great Price, which I began rereading. Also started the Old Testament for the first time, which took me longer because I was indexing it as I read.

A labeled photo of my bedroom's workshop showed a desk with two long files (made of cardboard) for index cards—one for 4x6 cards and one for 3x5 cards, with two small metal files. I was using thousands of cards to type quotes from the Standard Works.

On the wall above my desk was a large painting from Mexico of a slender *toreador*, my ideal type of man. My stepfather bought it in Tijuana as a surprise gift for me. Even though Mom obviously thought I had outgrown the homosexual tendencies she once observed in me, Wayne Hood knew better. At least, I think he did.

biblical patriarchs Abraham, Isaac, and Jacob, and adoptees, through baptism, into the House of Israel. Contemporary Mormons use the term "House of Israel" in referring to themselves as well as Jews. Armand L. Mauss, *All Abraham's Children: Changing Mormon Conceptions of Race and Lineage* (Urbana: University of Illinois Press, 2003).

CHAPTER SIX

INTERNAL CONFLICTS

1962–1963

28 January 1962–Witnessing a Miracle of the New Testament

From the account I wrote this evening about the dedication of Glendale's new stake center: "I had anticipated getting President McKay's signature on my leather-bound standard works the Sunday he dedicated the building. I also hoped to be able, as did the woman of Galilee when she touched the Savior's cloak, to have enough faith to shake the Prophet's hand and receive the strength I so much needed to supplant my gross weakness [my homosexuality], thus healing a grave infirmity of the soul.

"However, as the day arrived, I knew that my faith had been insufficient, and as the dedication service continued, I also realized my great unworthiness even to shake the hand of the Prophet, that so perfect man of God. I decided that I wouldn't even attempt to come near that beloved man, but my grandmother suddenly turned to me and said that I had better leave during the audience's singing of 'God Be With You 'Til We Meet Again' and get as close to the Prophet as possible, and perhaps enlist the aid of the stake authorities I knew to get him to sign the books.

"Despite my earlier feelings, I did so, and waited with many others outside the building for the Prophet to pass by. When he did, I followed him very closely to his car, being told by the Stake President that I should wait until he got there before asking him for autographs.

"As I walked along, unnoticed among the others, at his side, I was deeply moved as I saw him [McKay] eagerly shaking hands with the Youth of Zion who lined the sidewalk, in his utter defiance of his doctor's advice and the Stake authorities' caution to the people. The love that he radiated was gloriously reflected in the faces of those youth he so lovingly greeted. He shook the hands of adults, too, and their love for him was obvious without words.

"As he and his beloved wife got in the car, my still being at his side, a woman eagerly made her way through the crowd nearby saying, 'Oh! Brother McKay—Brother McKay!' When he seemed about to be getting

81

into the car, she said in a whisper next to me, 'Let me just touch his coat!', and she reached out and touched his sleeve.

"He turned with that wondrous glow on his face and spoke a few words with the woman, who in her joy had been weeping. He then began to walk around the back of the car to enter through the other door. ...

"At this point I, still being on the other side of the car, leaned down and asked his daughter-in-law, who was seated inside the car, if I could have the Prophet sign my books. She expressed hesitancy because of his extreme ill health, but voiced the question to his wife, Sister Emma Ray McKay. ... Sister McKay rolled down her window and reached out her hand for my books.

"When the Prophet entered the car, his daughter-in-law handed him the books. Despite the momentary frustration of the pen I gave him not working, he signed the books just as they were running the motor, and as soon as he gave them to me, I thanked him, reached out to shake his hand, but didn't quite make it. Then the car drove off, leaving me holding the only articles I think he autographed that day."

The above was the second entry I wrote in what would soon become my daily journal. I thought again of Matthew 9:20–22, as I saw President McKay somehow being aware of this woman's slight touch on his sleeve while he was surrounded by people in this tightly packed crowd.

In eight years, I would speak to a sacrament meeting in Munich, Germany, where I "related incidents of President McKay's life, showing that he is indeed a Prophet."

Early 1962–Warned about Sexual Suppression

One day, in Hoover High's class called "senior problems," matronly Miriam Turner gave a lecture about the psychological concepts of suppression and repression. She explained the difference between them and told us students that either of these defenses could damage a person's emotional growth. I didn't recall ever coming across those terms in the books I had read about homosexuality.

I thought: "No, no, no! Suppressing my homosexual feelings is what God wants me to do, and He wouldn't let that harm me." I silently repeated that argument, that plea.

4 March 1962–Performing Ordination

As a Priest, I conferred the Aaronic Priesthood upon my stepfather Wayne Hood, who had recently converted to the LDS Church. Then I ordained him to the office of deacon.

13 March 1962–Jesuits and the Hard Truths of Religious History

The plan for Hoover High School's honors seminar in the social sciences was for students to read aloud their research paper to the four advisers and other eight students. In addition, there would be a guest specialist for each student's topic, who would then critique the paper verbally. Then anyone could make comments and ask questions.

The topic for this school year was the Far East. I chose to research the Jesuit missions in China during the sixteenth century, especially in writings by Yale University's Kenneth S. LaTourette. I regarded the Ricci brothers as inspiring in their dedication as Jesuit missionaries. I greatly admired their brilliant strategy of using the European renaissance's humanist education as an indirect means to convert China's elites from Confucianism and Buddhism to Christianity.[1]

However, Mr. Gaines and Mrs. Shirley McDonnell told me that one of our teacher advisers was a devout Catholic who strenuously objected to my preliminary draft's introduction. Its first line was: "In the sixteenth century, the Catholic Church was in a state of decadence, and Europe was reeling from the impact of the Reformation and Counter Reformation." Miss Carroll Irwin, an English teacher, demanded that I drop that sentence or she would challenge it as anti-Catholic propaganda after I read my paper to the seminar.

As the first scheduled presenter, I refused to censor even one sentence of what I had written. Instead, I assembled quotes about the medieval church's decadent abuses. I researched them in the multi-volumed *Catholic Encyclopedia*, published decades ago as *Nihil Obstat* and *Imprimatur* by the American Catholic hierarchy. Having prepared this as a typed document titled "Corruption in the Catholic Church," I was ready for a confrontation with this teacher but told my two supportive advisers that I dreaded it.

Mr. Gaines and Mrs. McDonnell arranged for a Jesuit professor of history to be the respondent for my paper tonight. He was from Loyola University in Los Angeles. He defused the entire situation by endorsing my introduction. He said there were "all kinds abuses in the late medieval Church, which needed a reformation of some kind."

Despite her private expression of Catholic defensiveness, Miss Irwin remained silent during my Q&A period. I felt relieved that she didn't say something that required me to read my quotes from the *Catholic Encyclopedia*. This was hours of research that I was happy *not* to use—especially to defend just one phrase.

After my session ended, I declared effusive gratitude to the priest for his remarks. He replied that Catholicism was his devout faith, but that "as a historian, I must be honest about its past problems."

---

1. Matteo Ricci (1552–1610) was a prominent Italian Jesuit priest and one of the founding figures of the Jesuit China missions, opening the way for Christianity's introduction into China and East Asia.

This was five months *before* the opening session of the Second Vatican Council (Vatican II), which would officially endorse the kind of liberal openness this Jesuit professor was already expressing. On balance, he assured me, Catholic history had far more inspiring events than its embarrassments. From this evening onward, I admired Catholic intellectuals and Jesuit academics. They became my role models for open disclosure within religious history.

Mom praised my paper's introductory statement, which she regarded as a "very tame" summary of medieval Catholicism. Regardless, she didn't like my positive assessments of the Jesuits in China or in Los Angeles.

Last year, with Mom's encouragement, I did weeks of research at the Glendale Public Library about the history of the papacy. Her goal was for me to demonstrate all the dishonorable things they had done.

My 1961 report, "Notable Popes," was eight single-spaced typed pages (with endnotes) in which I named infamous and forgotten popes who had done something bad, which I itemized. Sodomy was among the items of Papal misbehavior I listed, fully aware of the irony.

"How can you praise the Jesuits?" Mom now asked, "since you *know* they sprouted from more than a thousand years of corrupt leaders who obviously had no priesthood!" I'd read enough to know that Catholics regarded their church and its ordinances as true and valid because of the purity and truth in the original conferral of authority by Jesus upon Apostle Peter.

A true Catholic Church didn't require pure popes or even good ones. But I knew better than to offer that explanation to my relentlessly anti-Catholic mother.

As usual, I just shrugged. This was a trait I regarded as uncomfortably close to Grampa's passivity.

April 1962–Fledgling Missionary

One of the LDS programs for young men was for us to accompany full-time missionaries occasionally. Usually in the evenings, I went with a young elder to visit people for proselytizing. Adhering to President McKay's repeated instructions for "every member to be a missionary," I also invited several of my non-Mormon friends at school to listen to missionary discussions in my grandparents' apartment.

From the memoir I wrote at twenty-three: "Since my non-Mormon friends who seemed the most receptive were in my Honors English class this last semester at Hoover High, I began asking several of them if they would like to learn more about the Mormon Church. Of those I asked, two fellows said that they would like to learn more.

"Bruce Parrott was a member of the Disciples of Christ; his father had been a minister in this faith for about twenty years, and Bruce himself was the Youth Coordinator of this Church for the entire Southern California area. In addition, Bruce was intending to become a minister of this faith. The other fellow who expressed interest was Dennis Rothhaar, an active Methodist, whose family had recently been chosen as the California Methodist Family of the Year.

"These two fellows were both active track and field athletes, and both were scholars in their class. Bruce later was the Valedictorian of the class, having received a 4.0 grade point average throughout high school, and Dennis' grades earned him a four-year scholarship to Stanford University. I had known each of these fellows since I entered junior high school and was hopeful of their conversion to the Gospel of Jesus Christ. ...

"Following our second meeting with the LDS missionaries, Bruce came up to me after our Honors English class. He seemed very disturbed, and he told me that he could not come to any more discussions [but] hoped this would not affect our friendship. ...

"Dennis Rothhaar accepted the discussion of the apostasy and restoration much better than Bruce, and wanted to learn more." Dennis would continue meeting with me and the missionaries but let me know privately that he was simply curious to understand my belief system.

13 May 1962–A Modern Apostle's Racism

Joseph Fielding Smith was the official visitor at conferences of the Pasadena Stake and of the East Los Angeles Stake today. I don't remember which location I attended, but his sermon was memorable.

Apostle Smith criticized church members in Southern California for using suntan lotion to darken their skin. He asked, "Why would you white-skinned children of Ephraim try to look like those whom God has cursed with a dark skin?" For the next several minutes, he quoted various scriptures which referred to dark skin as the sign of cursed people and white skin as the sign of righteous people whom God loves. I have no memory of my feelings as I listened to this sermon. As a brown-skinned LDS Chicano, did I feel empty? Dunno, but I've *never* forgotten his talk.

Afterwards, I went to the speaker's section and asked Apostle Smith to sign my Standard Works. He said he didn't have time to do so. With so many people crowded around us, we were awkwardly side-by-side for several minutes, but I didn't dare repeat my request. He just stood by me, silently waiting for a path to clear so he could leave.

A wonderful counterpoint to this apostle's talk occurred when I heard a liberal Mormon's comment while having lunch at the home of my friend Charlie Brown. His father, the professor-son of First Presidency counselor Hugh B. Brown, picked up a brown-shelled egg and said with mock solemnity: "I wonder what sin this one committed in the pre-existence to be born without a white shell." I laughed until my sides ached.

I wouldn't be laughing in seventeen months when *Look* magazine's managing editor, William B. Arthur, published what the senior apostle told him during an interview at LDS headquarters. Asked about the current restriction against Negroes receiving the priesthood, Joseph Fielding Smith replied, "'Darkies' are wonderful people, and they have their place in our Church."[2]

9 June 1962–Leaving Home

The day before I began several days of training to be a nursing orderly at the Glendale Adventist Hospital, I moved into the rec room of my uncle's house, which was within walking distance of work. I rarely stayed with my grandparents again, and never more than a few weeks.

I had always expressed my love effusively to Nana and was surprised at how easy it was for me to leave her. I was in my forties before I confronted the deeply repressed rage of my relationship with my grandmother.

I thought I was setting out on my own after high school. But I continued to live for the maternal approval of my grandmother and mother and the paternal approval of my church and father.

Homosexual fear governed my life: fear of hurting Mom (whom I regarded as a saint in the Catholic sense), fear of becoming another disgusting male to Nana, fear of being rejected by the homophobic LDS Church, and fear that I might do something to cause Dad to make me into a non-person as he had done with his Mexican parents and brothers.

13 June 1962–Mormons at Drunken Party

With 684 celebrating seniors and their dates, Hoover High's graduating class filled a banquet room at the elegant Biltmore Hotel in downtown Los Angeles. Our group of about twenty Mormons sat at adjacent tables, sipping water and soft drinks, while hundreds of our fellow graduates got increasingly drunk and boisterous during the meal, dance, and entertainment. Partway through this event, six couples came up to my table and asked: "Can some non-Mormon teetotalers join you?"

Dennis Rothhaar was the one who spoke. After this group gathered around us, he and his date chatted with me. I soon felt sorry that I had not even tried to socialize with him and the other non-LDS students who shared my ethical values and secular interests.

Tonight was my first awareness that Mormons are unnecessarily clannish.

---

2. See "Memo from a Mormon: In which a troubled young man raises the question of his Church's attitude toward Negroes," *Look Magazine*, Oct. 1963, 51–54.

Yet I would spend the rest of my life socializing almost exclusively with members of the LDS Church.

Probably the most clannish one of our Mormon group, I wouldn't attend a single one of my high school's reunions. By the time I regretted this virtual boycott, I would be too embarrassed to show up decades later to see those I still recalled fondly.

14 June 1962–Fledgling Nurse

From my newly begun journal of daily entries: "Today my first patient was an accident victim in the surgical unit. His shoulder was fractured, his hands were bandaged, and he had a urine tube—all of which made a bed bath and bed change unbearably hard for me. I was almost two hours doing it! He was very patient with me and complained only occasionally when I'd accidentally nudge his shoulder or hands."

After being observed by nurses during today's eight-hour shift at the Glendale Adventist Hospital while I tended to only this patient, I was assigned four to six patients each shift to care for on my own. Seemingly allowed to do much of what a registered nurse does, except administer medicine and assist in dangerous procedures, my months as a nursing orderly were eye opening.

Two of my patients had post-operative dementia. The first was a Protestant minister who, after abdominal surgery, saw bugs and soldiers marching in formation on the ceiling while he swore like a sailor. The other had a brain tumor, and his post-surgical hallucinations anguished his wife and terrified his young son whenever they visited. After a few days, both men resumed pre-surgery normality.

My emotions were in control at work, but sometimes I shed tears in my room when I couldn't stop thinking about certain patients or scenes of suffering. Nonetheless I still wanted to become a physician. Although some young men were my patients, I honestly felt no sexual attraction for them.

15 June 1962–Conditional Prophets

From my daily journal: "Tonight, on the phone, Lois Losee asked me if I believed *all* the things that the prophet and other Church leaders say. I told her that I sometimes disagreed with what I considered opinions of the authorities, but—although I didn't say it to her—when they are speaking or writing as prophets of the Lord to the members of the Church, I feel that their words should be heeded."

17 June 1962–Filial Payback?

From my journal: "Today was Father's Day, and Wayne, my stepfather was ordained a Teacher. We're all so proud and thrilled at his progress. Because of having guests over, I didn't get over to Dad's until 10:45 p.m. Despite my calling in the afternoon, he was hurt and irritated at my coming so late.

"I wonder if he remembers the times when he wouldn't see or call me for months. Oh, well. All that is in the past, and I've grown to love Dad quite a lot. Hope it'll all work out well."

Rereading this for the first time in my mid-60s, I felt astonished to discover how casually cruel I was toward Dad at eighteen. My self-pitying narrative was that I had always been an afterthought to him. I now wonder if my outrageously delayed visit on this Father's Day was revenge for decade-earlier neglect? It would be the 1980s before I heard a term for such behavior: passive-aggression.

13 July 1962–Scriptural Achievement

From my daily journal: "I continued reading the Old Testament. Within a week or so, I can say that I have fully read all the Standard Works of the Gospel."

2 August 1962–Researching Problems in Mormon Scripture

Despite his devout faith, my friend Charlie Brown showed me ex-LDS Arthur Budvarson's recent booklet against the Book of Mormon.[3] It empha-sized that there were thousands of changes in its text since 1830.

From today's journal: "After cashing and depositing all of my paycheck but my ten dollar allowance, I went to the Seventies Book Store and pur-chased a book by devout LDS researcher Wilford C. Wood which contains an exact reproduction of the 1830 edition of the Book of Mormon.[4] I will not accept any criticism of the Church on face value, but, instead search and study (and if need be, pray) to find the truth."

I was preparing to check Budvarson's allegations myself. My line-by-line comparison painstakingly verified that there actually had been thousands of changes since 1830. All but sixteen seemed of minor importance to me, and even those merely clarified some doctrinal statements.

I emphatically rejected this anti-Mormon's conclusions about such revi-sions in a sacred text. Therefore, I wrote to Joseph Fielding Smith, who was

3. See Arthur Budvarson, *The Book of Mormon: True, or False?* (Grand Rapids: Zondervan Publishing House, 1961). Budvarson (1909–91) and his wife, Edna (1911–96), co-founded the Utah Christian Tract Society, which later merged with the Mormonism Research Ministry, founded in 1979. The organization's purpose is to "evaluate the differences between Mormonism and biblical Christianity."

4. See Wilford C. Wood, *Joseph Smith Begins His Work: Book of Mormon 1830 First Edition Reproduced from Uncut Sheets* (Provo: Publisher's Press, 1958). Wood (1893–1968), was a busi-nessman who, primarily in the 1930s and 40s, acquired many artifacts and historic sites of the Restorationist movement, including the Nauvoo Temple site, Liberty Jail, Adam-ondi-Ahman, Newel K. Whitney Store, John Johnson Farm, and the Hale property in Harmony, Pennsylvania.

the official Church Historian, about these textual alterations. And got back a cantankerous reply that questioned my testimony.

Uncle Frank asked about Smith's letter, which he had noticed in the day's mail at his house. When I described it, he said that Apostle Smith didn't care who he hurt with his dogmatic attitudes.

I was stunned by this remark from my devout Mormon uncle, who was then a counselor in the bishopric of the Glendale East Ward. He had recently been very defensive of the Church when he noticed me reading Irving Wallace's *Twenty-Seventh Wife*, a book I thought was trashy for the most part.[5]

Uncle Frank explained why he had negative feelings about Elder Smith. There was no temple in California when he and Aunt Darlene married in 1948. The day after their civil ceremony, they made a two-day trip to Utah with official recommends signed by their bishop and stake president for them to be sealed in the Salt Lake Temple. Joseph Fielding Smith was the temple's president and initially refused to allow their ceremony. He sternly told them that they showed "contempt for the temple" by having "a gentile ceremony with all its pomp and circumstance" and then asking "to be sealed as an after-thought" on their honeymoon.

Following this stern lecture, he agreed to hear their tearful testimonies, humble apologies, and earnest pleas. Then Smith relented and allowed them to be sealed. Uncle Frank had never been able to forgive this apostle for putting them through such an ordeal to receive the sealing ceremony for which they had already submitted written recommends from their local LDS leaders.

I guess this is why I didn't regard Smith's letter to me as "the handwriting on the wall" of forbidden history. I just shrugged off his reaction as a personality quirk, while continuing my efforts to understand Mormon controversies so that I could help defend the church.

As a teenager, I didn't regard it as disloyal to say that there were problems in LDS scriptures. Since the late 1950s, I had read various articles about the Book of Mormon that had the word "problem" in the title as published by the church's magazine, *Improvement Era*. They were written by BYU religion professor Sidney B. Sperry, who would collect them in two years for a book titled *Problems in the Book of Mormon*.[6]

6 August 1962–Black Acquaintance

Despite more than ten years of hearing schoolyard jokes, watching TV

---

5. Irving Wallace, *The Twenty-Seventh Wife* (New York: Simon and Schuster, 1961), was a biography of Ann Eliza Young, a plural wife of Brigham Young who left him and Mormonism.

6. Sidney B. Sperry (1895–1977) was director of the Division of Religion and director of Graduate Studies in Religion at BYU.

news about Negroes, and silently objecting to my family's racism, I never had a significant encounter with a Black person until today.

From my daily journal: "Somewhat surprising myself, under the circumstances, I felt no different toward him than I did any other patient. I treated him no different—neither coolly, nor overly friendly, in that guilty, over-compensating way. To me, he was just another patient, not to be treated differently in any way." This clearly showed that I was a racist, because I regarded my Black patient as The Other. I felt a sense of wonder in chatting with him, getting to know him, recognizing his gentle kindness, and caring for his painfully human needs. Aside from the color of skin and texture of his hair, I *discovered* that he was like my neighbor, my LDS bishop, my grandfather, my father. I was racist, because *that* was a revelation to me.

I was also racist because I continued seeing African Americans as The Other, just as I knew that Anglos continued seeing Mexican Americans like me as The Other. My Black patient and I *were* different. In appearance, at least. I couldn't escape that feeling, that internalized racism.

But as soon as I perceived this Black man as an individual, I regarded his group as merely a collection of individuals. Some Negro individuals I might like, while some I might dislike. Some might like me, while others might dislike me. Some might be superior to me in certain ways, while I might be superior to some in certain respects. I wouldn't know any of those things until I was at least as well acquainted with those individuals as I was with this Black man at the Glendale Adventist Hospital.

Lacking that awareness, I could only reserve judgment and get along with everyone as best I could. In every group that was The Other to me.

My teenage journal didn't express it in those words, but that's how I felt. And how I tried to behave from this summer onward. Is it fair to call this my benign racism?

This led to my reading *Black Like Me*, a classic narrative of race identity and American racism.[7] Two weeks before I met this patient, a white LDS woman recommended it to my ward's MIA class. A wonderfully liberal Mormon!

Late August 1962–Writing about LDS Problem Areas

By this time, I had typed long summaries of my research about several problems in Mormon doctrine and history. In order of completion, their titles were (1) "Observance of the Jewish Sabbath Versus Sunday," (2) "The Bible and the Book of Mormon," (3) "Comparison of Book of Mormon

---

7. Journalist John Howard Griffin (a white man) based his book, *Black Like Me* (Boston: Houghton Mifflin, 1961), on experiences during six weeks of travel through the Jim Crow South with his skin darkened to appear black.

Names" (for which I used the King James Version of the Hebrew Bible to identify exact duplicates, close variations, and cognates), (4) "Major Changes in the Book of Mormon," and (5) "Plural Marriage in the Old Testament." This month, I stored them in a special three-ring binder to share with any Mormon I met who was disturbed about those matters.

I expected to do so only on a person-to-person basis. And only if the other person happened to mention that they had heard something disturbing about any of those matters.

Mid-September 1962–Fledgling Freshman

My high school Latin teacher was also my academic counselor, and had tried repeatedly to get me to apply for Stanford University. To no avail.

I didn't want to be a religious minority at school anymore, and applied only to BYU and the Church College of Hawaii.[8] Accepted at each, I chose the Utah campus because Lois Losee's sister Lelani (who had attended both LDS schools) said CCH was "a lot of fun" but that I would prefer the academics of BYU. Without her advice, I would have chosen Hawaii, because I didn't want to live in snow during winter.

Following our bishop's announcement of those who were starting at various colleges, I was surprised at the advice several gray-haired Mormons in the ward gave me. Their words were variations on a theme: "Don't let the church there disillusion you. Utah Mormons are strange." One regular-attending woman even said: "Remember, the *real* Church is here in California!" I didn't know what to make of that.

After a week of orientation tours and meetings with 5,100 other freshmen, I enrolled on September 22nd for the BYU courses I would take this semester. And I wrote in my journal what a thrill it was for me to be surrounded by Mormons—about 95 percent of this year's 12,400 students.

Living in Provo was a different matter. I had to suppress laughter whenever someone referred to it as a city. Even having a university filled with student transplants, its total population was two-thirds smaller than my hometown of Glendale, which I had always regarded as a town. As an incorrigible city boy who grew up in a mere bedroom community of Los Angeles, I always answered "LA" whenever someone asked where I was from.

Nestled against beautiful mountains and jagged peaks, BYU's campus was the only thing I liked about Utah's city of Provo. Whether from the metropolises of Southern California, or the Bay Area, or greater Phoenix, most of BYU's non-Utah and non-Idaho students felt the same.

---

8. The (LDS) Church College of Hawaii was founded in Laie, Oahu, in 1955. In 1974 it was renamed Brigham Young University–Hawaii.

Mid-September 1962–An All-Male Environment

As I recall, from his family's new home in San Luis Obispo, California, Clifton Jolley had suggested in a letter that we be roommates our freshman year at BYU. That invitation made me very happy.

Residing in BYU's Helaman Halls dormitories, I fell in love with nearly every guy in our ward's half of Taylor Hall—especially LA surfer David R. Francis. He had a perfectly toned body and sweet personality. Once we were alone in his room, and I struggled against the impulse to kiss him as we sat on his bed comparing the thick binders of genealogy we had each compiled. We didn't do much socially since he was a sports jock and I a bookworm. Yet I fantasized about him for decades as a beautiful, godly, unavailable lover.

Then there was David A. Eldredge Jr. from Colorado. Because he had a sharp sense of humor and was even more of a straight arrow than I was, we got along famously. I spent more time with him than with my roommate, Clifton, but felt no sexual attraction for this David.

During one of our discussions about God and the Gospel, Dave Eldredge confided to me that Denver Stake Patriarch Samuel L. Morgan had told him last April that Dave would one day become an apostle.[9] The patriarch said this after giving him the official patriarchal blessing. Turning off the tape recorder, Patriarch Morgan explained that he didn't want his secretary to hear such an apostolic promise, nor did he want anyone in Salt Lake City to read it in the transcription the patriarch sent to LDS headquarters.

Of course, I then told Dave about my own expectations of becoming an apostle. We thought we had a future of church service in common. I wonder now how common such an expectation/aspiration has been among teenage Mormon boys.

8 October 1962–Burnings of the Spirit

One of my most memorable encounters with God's Spirit occurred during a religion course I took from Professor Hyrum L. Andrus. He liked talking about deep doctrine, but I don't think this experience had anything to do with today's class. Rather than inspiring me, Andrus usually amused me by throwing pieces of chalk at students who fell asleep.

Today my common pattern of feeling the inner warmth of the Holy Ghost began slowly increasing, until it reached a level I had never before known. From my journal for today: "The sweet warmth continued growing within my heart until it reached a glorious climax during my scripture class at noon. It was as if fire burned within my bosom. The influence of the Holy Ghost was so intense I felt almost like weeping in joy or shouting praises to the Lord. I was overjoyed at this wonderful experience, since it has been literally years

---

9. David A. Eldredge Jr. did not become a church apostle or general authority.

since the Spirit has been that intense upon me." This day, I experienced a kind of oneness with the Divine that I've read about in the writings of medieval Catholic mystics who described their religious ecstasies.

Nonetheless, as an undergraduate, I admitted to myself and others at BYU that this kind of feeling state (in philosopher's jargon) could be non-metaphysical. In other words, its origins might simply be within my emotions, thought processes, brain chemistry, or other physiological processes. Likewise, since my teenage readings on existentialism, I had acknowledged that atheism was a legitimate, rational option of belief.

Whether a gift or a burden, I remained an ardent believer in the divinely external source of these burnings within—what I still call the Spirit.

15 October 1962–"12 Dances Slated for This Week"

Thus ran a headline in today's issue of BYU's newspaper, *The Daily Universe*. We students eagerly danced to the rock music of stomps sponsored on campus by the California Club and the Arizona Club. To dance the "twist," a smaller number of us carpooled from campus (where it was forbidden) to the Blue Terrace ballroom in Provo or to the Steelworkers Union Hall in the adjacent town of Orem.

Throughout the years I was an undergraduate, I would often be among the hundreds of teetotalling and non-smoking BYU virgins of both sexes who gyrated in the low-ceilinged Union Hall to "a loud, wild, primitive beat." That's how President David O. McKay would eventually describe our music when he formally asked BYU students to avoid "grotesque contortions of the body such as shoulder or hip shaking."

Even though the *Universe* would publish this explicit condemnation by the living prophet on its front page in 1965, we continued dancing to rock music.[10] Drenched in sweat and glad to be Mormon.

23 October 1962–Heritage of Dissent

Besides my awareness of Dad's anticlerical background, my reading today of *The Workman Family History* revealed a pattern of religious dissent in my mother's ancestry. There were Puritan English refugees settling in the Netherlands, Protestant Huguenots fleeing Catholic France after the St. Bartholomew's Day Massacre, Dutch-English pilgrims arriving in the New World, Mormon converts abandoning Evangelical Protestant Tennessee, a woman divorcing her polygamist husband in Utah to become the wife of a Canadian Anglican (Nana's grandfather), a different polygamist wife (my ancestral aunt Mary Ann Polly Workman) abandoning John D. Lee after his

---

10. See "Executive Council Votes to Abolish 'Fad' Dances," *Daily Universe*, Oct. 5, 1965.

locally authorized participation in Utah's Mountain Meadows Massacre, and LDS converts leaving a Swiss Catholic canton to live in Utah's Mormon Zion.

12 November 1962—Dramatics with Almost No Limitations

Concerning BYU's organization for students majoring in speech and dramatic arts, the *Daily Universe* quoted its president saying that the "Mask Club presentations are opportunities for dramatic artists to express themselves and create with almost no limitations."

Imagine my surprise to learn one day about a free showing of *Lysistrata* on BYU's campus! My high school's honors English class had read this ancient Greek comedy by Aristophanes about a city of men with permanent erections, due to all its women protesting a war by refusing to have sex.

I didn't know what to expect for this performance at BYU. The theater was standing-room only, and the audience howled with laughter as young men in Levi's said every line of the dialogue about sex and priapism.[11] I had to sit with dozens of others in the aisles, because there wasn't a vacant seat left.

Mid-November 1962—Violent Radicalism and Ideological Radicalism

Someone used a time bomb to destroy the east doors and windows of the Salt Lake Temple on November 14.[12] A week later, my journal noted: "Someone last night cut the power cables on the Temple Grounds, shutting off all the electricity in the temple. Again, the culprits were not captured or even seen." This infuriated me, and I filled my journal and dorm conversations with condemnations of anti-Mormons.

This explosion didn't cause me to have suspicious thoughts about the two chemistry majors who were roommates in our dorm. While visiting them a month earlier, they confided that they made pipe bombs, which they were detonating "for fun" in Provo's Rock Canyon. When I expressed skepticism, they locked the door and showed me a canister full of black powder. With curiosity, rather than fearful concern, I asked how they acquired so much. They explained that it was legal to buy small amounts of blasting powder in rural areas, so they made purchases at dozens of country stores.

It's inconceivable to me now that I didn't worry back then about an accidental explosion that could demolish Taylor Hall. And kill many of us. Somehow, I just trusted these church-going pipe bombers to be careful.

Only weeks after the 1962 Cuban Missile Crisis (which Democratic President Kennedy defused so masterfully by tough negotiations with Soviet Russia's leaders), this was a scary time politically. One of my dorm buddies was a New Yorker who praised the John Birch Society's crusade against

---

11. An erection that continues for an abnormally long period of time after sexual arousal.

12. The blast blew a five-inch hole in the oak doors on the east side of the temple and shattered seven windows. "Police Checking for Leads in Temple Blast," *Deseret News*, Nov. 15, 1962.

domestic Communism. One night, he told me in hushed tones that he had learned something important about the church and wanted to confide in me.

After I locked the door of my dorm room, this student said that BYU religion professor Glenn L. Pearson had talked with him privately about "Communist influence" in the church. Professor Pearson told him that Hugh B. Brown was "a socialist Democrat and a traitor inside the First Presidency."

I stunned my friend by telling him that "only a crackpot would say such a thing about President Brown," and this demonstrated that Pearson "is a fanatic." I warned this fellow student that such talk could lead to apostasy and undermine the faith of others in the church itself. Pearson was one of two right-wing zealots in the College of Religious Instruction. Reid E. Bankhead was the other, and they co-authored a book or two.[13]

This incident probably led me to confront Professor Pearson in the class I was taking this semester from him on missionary preparation. At one point in a lecture, he commented that all of us had raised our right arms to the square to sustain the Standard Works of the church. My hand immediately shot up, and there was irritation in his voice as he asked for my comment. "Maybe the church is different in California," I said with a smile, "but in every stake conference I've attended there, the Standard Works were never presented for a sustaining vote. So when does this vote occur?"

He glared at me and then with a sweeping motion of his hand toward the class, my religion teacher said: "If you don't want to join the rest of us in sustaining the Standard Works, Brother Quinn, you have the free agency to follow Satan's path." I was so humiliated and angry that my ears felt like they were burning.

I waited after class to talk alone with him. "Why did you say that and embarrass me in front of the class?" I asked. Pearson replied: "Sometimes I get out of patience with your questions, which seem designed to draw attention to yourself."

I said that my questions were sincere and that I didn't appreciate being attacked for asking questions. So I again asked when the Standard Works are sustained with upraised hand. Brother Pearson said, "That occurs during the endowment ceremony in the temple." I thanked my BYU professor, without adding that a direct and honest answer was all I asked for.

The Bircher controversy just got worse. It wasn't long before dorm buddies were asking me who was right about the John Birch Society—Ezra Taft

---

13. Glenn Pearson (1918–99) taught college religion courses at BYU for twenty-six years and wrote college religion manuals for students. Reid Bankhead (1911–2003) joined the BYU faculty of religious instruction in 1948, where he taught Book of Mormon and other religion classes for more than forty years. For their works, see Glenn L. Pearson and Reid E. Bankhead, *Building Faith with the Book of Mormon* (Provo: Joseph Smith Educational Foundation, 1994); and *Teaching with the Book of Mormon* (Salt Lake City: Bookcraft, 1978).

Benson or Hugh B. Brown. Initially or eventually that question became, "Is Brother Benson following God's will about this or is Brother Brown?" My answer was that Brother Benson and Brown were each following God's will regarding anti-Communism and the John Birch Society. This year at BYU (and for a decade longer), I affirmed this in my testimonies at fast meeting and in talks at sacrament meeting.[14]

Afterward, friends asked me how it could be possible that both LDS leaders were following God's will when they openly criticized each other and took opposite positions about anti-Communism and the Birch Society? My answer: "President Brown is following God's will *for him*, and Brother Benson is following God's will *for him*." Why should that seeming contradiction bother me if it didn't bother Heavenly Father?

Still, as a liberal Democrat myself, I accepted Hugh B. Brown's point of view on nearly everything. Likewise, I disagreed with Ezra Taft Benson's right-wing views on nearly everything.

30 November 1962–BYU Protest

Already unhappy about not being able to visit with their families on Thanksgiving, students from outside the intermountain area were outraged that BYU's administrators refused to extend Christmas vacation two days longer, as at other universities. Therefore, "almost 2000 students staged a rally in the football stadium Friday at 6 p.m."

I was one of these openly rebellious Mormons at BYU.

2 December 1962–Crusading Apostates

This Sunday morning at BYU, my journal noted that "advocates of the Church of the Firstborn were passing out literature in front of our Priesthood meeting.[15] The pamphlet was on the 'Adam-God Doctrine.'" All were returned missionaries, and they infuriated me by saying that David O. McKay was not God's prophet on earth. Their pamphlet got my serious attention, however, because it quoted extensively from a master's thesis on Adam-God by a BYU professor of religion, Rodney Turner.[16]

As a result, I read Turner's quotes from Brigham Young's many sermons that discussed the Garden of Eden's Adam as "*our* FATHER *and our* GOD, *and the only God with whom* WE *have to do*" (emphasis in original

---

14. "Fast and testimony meetings" are sacrament meetings held on the first Sunday of the month. Members fast from food and water for two meals on that day and are invited to share their personal testimonies of faith during the meeting.

15. Established by members of the LeBaron family in 1955, the Church of the Firstborn is a Mormon fundamentalist religion whose doctrine includes the practice of polygamy.

16. Rodney Turner (1922–2014) was a professor of religious education at BYU from 1956 to 1988.

as published in *Journal of Discourses* 1:51). Not just in that 1852 talk, but similar, more detailed statements were in his sermons for the last twenty-five years of this prophet's life.

I verified Turner's accuracy by double-checking the original sources he quoted. This *really* confused me. As Apostle Richards advised me a year earlier, I still kept the Adam-God doctrine on the shelf.

Mid-December 1962–Discovering Special Collections

This winter, those inquiries introduced me to the reading room of BYU's special collections and its curator, Chad Flake. After I overcame his initial skepticism that I knew anything significant about Mormon history, he was usually glad to assist me.

Chad sometimes criticized my fishing-expedition approach. I couldn't help it, because everything I read in special collections interested me in learning about other topics and in reading even more sources that seemed available only there.

My research kept stumbling across references to general authorities who had been excommunicated. For example, I learned that senior apostle Thomas B. Marsh didn't apostatize in 1838 over a dispute of his wife about milk strippings (cream), as dismissively claimed by members of the Twelve and First Presidency after George A. Smith's sermon in 1856 (see *Journal of Discourses* 3:283–84; Gordon B. Hinckley, *Faith: The Essence of True Religion*, 89). Instead, Marsh and Apostle Orson Hyde left the LDS Church because its secretive, oath-bound Danites were burning public buildings and non-Mormon farmhouses during the religious civil war that raged across four counties of Missouri from August to November of 1838.

Apostle Smith's own father, presidency counselor John Smith, had been a Danite, as were First Presidency counselor Hyrum Smith, and the martyred Apostle David W. Patten, and Apostle Smith himself. Increasingly, I was discovering that LDS leaders had shades of gray intermingled with flashes of inspiration and heroism.

As a latter-day echo of my study about infamous popes, I finalized a report about "Unfaithfulness in LDS Church Authorities" that I began last summer. Now more detailed, including photos, it was similar in length to my report about a far larger number of popes. In the mid-1970s, I would look back on this typed survey as a curious antecedent to my group biography of the Mormon hierarchy.[17]

I added this study of problems in LDS leadership to the papal study that was already in my special binder about problem areas. I soon wrote two more:

---

17. Quinn is referencing his book, *The Mormon Hierarchy: Origins of Power* (Salt Lake City: Signature Books, 1994).

"Some Early Church Denials of Polygamy," and "Some Revelations Received by Joseph Smith but Not in D&C."

19 December 1962–Writing about Suppression of Minorities

For English 118, I submitted a term paper on the incarceration of Japanese Americans from 1942 to 1946. Titled "Citizens Betrayed," it received an A grade from Professor Lee Farnsworth. Ever since Dad told me about his involvement in this, I had been critical of our government for committing such an outrage on a despised minority.

Like all of the collegiate term papers I would ever submit, I typed this as a first draft in an all-nighter before handing it to the professor the next day. I proofread and made ink corrections while walking to class on the day the paper was due.

14 January 1963–Confessing to Bishop

This evening, I confessed to Bishop Blaine L. Houtz my decade of desires, years of solitary masturbation, and near encounters with homosexual acts. This kindly, blue-collar worker wept with me and was totally reassuring. My daily journal commented: "Such a load and burden has been lifted from me. I have rededicated my life to Christ and must unfalteringly strive to be worthy of serving Him."

First Week of February 1963–Last Semester's Grades

I had planned since the age of ten to become a physician, but now washed out of the pre-med program. Like all other students, I received a copy of fall semester's grades at the in-person registration inside the George Albert Smith Fieldhouse, where we enrolled in the second semester's courses. I managed to get a D+ from the pre-med program's first required class in advanced mathematics and was grateful not to fail it as I had my first semester pre-med chemistry course.

Although I flunked his midterm exam last semester, Professor J. Bevan Ott had allowed me to withdraw from his chemistry course with a passing notation on BYU's withdrawal form. This avoided the recording of a failing grade on my permanent transcript.

Despite my desperate anxiety about grades, I refused to study on Sundays. I stopped doing homework in the dorm on Saturday nights at midnight and would not resume until the stroke of midnight on Sunday nights. Adhering to the letter of Mosaic LDS law, I then studied until 2 or 3 AM on Monday.

I knew I would never make it through the years of math and chemistry required to become an MD. Thus, eight years of medical hopes were at an end. Despite having proved last summer that I could cope with people's sicknesses, dying, and deaths, I would not become a beloved physician like Luke (see Colossians 4:14).

A man in BYU's advisement center said that I had an IQ of 125: "You're not brilliant, but you're smart and you work hard." After I took the vocational aptitude test this guidance counselor recommended, he said that my scores showed I was "best suited" to be a musician.

Aside from singing, I had no musical talents, and decided that the psychological test had actually identified my "artistic temperament" (i.e., my homosexuality). I didn't go back to that advisement center again.

My adviser in the honors program was Robert K. Thomas, a Columbia-trained professor of American literature. Giving up my dreams of becoming a physician was deeply painful, and I shed tears while talking in his office about what to do after this failure.

Literature and writing had always been my academic strengths, so I majored in English. As my decade-long hobby, history would have been the obvious choice for an academic minor, but I preferred the unfamiliarity and intellectual challenge of philosophy.

Studying a romance language for my BA degree should have also been an obvious choice. I had maintained a B+ average during six semesters of Latin in high school. Spanish was the language of my paternal grandparents. I grew up watching French and Italian operas, which were the languages I sang most often in four years of private voice lessons. Yet German fascinated me, and this semester I began studying the language of my Swiss maternal great-grandmother, Susan Barben Workman. I expected to go on a German-speaking mission.

I couldn't force myself to finish even one of the correspondence courses I repeatedly paid for to re-take college algebra at my own pace in order to improve my D+. I don't know if this was a mental block or sheer inability to comprehend higher math.

Late February 1963—Sex Surveys at BYU

My ex-girlfriend Lois Losee (now just a friend) and I sat together in a sociology course titled "Social Disorganization." After a few weeks, its graduate-student instructor Richard Sturgis handed out a multiple-choice questionnaire he said was prepared by the department's senior professor Wilford Smith for distribution in BYU's sociology courses.

I lied in answering the question about having homosexual feelings and figured that the other students in this large class would likewise not report or under report attitudes and behaviors that were disapproved by the LDS Church.

To the contrary, in announcing the aggregate results to us, instructor Sturgis said that we departed from the statistical trends of all other students who took the same survey this semester or in any previous year. He then rattled off the statistics, in which a far higher percentage of our course had engaged in masturbation, heterosexual petting, sexual intercourse, and homoerotic behaviors, as well as committing felonies such as rape and grand theft auto. More startling from his point of view, our girls were more active sexually and criminally than our boys. Hardly anyone made eye contact with another student as we left class that day.

It would be thirteen years before Wilford Smith published results from his three decades of surveying LDS students. Ten percent of Mormon male students reported homoerotic activities and two percent of LDS female students reported homoerotic experiences. However, his publication in *Dialogue: A Journal of Mormon Thought* would not include any statistics from the spring 1963 semester at BYU, when my class of students went off the charts in reporting sexual behaviors. His future article would specify that the above percentages were based on questionnaires completed by students in "1950, 1961, and 1972."[18]

Mid-March 1963–*Lawrence of Arabia* and Me

On March 14th, David Lean's beautifully filmed and wonderfully acted Hollywood epic had its "Mountain West Premier" in Salt Lake City's Southeast Theatre on 21st South. I saw it as soon as I could. The movie brought together intense feelings about elements of my youthful identities, desires, hopes, and fears.

First was the language prodigy T. E. Lawrence, as portrayed by rail-thin, blue-eyed, blond, chisel-faced, good-looking, smooth-chested Peter O'Toole.[19] Twelve years my senior, he had all the physical qualities I had yearned for in males since my early childhood.

Second, portraying the Bedouin chief, was Anthony Quinn saying: "Thou Tulip," to an effeminate Arab man. This was the kind of demeaning brush-off I feared from Dad, Anthony's childhood friend. Or were they cousins?

Third were the *Bedouin* teenagers who became Lawrence's servants, friends, traveling companions, and (I thought) boy lovers. I was especially drawn to the dark-complexioned, beautifully blue-eyed youth who ultimately lay dying in the arms of O'Toole just before he delivered an anguished *coup de grace*. An exception among Arabs, this teenager's blue eyes were common among North Africa's Berbers.

18. See Wilford E. Smith, "Mormon Sex Standards on College Campuses, or Deal Us out of the Sexual Revolution!," *Dialogue: A Journal of Mormon Thought* 10, no. 2 (Autumn 1976): 76–81.

19. Thomas Edward Lawrence (1888–1935) was a British army intelligence officer who fought in Arabia during World War I. See Scott Anderson, *Lawrence in Arabia: Deceit, Imperial Folly and the Making of the Modern Middle East* (New York: Doubleday, 2013).

Decades later, I would learn that the Berbers of Siwa in Western Egypt were famous for performing male-male marriages. "The feast of a man marrying a boy was celebrated with great pomp," wrote George Steindorff in 1904. This was just seven years before T. E. Lawrence arrived in Egypt, where he fell in love with Arab customs and with Arabs. In 1936, the year after T. E. died, anthropologist Walter Cline wrote this summary of his field work in the area: "All normal Siwan men and boys practice sodomy." Understated irony.[20]

The movie's fourth impact was Puerto Rican actor Jose Ferrer as an officious, homosexual Turk reviewing the young men that his military minions had rounded up. He was selecting one to be his sex partner for the night. At first I was titillated by the selection process in which Ferrer, as the officer, leered at and touched his potential conquests. One young man, like me, was obviously willing to be seduced.

In this crucial scene, Lawrence himself seemed initially agreeable, especially when the Turkish officer asked if he was "a Berber." Then T. E. switched to what has been called homosexual panic and struck his seducer. This resulted in the kind of male rape I had thought I was fighting off at age 11.

Fifth was my profound sadness in seeing Lawrence's emotional, spiritual, mental, and ethical decline after his rape. And yet I felt the Holy Ghost within me during my experience of watching this movie.

Shortly afterward, I noticed Lawrence's multi-volumed *Seven Pillars of Wisdom* on a bookshelf in the reading room of BYU's Honors Program.

I was stunned to find a homosexual subtext (including a shared orgasm of face-to-face male intercourse) as expressed in the book's dedication to Lawrence's servant friend. In a *double entendre* about S. A. that linked Saudi Arabia with his Arab boy, Lawrence wrote:

I loved you, so I drew these tides of men into my hands
And wrote my will across the sky in stars
To earn you Freedom, the seven-pillared worthy house,
That your eyes might be shining for me.
When we came.
***
Love, the way-weary, groped to your body, our brief wage
Ours for the moment. ...

This was the experience of male-male love I continued to abandon on my Mormon path. I could not read one more page of Lawrence's volumes. Ever.

---

20. See George Steindorff, *Through the Libyan Desert to the Oasis of Amon* (Leipsig: Velohgen and Klasing, 1904); and Walter Cline, *Notes on the People of Siwah and El Garah in the Libyan Desert* (Menasha, WI: George Banta Publishing, 1936).

25 March 1963–Words of Inspiration

Despite sharing my expectations of apostleship with dorm buddy Dave Eldredge, I struggled more than ever with what seemed to be the conflict between my spirituality and my homosexuality. My patriarchal blessing suggested that there might be compatibility between them, but I couldn't understand how that was possible. All I felt was contradiction. Wondered if I had forfeited my Godly potentials because of even having this kind of struggle, rather than being the pure kind of person I wanted to be.

From my journal for today: "This afternoon, the Lord made known unto me through the prompting of the Spirit that I should receive another blessing from a patriarch. I have wondered about this for quite a while, but I thought that it was wrong for me to desire such a thing. I have been praying about it quite a lot recently, and today the Lord answered my prayers with a great outpouring of His Spirit upon me. The words of the Lord came into my mind saying: 'Thy desires to have another blessing are righteous.' It was a wondrous experience, and the Spirit has continued with me throughout the day."

This was the first time I seemed to hear distinct words of revelation since my experience in the Oregon Caves at age nine. Tomorrow would be my nineteenth birthday. With ten years between hearing voices, I didn't question my sanity, but I felt reconfirmation of my faith in God as Revelator.

5 April 1963–More Anti-Mormon Terrorism

Whether the same perpetrator(s) as last November, or a less violent copy-cat, someone planted a second bomb on Temple Square in Salt Lake City. Attached to the north wall of the Old Museum, the phosphorus bomb "burned brightly but never exploded."[21]

6 May 1963–Second Patriarchal Blessing

Although receiving more than one officially recorded blessing had been very common in the nineteenth-century church, it was virtually unknown now. I received a second one by the kind intervention of Apostle Harold B. Lee, who had signed my Standard Works in Los Angeles the previous year.

West Utah Stake's patriarch J. Earl Lewis blessed me. He reaffirmed my former blessing and promised I would serve a full-time mission. He said my life's mission was "teaching thy fellowmen and bringing into their lives hope and salvation." I again felt confident about devoting the rest of my life to serving God and humanity through the church.

9 May 1963–Ribald Talent at BYU

This evening I went to BYU's Smith Fieldhouse to watch an all-freshman

---

21. The device was a coffee can filled with phosphorus and lit by a fuse. It was described as a "prank" by an explosives expert. "'Bomb' Stirs LDS Center," *Salt Lake Tribune*, Apr. 6, 1963.

talent show. One of its performances was described in two decades by an off-campus student newspaper and by two of its editors in their book, *Brigham Young University: A House of Faith*. BYU boys "dressed as women and did a can-can, reportedly concluding with participants bending over and flipping up their skirts to expose bare buttocks, framed by athletic-supporter straps, to the faculty sitting in the front rows."[22]

I howled with laughter at this display tonight.

23 May 1963–Spring Panty Raid and Riot

All winter, I heard that the boys of Helaman Halls had two rebellious traditions for the spring. First was a panty raid against Budge Hall, the adjacent dorm for girls. Second was a giant water fight in the grassy quad between the boys' dorms and the Cannon Center cafeteria. I happened to be away at a dance this night when both occurred.

The girls got tired of waiting for the boys to raid Budge Hall, so dozens ran through the male dorms of Helaman, entering unlocked rooms and rifling drawers for underwear. Armed with honey jars, some girls besmeared lots of briefs and boxers.

As for the big water fight, it turned ugly after BYU security showed up and started manhandling some of the hundreds of drenched young men. When students surrounded squad cars and commenced rocking them back-and-forth, the campus cops put in a call to Ernest L. Wilkinson. Showing up at 2:30 a.m. with a megaphone, BYU's president stood at the side of a cop car, where he was splashed by a water balloon that hit the car.

Dorm buddies involved in the fracas told me Wilkinson angrily announced through the megaphone: "Any student, who is wet and still in this area fifteen minutes from now, will be arrested and expelled!" When I returned from my date, the quad at Helaman Halls was still awash in water but deserted of students.

In its account on May 27th of this "Rumpus at Helaman," the *Daily Universe* mentioned water balloons, but didn't volunteer that one splashed Wilkinson before he gave his ultimatum. It added that the "mob-sized group of men spent several hours leading Provo Police, Fire Dept., and BYU Security on a merry rampage." This was the last reminder in my freshman year that BYU is not as straight-arrow as its PR often portrays.

Tonight's dance date was with one of three young women I was dating this semester, including a brunette from Central California and a blonde from Germany. Members of my ward, the three lived in the same dorm of

---

22. This story appeared in the *Seventh East Press* (Dec. 15, 1981) and in Gary James Bergera and Ronald Priddis, *Brigham Young University: A House of Faith* (Signature Books, 1985), 236.

Heritage Halls. I rarely kissed any of the girls I dated this school year. When we smooched, it was without my feeling sexual interest for them.

4 June 1963–Autograph of Official Church Historian

Without an appointment, I went to Joseph Fielding Smith's office on the third floor of the Church Administration Building, at 47 East South Temple Street in Salt Lake City. I asked this apostle's secretary if I could get his autograph on my Standard Works.

She said, "He's in his office and has no appointments, but he's in a terrible mood." I have no idea why she would make that kind of comment to some nineteen-year-old stranger. She consulted with him and then ushered me into his office.

I told him about getting the signatures of all current members of the First Presidency and ten of the Twelve Apostles on the blank front pages of my scriptures. Beyond those in Southern California, the rest signed after BYU's weekly devotional addresses. I didn't remind Apostle Smith of his abrupt refusal to do so at the California stake conference the previous year.

He took my Bible and looked at the autographs, first at one page and then the other. As he did so, his brow furrowed and he seemed agitated as he repeatedly turned back and forth between the two pages of signatures.

Finally, he put my Bible on his desk, thumped it with his index finger, and said: "Young man, these signatures are not in order of seniority!" I stammered an explanation that the others had signed at different times and wherever they chose on the pages.

He still wasn't pleased but added his own signature, anyway. Then I walked with my suitcase to the Greyhound terminal in downtown Salt Lake City.

It would take me three years to get Apostle Delbert L. Stapley's autograph, the only missing one before my mission.

4-5 June 1963–The Road Taken and Not Taken

As a teenager, I consoled myself frequently with Robert Frost's poem, "The Road Not Taken," and felt confident that I'd chosen the more difficult, but worthwhile, path of life's options. Yet I had second thoughts during the twenty-hour bus trip from BYU to California, where I was scheduled to be ordained an elder and enter the LDS temple.

I bought a paperback collection of O. Henry short stories at a bus stop and read his "Roads of Destiny." It plunged me into a few hours of depression at the thought that misery and futility might result whether I chose to pursue my homosexual needs or continued to follow my conformist needs.

The thought also occurred that equal happiness might result either way. Deciding God wouldn't do that to me, I continued on my Mormon path.

CHAPTER SEVEN

BASEBALL BAPTISMS AND DISBELIEF

1963–1964

6 June 1963–Factory Worker

I missed the opportunities to nurse the sick in Glendale Adventist Hospital but worked at Sunset Lamp Factory for higher wages. I needed to earn as much money as possible to pay for new clothes and other things required for full-time missionaries. At this time, missionaries also had to pay one-half of their transportation from home to their mission. The church paid the entire cost from mission assignment back to the missionary's hometown—if he or she was released honorably. If sent home dishonorably, the missionary paid the return fare.

I moved around this summer. Sometimes in the spare bedroom at the home of Uncle Frank and Darlene; sometimes in the spare bedroom of the apartment with Nana and Grampa; sometimes at the home in Glendale of my Dad, his wife Kaye, and my sisters Kathy and Patricia; sometimes on the couch in the apartment with Mom and Wayne. I was camping out with family before the first time I would be absent from them for two-and-a-half years in the foreign-language mission I expected.

8 June 1963–Pro-Jewish *and* Anti-Semitic?

From my journal, concerning: "the lamp factory where Mom works. It is owned by Jews and my boss or foreman is a Jew. I have always maintained that there should be no discrimination against the Jews and that prejudice against them is wrong. I even argued and discussed this point with some of the anti-Jew fellows in the [BYU] dorm.

"However, despite this background, the story seems to be different when I myself am now among Jews. I suddenly found myself, after only two days at work, viewing my foreman's irritating habits and personality traits and thinking to myself, 'Well, he's a Jew all right.' In doing this, I very much surprised myself. Here I was extending the irritating attributes of my Jewish foreman to all Jews in general.

"Here was prejudice—pure and simple! Although I could never see it

105

before, prejudice about the Jews is extremely easy to develop. I do hope that I may become less prejudiced and more tolerant."

14 June 1963—Temple Endowment

While at BYU, I prepared myself to receive the endowment by reading David O. McKay's unpublished talk, "The Temple Ceremony," which was available as a typed manuscript in special collections. His was a beautifully expressed summary. I had also read anti-Mormon descriptions of these rites as published from 1846 onward. Not something I would recommend to others, but the latter worked for me as preparation.

Recently ordained to the office of elder by my stepfather Wayne Hood (who had received the Melchizedek Priesthood while I was at BYU), I felt inspired and intrigued to experience the endowment ceremony today. I especially liked the mural on the walls of the LA Temple's Garden Room.

During the summer, I attended this temple on Santa Monica Boulevard weekly to be a proxy for others. For some reason, a member of the temple presidency called me aside after one session to chat, sitting side-by-side. After I answered his questions about my background, and he talked about his experiences as a temple worker, I decided to inquire about something I knew was controversial.

I asked whether the LA Temple had a Holy of Holies room, like the Salt Lake Temple. I had seen a photo of its special room in the first edition of Apostle James E. Talmage's *House of the Lord* that I had consulted in BYU's special collections.

I knew this was a sensitive matter, because that photo and the textual discussion of the room's purpose were deleted from recent editions of the book as published during David O. McKay's presidency. I thought that was strange, since the 1912 edition had been published by permission of the then-living prophet Joseph F. Smith.[1]

At first taken aback by my question, this silver-haired temple worker answered, "All temples have a *sanctum sanctorum*." He added that this room was "rarely used, except for special purposes."

The kindly old man was very flustered when I next asked if the second endowment was currently performed in the Los Angeles Temple's Holy of Holies. After an uncomfortable pause, he said that the correct term was second anointing, which was an ordinance performed only by instructions from the living prophet, David O. McKay. The temple's counselor wouldn't discuss what it involved.[2]

---

1. Joseph F. Smith (1838–1918) served the sixth church president, from 1901–18. He was a nephew of church founder Joseph Smith.

2. An extension of the endowment ceremony, the second anointing is the crowning ordinance of LDS temple rites. Joseph Smith taught that the ordinance ensured salvation and conferred

Mid-June 1963–Dating a Longtime Friend

Even though Suzanne Scherer and I dated only once or twice in high school, she was my steady girlfriend this summer. Aside from LDS dances, we went to restaurants, movies, Disneyland at night, a concert by comic pianist Victor Borge, and one by folksingers Peter, Paul, and Mary at the Hollywood Bowl. We often held hands. Sometimes, as in long lines for Disneyland's rides, I also held Suzanne affectionately in my arms as she stood in front and leaned back to me.

Perhaps to prove I was capable of it, I tried to kiss her open-mouthed late one evening. Suzanne pulled away, saying she didn't "want to kiss that way with anyone before marriage."

I was disappointed, because I felt a slightly erotic response toward her. It was the only time I had experienced that feeling in the company of any female since the night I danced with the buxom blonde four years earlier. Otherwise, I had just obligingly kissed girls on the lips—until this evening with raven-haired Suzanne.

Midway through my mission, she wrote me a "Dear John" letter. She eventually married a BYU graduate and had eleven children.

Late June 1963–Visiting Elderly Mormons

Lacking a formal position in the Glendale West Ward this summer, I volunteered for anything that Bishop Homer B. Reeder (who had replaced Reed Callister) might want me to do. He asked me to visit the Latter-day Saints who were permanent residents in nursing homes.

7 July 1963–Bishop Asks about Homosexuality

During my missionary interview with Bishop Reeder, he asked if I had ever had sexual experiences with another boy or man. I said, "I've talked about that fully with my bishop at BYU, who told me that it was not necessary to ever discuss this again."

Bishop Reeder seemed relieved not to pursue that avenue of questioning, even though he had departed from the standard question I had been asked since age 12: "Are you morally clean?" I wondered how Bart would answer our bishop's unexpectedly specific question to begin the missionary service

godhood. From the 1840s through the 1920s, the church regularly performed the ceremony for nominated couples, which continued less regularly into the 1940s. The ordinance is currently only given to a few select couples, recommended by top church leaders. Though it continues in small numbers, many modern Mormons are unaware of its existence. Gregory A. Prince, *Power from on High: The Development of Mormon Priesthood* (Salt Lake City: Signature Books, 1995); David John Buerger, "'The Fulness of the Priesthood': The Second Anointing in Latter-day Saints Theology and Practice," *Dialogue: A Journal of Mormon Thought* 16, no. 1 (Spring 1983): 10–44.

expected of LDS young men. Perhaps because of confessing his uninhibited sexuality, Bart didn't become a missionary until a year after I did.

Mid-July 1963–Listening to Jewish Convert

At one of our ward MIA's Tuesday evening meetings for young adults, I listened to the remarkable testimony of a visiting Jew who was a convert to the LDS Church. Raised Orthodox, Harry Howard had been president of the San Gabriel Valley's lodge of the *B'nai B'rith* Jewish fraternity in Pasadena. He tried to remain its president as a member of the church.

It took more than a year of his repeatedly explaining how he could remain a loyal, believing Jew as a loyal, believing Mormon. This included filing formal appeals from each Jewish leader's or council's decision against him. Finally, the highest decision-making council of *B'nai B'rith* ruled that he could not remain an officer in the local lodge.

I admired this man's faith, dedication, and patient resistance against the religious authorities whom he continued to regard with fondness four years after this saga began. It was inspiring to me.

2 August 1963–Disappointing Letter from Living Prophet

I excitedly read the letter containing my mission call from David O. McKay. But was stunned to see that he called me to the British Mission for two years.

I had been sure that I would be assigned to a German-speaking mission for two-and-a-half years (six months extra to learn the language). I thought this was virtually guaranteed due to my Swiss ancestry and my just-completed semester of German. Bishop Reeder had reported both in the recommendation form he sent to church headquarters.

At the least, I expected to be called to Mexico or other Spanish-speaking country. The recommendation form had also listed my Mexican ancestry.

But London? What a disappointment! It didn't matter to me that the British Mission was the oldest and most prestigious mission in the LDS Church.

From this day forward, the hymn "It May Not Be On the Mountain Height" had special poignancy to me. It was usually with a lump in my throat that I sang its chorus: "I'll go where you want me to go, dear Lord."

Uncle Frank and Aunt Darlene were paying all the expenses of my mission. This was not something I asked of them, but that they generously offered to do. Because of joining the Navy during World War II, Uncle Frank hadn't been a full-time missionary. He told me: "Your mission will be my mission."

8 September 1963–Farewell Testimonial

At this sacrament meeting in the Glendale West Ward, Clifton Jolley traveled from Central California to give the opening prayer. I didn't explain to

Quinn at the time of his LDS mission. *Courtesy Quinn family.*

anyone my very specific reason for requesting "It May Not Be On the Mountain Height" as the opening hymn by the congregation, nor for selecting "O Divine Redeemer" as an intermediate song by the ward's choir.

Then I noticed my former voice teacher and his wife in the audience. After the surprise of seeing these devout Catholics in our worship services, my next thoughts were of slender young men in front of Coffee Dan's on Hollywood Boulevard. I silently repeated Gounod's opening words to Jesus as Redeemer: "turn me not away, receive me, though unworthy."[3]

The meeting's speakers were Patriarch Edling, Uncle Frank Workman, former-bishop Callister, Grampa, Bishop Reeder, Mom, and me. I had invited Nana to speak, but she declined for fear that she would "sound like an uneducated fool." I even asked my non-Mormon father to speak, but he chose not to. My friend Charlie Brown gave the closing prayer.

Within a few years, LDS headquarters asked local congregations to stop devoting an entire sacrament meeting to the celebratory farewell for a

---

3. French composer Charles Gounod (1818–93) wrote "O Divine Redeemer," published in 1894.

full-time missionary. The disparity was too painful for the families of young men who were unable to serve the church in this way, due to being drafted to kill and be killed in the Vietnam War.

In my first trip on an airplane, I departed from Los Angeles International Airport for Salt Lake City late on the night of the 8th. Gripping the hand rests for my window seat as the plane taxied for take-off, I felt real fear to see the large wing moving up and down slightly. I didn't realize that this flexibility was aerodynamically necessary in its construction. A kind stewardess explained that to me, and I relaxed.

Following the stomach-clenching experience of my first rumbling take off, I gaped in wonder as this big metal bird ascended over the Pacific Ocean, then turned slowly around to pass over the bright lights of the seemingly endless megapolis I had previously seen only from cars on its streets and freeways. In its twinkling, nighttime glory, LA from the air was the most beautiful manmade thing I had ever seen. Yet it would pale by comparison a week later when I saw Greater London at night from another plane.

9-15 September 1963–Missionary Training

From my journal: "The plane arrived in Salt Lake City shortly after 2:00 a.m. I traveled to the mission home with five other missionaries who came on the [same] plane. It was after four before I finally fell asleep; then up at 6:00 a.m. for the mission home activities."

Before departing for our assigned mission field, we had a week of training in Salt Lake City. Devotional sermons alternated with practical instructions. We were repeatedly encouraged to tell the Salt Lake Mission Home's president "any problems" that we had not already confessed to a bishop. Because I had slipped back into masturbation during the summer, I dutifully and tearfully confessed this to the mission home president, Lorin L. Richards.

The odd thing was that he gave me no privacy to do this. Young men in dark suits, white shirts, and ties were lined up next to a long folding table in the mission home's entry foyer, with him at one end of it, signaling for the next confessor to sit next to him and speak *sotto voce*.[4] Like the rest of these nervous, young elders, I heard every word uttered by the confessor immediately in front of me. It was assembly-line repentance. I assumed that the lady missionaries had absolute privacy for their talks with President Richards. There were none in line to do so.

We missionaries-in-training ate meals in a special dining room of the Hotel Utah. One of the Black waiters called for our attention during a meal mid-week. Introducing himself as Monroe Fleming, he said that he was a convert to the church and that we should not feel negative about the restriction

4. *Sotto voce* is latin for a whisper or quiet voice.

against people like him receiving priesthood ordination and the temple endowment sealing.[5] He bore his testimony of God's love, of the restored gospel's truth, and of David O. McKay as Heavenly Father's prophet on earth. He expressed faith that one day he and all others would have full opportunity to receive every blessing of the priesthood, but that this must come by revelation from God. It was the week's most emotionally moving talk.

Even though I had regularly attended the LA Temple for months, the hours-long endowment session in the Salt Lake Temple on September 13 was eye-opening. First, unlike the filmed format I had experienced in Los Angeles, Utah's temples had living actors for the endowment's dramatized portions. Second was the Victorian gaudiness of the Salt Lake Temple's Celestial Room, which even had a sculpture reminiscent of Botticelli's Renaissance painting "The Birth of Venus." An equally well-informed missionary whispered to me: "Venus on the Half-Shell!" in surprise, and we both marveled at this echo of Roman paganism in the LDS temple.[6] Third was a question-and-answer meeting with apostle Joseph Fielding Smith in the huge Assembly Room on the fourth floor. He gave such a sour look at one missionary who asked a question, that I didn't dare raise my hand to inquire about the sculpture of Venus. I just concluded that it had the same significance as symbols of the Sun, Moon, Big Dipper, and North Star on the temple's exterior.

In a small room, Apostle Ezra Taft Benson set apart me and nine others for missionary service in England.[7] In blessing two of us, he said, "I set you apart as a missionary in the British Mission and any other mission to which you may be called." We two were also the only ones of these ten missionaries who eventually served in more than one mission during our two-year service. It was really faith promoting!

This was my testimony that Ezra Taft Benson was a prophetic apostle, which tempered my criticisms and mockery of his ultra-conservative politics.

---

5. Monroe H. Fleming (1896–1982) moved to Salt Lake by 1930 and began working at the Hotel Utah in 1945. He converted to the LDS Church in the 1950s and was one of the first Black men to be ordained to the LDS priesthood after church leaders lifted the restriction in 1978. "Monroe Fleming, One of First Black Mormon Priests, Dies," *New York Times*, Aug. 5, 1982.

6. Referred to as "the woman at the veil," a six-foot-tall statue above the Salt Lake Temple veil was modeled after an eighteen-inch statue that Salt Lake Temple architect Don Carlos Young bought in 1877 in Manhattan. He found young Italian boys carving Carrera marble and bought "the Angel of Peace" from one of them. The original had wings but when the larger copy was made for the temple, no wings were included. LDS sculptor Cyrus E. Dallin likely created the larger statue in the temple. Alonzo L. Gaskill and Seth G. Soha, "The Woman at the Veil: The History and Symbolic Merit of One of the Salt Lake Temple's Most Unique Symbols," in Kenneth L. Alford and Richard E. Bennett, eds., *An Eye of Faith: Essays in Honor of Richard O. Cowan* (Salt Lake City: Deseret Book, 2015), 91–111.

7. Prior to 1972, LDS general authorities blessed, or "set apart," missionaries as they began their missionary service. Beginning in October 1972, church policy changed so that missionaries were set apart locally before embarking in missionary service.

He could be divinely inspired about some things and absolutely wrong about others. Like all prophets and apostles, he was human before he was divinely called. And Elder Benson remained a fallible human thereafter.

After the Tabernacle Choir's morning broadcast on Sunday, the 15th, we departing missionaries (numbering more than 200) sat on the stand for a special meeting, while about a thousand of our families and friends were in the audience. President Richards invited us to come to the podium and "bear testimony of the gospel" briefly "as time allows."

In this week of conversations during meals and evenings with other missionaries, I learned who were the shy ones. So I kept whispering to encourage them to step forward to the microphone. When the meeting closed, I had not been among the testimony bearers.

As I happily greeted my grandparents and mother in the tabernacle before being bussed to the airport, Nana was trembling with anger: "We didn't drive nearly a thousand miles in hot weather to watch you give up your *only* opportunity to speak in the tabernacle! How could you do that to us? To *me*!" I tried to explain, but she remained angry—even more than an hour afterward, while roughly kissing me goodbye at the airport. By contrast, Mom hadn't complained and gave me a gentle hug-kiss. Grampa shook my hand warmly, tears in his eyes.

Just before I boarded the plane, Nana handed me her going away present: a man's gold ring with a flat black stone (obsidian?) and a diamond in the middle. I put it on my right ring finger.

Missionaries sat in the tail section of a prop-engine plane that stopped once on route to New York City. As we flew through a storm, it felt like the tail was rotating. All of us were nauseated, and some had to use their vomit bags. Sleeping wasn't easy.

Arriving Monday at what was then called Idlewild International, we slept for hours on the benches while waiting for our connecting flights.[8] Then ten of us boarded a jet operated by British Overseas Airways Company (BOAC). I learned why BOAC was known popularly as "Better On A Camel." Its flight was very bumpy.

Like most of the other elders, I was too excited to sleep while speeding across the Atlantic Ocean for the first time. BOAC's non-smoking section amused me—it was across the aisle from the plane's full-length smoking section! Only the first of English oddities I experienced.

17 September 1963–Missionary in England

Our flight arrived at Heathrow Airport late Monday local time, but it was the wee hours of Tuesday before the ten of us got through customs and

---

8. Three months later, Idlewild International Airport was renamed John F. Kennedy International Airport, after the president was assassinated in Dallas, Texas, on November 22, 1963.

baggage claim. Two of the British mission home's staff missionaries led us to an English Ford van which allowed twelve passengers.

While on the *left* side of every road, the driving elder weaved crazily around other cars at breakneck speeds through the maze of London's streets—both wide and narrow. Then checked us into a small bed-and-breakfast hotel.

The same two elders had to shout to wake us from our paltry hours of sleep on Tuesday morning. After washing up and dressing, we blearily had our first English breakfast of greasily fried eggs, limp bacon, fried toast, fried tomatoes, stale bread, and bitter orange marmalade. Afterwards, the two hustled us to our mission's headquarters.

It was at 50 Princess Gate, on the corner of Exhibition Road in London's posh Kensington District. This five-story mission home was the corner unit in a row of elegant, identically white mansions. Each shared a wall with its side-by-side mansions on the uninterrupted block-long building.

Each also had identical marble stairs leading from the pavement (sidewalk) to an identically columned porch. My perception of the mansion's narrow exterior belied the expanse of its interior as I entered.

In the large front parlor, we new missionaries fought against dozing from fatigue during hours of the morning's orientations. Then we were ushered into the second-floor dining room, where we met forty-one-year-old Marion D. Hanks, the general authority seventy who had been serving as the British Mission's president since January 1962.[9]

As one of the coincidences I didn't discover until doing research for this self-biography, twenty-three-year-old Hanks had blessed the sacrament in the Glendale West Ward a few months before Mom moved toddler-me there from Los Angeles. Recently released from his own mission, he was apparently visiting from his home in Utah. Small world!

As President Hanks, his wife, Maxine, and their missionary staff ate with us my first day in the opulent-looking mission home, I marveled. There were abundant portions of fish, chicken, roast beef, and perfectly prepared vegetables on silver platters, plus wooden boards with cheeses from Britain, Scandinavia, and Holland. I had never before dined in such elegance. The mission home's skillful cook was an English Mormon named Jack Tavener.

18 September 1963–Knowledge of LDS History Can Be Bothersome

After having individual get-acquainted interviews with President Hanks, we ten newly arrived elders were divided among as many different missionary

---

9. Marion Duff Hanks (1921–2011) was an influential General Authority of the church. He was an advisor to five US presidents sitting on the President's Council on Physical Fitness and Sports. He was also involved in the Sons of the Utah Pioneers, Salt Lake Cancer Society, the Boy Scouts of America and the Rotary Club. He later served as director of both the Correlation Committee and Priesthood Department, and as president of the Salt Lake Temple.

districts. As I traveled this afternoon from London in a van with the other elders of my Garden City district north of London, someone asked a common question among missionaries trained by Hanks: "How many times have you read the Book of Mormon?"

In my tally, I included the 1830 version. When asked why I had read the first edition, I explained that it was for a line-by-line comparison to see "if there were any doctrinal changes among the thousands of differences between the 1830 edition and our current printing." I cheerfully informed the other missionaries: "There were only sixteen doctrinal changes between the 1830 edition and our present one."

There was an awkward silence, and then Elder David W. Thomas said with sarcasm: "After my sixteen months as a missionary, Elder Quinn, you don't know how comforting it is to learn that the church made *only* sixteen doctrinal changes in the Book of Mormon!" After that, I avoided talking about what I had already learned concerning problem areas in the Mormon past.

I felt especially bad about this incident when I learned what Elder Thomas had experienced less than six months earlier. He watched his companion John V. Christensen die shortly after being struck by a car as they rode their bicycles in London.

19 September 1963–Tracting

Like most Mormon missionaries, my first day of tracting door-to-door was a jolting experience. Strangers considered it rude for us to knock on their doors and offer them religious pamphlets (tracts). Thus, nearly everyone was abrupt in expressing their lack of interest, often slamming the door in our faces.

On the other hand, one of my greatest shocks occurred when a friendly woman told us at the doorstep that she was "an R.W." Thinking she said "J.W.," I replied: "Well, you're the first Jehovah's Witness I've met in England." She laughed and said: "No, I'm a Registered Witch! There are more of us in England than Jehovah's Witnesses."

She explained that occult practitioners could officially register with the British government, and that she was a "white witch." My companion dragged me away before I dawdled longer in "useless conversation" with her.

Missionaries were supposed to wake up at 6:00 a.m., get dressed, study for an hour, eat, then start proselytizing at 8:00 a.m. Typically, we tracted four hours every morning and four hours every afternoon, except Sundays and Mondays. If we didn't have an appointment to teach someone in the evening, then we tracted another three or four hours in the dark before we were supposed to be in bed by 10:30 p.m.

Adding to the misery of getting a hundred or more rejections daily was tracting in the rain. That was a very common occurrence in England, which had the greenest countryside I had ever seen. We were able to get our clothes dry by standing in front of our ground-floor fireplace after lunch and supper. Then we returned to the streets for more hours of bicycling and walking in the rain.

Although often ill as a missionary, I rarely stayed inside. With my previous bouts of diagnosed bronchitis, it's amazing I avoided pneumonia.

26 September 1963–Counselor in Branch Presidency, Letchworth, Hertfordshire County, England

With too few members to be organized as a ward, the small branch here paid for using the Vasanta Hall of the town's theosophical society. I had never before heard of this organization, and was intrigued by its hall's mystical murals. Nonetheless, it would be two decades before I was sufficiently interested to read about theosophy.[10]

As counselor in the branch, I had my first experience in speaking what I regard as revelatory words to another person. Today I was in the middle of setting apart Daphne Joy Rice as the Primary president when I said, "You are accepted of the Lord." At the same instant, I felt at the center of my being the burning sensation I have always known as the Spirit of God. It was a glimpse of how patriarchs can utter pages of prophetic blessings by inspiration.

Elder Richard E. Swinyard, the branch president, was a great first companion for me. We got along fine, even after I learned that English law didn't require me (as a greenie missionary) to put an L-plate (for learning to drive) on my bicycle. It was required only for automobiles and lorries (trucks).

This was the first time I was in constant association with someone wealthy, at least by my standards. He seemed to have unlimited money to buy whatever he wanted and was a member of the University of Utah's elite fraternity, Sigma Chi.

Aside from his bicycle, Elder Swinyard had a Vespa motor scooter built for two. It was fun to putt-putt around town at the conservative speed he drove. Two of the elders in our district had a Triumph motorcycle that they let loose on diversion day each Monday.[11] I envied its speed until the front wheel locked, pitching them onto a highway and scraping them up from head to toe.

During this time, Elder Swinyard and I were staying in traditional British digs (a furnished spare bedroom, plus two or three meals daily) in a house. Its owners here were a forty-something couple who had no children. The wife was a registered nurse and a wonderful cook.

10. Russian-born Helen Blavatsky and others started the Theosophical Society in New York in 1875 to seek ancient wisdom. Today, the society's mission is to encourage "open-minded inquiry into world religions, philosophy, science, and the arts in order to understand the wisdom of the ages, respect the unity of all life, and help people explore spiritual self-transformation" (www.theosophical.org).

11. "Diversion day," later re-named "preparation day," was one day a week in which missionaries grocery shop, wash clothes, clean their living spaces, play sports, write letters home, and so forth.

My first English landlady's nights of roast lamb with Yorkshire pudding and gravy were to die for. One Sunday a month, she served English trifle for dessert. I loved its chilled layers of custard, sponge cake, fruit, and whipped cream. Yum.

Contrary to former tradition, we two elders didn't share a double bed. Nor was I aware of any young, unmarried missionaries doing so while I was in England.

Newly assigned to preside over the missions in Britain and Ireland early this year, Apostle Mark E. Petersen had required all their missionaries to sleep in separate beds, forcing digs-owners to buy new beds or lose their mission-ary renters.[12] At a March 1963 mission meeting, which several elders told me about, he announced this bed policy when he told missionaries not to see the movie *Cleopatra*. He condemned its star Elizabeth Taylor as "a wanton whore."

As another precaution against homosexual encounters at their digs, Apostle Petersen insisted that missionary companions should never be in the bathroom at the same time. To guard against masturbation, he also told missionaries to leave the bathroom door unlocked, to take quick, cold baths or showers, and not to look at themselves in the bathroom mirror until they had their temple garments back on.

I don't know how well all missionaries observed those rules, but I certainly needed a hot bath or shower in England's always chilly houses. And keeping the door unlocked didn't survive even one incident of a surprised landlady entering the bathroom or the toilet room while you were *in medias res*.

The missionaries who told me about attending that meeting also laughed about the outcome of Apostle Petersen's condemnation of the movie *Cleopatra*: "Within a month, every district of the British Mission had seen it, including the mission home's staff!" I had enjoyed watching it in LA two months before I entered the mission.

Movie-going was such an ingrained part of diversion day that the British Mission's mailed bulletins even recommended various films to see. On our full-day D-day (the first Monday of each month), some elders went to two movies in a row before the evening stage plays that every district attended in London.

President Hanks encouraged us all to experience English culture to the fullest extent we could. Nevertheless, my fellow missionaries wouldn't agree to watching operas.

The digs couple in Letchworth were members of the Spiritualist Church,

---

12. Mark Edward Petersen (1900–1984) became an apostle in 1944. Initially a reporter for the church-owned *Deseret News*, he continued to work there some sixty years, becoming an editor, and then president and chairman of the board. He wrote weekly editorials for the *Church News* section of the paper for many years. Besides expressing racist comments and homophobic beliefs, he also doggedly pursued modern polygamists. Petersen published some forty books on morality, doctrine, and faith.

and during the past several years the husband had accurately predicted the transfer of each missionary just days before the British Mission informed the particular elder of his transfer to another town/city. In like manner, he predicted Elder Swinyard's transfer. And mine. This Spiritualist was a kind, congenial man, who eagerly helped new missionaries to memorize the six proselyting discussions. He played the role of the investigator, Brother Brown, and knew all parts of the verbatim dialogue required by LDS headquarters.

Because of such positive experiences with our Spiritualist landlord, I eventually persuaded Elder Swinyard to make an evening appointment to teach another R.W. we met tracting. Her warlock husband didn't say a word as he sat in the background, glowering at us under a painting of an American Indian this Registered Witch said was her spirit guide. The visit felt creepier the longer we stayed. My companion had vowed that he wouldn't say a word, and he didn't. I was the one who made a lame excuse to leave.

When I mentioned this couple to our digs owner, he said that those two practiced "the dark side of Spiritualism—Black Magic." He warned us to stay away from them: "I wish you had asked me first—before even entering their house. Bad things can happen with people like them." It made this sleepy English town seem very Gothic, but he was serious. I didn't try it ever again.

On the monthly fast and testimony Sundays (when there was no LDS meeting in the afternoon or evening), British missionaries often attended the services of other churches. At our landlord's invitation, we went with him a couple of times to meetings of the Spiritualist Church, where I was impressed by the calmness and lightly physical touching of neck, shoulders, chest, and limbs in their healing ceremonies.[13] This was so different from the ecstatic shouting of the healing ceremonies in Evangelical Protestant services I had witnessed, and from the head-only touching of LDS ordinances I had participated in.

2 October 1963–Painful Announcement

From my journal: "Today we had a zone missionary meeting [in London] at which President Hanks solemnly informed us of the recent excommunication of an elder in the mission for fornication. The elder next to me, who knew the disgraced elder quite well, broke down in tears when President Hanks told the group. ...

"At the meeting, during the course of President Hanks's confidential discussion of the case, he mentioned that his uncle, Richard R. Lyman, who had

---

13. Spiritualism is a metaphysical religious movement that developed in the 1840s and peaked in English-speaking countries by the 1890s. Based on the alleged ability to communicate with spirits of the dead (usually through a medium), there was no formal organization for several decades. Women in particular were drawn to it, as religions generally at the time did not allow formal participation from them in leadership. Spiritualist churches and societies began to form in Britain in the 1870s.

been excommunicated as an apostle for a similar offense, had been baptized eleven years afterwards in 1954. I was glad to learn of his return and hope that this elder will do the same."[14]

President Hanks then warned us never to be separate from our companions. However, I soon discovered that it was routine for missionaries to travel alone by train whenever they were transferred from one town/city to a distant town/city. I always felt real anxiety whenever it was necessary for me to do so.

In less than seven months, this sad ordinance was repeated. Two companions were excommunicated, along with "one of the married sisters in the branch where these elders had been working."

10 October 1963–General Authority Becomes Mentor-Confidant

My district drove to mission headquarters for our routine interview chats one-by-one with Marion D. Hanks. For some reason, beginning today, he spoke about conflicts at LDS Church headquarters every time he interviewed me in his London office. He began by saying that, because of Bruce R. McConkie's doctrinal narrowness and dogmatism, "we have been at loggerheads" ever since President Hanks entered the First Council of the Seventy ten years earlier.[15]

Over time, he confided to me many details of his conflicts with the First Presidency's recently deceased counselor Henry D. Moyle about the youth baptism program. British Mission President T. Bowring Woodbury had inaugurated it soon after his appointment in 1958, but President Hanks officially announced its abandonment five days after replacing him in January 1962. He ended this baseball baptism program (as it was more commonly known) by private instruction from LDS President David O. McKay.[16] Nonetheless, Moyle was so angry that he then cut off all supplies to the mission.

---

14. Richard Roswell Lyman (1870–1963) remains the last LDS apostle to have been excommunicated. In 1943, the First Presidency discovered he had a relationship with Anna Jacobsen Hegsted, though he was legally married to Amy Brown Lyman. Apostle Lyman claimed he had secretly sealed himself polygamously to Hegsted. Gary James Bergera, "Richard R. Lyman: 'This Tragic Affair,'" in *Justice & Mercy: Studies of Transgression in the Latter-day Saint Community* (Salt Lake City: Lane-shine-house Press, 2021), 54–81.

15. Later called the First Quorum of the Seventy, the First Council of the Seventy was established by Joseph Smith in 1835. These seventy men were called "to be traveling ministers, unto the Gentiles first and also unto the Jews" (see Doctrine and Covenants 107:93–97). Similar to apostles, they are general authorities over the church and travel extensively to assist in missionary work, humanitarian aid, temple construction, and so forth. Unlike apostles, whose callings are for life, seventies are now released from this calling at age seventy.

16. Henry Dinwoodey Moyle (1889–1963) was an apostle and counselor in the First Presidency. He was responsible for excessive spending on the construction of church buildings, creating a large financial deficit of the church, leading to his being relieved of many of his administrative tasks. The "principal architect" of the controversial youth baptism program was T. Bowring Woodbury. Quinn later wrote an exposé on the infamous practice: "I-Thou vs. I-It Conversions: The Mormon 'Baseball Baptism' Era," *Sunstone*, Dec. 1993, 30–44.

I silently wondered how many other young missionaries had received these insights from Marion D. Hanks. Undoubtedly, those who were his trusted counselors and assistants, but why a "greenie" like me? Dunno.

Due to the secret embargo by the prophet's counselor, President Hanks told me that he had to beg other mission presidents in Britain for supplies and even for sufficient numbers of replacements for departing missionaries. Despite their own differences about baptism goals, President A. Ray Curtis of the Southwest British Mission was the most helpful to President Hanks in surviving what he called "Henry D. Moyle's effort to strangle the British Mission into submission."[17]

In the fall of 1963, most of this was new to me, but I had first learned about baseball baptisms during a talk by a non-general authority at a BYU devotional for all students, administrators, and faculty. The speaker stunned us by criticizing LDS missionaries in the Eastern States who organized a baseball game for non-Mormon boys in a public park. These elders had offered an ice cream cone to every boy over the age of eight who agreed to be baptized after the game. This seemed like an evil way to use secular bait for proselytizing.

President Hanks also recommended that all his missionaries should begin by reading a brief history of England. He also encouraged us missionaries to consult translations of the Bible other than the authorized King James Version. He especially liked a poetic rendering of the New Testament by J. B. Phillips, as well as Jewish rabbi Hugh J. Schonfield's *Authentic New Testament*, both of which I read several times. I copied some of Schonfield's passages into my New Testament as improvements on the KJV, which President Hanks also recommended we do.

Under his leadership, the British Mission was a cultural, intellectual, and spiritual paradise for young missionaries. It took me years to accept this fact, but in 1963 there was no better mission in the world for me. I could have served people beneficially elsewhere—as I wanted to do in a German-speaking country—but my personality and previous development were uniquely suited to gaining the most as a Hanks missionary. As he often said, "If you convert only one person, let that convert be you, and your mission will be a success."

18 October 1963–Anticipating Revelation about Blacks

From my journal: "This week, *Time Magazine*, an internationally syndicated publication, carried a page-long article on the Church's position on the Negro.[18] The article was highly sarcastic, critical, and defamatory. I see in this

---

17. A. Ray Curtis (1911–88) served as president of the Southwest British Mission and an LDS regional representative over the United Kingdom, the southern United States, Hawaii, and Utah. He also served as president of the Salt Lake Temple.

18. See "Mormons: The Negro Question," *Time*, Oct. 18, 1963, 83–84.

a very critical problem which may soon erupt. If the Church continues the policy of denying Negroes the priesthood, persecution is going to follow. I personally don't think the Lord is going to allow the Negroes to have the priesthood until after Christ's second coming ... .

"However, the Lord may see fit to allow the Negroes to have the priesthood before the Lord's coming. If this is so, then the revelation could conceivably even come during the next year." The race exclusion remained for nearly fifteen years.

22 November 1963–John F. Kennedy's Assassination

My companion and I were tracting when a woman answered the door and burst into tears as soon as she heard our American accents: "Oh, my boys, your President has been killed." Invited inside her house to watch the uninterrupted television coverage, the two of us hardly said a word. This was the day after President and Sister Hanks celebrated Thanksgiving dinner with all the British Mission's missionaries in the Epsom Branch's cultural hall.

The next weeks were especially surreal for Americans living abroad, where all flags were at half-mast. Contrary to their famous reticence, Brits came up to us on the street to express their sorrow. Sometimes tearfully. We missionaries were instructed to carry our passports and $50 worth of local currency at all times, in case of emergency evacuation to the USA.

9 December 1963–Flesh and Spirit

From my journal: "My heart is burdened with sorrow because of my flesh. I grieve because I am weak and subject to evil thoughts and feelings [of homosexuality]. Sometimes my heart feels near to bursting because of the sorrow I feel at my unworthiness. ...

"I am so far from perfection, so far from even being *good*, and so far from even being a *good missionary*! I pray that I may draw close to the Lord so that I may become what people seem to think I already am and to become what *He* wants me to be."

14 December 1963–Facing Death

After Elder Swinyard was reassigned, David W. Harris became my senior companion in Letchworth. Four years older than me, he was also the new supervising elder for the Garden City district. This gave him responsibility for its missionary van, which we used tonight to take some members of our branch to a meeting in London.

From my journal: "Elder Harris drove down and it was my turn to drive on the way back. I really didn't feel very well, and I didn't want to drive; but, rather than refuse the responsibility, I took the keys and started the van toward home. ...

"As we were approaching the outskirts of London on a motorway, going about 40 m.p.h., a little car in front of us made an unexpected complete stop to make a sudden right turn. To avoid colliding with him, I turned the wheel sharply—too sharply—and we skidded into the curb and hit a streetlamp.

"At the moment of impact, my door sprung [open,] and I was thrown from the van. (This was one of the few occasions that I had not put on the safety belt.) I remember the crash and the sensation of leaving the van. I must have landed on my back, my right arm taking much of the impact, although I don't actually remember hitting the ground.

"After landing in the street, I dazedly, numbly watched the van skid sideways after hitting the street post and impassively watched it as it started to roll over on top of me. It tilted over me, paused, then rocked back to its upright position.

"I can still remember the silhouettes of the other five persons in the van. This all took place in such a few seconds [so] that there was no real time to think or even to react. I didn't even have time to pray, but since those few terrible moments I have had much time to think and to pray about it. I only received a few cuts, bruises, and strains. The rest were about the same, except one girl who got a bloody nose and a cut on her knee. The Lord was with us that night."

I soon learned that my sternum had cracked from the impact of landing on my back. Don't know how I avoided a concussion or broken spine from that airborne tumble out of the driver's seat. After hitting the ground, I found myself lying perpendicular to the curb, with my head and back on the grass, my mid-section over the curb, and the lower part of my body on the paved road. If the heavy vehicle had actually rolled and crushed me, I would have been cut in half when it smashed against me on the curb. I realized this as I got up, dazed though I was.

The mission van's frame was twisted due to its hitting the pole at an angle. After the necessary time to answer questions from a London policeman (bobby), we all had to return to Letchworth by train, pooling our cash. I later reimbursed everyone.

In what I eventually realized was a form of post-trauma hysteria, I laughed or giggled at the least reason for hours after this accident. When we finally got back to our digs, Elder Harris—who didn't like me anyway—started to slap me across the face—because "you think everything is a joke." I just looked at him and he lowered his hand, muttering: "Damn you."

The tension with him continued to be so intense that the traveling elders perceived it during their visit. Zone leader James M. Richards privately asked: "How are you getting along with Elder Harris?" and I just said: "Okay." I didn't want to talk about it, but Elder Richards kept asking me to "describe your companionship." When I reluctantly did, he gave me a hug and said reassuringly that I would soon be reassigned.

I still felt awful about totaling the mission's vehicle, and made monthly payments of $50 to pay for it. After the third or fourth installment, President Hanks said I had paid enough.

13 January 1964–Training to Be Senior Companion, Chelmsford, Essex County, England

When I was transferred from Letchworth this day, it was a huge relief to leave the barely civil companionship of David Harris. My next assignment was in the east-of-London town of Chelmsford. My first companion there was a professional baseball player.

Six years older than me, Elder Charles R. Bennett had converted in his twenties while with Kansas City Athletics. His easy-going personality provided a wonderful return to the kind of enjoyable companionship I had known with Elder Swinyard. Chuck prepared me to become a senior companion.

In two weeks, he generously asked me to perform the baptisms for David and Janet Emberson, a couple he had been teaching for months. They were my first convert baptisms, and he did the confirmations.

26 January 1964–First Visit to a Bath House

From my journal: "We went in [to London,] with the supervising elder [and his companion] on business, but we came in late Sunday evening so we could stay all night at a Turkish bathhouse. It was quite an experience." Now, the details. My stomach knotted when I learned our destination, but I said nothing. Each given a white towel upon entering, we four missionaries stowed our clothes in lockers.

I felt self-conscious out of my temple garments and put the towel around my waist, as did my companion. By contrast, the other two young elders kept the towels around their necks and seemed utterly at ease walking around totally nude in the Turkish bath. Its other guests tonight were very old, very fat, or both. Elder Bennett was an athlete, but I had never been attracted to him. His tall, imposing frame intimidated me somewhat. However, the completely naked missionaries were shorter, slender, and drop-dead gorgeous. If I hadn't been so scared, I would have had an erection.

I tried to keep my eyes averted from their groins during the hours those two Adonises guided us through the exercise rooms, swimming pool, steam room, and dry-heat caldarium. Finally, the uninhibited elders led us to a large room filled with wooden cots, each separated from the others by white-sheet curtains hanging from horizontal rods. It felt like hours before I fell asleep, while listening to the soft breathing from adjacent cubicles of the three young men who seemed as innocent of bathhouse sexuality as they were oblivious to what kept me awake. For me the night was a bizarre experience.

27 January 1964–Hyde Park Chapel and a London Polygamist

The four of us didn't talk about the Turkish bath as we left it on Monday morning to attend a conference of all our missionaries in the Hyde Park Ward's chapel. My journal explained: "It is a special one to initiate the program of giving seven discussions after [each convert's] baptism." President Hanks required these as another way to avoid superficial conversions.

On Exhibition Road, this grandly modern chapel was the equivalent of two regular blocks from our mission home and the same distance from London's famous Natural History Museum. Non-LDS Brits were scandalized to learn from the tabloids that this "gold-plated" building had cost 1 million US dollars at its 1961 dedication.

One of its attendees was an Egyptian convert, Dr. Ebeid Sarofim, a multi-lingual lecturer at the University of London on Middle Eastern legal systems. Years afterward, I discovered through archival research that he resided in London with a plural wife at this time. Because they had married in Egypt, where polygamy was legal, the First Presidency approved this as an exception to their otherwise strict, international enforcement of the 1890 Manifesto. Without explanation, BYU's *Daily Universe* had announced his baptism in October 1962.

From the archival documents, I eventually learned that David O. McKay authorized this prominent polygamist's baptism and ordination to the priesthood because Dr. Sarofim promised to lecture on the Book of Mormon as an ancient Middle Eastern text. Without knowing this, I attended one of those lectures in the Hyde Park Chapel, and it was very faith promoting. He was a member of the ward's elders quorum.

President McKay even mentioned Dr. Sarofim as a guest during the October 1962 general conference, which I had also attended while at BYU.[19] I wonder if this Egyptian Mormon was sitting there with his plural wife, who was a daughter of Cairo's former mayor. That day in the Salt Lake Tabernacle, the rest of us had been oblivious to the backstory of the prophet's reference to this LDS-authorized polygamist.

30 March 1964–Sixties Activists

From my journal: "Today was our diversion day, and we went into London for a missionary meeting. We left a few hours early to see a few sights

---

19. See *Conference Reports of The Church of Jesus Christ of Latter-day Saints*, 132nd Semi-Annual Conference October 1962 (Salt Lake City: The Church of Jesus Christ of Latter-day Saints, 1962), 4.

before the meeting. While we were in Hyde Park, there was a demonstration by university students from all over England to 'Ban the Bomb' (and a host of other things).

"As I looked at the many bearded long-haired, rebellious youth, my mind was drawn to wonder just how much real purpose or satisfaction they have in life. My heart is a bit sad when I think that these youth are wasting their efforts on such campaigns[,] when they could be actively involved in the gospel. But this is their choice to make, not mine."

Reading this many years later, I'm appalled at my youthful self-righteousness, condescension, and glib dismissal of the social activism I would later applaud.

22 May 1964–Junior Companion's Complaints

Gary O. Laing was transferred to Chelmsford to be my first junior companion. Recently arrived from Lovell, Wyoming, but nearly a year older than me, he explained on May 1 "that he had never wanted to go on a mission and that his heart was just not in the work."

My journal added another perspective on May 23: "Last night I asked Elder Laing to tell me what it was about me or my personality that made him feel like rebelling. ... He said that the main problem was that I was extremely egotistical, in word and action. He also said that some of my personal habits irritated him....

"By this time, I already felt very sorrowful, but I wanted to know it all, so I asked him what else bothered him about me. He said that I acted like I was 'buttering up' the leaders in the mission with the aim of trying for a leadership position of prestige for myself. Well, I felt so hurt I could have bawled (and did, but tried to hide it)."

The reason he accused me of "buttering up" for leadership was that I was trying to be supportive of our new mission president, O. Preston Robinson.[20] He had been publisher of the Church's newspaper, *Deseret News*, and claimed to be an expert on the Dead Sea Scrolls. As had been the rule with President Hanks, missionaries were required to write President Robinson weekly, and I sent him long letters. By contrast, Elder Laing mailed a paragraph or two.

Missionaries devoted to President Hanks probably would have resented anyone who succeeded him, but they openly criticized President Robinson for letting his wife be co-president of the mission. She was the older half-sister

---

20. Oliver Preston Robinson (1903–90) married Christine Hinckley (1908–91), the half-sister of Gordon B. Hinckley (1910–2008). Robinson served as president of the British Mission from 1964–67. Prior to that, he was an advertising professor at the University of Utah, where one of his students was Thomas S. Monson. Both Hinckley and Monson were junior LDS apostles in 1964.

of apostle Gordon B. Hinckley, who had set them apart for this calling in the British Mission.

Monthly bulletins had letters from our mission president, sometimes signed as "The Robinsons." We soon learned from a few mission home staffers (who despised her and used only the name Christine) that Sister Robinson also read our personal letters to the President. She did so much administratively, that he appointed a lady missionary as her secretary. During their visits to missionary districts, Sister Robinson interviewed all the lady missionaries and half of the elders. She even asked each young man if he was masturbating. Some spoke of her with hatred.

I felt ambivalent. She seemed to be a genuinely sweet and kind person. Moreover, she obviously loved President Robinson. That was something my grandmother's negative example taught me to appreciate in a marriage.

The following year, after I was transferred into a new mission, I would learn that Elder Laing had become a zone leader in the British Mission. We met by accident, and the awkwardness was thick enough to cut.

This missionary, who had accused me of brown-nosing President Robinson, eventually became his chief assistant, the second-in-command over full-time missionaries. It seemed ironic.

Mid-June 1964–*Siddhartha* and Me

After being transferred from Chelmsford on June 12, I was trained for six days to be the presiding elder of Maidstone Branch, south of London. My trainer was the Tonbridge district's Supervising Elder George T. Harris, who often criticized me for reading Hermann Hesse's *Siddhartha*.[21] My mother had shipped it to me in one of her "care packages," writing that she thought I'd enjoy this book of "religious history." In view of its anti-institutional philosophy, I question whether she had actually read it herself.

Three years older than me, this disapproving companion probably observed a lustful expression on my face one day as I silently read the only sexual passage in this novel about the Buddha. "A penny for your thoughts," he said, "and don't clean them up." I made no response and kept reading, yet admired him for not grabbing the book out of my hands.

Late June 1964–Presiding Elder, Maidstone, Kent County, England

I began presiding at the Maidstone Branch's meetings in a rented room of the town's Corn Exchange building. There were six participating Mormons out of eighty formerly active members.

---

21. *Siddhartha* is a 1922 novel about a Nepalese man who becomes a wandering beggar. His best friend, Govinda, joins him, and eventually they encounter the Buddha. Govinda decides to follow the Buddha, but Siddhartha feels like spiritual enlightenment is an individual experience that cannot be taught by another.

I felt real love for my new companion, Rinehart Peshell. About my age, he was enthusiastic and gave me affectionate hugs. More straight-arrow than me, he didn't like it when I drank Coca Cola at every opportunity. I switched to Pepsi, but that didn't help.

He was constantly cheerful except when he received anti-church letters from his mother. She had been excommunicated with his father for their Mormon fundamentalist and polygamist beliefs in the little town of Hurricane, Utah. Elder Peshell told me that the Adam-God doctrine was what started his parents "on the road to apostasy." I understood why, in view of the BYU professor's thesis about it.

30 June 1964–Slouching toward Atheism

From my journal: "Tonight we [Elder Peshell and I] began the first of a series of events which will end in the excommunication of four families from the Church here in Maidstone."

Now, the backstory: By written instructions from Apostle Mark E. Petersen, mass excommunications had been occurring for more than two months throughout the British Isles and Ireland. He instructed the full-time missionaries to conduct in-person surveys of all the inactives in each branch or ward where the missionaries lived. This was his way of cleaning up the mess left by baseball baptisms.

The purpose was to ascertain their status and to recommend excommunication for those (1) who could not be reactivated or (2) who should not remain members by reason of personal preference or sin. The written recommendation for either fellowshipping or excommunication then went to the branch presidents (or their presiding missionary elders) and ward bishops. Since early May, I had been conducting those excommunication surveys in Chelmsford and in Maidstone.

However, now I was the twenty-year-old presiding elder over a branch that had collapsed into apostasy. As of June 30, I found myself in the position of preparing to conduct church court trials for twice the number of people I had baptized. I obediently went ahead with the excommunication process, but it nearly destroyed me. My journal shows that I woke up on July 1 "with feelings of disaffection toward the church."

For a brief time, I was an atheist as missionary. It seemed easier for me to think that there was no God, than for me to know that I was helping to cut off people from his eternal presence. This profound doubt was tearing me apart.

Despite all my intense religious experiences and their still-clear memories, I prayed: "Oh, God, if there is a God, help me to know it again." I was going to leave my mission and abandon the church itself if I could not regain faith.

I didn't confide my struggle to Elder Peshell, who seemed unaffected by these preparations, despite his parents' excommunication. He was a stronger spirit than me.

Faith is more difficult to explain or understand than disbelief, but—in its way—faith returned within two weeks. I again felt the daily influence of the comforting inner warmth I've always known as God's Spirit. Eventually, I was glad for this experience. Previously I had no understanding or empathy for those who said that they "could not" believe in God, or those who said that they had suddenly lost their testimony. Now I understood one more dimension of the human condition. At least in part.

Still, I would not want to know what it's like to experience months, years, or decades of doubt or of disbelief. One bitterly empty taste was enough to achieve empathy. I would be especially grateful for this experience when other missionaries asked me in tears why they couldn't "get a spiritual testimony" after studying, praying, and even fasting for it.

I began to understand faith as a mysterious gift. Especially *my* faith. As a spiritual gift, a testimony was not a measure of one's goodness, or of one's worth to God. Even atheists have his gifts—just different ones.

And as a concealed queer, I had my gifts. Faith was one. Empathy was another.

13 July 1964–Unusual Request to First Presidency

I had barely resolved my crisis of faith when Hugh B. Brown, first counselor in the First Presidency, visited our mission to speak at a thanksgiving service on July 12th for the recently completed Crawley Chapel near the temple. I had never gotten over my disappointment about not being assigned to a German-speaking mission, so met privately with President Brown in London on the 13th to ask that I receive a new mission call to Germany. Although I hadn't consulted my family about this request, I was sure that they would allow me to remain an extra year-and-a-half, so that I could serve the standard time in a foreign-speaking mission.

Adding to my disappointment since mid-1963, I had met five native-Germans who were serving in the British Mission. Every time I said their names or heard their accents, I wanted to be in their *Vaterland*.

From my journal: "Today Elder Peshell and I went to London so that I could talk with President Robinson and with President Brown. President Robinson was a little upset and irritated with me because I had sought to bypass him by going to President Brown directly and because he thought that I didn't like the British Mission or his leadership—since I explained to him my desire to be released from the mission and [be] called to another.

"He said that as far as he was concerned, it was out of the question because of the draft board, and because I had been called to England through inspiration to a prophet. He was really hurt, and it made me feel especially bad when he said, 'Well, when President Brown comes, you can talk with him and his decision will probably mean more to you than mine.' ...

"Then I was left alone with President Brown. He first asked me how I was and about my experiences in the mission field. Then I began to tell him about my desires to be called to another mission [in Germany] and be released from this mission. To make a half hour's discussion short, he said he would mention my request to the prophet. He said, however, that he had never known the prophet to change his decision concerning mission calls, except where circumstances beyond the missionary's control intervened. He gave me some very good advice. He said that I shouldn't try to counter the decisions of the Brethren."

From my journal a few days later: "Last Sunday we had a special missionary meeting with President Brown. He told of some wonderful experiences in his own life. The Spirit of the Lord was truly there. Afterwards I came up to him and explained that I'd been thinking a great deal of what he had counseled me and I had been reading over Alma 29, and I agreed with him and with Alma that it was wrong of me to desire more than my present calling. I apologized and thanked him and he said, 'God bless you, elder.'"

For a decade after my two years in England, I had a recurring dream of serving a second full-time mission in Germany. Typical of the silliness in dreams, I always parachuted out of a plane to begin this second mission. I awoke after landing on the ground with all my gear amid billowing, white nylon.

This dream persisted despite a new insight my former dorm buddy David Eldredge gave me about the LDS Church's current sink-or-swim method for learning new languages on a mission. Dave went to Finland, where (he told me in a letter): "I couldn't understand anyone except crying babies and barking dogs for six months!"

Not long after my conversation with President Brown, his grandson Charlie began serving in the British Mission. However, I saw this year-younger friend from my youth only a couple of times at mission HQ. Charlie surprised me once by volunteering that, according to President Brown, David O. McKay was faltering mentally as church president. Assuming this meant becoming forgetful, I didn't ask for details.

3 August 1964—Palmistry's Insight

Sister Avis K. Niblett, one of the few active members of the Maidstone Branch, was a sixty-five-year-old midwife who had lived in colonial India until it became independent. During a bus trip of our local district's members and missionaries to the beach on this diversion day, we talked at length about her experiences. She confided that she had a gift of reading palms and offered to read mine. "You have a long lifeline," she said and began to talk about something else.

I knew enough about palmistry to ask about my love line. "I see marriage there, but ..." And Sister Niblett looked very uncomfortable, "but male friends are more significant to you." Stunned, I gladly let her change the subject as we motored toward the sea.

7 August 1964—Vietnam War Looms Closer

Congress passed the Tonkin Gulf Resolution, which authorized US President Lyndon B. Johnson to wage war against Communist North Vietnam and to conduct combat operations against its Viet Cong insurgents in South Vietnam. My stomach knotted when I read about this closer approach of a war that could end the ministerial draft deferments given to LDS missionaries like me.

In thirteen months, LDS headquarters would establish a missionary quota that limited each ward in the United States to a maximum of two full-time missionaries serving at the same time. The US Selective Service Department required this for continuing to grant us draft deferments.

20 August 1964—Church Court

From my journal: "Today I presided at an elders court in Maidstone ... resulted in the excommunication of nine persons—five adults and four children."

7 September 1964—Depressing Diversion Day

Our missionary district's supervising elder asked me to arrange all the activities for this month's all-day diversion day. Even though I cheerfully did so, he would regret asking me to do it.

I arranged for our dozen missionaries to have a mid-morning tour of a special hospital for those who were permanently damaged mentally and/or physically. My longest-lasting memory was looking at a three-year-old hydrocephalic boy whose head was the size of a large pillow. I thought: "How could he survive so long in this terrible condition? And why did God allow such living tragedies for the innocent?"

After hours on the official tour of this facility by its director, the other missionaries were positively giddy to learn that we were going to a movie in London that afternoon. I took them to *Lord of the Flies*.

Mercifully, for the evening I had arranged for all of us to see the lavishly performed musical comedy *Camelot* in a West End theatre. Tonight, I noticed that the other missionaries laughed so hard at the performance's humor that they were sometimes in tears.

Not until two decades afterward would I see the parallel of this day to my grandmother's singing "sad morbid songs" as lullabies to my mother.

Even at the time, however, I recognized the stark contrast between my arrangements for this September and the exceptional all-day diversion day of last autumn, when my first supervising elder George D. Hessenthaler drove us missionaries to the Midlands. Following a quick lunch, we toured Coventry, Warwick Castle, and Stratford-on-Avon. In the evening, we watched a Shakespearean comedy as performed by its resident Royal acting company. We didn't get back to our digs until after 2:00 A.M. the next morning.

Why didn't I arrange for something that fun? It required my careful reading of *The Family Crucible* two decades later to understand. Really understand.[22]

16 September 1964–Penance

From my journal: "Last week I had the opportunity to speak with President Robinson. At that time I asked him if I might be released on September 8, 1965, since I will be entering school [BYU] on the 16th. He said yes, and I also asked him if I could spend eight of my next full-day diversions working at the mission home to in some way make up to the Lord for the days I'll lose in an early release. He said that this wouldn't be necessary, but that I could do it.

"I also told him that I did not want to serve as a supervising elder over a district because I didn't feel that I could adequately drive a mission van. He said that he would remember this when considering me for a leadership position. I said that if I had my choice of leadership positions, I would rather spend the rest of my mission presiding over branches. But he said that this isn't why we are on missions. I felt like saying that I'd rather not work in the mission home either but would rather be in active proselyting. However, I felt it best to not push the point.

"I also reviewed my activities and programs in Maidstone and requested that I remain here at least six more months. He said he would keep this in mind. I enjoyed the opportunity to discuss my feelings with him."

Concerning my upcoming all-day diversion day of work at the mission home, my journal noted: "They kept me busy and so the time passed fairly rapidly, but that type of work is a far cry from the proselyting work I would much prefer to do. I do hope that others will not think that I am trying to make a big impression by doing this."

12 October 1964–"Mainly Intellectual" Faith?

From my journal: "Yesterday I met with and was interviewed by one of the traveling elders of the mission.... He asked me if my testimony toward

22. *The Family Crucible* was written by therapists Augustus Y. Napier and Carl Whitaker, and treated scenarios from one's family's experience to deal with stress, scapegoating, blaming, identity diffusion, polarization, and so forth. Napier and Whitaker, *The Family Crucible* (New York City: Harper & Row, 1978).

the Church before I came on my mission was mainly intellectual and not spiritual. This has caused me to wonder why he asked this[,] so I am going to write him about it later."

I was obviously offended, but understand now why this missionary regarded my faith as too intellectual.

31 October 1964—Last Public Activity with Maidstone Branch

Now housed at the LDS Church's History Library in Salt Lake City, this English branch's manuscript history describes the event I arranged for this Saturday evening: "Bonfire & Firework Display Organised by Branch. All District to Attend. Proceeds to Medway Branch Building Fund." Six weeks earlier, I had also organized a related event: "Sept. 12—With the help of members from other branches throughout the district, the proposed chapel site was cleaned, grass cut, and etc."

My role in those positive events was how I wanted to be remembered, *not* for the Church courts and excommunications I conducted in Maidstone. But its British clerk Terrance P. Miles apparently wanted no one to recall my name, which is absent from his history of the branch since my appointment as its presiding officer.

On November 10, I returned from my new assignment residence in London to conduct the last court, which excommunicated four more of our baseball baptism boys. The branch's history gives their names, not mine. After all, this tragedy wasn't about me.

After excommunicating sixteen percent of its Mormons and reactivating three of its baseball baptism boys, I was happy to learn that Maidstone grew into such a thriving branch that it became a ward. With well-converted Saints, it became a stake in 1978.

Early November 1964—Traveling Elder, British Mission

As of the 1st, I became the traveling companion of a zone leader named Keith Rayner. We visited one missionary district a week, splitting up so that each of us worked with each missionary of assigned companions, to whom we gave suggestions about methods of proselytizing. If any of these missionaries wanted to talk privately, they did so with the zone leader.

One of the most embarrassing experiences of my mission occurred while I was a traveling elder. Accompanying a greenie elder while tracting in a posh area, I told him that "it seems to reassure people of your good intentions if you step back from the door—just as they open it—rather than standing too close to their faces." I said, "I'll now demonstrate this technique to you," as we ambled up a long, trellised walkway to the large door of an elegant house, with tall Chinese vases carefully spaced along both sides of the walkway. I rang the bell, and—as the lady of the house opened its door—stepped back.

In doing so, I knocked over a huge Chinese vase that I hadn't noticed behind me on the raised entry. After it shattered into dozens of pieces, I looked at the ashen face of the greenie, then turned to the anguished face of the woman staring at her vase. "So very sorry" wasn't adequate, and there was only one other thing I could think to say: "Would you believe that we represent a church?" I asked, while trying to suppress embarrassed laughter. "No!" she replied. "Good!" I answered, and dragged the newly arrived missionary away from this scene of ceramic devastation. I never again used the reassuring method of tracting.

The most startling experience occurred in a different city. While I was night tracting with an equally new missionary in an equally posh neighborhood, a car suddenly screeched to a halt next to us. Two men jumped out in civilian clothes, flashing badges. "Hands in the air!" one of them shouted. Arms above my head, I started to repeat a canned line we said at doorways: "We're two young Americans who've interrupted our college education ... " Cutting me short, one of the men groused: "You damned Mormons ought to wear signs!" And these plain-clothes coppers drove off.

I, of course, reported this during the next meeting of the zone leaders and their companions with President Robinson. Because he was obviously well-connected with the general authorities in Utah, I take partial credit for what became the church's new policy throughout the world: all full-time LDS missionaries commenced wearing officially manufactured, black plastic name tags prominently inscribed with their names and missionary status in white lettering.

On Saturday afternoons Elder Rayner and I drove back to London where all the traveling elders slept in bunk beds in our mission home's attic. One evening, Elder Rayner announced that we were driving to Leatherhead, Surrey, to visit Mark E. Petersen at home. Due to Apostle Petersen's excommunication program and his preventive instructions about missionary homosexuality, I had preconceptions about the kind of austere evening we would experience.

Instead, it was a delightful time of casual conversation, laughter, and relaxation. He greeted us wearing a sweater and no tie, his shirt open at the collar. The house was well-heated and his missionary assistants were in shirt sleeves. I had read a couple of the devotional books by his wife, Emma Marr Petersen, who was as sweet as could be tonight, with a quick sense of humor. She seemed like Norinne Callister in Glendale.

At one point, Apostle Petersen asked if Elder Rayner and I would like "thick strawberry malts." This was a treat unknown at this time to the British—who gave the name milk shake to a glass of milk mixed with a dollop of ice cream. Thus, the three of us talked casually in the kitchen as Elder Petersen made each malt.

It was a thrill for me to be in such casual association with an apostle. This dove-tailed with what I regarded as the relaxed informality of his knees-to-knees method of privately interviewing missionaries seated in front of his chair. To me, that seemed very congenial.

In 1971, however, I would be stunned by the comment of a Mormon researcher, to whom I expressed admiration for Apostle Petersen's approach. "That's a method the police use for interrogating criminals!" exclaimed Raymond W. Taylor, who had once been a cop.[23] That would make me feel very naive!

One weekend night in November 1964, as Elder Rayner and I returned to the traveling elders' digs on the mission home's top floor, I got a new perspective on aspiring for positions in the LDS Church. A couple of weeks away from returning to the United States, a twenty-two-year-old zone leader exclaimed: "Can my mother actually think I'd *enjoy* reading this letter?!" He quoted the part where she explained that she didn't want him to move back home—because their ward's bishopric had just been reorganized, leaving no opportunity for him to be called as a bishop's counselor.

Therefore, she and his father had rented an apartment for their son within the boundaries of a ward that had no recently returned missionaries and whose elderly bishopric would probably change in a year. She said this left a strong possibility for him to advance into that ward's new bishopric.

Despite not aspiring for church offices with such calculation, I felt embarrassed. I hadn't confided my apostolic expectations to him or to any other missionary, but I couldn't escape the feeling that my own hopes were being unintentionally criticized by this elder who complained about his family's aspirations for him.

23 November 1964—Mom's Second Divorce

From my journal: "This morning at 5:45 a.m., called Mom on the telephone. It was good to hear her voice."

This was in response to her letter that she had left my stepfather, Wayne, because of his adulterous affair. Mom could forgive almost anything from him (including lies—big and small), but she could not forgive the discovery of Wayne's infidelity. That ended all the feelings of romance that had kept her

---

23. Historians Raymond Woolley Taylor (1904–72) and his brother Samuel Woolley Taylor (1907–97), sons of Apostle John W. Taylor and grandsons of LDS President John Taylor, curated and archived their grandfather's letters, journals, and other records. At the time of Raymond's death, he was a police officer in Utah County.

happy, in spite of his other problems. She left their apartment and moved into the spare bedroom of her brother Frank's house, where I had stayed on and off.

My first thought upon reading the letter was that Wayne Hood would kill her. However, Mormonism had calmed his violent nature, as Mom assured me when I phoned. President Robinson also tried to comfort me in a very grandfatherly way about my mother's divorce.

13 December 1964—Exiled

From my journal: "Today I feel a little depressed and sad. I have received definite notification that I'll be splitting up from Elder Rayner and that I'll become the new district leader of the Garden City district (which now does not include Letchworth). The British Mission is also being divided shortly to form a new mission and Garden City will be in the new mission."

Now, the backstory: President Robinson had decided to exile me from the British Mission. It was clear that he didn't like my voicing concern in a zone leaders' meeting about his plan to give medals to missionaries who excelled in proselytizing. As diplomatically as I could, I cautioned that this "might become a false incentive for competitive elders." The formation of a new mission allowed him to reassign those who still clung to the Hanks philosophy of missionary work.

As traveling elders, we also discussed among ourselves the remarkable coincidences connected with this division of our mission. President Robinson was reassigning short timers to the new boundary, as well as every missionary who was lazy, rebellious, unbelieving, smoking cigarettes, or dating girls. I would learn from the new mission's president that President Robinson told him face-to-face that these were "the very best of missionaries," and didn't warn him about any problems a single one might have. Also, President Robinson transferred all the junk-heap vehicles into the affected area and put the newer ones into the area he was retaining.

Mid-December 1964—Others Are "Dealt with" for Candor

From my journal: "Also the traveling elders who were outspoken in their honest opinions about mission policies also have been dealt with. Elder Jacobsen, an excellent zone leader, was sent out into the field again the last two months of his mission. Elder Johnson, a dynamic and outspoken zone leader (or zone counselor), was suddenly sent back out into the field into one of the districts affected by the new mission. Elder Dutson, another outspoken zone leader, will be going into the new mission and also his companion, Elder Payne.

"And lastly me. I was traveling while a lot of these moves and some new mission policies were presented and on occasion I frankly stated my views to President Robinson in the meetings the traveling staff has weekly with him, and now I, too, am going into the new mission."

Initially, Elder Rayner was on the list to go into the new mission. Having only six weeks left before returning home, he was distraught.

In tears, he begged President Robinson to keep him and promised to enthusiastically support every change in policy. Thereby Keith stayed in the British Mission. He seemed embarrassed when he told me how he achieved this reprieve, but I was glad for him. If I had dared, I would have kissed him.

15 December 1964–District Leader, Garden City District, Hertfordshire County, British Mission

By the recently changed title for supervising elder, being a district leader was my first formal opportunity to counsel young men. Because concealing my sexual orientation was almost unbearably painful, I was eager to encourage others to reveal their innermost problems to me. Many were willing to unburden themselves to such a sympathetic listener. Others resisted my efforts to invade their own boundaries.

I told them it was harmful to "hold in" the cause of their apparent sadness, but I was unwilling to follow what I knew was good advice. In this and future church positions, I used counseling with others as vicarious redemption for myself and as my only intimacy with males.

24 December 1964–Ballet and Midnight Mass

Tonight I drove my district into London, where we joined other missionaries in watching *The Nutcracker*, my first ballet. I sat next to mission home secretary Jonathan P. West, an older missionary who seemed very sophisticated, intellectual, and liberal, yet outgoing and down-to-earth.[24] He was a grandson of the man who gave my grandmother her patriarchal blessing. Jonathan was also a son of historian Franklin L. West, who was once commissioner of education for the LDS Church.[25]

Many Mormons pay attention to who's related to whom. It goes deeper in the culture than merely doing ancestral genealogy for vicarious ordinances to be performed by proxy in temples. Family connections are of particular interest to those who have Utah pioneer ancestry.

After the ballet, we attended midnight mass in a Catholic Church. I was fascinated by its pageantry and liturgy ("the smells and bells" as some communicants call it). Because those were things that my anti-Catholic mother

---

24. Jonathan P. West became a professor of political science and director of graduate MPA and MPP programs at the University of Miami. He received his BS in Political Science at the University of Utah and earned his MA and PhD at Northwestern University. Much of his work involved ethics and integrity in public service.

25. Franklin Lorenzo Richards West (1885–1966) taught physics at what became Utah State University. He also was a high-ranking leader in the LDS Church's Young Men's Mutual Improvement Association during the 1930s, and was Commissioner of Education in the church from 1936 to 1953, authoring three manuals for the Church Education System.

regarded as "disgusting," I never told her about my occasional attendance at apostate worship services.

CHAPTER EIGHT

SPIRITUAL PROMPTINGS

1965–1966

13 January 1965–District Leader, Portsmouth District, Hampshire County, British South Mission

Organized on December 27, the new mission combined elders and sisters from rival missions that had been suspicious of each other ever since Marion D. Hanks ended all pressure and false incentives in the British Mission. Such phrases and views infuriated the Southwest British missionaries who now joined with us. They had been trained by President A. Ray Curtis to regard baptism goals and competitions as religious motivations for "the Lord's work."

The new British South Mission's president Don K. Archer (also trained by Curtis) was determined to create a "mission of love" out of the mutually antagonistic groups. He began this effort today by transferring every district leader in the previously British Mission area to preside over missionary districts in the previously Southwest British Mission area, and vice-versa.

I was successful in building trust and affection with missionaries in the southern harbor city of Portsmouth. I even got along with the former district leader's worldly companion, Elder Donald Ray Winn, who had been a professional blackjack dealer in a Las Vegas casino before going on this mission.

10 February 1965–Zone Leader, British South Mission

President Archer transferred me to mission headquarters in Reading, Berkshire County, several hours southwest of London. He appointed me as a zone leader, instructing me to "just love every missionary." My first traveling companion was Elder John S. Weymouth. The two other zone leaders at this time were Elders David E. Payne and Charles R. Teames. The latter soon became chief assistant to President Archer.

For a missionary talent show, Elder Payne and I performed a skit that mocked BYU's religion professors like Glenn Pearson and Reid Bankhead. Sadly, the latter would eventually become president of the British Mission.

The zone leaders reported back to President Archer and his missionary assistant Saturday afternoons at the mission's administrative offices. Those were hastily remodeled rooms in the Reading Branch's meeting house.

"Reading Gaol" was where playwright Oscar Wilde had been imprisoned from 1895 to 1897 for sodomy.[1] Wilde (the married father of two sons) and his young lover Lord Alfred Douglas "Bosey" preferred to call it "The Love That Has No Name." One day, I drove my missionary companion by this old penitentiary. "Out of curiosity," I said. And in earnest.

Unlike the elegance of London's mission home, this newly created British South Mission provided merely a leased bungalow in Reading for President and Sister Archer. As down to earth, working-class people, they were remarkably different from the Salt Lake elites I had previously known as mission presidents and wives.

For example, in contrast to even the semi-relaxed formality of President Hanks, Don Archer laughed about having to wear a white shirt and dark tie all the time. He was also proud of kissing his teenage son Kim on the lips when greeting him in public, a paternal affection that moved me. Far more than the intellectually inspiring, but somewhat aloof Marion D. Hanks, President Archer was a loving father figure to me. I thanked God that both men were able to bless my life so profoundly for nearly equal periods of time.

March 1965–The Qur'an and Me

On weekends, my traveling companion and I stayed in a spare bedroom at the house of branch clerk Tony Strong and his wife, Ann, who lived on the outskirts of Reading. Even though she cooked delicious meals for us on Saturday evenings and three times on Sundays, this young couple refused to accept any money from us.

One day, I noticed that the Strongs had an English translation of the Qur'an. I had consulted secondary works about Islam five years earlier, but hadn't read its holy book. Although I certainly encountered a lot of Islamic theology during the weekend I read one-third of the Qur'an, I was most impressed by its cadences and literary beauty.

4 April 1965–Weeping in Public, and More about My Family

From my journal: "Today was fast and testimony meeting. I stood and told of my family being partly active, partly inactive and partly non-members. I related the circumstances of my uncle's conversion and my aunt's reactivation.

"For the first time in two years I wept during my testimony. I felt a perfect fool since I lost almost all control of my emotions."

While I was in England, Uncle Vaude converted to Mormonism, immediately

---

1. Built in 1844 in the town of Reading, England, the prison was nicknamed the "Reading Gaol," meaning "jail."

gave up his two-pack-a-day habit of cigarettes, and re-activated his wife, Joy. After that, he couldn't contain his enthusiasm about anything connected with the LDS Church.

23 April 1965—Private Revelation

From my journal: "I have always considered myself a proud and aspiring person. Perhaps what I am going to write is a result of a proud and vain imagination—but I think not. As we drove, my mind was filled with thoughts of the mission I had been sent to earth to accomplish.

"The Spirit burned within me and it was as if my future service to the Lord here upon the earth was opened unto me. According to these impressions I will return home and shortly later be called as a counsellor in a bishopric, a few years later I will become a bishop, and after serving as a bishop several years, I will be called to be a stake president. After only serving as stake president for a relatively short time, I will be called as a stake patriarch, which position I will hold several years. Following this I will be called to serve three years as a mission president (*not* in England the Spirit impressed upon me.) Following my service as mission president, I will return home and be called as stake patriarch. I will serve in that position until I receive my call to become a member of the Quorum of the Twelve Apostles! The Spirit impressed me that if faithful I will become an Apostle at about 50 years of age or so."

Shortly afterward, George (my younger companion who had always seemed worldly) disappeared on a foggy Thursday night while we were working with some missionaries on the Isle of Wight. In a few hours, I discovered him in the arms of a woman on a park bench. Confronting him was very difficult for us both. After our abrupt departure by ferry and our silent, unscheduled drive back to mission headquarters, he confessed the indiscretion to President Archer on Friday, April 30. George was immediately released as my companion but remained a missionary. "Under a cloud," I thought.

Years afterward, I would learn that this young elder became a zone leader in our mission after my departure. That surprised me but was another example that the LDS Church of my youthful experience maintained its family-like long-suffering, rather than my way or the highway.

4 May 1965—A Companionship of Love and Promise of Apostleship

From my journal: "On Tuesday, May 4, the fasting, prayers, hopes, and desires of my heart were answered. Elder [Michael E.] McAdams and I became companions. So much had happened the four days previous and I was so thrilled to see him again that I could have broken down in tears and embraced him, but I restrained myself because we were in a train station."

Elder McAdams and I had developed an intense emotional bond while he was one of my missionaries in the Portsmouth District. During the six weeks that we now traveled together, we shared many spiritual experiences. Though I didn't initially tell him about my personal revelation of future callings, he gave me a blessing in which he said that God would help me overcome my reluctance to express love and that we would both one day be known as "apostles of love."

From then onward, we spoke to each other about one day serving together in the Twelve—or even as members of the First Presidency.[2] We continued to discuss these solemn expectations for more than fifteen years.

A favorite memory of my mission companionship with Mike McAdams involved the song, "We Shall Overcome." I taught it to him, and we often sang it while driving in one of the mission VW's to work with various districts of missionaries. He was a convert from Texas, and I loved hearing someone with a Southern accent sing this Black civil rights anthem.

All the while, I was fighting my old struggle with the desires of the flesh, which had gotten more intense during my mission, rather than less. As promised in my patriarchal blessing, I was having spiritual experiences with young men who knew the Lord as I knew Him, and I knew that my love for them had God's approval. On the other hand, I teetered at the edge of expressing sensuality that I had struggled against since age twelve. Especially with my companion Mike.

He was a college wrestler of bantam physique with every gentle, spiritual, and emotional quality I could hope for in a male lover. Yet I knew instinctively that he was completely heterosexual and that there was no erotic dimension in his hugging embraces and words of love for me.

I couldn't make sense of the situation, especially when this spiritual companion blessed me to "overcome the barriers that keep you from expressing love." He had no idea about the male-male love I wanted to experience with him.

Nonetheless, I was convinced that, despite everything else about me, I was destined to fulfill a mission of great service to God and His people. This kept me celibate, although I wouldn't claim to be pure.

30 May 1965–Again Opposing False Incentives

From my journal: "Just a note concerning our zone leader meeting [with the British South Mission's president and chief assistant]. A situation arose which caused some sharp disagreement. Elder Teames presented their plans for a July 24 pioneer contest for the mission. It would be in the form of a challenge to the mission. Those who had the best proselyting hours and who baptized the most people would get a free steak dinner at the July 24 get together.

"I suggested that baptisms be taken off the challenge and that there be

---

2. Michael E. McAdams did not become an apostle or member of the First Presidency.

no prize for those who had done the best. My reasons for this are deep felt ones. ... Missionaries shouldn't be working to achieve a pin, or a free dinner or special recognition. They should be working to serve the Lord, and the reward they receive should be the inward joy and satisfaction that they have worked hard, excelled, and baptized choice people.

"Elder Payne and Elder McAdams joined in strongly advocating the suggestions I had made. It was clear that President Archer, Elder Teames, and Elder Payne's travelling companion did not agree with us. Elder Teames said that they would reconsider our proposals and discuss it again in our next zone leader meeting.

"As I later reflected seriously upon this, I made up my mind about several things. If the mission adopts the policy of baptism pushes, challenges, and drives, coupled with what I consider false incentives, I will ask to be released from leadership. These programs may have merit, but they are contrary to my conscience, and I hope and pray that I will never act contrary to my conscience."

Late June 1965–Like unto Biblical Job

For the previous six months, I had been losing weight (about forty pounds). Then I began getting boils. This month, the first was on my right finger—under the ring Nana had given me. Its gold alloy had enough impurities to turn the skin underneath a greenish color. The boils seemed to stop in August—after I lost the ring by leaving it on the sink of the men's restroom in the Crawley Chapel one Sunday.

3 July 1965–Missionary Temple Ordinance Worker

From my journal: "On Saturday morning, Elder [Lewis P.] Marchant and I went to the temple. ...

"Some of the sweetest desires of my heart have been to do temple work. So far and especially on my mission, the Lord has given me many opportunities to do temple work. I have acted as proxy in baptisms, initiatory ordinances, the endowment, and sealings for the dead. The Lord has also allowed me to officiate in some capacity in temple baptismal sessions, endowment sessions, at the veil, and the washing and anointing sessions. I will always be thankful for these opportunities to serve."

After my appointment as zone leader in February, the London Temple's new president George England had asked me to serve as an ordinance worker whenever I could come to the temple.[3] With President Archer's permission, I went there with my companion whenever it was convenient, usually on

---

3. George Eugene England Sr. (1904–96) served as president of the North Central States Mission (1954–57), counselor in the Salt Lake Temple presidency, and president of the London Temple (1964–66).

Saturdays and Mondays. President England said that my setting apart as a full-time missionary was sufficient for me to be a regular temple worker to perform various ordinances. I didn't need to be set apart for that service, as was usual.

One day, he talked to me with great pride about how well his son Eugene was doing at Stanford University. In a year, graduate student Gene would co-found *Dialogue: A Journal of Mormon Thought*. A decade after that, I began meeting with Gene England, whom I revered as one of liberal Mormonism's greatest advocates and heroes.

I annoyed Elder Marchant once when I declined to stop at Arundel Castle in West Sussex as we drove by it on the way to the temple. I wanted to participate in *two* sessions of the endowment that day, but soon regretted my single-mindedness that deprived him of a cultural experience he had every right to expect me to allow for an hour on our Diversion Day.

3 July 1965–Presentation about LDS Race Restriction

From my journal: "In the evening we returned to Reading. I met President Archer and inquired about the study class I had prepared on the Negroes. He said that his first councilor [*sic*] had read it and said it was dynamite and shouldn't be sent out, in case it caused greater problems than it corrected. That stuns me a little bit, but I appreciated why he said it. Pres. Archer hadn't read it yet, but he said he would have it typed up and sent on to Pres. Mark E. Petersen.

"I feel that there is a need for this study class, but if it is decided not to use it, I will certainly heed the decisions of my leaders."

As foreshadowed by this entry, my suggested presentation for missionaries died after Apostle Petersen read it. Too much candor about a painful policy.

6 July 1965–Special Teaching Assistant to
the Mission President, British South Mission

Although President Archer said that I was his "special assistant," my role actually involved working with missionaries in the field Tuesdays to Saturdays. Glen E. Sommers and I were formally a teaching team.

In the mission office, the last week of this month, I read *Newsweek*'s story about LDS congressmen who declined to follow the living prophet's instructions on how to vote. In a private letter, David O. McKay had asked them to retain a provision of the Taft-Hartley Act that weakened labor unions. Instead, these Democratic leaders made his letter public, criticized this effort to influence their votes, and voted contrary to the explicit counsel of the LDS president and his counselors.[4]

---

4. See "The Right to Vote," *Newsweek*, July 26, 1965. The Mormon Democratic Congressmen who wrote the public letter were Senator Frank Moss (D-UT), Rep. John E. Moss (D-CA), Rep. Richard T. Hanna (D-CA), and Rep. Kenneth Dyal (D-CA). Rep. Morris K. Udall (D-AZ) joined his fellow Democratic Mormon congressmen in opposing church political meddling in an

I was mystified for multiple reasons. First, why did the prophet intervene in a political matter that didn't seem to have anything to do with religion? Second, how could faithful Mormons defy him? Third, my mother was a longtime member of Local 1710 in her union.[5] Why did the prophet want to weaken her California union and other labor unions which benefitted millions of blue-collar workers throughout the nation? Who gains from this?

I puzzled about those questions for a year, until I arrived at my own *modus vivendi* concerning matters of church and state. It generalized my previous conclusions about the political conflicts between apostles Ezra Taft Benson and Hugh B. Brown. Regardless, it was a major step when applied to the living prophet.

18 July 1965–Cultural Colonialism

I was impressed again this Sunday at how patient British Mormons were with the cultural imperialism of LDS headquarters. Throughout the world, English-speaking Mormons used hymnbooks printed in Salt Lake City, with no option for congregational singing of local hymns. At this time, Utah headquarters also specified monthly hymns for the opening services of Sunday School, including Thanksgiving hymns for that US holiday in November and songs celebrating Utah's Pioneer Day in July for that state holiday on the 24th.

Each of these months, it was somewhat sad to see English Mormons on Sundays obediently singing songs for American holidays. At this time, there was no option for non-US congregations to sing patriotic songs for their own national holidays.

29 July 1965–District Leader, Crawley, Sussex County, British South Mission

For the next five weeks, it was odd to speak at sacrament meeting in Crawley. I looked down from the pulpit at the active membership of the branch assembled in the center of the front three rows in a huge chapel. LDS headquarters in Salt Lake City had authorized its construction in this pre-designed new town a few years earlier, when Crawley was expected to become its own stake with thousands of Mormons. This was another result of President T. Bowring Woodbury's baseball baptism program, whose statistics had made him into First Presidency counselor Henry D. Moyle's favorite mission leader.

Nearly 2,000 visitors had been sitting in this chapel when Hugh B. Brown

---

addendum to the public statement. H. George Frederickson and Alden J. Stevens, "The Mormon Congressman and the Line Between Church and State," *Dialogue: A Journal of Mormon Thought* 3, no. 2 (Summer 1968): 121–29.

5. "Local 1710" was an assigned number of a local branch of a national labor union.

spoke here the previous year. That non-resident attendance concealed the local reality.

Its branch president, Peter R. English, and his counselors now sat in those front rows as an unusual effort to make forty to fifty attenders seem like more. He was also official recorder for the nearby London Temple, having been set apart to that position and ordained a high priest by David O. McKay four-and-a-half years earlier.[6]

The Crawley Branch had ceased to be a ward after Brother English (as its bishop) excommunicated hundreds of baseball baptism boys on its inactive rolls, in accordance with Apostle Petersen's instructions last year. It was with obvious melancholy that he told me about those boys and how they had been deceived into LDS baptism by American missionaries. In a few years, this gentle man would abandon Mormonism. He returned to the Church of England and became an Anglican vicar. Another casualty of baseball baptisms.

But there would be a happier side to this story. Crawley's active LDS membership gradually rebounded. It became a ward again, then its own stake in 1977.

12 August 1965–Riots in Los Angeles

News of rioting by Blacks in the Watts District of South Central unnerved me. Ten days earlier, I had recorded premonitions of impending death while writing letters to my family. If this street violence continued for a month, I thought, my family would need to drive near that area to pick me up at LAX airport. Lasting only six days, these riots killed more than thirty human beings and injured more than a thousand.

As a nation, we continued to reap the whirlwind of our historical racism and exploitation of Blacks. Although the 1830 census of Maryland and 1840 census of Tennessee showed my first Mormon ancestor John Workman (born in 1789 and baptized with his wife Lydia in 1839) owning no slaves, a published family history stated that John purchased slaves in Tennessee at an unspecified time (probably 1840–41). He sold them to finance his 1843 move to Nauvoo, Illinois. Moreover, Lydia's brother, Isaac Bilyeu, owned twenty-one slaves in 1840. Their father may have had slaves at his residences in the old South. Two branches of shameful slave-owning ancestry!

The year 1965 was nearly 350 years after British immigrants brought African slaves to North America. Fully 100 years had passed since a US Constitutional amendment ended slavery, yet white Americans used various methods of maintaining their supremacy and enforcing hopeless subordination of

---

6. A temple recorder is a priesthood position that ensures ceremonies in Latter-day Saint temples are properly performed and recorded.

Blacks. Democratic President Lyndon Johnson's recent Civil Rights Act had made barely a dent.

Today's riots also had a very personal dimension for me. Exactly twenty years earlier, my grandparents, Mom, and I had lived in South Central, whose Black residents she had once visited daily—alone, with total acceptance, and in complete safety.

1 September 1965—Passing the Love of Women

At a zone conference of missionaries in the Reading Chapel, I began crying at the speaker's podium when I mentioned my gratitude for Elder Mike McAdams. President Archer stood next to me, put his hand on my shoulder, and said (as recorded in my journal):

"This kind of love is different from the love a man feels for his wife, but it is just as Godly and enduring. The Lord has blessed Elder Quinn and Elder McAdams to find this kind of love for each other, and it is a blessing that they both will always cherish."

I thought of my patriarchal blessing at age fourteen, and of the Biblical words David said about his beloved Jonathan (see 2 Samuel 1:26).

7 September 1965—England to USA

I had asked the mission secretary to schedule an hours-long stopover in Texas during my trip westward from New York's recently renamed John F. Kennedy Airport. Mike's mother, Ruby McAdams, met me at the Dallas Airport today and took me to lunch, where she chatted energetically about him and our friendship as companions. During the next several years, she wrote to me far more often than Mike did.

Asking me to call her "Mom McAdams," her beautifully handwritten letters were always lovingly inspirational. Because of the odd circumstances in my maternal upbringing, I avoided the suggested title and called her "Sister McAdams" or "Ruby."

This was my first visit to Texas, the "one place in the United States" where Dad said he "never" wanted to go. When I, at about age ten, asked why, he replied: "Because *Texans hate Mexicans*!" Adding quickly: "and Negroes, and Indians, and Jews, and Catholics." It was the closest Dad ever came to almost admitting his ancestry to me as a kid.

After traveling in several jets from London this day, I was weary but overjoyed at the reunion with my family at the LA airport. Only later did I see it from the perspective of my father, who told me that he "felt like flying away like a bird. Because you left me holding your luggage, while you walked away talking happily with your mother, her sister Joy and brother Frank, your grandparents, and even your Uncle Vaude who seemed to be running the show."

For the first time, I saw my father-son disappointments from Dad's point-of-view. I began to realize that I pulled away from Dad as much as I tried to draw close to him.

Early September 1965–Nana and Grampa Are Still Strange

While I was growing up, she bought me blue jeans only under strenuous protest and refused to allow me to wear Levi's because they were "too sexual." When I bought some before leaving for BYU this week, Nana snapped: "So the Godly returned missionary wants the world to see his penis in bunched-up Levi's!" I grumbled but didn't argue. What was the point?

On the other hand, during my absence in England, Grampa threw away the stamp collection I had maintained for ten years. It had US stamps from the late 1800s onward, and twentieth-century stamps from everywhere else in the world. Including places I didn't pronounce correctly, like Seychelles. It had at least one full page of stamps for each country. When I discovered they were missing and asked why, Grampa said: "I got rid of them."

When I asked, "Why did you do that?!" in astonishment, he became silent and hung his head. He wouldn't tell me why. Complaining wouldn't accomplish anything, so I said nothing more after this first inquiry. I didn't tell Nana or Mom, but remained mystified by what Grampa had done.

At first, I thought he secretly sold all my stamps to pay for some financial crisis he and Nana experienced during the two years of my mission. Although this possibility made me feel better about my loss, I decided against that explanation. A stamp dealer would regard my collection as worthless. Since my stamps always fell off the temporary stickers recommended for serious collectors, I had permanently glued them onto the pages of my big album. Thus, I was stumped to understand why Grampa had disposed of it.

Years afterward, Mom would make an offhand remark that explained what he did. She said that he secretly rifled through her keepsakes and destroyed every photo of Wayne Hood that he could find, as well as every letter and love note that her ex-husband had written to Mom.

The large stamp album that Grampa threw away was a gift from Mom and Wayne to me, which had my ex-stepfather's signature on its front page. That was apparently why Grampa disposed of thousands of beautiful, vintage stamps from all over the world.

Rather than tearing Wayne's hated name from its front page, Grampa threw my stamp album away. I can't understand such blind hatred. Especially when it obviously hurts someone besides the object of hate.

Early September 1965–Former Stepfather

During the week I was in Glendale before returning to BYU (on a renewed student draft deferment), I wanted to visit Wayne. Notwithstanding all the problems in his marriage to Mom, I had grown to love him. His adultery and their divorce didn't change that.

When I went to his apartment, he seemed to answer the door reluctantly—even though I had phoned in advance to ask if I could visit. He kept backing away as I greeted him. The more I tried to talk casually, the more he stepped away.

Finally, I was standing in the middle of the apartment, while his back was against the farthest wall. He had hardly uttered a word, when I finally said: "Wayne, I still love you. I guess I'll be going." He remained silent as I quietly closed the door, saying: "Goodbye."

Never saw him again, nor heard from him. I understood but felt sad about it.

Early September 1965–Loan from A Weak Drunk

It was Nana, not Grampa, who arranged a meeting with one of his brothers to ask him to give me a much-needed loan to attend BYU this year. During their discussion, I was thinking: "You've called him 'a weak drunk' my whole life, Nana, and here you are groveling before him on my behalf—because he's the richest of your despised in-laws."

Uncle Ruben had typically arrived smelling of beer at the noontime Workman Family reunions I attended as a child. Now he seemed to be relishing his supremacy in dealing with his disapproving, poor sister-in-law.

In spite of all her problems, Nana's love for me was boundless. She did everything in her power for me. Uncle Rube loaned me the money.

12 September 1965–Missionary Homecoming Talks

I had given my mission report to the Stake High Council on the 8th. Tonight, the Glendale West Ward hosted a sacrament meeting homecoming for me and my longtime friend David Henry to give public reports about our missions. His immigrant father had Anglicized their surname, and Dave went to a German-speaking mission. However, I was struck by the emotionless, bland, and brief talk he gave our congregation.

Afterwards, he explained: "Judging by your talk, you had positive experiences on your mission. I didn't. My mission president hated me, told me I was the most rebellious elder he'd ever known, and said he wanted to tie me to a tree and bullwhip me." Dave smiled as he said this, but anger and pain were behind the words.

I thought back on the congenial and loving support I received from three mission presidents with very different personalities and styles of leadership. I didn't know what to say to this always independent and religiously devoted friend, who had been the first teenager in our seminary class to read the Book of Mormon cover-to-cover on his own. I saw my share of lazy, rebellious elders in England, but couldn't imagine that always hard-working David Henry had been that kind of missionary.

How could a church official say such things to anyone? I didn't doubt what my friend told me, and grieved that modern Mormonism had produced such a leader.

15 September 1965–"What Leadership Position Would You Like?"

After another day-long trip on a Greyhound bus, I returned to BYU. I was living in a dorm that was then named U Hall in the recently opened Deseret Towers.

From the memoir I wrote at twenty-three: "Tonight in the dormitory, the bishop, Richard Anderson, of the BYU 47th Ward called by to see me. ... He asked me to tell him of my leadership experience in the mission, and then he asked me what job I wanted in the ward. His question caught me off guard. ...

"I told him that I would prefer to be a teacher in one of the ward classes. He looked at me intently, smiled and said, 'It's great to be a teacher, but what leadership position would you like? ...

"Although shocked at this sudden thought of being in the elders quorum presidency, I quickly answered that I would still like to be an instructor in the ward. He smiled and said, 'Well, we'll see, Dennis.' Then we shook hands and he left the room."

I dismissed as ridiculous my strong inward impression that I would be called as a counselor in the elders quorum presidency. It happened on the 28th.

Mid-September 1965–Small World of Mormon Associations

Both now and in retrospect, this semester's membership in the BYU 47th Ward had more examples of how coincidental and interlinked Mormon associations can be at far-removed places and times. Most extraordinary was the fact that Antonio A. Feliz Jr. was one of the members of my BYU ward this semester. In twenty years, as an excommunicated, divorced bishop and actively homosexual father, he would become the founder and revelatory prophet of the schismatic Restoration Church of Jesus Christ of All Latter-day Saints. It would perform same-sex ceremonies of marriage sealing for time and eternity.[7] A decade farther along, and we would meet as openly gay authors/activists in San Francisco and Salt Lake City respectively. Neither of us would then remember this early association that is verified in the BYU ward's minutes.

---

7. Antonio A. Feliz was a high priest, Latter-day Saint bishop, and temple sealer who, on August 23, 1985, along five other members of the Los Angeles chapter of "Affirmation: Gay and Lesbian Mormons," founded The Church of Jesus Christ of All Latter-day Saints, which was later renamed the Restoration Church of Jesus Christ. The church dissolved in 2010.

Mid-September 1965–Speech Therapy

I decided to remedy my speech defect for three reasons. First, an English boy with a severe lisp deflated my ego a month earlier in Crawley by saying cheerfully: "You tawk jusht like Ah do, eldah."

Second, I planned to teach full time in the seminary program for high school students and decided that I should learn to form "s" sounds "normally." This would avoid ridicule from rebellious kids.

Third, speech therapy was free for BYU students.

Imagine my surprise when I met the assigned therapist and discovered that she was a friend from my teenage years in the Glendale Stake! Cathy Kearl and I cheerfully greeted and reminisced about the times she and her friends took me to beach parties. Her father, a physician, had been on the Stake High Council during those years.

Now she said: "It's great seeing you again, but what on earth brings you to the Speech Therapy Department?" When I explained that I wanted to overcome my bilateral lisp, she did another double-take.

After a pause: "Until this moment, despite my training, I never realized that you have a speech impediment. In our teenage years, I just thought you had a distinctive way of speaking, and that perception continued as we talked today." The same age as me, she was now a senior in speech therapy.

But, with Cathy's skillful assistance, I learned to make sibilants crisply with my tongue, rather than thickly through the sides of my mouth.[8] During that process, there was a strange period when I had trained myself not to speak the old way, but wasn't sure how to speak the new way, and so tried to avoid words with sibilants. It now reminds me of the sociological concept of *anomie* (being without norms).

I'll never forget the feeling of triumph and happiness the day I got praise for my correctly pronouncing "she sells seashells by the seashore" at regular speed. I was twenty-one.

Mid-September 1965–Return of Biblical Job

Shortly after my return to BYU, the boils returned. With a vengeance. Each armpit filled with a nest of boils, which a doctor at the student health clinic called a carbuncle. He said that I had a severe, systemic infection, which required anti-staph shots on Mondays, Wednesdays, and Fridays from mid-September until Christmas vacation. Twelve weeks!

He was right. After the injections ended in three months, a small boil developed but shrank before coming to a head. Then no more. I ceased being a latter-day Job.

When I complained to him once about my situation during this time, the

---

8. A sibilant is the sound of an "s" or "sh" in spoken English.

BYU physician said: "Just be grateful you're not like so many of the missionaries to Latin America. They come back here with damaged intestines from parasites or amoebic dysentery!" I *was* grateful for that, and stopped complaining about the boils and shots. Now I was glad that I didn't serve a mission in Mexico.

Early October 1965–Corresponding with Oscar Winner

After all the years of listening to Mom's memories concerning what Dad had told her about knowing Hollywood actor Anthony Quinn and after hearing all the denials by Dad, I decided to find out the truth in the only way I could. In care of a theatrical agent, I wrote to Mr. Quinn, asking him to clarify this if he possibly could.

My mother had suggested that I do this. She even provided a newspaper clipping that named his agent.

Recognizing my sincerity, Anthony answered in a two-page letter. The man I knew as Donald Peña Quinn was the boy Daniel Peña he grew up with in Los Angeles. He also verified knowing my grandmother Carmen and her older sons, whom Anthony didn't respect as he did my father, Dan.

In addition to this confirmation, Anthony explained how Dad acquired the name Quinn. He simply tacked it onto his own as a teenager, because he wanted Anthony's family to adopt him. This *simpatico* response to my letter made me wish I had introduced myself to the famous actor when I had the opportunity in my mid-teens.

More stunning was the letter's heartfelt tribute to my father as an unusual bookworm who introduced Anthony to good books, opera, and the wider culture of the world. With more details and some funny anecdotes, Anthony Quinn would publish such praise for Dan in the first installment of this Mexican actor's memoir, *The Original Sin*.

30 October 1965–Veil Worker at Manti Temple

From the memoir I wrote at twenty-three: "Today at 6:30 in the morning I met Dave Payne in the lobby of the dorm and we drove to the Manti Temple for an endowment session."

Golden sandstone made this the best looking of Utah's temples. The down-to-earth, affectionately back-slapping behavior of its farmer ordinance workers made the Manti Temple my favorite.

I rode there in my missionary friend's VW Beetle every week or two, when we served as proxies for an endowment session. We became well enough known as regular attenders from BYU, that a member of the temple's presidency gave us a special tour of the building one day. This included the circular staircase within each of its towers. Dave and I continued these trips for eighteen months.

2 November 1965–General Authority Warns Against CES Employment

From the memoir I wrote at twenty-three: "Today Dave Payne and I went to see President Hanks in Salt Lake City. We had arranged to meet with him to discuss our plans to enter the Church Seminary and Institute program of education. ...

"President Hanks related some of his experiences in the seminary system and in the institutes. He referred to both the advantages and disadvantages of teaching with the church. During our conversation he also mentioned J. Reuben Clark Jr., Joseph Fielding Smith, Harold B. Lee, and Bruce R. McConkie.

"When we left his office, the Church Office Building was nearly deserted, it being long after closing hours.[9] Our meeting with President Hanks had been very enlightening and rewarding."

And now, the details: Our former mission president (a general authority seventy) spent more than an hour telling us about the personal discrimination, politicking, and anti-intellectualism within the Church Educational System. His remarks about Elder McConkie's dogmatism were basically the same that he had expressed privately to me in the fall of 1963.

Suddenly, President Hanks interrupted himself by saying: "And I'm so sick and tired of Harold B. Lee acting as if he is the president of the Church. He isn't even the senior apostle! Joseph Fielding Smith is." I was stunned and, like my friend Dave Payne, said nothing.

Likewise, his anti-Clark anecdote didn't involve Church education. After J. Reuben was demoted from being first counselor in 1951, his replacement arranged to hire an unemployed friend for a job at LDS headquarters. The new First Counselor, Stephen L Richards, died eight years afterward, and the reinstated Clark fired the low-level functionary. President Hanks condemned this "outrageous abuse of power." He gave this hapless employee's name and job, but I don't remember them now.

Then he continued talking about the seminary and institute program, giving negative examples of various administrators in CES (whom he named), their arbitrary behavior, and prejudiced decisions. He told us that our combination of intellect, spirituality, and independence would "not survive the system."

Due to this candid talk with President Hanks, I reconsidered my plans to teach religion full time for the church. I'd flunked out of pre-med but had almost straight A's in English. If I didn't become a seminary teacher, I could become an English professor.

Still, I was very reluctant to again give up all prospects for an anticipated

---

9. Today's Church Office Building was not completed until 1972, so Quinn is likely referring to what is now called the Church Administration Building, where many general authorities have offices. Completed in 1917, the building is a neoclassical design, located at 47 East South Temple in Salt Lake City.

career. Next year, I took a BYU course in teaching scriptures. It was required for CES applicants, and I wanted to retain that option.

Although Dave Payne had read the Book of Mormon twenty-two times(!) before age nineteen, he now definitely gave up his dream of being a full-time seminary teacher. He became a sociologist, with a master's thesis on "Social Determinants of Leadership in the Mormon Missionary System."[10]

15 November 1965–Miraculous Healing

From the memoir I wrote at twenty-three: "Tonight I was called in to help administer to a young man who had gone blind. His blindness resulted from a diabetic condition. ... Now in a matter of days he had become blind in one eye, and almost completely blind in the other eye.

"Wally Hilmo, my elders quorum president, came into my room and asked me to join the administration in the fellow's room. When I entered the room, I was almost overwhelmed by the influence of the Spirit of the Lord. ...

"The stake president's first counselor, Brother [Carl D.] Jones, Bishop Anderson, and several others were there in the room already, and I can truthfully say that the Spirit of God burned within that room as I have rarely felt it before. Bishop Anderson anointed the afflicted young man and President Jones sealed the anointing. As I laid my hands with the other brethren, I felt (for the first time in an administration) the warmth of the Spirit enter my very fingertips.

"The young man was blessed [by Jones] that although he had to withdraw from school now he would return next semester. He was also blessed that through the power of God and the skill of man's power, his sight would be restored.

"At the time of the blessing three Utah doctors (two of them eye specialists) had told him that he was going totally blind and might as well start studying Braille.

"I left the room with a feeling of assurance that the blessing would be fulfilled.

"(Note: next semester the young man returned to school to resume his studies. Through an operation at his home state, his sight was very much restored.)"

Later, the BYU 47th Ward's minutes of sacrament meeting on 6 February 1966 announced "the return of Jim Miller with his sight."

Late 1965–Converting to Organic Evolution

During my honors program course in animal biology, a BYU professor progressively demolished every anti-evolutionary view I had maintained

---

10. David Payne became an American sociologist, trained at the University of North Carolina-Chapel Hill. He taught at multiple universities before becoming Provost at Sam Houston State University in Conroe, Texas. He retired in 2011.

since adolescence. This included Apostle Joseph Fielding Smith's arguments against the evolution of new species, concerning which zoologist Henry J. Nicholes triumphantly announced, "BYU botanists have been *creating* new species of plants for decades." From the age of the earth, to the mutability of species, to the "survival of the fittest," to the human connection with lower primates, I was gradually persuaded to become a reluctant Darwinist.

Whether I liked it or not, the Heavenly Father of all the spirits of humanity was creator-as-overseer of earthly processes that took billions of years to result in humans. Instead of special creation for "every living creature" (Genesis 2:19), Charles Darwin was basically right about incremental creation*s* by natural selection that originated spontaneously in the oceans and continued on land.

Professor Nicholes emphasized that *Origin of the Species* repeatedly expressed Darwin's abiding faith in God. Like Galileo, Darwin challenged his religion's views of reality, while remaining a believing radical. I'm not sure if that's exaggeration, since I've never read *Origin* and have heard that Darwin was an agnostic when he wrote it.

Nonetheless, I would get intellectual comfort a dozen years after 1965, while reading *Out of Chaos*. Its author, Louis J. Halle, found his decades-long atheism continually challenged by the statistical improbabilities required for completely random evolution in the cosmos and in living things. The seemingly impossible statistics required for the convergence of even two such coincidences troubled him. But I laughed out loud at reading the soul-searching involved in his maintaining the atheistic requirement for randomness when confronted with dozens of virtually impossible coincidences necessary for the evolution of life as currently understood by scientists in various fields.

Atheism, theism, and science involve cognitive dissonance. Social psychologist Leon Festinger was too limiting a decade ago, when he coined that term in *When Prophecy Fails* to describe people who maintain clearly contradictory beliefs of religion versus facts of reality. Logic and common sense can also fail.

Because I continued to maintain my own faith from 1965 onward in the reality of an *eventual* Adam and Eve of religious significance, I found myself thinking that Brigham Young might have been right that they "were first brought here from another planet" (*Journal of Discourses* 7:286). However, I still left that on the shelf, while concluding that the biblical author of Genesis was creatively symbolic.

On the other hand, while talking with BYU philosopher Truman G. Madsen in his office about President Young's Adam-God statements, I bristled as an undergraduate when this professor's secretary said: "What does it matter?"[11]

---

11. Truman G. Madsen (1926–2009) was a professor of philosophy and religion at BYU, as well as director of the BYU-Jerusalem Center for Near Eastern Studies.

My withholding judgment was not the same as saying that something doesn't *matter*. I can live with not understanding important things, but I cannot glibly dismiss the mysterious as insignificant to human awareness. Or as unworthy of efforts to comprehend. The life of mind is intertwined with the life of spirit—at least for me.

Late 1965–New Perspective on Vietnam War

A returned missionary from the North British Mission was my roommate in the dorm. Nearly three years older and a pre-med major, Garth W. Holyoak often commented about the difficulty of his courses, which made me feel better about my own failure in the field.

One day, Garth was depressed about a letter from his brother, who had been shipped to Vietnam with Idaho National Guardsmen after the Army paid for his dental schooling. Arriving in Saigon, his brother was assigned to be a field surgeon with those troops, despite being trained only in oral surgery. Yet that wasn't why Garth was depressed.

The letter described how this combat unit of southeastern Idaho farm boys cut off the ears and genitals of dead Viet Cong, then wore those body parts as trophies on their belts. Garth told me: "I knew these Mormons in Idaho and grew up with their older brothers. I can't understand how these boys could do such terrible things."

There was nothing I could say, but hoped that my Idaho cousins were not in Vietnam. I remembered Coy and the others fondly, yet had no contact with them now.

12 January 1966–Teaching Assistant for Book of Mormon

From the memoir I wrote at twenty-three: "I have been given the opportunity to be a teaching assistant in the Book of Mormon. Although I am only a sophomore, I was recommended by Robert K. Thomas, director of the honors program to Dr. Daniel Ludlow. After the meeting with Dr. Ludlow he hired me as his assistant.

"Brother Ludlow is in charge of the TV Book of Mormon classes. As his assistant I spend about 10 hours a week working for him. On Fridays I teach a discussion group in Book of Mormon, reviewing the week's lectures."

Daniel H. Ludlow, a member of the Correlation Committee at church headquarters, had pioneered this course of televised lectures at BYU.[12] They

---

12. Daniel H. Ludlow (1924–2009) was a BYU professor from 1955–72, where he served for a time as dean of Religious Education. He later became director of teacher support services for the Church Educational System and director of the church's Correlation Department. Church president Joseph F. Smith founded the Correlation Committee in 1908 to ensure all church publications conformed to official church doctrine. In the early 1960s, President David O. McKay charged apostle Harold B. Lee to form committees "to correlate the instruction and

were held twice weekly for hundreds of students assembled in the Joseph Smith Auditorium. In my discussion group, I answered questions and gave added information to students regarding the Book of Mormon.

16 January 1966–President of Young Men, BYU 47th Ward

Bishop Richard L. Anderson (a religion professor) told me that he was too busy writing a book to spend much time with the sixty or so young men of our ward who were in the Aaronic Priesthood. He instructed me to get to know them as if I were their bishop, since I resided in Deseret Towers with them. He also authorized me to do personal counseling he didn't have time to do.

Without public explanation of my actual role as substitute bishop for the ward's young men who weren't returned missionaries, its members sustained me on January 16 to be the Aaronic Priesthood general secretary. I also continued serving as counselor in the elders quorum until publicly released on February 6.

From mid-January onward, I averaged three-to-four hours each evening visiting with the young men of the ward. I continued this intense activity in the 1966–67 school year, even though Bishop Anderson's successor, D. Evan Davis, made a greater effort to know the young men in the dorm. This calling and my close personal association with missionaries in England were the two happiest periods of my LDS Church service.

In four decades, a man came to me at an academic meeting and asked: "Did you do religious counseling for the guys in 'U' Hall at BYU in the 1965–66 school year?" When I answered that I did, he said: "You're the reason I went on a mission." Hearing this—after so many years—made me feel very happy.

17 January 1966–What I don't Want to Be

As written on this day: "I am very unsettled in my feelings. I don't have the desire to 'be the best,' or to be an avid scholar. I just want to be me. I don't want to be looked up to as a great scholar or scriptorian, and have others look on in awe. I want to be down-to-earth, warm, simple, and not have so much respect that people are hesitant to be themselves around me."

2 February 1966–Scripture as Literature

Taught by English professor Robert K. Thomas, "The Bible as Literature"

curriculum of all priesthood and auxiliary organizations of the church." Under Lee, correlation took on a wider scope than just curriculum, including bringing the auxiliary organizations (such as the Relief Society, Primary, Young Women and Young Men programs, Primary, and Sunday School), directly under the control of the Quorum of the Twelve Apostles. *Church News*, February 13, 1993; Daniel H. Ludlow, "I Have a Question," *Ensign*, Mar. 1986, 50–55; "Ministry of Harold B. Lee: Priesthood Correlation is Created," churchofjesuschrist.org; "An Era of Correlation and Consolidation," in *Church History In The Fulness Of Times Student Manual* (2003), www.churchofjesuschrist.org.

was one of the most significant courses I took at BYU. With a brilliant mind, he was a spellbinding lecturer. From a believer's perspective, he introduced me to several dimensions of biblical criticism.

I was especially impressed by his analysis of ancient Hebrew poetry that was discernable in the English translation, due to ancient literary emphasis on parallelisms—synonymous, antithetical, and synthetic.

Beginning in the summer, I would follow this course with years of my own research into many different approaches toward analyzing the Bible. As a reader, I had loved the Old Testament's narratives since adolescence, but Bob Thomas showed how to use the King James Version to *teach* the Hebrew Bible as vibrant storytelling, mixed with scholarly exegesis. I also studied an interlinear Greek-English version of the New Testament for carefully comparing its use of three words for love: *eros, philia,* and *agape.*

By applying Thomas techniques to all the Standard Works, this would become my central approach as a Sunday school teacher in the Gospel Doctrine classes of various wards for nearly twenty-one years. Whether newlyweds or elderly temple workers, the Mormons in these classes were fascinated—not disturbed—when I explained J-E-D-P authorship,[13] second Isaiah, the Johannine Problem,[14] poetic parallelisms, and other textual insights into the Holy Bible. Whenever members of those classes praised me as a teacher, I felt that Bob Thomas deserved half the credit.

Early 1966–A Devout Freshman Shakes My Confidence

After my discussion with apostle LeGrand Richards in December 1961, I had felt confident of the traditional explanations by church authorities and LDS historians about plural marriages after the 1890 Manifesto. However, one afternoon Stephen E. Robinson (a religiously devoted freshman who was already studying the New Testament in Greek) confronted me in the BYU dorm with the accusation that his religion professor had willfully lied to the class that morning by claiming that anyone who married in polygamy after the Manifesto was an adulterer.[15] "My grandfather was a mission president who married two plural wives in Salt Lake City ten years after the Manifesto, and my family has a recommend for one of the marriages—signed by President Joseph F. Smith."

---

13. Many Bible scholars argue that the first five books of the Old Testament were written by four different unknown authors, each with a distinct writing tell—Jahwist (J), Elohist (E), Deuteronomist (D), and Priest (P).

14. The "Johannine Problem," refers to the debate about whether the apostle John wrote the Gospel of John and whether the text is literal history or a figurative, dramatic account of the author's experiences.

15. Stephen E. Robinson (1947–2018) went on to earn a PhD in biblical studies from Duke University. In 1986 he began teaching religion at BYU, where he remained until his retirement in 2012, serving six years as the department chair of Ancient Scripture.

By this time, Steve was yelling: "That religion teacher was lying! My grandfather was not an adulterer! He stayed mission president for years, and President Smith knew he married after the Manifesto." I spent an hour persuading this student that the religion professor wouldn't lie to the class, but obviously was unaware of cases like his grandfather's.

I was deeply disturbed by what Steve told me about his grandfather's post-Manifesto polygamous marriages. This didn't fit the explanation of apostle Richards and traditional histories by B. H. Roberts and Joseph Fielding Smith that people entered post-Manifesto polygamy without authorization of the First Presidency. I couldn't believe Steve's story and (without indicating my skepticism) asked for his grandfather's name to look into it.

The next weekend, I took the bus from Provo to the LDS Genealogical Library in Salt Lake City. There I found individually submitted family group sheets showing that Joseph E. Robinson married two plural wives in 1901 (during April and October general conferences). He remained president of the California Mission for almost twenty years, during which time he fathered children by all his wives. That day ended my confidence in traditional Mormon historians.

This BYU student set me on a quest to understand post-Manifesto polygamy and every other historical claim about the LDS Church made by anti-Mormons. In the process, I found that traditional Mormon historians were denying the existence of things that anti-Mormons could demonstrate even from Mormon sources. I felt that this was a great vulnerability for the average Mormon. I was determined to get to the bottom of every historical claim made by anti-Mormons and do what traditional historians had not been doing: acknowledge all the evidence and still come up with an explanation that was both honest and reassuring for believers.

Twenty-one years later, I published *Early Mormonism and the Magic World View* with that purpose, but ironically it would receive a vicious and dishonest review by Stephen Robinson in *BYU Studies,* when he was on BYU's religion faculty.[16] I'd had no contact with him since his freshman year.

Still, this religion professor would maintain some integrity about post-Manifesto polygamy. His Deseret Book publication of *Following Christ* told faithful Mormons: "My grandmother, Willmia Brown, for example, once heard an audible voice identify Joseph E. Robinson as her future husband, and it turned out to be so."[17] Even though he wouldn't publicly specify that his grandparents married polygamously in Salt Lake City a decade af-

16. See Stephen E. Robinson, "Review of *Early Mormonism and the Magic World View,*" *BYU Studies* 27, no. 4 (Fall 1987): 88–95.

17. Stephen E. Robinson, *Following Christ: The Parable of the Divers and More Good News* (Salt Lake City: Deseret Book, 1995), 104.

ter the 1890 Manifesto prohibited such marriages, Stephen E. Robinson wouldn't repeat the specific misrepresentation he condemned this semester. A polemical apologist's half-full glass of honest history.

Spring 1966–Warned against Controversial History

One day, graduate student Jeff Holland came to Brother Ludlow's office and stopped by the teaching assistant room. When he entered, both of the teaching assistants present were former British missionaries. The older TA, Kenneth H. Patey, had been there during what he called "the nightmare years of baseball baptisms."

While I was in the British Mission, President Marion D. Hanks had often spoken in glowing terms of Elder Holland, his zone counselor who returned to the United States a year before I arrived. In England, several elders had told me they thought he was the missionary that Hugh B. Brown was referring to when this First Presidency counselor prophesied at an all-mission meeting in London that one of the missionaries there would become a member of the Quorum of the Twelve Apostles.

However, this was their conflation of memory. When I checked the mission's manuscript history in preparing this self-biography, I found that President Brown had made a prediction that "there were those in the room who would one day sit in the presiding councils of the Church" in October 1962, a month *after* Elder Holland returned to the USA. This general authority's only other long sermon to British Missionaries had been a month *before* the young man arrived in England in 1960. The only other possibility was a meeting in February 1961 (when Elder Holland certainly attended), where the typed history noted (without details) that Counselor Brown "delivered a most remarkable and inspirational address" for only a few minutes—in deference to President McKay, who was giving the main talk to the missionaries that day. The mission's history mentioned no prediction at this 1961 meeting. Nonetheless, the prophetic expectations expressed to me in 1963–64 about Jeffrey R. Holland's apostleship would be fulfilled.

After sharing our mutual admiration for President Hanks this spring of 1966, I asked Jeff how his graduate program was going. He suddenly became subdued, explaining that he was having difficulties with religion professors and with BYU's administrators about completing his master's thesis on textual changes in various editions of the Book of Mormon. He didn't specify who was delaying his thesis, but I doubt that it was his thesis chairman, Professor Ludlow.

"Never write about a controversial subject in Mormon history, no matter how interesting and worthwhile you think it is," Jeff Holland advised me during our 1966 conversation. "It'll bring you more trouble than it's worth."

His controversial MA thesis was approved in the summer.[18] Meanwhile, I remained Brother Ludlow's teaching assistant for nearly two years.

16 May 1966–Advocate for American Communist Party

To my pleasant surprise, there was enough academic freedom at BYU for today's *Daily Universe* to publish an op-ed by Bob King advocating legalization of the Communist Party USA.[19] This seemed like good public policy to me, since the Communist Party had previously appeared on the ballot in Utah and other states, and especially since it was currently a legal political party in Britain and in the free countries of Western Europe (excluding still-fascist Spain, for example).

In four years, Robert R. King and I would become friends in Munich, Germany, where I would be engaged in combating "the international Communist conspiracy." He'd later work there for Radio Free Europe. Mormon culture can be both small and ironic.

5 June 1966–"Strangers in the Night"

After returning from BYU, I commenced working at Glendale Adventist Hospital for the second time. There were limited openings for nursing orderlies this summer, so I sat around most of the time doing nothing in the hospital's central supplies section.

My enduring memory of this experience was sitting in the central supplies room when I first heard Frank Sinatra singing "Strangers In the Night." It bowled me over.

In spite of knowing he was hetero, I was sure that the song was about two homosexuals exchanging glances—possibly in the kind of gay bar I had seen depicted in the 1962 movie *Advise and Consent*. In contrast to that homophobic film, this song affected me deeply as a suggestion of gay romance in popular music.

In two decades, I would begin purchasing music albums that more openly presented same-sex love—songs by Perry Blake, Bronski Beat, Communards, Death Cab for Cutie, Depeche Mode, Duran Duran, Erasure, Melissa Etheridge, Jason and DeMarco, Elton John, K. D. Lang, Paul Lekakis, George Michaels, New Order, Nirvana, Pet Shop Boys, Red Hot Chili Peppers, Soft Cell, Village People, and Rufus Wainwright. Their singers were either gay, bisexual, or gay-accepting heteros.

18. See Jeffrey R. Holland, "An Analysis of Selected Changes in Major Editions of the Book of Mormon, 1830–1920," available at scholarsarchive.byu.edu.

19. Established in 1919, the Communist Party USA (CPUSA) played a large role in American politics before the Cold War and McCarthyism marginalized it. The CPUSA was influential in the US labor movement, especially for its outspoken opposition to racism against Black Americans.

Same country. Same culture. Same old me. But a different world. A better one, I think.

Mid-June 1966–Former Bishop Asks My Advice

Scheduled to move to London in six months as the new president of the British Mission, Reed Callister asked me to give him information and counsel that might help prepare him for the challenges. I was deeply moved by my former bishop's interest in getting my views.

I talked to him about the effects of baseball baptisms, which I blamed on the common practice of giving baptism goals to missionaries and stressing statistics. I spoke about the devotion of British Saints, and the problem of their being treated like colonials by American missionary leaders. I also confided to him my perceptions of problems in the leadership of his immediate predecessors in the mission home, O. Preston Robinson and his wife, Christine.

It was an earful, and at times my candor seemed to surprise Bishop Callister. Nonetheless, he repeatedly thanked me for the insights and suggestions.

8 July 1966–Occupational Adventure

Getting the go-ahead by phone today, I abruptly quit my job at Glendale Adventist Hospital and moved to Salt Lake City. There I planned to begin high-paying work in freeway construction. I had arranged this through Irvin H. Jacob (one of my Aaronic Priesthood boys in the BYU ward), whose brother was a senior officer in the construction company.

I hadn't been able to do this during the previous month because of a labor strike, which the older brother now said was about to end. Solely as a favor, he promised me a post-strike job and told me to join the Iron Workers Union as a summer temp when I arrived.

After another Greyhound bus trip, I began staying rent free in a spare room of the Sugarhouse apartment occupied by Grampa's second cousin, Arnold Burgener and his wife, Jane. They had attended the Glendale West Ward during my first years growing up in that congregation.

Because I would be a temp laborer in building freeway overpasses at various locations, I needed a car. From savings, I paid bottom price for a ten-year-old Mercury—the first car I could call my own.

It was a gamble to abandon my secure, low-paying job in Glendale, but Mormon associations of family, BYU ward, and mission made it possible to earn lots of money. I also found myself depending on the kindness of strangers in Utah.

Mid-July 1966–*Who's Afraid of Virginia Woolf?*

I hadn't yet read any of the novels by this English lesbian, married to a man, who mixed her painfully empathetic view of people's inner conflicts with stream-of-consciousness narratives. Thus, I had no appreciation for the multi-level ironies in the title of Edward Albee's play, which I had never heard of. I was simply eager to see the extremely talented Elizabeth Taylor and Richard Burton in another movie. It was their first together since *Cleopatra*, and this film's title just sounded fun.

But fun is not the way to describe what I saw at Sugarhouse's Southeast Theatre on 21st South. The venomous insults and vicious hatred spewed by the movie's husband and wife reminded me of growing up with my grandparents. I left the cinema feeling shell-shocked.

I couldn't get those scenes out of my thoughts for weeks. The movie's acerbic husband was certainly not passively benign Grampa, but (with her own reasons for bitterness) its caustic wife was far too close to portraying Nana. They had been my decades-long negative examples of Mormon family life, and Albee now provided me with negative examples in the marriage of an English professor—which I was preparing to become.

I again vowed that I would never, *never* allow my future marriage to degenerate into even one such argument. No matter what our differences or conflicts, I would always treat my wife with the utmost dignity, respect, and love. I *had* to find a young woman who would treat me the same. I prayed to God to give both of us at least that minimum quality of matrimony.

1 August 1966–Fledgling Construction Worker

From the memoir I wrote at twenty-three: "Having finally gotten clearance through the iron workers local, I started work today in constructing freeway bridges. It is the toughest work I have ever done. Within an hour after starting I fell while carrying the long iron rods (called 'punking iron'), and ripped my left leg. After going to a doctor to be patched up, I went back to work.

"By quitting time my muscles throbbed, I was having cold chills and dizzy spells from the blazing sun, and I had scraped off most of the skin from both of my shoulders by punking iron. I came home feeling worse than I can ever remember, but having earned over $30 in the first day." Sweating profusely in the oppressive heat, I struggled through a second day on the partially completed overpass. This work was more strenuous than I ever imagined.

3 August 1966–Fired

From the memoir I wrote at twenty-three: "Today I was laid off from the construction job. I had scraped the skin off my shoulders so badly that there was only raw flesh left. I couldn't carry the iron on my shoulders and was told that if I didn't carry it on my shoulders, that I'd better quit, so I did.

"All my plans of saving hundreds of dollars this summer were shot. At almost $5.00 an hour I could have done it. But now I have no job in Salt Lake, no job to return to at Glendale, almost no money since I had been required to buy a car in Salt Lake in order to get the construction job, and only a few weeks before school started.

"I was so depressed about losing my job I felt like going out and getting drunk, and I almost did. But instead I got the biggest bottle of Coca Cola I could find, parked my car, and tried to drown my sorrows as best as I could." Thus ended my hopes of netting enough money from this summer's job to avoid loans for attending BYU.

I felt tremendous admiration for the sweating laborers who sometimes risked their health and lives on various job sites. Thus I became an avid supporter of labor unions—even the corrupt teamsters and longshoremen. While supporting governmental prosecution and imprisonment for corruption within labor unions, I honored all strikes and refused to cross picket lines. As always, I wanted checks and balances on power in all facets of social interaction. For *everyone*.

I no longer cared what the living prophet had written in his 1965 letter against unions and for the Taft-Hartley Act. Hard-working women and men needed protections and benefits, plus power against the onslaught of slash-and-burn corporations.

9 August 1966–Tailspin

From the memoir I wrote at age twenty-three: "I have been so depressed the past few days that I can barely endure it. I do not know why I am here in Salt Lake City. After losing the job with the construction company I began working as a salesman with my distant cousin Bob Burgener in his music store. But although I thought I would have done well in soliciting and sales presentation [to acquire new students for music lessons], I have not.

"I feel like a failure and also like a fool for coming up here. I had felt that the Lord wanted me to come to Salt Lake City but everything has gone sour since I came here. I have begun to doubt that the Lord really wanted me here, yet I know that He did."

15 August 1966–A Friend's Spiritual Impression

From the memoir I wrote at twenty-three: "At 6:30 in the morning there was a knock at the door. I quickly arose and answered it. To my surprise there stood Martin Diestler and his recent bride, Joy. They had driven all the way from Provo to see me. I went out to the car to greet Joy (who had been in the mission field with me in England at the same time he was there), then Martin and I began walking down the sidewalk talking at that early morning hour.

"Martin and I talked together for about an hour. He had not received and opened my letter until the midnight before, since I had forwarded it through David Payne. He was so concerned at the depressed tone of the letter that he decided to drive to see me that very morning, after only about five hours of sleep.

"As we talked together the Spirit of the Lord burned within me, and he commented on how he could also feel within himself the intensity of the Spirit that glowed within me. We discussed my coming to Salt Lake, the disappointments, and my spiritual depression.

"He chided me for doubting the Lord's prompting that led me to Salt Lake. He said that he did not know why the Lord had called me here, but he said that he felt that the Lord's purposes were to begin their unfolding perhaps this very week."

16 August 1966–Guide on Temple Square, Salt Lake City

From the memoir I wrote at twenty-three: "Today it occurred to me to inquire if I could become a guide at Temple Square. Marion D. Hanks had written a letter to me on July 20 about my expressed desire to be a guide at Temple Square. He said that the guides for the summer had been selected in April and had been at work for several months, and that there were hundreds who would like to be guides.

"I decided today to ask him what I should do to apply. I went to the Church Office Building and met him just as he was leaving the building. He said that he didn't have time to talk with me, but told me to see President Ted Jacobsen at the new visitors center.

"After leaving President Hanks, I went to the visitors center in search of President Jacobsen. He wasn't there so I called at his construction company. He said that nothing could be done for me for at least a year and perhaps longer. But he said to see Mrs. Viola Clawson at the old bureau of information and fill out an application to be a guide. With my hopes pretty well diminished, I went to see Sister Clawson.

"At the bureau of information I met Sister Clawson and asked for an appointment and application form. After I completed it, she looked it over quickly as we talked. When she noticed that President Hanks was one of my mission presidents, she said, 'You know I just think that he is the finest man. But I think he sends almost every one of his missionaries here.' We talked for a few minutes, then she said, 'You know, Dennis, I have a stack of applications three inches thick. But I have a feeling about you.'

"She paused and then told me to go on as many guided tours today and tomorrow as I could, and that I could substitute for a guide on a Thursday evening tour. The Spirit of the Lord burned within me as I realized that my hopes and prayers were realized."

17 August 1966–Surgical Orderly

From the memoir I wrote at twenty-three: "Today I felt prompted to apply for work at the LDS Hospital in Salt Lake City. ... Bob Burgener's mother, with whom I was living suggested I try the hospital again. I didn't hold out much hope, but I thought I'd try today.

"As I drove up to the hospital, the Spirit of the Lord burned within me. I felt that this is what He wanted me to do.

"In talking with the personnel manager, he said that the surgery department needed orderlies but that he was sure the surgical supervisor would not hire me for just the five weeks before I would leave for school. As he said this, I felt the Spirit of the Lord with me, and I knew that if I could talk personally with the surgical supervisor I would be hired. I told him that I would like to talk with her in person. He shrugged and telephoned her, explaining that I wanted to work for less than five weeks.

"I heard her say 'Absolutely impossible!' in response, but [I] indicated to the personnel manager I still wanted to see her. He asked if I could come up, and she said I could but that it wouldn't do any good. As I took the elevator up to the surgery floor, the Spirit of the Lord continued strongly with me.

"Miss Thomas was abrupt as we met, but asked me to step into her office. When she came in, I began telling her about my hospital experience and my job experiences this summer, that Mr. Terry the personnel man had said that surgical orderlies were very much needed. She agreed but said that hiring one for only five weeks wouldn't be much help.

"Then she hesitated and then said that she sensed something about me that she felt confidence in, and she said that I could have the job. As I left the hospital, I felt that the Lord's prompting to me that I come to Salt Lake in July was beginning to reach its fulfillment."

With on-the-job training instructions from orderly David M. Cockayne (who had just turned 18), I began putting patients in gurneys and wheeling them to operating rooms. During down times, Dave and I talked a lot. Meeting him by accident in six years, he would tell me that I was "the main reason" he decided to go on an LDS mission (at age 20). I don't know why I had such an impact. Ironically, he would also serve as a missionary in England.

One day in a corridor, Dave motioned toward a semi-conscious, elderly patient on a gurney. "He's a general authority named Anthony R. Ivins." I knew at the time that his actual name was Antoine, but not until decades later would my research for this self-biography alert me to the fact that he had once attended Church services weekly in LA with my grandparents and Mom.

My biggest surprise occurred one morning when I wheeled a patient into an OR and saw Brent Pratley, a new MD. Most surgeons have some kind of music playing during their procedures, but he filled the OR with laughter by the anesthesiologist, RNs, and me at his very funny jokes. At first, I wondered if the unconscious patient could somehow enjoy the humor.

Then he crossed the line by referring to this obese woman as a "whale." Recalling what he had said when we were ward teachers, I left the OR as soon as possible. Pratley eventually became the physician for BYU's football team.

18 August 1966–Religious Tour Guide

From the memoir I wrote at twenty-three: "Today, I took my first tour on Temple Square. About fifty people were on the tour, and I was a little shaken at the new responsibility, but the Lord was with me.

"Sister Clawson told me that I would be substituting for tours for the rest of the summer. I was also given the 5:30 Sunday afternoon tour on a regular basis."

Each tour had from 50 to 300 people, and I continued guiding tours whenever I resided in Salt Lake City during the next seven years. Among the letters of appreciation I received from these tourists was one from a general in the US Army.

30 August 1966–Holy of Holies and Apostolic Council Room

From the memoir I wrote at age twenty-three: "Today I attended the sealing of Peter and Helen Van Orman at the Salt Lake Temple. Peter and I had been missionaries under President Hanks in England. President Hanks gave them some wonderful and inspiring counsel before sealing them as husband and wife.

"I wanted to talk with President Hanks about the possibility of getting a scholarship from the Church, since I was in such poor financial condition to start school. I waited for him to perform another ceremony, then asked if I could talk with him. He said, 'Elder, I am already late for a meeting but if you want to talk with me, I'll take you to a part of the temple you've never been in.'

"So I followed him to an elevator and we entered an upper floor of the temple where the council chambers of the general authorities were. He said I was free to look through them while he changed his clothes. I felt a deep sense of awe as I looked through the various council rooms. As I proceeded to the locker area, I saw a strange circular hump in the floor which appeared to be the ceiling of the room below.

"I felt that it was the roof of the Holy of Holies, which President Hanks confirmed. I said that I understood that it was here that the Second Anointings were given and asked him if he knew if it had been used for that purpose often in recent times. He said that he didn't think it had been used for that purpose since President McKay had become the prophet.

"We talked briefly about my desire to have scholarship aid, and he advised me to apply through BYU again, since the Church itself granted no scholarships."

And now, more details: Surrounding this floor's circular protrusion (and guarding it against too-close approach by foot) was a circle of tall light fixtures whose bulbs were directed downward to the interior of the Holy of Holies and its altar.

Downstairs, at a subsequent time, I saw the back wall of the Holy of Holies, which is a glass mosaic of Joseph Smith kneeling before God and Jesus in the Sacred Grove near Palmyra, New York. The room is the same size as an adjacent one used for performing sealings of marriage for time and eternity, but the Celestial Room's entry door to the Holy of Holies is locked during the temple's regular hours of operation.

Back to this day on the Salt Lake Temple's third floor, Marion D. Hanks took me into the small council room of the First Seven Presidents of the Seventy, which was his echelon of the LDS hierarchy. He then pointed me to the very large council room of the First Presidency and Quorum of the Twelve Apostles, with its high-backed chairs in a semi-circle around a prayer altar, its walls filled with oil paintings of former prophets and apostles.

President Hanks invited me to walk into the apostolic council room, which I did for a few minutes of solemn reflection. He didn't enter it himself, but waited patiently. For some reason, he no longer seemed rushed.

1 September 1966–An Apostle's Anger

One of my missionary companions, John Weymouth, was a convert to Mormonism and invited me to be a witness for his wedding and sealing in the Salt Lake Temple today. His fiancée, Lucy was also a convert, and they alienated both sets of parents by insisting on marrying in an LDS temple—which their non-Mormon parents were prohibited from entering. These two young Mormons traveled alone from different parts of the country to be sealed in the Salt Lake Temple.

After a few moments of conversation today, I discovered that I would be the only other person John knew at the ceremony. I met his bride this morning. A male temple worker would be the other official witness. John had arranged by mail for apostle Harold B. Lee to perform the ceremony, but they had never met.

While the three of us whispered quietly outside the sealing room, the gray-haired woman attendant began pacing back and forth. With motherly affection, she had given constant attention to this young bride, frequently adjusting Lucy's veil and wedding gown, telling her how beautiful she was, and commenting what a wonderful couple they were. Now she manifested nervous anxiety as she frequently left us to make whispered inquiries with other temple workers.

Another five minutes passed, and she came back to tell us that the temple president had phoned Elder Lee's office and that he should be here shortly.

Fifteen or twenty minutes afterward, he arrived. It was immediately apparent that he was furious. With hardly any words of greeting—and no comment about being more than thirty minutes late—he ushered the three of us and a male temple worker into the sealing room. After the man and I took our places in the witness chairs on either side of Elder Lee, he asked John and his bride to kneel at the altar and clasp hands. He pronounced the required words in a rapid monotone and said: "You may now kiss over the altar." Then Harold B. Lee strode out of the sealing room without another word.

My former companion looked at me blankly, and I think we were in shock. The other witness warmly shook hands with the newly married couple, congratulated them, and said a few words of encouragement about their future. After he left, I made small talk briefly with John and Lucy, but all I could think of was the several minutes of gentle words and counsel the officiator gave in every other temple wedding I had attended.

None of us spoke about today's ceremony or Elder Lee. To say anything under these circumstances would have been speaking evil of the Lord's anointed within the temple itself.

2 September 1966–Meeting Future Wife

From the memoir I wrote at twenty-three: "This morning I met a cute blonde girl while I was coming to get a patient for surgery at 7:30 am. I don't remember ever seeing her before, but I was particularly struck with her. Before I left work at 3:30 I asked her to go with me to the singing concert of the Beach Boys at Lagoon. Her name is Janice Darley." This was her starting week on the job.

Our first date was the evening of September 10. The performance space at Lagoon was so small, that only about fifty of us were in the standing audience. The Beach Boys were all drunk on stage. They even forgot the words to some of their songs. But they were happy drunks, and we enjoyed it.

Jan and I triple-dated here with two of last semester's Aaronic Priesthood boys—John Haymore and Craig Moffat. Their parents lived in the Salt Lake Valley.

The Moffats weren't happy at overhearing me tell Craig that I drove on Interstate 15 from Provo at 100 mph. My old Mercury had a lot of horsepower, and it was way too easy to accelerate.

For some reason, Utah's highway cops rarely patrolled from Provo to Salt Lake City in the mid-1960s, and I often drove northward at 100 mph until the 53rd South exit. At this time, there was a gap in the completion of the freeway from that exit until nearly downtown Salt Lake City.

18 September 1966–Second Date

From the memoir I wrote at twenty-three: "Tonight I went up to Jan's home for dinner. Her father is Roy M. Darley, the tabernacle organist. Tomorrow classes begin at BYU." On Thirteenth Avenue of Salt Lake City's upper avenues, the Darley family's house had a panoramic view of the valley's lights.

19 September 1966–Meaningful Friends

From the memoir I wrote at twenty-three: "Tonight while I was calling on fellows in the dorm who might be Aaronic Priesthood, I met two fellows who had been in the British Mission while I was there. Dick Lambert and Jim McConkie had both been released from their missions this summer. Our meeting tonight began an association which has been rich, spiritual, and meaningful."

Richard N. Woodruff Lambert and James Wirthlin McConkie II both had general authority ancestry, were avid students of Mormonism, and had a unique mixture of devotion and sacrilegious humor. We were instantly drawn to each other in friendships that have remained strong and supportive to the present.

Allen D. Roberts was one of my Aaronic Priesthood boys this semester. In less than ten years, we would meet by accident on Salt Lake City's Main Street. He told me about *Sunstone*, a new magazine started by young Mormons. Although Allen became an architect, this subsequent meeting led to our decades of association in what became known as the New Mormon History.[20]

25 September 1966–Suggesting Marriage on Third Date

From the memoir I wrote at age twenty-three: "Tonight I returned to Salt Lake City to see Jan. She was working up at the LDS Hospital; it is Sunday evening. I went there and spent over an hour talking with her. I felt a freedom of conversation with her that never before have I experienced with a girl.

"I felt the Spirit strongly with me as we talked, and I felt right about suggesting the possibility that we could be married next June. She seemed hesitant but I felt good about suggesting the possibility."

And now, the backstory: Following my return from my mission, I dated extensively—often with three young women at a time at BYU during last school year, in Glendale this June, and in Salt Lake City during July and

---

20. After Mark Hofmann's bombing murder of Allen Roberts's friend, Steve Christensen, Roberts and co-author Linda Sillitoe wrote a bestselling book about the Hofmann case, *Salamander: The Story of the Mormon Forgery Murders* (Salt Lake City: Signature Books, 1988). Sunstone is an organization named for an architectural symbol from the Mormon temple in Nauvoo, Illinois. Sunstone published its first magazine issue in November 1975 and began holding annual conferences in 1979. The "New Mormon History" movement focused on presenting history in a more scholarly way, departing from previous approaches to prove truth claims of Mormonism. See Quinn, ed., *The New Mormon History: Revisionist Essays on the Mormon Past* (Salt Lake City: Signature Books, 1992).

August. Jan Darley was the first for whom I felt immediate sexual attraction. For a gay boy like me, that was enough to seriously consider marriage.

Fall 1966–*Moby Dick* and Me

During a lecture in Richard G. Ellsworth's class on nineteenth-century American literature, Professor Ellsworth suddenly announced: "And I know that the rumors are false about Patriarch Joseph F. Smith being released as a general authority in 1946 for homosexuality. I shared a bed with him on a camping trip when I was sixteen, and he didn't try to touch me even once!" You could have heard a pin drop in class at that moment.

Professor Ellsworth thought that his limited view disproved the married patriarch's homosexuality.[21] But I would eventually verify it in documents at LDS Church archives and by cross-referencing the interviews of others. Multifaceted evidence trumps one person's perception.

19 November 1966–God Tells Me to Get Married

From the memoir I wrote at twenty-three: "Today I went to the Manti Temple with Dave Payne. While in the session my thoughts were about Jan Darley as they have been for weeks. I felt I had to know if I should marry her, and this was the main reason I came to the temple today.

"During the session, I made a very specific and earnest prayer to God, asking if it was His will that I ask Jan to marry me in June. By the power of the Holy Ghost the Lord revealed that I should. I felt the peace and comfort of the Lord with me."

Four evenings afterward, "as we were alone in the living room of the Darley home, I asked Jan if she would be my wife. She accepted my proposal. I felt hesitant in making this step, but felt that it was right."

On November 29, "I wrote Jan a letter and proposed to her a second time. When I had asked her to marry me last week, I wasn't really sure if the love I felt for her was the kind of love that marriage must be built on. ... I proposed to Jan again in the letter, because the first proposal came because I knew it was right by the Spirit, now I wanted to propose again for the reason that I loved her and knew I loved her and wanted to give her that love throughout eternity."

---

21. The son of LDS apostle Hyrum M. Smith and Ida Bowman Smith, Joseph Fielding Smith (1899–1964) was ordained as church patriarch in 1942 by President Heber J. Grant. In 1946 the church reported he had resigned because of "ill health," but he was released due to the discovery of his homosexual affairs. Church president George Albert Smith called the scandal "a sad happening" in his diary, describing himself as "heartsick" about the events and of releasing Smith as patriarch. D. Michael Quinn, *Same-Sex Dynamics among Nineteenth-Century Americans: A Mormon Example* (Urbana: University of Illinois Press, 2001); Gary James Bergera, "Transgression in the LDS Community: The Cases of Albert Carrington, Richard R. Lyman, and Joseph F. Smith, Part 3: Joseph F. Smith," *Journal of Mormon History* 38, no. 1 (Winter 2012): 98–130.

Thanksgiving Day, 1966, the day after Quinn and Jan
Darley became engaged. *Courtesy Quinn family.*

Jan had been facilitating my weekend visits to Salt Lake City by arranging for me to sleep in a guest room at her Aunt Margaret Latham Gardner's
house above Thirteenth Avenue.

On Friday evenings during the fall of 1966, I took Jan on a date or spent
the time at home with her and her parents. Saturdays I did homework before
that night's date, then stayed again overnight at "Aunt M's" before returning
to Provo in time for Sunday morning's meetings of my BYU ward.

Because of my lifelong love for piano music, I felt real joy in watching
Jan play the Darley family's grand piano. Sometimes she and her English-
professor mother jointly performed one of Dvorak's Slavonic dances. Other
times, Jan played sonatas just for me.

She had all the qualities I had ever hoped for in a wife. I had even prepared
a long list last year, and now Jan matched every category. Every one!

Still, the thought of marriage scared me. Looking back on it now, I realize
I was facing the same alternatives I confronted when I was twelve: seeking
homosexual fulfillment, or conforming to what family, friends, and church
demanded. However, after the confirmatory revelation in the Manti Temple
this November, I no longer had misgivings about marriage.

Several years would pass, when it became evident that the homosexual
struggle I thought I could endure alone had created a marriage of love, devotion, frustration, pain, and increasing despair for us both. Plus there was
growing resentment on Jan's part against me. This was a heavy price for a girl

to pay to fulfill a Mormon boy's sense of duty to family and to church. Not necessarily to God.

I knew that He accepted me unconditionally, but church service was the best way I knew to serve him. And that required me to be married, if I was going to preside in any capacity within Mormonism.

Early December 1966–Another's Inspiration

From the memoir I wrote at twenty-three: "Early this month, Dick Lambert came to me one morning and told me that he had had a dream about me in the night which he thought was of the Lord. He said that in this dream he saw me in Texas and I was performing a ministry for the Lord among the people."

Beyond any anticipation he or I could have had in 1966 (nor when I wrote the above memoir a year later), I would go through Army basic training in El Paso at age twenty-four. During those months, I would tell many of the Tex-Mex recruits in my barracks about the LDS Church and its gospel. These Texas Chicanos nicknamed me "Chaplain."

CHAPTER NINE

ACCELERATING RELIGIOUS PATH

1967–1968

12 January 1967–Blessing a non-Christian

As written late this night: "Mike Bailey (one of the Aaronic Priesthood boys, who had been ordained an Elder) told me that his Muslim roommate wanted an administration. Fredoun Bassir, his roommate, had fallen down the stairs a few days ago and now was having severe headaches and nausea. The first thing I thought of was that he might have a concussion.

"The request disturbed me for two reasons: first, because Fredoun was not a Christian and therefore could not be healed by virtue of his faith in Christ, and second because my usual hesitancy of faith was even more evident in such a situation. But I knew that no man would be held guiltless who denied a person a request for a blessing, so I knelt and earnestly plead for the Spirit of the Lord.

"I went to Fredoun and asked him if he wanted a blessing. He said that he did. Feeling special need for the Lord's guidance, I asked Fredoun if it would be all right if we knelt in prayer. He asked me to pray. Afterwards Mike Bailey anointed him and I sealed the anointing.

"In the blessing I promised him that he would be healed because of his faith in God the Father of all men and because he had turned to those who held the priesthood. I promised him that his headaches and nausea would cease in a short while and that he would have no further problem.

"A short while after leaving his room, he was seized with the most violent nausea and severe headaches he had so far experienced. When I heard about this development, I was heart sick to think I had promised something that was not to be fulfilled.

"A few hours later, I was almost afraid to inquire about his condition. But upon inquiry I learned that he had gotten up from his bed and had gone to eat. To my knowledge he had no further headaches nor nausea from that hour."

This non-Christian's request had startled me, but I thought to myself:

"Why not?!" Words I suddenly recalled from Apostle Matthew Cowley's sermon, "Miracles," which I had heard in tape recordings as a teenager.[1]

I regarded this Muslim's faith as more important than LDS procedures. While feeling the burning of God's Spirit within me, I sealed the anointing by closing my prayer "in the name of Allah."

25 January 1967–Marital Choices

Jan visited me at Deseret Towers, and in an endearing display of affection, dozens of my Aaronic Priesthood boys rushed down to the lobby to meet her. They were curious to see the girl I had chosen. And who chose me.

Her choice hadn't been easy. Before we met, Jan was seriously dating a Catholic younger than me. She loved him but feared that her parents would disown her if they married. Her father had threatened to.

Bob was in Army basic training when she accepted my proposal and wrote him about it. As soon as possible, he took a flight to Salt Lake City to persuade her to break our engagement and marry him. She let me read his letters and told me about their planned meeting to discuss it. This kept me on edge for days about which of us she would choose.

12 February 1967–African American Speakers in BYU 47th Ward

At my suggestion, Bishop D. Evan Davis invited the Hotel Utah's waiter Monroe H. Fleming to speak at a fireside about "Negroes and the Priesthood" this Sunday evening. Jan and I picked up him and his wife, Frances Leggroan Fleming, from their home on Second Avenue in Salt Lake City and drove them to Provo.[2] Sister Fleming spoke briefly about growing up as "a Negro Mormon" in Utah, and he spoke at length about his adult conversion to the LDS Church. They both gave stirring testimonies of its truth, of David O. McKay as a prophet, and of their patiently waiting for "the Lord to open the way" for them to receive the priesthood and its blessings. It was truly inspiring.

Afterwards, Jan and I drove them back to Salt Lake City. In ten years, we purchased a house one block north and one block east of where the Flemings resided at this time.

More significant, the otherwise detailed minutes of the BYU ward's priesthood meetings and sacrament meetings made absolutely no comment about these African American visitors. Even though ward clerk Dennis T. Earl acknowledged that the Bishopric announced this fireside in advance at

---

1. Matthew Cowley, "Miracles," given February 18th, 1953, at Brigham Young University.

2. Frances Leggroan Fleming (1906–97), a great-granddaughter of early Mormon pioneer Jane Manning James, was born in Idaho and raised by her Mormon parents in then-rural Mill Creek, Utah. In 1930, she married Monroe Fleming, who converted to the LDS Church in 1935. They were leaders among the Black Mormon community.

those meetings, he omitted any reference to its topic or its speakers. Likewise, Earl's officially required "Quarterly Historical Report" for March 31, 1967, made no reference to this fireside among the events he listed for the ward from January 7th to March 26th.

By contrast, a different clerk noted in his minutes for the MIA on February 7th: "Fireside Sunday at 7:00 Monroe Flemming [sic] speaker." This remarkable silence in the BYU 47th Ward's main minutes reminds me of Ralph Ellison's book concerning this oft-repeated silence about the African American experience: *Invisible Man*.

Early 1967–Heresy Misperceived

I was stunned at how two friends misperceived what I intended to be a heretical poem about a conversation between God and the Virgin Mary. I structured "Epiphany" as an unidentified speaker persuading an unidentified woman to accept his proposal of a sexual tryst. This encounter would deceive her boyfriend Joseph and result in a child identified as Immanuel in the last line. I thought the ending was heavy-handed in revealing my radical view of the Virgin Birth, but still liked the audacity of what I had written.

I gave my poem story to Jim McConkie and Richard Lambert, expecting them to recognize the dialogue as my literary version of Brigham Young's infamous rejection of the Virgin Birth (*Journal of Discourses* 8:115). I thought it would be obvious to them, since we had previously discussed his view that baby Jesus resulted from sexual intercourse between our Heavenly Father and Mary, which Brigham's sermon had described as natural action. Still, I half expected these more conservative friends to be offended by my presenting God as seductive.

Instead, they both thought I was writing about a *homosexual* seduction involving two men! I couldn't understand how they could perceive such a thing in what I had written, and wondered if my homosexual secret was so transparent. I reread my fictional dialogue several times and still couldn't see any suggestion that it was a male speaking to a male.

I decided not to show this creative fiction to anyone else, but kept it among my personal papers.

Early 1967–Not Confiding in Fiancée

Ever since my spiritual impression last November to marry Jan, I had questioned whether I should confide to her that I had been homosexually inclined since childhood. I was afraid that such a disclosure would scare off the young woman I loved and who seemed so right for me to marry in every other way. Ultimately, two things decided me against disclosure.

First was one of the marriage preparation articles I was reading. It asked a rhetorical question, something like: "Should you confess everything to your intended spouse?" The author weighed the pros and cons of volunteering prior sexual activity and concluded that (unless the person felt incapable of monogamy) it was unwise to disclose prior sexual behavior to an intended spouse. Be truthful if asked the direct question, it advised, but don't volunteer what's not asked.

Jan hadn't asked, and I thought: "I haven't *done* anything! Why should I invite the problems this article mentions by volunteering *how* I've been tempted?!"

Most influential on my decision was a "counseling" experience. I was living in one of U Hall's single-occupant rooms at the end of each floor when I was awakened in the middle of the night by knocking at the door. In tears, a young man said that he needed to talk with someone. Technically, he had been one of my Aaronic Priesthood boys last semester, in spite of being in his twenties and engaged to be married. Recently ordained an elder, he had just received his temple endowment.

Now he was distraught about his very active sex life from mid-teens until the previous year at BYU. Since then, he had resumed church activity and had become celibate in order to marry his devout LDS girlfriend in the temple.

"The bishop and stake president both told me that God has forgiven me and that I should forget the past," the young man said, "but what about my fiancée? Doesn't she deserve to know?" He was sure that she would stop the marriage if he told her about the dozens of females he had bedded. "I don't want to lose her," he said through tears. "I love her so much, it hurts!"

This was uncomfortably close to my own quandary, and I found myself repeating to him what I had read. We talked about maintaining his silence, prayed about it one by one in my room, and he decided to follow what the bishop, the stake president, the marriage-prep article, and I had unanimously recommended.

This experience finalized my own decision to say nothing to Jan about my celibate homosexuality. This *seemed* right, but I don't recall praying about it.

1 March 1967–Spy Ring Against Liberal Professors

To the consternation of BYU's administration, its student-operated *Daily Universe* ran today's front-page story about accusations that students had been reporting to BYU president Ernest L. Wilkinson for nearly two years about liberal professors in various departments. Predictably, Wilkinson issued an immediate denial to the *Salt Lake Tribune*, not knowing that targeted professors had already assembled confessions from the student spies.

This led to the *Provo Daily Herald*'s front-page headline in two weeks: "Wilkinson Admits 'Spy Ring' Existence." Likewise on March 15, the *Daily Universe*'s front page published his formal apology for this "Spy Ring."

Professed innocence and plausible denial had backfired. I would painfully remember this nearly eleven years later.

These LDS student spies were officers and members of BYU's chapter of the ultra-conservative organization Young Americans for Freedom (YAF).[3] They were also members of the John Birch Society's Provo chapter.

Identified by the campus newspaper as instrumental in forcing Wilkinson's acknowledgement and apology were the officers in BYU's chapter of the American Association of University Professors. Among the listed AAUP officers was Ted J. Warner, from whom I had already taken the two-semester honors course about US history, 1600s to 1960s.[4]

All this shocked me deeply, even though I had known about BYU's right-wing zealots since my freshman year. From now on, I grimaced whenever I saw announcements in the *Universe* for activities of the John Birch Society, YAF, and the ultra-conservative speakers favored by BYU's administrators, such as Hyrum Andrus, Reid Bankhead, Reed Benson, Barry Goldwater, Paul Harvey, Kenneth McFarland, George Mardikian, Jerreld L. Newquist, Glenn Pearson, Herbert Philbrick, Max Rafferty, Chauncey Riddle, General Carlos Romulo, W. Cleon Skousen, Richard Vetterli, Ernest Wilkinson, and (of course) apostle Ezra Taft Benson. They constantly warned of "left-wing conspiracies," but the only real conspiracy at BYU was by its political conservatives. I felt embarrassed revulsion.

With his unfortunate first name, BYU student Adolf Fritz Becker reinforced those negative perceptions. Even after the exposure of the spy ring, his op-eds and letters to the editor in the *Universe* continued to defend the John Birch Society, the Young Americans for Freedom, and conservative politics.

Mid-March 1967–Democratic Socialist

Aside from my negative reaction to BYU's conservative spy ring, I discovered that I was more than a left-wing liberal—after reading and discussing the texts assigned for this semester's honors course "Man in the Contemporary World." I found myself not only condemning the Birch Society's *Blue Book* and its founder Robert Welch's *The Politician*, but also disputing the moderate views of Russell Kirk's *A Program For Conservatives*.[5]

---

3. Young Americans for Freedom (YAF) was founded in 1960. The acronym now stands for Young America's Foundation and states its purpose as "bringing conservative speakers to campus." See www.yaf.org.

4. Ted J. Warner (1929–14) was a professor of history at BYU, specializing in the Spanish Borderlands of the American Southwest.

5. Robert Welch's *Blue Book* (Belmont, MA: Western Islands, 1961) laid out the main tenets of the newly formed John Birch Society, an ultraconservative organization dedicated to rooting out communism in America and shrinking the US government. *A Program for Conservatives* (Chicago: Henry Regnery Co., 1954) warned against rapid societal change and advocated for gradual change, guided by the wisdom of Western traditions.

By contrast, I embraced the social justice perspective in Michael Harrington's Marxist examination of poverty in *The Other America* and admired the activist environmentalism in Rachel Carson's *Silent Spring*. I even liked much of the American Communist Party's political platform, even though I despised the Soviet repression concealed behind the CPUSA's pleasant ideals. Without those reservations, I also admired democratic Sweden's socialism as described in magazine articles I read beyond the assignments for this BYU course.

Now I had an informed answer for the question: "Would you rather be dead than Red?" My reply: "I'd rather be a member of the American Communist Party than be a member of the John Birch Society—because I've read their platforms."

Three years ago in England, I had mocked the weaknesses of its dole, of its free/subsidized housing for the poor, of the waste in its government's employing three men to watch one man dig a ditch (which I had photographed), and of its National Health Service's waiting periods for non-emergency surgery. Nevertheless, having myself benefited from the NHS as an often-sick and once-injured missionary, I gradually realized how profoundly the poor and working class needed Britain's socialism. By mid-March 1967, I was a critic of America's brutal survival-of-the-fittest capitalism. The Swedes have demonstrated that wealth and upward mobility do not require Social Darwinism, but they can exist within democratic socialism.

Having also read Karl Marx's *Communist Manifesto* and much of his *Das Kapital* (in English translation), I'm *not* a Marxist. I accept perspectives by Marxists like Harrington, but regard Marxism as too rigid philosophically, too willing to endorse violence, and too satisfied with "dictatorship of the proletariat." Whereas Western Europeans live freely in various forms of democratic socialism, all Marxist regimes are non-democratic and repressive for their citizens.

23 April 1967–Sermon on Spiritual Independence

At the BYU 47th Ward's sacrament meeting, I gave a radical sermon. It began with a discussion of options we have as Mormons for decision making: (1) automatic obedience to scriptural commandments and/or to the living prophet, (2) living only by personal revelation, (3) seeking a middle way between those two options. Noting that each approach has benefits and risks, I quoted revelations in Doctrine and Covenants 58:26–27 and 93:30 about the need for each of us to act independently. Brigham Young called such decision making "the true independence of heaven," after he condemned blind obedience to religious leaders (*Journal of Discourses* 1:312).

At the superficial level, God doesn't care which brand of toothpaste we use. Nor do the Prophets care. At the fundamental level, citing examples when God has allowed exceptions to each of the Ten Commandments, I announced to the BYU congregation: "There is no absolute moral law, except to obey the will of God for you." Written revelations, scriptural commands, and pronouncements by the living prophet, I argued, "provide *guidelines* for our happiness, but not inflexible absolutes that apply to all people in all circumstances at all times."

We must pay close attention to those guidelines, yet seek our own revelations. Without using the term "antinomian," I acknowledged that such an approach has risks of self-deception and anarchy.[6] Nonetheless, without taking such risks (Brigham said), people "will never be capable of entering into the celestial glory."

As my final scriptural citation, I quoted the words of Paul: "Where the Spirit is, there is liberty" (2 Corinthians 3:17). In the memoir I wrote later this year, I noted that my concluding words then urged the congregation tonight to seek "the true freedom of the Spirit which I pray we might all seek and live by."

Beforehand, I had about twenty minutes to re-think whether I should abandon my prepared talk. Due to unforeseen circumstances, it would have the appearance of being a direct rebuttal to the remarks that preceded it.

First, I had not known that the bishop was going to begin the meeting by reading the First Presidency's letter "about Law Day being May 1, 1967," as recorded in this sacrament meeting's minutes. Second, the speaker before me addressed the topic of "Following the Inspiration and Guidance of Our Leaders."[7]

In silent and earnest prayer, I asked the Lord if I should give what might appear to be an assault on the First Presidency's letter *and* on the first speaker. I wanted to provoke thought and reflection, not outrage. Regardless, I felt the inward burning of the Spirit, and gave the talk anyway.

I was aided in that decision by the musical number that separated the first speaker from me. Decades-long friend Charlie Brown (a violinist) and new friend Jim McConkie (a cellist) performed a duet of Eliza R. Snow's best-known Mormon hymn, "O My Father." I had previously told dorm buddy Jim about what my talk would say, and he whispered: "Now preach the doctrine to them," as he passed me following his performance.

After the meeting, Bishop Davis said: "You gave us strong doctrine tonight." However, I wasn't in trouble.

---

6. Martin Luther coined the term *antinomianism* during the Reformation to criticize extreme interpretations of doctrines of salvation.

7. Established in 1958 by President Dwight D. Eisenhower, Law Day is observed on May 1 in the United States, "to celebrate the rule of law in a free society."

7 May 1967–Special Blessing

The BYU 47th Ward's manuscript history states: "7 May Bishop D. E. Davis, assisted by his counselors, pronounced a special blessing upon Bro. Dennis Michael Quinn at the latter's request, as he leaves school to enter marriage and a vocation."

Afterwards, I rushed back to my room in Deseret Towers and immediately typed a long summary, abbreviated here: "Bishop Davis began the blessing by commending my desire to seek the will of the Lord for the conduct of my life which was to be itself a life of ministry in the Gospel. ... He blessed me that I would be a strength to the people in those times and that as did young Moroni, I would lead and inspire the opposition to wickedness in those days. He blessed me that I would endure and be protected from those attacks, divisions, and doctrinal disputes to come. He blessed me that those promises revealed to me at specific times in the past were reconfirmed upon my head in this blessing. He said that specifically I would be blessed to declare the will and word of the Lord to the people with power and the Spirit and that I would be a blessing to them ... in that ministry which would be with me twenty-four hours a day. He blessed me in my relationship with my wife. ... He assured me that I would yet serve in high leadership and that I was to be blessed in that ministry. He sealed the blessing by the power of the Holy Priesthood and in the name of Jesus Christ."

I felt comforted by the bishop's words about my upcoming marriage, but I regarded his blessing as having paramount importance for another reason. I perceived four separate instances where he reconfirmed my expectations to become an apostle. I had never confided that to him, nor had I even implied it.

27 May 1967–Accelerating Steps on My Religious Path

The day after I started working with the bureau of information at Temple Square as a full-time summer job, I was stunned to receive a letter from BYU's College of Religious Instruction. It gave me a graduate assistantship for the 1967–68 year. As I wrote this day: "Nothing could have surprised [sic] me more than receiving this award." Beginning in September, I would be in the senior class, with a "graduate" appointment.

20 June 1967–Time and Eternity in Salt Lake Temple

From my journal: "In the sealing room with us were Pres. [Evan O.] Darley (Jan's grandfather), his wife Jessie [stepmother of Roy M. Darley], Jan's parents, my mother, Vaude and Joy [my uncle and aunt], Bob and Margaret Kirkham [Jan's brother-in-law and sister], Karen Workman [my 2nd cousin], Brother and Sister Daniel Ludlow, Charles Brown, and Jim McConkie.

"After several minutes, President Hanks entered the sealing room and shook hands with everyone. ...

"After speaking to us for this period of time, he had us kneel across from each other at the altar, and with Vaude and Pres. Darley as the official witnesses, President Hanks performed the sealing and blessing of our marriage for time and all eternity. As he spoke the inspiring words of that ceremony and as I looked into the face of my beautiful wife, tears came into my eyes and trickled down my cheeks.

"Afterwards, President Hanks had us exchange rings and the simple ceremony was completed. It was an occasion I shall always remember."

20 June 1967–Commanding the Elements

From my journal: "As we left the temple the sky was clouded over and beginning to lightly drizzle. We had been worrying about the weather because all the arrangements had been made for us to have an outdoor reception at Jan's Aunt Margaret's house. Jan had her heart set on having this outdoor reception. As we had the wedding lunch up at Jan's parents, the sky became very black and it began to rain torrentially. The more it rained the more depressed I became for Jan. ...

"In accordance with the promptings of the Spirit, I arose and with full confidence brought my right arm to the square and said words to this effect: 'In the name of Jesus Christ, and by the authority of the Holy Priesthood I command you, ye elements, the wind and rain, to disperse from this valley from this moment and not to return throughout the duration of the day. This I do on authority of God, in the name of His Son, Amen.' As I concluded I felt the comfort of the Spirit that my words would be fulfilled and I felt no more concern about the success of the reception in the evening.

"Shortly afterwards, I left the apartment to pick up Jan at the hairdressers. As I left, I noticed that the clouds were dispersing and the sun was shining."

20 June 1967–Our Marital Union

From my journal: "When I returned with Jan to the apartment, we were both filled with excitement and anticipation. We had agreed that we wanted to spend this afternoon alone, in the privacy of our apartment, so that we could consummate our marriage in the relaxation of an afternoon rather than in the tired moments of the late hours of the night after the wedding reception."

Aside from some adolescent fondling with same-age boyfriends eleven years earlier, I had no previous sexual experience and felt supremely happy this day. My bride also seemed happy in the afterglow of lovemaking. I was pleasantly surprised to discover that I was spontaneously capable of intercourse with Jan, and I would likewise be "virile" nearly every time we actually made love throughout our marriage.

Years later, the increasing intervals between those acts would become a major problem, but perhaps less than the feeling she eventually expressed to me. From our wedding night onward, I seemed somehow "absent" or distracted even after I told her face to face how much I loved her as we merged to make what Shakespeare called "the beast with two backs." (*Othello*, Act I, Scene 1, line 117)

I *was* distracted. Thinking of some young man on Hollywood Boulevard, or in Utah, or on television.

20 June 1967–Wedding Reception in Salt Lake City

Mom, Aunt Joy, and Uncle Vaude were the only members of my immediate family at our wedding reception in Utah. Nana said that she and Grampa would not be able to get temple recommends. I didn't ask why. On the other hand, my Catholic father decided not to attend after learning that he was prohibited from witnessing my wedding in the temple. They would all be at our reception in California.

Among the Darley family's friends who attended our Utah reception were apostles Ezra Taft Benson, Mark E. Petersen, and Richard L. Evans, plus seventy's president S. Dilworth Young. I felt that this was the beginning glimmer of my future association with the general authorities.

The panoramic photos of our outside reception showed cumulus rain clouds hovering in the background, but not a drop of rain fell on us that evening of slight breezes. This confirmed the minor "miracle" of my commanding the elements.

A sad coincidence in timing was that our wedding occurred the same month as the death of eighty-five-year-old Arnold Burgener. Despite being only a distant cousin of mine, his allowing me to stay at his apartment in 1966 made it possible for me to meet Jan in Salt Lake. Even then, I wouldn't have seen her at LDS Hospital if his wife Jane hadn't urged me to apply for a job there.

On the lighter side, Jan and I suppressed laughter this summer whenever we saw someone wheezing in the doorway of our attic apartment, after ascending steep flights of stairs in our building's sweltering heat.

21 June 1967–Honeymoon in California

From my journal: "We drove steadily until we reached Las Vegas, Nevada. We spent a little time there, grabbing a bite to eat, and wandering through the magnificent new Hotel Casino Caesar's Palace. Then we took off again for Los Angeles.

Wedding reception of Michael and Jan, at the Salt Lake City
home of Jan's aunt, June 20, 1967. *Courtesy Quinn family.*

"We arrived at Uncle Frank's home in Glendale after midnight. Uncle
Frank and Darlene were in Salt Lake City for June Conference, so they let us
use their home for our honeymoon."

23 June 1967–Mad Dash to the Temple

From my journal: "In the late afternoon, we met Dad and spent a while at
his apartment, and then went out to dinner with him. ...

"We had been planning to go to the Los Angeles Temple tonight, and we
had less than thirty minutes to get there from Glendale in time for the last
session, a trip that usually takes over forty minutes. As I started to drive there,

I prayed that we would be protected from accident and from arrest, since I knew I would have to speed on the freeways to make it in time. It was a mad dash—at times we were driving 100 miles an hour on clear stretches of freeways—but we made it to the temple."

24 June 1967–Polarized Family Comes Together

Our wedding's "open house" in the Glendale West Ward was the first time when so many of the polarized elements of my extended family got together. Milling about were Dad, his first ex-wife (Mom), his second ex-wife (Kaye, who had recently divorced him), her daughters Kathy and Tricia (my half-sisters, who were Lutherans), Dad's only acknowledged brother Jimmy and wife Marge, their daughter Linda (one of my Catholic cousins), Grampa and Nana, some of Grampa's alcoholic brothers and sisters, his straight-arrow sister Lillian, Nana's Idaho grandniece Linda, Mom's sister Joy and her convert husband Vaude, Mom's sister Norma, her Catholic husband Lee, and their two children, Steve and Sue (my other Catholic cousins).

The obvious absence was Wayne Hood, my ex-stepfather. He still lived in Glendale, and I would have been glad to see him again. But I knew better than to invite him.

Most of the girls I dated in junior high or high school were at our reception, as were all of my strappingly heterosexual boyfriends from the ward. One surprise guest was Clifton Jolley, whom I hadn't seen since September 1963.

Early July 1967–The Rarely Seen Tabernacle and Its Spittoon

Because he was one of its permanent organists, my father-in-law could go wherever he wanted in the Salt Lake Tabernacle. One day, after Roy Darley's noon recital, he took me into the massive attic between the ceiling and roof. He showed me its remarkable lattice work of beams and wooden plugs that I touched in admiration of the Mormon pioneer builders who had insufficient nails and bolts to use in the 1860s. I also looked closely at the leather straps they had wetted, wrapped, and allowed to dry for securing many of the joints. Prior to this day, I had seen only photographs.

I also laughed about a pioneer artifact that Roy kept at his house. It was one of the Salt Lake Tabernacle's spittoons that tobacco chewing LDS leaders and regular Mormons had spit into during general conferences and other meetings. This was in the decades before there was widespread compliance with the Word of Wisdom's 1834 "advice" not to use tobacco.

16 July 1967–Enjoying Applause

From my journal: "This Sunday evening while I conducted a tour of Temple Square something occurred which made me pause for thought. At the end of the tour as I finished my remarks ... the group I had guided began to applaud me.

"I felt uncomfortable and acted ill at ease and indicated that applause was not expected. But despite my surprise and my discomfort, I *enjoyed* the applause. I came to realize tonight what I have before only glimpsed—that I thoroughly enjoy the adulation of a crowd and the praise of an audience.

"I recognize that I have certain abilities of persuasion, public speaking and charm, and I know that I can sway an audience—if not to action, at least to admiration.

"Being aware of my abilities is not wrong, in fact it is necessary. But I must also always be aware of the potential dangers of my enjoyment of public approval and my ability to sway an audience."

Late July 1967–Long-Lost Friend Asks Why I Got Married

Shortly after Pioneer Day, I was browsing LDS publications at Deseret Book in Salt Lake City, when someone called my name. To my surprise, it was Bart, the sexually aggressive guy from my deacons quorum in California. During our teenage years, he never socialized with our same-age friends in the ward, and I hadn't seen him since my missionary farewell.

He and his main boyfriend in our ward had both gone on foreign missions. Now he was acting like we were buddies and introduced me to the young man at his side, whom he referred to as "his friend."

When Bart asked what I was doing up here, I said that I had just gotten married. His smile vanished: "Why did you do *that*?!" The abruptness and intensity of the question caught me off guard. I glanced at his shirt, realizing that he wasn't wearing a temple garment underneath—barely a year after returning from his full-time mission. His friend blushed when I glanced at him. Then I understood. I stammered out something about how great it was being married and how much I loved my bride.

Bart looked at me in disbelief, shrugged, and said, "Well, good luck!" And the two slender studlees left. As I walked to the nearby apartment I shared with Jan, my mind was reeling. While growing up, I had thought I was the only regular acting homosexual in my ward. Bart was such a tough guy that I always assumed his early sexual behavior was simply the temporary phase of homosexuality that psychology books said all normal boys go through.

Now I wondered if I had been wrong in assuming that three effeminate guys in my California ward were homosexuals. One was a close friend my same age, and the second was the older brother of one of my good friends. I didn't really know the third—a middle-aged bachelor who led the choir. The latter had been the subject of occasional comments ("his poor mother") from my grandmother as I was growing up. Yet these three males might have been heterosexual despite being effeminate.

And now, a Mormon who acted like the Marlboro Man had just introduced me to his homosexual lover! Or so it seemed.

Early August 1967–Censoring Diaries

I think that in some way this talk with Bart led to my decision to remove any hint of homosexuality from the personal journals I had kept daily from age eighteen until after my mission. My bride was willing to type them in edited form.

To conceal the real purpose, I told Jan that I wanted to remove all the boring stuff, as well as certain entries about other people. In fact, I *did* line-through all the routine stuff and the negative comments about other people.

More important to me, though, I lined-through the many indirect references to my homosexuality. This included my comments about being "different" from other guys, my fasting and praying "to change," my frequent depression, etc.

I asked Jan not to read the sections I deleted. And (bless her heart!) she also agreed to that request. These deletions totaled ¾ of my original journals.

10 August 1967–The Marriage of Significant Friends

From my journal: "Today I went to the Salt Lake Temple on my lunch hour from Temple Square in order to attend the sealing of David Eldredge and his bride, Mary."

For tomorrow: "I went to the temple to attend the sealing of James McConkie to his wife, Judy. ... Pres. Bruce R. McConkie, Jim's uncle, officiated at the ceremony."

In two months, "Jan and I drove to Salt Lake to be with Mike and Sylvia McAdams for their Temple sealing."

I saw real significance in the fact that we all married this year. I fully expected that David, James, Mike, and I would become apostles in future decades.

Late August 1967–Early Mormon Polyandry

At this time, for my own use, I typed a several-page summary of my research into the most controversial aspect of Joseph Smith's polygamy. I titled it: "The Principle and Practice of Marrying Other Men's Wives." The only person I showed it to was my philosophy professor, Truman G. Madsen. He asked permission to photocopy it for his own files.

Fall 1967–Leaving Provo

Although we had moved to Provo, neither Jan nor I wanted to live there. We rented half of an old house south of campus at 326 North 400 East, but our side was mouse infested. In the other side, our neighbors were trapping rats, which we expected to invade our side any day or night. More than once we were awakened by the snap of a mouse trap, followed by painful squeaks.

In addition, the house's leaky roof had left a huge bulge of rotting plaster in the wall next to our bed. I covered the unsightly mess with a poster of the Disneyland-like exterior of Neuschwanstein Castle in the foothills of southern Germany's Alps. Neither Jan nor I dreamed that in three years, we would visit this third castle built by Bavaria's "Mad King" Ludwig II. Just now, we were more concerned about what would happen if it rained in Provo. It did, and the bulge got squishy from ceiling downward.

After Jan unsuccessfully applied for *fifty* jobs on campus and off-campus in Provo, she almost immediately got a good-paying position in Salt Lake City. We gladly broke our lease and moved into the basement of Aunt Margaret's home on October 19th.

Dorm life and the campus were all that I had ever liked about Provo, and I happily commuted to BYU for most of my senior year. Nevertheless, I soon joined a carpool due to Jan's need to drive the old Mercury for her work.

During the six weeks we resided in Provo, we were members of the BYU 24th Ward. Ironically, its bishop was Glenn L. Pearson. I don't know if this right-wing idealogue remembered me, but I had never forgotten the unpleasant experience with him five years ago.

Late December 1967–Resigning as Graduate Assistant

I spent three months preparing a questionnaire to assess the significance of Daniel H. Ludlow's TV courses on the Book of Mormon. After examining various surveys administered by BYU's College of Education and reading books about such surveys, I selected their questions that seemed relevant to the format of his course. Then I puzzled over devising multiple-choice questions that were tailored to the specifics of his course. Then I carefully examined each question to be sure that there were no ambiguities. Then I timed how long it took for Jan to fill out each version of the questionnaire I devised—to settle on one that students could complete in the time allotted.

Finally ready in mid-December, I gave my rough draft of it to Brother Ludlow's secretary to type. I expected his review, suggestions, and critiques—then approval. To my shock and dismay, he notified me that he had "never expected" me to devise my own questionnaire. Instead, he wanted me just to hand out to his large classes (at the end of term) the same multiple-choice survey that he had been giving for years. This seemed to contradict everything he had said to me in mid-September.

I was dumbfounded. When I asked what he thought I had been doing all semester for the salary of my "graduate assistantship," he said he thought I understood that it was his unofficial grant-in-aid for which I could do anything

I wanted. I didn't need to spend any time in the College of Religious Instruction, either this semester or next. This stunned me, because he had told me in September that he would assign me to another professor if I chose to do my own research project on the Book of Mormon or on LDS history.

His statements this December were absolutely inconsistent with what he had told me so emphatically last September. Aside from his own expression of disappointment this December, he seemed very uncomfortable explaining to me that he had used his position as the newly appointed dean to give me a monetary gift under the guise of a "graduate assistantship."

Rather than gratitude, I felt uncomprehending frustration and humiliation. For months, I had told everyone I knew that Professor Ludlow asked me to devise a new questionnaire to assess the success of this course. Instead, I now had to admit to anyone who inquired that my months of work had been a waste and that my "assistantship" had been a sham to conceal charity.

After mulling over the situation, I decided to resign this graduate assistantship. In view of our strained finances, Jan was understandably unhappy about my decision. Had I known from the beginning what it really was, I would have joyfully accepted this income while giving my full time to getting straight A's my senior year.

Regardless, in view of what happened, I just couldn't continue a charade—no matter how well-intended on Professor Ludlow's part. So I typed a letter of resignation, which he accepted graciously.

21 January 1968–General Secretary and Adviser of Adult Aaronic Priesthood, University 3rd Ward, Salt Lake City

Having served as adviser for the ward's adult Aaronic Priesthood members since December 3rd, I now had primary responsibility for them. Also today, Jan was sustained as secretary to Bishop Orson D. Wright. My former missionary companion Keith Rayner and his wife were likewise members of this ward.

Jan's work as legal secretary in a law firm since October provided enough money for us to move from Aunt M's this month to a tiny basement apartment on Twelfth Avenue, almost directly south of her parents' house. It required only a six-month lease, which turned out to be exactly the duration we needed.

The reclusive owner also rented out the main floor and lived in some kind of cubby hole he had built in between our walls and the basement's furnace room. We discovered that he was entering our apartment while we were gone and using its shower. We put up with this creepy situation for the months necessary.

31 January 1968–Tet Offensive and End of Draft Deferment

Shortly after the Communist Viet Cong's Tet Offensive commenced today in supposedly "safe" cities throughout US "controlled" South Vietnam, the draft board in California cancelled my student deferment.[8] Since 1965, married men without children were ineligible for draft deferments based on marital status alone. It seemed obvious that the Selective Service Department was preparing to conscript me.

I was desperate to avoid being drafted to kill people. Anywhere. I was a pacifist, even though I regarded some wars as both necessary and just. Whether I could ever kill someone in a just war was a choice I never faced.

Selective conscientious objectors have always had a rough time in various countries, because they (we) don't accept *any* authority as the absolute answer about whether to go to war or to abstain from war. Neither Bible verses, nor governmental proclamations, nor pro-war sermons are enough. Ethical relativism doesn't get much praise in any society, unless the leadership is the one exercising flexible ethics. Then it stages patriotic rallies.

Still, there was a military tradition in my family. Nana's father had served as a volunteer in the Spanish-American War and its resulting Philippine insurrection. Grampa's brother had died in the trenches of northern France during World War I. In the Second World War, my father and his brother had served in the Army, while Uncle Frank and stepfather Wayne did in the Navy. Uncle Lee had piloted planes on bombing missions over German cities, and I grew up praying nightly for "our soldiers who are fighting in Korea."

On the other hand, similar to my great-grandfather's anti-war views while he was stationed in the Philippines, I regarded the Vietnam War as an evil attack on the freedom of the Vietnamese people. Dwight D. Eisenhower's recently published autobiography acknowledged that this Republican president began the US policy of preventing free elections in South Vietnam. His advisers had informed him that eighty percent of its people would freely vote for a Communist government!

So we maintained an American puppet government and dictatorship in South Vietnam for our national self-interest, and against that of the common Vietnamese.

Then there was what I knew about the Idaho farm boy soldiers there. Mormons turned into monsters.

I had read enough personal accounts about World War II to have no illusions about heroism or surviving Vietnam's combat unscathed. I expected to die a sniveling death or to be permanently shell-shocked by what I saw and did there.

In the early months of 1968, I was preparing to volunteer for military intelligence in the hope of decreasing the likelihood of Vietnam service. At

---

8. The Tet Offensive took place over several months in 1968 when North Vietnam attacked South Vietnam with coordinated strikes in a number of areas. The offensive ultimately failed, but the high losses on both sides tipped US sentiment against the war.

the same time, I considered moving to Canada as a draft dodger. It may sound stupid, but the thought of never being able to attend LDS general conference in Utah as an ex-patriot was what inclined me against draft dodging.

But my wife made the decision for me. As I would write in 1972, "I continued thinking about the possibility until Jan told me she could never do it."

Early April 1968–Riots and Reflections about Race

Like most white Americans, I was transfixed by the televised coverage of the riots that erupted in Black neighborhoods of American cities after the assassination of Reverend Martin Luther King Jr. on April 4th. But probably few whites felt the grim satisfaction I did. As a devoted reader of *The Fire Next Time* by James Baldwin, I regarded these riots as the smallest kind of payback for centuries of white domination, suppression, and indifference to African American suffering.[9]

This was less than two months after white South Carolina policemen shot thirty Black students who were peacefully milling around a bonfire on a college campus, protesting exclusion from the small town's whites-only bowling alley. Among the dead was a sixteen-year-old Black passerby walking from a high school's sporting event.

This became personal for me the previous year, after African American Monroe Fleming gave his extended testimony of the restored gospel to my BYU ward. While Jan and I drove Brother and Sister Fleming back to Salt Lake City, they told us the other side of their story.

They had experienced horrendous discrimination from white Mormons in some LDS congregations they had attended. I was particularly shocked at their experience in a Los Angeles ward while on a month's vacation: no matter if these devout "Negro Mormons" sat in a middle row or back row, the white Mormons got up and moved elsewhere in the chapel. This left the Flemings sitting in a suddenly empty row. Outrageous!

And yet these devout Black Mormons maintained their faith in a church whose local leaders allowed such public cruelty to continue unopposed. Upon witnessing such discrimination, the ward's bishop or one of his counselors should have immediately sat with the Flemings throughout the rest of the meeting. This would be a silent example of the Christian fellowship that Latter-day Saints should eagerly give to all people.

But not in the United States of America during the 1950s and 1960s. Not in my generation of Mormonism. Not even in "liberal" Los Angeles! Swedish

---

9. James Baldwin (1924–87) was a Black American writer and activist. His book, *The Fire Next Time* (New York: Dial Press, 1963) was one of the most influential works on race relations published in the 1960s, dealing with both the place of race in American history and the intertwining of religion and race relations.

sociologist Gunnar Myrdal called this *An American Dilemma* in 1944, the year of my birth.[10]

I thought to myself in April 1968: "We deserve these riots here in Salt Lake City more than they do in Newark." As usual, however, I remained a silent, armchair radical.

2 May 1968–LDS or LSD?

For my senior-level survey course in modern philosophy, my term paper did a philosophical analysis of visions produced by the hallucinogenic drug LSD. Titled "William James and Chemical Epiphany," it concluded that phenomenologically (i.e., in terms of their external manifestations, or reports thereof), LSD drug visions had the same characteristics as traditionally religious visions reported by the Bible, by Catholic saints, by Protestant charismatics, and by Mormon prophets. Furthermore, I noted that such "mind-oriented experiences have produced some of the fruits of regeneration traditionally connected with religious conversion." Thus, as external phenomena, LSD-induced visions were as philosophically "valid" as LDS visions.

The most significant differences would reside in their internal dynamics or metaphysical origins, which were the domain of psychology, neurobiology, and theology. However, no academic discipline could give final judgment about the metaphysical truth of any vision. It was a matter of faith.

This was very dangerous ground at BYU. From the result of my freshman sociology paper, I knew I risked receiving a lower grade simply because of my uncomfortable analysis and unorthodox conclusions about recreational drugs.

Although I regarded the topic as legitimate for investigation, I also wanted to see whether a full professor of philosophy had more respect for academic freedom at BYU than a graduate-student instructor of sociology. A devout Mormon and Southern gentleman, Professor David H. Yarn gave me an A on this paper and a solid A in this four-unit course. I was ecstatic![11]

As one who also taught devotional classes in religion, Professor Yarn seemed to be a conservative's example of how BYU could become the Notre Dame University of Mormonism— rather than its Bob Jones University.

Late May 1968–Another Blessing of Inspiration

While Jan sat nearby, my friend Richard Lambert gave me a special blessing. In regard to my fears that I would end up in Vietnam after joining the

---

10. Gunnar Myrdal (1898–1987) was a Nobel Prize-winning economist whose nearly 1,500-page work, *An American Dilemma: The Negro Problem and Modern Democracy* (New York: Harper & Brothers, 1944) detailed the obstacles that Black Americans face to fully participate in American society. The book sold well over 100,000 copies.

11. David Yarn (1920–2012) was a professor of philosophy at BYU and the first dean of Religious Instruction. He served as the general editor of the J. Reuben Clark papers collection.

Quinn standing in front of BYU's Harold B. Lee Library on his
graduation day, May 31, 1968. *Courtesy Quinn family.*

Army next month, "he told me that he saw or felt impressed that I would
minister among the Saints of Germany." A remarkably fulfilled prophecy!!

31 May 1968–Graduating from BYU

Graduating *cum laude*, instead of *magna cum laude*, was the last in a string
of academic disappointments. The five units of D+ in my freshman semester
had dogged me all my undergraduate years. That D grade kept me from getting a cumulative GPA of A- and from being *magna cum laude* at graduation.
I had been admitted to the honors program as a freshman, but didn't receive
a scholarship until my third year.

I've always remembered one question in the oral exam for graduating from the honors program. C. Terry Warner, a recent PhD from Yale in philosophy (my minor), asked me: "Is mankind free or determined?"[12]

I answered: "Both—because humans have free agency within circumstances that are out of their control and therefore already determined." People raised in a slum, I explained, have less free will of thought and free agency of action than people raised in a penthouse. Economics and education determine the range of choice.

Professor Warner replied: "That's simplistic and you can't have it both ways. I hope that one day you'll learn to confront complex ideas better than this."

I was furious and felt like saying *he* was the one who offered a simplistic dichotomy. Instead, I was appropriately contrite.

I was in no position to challenge a professor. The previous December, I learned I was in the lowest one-third of those who took the advanced English exam for the Graduate Record Exam taken by college seniors nationally. My scores had always been above the ninetieth percentile in verbal and general aptitude exams I had taken in high school, and my GRE general aptitude and verbal scores were also above the ninetieth percentile. I felt humiliated to do so poorly in a standardized national exam about English literature, since I had completed fifty-two semester hours of its course work. I should have been proud of what I had achieved in college, but felt like a failure at graduation.

In a dozen years, I would renew association with two young women who had also been English majors in several courses I took. One of them, Camilla Eyring, would later introduce me to her husband, George D. Smith Jr. Several years older than me, he was heir to a stockholder's fortune amassed by his accountant father with the United Parcel Service (UPS).

George Jr. would underwrite most of the costs of the liberal Mormon media, including *Sunstone* magazine, for which my other fellow student, Susan Staker, would become an editor. In 1982, George would ask me to join the board of directors for a liberal Mormon publishing house he founded in 1981 and named Signature Books.

A decade after graduating from BYU, my archival research would uncover a disturbing perspective of Professor C. Terry Warner's views about free agency and academic freedom. In a "confidential draft" he had sent to BYU's President Ernest L. Wilkinson in June 1967, the Yale-trained professor of philosophy and BYU professor had written: "freedom of speech as it is

12. C. Terry Warner joined the BYU faculty in 1967. During his tenure there, he served as chair of the philosophy department, director of the honors program, and dean of the College of General Studies.

known today is a secular concept and has no place of any kind at the BYU."[13] An Ivy League education had been wasted on an intellectual fascist!

Early June 1968–Writing Summary of Post-1890 Polygamy

For the past six months, I had spent most of my spare hours "finalizing" research into the instances of post-Manifesto polygamy that had apparently been approved by LDS general authorities. Adding it to my binder about "problem areas," I titled this: "Violations of the 1890 Manifesto."

Early June 1968–Quick Trip to Parents in Glendale

We were disheartened by the assassination of Robert F. Kennedy in LA's Ambassador Hotel on June 6th. I had disliked the political opportunism of his late-starting campaign for the Democratic Party's nomination as US presidential candidate. Competing candidate Eugene McCarthy seemed more principled in his long-standing opposition to the Vietnam War. Yet RFK was a spellbinding speaker in his recent talk to BYU that I had attended, whereas McCarthy sometimes mumbled and seemed less likely to triumph over a flag-waving warmonger from the Republican Party. I agreed with RFK's views, and would have gladly voted for him.

Mom wouldn't have. "He was a radical," she said, "but another assassination is a tragedy for our country." This was the explanation she gave for driving with her car's headlights turned on during daytime as a sign of solidarity in mourning Robert F. Kennedy's death.

When Jan and I went to Dad's apartment, I noticed that the name tag on his door said: Donald L. Quinn. I thought: "What happened to P. for Peña? and where did this L. come from?" I would eventually learn that Dad had adopted yet another alias, Donald Lawrence Quinn. I never learned why, but discovered five years after this visit that he was also registering his car in California by the alias Donald Patrick Quinn. *Quien es, Papa? Quien eres?*

---

13. An examination of Ernest L. Wilkinson's diary reveals that Quinn misattributes Wilkinson's summary of his conversation with Warner to words written by Warner in a letter: "I had separate conferences with Roy Doxey, Terry Warner, Sterling and Wheelwright, asking each of them to give me a confidential draft on freedom of speech at the BYU. I was extremely impressed with Terry Warner. He made the comment that freedom of speech as it is known today is a secular concept and has no place of any kind at the BYU. I really expect he will come up with something." Ernest L. Wilkinson Diary, June 22, 1968, L. Tom Perry Special Collections, Harold B. Lee Library, Brigham Young University, Provo, Utah.

CHAPTER TEN

COUNTERINTELLIGENCE IN GERMANY

1968–1969

18 June 1968–US Army

Duke University had accepted me for a PhD program in English literature, but I joined the regular US Army three weeks after BYU graduation.
It seemed the best alternative for me this year. Jan tearfully moved back
with her parents for the time being. For my now-pregnant wife, this was an
anguished six months of separation, while I remained stoic.

When I entered Salt Lake City's induction center on June 18 to swear
the required oath, I was stunned to see my former missionary companion
Rinehart Peshell. Soon after, he and I boarded a drab-green bus to connect
with our military flight to Ft. Bliss in El Paso, Texas.

24 June 1968–Praying to Have a Black Boss

From my journal: "As I looked over the various drill sergeants at our
barracks, they all seemed to be arrogant, hard, harsh, and unnecessarily
mean, except one. This was a drill sergeant named [Lee G.] Sharp. He was
a Negro, and seemed to have a warm, genuine, friendly manner about him.

"The first time I saw him, I decided that he was the man I most wanted
to be my drill sergeant, because I felt he would help toughen me up and
orient me to the rigors of Army life without trying to treat me like an animal or a clod of dirt. That Monday night, as I went to bed, I prayed that
if it were according to the Lord's will for me, this Negro would be my drill
sergeant for basic.

"In the division that followed, I found, to my surprise, that my drill
sergeant was to be the Negro whom I had prayed about."

18 July 1968–Death of Aunt Darlene Workman

Because rheumatic fever had damaged my aunt's heart as a child, she
had had open-heart surgery a few years earlier to install an artificial valve.
It failed today, and she died at age 41 while shopping with my cousins Pam
and Donna.

Two days later, I wrote my wife: "I did not learn about Darlene's death
until this morning. The Protestant chaplain came out to where we were

drilling, called me aside and gave me the message my family had sent through the Red Cross. I feel a little depressed, of course, but the love I had for Darlene is still with me and with her. I was always her 'Little Sugar,' and she and Uncle Frank have always treated me as they would a son. I will miss her, but I feel no grief. I am comforted by the knowledge of the eternity of the spirit and of family relationships."

28 July 1968—Ministering to Texas Draftees

Today I wrote: "Although the fellows don't encourage me to explain Mormonism very much, all of them seem to highly respect me. Some, as long as three weeks ago, nicknamed me 'Chaplain,' and others have asked me if I was going to become a preacher." Nearly all the young grunts in our barracks were draftees, and almost half were Chicanos from Texas.

Most of the talks that Rinehart and I had with them about Mormonism began in the same way. One at a time, guys sheepishly asked about the "strange underwear" he and I wore instead of the Army-issued boxer shorts that everyone else had to sport in the often-undressed culture of barracks life. Both of us wore our temple garments throughout boot camp.

This led to my Black drill sergeant's defending me when our barracks were being inspected by a high-ranking officer. Upon seeing neatly rolled temple garments in my foot locker where the military-issued shorts were supposed to be, our Commanding General Robert H. Stafford angrily asked me: "What the hell is this?!!" Sergeant Sharp immediately whispered: "Sir, those have religious significance to this soldier." The general backed off like he'd been punched.

22-24 August 1968—Jan Visits El Paso

Toward the end of basic training in this blistering summer of 1968, we had more freedom on weekends. One Saturday, the Army trucked us recruits into New Mexico for a tour of Carlsbad Caverns. Those were the most spectacular caves I've ever seen, but I couldn't stop thinking about my childhood experience in the Oregon Caves.

The night before our graduation ceremony, Jan flew to El Paso, where I was allowed to stay with her. Another kind sergeant, Paul L. Price, picked her up at the civilian airport and dropped us at a motel near Fort Bliss. At the mid-morning graduation ceremony on August 23rd, Rinehart and I were among the few who were promoted to private first class. Then I returned to the motel, where I spent that day and night with Jan.

From my journal: "When it came time for me to report for our plane assignment, Sgt. Price said Jan could walk with me to the area where the men prepared for disembarking." Six-months pregnant, she was sobbing as I boarded a military flight for the East Coast.

Private Quinn upon his August 1968 graduation from Army basic training at Fort Bliss, El Paso, Texas. *Courtesy Quinn family.*

26 August 1968–Saved Twice by a Clerk

After arriving at Fort Holabird, Baltimore, Maryland, on the 25th, I discovered that my assigned specialty in its Military Intelligence School was to be an area specialist (undercover spy). Therefore, I immediately requested reassignment for training in the more routine job of counterintelligence (CI) agent. I had specifically signed an Army contract to be a CI agent *only*.

I wanted nothing to do with cloak-and-dagger stuff, primarily because of my teenage conversation with an LDS former spy. After speaking to a fireside in Glendale, he had told me and Clifton Jolley about how it felt to shoot someone in the face at point-blank range. It didn't appeal.

Clerks run the military, and the one I asked about this said: "No problem. We have too many scheduled to start the September class for Area agents and need to reassign some as CI agents. I'll put this in your file as an automatic transfer, and you won't even have to ask your commanding officer about it."

Also thanks to this paper-pushing clerk, I got written permission to visit my wife in Salt Lake City for the week before classes began. After borrowing $150 from the Red Cross office at the fort, I bought a round-trip ticket. The kindness of strangers.

Thus, my journal noted for the next evening: "At 10:00 S.L. time, the plane landed and I was greeted by my lovely wife. We returned to her parents' house to see Roy and Kay [Darley]. Aunt Margaret [Gardner] is in New York, so we will be spending the week in her home. Being with Jan is a fulfillment of life and happiness for me."

28 August 1968–Days of Rage

Barely starting this week-long visit to Utah, I could hardly take my eyes away from television's live coverage and stark reruns of the Democratic Party's national convention. On the streets outside, anti-war activists clashed with Chicago's police, who went on a rampage of beatings. I hadn't seen anything like it since the 1950s TV images of Southern cops attacking peacefully marching Black civil rights activists.

A kind of comic relief occurred during tonight's televised confrontation between arch-conservative William F. Buckley Jr. and arch-liberal Gore Vidal. After Vidal called him a "proto-crypto Nazi," Buckley lashed back: "you queer!"[1] I laughed but was appalled.

Less than two years earlier, my friend Jim McConkie, also a liberal, had encouraged me to read Buckley's syndicated editorials. We both agreed that he was a brilliant, eloquent conservative, and I enjoyed his carefully crafted prose. Tonight was not his best hour.

Despite his homophobia, I continued reading Bill Buckley's editorials for decades. Not to mock or be dismissive, but to understand political conservatism as presented by its most intelligent spokesman.

Meanwhile, the anti-war protests by long-haired hippies and radicals like Tom Hayden (whom I admired) scared most Americans and led to this year's election of Republican presidential candidate Richard M. Nixon.[2] Aside from devastating Southeast Asia in order to save it from Communism, "Tricky Dick" would be a political and moral disaster for America. While US soldiers continued to be non-Asian victims of an immoral war.

30 August 1968–Mormon Eye Candy Bites Back

My father-in-law had a membership with the Deseret Gymnasium—just north of Salt Lake's Temple Square, and he took me there for a game of racquetball. This Friday afternoon, the locker area was nearly deserted. After we

1. William F. Buckley Jr. (1925–2008) launched *National Review* magazine in 1955, catalyzing the US conservative movement. Gore Vidal (1925–2012) was a bisexual writer who often focused on sexual liberation themes. The two men traded insults in ten debates televised during the 1968 national political conventions.

2. Thomas Emmet Hayden (1939–2016) was a prominent civil rights and anti-Vietnam War activist during the 1960s. He was married to actress Jane Fonda for seventeen years and served in the California State Legislature for eighteen years.

changed into gym clothes, Roy was talking to me about something that I was barely listening to. Instead, my concentration and glances focused on the naked bodies of two slender studlees who had just emerged from the showers behind him. After a few minutes, one of the still-naked guys said to the other: "Didn't think they allowed spectator sports here." I immediately shifted eye contact to Roy Darley, who seemed oblivious, and we soon left the locker area for the racquetball court. I admired the deft manner in which the young man made his point without making a scene.

4 September 1968–Fledgling Agent

Concerning the start of my training at Fort Holabird to be a counter-intelligence agent, my journal noted today: "There are fifty students in the class, ranging from buck privates to master sergeants."

From September through December, Rinehart and I lived in the same barracks with the lower-ranking agents-in-training. There were about forty young men, mainly under twenty-three-years-old. In an irony the military didn't recognize, most of these college graduates were anti-authoritarian rebels, were privately opposed to the Vietnam War, and were political and social liberals.

We two Mormons also continued wearing our temple garments. We soon learned this was also the case with the returned missionaries who lived in other barracks here.

9 September 1968–Endorsing Interracial Marriage

Without specifying what triggered these meditations, I wrote to my wife: "As I think about the Negro problem in America, it seems to be insoluble. I feel I have to agree with William Faulkner's attitude that slavery was an evil growth which has cancerously infected America far beyond the reach of the Emancipation [Proclamation] and Civil Rights."

Farther along in this letter: "I am afraid, Jan, that we will live through a period when many will try to resolve the problem by ending it in bloodshed or perhaps by dissolving it in general intermarriage among the races. The beginnings of both efforts are with us now. In this respect, my Love, we must strive to teach our children unprejudiced love of fellow men and also the importance of Temple Marriage. ...

"If the Lord alters certain existing restrictions, our children will have my support if they do happen to marry within the Temple those who are presently unable to receive those higher ordinances, even though my preferences might be otherwise. Although I am subject to the prejudices of my times and culture, I feel little racial superiority."

September 1968–Preparing for PhD in Literature

Even during basic training at Fort Bliss, I had been reading classic novels as part of my expectation for getting a doctorate in literature. Because I planned on specializing in stream-of-consciousness works, I read five or six more of William Faulkner's novels, and a few more by Virginia Woolf, Tolstoy and Dostoevsky. I read all of Proust and reread James Joyce's *Ulysses*, but gave up on his *Finnegans Wake* after two tries. Clearly *not* stream-of-consciousness, J. R. R. Tolkien's *Lord of the Rings* was just for enjoyment.

In a letter from Fort Holabird this fall, I told Jan: "I think I would like to obtain my PhD at Columbia or Berkeley. But it will be two years before I will apply, and during that time I will continue to read and study and hope I can get in the 90s on my next try at the GRE literature test."

27-29 September 1968—Attending Synagogue, LDS Services, and Mass

From my journal: "It has been five years since I first attended a Jewish service—in a reformed Synagogue. The one on Friday was at a Conservative Synagogue. I thoroughly enjoyed the service, wearing a skull cap, and repeating the congregational response with the others in the Synagogue.

"There was quite a bit of singing and prayer in Hebrew, and the only Hebrew I was able to say was the translation of 'Hear O Israel, the Lord your God Is One.' However, Chuck was so surprised to hear me chanting even this much Hebrew that he nearly fell off his seat."

Riding with blond, blue-eyed Chuck Miller in his Volvo to weekly services of *shabbat* for the next three months, I was soon able to repeat back the Hebrew of several group responses. I felt more at home in synagogue than in any other religious setting outside the LDS temple.

And the congregation's Jews enthusiastically fellowshipped their *goy* (gentile) attender. They gave me a silk yamulka and often invited me to bar mitzvah banquets.

Meanwhile, every Sunday, Rinehart and I took a bus to LDS meetings in Baltimore. Occasionally I walked to Catholic Mass in the evenings at Fort Holabird. Allowed by the reforms of Vatican II, this was often a modern Mass with guitarists, tambourines, and folk songs.

Until recently, I looked back at this period as my somewhat odd submersion in organized religion. It was decades before I realized that I used these multiple religious activities to compensate for my introduction to the amoral and immoral world of the American intelligence community.

Early October 1968—Investigative Files and Official Terrorism

Nearly all our intelligence orientations had the government security classification of Official Use Only or Confidential. Two had the more strenuous classification of Secret.

In the first, our group was taken to a large warehouse where we saw aisle after aisle of towering metal frames, filled with document storage cartons stacked almost to the ceiling. Our guide told us that these were investigative files that US Military Intelligence maintained on American civilians. He didn't explain what circumstances might trigger such surveillance or who had the authority to initiate these investigations.

As an example of an inactive case, he produced folders (about four inches thick, in all) for then-deceased actress Marilyn Monroe. The active case he showed us was for singer Frank Sinatra, whose surveillance file was about a foot thick.

He showed us no specific documents. We didn't have the "need to know"— the expression in the US intelligence community for denying access to snoops like me.

A few years afterward, I read a newspaper report that the Pentagon denied to Congress that such files exist. Americans tend to believe whatever the brass says.

The next secret orientation we received was about the Phoenix Program in South Vietnam.[3] The lecturer—in full military uniform, with a chest of commendation ribbons and medals—explained that South Vietnam's society was filled with Communist agents, subversives, and their sympathizers. Therefore, to ensure American victory in the war, our government maintained investigative files and surveillance on any of our Vietnamese allies who were suspected of disloyalty.

When the evidence was sufficient, appropriate authorities gave orders for the person to receive "termination with extreme prejudice." The lecturer said "special interrogation" might precede a termination in order to discover the identity of other subversives.

When the lecturer invited questions from our group, someone asked what kinds of people were targeted for torture and assassination. "Spies and subversives" was the reply. "So you mean just in the South Vietnamese government and military," our classmate said.

"Negative," responded the officer. "Termination orders involve teachers, university students, Vietnamese employees of our government, waiters in Saigon restaurants, prostitutes throughout the RVN. You name it. Subversives are everywhere." No one asked another question.

At the time I received this classified information, US government documents stamped as Secret were automatically reclassified to Confidential in twelve years. In twelve more years, such documents were reclassified as Official Use Only. In the meantime, the *New York Times*, *Time* magazine,

---

3. The Phoenix Program was a CIA-initiated program launched in South Vietnam to root out Viet Cong members. More than 21,000 people were killed during the five years of the program (1967–72). See Douglas Valentine, *The Phoenix Program: America's Use of Terror in Vietnam* (New York: William Morrow & Company, 1990).

and *Newsweek* magazine exposed the operations of the Phoenix Program. Although what I learned was verbal, I kept silent about my personal knowledge of it for four decades.

Years later, Jan and I watched Robert Redford's movie *Three Days of the Condor* in a theatre. It was slashingly critical of the US government's Central Intelligence Agency (CIA) and of the murderous behavior that's possible in "the intelligence community," a term Redford's character mocked. I loudly applauded at the end, and we decided to watch a second showing of it immediately afterward.

Early October 1968–Blood and Plasma

Because the Army was sending my monthly checks to Jan, who was living with her parents, I didn't have much cash to spend. Married men were getting free housing in the barracks and free food in the mess hall, so the payroll officer handed me $10 monthly as spending money from my pittance of a salary.

The oldest of us agents-in-training, a bachelor, suggested to our group that we sell our blood for extra income. He charged several of us a dollar each to ride in his car from Fort Holabird to the nearest donation center in Baltimore. We discovered that it was possible to sell a pint of plasma twice weekly in addition to selling our blood every couple of weeks. I did both regularly until the end of training.

In the process, I learned for the first time that I had an unusual heart rate and body temperature. My steady pulse hovered around forty beats per minute, and I sometimes had to run in place in front of the donation center before my heart rate reached the level where I could be approved to give blood or plasma.

On the other hand, my healthy temperature was neither normal nor fixed. It usually fluctuated between 95 to 97 degrees.

This was the answer to why I felt that I was burning up with fever as a child, only to be told by nurses that my temperature was "barely above normal." It also explained why I felt chilled when others thought the outside temperature was comfortably cool.

By my sixties, my heart rate was in the 60s. But 98.6 on the thermometer has always been a significant fever for me.

Mid-October 1968–Glad for Missing German-Speaking Mission

One Saturday, a Mormon came to my barracks to talk. We had met at LDS services, but I hadn't seen him at Fort Holabird until today. That wasn't surprising. There were hundreds of young men in training there.

When he thought we couldn't be overheard, he said he didn't like his preparation as an undercover agent. And worried about his future assignment.

"There are eight of us in training to infiltrate East Germany, and we all were missionaries in West Germany or Switzerland," he said. "The others seem to like the challenge of moving to Berlin and pretending to be left-wing students or bribable businessmen. But they're all single, and I'm married with a kid on the way. My wife will have to stay in the States and if I blow my cover, the Communists will execute me as a spy. I'm really scared."

I listened sympathetically, which was all I could do. American intelligence agencies like employing Mormons as squeaky clean agents who've been trained since childhood to follow orders without question. I wasn't that kind of Mormon and didn't tell this young man how glad I was that God didn't answer my prayers to be a missionary in Germany.

26 October 1968–Voting against Instructions from LDS HQ

For six months, general authorities had been leading a campaign against a ballot measure that would allow liquor by the drink in Utah. This included articles in the Church's official magazines, talks at general conference, and official statements by the living prophet and his counselors in the First Presidency.

Aside from a ladle full of cooking wine that Nana forced me to drink as a child, I had never tasted alcohol. Even after Dad taught me how to pour his beers at an angle from the bottle into a glass while visiting him as a kid, I never accepted his invitation to take a sip.

Nevertheless, I regarded this political campaign as a violation of the LDS Church's teachings about free agency. According to Mormon theology, it was Satan's plan in the pre-existence to take away all opportunities for mortals to sin. By contrast, Christ's plan was to allow every opportunity for mortal sin, as central to the Plan of Salvation—which provides for unrestricted choice, Christ's Atonement, human repentance, and divine redemption.

I regarded it as spiritually misguided for LDS leaders to attempt to remove temptation from Utah's entire population. I also resented how LDS headquarters had turned this election into a test of faith. Therefore, with an absentee ballot in Baltimore, Maryland, I cast a teetotaler's vote for liquor by the drink in Utah.

In a letter to Jan, I summarized her reaction when I mentioned this during our phone call the evening of October 26: "You said that you could not understand why I had done so, when the Prophet has made such an explicit stand against the proposal and has encouraged the members of the Church to vote against this liquor proposal. You said that you were not only disappointed in me, but you were ashamed of me for my decision and action."

She had been trained by her parents to believe that all faithful Mormons should respond with lockstep obedience to any instruction from LDS headquarters. That had not been my training, nor my understanding of the gospel.

When I re-affirmed that I would follow my own conscience in voting, Jan began sobbing and condemning me for being "a liberal Democrat." She was parroting what I had heard her Republican parents say about their friend, J. D. Williams (a bishop and a professor of political science at the University of Utah), but I didn't make that reply.[4] I just reaffirmed my love for her, for the church, and for God's revelations that each of us must act independently.

As I recall, my pregnant wife hung up on me. As for Utah, its Mormon voters overwhelmingly defeated liquor by the drink.

Mid-November 1968– Witnessing Homoerotic Act

About four o'clock Saturday morning, three young soldiers in our barracks came back drunk, and one of them performed oral sex on another. The third (thoroughly straight himself) encouraged the other two.

From comments I heard the next day, their drunken noise woke everyone else up. Like myself, all the sleeping guys in the barracks were listening or watching. But none of us agents-in-training would snitch on another. A week or so afterward, everyone in the group exchanged glances as we watched the mock interrogation of an actor who played an officer accused of committing a homosexual act.

Another irony occurred when it was my turn to be the interrogator in one of these free-wheeling scenes that portrayed Personal Security Investigations (PSIs). I was supposed to be doing a Background Investigation (BI) interview about someone who was applying for a Top Secret clearance. At one point, this actor mentioned that he was reading the *Kama Sutra*.[5] I didn't know what that was and said so. Staying in character, the actor replied: "Oh, I think *you* would be *very* interested in it!" and winked. Which got a laugh from our audience of agents-in-training.

The next Saturday, I went alone to Baltimore's Public Library where I read the *Kamasutra*'s multiple methods of oral sex with fascination. And a hard-on.

The fellator in our barracks was a short, slender, blond guy I had lusted for since the day I arrived. He filled my sexual fantasies for months after his drunken night of fun with the tall, slinky guy.

29-30 November 1968–Thanksgiving Trip for First Child's Birth

Fort Holabird's rules allowed its agents-in-training to make a roundtrip flight anywhere on weekends. Because Jan was nearly full term, I phoned early

4. J. D. Williams (1926–2007) was a professor of politics at the University of Utah for forty years and a prominent Utah Democrat. Stanford- and Harvard-educated, he was the first director of the university's Hinckley Institute of Politics.

5. The *Kama Sutra* is an ancient Indian text (200–300 CE) about courtship, love, and sex. Originally written in Sanskrit, the primer has been translated into English and other languages. Wendy Doniger, *Redeeming the Kamasutra* (New York: Oxford University Press, 2016).

on the Friday morning after Thanksgiving Day to ask if she thought she could give birth during my school break for the weekend! She said for me to make the trip, and she would ask her physician to induce labor that day. It worked!

After my arrival at the Salt Lake airport on Friday afternoon, Jan and I watched TV in the Darley Family's home as her contractions progressed. Twelve hours later, early Saturday morning on November 30, she gave birth to our first child, Mary. After some much-needed sleep, the three of us visited for the rest of Saturday. Then I took a Sunday morning flight back to Baltimore. Whirlwind childbirth.

Mary was born in Salt Lake City's Holy Cross Hospital, despite Mom's repeatedly urging me to avoid Catholic hospitals. "If there is a life-threatening problem with the birth," she warned, "Catholic doctors will not abort the baby and will allow the mother to die." In such dire circumstances, Mom was in favor of what would subsequently be called partial-birth abortion. Because, she said, "the woman's life is more important than a fetus, and she can always have another baby." Thus spoke my *very* conservative LDS mother.

Jan and I stayed with Holy Cross only because that was the hospital her ob-gyn was on staff for, and we trusted that such a life-and-death choice wouldn't occur. The Army paid for this childbirth.

Late December 1968–Unexpected Meeting

Several days before Christmas, both Rinehart Peshell and I graduated from Military Intelligence School at the top of our class, earning promotions to corporal. Our high scores on the Army's language-aptitude test had different results. Assigned to the Language Training Institute in Monterey, California, Rinehart would study Vietnamese for eight months before going to a war zone. My assignment was to study German for eight months in preparation for peacetime Europe.

Arriving at Chicago's O'Hare Airport, I discovered that dozens of connecting flights had been cancelled due to bad weather this night. I was just one of thousands of stranded passengers (and scores of uniformed soldiers) running from one airline's desk to another, hoping for an open seat or signing up for standby.

Amid this chaos, Richard Lambert walked up and gave me a hug. He had visited with Jan, our infant Mary, and the Darleys in Salt Lake before he boarded a flight that was supposed to end up in Boston. He often received spiritual impressions and, upon arrival at O'Hare (after being diverted from nearby Midway Airport), he felt impressed that I was in this huge airport. Before he joined the scramble for a substitute flight, he prayed to find me. And he did.

Because of the chaos at the Baltimore airport from which I had traveled on standby, there was no way Richard Lambert could have known in advance about which airline or which connecting city I would be using.

24-25 December 1968–Mary's First Christmas with Grandparents

Mom and Dad traveled separately to Utah to see their first grandchild, Mom staying with Aunt Margaret and Dad in a motel. They were with Jan, Mary, and me on Christmas Eve and morning at the Darley home. Since the age of three, this was the first Christmas I spent in the same room with both of my parents.

Dad's first words upon seeing his infant granddaughter: "Her eyes are blue, aren't they!" And I realized why he had fathered a son and daughters by two redheads. Blue-eyed, light-skinned grandchildren would be proof that he was *not* Mexican, but Irish.

Last Days of December 1968– Visiting Historical Sites

A day or two after Christmas, I packed all our clothes and household goods that would fit into my old Mercury and started driving east on Interstate 80 in heavy snow. Jan and baby Mary would join me later. The destination was Washington, DC, site of my next military assignment.

After hours of white-knuckle driving in blizzard conditions, I turned south to Interstate 70, hoping for more moderate weather. Once on this southerly freeway, I decided to tour locations important to early Mormon history that were near its route.

After visiting the site of a divinely designated (but never built) temple in Independence, Missouri, I drove to the town of Liberty.[6] In its old jail, Joseph Smith and other LDS leaders had been imprisoned for six months after November 1838.

In the partly restored Liberty Jail's LDS visitor's center, I had a humorous conversation with an Idaho farmer who was a missionary guide there with his wife. I told him that I was going next to the valley of Adam-ondi-Ahman, where the first man gathered his posterity anciently (see D&C 107:53–54). "Oh, you don't want to go there now," this old guide said, "they haven't re-built Adam's altar yet."

To the uncomprehending "What?!" that he obviously expected from me, the guide continued: "Ya see, nearly every Utah Mormon who visits the place takes a souvenir rock from Adam's altar, which is nearly gone by each October. So in the spring, workers drive a pickup truck of rocks to Adam-ondi-Ahman

---

6. Joseph Smith dedicated this temple lot in Independence in August 1831, to be the center of the Latter-day Saint New Jerusalem or "City of Zion." Though the original temple lot remains unoccupied, the Independence Temple of Community of Christ, adjacent to the temple lot, was dedicated in 1994.

and dump them next to the sign." He added with a smile, "Idaho Mormons ain't that gullible."

Adam-ondi-Ahman was profoundly disappointing to me, but for different reasons. I was expecting a wintry version of Mormon artist Alfred Lambourne's 1890s painting of high bluffs at the river, with a hill about 500 feet above. Instead, I found no bluffs, nor tall hill, but only frozen fields of denuded cornstalks amid cows chewing cuds. I had felt the Spirit while visiting the empty temple sites in Independence and Far West, Missouri, and even while looking at amateurish mannequins of the Prophet Joseph and his co-sufferers inside the Liberty Jail, but I felt no spirituality in this place. It didn't help that a bull chased me and that my car got stuck in the snow at Adam-ondi-Ahman.

I eventually discovered a similar discrepancy between the plain reality and Lambourne's 1890s painting of the Hill Cumorah in western New York. There, Joseph Smith had spoken face-to-face with the Angel Moroni annually from 1823 to 1827. Instead of what this LDS artist portrayed as a 1,000 foot, volcano-like precipice in his painting, the real hill ascended a mere 140 feet above Palmyra's farmland. Both of Lambourne's romantically inflated images of Mormon history were hanging in the Salt Lake Temple for the most faithful Saints to see.

From Missouri I wended my way north to Nauvoo, Illinois, with its scattered buildings that have survived since Mormons were forced to abandon their church's headquarters in February 1846. Looking at the icy Mississippi, it was easy to imagine my ancestors crossing the frozen river in wagons. They left my ancestral Mormon mother, Lydia Bilyeu Workman, in Nauvoo's cemetery.[7]

She had died in 1845 after being burned out of her farmhouse by anti-Mormon mobs. With no twins, she had borne twenty children, with five minors at her side as she lay dying in Nauvoo. And loving Mormonism.

Next I visited Kirtland, Ohio, near Cleveland, but the temple at Kirtland was closed to tourists due to a flu epidemic. Nonetheless, I felt spiritually inspired, even just standing outside of this sacred building where Jesus and various angels had appeared to Joseph Smith and others in 1836 (see D&C 110:2–13; 137:1–5).

Mid-January 1969–Eight Months of German in Washington, DC

As a hurriedly established, Eastern Seaboard version of the filled-to-capacity Defense Language Institute in Monterey, California, this facility operated out of leased space in Washington, DC, near the Key Bridge. Although hundreds were studying various languages here, we were in classes of

---

7. Lydia Bilyeu Workman (1793–1845) died on September 30, 1845, in Nauvoo at the age of fifty-two. She was buried in the Old Nauvoo Burial Grounds cemetery.

about ten each for maximum conversation. During the thirty-two weeks, my group's teacher was a young Swiss woman from Basel.

The Army required enlisted students to assemble in formation once a month at the nearby Fort Myer to answer roll call, dressed in uniform. It was just the Army's reminder that we remained part of its Green Machine—referring to the drab-green fatigue uniform soldiers wore for manual labor and for combat.

Because classes at this Defense Language Institute ended at 3:00 p.m., I started a second job to increase our lowly income. I worked as an evening teller at a bank in Arlington, Virginia, across the Potomac River, from 5–9 p.m., Monday through Friday. This gave me enough time for an early dinner with my family before going to work. I did German homework and memorization in spare moments each week between thirty hours of school and twenty hours of evening work.

We lived in a furnished apartment within a huge complex of ugly buildings facing Duke Street and the Shirley Highway (I-395) in Alexandria, Virginia. Filled with lower-ranking enlisted military families, our best friends in the complex were a young Catholic couple.

When they came to our apartment, they were deeply offended by a poster on our bathroom wall above the toilet. Under a cartoon caricature of Pope Paul VI wagging his finger were the words: "The Pill is a No No," a sardonic reference to his recent encyclical, *Humanae Vitae*. Jan and I thought it was a hilarious reference to her own use of the contraceptive pill, since birth control was also disapproved by Mormon leaders.[8] We didn't even think of how offensive this poster would be to devout Catholics.

Aside from its restored colonial section with cobblestone streets, Alexandria's best attraction was its very tall Masonic Memorial Building. Inside was a giant statue of George Washington dressed in the regalia of Freemasonry. We saw it several times.

On weekends, we took infant Mary wherever we went. One day, I walked up every step to the top of the Washington Monument and down again, carrying her in a soft corduroy backpack.

Every weekend for eight months, we explored DC's museums, monuments, White House, halls of Congress, its Library, the National Archives, and other tourist sights, plus operas, symphonies, stage plays, and restaurants.

Jan and I often returned to the National Gallery, where my favorite work

---

8. Beginning in 1916, Mormon leaders explicitly condemned the use of artificial contraception. Beginning in 1983, the church softened its stance until it reached its current policy that it is a private matter. Taylor Petrey, *Tabernacles of Clay: Sexuality and Gender in Modern Mormonism* (Chapel Hill: University of North Carolina Press, 2020), 130–34.

of art was Salvador Dali's *Last Supper*. I sometimes viewed it silently for half an hour, meditating.

Early 1969–Husband-and-Wife Blessings of Priesthood and Faith

Like all babies, Mary got sick and sometimes had a fever or vomiting that worried us. Like all Mormon couples, Jan and I turned to blessings of the priesthood, in which two ordained men performed a two-stage LDS ordinance of healing. First, one anointed the sick person's head with consecrated oil, saying the words: "by the power of the Melchizedek Priesthood which I hold." Next, both men joined in the separate ordinance of laying their hands on the head to seal the anointing and offer a spontaneous blessing, by the power of the Melchizedek Priesthood we hold.

Unlike our experience in Salt Lake City, there wasn't another Melchizedek Priesthood holder within walking distance of our apartment. Nonetheless, under normal circumstances, I phoned another man in our ward in the daytime or evenings, asking him to drive to our apartment to join with me in the ordinances.

Yet when our child awoke in the middle of the night with symptoms of severe illness, I usually performed the ordinances of healing by myself. This had been authorized as an emergency procedure by apostle John A. Widtsoe's officially endorsed *Priesthood and Church Government* since the 1930s, in the LDS HQ's periodically published *General Handbook of Instructions*, and by instructions I had been given as a missionary and by my elders quorum in various wards.

At some point, as Jan sat nearby while I performed the healing ordinances for our daughter, I began thinking of my previous experience with the Muslim student at BYU. Because of his faith in Allah and his sincere request for an LDS ceremony of healing, I had omitted the formal requirement of closing the prayer "in the name of Jesus Christ." Feeling the endorsement of the Spirit within me, I decided that I would again follow the inward inspiration the LDS Church's second president called "the true independence of heaven."

The next time I needed to administer to our sick child, I asked Jan to also place her hands on Mary's head. Because there were no set words for the ordinance of blessing the sick, I said in the prayer of sealing the anointing that my wife and I were performing this ordinance "according to *our* faith and by power of the Melchizedek Priesthood which *I* hold." This seemed so consistent with the gospel and with LDS procedures, that it never even occurred to me to ask a bishop or other LDS official if it was okay for my wife to join in giving a blessing of healing to any of our children.

As Matthew Cowley had said in his sermon to BYU's students: "Why not?!"

Spring-Summer 1969–Young Men's Teacher and Dance Director, Alexandria Ward, Potomac Stake

This was a joint calling with Jan, who had the same titles in the Young Women's program.

One of the young men I taught was high school senior Courtney J. Lassetter. He would eventually become a BYU instructor of religion and a contributor to the multi-volume *Encyclopedia of Mormonism*, published by Doubleday.

In early summer, Nana, Grampa, and Mom visited us. We traveled with them in sweltering heat to George Washington's Mount Vernon, Jefferson's Monticello, colonial Williamsburg, and the site of old Jamestown, Virginia. As I held our daughter Mary, Jan took a picture of four generations of my family sitting on a park bench.

I have never seen a more impressive Independence Day. The evening of July 4, we sat on the steps of the Lincoln Memorial and watched fireworks above the Capitol, mirrored in the Reflecting Pond.

I had to take one weekend trip without Jan, because it was arranged by the Army for those in language training. Buses drove us to Lancaster County, Pennsylvania, where we gawked at the Amish, their closed carriages, and picture-perfect barns. Glad for the experience, I felt sorry for very private people having to endure our stares.

20 July 1969–Watching Moon Walk

This was another one of those days when people around the world have a distinct memory of exactly how they experienced an event. Jan and I joined BYU friend Richard Lambert and about twenty other Mormons to watch the televised moon walk of astronaut Neil Armstrong.

Richard was sharing a large house in McLean, Virginia, with several returned missionaries who were promoting a cordless microphone system in the DC area. Among them was Sterling Van Wagenen (the Mormon brother-in-law of Hollywood actor Robert Redford) and Hyrum W. Smith who was in the British Mission at the death of his father (the former patriarch who was released in 1946 for homosexuality).[9] I recall seeing Hyrum in grief at the

---

9. Sterling Van Wagenen (1947–) is an award-winning film director and producer who co-founded, with Robert Redford, the Sundance Film Festival and Sundance Institute. Sterling's employers included BYU and the LDS Church. He directed three films that were used in the church's temple endowment ceremony from 2013 to 2019. In 2019, a Utah court sentenced him to six years to life in prison for sexual abuse of a teenaged boy. Hyrum W. Smith (1943–2019) was a businessman who created the Franklin Planner and later co-founded Franklin Covey (with Stephen R. Covey). He held many leadership positions in the church, including mission president. Smith's book *Pain Is Inevitable: Misery Is Optional* (Salt Lake City: Deseret Book, 2004), recounts his excommunication for infidelity and his later rebaptism.

Quinn with his grandparents, Frank and Coila Workman; his mother, Joyce; and his daughter, Mary, early summer 1969. *Courtesy Quinn family.*

mission home shortly after he learned about his dad's passing. At the time, Hyrum was one of the two special assistants to West European Mission President, apostle Mark E. Petersen, living in Leatherhead, England.

Mid-August 1969–Miracle at Mormon Pageant

Jan and I took this summer's longest trip a few weekends before we moved from northern Virginia. LDS friends, Curtis and Mary Hawkins, babysat our Mary. I had met Curt in the BYU dorm four years earlier.

Missionary friend Dave Payne and his wife traveled to DC from graduate school in North Carolina, and we rode in their VW Beetle to the town of Palmyra in western New York. From the memoir I wrote at twenty-eight:

"When we went to the Hill Cumorah about 45 minutes before the performance, the sky was dark and menacing.[10] Within moments it had started to rain, and it really began to pour. Dave and I had our wives take shelter while we sat on the grass and kept our front row, center places.

"Dave and I each prayed earnestly that the rain would stop and not ruin

---

10. The Hill Cumorah Pageant was an annual production of the LDS Church, staged at the foot of the Hill Cumorah in Palmyra, New York. Premiering in 1937, it depicted Joseph Smith's retrieval of the golden plates at Cumorah, which he translated as the Book of Mormon, and a dramatization of the events recorded therein. It was the church's flagship pageant, featuring more than 700 cast members and averaging more than 35,000 viewers annually at its peak. Its final performance was in 2019.

the performance or disappoint the thousands who had come to see it. Still the rain continued in a tremendous downpour.

"At a certain time, they began the tape welcoming the audience to the pageant, which was greeted by a few comical laughs. The taped voice of apostle Richard L. Evans announced that one of the elders would give the opening prayer. As the young man (probably a missionary) began the prayer, the downpour increased in intensity. My hopes for a successful performance were nearly dead, yet I prayed that the Lord would stop the rain for the performance. During his prayer, the young Elder asked the Lord to 'temper the elements.'

"When he said these words, a woman behind me gave an audible laugh of ridicule. But when the young Elder uttered the words 'In the name of Jesus Christ, Amen,' the steady downpour abruptly ceased.

"The effect of this was electrifying. The woman behind me, who had laughed so derisively, whispered almost reverently, 'Oh, my God!' From under the shelter of trees and parked cars, people streamed to the area for audience seating.

"Jan and I watched the performance with the Paynes on the front row. Occasionally I looked around and saw lightning and apparent rain in the distance surrounding us, but no rain fell during the performance. At one time Jan and I looked above us and the sky was crystal clear and the stars twinkled brightly. In the middle of the last sentence of the pageant, however, a few drops of rain fell and before we could leave the area the downpour had resumed."

29 August 1969–Graduating from Language Training Institute

I was promoted to sergeant, then Jan and Mary flew to Utah while I cleaned our apartment and prepared for my military flight to Germany. While alone, I went to a seedy theatre in DC to see my first semi-pornographic film, Andy Warhol's *Lonesome Cowboys*.[11]

I went for its homosexual emphasis but didn't like Warhol's style of filmmaking. Still, actor Joe Dallesandro, with his hairless chest and six-pack abs, would fill my dreams for years.

I don't know why now, but at least once I walked alone through the Black ghettos of DC. The one occasion I remember, it was nearing dusk. I didn't try to chat with anyone, but nodded toward the men and boys who were sitting on stoops as I passed. They nodded back and resumed their conversations. Did I do this because it was the fourth anniversary of the Watts Riots in LA?

Early September 1969–Bremerhaven? or Munich? or Vicenza?

During my first week at headquarters of the 511th Military Intelligence

---

11. *Lonesome Cowboys* was a 1968 film satirizing the Hollywood Western genre, directed by famous gay artist Andy Warhol. The film was controversial for its explicit sexual content and Warhol's polarizing art-house approach to filmmaking.

Group in Munich, Bavaria, West Germany, I had the good fortune to be in the same barracks with a returned missionary from the Central German Mission. A year older than me and also married, Glenn L. Cox was stunned to learn that I had been assigned to be an agent at the military intelligence station in Bremerhaven on the North Sea, whereas he was assigned to be an agent at the MI station in Munich, which had a large branch of German Mormons.

Instead, he wanted to have my assignment, so that he could help Bremerhaven's very small branch of Germans. By contrast, I felt that Jan's life with me would be far easier in Munich, where there was a large English-speaking branch for LDS servicemen and wives.

Glenn and I shined our shoes, polished the brass on our khaki uniforms, and took our multilith-printed orders to the sergeant major in charge of transfer assignments for enlisted personnel at MI HQ. With appropriate obeisance, we asked him to switch our assignments. This senior NCO mulled it over silently, then said that he would change the other young agent's assignment to Bremerhaven. "But you look Italian," he said to me, "and you're the kind of agent we need in the Vicenza Station of Northern Italy."

My heart sank, and I stammered: "But, Sergeant Major, the Army has trained me for eight months in the German language! I can speak German and even think in German."

Now it was his turn to look disappointed. "I thought you solved our Vicenza problem, but the language training leaves you eight months less of your enlistment to work with the Italians, who hate German speakers!" He gruffly reminded us that we'd "damn well" go wherever he assigned us, but I stayed in Munich and my erstwhile friend Glenn went to Bremerhaven.

In two months, its German branch's minutes summarized his wife's remarks about her gratitude that she and her husband were able to be there. The clerk quoted her once: "*Gott erhoert unsere Gebete*" (God hears our prayers). He heard mine to remain in Munich.

Mid-September 1969–Refusing a Direct Order

The day I reported for duty in the Munich station, the unit received orders from Washington, DC, for all of us counter-intelligence agents to go undercover in Munich's homosexual bars to locate a Czech spy. He had seduced a lieutenant working here at MI headquarters. I looked at a photo of this young Czech and knew that I would be unable to take my eyes off the face and body of such beautiful studlees in a gay bar.

I refused to participate in this assignment. My excuse was that I was an ordained minister. Therefore, I could not drink the alcohol necessary for being inconspicuous inside a bar and could not risk being seen going into a gay nightclub by local Mormons. After I offered that explanation to my unit's commander, he congratulated my piety and then gave me "a direct order" to go with other agents into the bars. He was stunned when I said that I had to "respectfully decline to obey." Sternly reminding me that this "is a court martial offense," he put me on suspension for several weeks.

During this time, I had charge of the motor pool for agents. While there, I also took the opportunity to qualify for driving one of the Army's big trucks. Rumor was that HQ was cutting orders to send me to Vietnam for combat service. All this was beyond my worst nightmares, and I prayed non-stop. I didn't tell Jan about this, hoping against hope that God would spare us both from what such re-assignment would mean.

I was saved by a senior agent (an area specialist spy) who had taken a liking to me while an older CI agent and I visited his safe house outside Munich. Highly regarded, this undercover agent intervened with my commanding officer and with MI HQ to prevent my being transferred out of the unit and sent to Vietnam. He also secretly obtained my 201 Personnel File and destroyed all reports in it about this incident. The kindness of strangers.

The day he privately explained those things to me, this American spy said that he admired my religious commitment but that it was often necessary to violate moral principles in service of the US government. He related his own experiences with the Phoenix Program of assassinations in Vietnam, one of which involved his seducing a South Vietnamese woman suspected of being Viet Cong, living with her for weeks, then killing her (by direct orders from US command in the Republic of VietNam). I expressed gratitude to him for his intervention, but his confidences persuaded me to become a military deserter if I ever received orders to Vietnam. Gratefully, I never faced that choice.

Mid-September 1969–Put Under Covert Surveillance

The Department of the Army Civilian (DAC) who headed our unit's counter-subversive operations, Kenneth VanBuskirk, made it clear that he suspected I was homosexual. My refusal to look for "a Commie queer" had triggered both his right-wing paranoia and his homophobic suspicion. Fluent in German and its Bavarian dialect, he was foulmouthed in several languages and often made "fag" jokes around me.

The fellator in the Baltimore barracks incident was also assigned as an MI agent in Germany, but not in Munich. A year afterward, I would be shocked to learn that this blond bombshell had married a woman. I thought only Mormon homosexuals did that in the 1960s.

VanBuskirk also hinted that he had opened a file on me and had his civilian operatives keeping me under surveillance. This covert information must have bored him. When I wasn't working as an MI agent, I was either with my wife or doing church work.

Although I had been trained to spot surveillance operatives, I didn't bother trying. And I didn't tell Jan about the situation. She had enough to worry about. No use spreading paranoia to the innocent. I was accustomed to dealing with stress. With God alone.

Mid-October 1969—Activities as a Military Intelligence Agent

For a year and a half I continued as a counter-intelligence agent in Munich. For more than a year, my primary responsibility was to inventory all top-secret documents at US facilities throughout southern Germany. These were documents generated by the US Army and by NATO, such as contingency plans for first strikes, retaliatory strikes, invasions, evacuations, and documents of similar sensitivity. Once I finished that page-by-page inspection, I joined my team in using various items of equipment to perform technical inspections (sweeps) for listening devices (bugs) at the facility.

The commander of my MI unit had already informed me that all the phones in our offices and residences were tapped by at least one foreign intelligence agency. Either the Czech Communists or our West German allies. And our own Army Security Agency (ASA) also tapped them.

Walking outside, we always notified the unit's commander about this electronic surveillance. This might have disappointed ASA about the change in the quality of its intercepted conversations. And then there were the listening capabilities of a facility of the National Security Agency (NSA) near Munich. In the American intelligence community, no one trusts anyone. And with good reason.

Potentially far more serious during our inspections of various units was my finding that top-secret documents were missing at a facility—as they often were. Local commanders went pale every time I verbally informed them. They were in trouble even if this absence resulted from the failure of a lowly clerk to keep the unit's copies of required forms for document transfer or destruction. I always assumed that was the case, but my written reports simply described the missing documents. The resolution and consequences were out of my hands.

I thank God that I had no real-world experience of my tested skills as marksman with an M-14 rifle, nor as sharpshooter with .38 and .45 caliber handguns. I spoke German at the various hotels and restaurants our team used while on temporary duty (TDY) away from Munich.

From the memoir I wrote at twenty-eight: "It was pretty interesting work which gave me the opportunity to travel and earn extra TDY money. My supervisor was a Black named Emmett Johnson, who was a thirty-four-year-old career Army man. He was one of the finest men I have ever known.

"We had many conversations about race, politics, and religion (especially the LDS) but he never once asked about the LDS restriction on the Blacks receiving the Priesthood. I am sure he knew about it, but he never raised the question, nor did I."

He was aware of VanBuskirk's suspicions, and Emmett let me know later this year that he protected me once from that homophobe's efforts to entrap me.

Emmett's mother-in-law had a room in his three-bedroom apartment in the *Perlacher Forst* section of US military housing. She helped take care of her two grandsons while their mother worked in the US military's buildings (the *Kaserne*). I will never forget the shocked expression on the grandmother's sweet Black face when I mentioned that I was Mormon. I understood her reaction, and I felt shame for the LDS Church's Negro policy.

19 October 1969–Gospel Doctrine Teacher, American Servicemen's Branch, Munich, Germany

With about 170 members, this was the oddest LDS congregation I have ever known. Branch President L. Larry Boothe was a CIA officer, and his first counselor Marvin M. Poulton was an officer with Air Force intelligence (Office of Special Investigations—OSI).[12] One of the men who served as Larry's second counselor during my time here was supposed to be an American businessman in an import-export firm. This was a common cover for CIA operatives, so I don't name him here.

Because the maiden name of branch member Stephen G. Wood's wife, Mary Anne, was Quinn, she asked if we were related. I explained that we weren't, due to my father's name change. However, Mary Anne Quinn Wood told me that her grandfather Carl A. Badger had been apostle-Senator Reed Smoot's private secretary from 1903–07.[13] She said that her grandfather had kept records of those years and that his daughter (Mary Anne's mother) stored those manuscripts in the family's home in Bountiful, Utah. This led to my eventually reading and taking extensive notes on those revealing documents. Years later, Steve and Mary Anne both joined the faculty of BYU's law school, after which dozens of people asked me if she and I were related.

Half of the men in the branch were uniformed soldiers working with Military Intelligence. The rest worked for the Army Security Agency, or for the

---

12. L. Larry Boothe (1939–2018) worked for the CIA for thirty-one years, the last three as an Officer in Residence at Utah State University teaching intelligence courses.
13. The election of Apostle Reed Smoot as a US Senator in 1903 sparked a four-year battle in the Senate. The Smoot Hearings were held to determine if Smoot should be seated given his position in the Mormon hierarchy and some Latter-day Saints' continued practice of polygamy. The hearings led church leaders to further distance the official institution from the practice, including in Mexico and Canada. Badger's journal provides primary documentation on the controversy and contemporary Mormon reaction to the hearings. Kathleen Flake, *The Politics of American Religious Identity: The Seating of Senator Reed Smoot, Mormon Apostle* (Chapel Hill: University of North Carolina Press, 2004).

National Security Agency, or for the CIA's Radio Liberty and Radio Free Europe. The *New York Times* eventually unmasked these CIA radio stations, and this exposure would be circulated to millions internationally by *Time* and *Newsweek*.

The Cold War was a conflict of information. Both dangerous and inconsequential, it was concealed, researched, revealed, denied, repackaged. Forgotten.

Branch President Boothe told me a lot about the CIA during administrative meetings I attended with him. As a senior accountant for company activities in southern Germany, he lived in light cover, meaning he maintained his real name while working for an import-export firm next to the McGraw *Kaserne*.

While in Munich, he told me that only ten percent of the CIA's total employees were actually spies. The other ninety percent were either desk-bound administrators, or functionaries in routine roles like his own, or technical experts who processed interpreted classified information as relayed from the few who were CIA agents in deep cover and running spies or double-agents of their own throughout the world. I once asked if he personally knew any deep cover CIA operatives, and Larry changed the subject.

He did volunteer, however, that he was able to bypass customs officials of US allies and neutral countries because of his black diplomatic passport. Thus, he carried $1,000,000 of cash inside a briefcase on his most recent flight from Washington, DC, to Germany. He said that light cover CIA operatives like himself did not transport contraband into nearby Czechoslovakia or other Communist countries. The CIA used different methods to move cash and other contraband into such regimes.

The most vocal about their work were young Mormons in the Munich Branch who served as clerks at MI HQ. Junior enlisted men like Theo R. Larson used the phrase Mormon Mafia to describe their participation in a network of LDS clerks inside US government offices extending from West Berlin to Washington, DC, to Honolulu to Saigon. They pulled strings to benefit Mormons in Munich or elsewhere, and arranged with the personnel office to get LDS replacements for Mormon Mafia clerks who were being transferred.

From the memoir I wrote at twenty-eight: "While Jan and I were in Germany we did as much missionary work as we could. During the first six months, the missionaries held meetings in our home twice a week. We had several different people in the home for discussions, but the only one that proved successful was Mark Geiss."

Late October 1969–German Mission President's Unusual Testimony

This was my first attendance at the annual meeting of Mormon servicemen in the town of Berchtesgaden, formerly the residence of Adolf Hitler.

We met in the General Walker Hotel that had originally been the quarters for Wehrmacht soldiers and SS *(Schutzstafel)* officers who protected the Nazi Fuehrer. Before the sermon of First Presidency counselor Hugh B. Brown, at this meeting, each of the mission presidents in Europe spoke briefly.

One was the recently appointed, native German president of the Central German Mission, headquartered in Duesseldorf. A decade-long resident of the United States, forty-five-year-old Walter H. Kindt began his remarks in English this way: "As a member of the Wehrmacht, I once proudly served my Fuehrer. Now, as a member of the Church, I proudly serve another Fuehrer."[14] There were audible gasps from this audience of American servicemen and their wives. As one of the few who said: "Amen" after this German Mission President spoke, I felt ambivalent. He had joined Hitler's army at age 17.

Mountain-filled Berchtesgaden was the most beautiful place I had ever seen. I felt overwhelming and hopeless love for Jan as we walked hand-in-hand along the shore of an Alpine lake (Koenigsee) until we saw its island chapel. Back in the hotel, we made love and both shed tears (I think for different reasons). Eight months later, our second child was born.

21 December 1969–First Assistant to Elders Quorum Group Leader, American Servicemen's Branch, Munich

Enlisted man Charles L. Sonntag was the group leader who chose me as his assistant. This was equivalent to the elders quorum presidency in a ward. In their mid-twenties, he and his wife, Joan, were among the closest friends Jan and I had in Munich. After being sustained to the position with the elders, I also continued teaching the Gospel Doctrine class in Sunday School for ten months. I was glad to do so, because I *loved* teaching.

What I liked most about this branch on Rueckert Strasse was how accepting its primarily military members were of the diverse Mormons who attended. One of the wives was a feminist who had joined bra-burning demonstrations in Manhattan, and who was obviously braless whenever she attended LDS services. Summer tourists who entered the chapel were often bearded and barefoot or in halter-tops and short-shorts, but they were fellowshipped as enthusiastically as were church dignitaries who visited.

---

14. Walter H. Kindt (1923–2010) immigrated to the United States after World War II and became a bishop in a Chicago stake. He later served as part of a stake presidency, as president of the Central German Mission, as a regional representative over Europe, New England, Ohio, and Minnesota, as a counselor to four different mission presidents, and finally as a sealer in the Chicago Temple. Translated in German, *Führer* means "leader" or "guide."

CHAPTER ELEVEN

NEW MORMON HISTORY

1970-1972

January 1970–Changing Directions

During this year in the Army, I made the transition from planning on a career in English literature to wanting to be a professionally trained historian of the Mormon past. Stream-of-consciousness writing continued to appeal to me, but it would be just a hobby from now on.

With nothing to do at Munich Station in the days between my team's assignments to conduct MI inspections at various facilities, I had time to read whatever I wanted. As long as I remained at my desk—ready "at a moment's notice" to respond to "an Army Intelligence emergency!"

In-house joke. We often said: "Military Intelligence is a contradiction in terms." I didn't bother saying "oxymoron." The kind of sesquipedalian term I try to avoid. Har!

I commenced re-reading the six-volume *Comprehensive History of the Church*, by B. H. Roberts, and did a superficial index. Also finished the twenty-six-volume *Journal of Discourses* while indexing it on 3x5 cards. Then I wrote extensive notes and long quotes from the four published volumes of testimony transcript from the US Senate's 1904–07 investigation of apostle Reed Smoot, the LDS Church, and its post-1890 polygamy. I was turning my hobby of Mormon history into a serious endeavor, a "profession in waiting."

My former bishop, Richard L. Anderson, arranged for BYU's library to send these volumes to me at no charge. In one letter of our frequent correspondence, this religion professor wrote that his emphasis on early Mormonism didn't have any controversies like my research in post-Manifesto polygamy. Seventeen years later, I think we would both see the irony when I published *Early Mormonism and the Magic World View*.

By Professor Anderson's request in 1970, I did research in the University of Munich's library about Wilhelm Ritter von Wymetal, a former correspondent reporter for a Berlin newspaper. By the pseudonym of "Dr. Wyl," he published *Mormon Portraits* in 1886, based on his interviews of several who claimed personal knowledge of Joseph Smith's polygamy during the 1840s.

Beyond my fascination with this topic and interest in learning about Wymetal, I got an unexpected insight. While examining the university library's catalog, I came across many entries which said that the particular book had been removed from the library during the Third Reich. Then I remembered seeing 1930s images of book burning in Munich and elsewhere in Nazi Germany.

In fact, this residential experience allowed me to visit many surviving remnants of the Third Reich. Before Jan's arrival in Munich, I explored several floors of a concrete bunker (four stories tall, as I recall) that the Nazis had built there. This anti-aircraft structure was too massive to demolish economically and yet was presently unknown to nearly all tourists. Aside from staying in the former *SS* headquarters at Berchtesgaden last October, Jan and I also ascended Hitler's mountaintop Eagle's Nest in the elevator constructed by his henchman Martin Bohrmann.

Like most of Munich's visitors, we often ate *Weisswurst und Rotkohl* (white sausage and red cabbage) at the *Hofbraeuhaus* restaurant, where Hitler had launched his unsuccessful putsch in 1923. Likewise, we toured the austere-looking *Haus der Kunst* art museum that he commissioned eleven years afterward. We also visited the exhibit rooms and small gas chamber of Hitler's concentration camp for political prisoners in Dachau, on the city's outskirts.

Our creepiest experience occurred one night when we tried to attend the movie theater at Dachau's camp, most of whose buildings were being used by the US Army. Slowly driving our Volkswagen in the thickest of fog, Jan and I were lost in the *Nacht und Nebel* of Dachau. Moving carefully through the large camp's narrow, deserted streets, I thought of its starved, hanged, beaten to death, experimented upon, shot, and gassed Communists, Socialists, non-Nazi conservatives, labor leaders, Jehovah's Witnesses, dissenting clergy, academics, intellectuals, gypsies (the *Romani*), homosexuals with pink triangles, and those Jews who weren't sent to extermination camps in Nazi-occupied Poland.

During one of our trips to Nuremberg to attend LDS district conference, Jan and I also walked through that city's old stadium where the Nazis had staged the visually stunning rallies shown in Leni Riefenstahl's classic film of propaganda, *Triumph of the Will*. Two of the city's gray-haired residents—in different neighborhoods—professed to have no knowledge of *das alte Stadion* when I asked for directions. By contrast, farther along, a young German knew immediately and directed me to its derelict site. The older generation had historical amnesia about their embarrassing past.

Speaking of which, my other history correspondent during this time was Samuel W. Taylor, whose family memoir I had read at age seventeen. His wry sense of humor added even more spice to the tidbits he shared about

Mormon polygamy. Which Sam called "the crazy aunt in the attic that no one in the family talks about."

From him and his brother Raymond, I learned how difficult it was for researchers during the fifty years that apostle Joseph Fielding Smith was the official Church Historian before he became church president in January 1970. Moreover, the still-serving Assistant Church Historian, A. William Lund, was notorious for denying requests, for demanding to see whatever notes researchers had written about what he had allowed them to examine, and for confiscating their notes if he saw a quote or paraphrase he regarded as sensitive or controversial. This made me wonder in 1970 if I would ever be able to do research in the Church Historian's Office about polygamy. Which Sam Taylor said was "the most forbidden subject" to apostle Smith and his research overseer, Will Lund.

Therefore, while in Munich, I prayed almost daily (and fasted weekly) for God's special intervention when I got out of the military. I asked him to give me access to the documents of the LDS Church that would provide understanding of the internal operations of the general authorities and their activities, particularly regarding polygamy. Amazingly, that's what happened as soon as I began graduate study in history the following year.

Another of my correspondents in 1970 was Nora Taylor Burgener, who had secretly violated both the LDS Church's 1890 Manifesto and its so-called Second Manifesto of 1904 by becoming apostle Matthias F. Cowley's plural wife in September 1905.[1] After her childbirth and divorce a few years later, she married Grampa's second cousin Walter Burgener. His brother Arnold told me in 1966 that ex-apostle Cowley met them once by accident and reportedly said: "You're together now, but she's *my* wife for eternity!" Her 1970 letter described their post-Manifesto ceremony by a patriarch in Canada.

Early months of 1970–Manuscripts and the New Mormon History

I began writing to all the manuscript libraries in the US and Canada, asking what documents they had about Mormons or Mormonism. The army's library in Munich had a directory of such repositories, and I read it page by page. I sent over three hundred letters. This was part of my plan to drive my locally purchased VW station wagon from New York to Utah, doing research at various archives on the way.

In response, Cornell University sent me photocopies of a German American minister's 1830 letter about Mormonism in Palmyra, New York.

1. Matthias Foss Cowley (1858–1940) was ordained an apostle in 1897. Cowley performed many post-Manifesto polygamous sealings. In 1906, Cowley and John W. Taylor resigned their positions in the Quorum of the Twelve Apostles. Though church leaders suspended the priesthood of both men, Cowley's priesthood was restored in 1936.

I thought this was an extraordinary discovery and began transcribing and translating Reverend Diedrich Willers' very difficult German script. This became one of the first academic articles I would publish.

For nearly thirty years, my translation would remain the only one cited by historians—conservative Mormon, liberal Mormon, and non-Mormon. Then Dan Vogel published an improved translation of the 1830 document.[2]

This would be two decades after he became a close friend of mine in the mid-1980s. As a former missionary in England and then workaholic researcher writer about early Mormonism, Dan would understand me pretty well. As a brief atheist while on my own mission there, I would have empathy for his disbeliefs. Despite the persistent conflict between my view of Joseph Smith as a fallible prophet of God with real visions and Dan's view of Joseph as a "pious fraud" of cunning duplicity, we would continue as good friends.

In our joint relationship to what would be called the "New Mormon History" by its advocates (or "The Acids of Modernity" by its chief critic, Louis C. Midgley), I would think of an aphorism from the Protestant Reformation.[3] It involved two men who admired the cultural and intellectual roles of Humanism, but who diverged about its applications.

Ever-devout Catholic priest Erasmus of Rotterdam had nonetheless been a longtime critic of the human abuses he saw in late-medieval Catholicism, which he published as *In Praise of Folly*. Even though the Dutch Humanist ultimately rejected the Protestant revolt of Martin Luther from Holy Mother Church, his contemporaries said: "Erasmus laid the egg, and Luther hatched it."

This was the connection that some would see between my decade-from-now analysis of *Early Mormonism and the Magic World View* and Dan Vogel's seventeen-years-later biography, *The Making of a Prophet*. Neither of us would ever have the stature of an Erasmus or a Luther, but I like the parallel.

Although I delay its explanation, there is a more apt application of the analogy. It would involve crucial developments in Salt Lake City after this year served as catalyst for bringing the New Mormon History to LDS headquarters. In 1970, apostle Howard W. Hunter laid the egg, and historian Leonard J. Arrington hatched it.[4]

---

2. See Dan Vogel, ed., *Early Mormon Documents, Volume 5* (Salt Lake City: Signature Books, 2003).

3. Louis C. Midgley (1931–) was a political science professor at BYU and a leader of the conservative LDS apologetics movement. See Midgley, "The Acids of Modernity and the Crisis in Mormon Historiography," in George D. Smith, ed., *Faithful History: Essays on Writing Mormon History* (Salt Lake City: Signature Books, 1992), 189–226.

4. Leonard James Arrington (1917–99), was a Utah State University professor before he served as Church Historian from 1972 to 1982, appointed under the direction of apostle Howard W. Hunter. After the 1840s, he was the first non-general authority and professional historian to be Church Historian. His tenure has been called the "Camelot years" for the open access scholars had to the church archives. In 1982 he was released and reassigned to BYU to be the director

Remarkably, in two years, I would be present at the creation.

Late March 1970–Traveling to Italy

This year, the army gave me more than three weeks of continuous vacation leave. Jan and I decided to drive to sunny Italy. Five-months pregnant, Jan was as adventurous and eager for these travels as I was. LDS friends Royce and Rhonda Richins generously took care of eighteen-month-old Mary in our Munich apartment for these weeks.

Aside from stopping overnight in Verona, where we walked around its wonderfully preserved Roman arena, we drove straight to Rome. Entering this Eternal City on the *autostrada*, I laughed out loud at the sight of a tall industrial smokestack inscribed vertically with the word MORONI in large letters. Until that moment, I had no idea that this Book of Mormon name was also Italian.

Staying in a cheap little *pension* (breakfast-only accommodations, with small sleeping rooms and a bathroom down the hall) by the train station, Jan and I toured Rome's major sights for five days.

I was awed by the Vatican's Sistine Chapel, where a reluctant painter had presented the awesomely divine love of God touching the outstretched finger of Adam. The creation theology of that image didn't please Brigham Young. Nor, for that matter, did its anthropomorphism please Catholicism's Nicene Creed. However, Michelangelo's scene on the ceiling captured my deeply felt love for God as Heavenly Father.

I was amused by his somber *Moses* in the Church of St. Peter in Chains—because of the statue's head horns. Devout Michelangelo had included them due to the Latin Vulgate Bible's literal translation from the Hebrew that the face of Moses scared people because it was horned. Which the King James Version more rationally rendered as "the skin of his face shone."

Jan and I wanted to return one day to a city we immediately loved. Thus, adhering to the Roman practice of good luck and white magic, we threw coins over our shoulders into the Trevi Fountain. It worked in exactly thirteen years.

From Rome, we drove to the US Air Force station outside Naples, arriving two hours in advance of its military flight for Greece. As the only standbys, we were just about to board the plane, when a civilian-clad general and his wife showed up. "RHIP" (Rank Has Its Privileges), the sympathetic airman whispered to me, as he took our boarding passes for the once-a-week departure and handed them to the elite interlopers.

---

of the Joseph Fielding Smith Institute for Church History, where he served until 1986. For Arrington's annotated journals, see Gary James Bergera, ed., *Confessions of a Mormon Historian*, 3 vols. (Salt Lake City: Signature Books, 2018).

There were only three standby seats on this flight, so Jan suggested that I take the remaining one and leave her in Italy for a week! I couldn't believe that my pregnant wife was serious, but she seemed to be. Feeling overwhelming love, I assured Jan that I wanted to be at her side wherever I toured.

Losing our military flight to Greece was a huge disappointment, but I had planned a fallback itinerary of remaining extra days in Italy and getting to ancient Attica by overnight ferry. Thus, Jan and I stayed in a nice *pension* in Naples, while we toured its waterfront and museums, then spent a day at the nearby ruins of Pompeii.

Jan and other women were miffed that, even when given the required bribe for showing tourists the ancient city's pornographic murals, the Italian guide at each site didn't allow them to join the men in gawking. Aside from some in Pompeii's *bordello*, these images were humorous for their phallic exaggeration, rather than conventionally erotic. That was particularly true of residential murals, such as the scale-tipping phallus in the House of the Vettii. I think that Roman parents and their children regarded such murals in their homes with pagan amusement they were glad to share with all visitors. Not so for their uptight descendants in modern Italy. Christianity has its discontents.

Driving southward to the Amalfi Coast, I sang the Italian words of "Torna a Sorrento" that I had learned as a teenager. The view was spectacular of white stucco buildings next to sheer cliffs dropping into the Mediterranean. We drove fifty miles south of Naples to walk around the nearly intact Doric temples of the ancient Greek colony at Paestum.

We also picnicked one day with families who tired of waiting in their cars for a long, slow freight train to pass a rural railroad crossing. They gestured for us to join them on the nearby grass for bread and cheese. At a countryside restaurant, a different group invited us to sit with their wedding party. I *love* the Italians!

I planned to drive to Brindisi on the Adriatic Sea. From there we could take a ferry to Piraeus, but Jan and I decided against it. Greece would just have to wait.

Returning northward at a leisurely pace, we stopped in Rome for more sightseeing. This included the stunning Pantheon, Baths of Caracalla, the Christian Catacombs, and Emperor Hadrian's villa in nearby Tivoli.

While attending the LDS branch one Sunday, we met Eileen Davies, a British convert who had been a Catholic nun (Sister Mary Francesca) for more than thirty years. This included six years of service in the Vatican. Now heading a private school, she was delighted to learn that Jan spoke French, so this former nun switched to the beautiful language of God to continue the conversation with her.

Traveling north, we stayed in a rustic hotel near Fiesole and toured Florence several days. On the comic side, while I was bargaining in bad Italian at the Tuscan city's open-air market, I made a counteroffer that was far too low. Putting hand on hip, the woman selling marble carvings snapped in English: "This is Florence, not Naples!"

The city was filled with artistic wonders, but I gazed with an unspoken thrill at Michelangelo's statue of the naked David. Thinking back on Irving Stone's biographical *The Agony and the Ecstasy*, it was difficult to believe its glib dismissal of the homosexual rumors about his hero.

To me, the novel's beautiful description of Michelangelo's sexual intercourse with a woman seemed like a fanciful illusion by a homophobic author. Decades afterward, I would find this verified in the unexpurgated printing of the sculptor's notebooks and poems. Their originally male love objects had been changed to female names and pronouns throughout centuries of hetero-censored publications.

From Florence, Jan and I made a day trip to Pisa to see its leaning tower. I photographed it with abandon, while very disappointed that we weren't allowed to ascend its winding steps.

We finished our Italian adventure with visits to Venice and Milan. Having been warned by disillusioned Americans in Munich that the City of Canals was dirty and smelly, Jan and I instead found Venice to be romantic. As we traveled in a public transport *vaporetto* on the Grand Canal, the setting sun turned filthy canals into golden streams.

We couldn't afford a gondola ride, but were lucky enough to see a radiant bride and groom floating by in one. Seventeen years later, I would remember this while watching a somber dream sequence in the movie *Maurice*.

At a factory on the Lido, we bought a beautifully colored blown-glass vase. Its narrow neck allowed a single bud stem, which Jan preferred to be a rose—pink or yellow, if she didn't get a hot red one. Our vase was only slightly golden, but it reminded me of Henry James' *The Golden Bowl*.

I felt the thrill of history when Jan photographed me standing by the bronze horses that had been rescued from the Muslim conquest of Constantinople and placed on St. Mark's Basilica. My awestruck appreciation for its Byzantine architecture was repeated as we visited the wonderfully different gothic cathedral of Milan.

An unexpected treat for Mormons like us was touring that cathedral's basement and viewing the original, ancient structure's underground baptistery. It had waist-high walls, with stone steps, and I was thrilled to hear the priest guide explain that Milan's early Christians practiced baptism by immersion. Just like the LDS Church!

Late April 1970–Ancestral Home

On a long weekend, Jan and I drove from Munich westward and visited Switzerland for the first time. Such days off were routinely allowed by MI headquarters for one Friday/Monday of administrative leave monthly.

After arriving in Switzerland, we served as proxies for an endowment session in the LDS temple near Bern. Great-grandmother Susan Barben Workman was from this area.

At one point in this sacred ceremony, I was speaking English, as I heard other Mormons saying the lengthy phrases in German, French, and Italian. It seemed like polyglot heaven, yet regimented in the Mormon way.

On route to ascending Jungfrau mountain in an Alpine cable car, we drove through the area where my Swiss ancestors lived for centuries. I had never seen photos, so was unprepared for the spellbinding view of massive Alps ascending without foothills so close to the lakes. In between were nestled my ancestral villages of Spies, Thun, and Interlaken.

I shed tears while thinking of the Barbens and Burgeners exchanging this gorgeous place for the desert country of Zion. Utah had mountains and Idaho had richly volcanic soil, but what a loss! To them, however, the LDS gospel was worth it.

Early May 1970–Expansion of Vietnam War

This month ended any lingering ambivalence I still felt about the Vietnam War. After President Nixon expanded the war by invading Cambodia on May 1, college campuses erupted in protest and the Ohio National Guard murdered four students at Kent State University on the 4th. The *New York Times* had already exposed the My Lai Massacre (in which a returned LDS missionary was an enthusiastic participant), and I felt humiliated to be serving in the US military.[5] But I remained the good soldier in civilian clothes.

What could I do or even say in my position? Counter-intelligence agents are notoriously anti-authoritarian, but condemning the Vietnam War to a fellow agent or to one of the spooks in Munich's LDS branch could be a sure ticket to Saigon.

Moreover, my unit commander had warned me that MI headquarters here monitored our personal mail and that I should assume my apartment on the military base was bugged. And then there was the MI unit's proto-Nazi VanBuskirk, who had me under surveillance as a suspected homosexual and was just aching for the opportunity to file charges against me.

---

5. Michael Terry and Greg Olsen, both active Latter-day Saints when they served in Vietnam, said they arrived in My Lai shortly after the carnage was over. Terry said he and others came across a ditch where many villagers had been shot. "We shot and killed a couple that were wounded; we just assumed they would die. We shot them to put them out of their misery. It was the right thing to do." See "2 Utah Veterans of My Lai Tragedy Have Found Peace," *Deseret News*, June 11, 1989.

So I kept dissenting thoughts to myself and tried to forget how much I hated the Vietnam War. This worked until I was visiting the branch president and picked up at random one of Larry Boothe's back issues of the *Salt Lake Tribune*. For some reason, I turned to the obituaries—something I never did before then—and saw the photo of Roy Lee Richardson, a missionary I had dearly loved in England. This gentle young man went into the Army and died invading Cambodia on May 9.

After the shock wore off, I cried and cursed for days. When I sent a letter of condolence to his mother, she wrote back that Lee had more convert baptisms in the army than he did in the British Mission. Somehow that didn't comfort me, and I have felt occasional pangs of grief for Elder Richardson ever since.

Subsequently, I clapped my hands in praise when I learned that another missionary associate, Richard W. Glade, became a war protester and fled to Canada. Grandson of Salt Lake City's former mayor, he would publicly refuse to return after US President Gerald R. Ford gave amnesty to all expatriot war protestors.

Decades have passed, yet I'm still angry at those who supported America's participation in the Vietnam War. By default, I allowed myself to be a war supporter since I did absolutely nothing to oppose it. The closest I came to protesting the Vietnam War was giving a Gospel Doctrine lesson about individual conscience and war to nearly all the active adults in the Munich Serviceman's Branch. From the Book of Mormon (and without a word of reference to Vietnam), I demonstrated that God praised conscientious pacifists who refused to participate in a war they knew was just, and he also praised military men who refused to participate in a war they knew was unjust.

From the Standard Works alone, I also demonstrated that God had often authorized participation in just wars. I had to turn to the First Presidency's World War II statement as proof that faithful soldiers were free of responsibility for conscientiously participating in war waged for the wrong reasons and promoted by evil leaders. Army lifers and their wives came up and warmly shook my hand afterwards, but I noticed that one young man seemed to wait for the others to leave.

When we were alone in the classroom, he said: "I was drafted before I was old enough to go on a mission, and I killed a lot of civilians in Vietnam. One was trying to breach our camp's perimeter at night. In the morning, I found the body of a Vietnamese boy—about nine years old—that I'd blown in half with a Claymore." Tears filled this soldier's eyes. "I've stayed in the Army, but I can't bring him back. I can't bring any of those people back. What hope can I have for forgiveness?"

The only words I could choke out: "You have God's hope and His love."

And I hugged this young soldier with the kind of tender and chaste embrace I used to give Elder Richardson as a missionary.

I thought fondly of Hemingway's *A Farewell To Arms*, rather than his militant *For Whom the Bell Tolls*. Though I enjoyed imagining that Grandma Carmen was like its fiery Spanish socialist partisan and woman soldier, Pilar. However, that was the role that Anthony Quinn's mother had fulfilled with his *Mestizo* father as Zapatistas during the Mexican Revolution, while Carmen and Ysmael fled to Arizona.

28-29 June 1970–Run-In with LDS Official about Historical Truth

At the suggestion of full-time missionaries who were teaching the discussions to a non-Mormon in our apartment, I agreed to give a presentation about the history of plural marriage. They invited other missionaries, and the branch's minutes stated on June 28 that I would "speak on polygamy in the Church" that night at a fireside where Jan and I resided in the *Neu Harlaching* area of US military housing.

We ended up with about thirty people at this informal meeting. I talked about Joseph Smith's plural wives, how polygamy moved from secret practice in Nauvoo during the 1840s to a public way of life in Utah, the government's crusade against it throughout the 1880s, the 1890 Manifesto, and the occurrence of some authorized plural marriages until the Second Manifesto of 1904.

On Monday evening, mission president Orville Gunther phoned me at home, asking me to meet with him.[6] I did so and learned that he had overheard some elders talking in the mission office about my presentation. He was emphatic that I should not tell missionaries about polygamy. I said that I wasn't promoting plural marriage, but simply talking about Mormon history. He questioned me about some of the details he had heard through his missionaries, and I explained that these were "true facts according to my research."

Then President Gunther gave me some interesting advice about "telling the truth" concerning what happens in the church. He said that it wasn't always good to tell the truth and that sometimes it was necessary to conceal the truth to accomplish a greater good. "On more than one occasion, I've met with other members of the Utah Legislature and have showed them a letter from the First Presidency indicating a wish that the legislators should vote a particular way on certain bills." He explained that he had "Church authorization" to do this as a legislator, but showed such letters only to men he knew were loyal to the church and would know how to vote after seeing a letter of this kind.

---

6. Orville Gunther (1912–2007), a businessman from American Fork, Utah, served as president of the South German Mission, regional representative, and president of the Provo Utah Temple. He was a Republican state representative in Utah from 1953–57.

"What I have told you is true," Gunther said, "but if you told anyone else I said this to you, I'd deny I ever told you such a story, and I'd deny it ever happened." Up until this point, I had understood his line of argument about not volunteering information about Mormon history to investigators or new members that could injure their faith, but I was amazed that he used this story as an illustration.

Nevertheless, this mission president's advice had its impact on me. I decided not to impose my understanding of the past on church members. I wouldn't speak about Mormon history in sermons or Sunday School lessons, unless the branch president or ward's bishop specifically asked me to. But I would start receiving such invitations in two years.

Early July 1970–Wife Nearly Dies

Jan gave birth to our second child, Lisa, in Munich's US military hospital on July 1, and came back to our apartment within days. Shortly afterward, while on assignment in another part of the city, I got a panicky phone call from Jan. Hemorrhaging badly, she was going to the emergency room, while Relief Society President Jane Langdorf took care of our children.

Returning to our apartment, I was stunned to see a trail of blood in the hallway and in our living room. Discovering that the bathroom was awash in my wife's blood, I began sobbing. While cleaning it all up, I prayed nonstop for Jan to survive and to regain full health. I cried a lot that week.

It required a D&C procedure to scrape the uterus, and bed rest for her to recover from an army doctor's mistake. After the birth, he had failed to remove some of the placenta. Jan almost needed a transfusion, for which an LDS man had donated a pint of blood to replace her rare type.

Now I understood on an existential gut level why so many women had previously died in childbirth or shortly thereafter. Women's history was no longer academic to me.

On emergency leave for a week, I visited Jan in the hospital, while also taking care of newborn Lisa and toddler Mary. Then I cared for Jan upon her return. In the midst of this personal chaos, the branch sustained me on July 5 as the elders quorum group leader.

With her own children in tow, big-hearted Joan Sonntag spent hours daily at our apartment to assist. An extraordinary gift.

Now and in the future, our daughter Mary made this much easier by being very considerate and motherly toward her younger sister. Having been raised as an only child, I would often be a surprised observer of my children's relationships. I hadn't been aware of sibling dynamics during the infrequent visits with my half-sisters while I was growing up.

August 1970–Encouraging Non-LDS Sister to Attend BYU

After Kathy completed a brief intensive-language program in north Germany, she visited Jan and me in Munich. We talked about her plans for college, and I strongly recommended that she apply to BYU. Even though I didn't tell her this, I was sure that my sister would convert to Mormonism during her freshman year.

Meanwhile, our dad continued to be secretive and strange as ever. He wrote me a letter, saying that he "might" soon have important news about a woman he had been seeing. His next letter announced that he had married middle-aged Beverly Hill, but I discovered that their wedding occurred even before the date of his letter about "might." Decades later, Dad would repeat this after-the-fact reporting about her.

Among the tourist spots that we took Kathy during her visit was the Herrenchiemsee Palace of "Mad King" Ludwig II. On summer weekends, there was an evening recital of chamber music in the palace's Hall of Mirrors, lighted only by the hall's standing candelabra. To get to this performance, attenders walked through small rooms of gilded walls, ceilings, and draperies which were illuminated by the candles burning in chandeliers. The amber light of each room was so suffused, so diaphanous in appearance, that the air seemed to have substance you could touch.

Watching the performance of chamber music by Beethoven and Brahms in such a setting caused me again to ponder the contradiction that a land of such beauty and cultural sensitivity had given birth to Nazism. Any evil is possible.

In any place. At any time. For any people.

No one can honestly say: "*We* would never do that!" or "It can't happen *here*!" Let me count the ways.

2 September 1970–Reacting against Pro-War General Authority

Seventy's President Hartman Rector Jr. held a special mid-week meeting with our branch this evening. He opened his remarks by saying: "Unlike student wards in the United States, I know I don't have to persuade you in this American branch about the righteousness of the Vietnam War. I just want to tell you that, despite death and suffering, the Vietnam War is doing wonderful things for the growth of the Church in that land and among our servicemen."

Still filled with grief and anger about this war, I felt like vomiting when I heard those words. After that feeling passed, I wanted to stand up and interrupt his talk: "Shut the hell up, you war-mongering bastard!" But I said nothing.

Jan suggested that we go up afterwards and say hello to this general authority, since her parents knew him. I then shook President Rector's hand and actually *thanked* him for speaking to our branch! This was consistent with my pattern of being a pleasant peacemaker. Homosexual desires are not the only feelings I've spent my life suppressing. Anger is another.

Eleven years later, I would speak in Elder Rector's living room about the controversies of early Mormon succession. It was for a student fireside arranged by his openly liberal son, Daniel. On that occasion, I would be deeply impressed by this general authority's kindness, openness to discussing alternate points of view, and his frank comments about the fallibility of the living prophet. This would leave me feeling embarrassed at the ill-will I had harbored against him since his pro-war talk in Munich.

Mid-September 1970–Visiting Old and New Friends

One weekend, I traveled alone to meet Dr. C. Jess Groesbeck, a Jungian psychiatrist who was currently president of the Wuerzburg Servicemen's Branch.[7] We had a shared interest in Mormon history, which would bring us together at many academic conferences in the following decades.

During this first conversation, Jess told me of the rumor that LDS historian Brigham H. Roberts had been an alcoholic. That shocked me, but within a year (in the LDS Church's archives) I would read the journal of Seymour B. Young who commented on the alcoholism of his associate in the Seventy's Presidency.[8] The journal of general authority J. Golden Kimball did likewise. This didn't make me respect Roberts less, nor devalue his many contributions. He was human, as were his disapproving associates.

In 1980 I would be saddened to read the mental gymnastics involved in Truman G. Madsen's biographical defense of B. H. Roberts against the claims that he drank alcohol as a general authority.[9] Madsen had been my favorite professor of philosophy at BYU. It was disappointing to read his argumentation that carefully avoided the available evidence in diaries by other members of the First Council of Seventy who commented on Roberts as a heavy drinker.

Regardless, I would feel admiration for Madsen as a biographer. He discussed this very sensitive controversy that virtually none of his faithful

---

7. Clarence Jess Groesbeck (1934–2009), was a physician and forensic psychiatrist. He later examined Ron Lafferty after Lafferty murdered his sister-in-law, Brenda Wright Lafferty, and Brenda's infant daughter, Erica, in American Fork, Utah, in 1984. Groesbeck was medical director of the Utah State Hospital.

8. Brigham Henry Roberts (1857–1933) served as an LDS general authority in the First Council of the Seventy, including as one of its seven presidents. He was elected to the US House of Representatives as a Democrat in 1898 but was never seated because of his being a polygamist. Roberts edited the seven-volume *History of the Church of Jesus Christ of Latter-day Saints*. Seymour Bicknell Young (1837–1924) was also in the presidency of the First Council of the Seventy, a general board member of the Deseret Sunday School Union, and a physician.

9. See Truman G. Madsen, *Defender of the Faith: The B. H. Roberts Story* (Salt Lake City: Bookcraft, 1980).

readers knew about until he brought it up. That's an honesty not characteristic of old-style Mormon history.

31 December 1970–Convert Baptism

Army corporal Mark Geiss had been studying the gospel in our apartment for more than a year on and off. Sometimes with the missionaries, but often with Jan and me alone. Tonight, I baptized Mark. We were all very happy.

Early January 1971–Abrupt Decision to Leave the Army

For months, Jan and I had planned to take a month-long vacation this coming May. Our main goal was to tour Greece for at least two weeks, with possible side trips to Turkey, Libya, Egypt, and/or Israel. Our plans were serious enough that we obtained visas from the Libyan embassy.

After returning to Munich, we would pack for Jan and our girls to move to Salt Lake City by June 17. That was the scheduled release date of my original enlistment contract. Then I would drive our car from New York City to Utah, while doing research in the Mormon manuscripts I had located last year in libraries of various states.

This month, however, I felt spiritually impressed that I *must* leave the army in March and enroll at the University of Utah. Its Department of History had already accepted me for the fall 1971 term.

Through quickly scouring the AR's (army regulations), I found that I could apply to end my enlistment three months early to attend college. Because the graduate school didn't enroll new students until the fall, I decided to simply start attending the University of Utah on a non-matriculated basis. I just prayed for everything to fall into place.

I waited nervously for MI headquarters to approve that application. In September 1968, I had signed a contract to remain in the army six months longer than my original enlistment—if given the language training of my choice. Eight months of military instruction in German saved me from Vietnam, but contractually extended my service to December 1971. That is, if the contract was actually enforced.

I was hopeful that it wouldn't be. I had been saved in 1969 from assignment to Italy—partly because the sergeant-major didn't realize I had extended my enlistment to get into German-language school. I didn't volunteer that information then and didn't now.

The form required for early release had no space to describe a pre-existing contract to extend one's enlistment. I hoped that the clerk in charge wouldn't notice the earlier document in my 201 personnel file or wouldn't act on it.

I handed my request to a Mormon Mafia clerk at HQ. We didn't discuss it before or after, but I assume that Fred Higley saw the contractual extension, then ignored it and processed my early release for March. Beyond gratitude.

17 January 1971–Speaking about Different Priorities

According to the minutes of this evening's sacrament Meeting in the Munich Servicemen's Branch: "Janice Quinn spoke of Eternal marriage. She noted that it was necessary to gain entrance into the Celestial Kingdom, also went over the blessings of Eternal marriage and responsibilities connected with it.

"Dennis Quinn spoke of some of his experiences that had helped his testimony grow. Of a Nun who was at one time in charge of all the Nuns in the United Kingdom and then became disillusioned with the Catholic Church and joined the Mormon Church, and how it came about.

"He also told of an experience that happened to Joseph Fielding Smith in connection with helping a Negro congregation in Salt Lake City construct a new building, and of his (Bro Quinn's) missionary experience in the Military."

February 1971–Complications in Departing Germany

In contrast to the months of careful preparations for our now-canceled grand tour this spring, Jan and I were in a last-minute frenzy. This was my usual pattern.

Another obscure AR allowed her and our daughters to travel for free as the only civilians on a military cargo flight from Frankfurt to the United States. I was barely able to get the required approvals for last-minute paperwork, and Jan left on two-days' notice.

In a similar flurry of signed documents, I got the army to ship my VW to New York free of charge. The port of shipment was (the irony!) Bremerhaven.

To defray the costs of driving the car to north Germany and coming back to Munich by public transport, I advertised for riders. Thus, an enlisted man, his wife and small child were in my car when black ice caused it to spin out of control on the *Autobahn* in central Germany. As the mother and child screamed, the car did 360-degree rotations in front of the adjacent lane's speeding truck, which nearly hit us before we crashed into the median.

We were only shaken up, and the car still functioned, but continuing northward was out of the question. So I returned the passenger money to this hapless family and drove them back to Munich. I thanked God day and night for weeks that I didn't injure or kill anyone in the accident.

Barely getting my VW repaired in time to pass the customs inspections, I paid a German shipping company to transport it from Munich. Canceling June's departure also ended my plans for driving alone from New York to Utah for a summer of research before enrolling at the University of Utah this fall. Thus, I paid for my VW to be shipped to Los Angeles by slow boat, the cheapest I could find.

And passing the required inspection of my three-bedroom, furnished apartment was an ordeal. The inspectors were German employees of the US Army, were notoriously difficult to please, and seemed determined to make me suffer for having had this virtually free housing within two blocks of my office.

I spent hours re-cleaning the apartment after each of three rejections. They even made me scrape rust from the pipes under sinks.

The fourth English-speaking inspector also told me that my apartment had failed. Switching to German and addressing him in the familiar "Du" form as a maximum insult, I said that his inspection was as much of a *Schwank* (farce) as were the previous three. Then I asked for his supervisor's name, and this German inspector's face blanched. He immediately changed his report to approved.

Both depressed and lonely one evening amid those inspection rejections, I took a public tram from the military base to downtown Munich to see my first explicitly pornographic movie. Rather than the crowd of single men I expected, an audience of mainly female-male couples watched *Variationes der Liebe* (Variations of Love) with me in the upscale cinema. I thought this Technicolor film was beautifully presented, with beautiful people.

I didn't care whether VanBuskirk's spies had followed me there.

Mid-March 1971–Leaving the Army

As a mirror image of my 1969 arrival in Germany, a massive C5-Transport flew hundreds of us soldiers from Frankfurt to Fort Dix, New Jersey. It was such a relief to be out of the military, away from the potential of being sent to Vietnam—as I nearly was. Away from the likelihood of imprisonment for disobeying a direct order—as I had. Away from spies who wanted to entrap me as a homosexual—as they almost did, despite my being a celibate queer. Away from the possibility of a dishonorable discharge.

From Fort Dix, I eagerly went to New York City to do research. I first met with corporate executive Mark W. Cannon, to examine his research notes from First Presidency counselor George Q. Cannon's diaries of 1860 to 1901, which this grandson had quoted in his doctoral dissertation at Harvard. Mark later became the administrative assistant to Chief Justice Warren Burger on the US Supreme Court.

In seventeen months, Mark Cannon would write a letter asking the First Presidency to give me access to the George Q. Cannon diaries that were in its vault. Mark was a mensch, but his request would be denied.

For nearly three days, I read and took notes on every manuscript about Mormonism in the New York Public Library. In the evenings, I watched gay porn that was featured in the sleazy theatres and video booths on 42nd Street. There and in Times Square, I politely declined all invitations by street hookers and male hustlers (rent boys). This was the first time since adolescence that I was getting sexual invitations from males.

I felt sad for the prostitutes, but not self-righteously superior. Who was *I* to judge anyone?

During this visit, I stayed at the low-priced Midtown YMCA, many of whose residents were very appealing. Still, I declined the various opportunities to explore sexuality.

20 March 1971–Back to Utah and Its Uncertainties

Arriving in Salt Lake City on a civilian flight arranged by the army, I reunited with my wife after our first prolonged separation in more than two years. Until Jan and I settled into a new apartment, we and our girls stayed in the basement of her parents' home.

I quickly registered at the University of Utah on a non-matriculated basis for spring term. All the Veterans' Administration needed was a statement from the registrar that I was enrolled in enough courses to be a full-time student. This qualified me for a monthly VA stipend, which I desperately needed now that I was unemployed.

Although I was technically not enrolled as a graduate student until this coming fall, the history department assigned Professor Davis Bitton as my unofficial adviser until then.[10] This was a pleasant surprise, because I had corresponded with him while living in Germany.

Last year, I shared information with him about the diaries that my letter survey had found in libraries outside Utah. I had read about his Mormon diary project in the weekly *Deseret News's Church News* section, which we received by mail in Munich. Writing him without any anticipation that I would become his student, my 1970 letter alerted Professor Bitton that I was an unusually avid researcher of Mormon history.

April 1971–Probing LDS Church's Archives

To further a guide he intended to publish as a reference book, Davis Bitton employed me as his chief research assistant for examining hundreds of diaries in the LDS Church Historian's Office (CHO). I quickly learned that, as the recently appointed Church Historian, apostle Howard W. Hunter had opened the archives to all researchers by the end of last year. Assistant

10. Ronald Davis Bitton (1930–2007) taught history at the University of Utah from 1966–95. He served as an official Assistant Church Historian to Church Historian Leonard J. Arrington from 1972–82. Bitton was also a charter member and early president of the Mormon History Association.

Church Historian Will Lund had also died this past February, and his previous pattern of research restrictions was nowhere in evidence now.

For example, one day I sat at a table—typing extensive notes from the daily journal of apostle Heber J. Grant—while next to me sat non-Mormon researcher Henry J. Wolfinger.[11] Reeking of cigarette smoke, this Princeton doctoral student was typing notes from files of the First Presidency that happened to be in the CHO.

Neither he nor I was asked to show our notes to a staffer at the Church Historian's Office. It was a seemingly unrestricted archive in 1971, and there was palpable excitement among its visitors. For researchers in Mormon history, every day was Christmas morning!

Although the church furnished only clunky old typewriters to researchers, I had qualified in the army at 100 wpm on such clattering machines. Thus, I usually left the archives with twenty to thirty pages of single-spaced typed notes during eight or nine hours of reading every entry of entire diaries. I usually skipped lunches while doing research.

In exactly three years, I would write in my journal: "I said that I had read about 500 Mormon diaries in connection with Dr. Bitton's project. I am not sure if that is accurate because I kept no exact count. But I know I read several hundred diaries, many of which comprised several volumes and thousands of pages, so I guess the number 500 is good enough."

In 1971 I was sure God was opening the way for me to understand the deep things of the Mormon past. I knew that this was somehow part of my mission to his church.

For the next fifteen years as a graduate student and publishing historian, I burrowed into previously restricted documents of Mormon history and typed literally *tens of thousands* of single-spaced pages of notes and verbatim transcriptions. All the while, I asked God to help me get access to even more at LDS archives.

1 May 1971–West Side Story in Salt Lake City

By this time, I had taken a flight to Los Angeles, where I picked up my VW station wagon from its storage lot in San Pedro. It had traveled for months on a freighter from Bremerhaven through the Panama Canal, and I worried that it might not start. It did, and I drove from LA to Salt Lake City without any problems.

Through apartment listings in the newspaper, I discovered a low-priced

---

11. Henry Wolfinger may have been working on his article, "A Reexamination of the Woodruff Manifesto in the Light of Utah Constitutional History," *Utah Historical Quarterly* 39, no. 4 (Fall, 1971): 328–49. Wolfinger went on to become an archivist at the National Archives.

two-bedroom unit for rent. Managed by Richards-Woodbury Realty, it was federally subsidized housing for low-income families.

I was grateful for Democratic President Lyndon B. Johnson's war on poverty, despite the tragedy of his war on Vietnam. And his promotion of the Civil Rights Acts from 1964 to 1968 earned LBJ (a Texan!) my utmost respect. Still, because of the Vietnam War, I felt no regret when he declined to stand for re-election in 1968.

Because of my fixation on LDS general authorities, I clearly remember my interview at the apartment's management firm to qualify for federal subsidy. Its senior partner Franklin D. Richards was then an Assistant to the Quorum of Twelve Apostles.

Subsidized housing and my veteran's education subsidies didn't lower our expenses enough. Jan struggled with our necessity of alternating which bills to pay late, whereas I resumed selling my blood and plasma to earn extra money.

By following last January's spiritual prompting, I now lost three months of Army salary, its lucrative TDY allowances (which had supplemented my salary), paid vacations, free medical care, virtually free housing, plus subsidized food and goods at the PX.

From the memoir I would write next year concerning mid-1971: "We couldn't buy clothes, we couldn't afford medical insurance and at times when we needed medical treatment we could not afford to see a physician."

In spite of my growing up in the poor side of town in California, I was surprised at how Salt Lake's east bench Mormons regarded West Temple Street as a social dividing line. Our newly built, very attractive apartment building was only five blocks northwest of the Salt Lake Temple, yet we now resided in what Jan's family and friends saw as "a blighted, dangerous neighborhood." I would eventually learn that our new apartment was only a block from where my grandparents had lived in 1927–28 before they moved to LA.

Compounding its reputation as a geographic Other to the generally more affluent east-bench Mormons, Salt Lake City's north and west had an odd system of street names in 1971. In its logical system of street numbers, 200 South Street was also called Second South Street and 200 East Street was Second East Street. By contrast, our apartment was on the only street running parallel to Temple Square at 200 West, but it had the perplexing name of First West Street at this time. Likewise, our nearest cross street was the only street running parallel to Temple Square at 300 North, but it had the odd name of Second North Street.

Notwithstanding our apartment's close proximity to the temple and to the ZCMI department store, where her family and friends shopped, all of Jan's same-aged friends got lost whenever they tried to visit us the first time.

Likewise for nearly all the young couples in our University 3rd Ward, which we had resumed attending.

Two of our new friends who didn't get lost were Omar Kader and his wife, Nancy, who resided on Darwin Street on the west side of Capitol Hill bordering the industrial area of Beck Street. A Palestinian convert to Mormonism, Omar would ultimately get his PhD in international relations from the University of Southern California and become executive director of the Arab-American Anti-Discrimination Committee (ADC). Nancy Kader, a registered nurse, received her PhD in bioethics from the University of Maryland at College Park and became a staff officer with the National Institutes of Health. Between now and then, our paths would cross for several years while he and I were teaching at BYU.

Because even native Salt Lakers seemed mystified by the street names in their city's north and west in 1971, I wrote the new mayor, Jake Garn.[12] Explaining our experience, I recommended that he change the system.

Mailing him a hand-drawn map, I proposed that he begin by dropping the street names First North and First West. Then I said that he should re-title all the numerically named streets north of North Temple Street as Second North and so forth northward, while renaming those streets west of West Temple as Second West and so forth westward. Thus our 200 West would become the more understandable Second West, and our 300 North would be Third North.

I don't recall receiving any reply from this Republican mayor's office, but I privately took partial credit when Salt Lake City made the exact changes I had recommended to Garn. More of my pride.

Late June 1971–*Ryan's Daughter*, Me, and Jan

David Lean's beautifully filmed movie of forbidden female-male love in Ireland had been showing in Salt Lake City. We went to it one evening a few days after our fourth anniversary—before its last performance at the Century 22 Theatre. Aside from hearing that it was a great movie, Jan and I knew nothing about it.

This night of movie-going was a profound experience for both of us. In painfully different ways. Just after Jan and I settled into our preferred seats at the center of the middle row in the theatre's center section, an equally young married couple sat to my left. As the slender, young husband settled himself

12. Edwin Jacob Garn (1932–) was elected mayor of Salt Lake City in 1971 and a US Senator from Utah in 1974. He served three terms. A former Navy and National Guard pilot, Garn became the first sitting member of Congress to fly in space when he flew aboard the Space Shuttle *Discovery* in April 1985.

into the seat next to me, we had momentary eye contact. He smiled, then turned to chat with his young wife until the lights went down.

Partway into the movie, he moved his leg gently against mine. When I didn't pull away, he pressed more firmly. My heart raced. Then he casually lifted his right arm to our shared armrest and pressed it against mine.

For what seemed like an hour, we each pressed leg against leg, arm against arm. Released slightly, pressed them gently again, then firmly. It was difficult to keep my breathing steady.

All the while, I kept my eyes resolutely on the large screen—aware of nothing but *him*. The movie's dialogue seemed muffled, the screen a blur, the plot obscure, its characters unimportant ciphers.

Then a scene loomed into my awareness. A fully nude hero was having intercourse with another man's wife in a grove of trees. It was wordless, beautiful intimacy.

And I was yearning to be intertwined with the young husband at my left, when I felt my wife's fingers squeezing my right hand. Suddenly I realized that we had been holding hands throughout the movie. My right hand was in hers, which now feverishly pressed against mine.

Reluctantly moving my left leg and arm away from *him*, I shifted toward Jan for the rest of the movie.

Afterwards, I got up without even glancing in the young man's direction. I assume he did the same. We left our seats in opposite directions, each with his respective wife. Respectfully. Affectionately. It would be nearly twenty years before I would experience anything close to the male-male touching I had just shared with this equally young husband. But the damage was done, at least for me.

When Jan and I returned to our apartment, she wanted to make love. I refused.

Coward that I was, I *couldn't* tell my wife that I didn't want to give up the afterglow I felt from touching and being touched by another, eager man. That young studlee was my ideal type.

Jan was uncomprehending. Distraught. Angry. Pleading. Nearly desperate with unfulfilled desire after watching the most erotic movie she had ever seen. She cried herself to sleep next to me that night. This was the cruelest thing I had ever done in my life. To the person I loved most in the world.

Yet I didn't want to make Jan into a substitute lover this night. Better to merge with her when I felt less passionate, but adequate enough to rise to the occasion—even if our union lacked the breathtaking thrill of merely sitting next to *him*.

Four years of homosexual yearnings as a married man should have signaled this to me long before now, but I had lived with my wife in denial. After this night, I *knew* our gay-straight marriage was doomed.

Yet it was sealed for time and eternity, and already blessed with two children I loved dearly. Really *blessed*. And really tragic—at least for Jan.

I was the anti-hero in this script. One I started when I proposed marriage to her, with the best of intentions.

July 1971–Meeting Leonard J. Arrington

Through Richard E. Bennett I met Leonard Arrington, Utah State University economic historian and author of the famous *Great Basin Kingdom*.[13] A Canadian Mormon, Richard was his research assistant at LDS archives, and Leonard took us to lunch at the Hotel Utah one day. It was a rare occasion for me to interrupt archival research to have a meal.

Dr. Arrington seemed quite interested in my background and research interests, which pleased me. I was stunned a month afterward to learn that he wanted me to replace Richard, who would start graduate school in Canada in September. I declined because of my prior commitment to be Davis Bitton's research assistant.

August 1971–Learning of Dad's Spanish Language Avoidance

Mom sent me some twenty-four-year-old letters she discovered in a box of correspondence she had forgotten about. While visiting a sister in Sinaloa, Mexico, my grandmother Carmen B. Peña wrote two letters to Dad, agreeably addressing them to his fake surname as Dan P. Quinn. Our closest friends in the apartment building on 200 West were a Chicano couple, whom I asked to translate these Spanish-language letters. In one, my grandmother wrote to Dad along these lines: "You ask me to write you in English, but it is very difficult to find someone here who knows English."

When I read my friend's translation, I regarded Grandma Carmen's letter as evidence that Dad never learned Spanish very well. He had indicated this in my mid-teens when I slyly asked him to translate a Spanish letter that was on display in an Exposition Park museum that he took me to visit in South-Central Los Angeles. He had haltingly translated scattered words, as if he were depending on cognates to piece together the letter's general meaning.

My Mexican grandmother's letter would have new significance to me decades later, when my cousins Susan and Linda Quinn told me about their

---

13. Richard E. Bennett (1946–) was head of the Department of Archives and Special Collections at the University of Manitoba before he became a professor of Church History and Doctrine at BYU. He has served as president of the Mormon History Association and as director of the LDS Church's historic site at Winter Quarters, Nebraska. Leonard Arrington's *Great Basin Kingdom: An Economic History of the Latter-day Saints, 1830–1900* (Cambridge: Harvard University Press, 1958), is a classic in Mormon and Western American History.

father's final illness. During his decline, Uncle Jimmy's Anglo wife hired a Mexican American nurse. To Aunt Marge's shock, her husband of fifty years began speaking fluent Spanish with this nurse.

Because Grandma Carmen's youngest son totally concealed his fluency in Spanish as an adult, so did Dad. I knew since the late-1950s that he had persuaded Uncle Jim to adopt Dad's alias of Quinn, but fluency in Spanish gave new insight into their concealed identity. When Dad asked his mother to write him only in English, he was able to read every sentence she wrote in Spanish. I was stunned to learn this aspect of my father's radical Americanization.

With this insight into Dad's brittleness, I better understood the only words in English that Grandma Carmen said to Mom when he first introduced them—after my birth. She whispered, *"Lo siento por ti."* (I feel sorry for you.)

Mid-September 1971–Mentor in History

Beginning with this term's class at the University of Utah, Davis Bitton greatly expanded my perceptions of historical inquiry and analysis. First, he introduced me to the crucial concept that there are fundamental differences between the past and history.

The past is infinite. All-inclusive of every conversation, every act, every source, everywhere at every moment. History is a finite, human, incomplete, imperfect effort to understand the past on the basis of the extremely limited sources that have survived.

The past remains unchangeable, while history is ever-changing as new evidence, new methods, new interpreters, new perceptions arise and compete with each other in the human task of trying to comprehend the infinite past. Only an infinite observer (God) can have a truly objective view of the past.

History—by its very nature—is humanly subjective but should be as complete and balanced and fair as humanly possible in assessing the available sources. The latter approach is often loosely called objectivity—albeit philosophically and practically, pure objectivity is fundamentally impossible for the human endeavor called history.

Likewise, everyone sees the world through filtered lenses of bias. The most highly trained and objective scholars have biases of gender, nationality, ethnicity, social class, memory, and numerous other factors which filter our perceptions. The scholarly obligation is to recognize our biases and compensate for them as much as humanly possible in research and in assessing the limited sources available. The result is often loosely called unbiased reporting, but practically speaking, no human can be unbiased. Multifaceted observations and rigorous efforts to be balanced are the goals.

Historians of the twentieth century to the present know those things about objectivity and bias, but their polemical critics claim otherwise. Particularly BYU political philosophers Louis C. Midgley and David E. Bohn in their slash-and-burn critiques of Mormon historians and of the New Mormon History.[14]

Equal in importance to the research access he gave me in 1971, Davis Bitton also introduced me to various modern approaches of the New History for understanding and presenting the past. This included social history, quantitative history, psychobiography, oral history, and a kind of group biography pioneered as prosopography by Sir Lewis Namier for the English Parliament's membership.

The last became my academic approach toward LDS general authorities and their echelons of leadership, the Mormon hierarchy. A term paper for Bitton's class in historical methods evolved into my life's work.

Fresh from my eighteen months in Munich, I gave the principal term of my research a German pronunciation. Davis tried not to smile when correcting my classroom comment about heerarchy. In this academic diplomacy, Professor Bitton reminded me of my junior high school teacher, Leonard DiGrassi.

26 September 1971—Elders Quorum Presidency, University of Utah 3rd Ward, University 1st Stake, Salt Lake City

A week after Jan was sustained as the ward's Primary president, I was sustained and set apart this day as second counselor in its elders quorum. Exactly two weeks later, the elders president advanced me to be his first counselor. Jan and I served in those callings for five months. Jan and I would relocate eight times during the next six years (including four cross country moves), and then buy a house in Salt Lake City's Lower Avenues.

October 1971—Destroying Uncensored Journals

After four years of on-and-off typing, Jan completed the edited version of my personal journals. It had been a labor of love, but she objected when I said that I would now destroy the originals.

She said that I might change my mind about the need to delete 3/4 of the entries. I countered that I wanted my children or others to read the *edited* diaries as a faith-promoting record of my life. I didn't want them to be distracted by all the boring stuff or by unkind things I had written about other people.

One evening, I tore up every page of my original journals into small pieces

---

14. A protege of Midgley's, David Earl Bohn (1942–) was also a professor in BYU's political science department, where he taught for thirty-five years. His essay, "Unfounded Claims and Impossible Expectations: A Critique of New Mormon History," is published in George D. Smith, ed., *Faithful History: Essays on Writing Mormon History* (Salt Lake City: Signature Books, 1992).

and threw them in the dumpster of our apartment building. Jan just shook her head.

It wasn't long before I realized she was right. I also saw the historical irony of a decision I soon regretted. As a result, the personal journals I kept daily from the next year onward were increasingly candid and detailed.

But irretrievably lost were those daily notations that demonstrated a fuller view of me as a teenager and young adult. Both God and the Devil are in the details, and I should have allowed the future readers of my youth's original diaries to decide where they saw one influence or the other. Or perhaps both. Too late my awareness, which I've tried applying to this self-biography. Let the chips fall where they may.

November 1971–LDS Conversion of Half-Sisters

I had no role in teaching the missionary lessons to my sisters, but I baptized Kathy in Provo shortly before Thanksgiving. Having investigated various fellowships after leaving their Lutheran congregation, her sister Tricia and their mother were baptized into the LDS Church in Glendale, California, just weeks after Kathy's baptism as a BYU freshman.

Late December 1971–Research Assistant for Professor Arrington

Giving me thirty days' notice, Professor Bitton had notified me that his research funds were ending. He discontinued my employment this month.

I informed Leonard Arrington, who employed me as his research assistant, beginning the last week of December. During the next few weeks, he had me write a chapter for a Utah history text in which I presented an economic history of the Latter-day Saints, 1847–1900. I also wrote an article on the entire history of the LDS Church for a new encyclopedia on Western history, and wrote shorter articles for the same encyclopedia. My checks as his ghostwriter came from USU, but I never went to Logan this year.

Leonard expressed surprise at the speed with which I completed the compositions he requested. And he complimented me on their "high quality."

Early January 1972–Former Mentor's Backhanded Recommendation

As a natural-born snoop, I was intrigued to see a drawer labeled Graduate Student Files in the office of the history department's secretary. Noticing that it was unlocked one day when she was gone, I opened the drawer and looked at my file. With pride typical of me, I wanted to read the glowing report I expected that BYU's Robert K. Thomas had written to the University of Utah in support of my application.

I found the praise I expected him to give for my intellectual curiosity and academic achievements but was stunned to see that Professor Thomas had also expressed "hope" that I had outgrown my "emotional immaturity and disturbances." At first, I couldn't imagine what he could possibly have meant concerning the four years he was my adviser in BYU's honors program, or when I got a solid A in his course on the Bible as Literature while I was a second-semester sophomore.

Then it hit me: he was referring to my crying in his office as an eighteen-year-old freshman flunking out of pre-med. "What a condescending jerk!" was my assessment as I shoved his letter back into its official folder and shut the drawer.

I maintained a cordial demeanor in future conversations with Bob Thomas, but never asked him to write another letter of recommendation. I no longer trusted him.

Late January 1972–Stunning News

From the journal I resumed this year: "The last week in January Dr. Arrington gave me some news I could hardly believe. I was studying at the U of U on a Saturday—working on a paper for Dr. Arrington, in fact. When Jan picked me up from the Library, she told me she had exciting news. Dr. Arrington had telephoned from Logan, telling her that there was going to be a change in the Church Historian's Office.

"Being appointed as the Church Historian, he was submitting to the First Presidency a proposal for new personnel. He said that he was submitting my name. I could hardly believe it.

"I returned his call when I got home and was thrilled to hear him make the offer [to me]. He seemed as excited in telling me as I was to hear the news."

Leonard Arrington was the first PhD to serve as official Church Historian and the first who had already published about Mormon history with academic presses. Following Church Historian Joseph Fielding Smith's advancement to be LDS Church president in January 1970, apostle Howard W. Hunter had been his successor until now.

After Leonard's appointment by the First Presidency in January 1972, he asked historians Davis Bitton (of the University of Utah) and James B. Allen (of Brigham Young University) to be his Assistant Church Historians. The three were publicly sustained in those positions at the general conference in April.

As the first member of his research staff, he appointed Dean C. Jessee.[15] He was the first person with a graduate degree in history whom Joseph Fielding Smith had hired in the old Church Historian's Office.

Leonard told me that I was the next person he asked to serve on his staff

---

15. Dean Cornell Jessee (1929–) is an author, historian, and leading expert on Joseph Smith's writings. Before his retirement he served as general manager, along with Richard Bushman and Ron Esplin, of the Joseph Smith Papers Project in the LDS Church History Department.

of researchers and writers. It was called the History Division in the newly formed Historical Department of the Church (HDC).

Mid-February 1972–Fledgling Historian and Renewed Diarist

Dr. Arrington told me that I had been approved with the others—subject to the final interview with one of the general authorities. I was interviewed by Alvin R. Dyer, an apostle who currently served as an Assistant to the Twelve. My appointment was officially dated as of March 1, and my pay was $3.50 an hour for 1/2 time work (twenty hours weekly). That was a forty percent increase over my previous salary.

I started working all day every Tuesday and Thursday in Arrington's small staff on the third floor of the Church Administration Building (47 East South Temple). It was a wonderful experience of research, discovery and writing for me, but I was an employee for less than eighteen months. That was the shortest service for anyone in his History Division. As a graduate student, I was full-time on Leonard's staff for only the last three months.

Davis Bitton later compared the experience of Leonard's History Division to legendary King Arthur's Camelot. In retrospect, it was as wonderful, as exuberant, as dream-like. And as short-lived. For me, it was life-changing, which is why I soon resumed making daily entries in a journal.

1 March 1972–Youth Sunday School Teacher, Valley View 4th Ward

Jan and I moved so far from the Art Deco chapel at University and Second South, that we decided to join our resident ward in the Salt Lake Valley. That seemed better than commuting a long distance to attend a university ward, as many LDS students did. In April, the Valley View Fourth Ward's bishop called me as Sunday School teacher for sixteen-year-olds.

14 April 1972–Access to Manuscripts at LDS Church Archives

From my journal: "Today I am at the University of Utah Library studying for my classes. I find it difficult to concentrate on my assigned schoolwork. I find that my mind often wanders to my research projects.

"The Lord has, I believe, blessed me greatly in having access to important documents relating to post-1890 polygamy. ... I have found important MSS which show the role of George Q. Cannon in advocating post-1890 polygamy, which show the manipulations and strategies involved in the Smoot Case and resultant resignations of Cowley and Taylor, and which have highlighted other aspects of post-1890 polygamy. During 1971, I verified that Heber J. Grant and Francis M. Lyman (traditionally considered as implacable foes of post-1890 polygamy) had each performed a few plural marriages after 1890, and that Heber J. Grant unsuccessfully tried to marry a plural wife after 1890. I also found other tidbits of importance to this subject during 1971.

The Church History Division, in the recently completed Church Office Building, 1973. Left to right: Ronald Esplin, Gordon Irving, Flore Chappuis, Richard Jensen, possibly A. Glen Humphreys, Maureen Ursenbach (Beecher), Pat Jarvis, Michael Quinn (seated), Davis Bitton (standing), unidentified, Dean Jessee (standing in doorway), Christine Croft (Waters), Pearl Ghormley, James Allen (standing), Edyth Romney (seated), and Leonard Arrington (standing). *Courtesy Susan Arrington Madsen.*

"After I became a member of the HDC a few weeks ago, my ability to pick up information increased. Being a staff member I could wander through the stacks of MSS without supervision.

"This gave me the opportunity to find what I could by snooping around. In this way I located the sealing records of Patriarch Alexander F. Macdonald of Juarez Stake (1900–1903);[16] the record of some plural marriages performed by Apostle Marriner W. Merrill[17] between 1894–1903, and a record called Temple Book B, which recorded over 300 sealings performed outside the temple from 1891–1903 (at least 9 of which were polygamous marriages—including that of [apostle] George Teasdale performed [in 1897] by Apostle Anthon H. Lund)....

16. Alexander Findlay Macdonald (1825–1903) was a Latter-day Saint convert from Scotland. In the early 1880s, Macdonald was sent to Mexico to explore possibilities for colonies for polygamous Latter-day Saints to avoid anti-polygamy prosecution in the United States. He was authorized by LDS Church leaders to perform polygamous sealings in Mexico and served as patriarch of the Juarez Stake from 1895 until his death.

17. Marriner Wood Merrill (1832–1906) helped settle Cache Valley, Utah, in the 1860s, was president of the Logan Temple, and became an apostle in 1889. He was arrested once for unlawful cohabitation and married polygamously after the 1890 Manifesto.

"I feel [that] the Lord has allowed me to find as much information as He has for a purpose. I believe that this purpose is for me to write a detailed and comprehensive history of this era [of post-Manifesto polygamy]—why I do not know. But I will never attempt to write such a history unless I have researched those additional sources I regard as absolutely essential to understanding the full story of this period of quiet and secret continuation of polygamy."

I didn't tell *anyone* about such discoveries. But I could hardly contain my excitement upon finding all the nineteenth-century records of polygamous marriage sealings.

Like the sealings of the Nauvoo Temple in 1846, the bound volumes of living sealings in the Salt Lake Endowment House had both polygamous marriages and monogamous marriages interspersed from 1853 to 1889. Those records at HDC seemed to be the original versions of what was on microfilms at the LDS Genealogical Library (subsequently called the Family History Library).

By contrast, my years-earlier research found that individually prepared family group sheets often reported that an ancestor's polygamous sealing of marriage in one of Utah's temples could *not* be found in the microfilmed records at the Genealogical Library. One reason for that apparent absence was that such marriages violated federal laws passed since 1862.[18]

As a result, current Mormons often concluded that Utah's temples kept no records of their polygamous ceremonies. However, that would violate revelations about the necessity of recording every ordinance—especially temple ordinances (see D&C 128:2–4, 8).

What I discovered at HDC was contrary to those common beliefs. It was also contrary to what rank-and-file Mormons were told by personnel in the Genealogical Department and at the LDS Family History Library. Starting with the St. George Temple's opening in 1877, each temple recorded its relatively few polygamous marriages of living couples in a volume separate from those used for monogamous marriages. I also found records of marriage sealings (including polygamous) performed outside the Endowment House and outside the temples. I typed complete transcripts of those.

Despite my ability to do personal photocopying for two cents a page as an employee of HDC, I preferred to type detailed notes. Because I rented safe deposit boxes to store backup copies of my precious notes, photocopies were inefficient for storage space. Also, even two cents a page would add up significantly for someone with my limited finances.

Thus, compared with the tens of thousands of pages of research notes I typed, I probably Xeroxed fewer than fifty pages of manuscripts at the LDS

18. Quinn is referring to Congress's Morrill Anti-Bigamy Act of 1862.

archives. Over the decades, other researchers (never employees of HDC) sometimes gave me copies of *their* personal photocopying of manuscripts, but I did little of it myself.

As a result, I could kick myself now for not Xeroxing every one of the records for polygamous marriages of living couples in the temples of St. George, Logan, and Manti, Utah. Instead, with my tunnel-vision emphasis on the general authorities and post-Manifesto polygamy, I Xeroxed only the post-1890 entries in the last page or two of small books maintained for the Logan Temple. I did so only because those polygamous marriages involved apostles Marriner W. Merrill and Matthias F. Cowley. I didn't even look for the names of general authorities among those who married plural wives in the Logan Temple from 1884 to 1890, even though I knew this included apostle Merrill's childless marriages for which his descendants had only approximate dates!

I also didn't take notes on the few polygamous marriages of living couples in the Manti Temple's book from its dedication in 1888 to 1890. Likewise, I didn't even skim entries in the St. George Temple's books of polygamous marriages because they didn't go beyond the 1880s.

If I had bothered to do that, I would have discovered the record of a little-known polygamous marriage of apostle Wilford Woodruff to a living daughter of Brigham Young in the St. George Temple in 1877.[19] I learned about it only after someone deciphered shorthand entries in Woodruff's journal. How many others did I ignore? At the least, there were details for the polygamous marriages that apostle Erastus Snow entered there—one of which had been hinted in his family group sheets and published history.

Of all the regrets I could have in my life, the one I have never been able to forgive myself is my thick-headed failure to make at least typed copies of *all* those incomparably important records of Utah's plural marriages for living couples in LDS temples from 1877 to 1890. Millions of their modern descendants have been told that such records don't exist but have likewise been instructed by LDS headquarters to verify from the original records *every* ordinance received by their ancestors. This is just one double-bind in modern Mormonism.

If I had followed the opportunities and promptings given to me by the Lord, I could have aided those Mormons by publishing my complete notes from these hidden records of temple-performed polygamy. But I didn't. Dammit!

20 April 1972—Transitioning from Ghostwriter

From my journal: "Today I began doing research on the L.D.S. Washaki

19. Woodruff married Eudora "Dora" Lovina Young Dunford on March 10, 1877. She was sealed to Woodruff by her father after her first marriage to Frank Morley Dunford ended in divorce. Her marriage to Woodruff also ended in divorce. She went on to marry a Catholic man and leave the LDS Church. Romney Burke, *Susa Young Gates: Daughter of Mormonism* (Salt Lake City: Signature Books, 2022), 277–78.

Project, or Indian Farm near Malad, Idaho. Dr. Arrington wants me to do this under my own name and have it published, perhaps in an Idaho journal of history.

"Up to now, most of what I have written will be published under Dr. Arrington's name. But at $3.50 I can't complain. Dr. Arrington has frequently given me lavish praise (in front of others) on my writing ability.

"I always have thought my style was a bit dry, but I am pleased to know he likes it. I think it was my narrative style which led Dr. Arrington to recommend me for this position at the HDC."

However, my Washaki article never got published.

23 April 1972–Cascading Insights about Mormon Hierarchy

Undoubtedly because of my official appointment at LDS headquarters, my father-in-law, Roy M. Darley, became increasingly candid in talking with me about his personal knowledge of inner workings within the LDS hierarchy. He had been in close association with the general authorities since his full-time appointment in 1947 as an organist in the Salt Lake Tabernacle. I wrote many of those disclosures in my journal within hours of hearing his narration.

A few I record now from memory, such as the following: One of my father-in-law's favorite stories concerned general authority Marion D. Hanks. Roy referred to him as "Duff," but to me he has always been President Hanks. One day in the 1950s, President Hanks came into a back room of the Salt Lake Tabernacle where Roy was preparing for the noon organ recital. He was obviously agitated, paced back and forth momentarily, and then said: "Darley, do you know what's wrong with this damn place? There's too many chiefs and not enough Indians!" Roy liked him a lot.

And now from my journal for April 23: "While Roy was visiting us, he and I began talking about some of the inner workings of the Church leaders. I told him that in discussing my proposed thesis on the Mormon hierarchy, Dr. S. Lyman Tyler at the University told me of some of the power struggles that have occurred in recent years.

"Dr. Tyler had been an adviser or secretary to the Quorum of the Twelve a few years ago and picked up some of the undercurrents of the Church leadership. He told me that during the latter years of David O. McKay's Presidency, several of the general authorities felt that Harold B. Lee was assuming too much authority. Some members of the Quorum felt this, but more important members of the First Presidency felt that Harold B. Lee was attempting to assert the power of the Quorum of the Twelve against that of the First Presidency. Dr. Tyler said that when Pres. McKay brought in his three additional counselors (Joseph Fielding Smith, Thorpe B. Isaacson, and Alvin R. Dyer) that it was not so much to relieve the burdens from Pres. McKay and his counselors, as it was to expand the power of the 1st Presidency in opposition to the growing rivalry with the Quorum of the Twelve as spurred by Harold B. Lee.

"Roy said that he hadn't heard this, but that it was consistent with certain alignments among the general authorities. He said that David O. McKay, Hugh B. Brown, and Alvin R. Dyer had been a close knit group; and that J. Reuben Clark Jr., Joseph Fielding Smith, and Harold B. Lee were another somewhat opposed alignment. ...

"Roy also said that at one time Jessie Evans Smith told him that when [her husband] Joseph Fielding became president, Harold B. Lee would never be his counselor. Brother Lee had been abrupt with her during a semi-annual conference, and she felt resentful toward him and had told Joseph Fielding of Lee's actions. Jessie Evans had also told Roy that neither Hugh B. Brown nor N. Eldon Tanner would be Joseph Fielding's counselors when he became president. Because of this, Roy was quite surprised when Joseph Fielding Smith chose Harold B. Lee as his first counselor and retained Tanner.

"Concerning Hugh B. Brown, Roy said relations between President Brown and Joseph Fielding were so strained that Hugh B. Brown would not have been retained even had he been in good health.

"As with this other information Roy learned through his close association with the Smiths (especially with Jessie Evans during her life), he had some interesting insights concerning Alvin R. Dyer. Alvin Dyer was a nephew (or some close relation) to Clare Middlemiss, the private secretary to David O. McKay. During the last years of David O. McKay's life[,] he was often unapproachable by the other general authorities. When Harold B. Lee or even Joseph Fielding Smith came to President McKay's office to see him, they were often turned away [by secretary Middlemiss]. Yet Alvin R. Dyer always had easy access.

"Although Brother Dyer may have been unaware of this preference shown him against Brothers Smith and Lee, they both felt the snub keenly. Roy said the feelings on the part of Joseph Fielding and Harold B. Lee were sufficiently strong concerning this preference shown Alvin R. Dyer, that neither would ever call Alvin R. Dyer as a member of the Quorum of the Twelve, even though he had been ordained an Apostle by David O. McKay.

"Concerning all these undercurrents among the Authorities, Roy and Kay Darley certainly have their own biases. They were both extremely close with J. Reuben Clark Jr. and with John A. Widtsoe. Their closeness with J. Reuben I think tended to bias them in his favor concerning the frictions between J. Reuben and David O. McKay.

"J. Reuben gave Roy to understand that during the administration of Heber J. Grant, David O. McKay felt extreme resentment at being the 2nd

Counselor when J. Reuben (initially a High Priest) was the 1st Counselor. Roy said that President McKay upon becoming president, made his own resentment clear when he demoted J. Reuben from 1st to 2nd Counselor.

"Roy and Kay have on several occasions felt the sting of David O. McKay's temper, and so they do not share my somewhat blind adoration of David O. McKay. I knew him as a symbol and they knew him as a man; the two viewpoints are bound to clash on occasion. No matter how high in station a man attains, he still carries with him the frailties of mortality."

Although not recorded in my journal, my favorite story concerned the homemade root beer that Roy had given for decades to apostle Joseph Fielding Smith and his wife Jessie Evans Smith at each Christmas season. Joseph Fielding complained if his yeast-brewed root beer wasn't strong (aged until it was nearly alcoholic). One year, Roy let a batch age so long, that every bottle exploded in the basement of the Darley family's home!

For another dozen years, Roy Darley volunteered many such anecdotes to me. Some involved humorous incidents at the Logan Temple, where his father Evan O. Darley was a counselor in its presidency.

Roy's father (born in 1891) was named after Evan Stephens, a prominent musician in Cache Valley for decades before becoming the Salt Lake Tabernacle Choir's director in 1890.[20] In twenty-four years, the University of Illinois Press would publish my book which examined the significance of the boy chums of bachelor Stephens from his teens to his sixties. It would be two decades from now before I knew about those relationships.

29 April 1972—The Mormon Underground of History

Word got around quickly about how I was burrowing into previously unavailable/unknown documents of extraordinary historical importance. Thus, British convert and researcher Guy F. Potter glommed onto me, as my journal first recorded for this date.

He was a new wheeler-dealer in the long-operating "Mormon Underground" of trading research notes among history buffs. Begun decades ago by well-connected Stanley Snow Ivins, the Mormon Underground went into overdrive a few years after his death, when apostle Hunter opened the LDS Archives in late 1970.

Now the only restraint on the Mormon Underground was the secretive possessiveness of research notes by professional historians. Each wanted to be

---

20. Evan Stephens (1854–1930) was a Welsh composer, hymnist, and singer. In polygamous Utah, he never married but boldly claimed a series of young men were his "life companions." He also sang in drag at the Salt Lake Tabernacle in 1884 and the Malad Stake Tabernacle in Idaho in 1918. Quinn believed Stephens had same-sex relationships and wrote about this in *Same-Sex Dynamics Among Nineteenth-Century Americans: A Mormon Example* (Urbana: University of Illinois Press, 1996).

the first to publish something. And, while just a graduate student, I became infamous as one of those holdouts.

Because he was a recent research assistant for BYU religion professor Hyrum L. Andrus, Guy Potter was deep into that community of document exchangers by the time he introduced himself to me. He constantly pestered me to trade my incomparable notes for his merely interesting ones that he had obtained from Andrus. I could easily examine the originals on my own if I wanted to take the time, but Guy could also be helpful in alerting me to sources I didn't already know about. So I tolerated his incessant requests for me to share my notes.

Today was my first meeting with his then-fiancée Margaret Merrill, but I would have a much more significant association with her a decade later. This would be long after their divorce, following which she married Catholic convert Paul J. Toscano in the temple. Paul was as rigorous and original a thinker as Margaret.[21]

As for Guy Potter, I periodically gave him some of my routine notes from Bitton's diary project, for which he exchanged Xeroxed notes from Andrus's research. Typically, Guy made empty promises about sharing sensational findings of various kinds, and I became impatient and uncooperative. Eventually, he left the document-exchanging world of the Mormon Underground. At least as far as I knew about it.

This experience made me even more resistant to sharing my research notes with *anybody*. Even with academically trained historians and colleagues, I shared only excerpts—usually after their repeated requests. This was professionally stingy, but necessary in my view.

30 April 1972–Invited to Marion D. Hanks's Monthly Study Group

President Hanks could be as blunt in what he told me about his personal circumstances as he was about LDS headquarters. One evening when he invited Jan and me to his home (previous to this year), he took me aside for one of our *mano a mano* talks.

Out of the blue, he said: "My church salary isn't enough for me to send my children to college." He told me that their only hope for higher education was the free tuition and fees they were entitled to receive at BYU because of his being a general authority. If they had to attend a Utah school, however,

21. Paul Toscano is a lawyer and author in Salt Lake City. Margaret Merrill Toscano is department chair of World Languages and Cultures at the University of Utah. Together they authored *Strangers in Paradox: Explorations in Mormon Theology* (Salt Lake City: Signature Books, 1990). In September 1993, Paul was excommunicated as one of the September Six scholars and feminists who were excommunicated or disfellowshipped, as was Quinn. Margaret was excommunicated in 2000.

he wanted them to go to his *alma mater*, the University of Utah. He was very frustrated.

In his study group (but more often in our private chats), Marion D. Hanks remained my religious mentor and confidant for decades.

1 May 1972–Resuming Regular Tours on Temple Square

Since my return from Germany, I had been a substitute guide at least once a week for tours on Temple Square. This was thanks to my friendship with Viola Clawson.

Leaving Temple Square tonight, I thought about the LDS Church's official position that "the Lord has not yet authorized the bestowal of Priesthood on those with Negro blood." ("Melchizedek Priesthood," *Improvement Era*, Jan. 1955). However, my journal gave no clue for what actually triggered the following meditation: "If I were ever to discover in my Mexican ancestry a Negro, I would keep it to myself. That would be a matter between me and the Lord. Having received the Priesthood and had the assurances of the Spirit that he was exercising it validly and in righteousness, any man would be a perfect fool to give this information to those who would demand him to stop exercising the Priesthood.

"There are times when the Letter of the Law must yield to the Spirit, and that is one of those times. If someone came to me with such information, I would refuse to hear it and would counsel him to forget it."

Ironic postscript: Due to the twenty-first century's advances in DNA analysis, I've learned that about one percent of my ancestry derives from West Africa. Thus, more than six generations ago, one of my slave-owning Southern ancestors had sex with a mulatto "Negress" and fathered a light-skinned child who was attributed to the slave owner's wife and raised white.

Somehow in May 1972, I accurately sensed that I possess the "one drop" of Negro blood that allegedly disqualified *anyone* from receiving the Priesthood of God (Harold B. Lee, *Decisions for Successful Living*, 168). I'm glad that I've known since the 1970s that the LDS Church's policy violated Joseph Smith's example of authorizing the ordination to the Melchizedek Priesthood of free Blacks like Elijah Abel in 1836 and others in the 1840s. In announcing the priesthood restriction in 1852, Brigham Young was simply a Northern racist who ignored the founding prophet's example and violated the 1830 Book of Mormon's statement that "he [God] denieth none that come unto him, black and white, bond and free" (see 2 Nephi 26: 33).

16 May 1972–Wife Learns about My Homosexuality

From my journal: "In the evening, I weeded for an hour, although I am pressed with many heavy school pressures. I spent most of the evening talking with Jan about our lives past, present, and potential."

And now, the unrecorded details: Since March 1, Jan and I had been working as apartment managers for free rent at a large complex (Georgetown Square) in the Millcreek area of the Salt Lake Valley. But Jan was doing most of the onsite work, due to my being a full-time student with a part-time job at LDS headquarters. Those strains of time and finances were not the main reason that our marriage had been in crisis for nearly a year.

Even without indulging in pornography, my thoughts were filled with homosexual lust on a daily basis. Sometimes hourly. Other times, minute by minute. The aching frustration of my unfulfilled homosexuality was making it difficult for me to respond emotionally or sexually toward my wife. When I did merge with her, I had post-coital dreams about being caressed by a man. And cursed myself silently upon waking. Having sex with my wife actually *increased* my longings to have sex with men. That is the fatal flaw of encouraging homosexually inclined males to marry women. It was less painful to try deadening myself sexually by delaying intercourse as long as I could postpone it. Until Jan could endure no longer.

Adding to my guilt, she sometimes blamed herself for not being "sexy enough" or "pretty enough." This was heartbreaking for me to hear. More often, she rightly saw me as the problem. Tonight, she said that "we should make an appointment to see a doctor." And I finally told her the truth.

After the initial shock, Jan was determined that we would work out the situation together with our mutual love, devotion, and religious faith. I eventually learned that this is the universal approach by unfulfilled spouses of homosexually oriented Mormons. The *unresolvable* plight of such wives was something I couldn't recall encountering in my extensive reading about male homosexuality from age twelve until my marriage. Would such knowledge of their almost universal despair have changed my decisions? I don't know.

Mormonism teaches that any sacrifice is worthwhile for service to God and the LDS Church. Spencer W. Kimball's 1969 *Miracle of Forgiveness* instructed each homosexually inclined male to just forget his desires and "force himself" to date the opposite sex and marry a woman in the temple for time and eternity. In 1971, the church officially published his pamphlet *New Horizons for Homosexuals* (subsequently called *A Letter to a Friend*), which had a section titled "Multiply and Replenish" as a step in repenting from homosexual activities.

In effect, such counsel has turned generations of females into therapeutic sex objects to redeem homosexually oriented males, whose priesthood service to the LDS Church is more important than the happiness of their wives on earth. Women aren't expendable in Mormonism, but their personal fulfillment is less important than male achievement in the LDS Church. How can religious people think that Heavenly Father is pleased with this?

Within two decades, I would see irony in the fact that we were now attending ward and stake meetings in the chapel on Evergreen Avenue when I told Jan of my sexual orientation. Evergreen International would become the name of the headquarters-approved LDS support group for "those who struggle with same-gender attractions."

I never affiliated with this organization for several reasons. First, it tried to get its male participants to do exactly what I had been doing all my life: act heterosexual, engage in manly sports, pray for God's strength to avoid homosexual intimacy, participate fully in LDS activities, get married to a woman in the temple, and be sexually faithful to her. Second, its claimed successes in reparative therapy to change a male's homosexuality into heterosexuality were based on his ability to have sexual intercourse and produce children. In those two respects, I could be a poster boy for Evergreen. However, third—and most important—such success nonetheless overwhelmingly failed to eradicate homosexual attractions and desires.

If you look only at the *quantity* of children, then reparative therapy succeeds in nearly all gay-straight marriages. If you look at the *quality* of husband-wife dynamics and happiness, then reparative therapy of homosexuality fails in nearly all marriages of mixed orientation, despite the earnest love between spouses. As reparative therapy fails those parents, it fails their children.

Those are tragedies upon tragedies. And Evergreen just compounds them by encouraging false expectations of heterosexual bliss in its homosexually inclined men and women, who desperately reach for any straw of hope. To become normal. To be accepted by a homophobic church.

During the ten years after Jan learned of my homosexuality, she played the piano whenever I sang Gounod's "O, Divine Redeemer" in each ward we attended. On a technical level, she liked the intricacies of its accompaniment which demonstrated her skills as a pianist, and I liked to show off my vocal range by sustaining its highest and lowest notes. At a personal level, we both had a special affinity for my singing its lyrics.

CHAPTER TWELVE

HISTORICAL BREAKTHROUGHS

1972-1973

18 May 1972–Discovering Polygamy Revelation at HDC

From my journal: "I asked Dean Jessee if he was aware of the letter revelation of Joseph Smith to N. K. Whitney in 1842. Dean is preparing a book (the 1st in the Heritage Series by HDC) on holograph writings of Joseph Smith.

"I explained that the letter was instructing N. K. Whitney on the manner in which to perform the ceremony uniting his daughter to Joseph Smith as a plural wife. Dean hadn't heard of the letter."

7 June 1972–Manuscript Acquisitions

From my journal: "At HDC. I finally decided to contact one of Matthias F. Cowley's daughters today, Mrs. Carole C. Dame. Elva Cowley (widow of Matthew Cowley) had told me a few months ago that she had given Sister Dame the diaries written by M. F. Cowley's first wife.

"I left her home with her brother's journal of his mission to Hawaii, and the scrapbooks of her sister and mother, plus some family photographs.

"Dr. Arrington was quite pleased at the acquisition, as well as Max Evans, who is in charge of cataloging at HDC.[1] He is quite excited about acquiring new MSS and is perturbed that the people technically assigned to Acquisitions do not seem to be going out of their way to acquire new MSS.

"Therefore, Max encouraged me and said he was willing to bypass 'channels' as long as I keep bringing in MSS. ... I am quite anxious to bring as many MSS as possible to CHO, especially if they aid my own research."

Elva Taylor Cowley and Jan became acquainted at Jan's job before our marriage. Because of my friendship with Sister Cowley, I became an official representative for the Historical Department of the Church to acquire important manuscripts from families currently possessing them. These were sometimes called "field acquisitions," because they were outside the usual channels of official acquisition from within the organizational structure of Mormonism.

---

1. Max J. Evans went on to become director of the Utah State Historical Society and then executive director of the National Historical Publications and Records Commission of the National Archives, before returning to the LDS Church History Library as an archivist in 2007.

Thus, I was sometimes called "a field representative" for acquiring manuscripts that originated with individuals. Aside from spontaneous donations by such persons and their families, the old Church Historian's Office had depended on passive acquisition from units of the church and from units of its administrative outreach, such as businesses.

Until the spring of 1972, there had been no active effort at LDS HQ to make acquisition contacts with descendants of prominent persons. I changed that. In March 1973, I made twenty-six percent of HDC's reported acquisitions.

During the next ten years or so, I brought to LDS archives dozens of manuscripts, several written by already deceased general authorities. Others were by Mormons who had once been prominent in various capacities. As in my research, my effort at acquisitions emphasized the LDS elite of the late-nineteenth century and early twentieth century.

By happenstance rather than design, I provided similar service to the libraries of Brigham Young University and University of Utah. But most manuscripts I brought in were for LDS Church archives. Meanwhile, each of those repositories appointed staff members to do this kind of field acquisition at least part-time.

As would be true with many other people I later contacted, Elva Cowley expressed surprise that the church might want to have documents she regarded as of interest only to the immediate family. And she was understandably reluctant to part with them. Then I offered (as impromptu ideas) the inducements I would repeat with others. It was as if I were reciting the canned lines of a missionary while tracting:

First, I was "sure that the Church archives will give you complete photocopies in exchange for the right to maintain the originals." Second, in its new facility, LDS archives "will maintain the documents in fireproof, humidity-controlled rooms, so that your precious documents will be preserved without the dangers they might experience from fire or floods in your home." Third, "if these documents remain in your possession until you die, your children will probably divide them up, which will make it more difficult for another descendant to have access to read them." Fourth, "the dividing up of these precious documents will continue after your children's deaths." Finally, a donation to HDC "will guarantee that all descendants can see these precious documents of their ancestor whenever they want—in one safe place."

As others often did, Elva expressed concern that the Church Historian might make her general authority husband's diaries "unavailable" to the public after she donated them. For example, the Mormon Underground had been circulating copies of a letter by BYU's religion professor Hugh Nibley, who admitted that he had been denied access to his great-grandfather

Alexander Neibaur's journal after Nibley donated it to Church Historian Joseph Fielding Smith.[2] I replied to those legitimate concerns by saying that I was sure that the *new* Historical Department would be willing to accept a written requirement that all donated materials would always be available to their creator's descendants.

Eventually, Elva agreed, and let me carry apostle Matthew Cowley's diaries, scrapbooks, and letters out of her residence in the old Gateway Apartments. I immediately took them to HDC across the street.

Besides things of lesser import, I was able to acquire for HDC the collections of general authority seventy Rey L. Pratt, apostle Hyrum M. Smith, apostle Marriner W. Merrill, apostle Abraham Owen Woodruff's post-Manifesto plural wife, and mission president Joseph E. Robinson. I was most interested in the last three collections because of their oblique references to post-1890 polygamy.[3]

Moreover, delayed success in acquisitions followed my being allowed to type hundreds of pages of detailed notes from manuscripts in the possession of descendants. Years after my encouragement, various families donated to HDC the diaries of Seventy's President J. Golden Kimball, of presiding bishopric counselor John Wells, of First Presidency counselor Henry D. Moyle, and of Harold B. Lee. Apostle Rudger Clawson's diaries and First Presidency counselor Hugh B. Brown's papers would go to the Marriott Library of the University of Utah. BYU would get the diaries and accounts of Patriarch Hyrum Smith, one of apostle Abraham Owen Woodruff's diaries, and Carl A. Badger's letter books while he was apostle Reed Smoot's private secretary throughout the US Senate's investigation of post-Manifesto polygamy.

In addition, on June 10, 1972, I persuaded Nana to donate to the Marriott Library the letters her father wrote during the Spanish-American War and start of the Philippine Insurrection against US colonialism. Reminding me again that George P. Simpson was "a brutal beast" who beat her repeatedly as a teenager, her only objection was: "Why should I let him be known to anyone who doesn't remember what a cur he was?"

I countered that giving his letters to the University of Utah would allow researchers to learn more about the Philippines. Nana shrugged, sneering as she said: "Take them off my hands, and good riddance to the mean bastard."

---

2. Hugh Winder Nibley (1910–2005) taught foreign languages and Christian church history at BYU, starting in 1946. An LDS apologist, he wrote extensively about Joseph Smith and LDS scripture and doctrine. Alexander Neibaur (1808–83) was a native of Germany, Utah's first dentist, and the first Jewish person to join the LDS Church, which occurred after he moved to England.

3. Ray Lucero Pratt (1878–1931) was president of the Mexican Mission for twenty-three years and a general authority of the First Council of the Seventy for six years. Hyrum Mack Smith (1872–1918) was a son of President Joseph F. Smith and became an apostle in 1901. Abraham Owen Woodruff (1872–1904) was a son of President Wilford Woodruff and became an apostle in 1897.

I wondered if giving up his handwritten manuscripts when she was seventy-seven would allow Nana to finally let loose of some hatred. Never could tell.

11 June 1972–To Be Healed of Homosexuality?

Almost a year before I confided my homosexuality to my wife, I had written a letter about it to my closest friend, Mike McAdams. This is how my journal described his visit to us from Oklahoma on this Sunday:

"After the three of us watched the slides I have of England, it was 10:30 p.m. Jan went to bed while Mike and I continued to talk. Mike gave me a blessing, after we had kneeled in prayer. He told me that I had been cursed by Satan in the pre-existence because of my opposition to him in the war in Heaven. He said that Satan hated me and was trying to destroy me in any way he could.

"Mike raised his arm to the square and commanded Satan to depart and rebuked the curse. He blessed me with peace and a new ability to achieve my highest potentials."

His words were both comforting and burdensome for me.

12 June 1972–Matthias F. Cowley's Original Journals

From my journal: "At the HDC. I telephoned Mrs. Laura Brossard, a daughter of M. F. Cowley and she was quite abrupt, telling me her brother Joseph now had the journals and papers of her father and added that they were going to keep them. ... I located her brother's address and drove there, hoping that I could at least talk with him. His wife met me at the door, said he was sleeping, and told me Mrs. Brossard had already telephoned that I might be by. In effect, I had the door slammed in my face by both. It was quite depressing."

14 June 1972–Future Service in the First Presidency?

From my journal: "He [Mike McAdams] and I, feeling desirous of the opportunity to serve despite our personal limitations, are impatient to become Apostles. We both think it is almost laughable to talk about becoming Apostles, yet neither of us can deny our feelings and previous impressions which indicated we would attain the Apostleship. ...

"After Mike had told me of his impression, he said he felt sure that both he and I would serve together in the First Presidency, and that one of us might become the president and Prophet of the Church. That nearly bowled me over! ... I can regard such thoughts about myself in the same light as I do my fantasies when I was ten years old or so. I distinctly remember thinking or fantasizing at that time that I would be an Apostle and eventually the president of the Church. Those thoughts did not even have the attendant impressions of the Spirit and I can regard them only as childish dreams. My more recent thoughts about Church callings may be equally childish and unfounded, but they have consistently been accompanied by the confirmation of the Spirit."

16 June 1972—Apostle Matthias F. Cowley's Abridged Journals

From my journal, concerning another visit with Carole Cowley Dame: "While talking with her, I discovered that she had the abridgement which M. F. Cowley had made of his 50 volume journal. I asked to see these abridgements, and found they were handwritten and covered the period 1890–1938. I could hardly suppress my excitement.

"I asked her about donating these to the Church, but she said she could not do so as long as her sister Mrs. Brossard felt as she did. So it seems that everything hinges on Sister Brossard. I pray that I may be able to obtain these records for the Church, or at least obtain access to them myself."

18 June 1972—Frustrated Aspirations

From my journal: "We lived in the University 4th Ward boundaries and attended their S. School at 10:30. While there we heard the announcement that the First Presidency was changing all university and college wards into branches to avoid ordaining young men [to be] High Priests who later find themselves in High Priest quorums composed primarily of elderly men. This news promptly made me decide that we may as well attend our resident ward.... Frankly I see no reason to bother with the university 'branches' if there is no opportunity for me to have even the possibility of Priesthood advancement [as a High Priest in a ward's bishopric].

"In the evening we attended the Sacrament Mtg. at our resident ward, the Douglas Ward."

21 June 1972—Minutes of LDS Church's Highest Quorums

From my journal: "At HDC. Still working on [typing detailed notes from] the minutes of the First Council of Seventy. I plan to go only to 1940, and hope to finish tomorrow. Then I think I will try for the minutes of the Council of the Twelve Apostles which are sketchy for most of the nineteenth century but apparently complete for the period 1887 to 1914. These last are, of course, of particular interest to me.

"If the Lord wants me to have the access, I know He will provide the way even though it might otherwise be impossible."

22 June 1972—Apostle as Grand Inquisitor

From my journal: "From what I know or have heard of Mark E. Petersen in this regard, he seems to be somewhat of a fanatic in seeking out and attacking real or imagined polygamists and other apostates. He seems to have something of the burning zeal of an Inquisitor, and the thought that I might one day have a run-in with him or someone like him chills me. ...

"I only pray that God will spare me such an ordeal. If it comes, He will be my only refuge and hope of avoiding bad consequences."

Six days afterward, "Jan and I attended the wedding at the Temple where Mark E. Petersen sealed Van [Gessel] and Elizabeth," Jan's younger sister.[4]

29 June 1972—I Type My Copy of the Twelve's Minutes (1887-1914)

From my journal: "At HDC. I spent the entire day, 8:00 to 5:00 working on the minutes of the Quorum of the Twelve Apostles."

3 July 1972—End of an Era

From my journal: "This morning while on the way to HDC, I learned that President Joseph Fielding Smith had died of a heart attack last night. ... He was an energetic man and had been in relatively good health his entire 95 years."

He was the last of those general authorities born during the long administration of Brigham Young. Even though three of Joseph Fielding's presidential successors were also born in the nineteenth century, he was the last member of the Mormon hierarchy to reach adulthood before 1900. A link with pioneer Utah had passed, and I thought of the day I persuaded him to autograph my Bible.

Again from my journal for this day: "As I entered the Church Office Building, I saw Harold B. Lee walking down the hall toward his office. His face was bright and he had a big grin. I can hardly blame him for his happiness at having the Presidency of the Church at his door."

4 July 1972—More Perspectives on Presiding Quorums

From my journal: "After dinner at Aunt Margaret's, Roy [M. Darley] and I got to talking about the Church and the Authorities, as we sometimes do. Roy made the comment that in leading the Church these past 2 1/2 years, Harold B. Lee had seemed to do his best to lead it as Joseph Fielding Smith would have wanted it.

"Roy said that during the latter years of President David O. McKay's Presidency, his counselors often led the Church in directions other than those which Pres. McKay wanted. Roy said, 'And I'll give you a few examples of how the Counselors sometimes went contrary to David O. McKay's own directions or intentions.'

"A prime example, Roy said was the conduct of the missionary work under

---

4. Van C. Gessel (1950–) earned a PhD in Japanese language and literature from Columbia University. He taught there and at Notre Dame and UC Berkeley before finishing his career at BYU, where he was a professor, department chair, and dean of humanities. He retired in 2020.

Henry D. Moyle's direction. 'I'm sure,' Roy said, 'that President McKay did not know what Henry D. Moyle was doing in the missionary program, and I'll give you one reason why I believe that.' Roy said that as he was about to leave England [in the summer of 1962] after one year of playing the organ at Hyde Park Chapel, Marion D. Hanks took him aside for a private talk. Pres. Hanks said, 'I have a message about the missionary work situation I want you to deliver verbally to no one but Joseph Fielding Smith.'

"Roy said he was puzzled that Pres. Hanks would not use the telephone or mails, and was especially puzzled that Pres. Hanks would send a verbal message of apparent urgency to the president of the Quorum of the Twelve rather than to the First Presidency. I asked Roy what the message was, and he said he wished he had written it down because he could not now remember it. But Roy said it was about the bad state of the missionary work which had 'gone wild' (Roy's words).

"He delivered the message to Joseph Fielding, and a short while later Joseph Fielding was made an Assistant Counselor to the First Presidency and was put in charge of missionary work, and Henry D. Moyle was 'stripped of his authority' over the missionary program. This was one fact of the 'New Era' of the British Mission and the Church missionary program which I did not know of.

"Roy said that Henry D. Moyle's daughter, who works with Roy on the MIA General Board, told him that Henry D. Moyle said just before going to Florida [in September 1963] that the Church no longer needed him and that he was of no further use to the Church. He died suddenly while in Florida.

"The fourth example Roy gave of the apparent conflict of interests between President McKay and his 1st and 2nd counselors occurred about this same time [actually in June 1966]. David O. McKay made a trip to Independence, Missouri, and Adam-ondi-Ahman, accompanied by Joseph Fielding Smith and Alvin R. Dyer. He not only failed to include either his first or second counselors (Brown & Tanner) but he also left Salt Lake City without telling either of them that he was leaving the city, the destination, or object in view. Hugh B. Brown learned of the matter after Pres. McKay had departed, when he telephoned Pres. McKay's apartment at the Hotel Utah.

"The French maid told Pres. Brown that Pres. McKay was out of town. When Hugh B. Brown inquired about his whereabouts, the maid told him that President McKay was in Jackson County, Missouri, with Joseph Fielding Smith and Alvin R. Dyer. As Roy put it, 'Hugh B. Brown learned about it through the grapevine.'

"Roy said that he felt the Presidency were not always united as they should have been—during the presidency of David O. McKay's last few years. It was his opinion that there had been great unity in the Presidency of Joseph Fielding Smith.

"We were speaking later about last week's announcement of the First Council of Seventy's assuming control of all missionary work. Roy said that it was a proper change to make since the responsibility of missionary work fell naturally within the domain of the Seventies.

"He said that for a time the Quorum of Twelve and First Presidency had nearly taken away all of the responsibilities of the First Council of Seventy. S. Dilworth Young had told Roy that for a long period of time he had absolutely nothing to do as a member of the First Council of Seventy.

"Bro Young would come into his office, sit at his desk and put his feet up on the desk and stare at the walls. For diversion he would get a small mirror and catch the sun's reflection in it and shine it into the office of the president of Deseret Book Company across the street. Bro. Young would reflect the light into the office to catch the attention of the man, who was a friend. It was during this period that S. Dilworth Young composed much of his poetry which he has since published."

11 July 1972–Discovering a Treasure Trove

In January 1970, former Church Historian Joseph Fielding Smith had taken a safe full of the most sensitive documents with him from the third floor of 47 East South Temple to the First Presidency's Office on its main floor. Still, the Church Historian's Office (CHO) remained a treasure-trove of Mormon documents that apostle Howard W. Hunter had made available to the public two years earlier. Because its old-guard employees were accustomed to decades of apostle Smith's closed-archives policies, Elder Hunter's decision for openness had blindsided them in late 1970, as did Leonard Arrington's appointment as Church Historian in 1972.

This afternoon, I went to the CHO annex in the basement to ask Lauritz G. Petersen about some documents I found listed in old inventories, but that could not be located on the third floor.[5] As one of the old guard, he openly expressed to me his opposition to recent changes. When I commented that the old catalog listed as restricted some anti-Mormon newspapers that anyone could read at the University of Utah, Lauritz snapped, "Then they should go to the U to read such trash, not to the headquarters of God's church!"

Not wanting to prolong our disagreement, I asked if he knew where the missing documents might be. He waved toward a dimly lit expanse of the basement and said: "Maybe over there." When I asked if it was okay for me

---

5. Lauritz George Peterson (1916–99) was employed by Church Historian Joseph Fielding Smith. According to his obituary, "he worked as an Historical Researcher for the LDS Church." *Deseret News*, Feb. 20, 1999.

to browse around the area, Lauritz forced a smile: "You do pretty much what you want, anyway, don't you, Mike? Brother Arrington has control of you. I don't." That was enough for me, and off I went into the recesses of the basement. Then *eureka*!

What a discovery! Covered in dust, stacked against the walls and in tall piles across the floor, were hundreds—perhaps *thousands*—of leather-bound volumes in various sizes. As I leafed through them at random, I found that many were Brigham Young's financial records. I knew Leonard would be interested in those, but I wasn't.

Continuing to snoop around, I was drop-jawed to find what looked like daily minutes of the First Presidency's Office during John Taylor's presidency in the 1880s. Those were of profound interest to me, and I had to drag myself from reading them—to do a cursory survey of whatever else was in this dusty treasure trove.

Among the other things I found were filing cabinets that had apparently been removed from the office of Brigham H. Roberts shortly after he died in 1933, and then simply stored in the basement. In view of their contents, it's understandable that his longtime antagonist Joseph Fielding Smith consigned them to oblivion. Luckily, at ninety-three years of age, he forgot about Roberts's papers in the basement when he transferred other hidden documents from the CHO's vault to the First Presidency's vault.

In one of the drawers was a 1928 typed manuscript titled "The Truth, the Way, the Life: An Elementary Treatise on Theology." Roberts regarded this as his magnum opus. Also there were his far more controversial manuscripts: "Book of Mormon Difficulties," and "A Book of Mormon Study," and "A Parallel."

In three years, LDS headquarters would allow Truman Madsen to quote sections of the first in an article published by *BYU Studies*. Roberts's other three treatises would be printed in full by the University of Illinois Press thirteen years later—but only because Roberts's children had their own copies, which they authorized to be published. That eventually led to competing editions of a complete *The Truth, The Way, The Life* in 1994, one from BYU (with Leonard's Assistant Church Historians James B. Allen and Davis Bitton among its numerous coeditors) and one from Signature Books, the independently liberal press of George D. Smith Jr. (with Leonard among its numerous coeditors).[6]

Those dueling editions of the mid-1990s would symbolize a crucial split among LDS intellectuals about the New Mormon History. That was

---

6. See *The Truth, the Way, the Life: An Elementary Treatise on Theology* (Salt Lake City: Signature Books, 1994).

something no one anticipated this year—whether friend or foe of Leonard Arrington. Sadly, I became a principal wedge in the split.

Anyway, today I lost all track of time while exploring the seemingly un-known section of 47 East South Temple. I spent four hours sampling this candy store of Mormon historical documents. It was about 7 PM when I fi-nally dragged myself out of the area, left the basement, and walked out the Church Administration Building past puzzled guards. They relaxed when I showed them my church employee's ID.

The next day, I announced my discovery to Leonard Arrington. He rushed with me to the basement, where he quickly surveyed the documents in wide-eyed wonder.

Less than three weeks afterward, he said that the HDC processing staffers "have filled over 80 large boxes with the materials," after which my journal continued: "Dr. Arrington told me that next to his own call as Church His-torian and the establishment of his history writing staff, the discovery of these MSS is the most important development for the history of the Church in a century."

12 July 1972–My Daughter's Black Friend and Our Wild Renters

Having been fired on May 7 as the managers for Georgetown Square (with two months to vacate), Jan and I were hired today by Grayson Wright to be resident managers for La Castellana Apartments on Twelfth East. Most of the renters were undergraduate students at the nearby University of Utah.

The only child of renters was an African American boy named Maurice, a year older than Mary. They were inseparable, and I often wondered if my old-est daughter would eventually marry a Black. In principle, I had no objection to that—for her or any other child of mine.

Trying to keep order in a twenty-unit complex mainly occupied four to a unit by seventeen-to-twenty-year-old boys was a trip—in 1970s slang. Whether or not of LDS origin, they drank like fish and sometimes pissed in the elevator.

Because all bedrooms had glass walls facing the pool, the sleeping resi-dents were easily disturbed by late-night noise from the back. We kept the pool's water warm year round, so hardly a week went by that I didn't have to stand poolside in my robe in the middle of the night—waiting for every skinny dipper to walk inside.

In the spring of next year, we discovered marijuana plants in our garden—which I thought was amusing as I churned through them with the power mower. All in all, I loved this youth-dominated place as much as I disliked be-ing the hired help of its management company, which never seemed satisfied.

23 July 1972–Reconciled Companionship

As one of the small-world coincidences in Mormon culture, my second companion in the British Mission was a member of the Douglas Ward. When David Harris greeted me with such surprised delight and genuine warmth, I felt guilty about thinking of our tension-filled companionship nearly nine years earlier.

From my journal for this Sunday: "After Priesthood I talked with my former missionary companion David Harris. He is in the ward and is concerned about a friend who seems to know a lot about the Church's history, but seems to relish the negative.

"I talked with Dave about my own views of a balanced approach to our history. Dave said he wanted me to be the fireside speaker in this other fellow's ward and to talk about this. I said I'd be glad to."

28 July 1972–Church Historian Indicates His Plans for Me

From my journal: "Dr. Arrington asked if I could give him a ride home, which I was glad to do. ...

"Just as I stopped the car in front of his house, Dr. Arrington said an interesting thing. 'The only way I could boost your salary appreciably would be if you became an Assistant Church Historian.' ...

"This last bit of our conversation was really a surprize to me. It dumbfounded me that he even suggested the possibility of my becoming an Assistant Church Historian."

Not until eleven months had passed, would he confide this to his currently serving Assistant Church Historians.

28 July 1972–LDS Succession Crisis of January 1970

From my journal: "We had Jim and Judy McConkie over for dinner. During the evening James told me some very enlightening, and somewhat disturbing things about Joseph Fielding Smith's presidency of the Church. These things he learned through his uncles Bruce R. McConkie, Britt McConkie, and Oscar McConkie, as well as through Wilford W. Kirton Jr., the Church's top legal adviser.

"At the death of David O. McKay there was a movement to choose someone else besides Joseph Fielding Smith as the Prophet. This would have ended the previous practice of automatically advancing the senior member of the Quorum of Twelve Apostles to be the next president. What is most disturbing to me is that this movement came within the Quorum of Twelve itself.

"Bruce R. McConkie, being Joseph Fielding's son-in-law, heard rumors that such a movement was underway. Spencer W. Kimball (at that time the 3rd ranking member of the Apostles) told Britt McConkie that now that

David O. McKay was dead, 'We'll have a *younger* Prophet now, instead of an older Prophet.' In bypassing Joseph Fielding Smith, the other Apostles were presumably going to choose Harold B. Lee (who was certainly not young in a strict sense, but was over two decades younger than Joseph Fielding).

"Bruce R. McConkie was adamant that his father-in-law should become the Prophet by right of his seniority. Jim says that Bruce R. held special family nights for the McConkie Clan at which he forcefully preached the doctrine of succession by seniority.

"After his conversation with Apostle Kimball, Britt McConkie was shaken about the prospects of this succession crisis. He began fasting and praying about this and after a period of time, he received a direct revelation from the Lord in which God told him that the new First Presidency of the Church would be Joseph Fielding Smith, with Harold B. Lee and Nathan Eldon Tanner as counselors. The Lord told Britt that this was His will.

"The revelation to Britt on the composition of the First Presidency was itself surprising to him. Jim says it was known in the McConkie Family that a Brother Garff had become a favorite of Jessie Evans Smith and that she wanted him to be her husband's counselor in the First Presidency, even though he had never been a stake president. Joseph Fielding had privately indicated to the McConkies that this man [Mark B.] Garff would be his counselor.[7]

"And yet there was the movement within the Quorum to reject Joseph Fielding and choose Harold B. Lee instead. What was the intention concerning Joseph Fielding Smith in this situation is not clear.

"Anyway, Britt later learned that the night he had this revelation, Harold B. Lee took Joseph Fielding Smith to the Temple for a private consultation. If there was sufficient support among the Apostles to reject Joseph Fielding, the nature of this meeting was certainly momentous. Following their meeting, Jos. Fielding indicated Harold B. Lee and N. Eldon Tanner would be his counselors, and the traditional succession was observed in the subsequent choice of the First Presidency.

"This was a situation of no ordinary significance to the Church. In one respect, it does not matter whether the succession to the presidency of the Church is automatic, as long as a good man is chosen. But believing as we do that the Prophet is indeed God's mouthpiece, changing the tradition of succession would be dangerous.

"If it were not automatic, if the Apostles could choose any of their number

---

7. Mark B. Garff (1907–95) was a senior partner in Garff, Ryberg & Garff Construction Co. In 1937 he became president of the Danish Mission and in 1939, he and Joseph Fielding Smith organized the evacuation of the missionaries from Europe via Denmark. In 1965 he became chairman of the LDS Building Committee. He helped build Salt Lake City's Church Office Building and the Washington DC, Ogden, and Provo temples.

to be the new Prophet, this would lead inevitably to power struggles within the Quorum, intrigues, and compromises on 'dark horse candidates' between opposing factions within the Apostles. It would bring disunity and perhaps even schism of the Church—not at first, but perhaps decades after the automatic succession was discarded.

"After telling me of the movement to reject Joseph Fielding as the next Prophet, Jim then told me some things about Joseph Fielding Smith's presidency that were disheartening. Although Joseph Fielding seemed strong in public appearances, he was in a state of advanced senility throughout his administration.

"The legal counsel for the Church, Bro. Kirton, attends all meetings of the First Presidency. He said that at these meetings, counselors Lee and Tanner discussed all the propositions between themselves and then made a decision. At the end of every decision, they asked Joseph Fielding if that decision met with his approval. He would answer 'Yes, it is.' Bro. Kirton told the McConkies that in all the meetings of the First Presidency during the administration of Joseph Fielding Smith, Pres. Smith never took an active part, aside from assenting to decisions which his counselors had made.

"Moreover, what is more disturbing, Joseph Fielding Smith was so senile that he often forgot he was the Prophet. Once in California, after becoming the Prophet, he was setting apart the new officers in the Temple Presidency in the Temple at Los Angeles. He repeatedly said in his settings apart that he was doing so by virtue of authority given him by Pres. McKay. Harold B. Lee repeatedly nudged him and had him correct himself to say, by authority as president of the Church.

"Jim said that in the home of Bruce R. McConkie, Joseph Fielding often spoke as though David O. McKay was still the Prophet. On one occasion, Stan McConkie (Bruce's son) asked his grandfather Joseph Fielding how it felt to be the president of the Church, to which Joseph Fielding replied, 'Yes, President McKay is a good man.'

"Recognizing this, I can see why the Apostles seriously considered bypassing him."

9 August 1972–Confiding My Aspirations to a Longtime Friend

From my journal: "So I told him [Clifton Jolley] that I have had impressions of several years' duration that these men would become Apostles and that I myself would become an Apostle. Clifton was almost speechless with surprise at my words."

11 August 1972–Overtime without Extra Pay

From my journal: "In the past month I have worked over 110 hours on HDC matters" as a half-time employee.

13 August 1972–Sermonizing about LDS History

The sacrament meeting's minutes of the Douglas Ward state that I "told about the research being done to bring Church history on a professional level. [I] said that personal diaries can reveal much information which is needed to update the history of the Church and [I] encouraged all to keep diaries."

Aside from briefly encouraging members of the Valley View Fourth Ward last April "to donate their ancestors diaries to the HDC," tonight was my first devotional talk about history. Beginning soon with the Ensign Fourth Ward, several bishops would invite me to talk on the LDS past.

Nonetheless, I still preferred speaking to congregations from the scriptures alone—both at the pulpit and in Sunday School classes.

15 August 1972–Druthers

From my journal: "As much as I love my research and want to establish a reputation as an eminent LDS scholar and historian, I would gladly give those opportunities up if I could devote my life to counselling the distraught, blessing the Saints, and strengthening the Church. In the absence of such an opportunity, I will continue along my present lines."

23 August 1972–Mormon Hierarchy as an Extended Family

From my journal: "Spent the day at the Genealogical Library researching marriage & kinship relationships among the general authorities."

26 August 1972–Primitive Beat

Jan and I danced together at a University of Utah stomp. From my journal: "It has been 6 years since I have been to a rock stomp. I loved it. The primitive beat of the music is in my blood and I enjoy it thoroughly."

30 August 1972–"Propaganda of Well-Intended Mythmakers"

From my journal: "It seems the *Ensign* magazine, despite its show of a new, forward-looking image, is not going to allow forthright history. Today, Bill Hartley received back from the editors his article on the development of the Seventies.[8]

"Apparently the editors want him to remove the examination of the tension between the Quorum of Twelve and 1st Council of Seventy, to delete any suggestion that any changes made were not always for the best, and avoid the suggestion that the Seventies were ever dissatisfied with the declining

---

8. William George Hartley (1942–2018) was an author and historian. At the Church History Department he was director of the James H. Moyle oral history project. In 1980 he was transferred to the Joseph Fielding Smith Institute for Latter-day Saint History at BYU.

stature of the Seventies at specific times in our history. Dean Jessee observed that the *Ensign* apparently prefers the 'pablum approach' to history.[9]

"As long as the self-assured guardians of the Church's image refuse to present our history as it is, our people will continue to become disenchanted and disappointed to learn that our history has been full of false starts, doctrinal evolution, and human leaders.

"I wish that we took the Hebraic approach to our history, as can be found in the Old Testament, New Testament, and to a lesser degree in the Book of Mormon. The great Prophets and spiritual leaders were shown as being human with human foibles and who made mistakes. The Hebrews could identify with such heroes and thus have hope that they, too, might overcome their weaknesses to become valiant servants of God.

"It is difficult for us to identify with the demi-gods we have made out of Joseph Smith and David O. McKay and most of our other leaders. They, too, were men capable of sin and who *did* sin as every man does.

"Thank God for leaders like Brigham Young, Heber C. Kimball and J. Golden Kimball whose rough humanity is hard to ignore or gloss over. And yet public relations men in our Church insist that the Church and its leaders—past and present—be regarded as pristine, ever faithful, ever right, and always progressive.[10]

"I hope I live to have the opportunity to thrill the Saints with the awareness of our Church's vitality and tradition and help them to realize the Church is more believable and inspiring when you discard the lying fantasies and propaganda of well-intended mythmakers."

Without that incendiary last phrase, I would express most of the above ideas in a talk to BYU students and faculty. I waited nine years to say those things publicly.

31 August 1972–Purchasing Income Property with Little Money

While still working as resident managers on Twelfth East, my journal noted that today Jan and I "drew up the papers, offering $22,500" for a house on Lincoln Street, near Ninth South and Ninth East. We even had to borrow the ten percent down payment. This was Jan's daring idea, which I reluctantly went along with.

Her plan was to convert its finished 3/4 basement into a separate apartment of two small bedrooms that we could rent when we moved there. Until that time, we would also rent the top floor for even more money. This would

---

9. The "pablum approach" refers to sharing with people a simplified, easy-to-digest form of a challenging concept.

10. Heber Chase Kimball (1801–68) was ordained one of the original LDS Twelve Apostles in 1835. In 1847, President Brigham Young made Kimball his first counselor in the First Presidency.

make the heavily mortgaged house into a self-sustaining investment. Jan always had better business sense than I ever did.

Also thanks to her plan, I had a late-life opportunity to work closely with Grampa, who had once built entire apartments on his own. Beginning with our basement laundry room, he and I would soon install two-by-fours, wall-in the area with wood paneling, lay new carpet, and install plumbing, sinks, drainboards, and cabinets. My eighty-year-old grandfather helped create a nice little kitchen for our downstairs apartment.

My grandparents and Mom had moved to Salt Lake City from California the previous year, so that they could have frequent association with me and my children. He and Nana bought a tract house on the southwest side of the Valley.

More than a month later, according to my journal: "I urged Mom for her own benefit to move away from Nana and Grampa and into an apartment of her own." In ten days, she had her own apartment on Third South, just two blocks from the agency where she worked as a very successful employment counselor. Nonetheless, Mom continued to live under Nana's domineering personality and emotional control.

5-6 September 1972–Olympic Terror and Thoughts on Israel

With my decades of pro-Jewish sympathies and recent residence in Munich, it was gut-wrenching to watch televised images of the kidnapping and murder of eleven Israeli athletes by Palestinian terrorists calling themselves Black September. I didn't agree with many actions by the state of Israel, but affirmed its right to exist as a nation, and I abhorred such terrorist acts.

Nonetheless, ever since seeing the movie *Exodus* as a teenager and reading the novel on which it was based, I also recognized some bitter facts. Jewish groups *Hagana*, *Irgun*, and (ironic for Mormons) *Lehi* had waged terrorist attacks that led to the creation of the Jewish state of Israel in 1948. This displaced thousands of Palestinians who fled to surrounding countries, and Israel's army had occupied more Palestinian land after the Six Day War of 1967.

Conquest, victimization, self-determination, terrorism, and justice were slippery concepts in the Middle East. My friend Omar Kader emphasized this in our conversations, which moderated what might have been an exclusively pro-Zionist position on my part. The plight of stateless Palestinians in refugee camps was an existential fact. It demanded a remedy that was both compassionate and just, even if highly unlikely in the winner-take-all culture of the Middle East. There must be a Palestinian State coexisting peacefully next to the State of Israel.

11 September 1972–Fallacy of Passively Awaiting Revelation

From my journal, concerning the LDS Church's policy of denying priesthood to those with Black African birth or even far-distant ancestry:

"But it seems as though the Brethren are afraid to meet the issue head-on with the Lord, and so they retreat into the tradition of the Church, which has limited scriptural or revelatory basis. It is hardly better than the mindless apologies of the Catholics.

"I feel the Prophet should fast and pray about it, and then come to a definite decision, rather than passively awaiting some detailed revelation. If the Prophet in fasting and prayer, went to the Lord with the proposal to give worthy Negroes the Priesthood, *then* I feel the Lord would give a definite revelation or impression to the Prophet."

I soon expressed this to David Goates, a member of our ward, and he was deeply offended. He insisted that his grandfather, Harold B. Lee, was "*not* passive," was very concerned about the question, and had asked the Lord about it. Dave and I would both learn things after 9 June 1978.

23 September 1972–Daydream Theophany

Concerning my participation with an endowment session in the Salt Lake Temple, my journal said: "I sort of day dreamed about entering the Celestial room and going up to the locked doors of the Holy of Holies. In this day dream I tried the doors and they parted at my touch, and I entered the Holy of Holies and closed the doors behind me. In this day dream, I knelt at the altar and offered up the signs of the Holy Priesthood in the true order of prayer.

"At the conclusion of my prayer, the Lord appeared before me in this day dream, and I reached out and touched Him and then embraced Him. Like so many other of my day dreams concerning spiritual things, I wonder if I will ever experience the reality."

7 October 1972–Prophesying Death of New Church President

From my journal: "After dinner [Jim McConkie, Richard Lambert, and I] went to the Tabernacle for the Priesthood Session. Through Roy [M. Darley], we were able to have seats in the choir section and sat immediately behind the First Presidency.

"Soon after the Prophet began the session, I began looking at Pres. Lee closely and found myself feeling [like] I was gazing upon a corpse! His complexion seemed to be that of the dead and it rather unnerved me to find myself wondering how much longer he would be alive. Eventually, I dispelled this strange thought.

"After the session, I mentioned to Dick my observation and feeling. He had shared the same experience. We both concluded that it must be that Pres. Lee merely has a very pale skin compared to the other elderly general authorities."

Nonetheless, I told Richard Lambert something that I didn't have enough faith to write in my own journal for this day. I had felt a distinct impression that President Lee would be dead within eighteen months. I was skeptical because Harold B. Lee was the youngest president of the LDS Church in more than forty-three years.

12-16 October 1972–Visiting Yale University

Leonard Arrington invited me to attend the Western History Association's annual conference at HDC's expense. Meeting this year in New Haven, Connecticut, all of the WHA activities were on Yale's campus, which I fell in love with.

Leonard encouraged me to apply for its doctoral program in history and arranged for me to interview with Howard R. Lamar.[11] A Southern gentleman and notable scholar of the American West, Professor Lamar was enthusiastic about my enrolling in Yale as one of his graduate students.

During the first night's banquet, I was seated next to Richard L. Bushman and his wife, Claudia. I had first met Professor Bushman during my freshman year, when he and Richard D. Poll were assistant directors of BYU's honors program. After I described the social history and group biography of the LDS general authorities that I planned for my MA thesis, Claudia said: "That sounds like a decades-long study!" A feminist and scholar, she was prophetic.

Another historian seated at this dinner table was Jan Shipps, a Southern Methodist who was fascinated by religious studies and Mormonism.[12] She became one of my decades-long mentors and academic advocates.

At a banquet the next evening, I sat next to Princeton librarian Alfred Bush, an ex-Mormon and delightfully gay scholar of North American Indians.[13] Twenty-six years later, I would accept his invitation to move to San Cristobal de Las Casas in the State of Chiapas, Southern Mexico. There I occupied his hacienda that was scrupulously maintained by Maya employees during his absences for most of each year.

17 October 1972–Chatting with Senior President of Seventy

From my journal: "On the flight from Denver to Salt Lake City, I sat

11. Howard Roberts Lamar (1923–2023) was a renowned historian of the American West. He earned his PhD in history from Yale, was acting president of Yale from 1992–93, and in 1994 became Yale's Sterling Professor of History—the highest rank awarded to a faculty member considered top in their field.

12. Jo Ann "Jan" Barnetts Shipps (1929–) is a historian specializing in the Restoration movement. She wrote several books and articles on Utah and Mormonism and was the first woman elected as president of the Mormon History Association, serving from 1979–80. She was also president of the John Whitmer Historical Association (2004–05) and the American Society of Church History (2006–07).

13. Alfred Lavern Bush is a BYU graduate who for forty years was the Curator of Western Americana at Princeton University Library. An early member of the Mormon History Association, in 1980 he designed and printed MHA's first professional program for its annual conference. In 2019 he received an honorary lifetime member award by the Western History Association.

across from S. Dilworth Young and his wife. Sister Young had been at the Ensign 4th Ward when I spoke, and she urged me to convert Pres. Young to keeping a daily journal.

"I talked with him about the importance of personal diaries to the history of the Church. ... He said when he became a member of the Council of 70, he decided against keeping a diary because if he did he would write some personal comments against other members of the general authorities."

20 October 1972–Questioning Policies of LDS Temple Work

From my journal: "In the afternoon Jan and I went to the Temple where Jan acted as proxy for the endowment and sealing to parents of my grandmother Carmen Buelna Peña.

"I cannot see how Carmen can be sealed to her parents when they have not been sealed [in marriage by proxy] or even baptized by proxy. I feel that this policy is in error and that either the Lord will wink at our stumblings or many sealings will have to be redone."

20 October 1972–Leonard J. Arrington's Successor?

From my journal: "Jan feels that Dr. Arrington is priming and preparing me to become his successor as Church Historian. The idea is flattering but unlikely, even in 20 years."

However, on 18 June 1973 and 31 August 1974, I would learn that this actually seemed to be Leonard's plan.

22 October 1972–Designated Murderers in "Free" South Vietnam

From my journal: "After Church we had Chuck Pledger and his wife Lina over for waffles. We talked about many things. He had been in Vietnam five years ago, and his experiences there reconfirmed me in my opposition to this immoral war.

"He was an airborne soldier, and commented that the 101st Airborne Division took no prisoners. He said one man in each company was appointed to murder the prisoners. ...

"[When] I described the [Phoenix] program as one of murdering people (usually village, hamlet, or town leaders) who were suspected of sympathizing with the V.C. [Viet Cong], he recognized it. He said it was a routine activity and that usually the people were killed with grenades, so that U.S. military authorities could claim that the person had tried to throw a grenade at U.S. soldiers and had been killed in the attempt.

"Our nation has entered this war for selfish purposes, and an entire generation of men has committed crimes hardly less horrible than those of the Nazi SS and Gestapo. Even in defeat we will not have our Nuremberg trials, but we will pay the price by having a generation of men who learned murder while receiving the praise of our nation. What a price to pay for 'national interest.'"

In thirty-three years, I would think of this upon hearing James Blunt sing "No Bravery" during another US war for freedom. It would be an invasion of Iraq, launched by war-mongering Republicans, with support by unthinking Democrats.

30 October 1972–Moving HDC

The recently formed Historical Department of the Church moved from the old Church Administration Building to the new twenty-eight story Church Office Building at 50 East North Temple. Instead of cramped offices and inadequate space for its manuscripts and publications, HDC now had all four floors of the new building's east wing.

From my journal: "At HDC this morning before 8 A.M. Found out that the pay for our moving shelves, unloading trucks, and building shelves in the new building was $12.00 an hour. I am dumbfounded. Of a possible 30 hours on this project, I worked only 10 hours. Had I known the rate of pay, I would have hired a babysitter for the times I took care of the kids instead of working. Oh well."

7 November 1972–Prophesying against US President Richard M. Nixon

After the Watergate break-in of June, but before President Nixon's re-election, my feelings toward him changed from simple dislike to a conviction that he was the most dangerous man in America.

Today I wrote in my journal that "the overly powerful executive branch of US gov't is in the hands of a man who will not only abuse those powers dangerously but will aggrandize even greater power to himself."

15 November 1972–Psychoanalytic Study of Brigham Young

From my journal: "I told him [graduate student John Pitts] that there is choice material for a psychoanalytic study of Brigham Young in the 25 or more dreams which he recorded in his personal diaries and in the Historian's Office Journal. The dreams, as recorded, span several decades and are quite detailed.

"They would provide a legitimate basis for a psychoanalytic study, and I think the study would be a valuable addition to the literature on Brigham Young. I have my own reservations about psychoanalytical studies, but I feel that pluralism in approaches to history and religion is necessary and valuable. I would welcome such a study if done knowledgeably and sympathetically."

14 December 1972–Second Thoughts

From my journal: "Perhaps my attitudes toward the conduct and writing of LDS history are not according to His will. Perhaps the Church *does* need to be protected from its own history, but it will be a difficult process for me to accept such a position if it is required. Still, I know the Lord has opened the way for me to be where I am now.

"For over a decade I have researched out areas—problem areas—in LDS Church history, so that I might understand them thoroughly and be able to explain them with honesty and love. The Lord has sustained me in this effort, and I feel that He will open the way for me if my desires are right before Him."

11 January 1973–Power Corrupts

As a part-time employee at LDS headquarters, I had a temporary parking pass that I showed to the security booth each time I drove into the underground lot. From my journal for today: "I was ordered to leave the parking lot by a belligerent parking attendant, merely because I asked if I could go down to the lower levels (which they had blocked off) to see if any places had been vacated. I had to pay to park across from the temple."

While parking, I thought: "If I had the power, you'd be out of a job by 5 this afternoon, you twerp of a parking attendant." The significance of that sentiment hit me immediately, and I whispered: "My God!" No better than any of the petty tyrants I had privately condemned, I was amazed at how easily power could corrupt me. Lord Acton was right: "Power corrupts."

How can I criticize *anyone* who has actual power and abuses it? Yet I do.

23 January 1973–President Spencer W. Kimball Blesses Me

Although my tension-filled marriage and conflict-ridden personality should have killed any hopes I had of becoming an apostle, the dream wouldn't die. I wanted to be free of the aspiration and self-delusion. I thought if anything would help me to escape my oppressive sense of mission, it would be for the president of the Quorum of the Twelve Apostles to solemnly tell me that I was completely wrong to think of becoming an apostle. I got an appointment.

From my journal: "I told Brother Kimball of my lifelong acquaintance with the Lord and His Spirit, and how I have experienced the revelations and presence of the Holy Ghost since early childhood. I told him that eight years ago I had had an experience while on my mission in which the Lord seemed to reveal to me that one day I would become a member of the Quorum of the Twelve Apostles. I watched his face for some reaction of surprize or consternation (which I expected) at this last remark, but there was none. ...

"Pres. Kimball then said: 'Now I have given you examples on both sides of the issue at hand. I don't know in your case which would apply. If the Lord gave you that prompting, then it is within your power to become an Apostle. But you must not despair because of the passage of time in its fulfillment.'

"I told him that I knew that my experience with the Spirit had come to me not for any special worthiness on my part, but as a special gift. I said that I was very aware of my personal weaknesses and had to combat the lusts of the flesh, and that this recognition of my fallibility also caused me to wonder how I could be given the prompting of one day becoming an Apostle. I said that I did not want to be thinking about this prompting if it were actually a self-delusion or product of pride and vain aspiration. I said that I would like to receive a blessing from him and that if he felt inspired that my prompting was false, then I would forget it.

"President Kimball talked with me in great earnestness for a few minutes. He encouraged me to magnify any call I receive as if it were the last and only call I was going to have—whether it be chorister, home teacher, or elders quorum president. He looked at me penetratingly with his kindly eyes, and said: 'You are a fine looking man, really a fine looking man.' He told me that he admired my coming to see him and hoped that I would feel no embarrassment about confiding in him. ...

"Then he arose and laid his hands on my head for a blessing. In the blessing he commended me repeatedly for my integrity and faith. He admonished me to keep myself worthy at all times for the call which I anticipated. He admonished me also to serve diligently in whatever calling I might receive. He concluded the blessing with the promise that if I fulfilled God's expectations of me I would receive the calling which I had been promised by Him.

"After giving the blessing, Brother Kimball put his arms around me and gave me a hug. As we walked to the door he said 'Be sure to come back whenever you feel like talking with me.'"

Although not in my journal, I remember that after the blessing, President Kimball told me not to work for the office, nor try "to curry favor" with the church's leaders, but just to live as I felt the Lord desired for me. This didn't make life easier.

Jan sobbed when I told her what he had done. My sense of mission was as much of a burden to her as it was to me.

Shortly after today's meeting with Elder Kimball, I had another inward impression: he would soon become president of the church. Again I smiled at the improbability. Without exaggeration, of the living apostles, he was the most likely to die within a short time. He had already barely survived throat cancer and heart attacks. Moreover, President Lee was so physically vigorous, that any rational person would expect him to outlive the next-senior apostle Kimball.

As my journal would state in six-and-a-half years: "I mentioned [to Ron Walker][14] some of my spiritual impressions (which I disbelieved at the time)

14. Ronald Warren Walker (1939–2016) began working at the LDS Church history division under Leonard Arrington in 1976, earning his PhD from the University of Utah the following year. When the division was dissolved in 1980, he became an inaugural professor of the Joseph

concerning the death of Harold B. Lee and the eventual presidency of Spencer W. Kimball."

1 February 1973–Asking an Apostle to Rescue Manuscripts

From my journal: "At HDC at 9 a.m. Dr. Arrington had given me a referral for possible acquisition over a month ago, and I decided to try to make the contact today. The man's name is Adrian Hepworth. ...

"Since Mr. Hepworth lived in Bountiful, I decided to telephone him before making a long icy drive. That probably was a tragic mistake. On talking with him, he told me that he had discovered these MSS in the attic of a house he bought 6 years ago. He said that the things that were written should never have been written down, or if they had been written down they should have been burned immediately after being read.

"He refused to tell me either what the materials concerned or who wrote them. He said they were damaging and he and his wife had decided to burn them. I did everything and used every argument I could to dissuade him from destroying them. ... Feeling it was hopeless I ended the conversation—so depressed I could have cried.

"Did some research on my thesis, finishing at 3 p.m. I telephoned Howard W. Hunter, who had just left the temple, and told him about my conversation with Hepworth. I gave him the telephone number and address and urged upon him the importance of his using his influence to try and stop the destruction of the MSS. He seemed quite anxious to do so." I never learned if he tried or succeeded.

16 February 1973–Witch Hunt for Historians

From my journal: "If Lauritz Petersen or someone else is trying to initiate a witch hunt to root out 'untrustworthy' employees at HDC, I may find myself on the hotseat because I have been quite vocal about the need for honesty in our Church history, particularly with reference to the history of polygamy as it relates to the current polygamy problems.

"If my position became in jeopardy, I can only trust on the Lord. He gave me my present opportunities, and if it is His will that they be removed, I accept it."

6 March 1973–Response to Fundamentalists

This was the first draft's date for my signed letter to "Dear Brother Shaw," titled "Some Notes on Polygamy, before and after 1890." I wrote it for a

---

Fielding Smith Institute for Church History, at BYU. Arrington called him "one of the church's most sophisticated writers." Arrington, *Adventures of a Church Historian* (Urbana: University of Illinois Press, 1998), 86.

specific member of the Church at the request of Ron Esplin, one of the full-time researcher writers in Leonard's History Division.

Six days afterward, I wrote in my journal: "Dr. Arrington said that he was very impressed with my letter on present polygamy. He was especially intrigued by my interpretation. He wants me to provide footnotes, and to eliminate my name from it. He feels it would be valuable if sent out [anonymously] in xerox or mimeograph form to all stake presidents who are in areas where these problems arise. ... Leonard said he wanted to show a final copy to Joseph Anderson for his recommendation on its use."

As Leonard asked, I revised it to become the anonymous "Response to a Mormon Fundamentalist," addressed to "Dear Brother _____". During the coming weeks, my journal would mention that nearly every member of the History Division sent copies of it to friends and local leaders.

Sixteen months later, my journal would state: "This morning a fellow who has gotten a Xerox copy of my 'Letter to a Fundamentalist' (with Leonard's O.K.) told me that the letter had seemed to shake the faith his relative has in Fundamentalist teachings. I am pleased to hear this."

15 March 1973–Wife's Business Activities.

From my journal: "In the eve., at Jan's prodding, I attended a promotional organizational meeting for Shaklee Products. Long meeting, but an impressive program. I cannot take the time to become very involved, but I will support Jan's participation."

During the next decade, she became a senior distributor with this nationwide Shaklee Foundation, and later with its spinoff and short-lived rival called Enhance Products. I enjoyed the role-reversal of being the subordinate and supportive spouse. I was very proud of her and had to hide my quiet amusement at being introduced at various business meetings: "and this is Jan's husband, Mike."

Through those enterprises, we associated often with the Logan, Utah, former legislator Frank W. Gunnell and his wife El Marie. She was Jan's mentor for another ten years.

18 March 1973–Gospel Doctrine Teacher, Douglas Ward

Six months after Jan was sustained as counselor for the ward's Young Women's program and after I became instructor for its elders quorum, I was also sustained today as a teacher in the ward's adult Sunday School, which was studying the Old Testament.

I remained in both positions of teaching for four months, and then Michael D. Rhodes became my replacement in the elders quorum.[15] A month

---

15. Michael Dennis Rhodes became an Egyptologist and associate professor of ancient

afterward, this congenial and brilliant Egyptologist-in-training also replaced me as gospel doctrine teacher when we moved from Salt Lake City.

My journal would state at that time: "In my Sunday School class I gave a final lesson—a special one of appreciating the Bible as literature."

23 March 1973–Those Who Burn Controversial Documents

From my journal: "I asked El Marie [Gunnell] about the work she had done for Emily Smith Stewart. El Marie said Mrs. Stewart had lived at the Hanson's home for several years, and that El Marie had helped her sort through the papers of George Albert Smith. This had taken them five years. El Marie said there were many things that were not donated to the University of Utah which Mrs. Stewart burned.

"El Marie said that Mrs. Stewart destroyed those things she felt would be damaging to others, particularly prominent leaders of the Church." This referred to Emily's massive collection of the papers of her father, apostle and LDS President George Albert Smith, of apostle-counselor John Henry Smith, of apostle-counselor George A. Smith, and of counselor-patriarch John Smith.

Not only depressing, this disclosure was stunning in view of the controversial documents that survived to be included in the George A. Smith Family Papers now housed in the University's Marriott Library. The mind boggles to think of what things could have been so much more controversial as to merit the flames of censorship and protectiveness.

7 April 1973–Prophesying a Future Dictatorship in the USA

From my journal: "During dinner, the McConkies and I expressed our distrust for Richard Nixon and I expressed my believe that perhaps as no other American leader, Pres. Nixon represents anti-Christ and he is laying the foundation for a dictatorship within the United States. Dick [Lambert] was appalled at these sentiments, and we had quite a spirited discussion at the dinner table."

20 April 1973–Future Downfall of American Government

From my journal: "I may as well record here the conversation I had with Jan last Thurs. evening [April 19th] about my reflections on the current political situation and future developments. As I stated in my private journal last fall, I regard the election of Richard Nixon in 1972 as the beginning of the downfall of the American govt. ... not dissimilar to that of Adolf Hitler in Germany 40 years before. ...

"This 'Watergate' scandal will bring us to a constitutional crisis. I am sure the evidence will continue to implicate Nixon in these illegal activities.

---

scripture at BYU. He wrote several articles about the Book of Abraham for the Foundation for Ancient Research and Mormon Studies (FARMS).

Congress will then have the alternative of whitewashing Nixon's guilt, or impeaching him."

Today's journal continued with my apocalyptic expectations for anarchy in America. Gratefully, such things have not occurred.

26 April 1973–Publishing Scholarly Analysis of Mormon Past

From my journal: "When I got home in the eve, I found a copy of the *Utah Hist. Quarterly* with my article on Young University [in Salt Lake City during 1892–95]. It was a real thrill to see my first article in print."

Five of my articles were published this year. Aside from the above one, they included a routine survey of pioneer Utah history coauthored with Leonard Arrington for a book, articles of surprising documentation and non-traditional (revisionist) interpretations with my sole byline in *New York History* and *BYU Studies*, as well as a revisionist article about the evolution of the presiding bishop's office in the *Ensign* magazine.

I had followed the same process for those and all my future publications in Mormon history. At every stage, I asked God's guidance for me to know how to tell "the truth in love" (Ephesians 4:15). I felt that this would be a strength to Mormons and a resource for LDS leaders.

Yet it's fair to ask why I chose to research and write about controversial topics of the Mormon past? At the time, I felt that I was simply trying to understand problem areas and provide a means for faithful understanding.

But I now realize that there were subconscious factors operating in my choices as a Mormon historian. First, I sought out areas of apparent ambiguity or contradiction in the LDS Church's past and tried to resolve them. That was something I hadn't been able to do with the ambiguity and contradiction within me.

Second, I now recognize that I saw my father reflected in the church's official concealment of its controversial past. I was as determined to uncover the secrets of the Mormon past, as I was to discover those of my father's Mexican heritage. After all, the leaders of the LDS Church had been an earthly father substitute for most of my life.

Third, I also realize that I saw the LDS Church in my own situation— outwardly happy and prospering but burdened with unspoken secrets and wounds that needed to be opened for the process of healing and health. Guess I hoped to obtain some vicarious comfort by bringing a resolution for the Mormon experience that I couldn't give to my own life.

While I must admit that there has been a lot of subconscious projection in my choices as a Mormon historian, I have always done my best to recreate the Mormon experience as accurately and fully as the available sources allowed. I have hoped that Jesus, Joseph, and Brigham would approve of my efforts. I still do, even though current LDS leaders would eventually make it clear that they didn't like my stirring up the past. Another echo of Dad.

3 May 1973–Fired Again

From my journal: "Had Mom over for pizza dinner. Just as we were finishing the new property manager came by and said he wanted to talk with us alone. He gave us notice to terminate our employment."

Then, on the 17th: "When I got home, Jan told me Stewart Van Wagoner had asked us to stay on as managers. I telephoned him later, and he is quite anxious for us to stay. Curious."

In retrospect, his reversal saved my graduate program at the University of Utah. I would never have received my MA degree in August if I had needed to devote time to moving from La Castellana Apartments while writing my thesis from scratch.

18 May 1973–Continued Formula for Writing

From my journal: "He [Leonard J. Arrington] came up to me during the day and asked if he had heard me actually say two days ago that I had not even started Chapter One of my thesis. I said, yes. He was appalled."

As a publishing historian, I didn't change the formula for research and writing that I had used for undergraduate term papers. Between the start of an academic publication and its completion, I usually devoted ninety percent of my time to research and ten percent to writing. Sometimes the ratio was ninety-five to five. My first draft was often the version I submitted as final.

30 May 1973–Getting into Yale

Because of Howard Lamar's emphatic support of my application and the Yale History Department's recommendation for my acceptance to its PhD program, he was "dumfounded" that the Graduate School rejected me in March. At the first of this month, he "told Leonard that he had officially protested to Yale's administration." Even though UCLA accepted me, I turned down its offer.

I decided to remain on the staff of the Church Historian, and Yale was the only other option I'd consider. I thought that I would apply there again next year.

For months, Leonard had said that he wanted me to be his acknowledged coauthor on an upcoming book for Knopf in New York City, but he was puzzled by Yale's rejection. He wrote a letter of inquiry to its graduate school, and my journal for today summarized the outcome:

"Leonard told me that on Saturday he received a telephone call from [Donald W. Taylor,] the dean of the graduate school at Yale University. He received the call at home. The dean explained that I had not been accepted to Yale because my financial statement indicated I could not finance my own way without financial help.

"The dean told Leonard that my chances next year might be no better because Yale was going to lose several million dollars of aid. He told Leonard that he could not commit himself in any way but that if I informed Yale I could meet half tuition that it was possible that Yale would grant me a scholarship for 1/2 tuition."

After learning of this unusual, backdoor offer, I still wanted to continue with Leonard. Paying half-tuition would require me to borrow many thousands of dollars to attend Yale. I decided to reject its offer, even though Jan strenuously urged me to "go for this adventure!"

In five days, I accepted her advice and notified Yale. Two weeks later, I received its letter formally offering me admission as a graduate student, with a ½ tuition fellowship. A gentlemen's agreement was now in writing.

1 June 1973–Scholarly Article on Priesthood Restriction

From my journal: "I met Lester Bush who has written an 80 page analysis of the historical development of our position on the Negro. I directed him to one statement [recorded verbatim in an unpublished manuscript of early 1852] in which B. Young indicated that if no other prophet had ever restricted the Priesthood then *he* was doing it.

"Bush was real excited about it. His article will appear in the next issue of *Dialogue* which will be a special issue on the Negro."[16]

2 June 1973–Utah's Zion Curtain and Its Spiritual Decline

From my journal: "I am appalled at the controlled society in which our Church leaders put us at times. *The Ensign* has been instructed to blackball Carol Lynn Pearson because she has openly supported the Equal Rights Amendment! I find in so many ways disturbing parallels between the trends of our Church and the history of Roman Catholicism."

In almost exactly seven years, I would state that last sentence privately to my associates in the New Mormon History. And that would startle them into temporary silence.

8 June 1973–My "Devastating" Narrative

From my journal: "He [Leonard Arrington] said that nobody has ever attempted what I am in the process of doing regarding the Mormon hierarchy. He said that the material I present, especially in the 3rd chapter, is like a barrage

---

16. See Lester E. Bush Jr., "Mormonism's Negro Doctrine: An Historical Overview," *Dialogue: A Journal of Mormon Thought* 8, no. 1 (1973), 11–68. The landmark article provided a comprehensive history of the LDS Church policy on race, demonstrating that the priesthood and temple restriction for Black people was not consistently taught and did not originate with Joseph Smith.

of unrelenting gunfire or like the constant dripping of the Chinese water torture. Without some kind of change, he said, the effect was devastating. ...

"He indirectly suggested that I not submit my work on the hierarchy as a Master's Thesis, but instead print portions of it in larger studies.

"As Leonard spoke, I sat leaning on my typewriter listening and saying nothing. When he had finished, I reminded him that I had worked two years on the thesis and I had every intention of graduating with my M.A. I said I '*had*' to finish my M.A. ... [and] that I would have to do [its thesis as] my prosopographical study on the hierarchy."

I aspired to be the Sir Lewis Namier of Mormon studies, but Mormonism's first professionally trained Church Historian seemed to want me to go beyond that.[17] He feared that my controversial master's thesis would jeopardize his plans, as I wrote this day: "Leonard seems to be more than a little concerned about the reverberations that will result from my thesis."

15 June 1973–Researching LDS Prayer Circles

From my journal: "Leonard said the first project he wanted me to work on in my halftime was an analytical history of the prayer circles in the Church, dedication of rooms for their use in stake houses, etc. I told him I admired his courage, for I regarded that topic as far more explosive than he seemed to think my hierarchical analysis is.

"Leonard smiled and said: 'That may be, but I want you to research and write it. If we have to wait 70 years to publish it, all right. But one day our Church will have to be ready to have its history told in a forthright manner.'"
This special form of prayer was connected with the endowment as administered in LDS temples.

My journal says seventy, but now I can hardly believe that Leonard was so pessimistic at this time. In retrospect, "seven years" would seem more accurate for indicating his optimistic projections in 1973. In fact, I would publish the study six years after this assignment.[18]

18 June 1973–Leonard Arrington Tells Others of His Plans for Me

From my journal about a private meeting at HDC: "Then Leonard said something that caught us all off guard. After Davis [Bitton] and Jim [Allen] had assented to the wisdom of my obtaining a Ph.D., Leonard added: 'And

---

17. Sir Lewis Bernstein Namier (1888–1960) was a British historian who deeply researched eighteenth-century British political figures to form new conclusions. His innovative process was dubbed "namierism" and influenced a generation of British historians. John Cannon, "Namier, Sir Lewis Bernstein (1888–1960) in *Oxford Dictionary of National Biography* (Oxford: Oxford University Press, 2004).

18. See D. Michael Quinn, "Latter-day Saint Prayer Circles," *BYU Studies Quarterly*, 19, no. 1 (1979), 79–105.

when the time comes that we need a new assistant Church historian, he will have to have a Ph.D. won't he?' Leonard asked the question in all seriousness. The surprise on Davis' face at Leonard's quite explicit suggestion was marked.

"There was an awkward pause, and then Jim said: 'Well, I think that is one of the settled things, now isn't it, that the assistant Church historians will have doctorates?' The subject quickly passed on, but I was amazed at Leonard's undisguised suggestion that I might become one of the assistant Church historians.

"Leonard ... said that it would have to be a gentlemen's agreement between the three of them and me that they would consider me only on a leave of absence [while at Yale] and would therefore hold my position open for me."

6 July 1973–Confrontation with Leonard Arrington

From my journal: "He had me meet with him and Davis [Bitton] to discuss the issue. ... I became increasingly concerned that he was regarding my thesis as a product of HDC rather than a graduate thesis. I said I did not feel I should be penalized in my use of sources merely because of my position with HDC.

"I resented the possibility that I might not be allowed to use sources which even non-members have had access to. I also spoke about my concern that my thesis might be emasculated. Davis agreed with me but I could tell Leonard was becoming irritated.

"He was so agitated that instead of addressing me, he directed remarks for my benefit to Davis. Thus, Leonard said to Davis 'Now, if this was me, I would appreciate someone watching out for my interests' and later he exclaimed: 'Doesn't he trust us to review his thesis without acting as censors?' I tried to mollify the situation and felt very bad that I had angered Leonard. However, I felt it necessary to express some of my concerns.

"He told me to have his secretary Chris [Croft Waters] type my thesis while he was gone. He said she could do at least the first two chapters, if she had time." She incorporated into a polished draft all of Leonard's red ink changes on my first draft.

I left the Historical Department this day with a profound awareness that my commitment to full disclosure in writing the history of the LDS Church was more extreme than the kind of openness Leonard advocated. The New Mormon History meant something different to me than it did to Leonard Arrington, its chief architect.

It was so odd for me to feel religiously conservative and yet to be regarded as some kind of radical. I would eventually learn that this was Leonard's quandary, too.

28 July 1973–"Jurisdictional Conflicts of the Mormon Hierarchy"

From my journal: "Leonard also told me that he had finished reviewing chapters 3 and 4, plus the first half of Chapter 5. He said since I was not going to put the 3rd chapter on conflicts into my thesis, then he had made no substantive changes.

"I asked if I could present the chapter on conflicts in its present form for a Yale seminar paper. He said I could, but said he wanted to review it before I actually put it in a dissertation or published it."

5 August 1973–Submitting to the University of Utah My M.A. Thesis, "Organizational Development and Social Origins of the Mormon Hierarchy, 1832-1932: A Prosopographical Study"

Yesterday, Saturday, Kay Darley and my mom did a total of eight hours in proofreading the final draft of my thesis chapters, bibliography, and the appendices that Chris Croft Waters had typed at her desk in the History Division. Jan then typed page corrections until 10:30 PM, when "she ran out of energy."

My journal continued: "Feeling that I must finish the thesis now at all costs, I continued to work through the night. As Jan had predicted, I did not finish the [long appendix of] bio profiles until 230 a.m. I then typed in the unfinished table of contents and preliminary pages. From about 4 a.m. until nearly 8 a.m. I reproduced 3 xerox copies of my 312 page thesis, so that I could give them to my committee members. ...

"When I got to Dr. [David] Miller's house [this morning,] I apologized for bringing him the thesis only three days before my oral defense."

Like all term papers I had submitted, my MA thesis was a last-minute all-nighter. My graduate committee was pleased with the final product, however, and I passed their oral exam with distinction. In this graduate program, I got straight A's (4.0 GPA), with a few "incompletes." The MA thesis was my first expression of the warts-and-all view of God's modern leaders, a perception I have had ever since my teens. I presented LDS leaders with the calm candor I have expressed about biblical prophets and apostles, while teaching Sunday School classes, youth groups, and Priesthood quorums.

I feel equal affection for those of both epochs. Abraham saw God face to face, yet cast out his wife Hagar and son Ishmael into the desert (all to keep peace with his first and favorite wife, Sarah). Should I ignore this crucial event of his life and family life? Should I pretend it's an example of being a good husband and father? Or should I simply present this according to the available evidence?

I chose the last approach for Abraham and for latter-day prophets. It was my method ever after.

8 August 1973–Apostle to Read My Article

From my journal: "Leonard told me that he wants me to complete the prayer circle article as soon as possible because Delbert L. Stapley has been asking HDC for everything we have on it (which isn't much). Brother Stapley has been assigned by the Quorum of the Twelve to give a report on the history of the prayer circle to an upcoming Thursday meeting of the Quorum of Twelve and First Presidency.

"Dave Mayfield, of the Library Division of HDC, let the cat out of the bag that someone in Leonard's division was preparing a study of the prayer circles. [19] Brother Stapley had asked Leonard about it.

"Leonard did not mention my name, but asked Brother Stapley if it would be alright if the researcher's name appeared on the study. Apostle Stapley said that was fine with him; he was concerned only about having the information. Leonard told me he wasn't sure he would show the authorship, but if he did, he would indicate (for my protection) that I prepared it at the direction of the Church historian."

Delbert L. Stapley was another general authority whom my father-in-law didn't like. The only time I ever met this Arizona apostle was the day he autographed my Bible in April 1966.

It was decades before I learned that he was bigoted against African Americans. He had condemned proposed legislation on their behalf in a January 1964 letter to liberal Republican George W. Romney. Warning Michigan's governor that God had brought about the death of those who "were very active in the Negro cause," Apostle Stapley wrote that it would be "vicious" to outlaw residential segregation. It was his letter that was vicious. [20]

13 August 1973–Last Day as Employee in the History Division

From my journal: "At HDC I worked on article on the prayer circles in the Church. I submitted the first draft of the article to Leonard."

After his secretary typed a clean copy, he sent it (with my name listed on the byline) to Delbert L. Stapley. Even though he lived five more years, I never learned of this apostle's reaction to my article.

19. David M. Mayfield (1942–) went on to become director of the Church Genealogical Library and director of member services for the Family History Department. *LDS Church News*, Oct. 20, 1985; David M. Mayfield, "I Have a Question," *Ensign*, 1992.

20. Delbert L. Stapley (1896–1978) was a wealthy businessman before he was ordained a Latter-day Saint apostle in 1950. The letter Quinn is referring to was written on his official church letterhead to Michigan Governor George Romney after listening to a pro-Civil Rights speech by Romney. "I fully agree the Negro is entitled to considerations also stated above, but not full social benefits nor inter-marriage privileges with the Whites, nor should the Whites be forced to accept them into restricted White areas. In my judgment, the present proposed Bill of Rights is vicious legislation." A digitized photocopy of the January 23, 1964, letter is available at archive.org.

20 August 1973–Henry E. Huntington Library

During my week with Jan and our daughters in Southern California to visit my extended family, I did research at the Huntington Library in San Marino, next to Pasadena. Leonard arranged for me to begin examining Mormon manuscripts in its extensive collections about the American West. Fifteen years later, I became one of its full-time senior fellows.

29 August 1973–Another Cross-Country *Hejira*

Three days after Jan bore a farewell testimony in fast meeting at the Douglas Ward, we began driving with Mary and Lisa in our engine-troubled VW station wagon to attend Yale University in Connecticut. At Fort Collins, Colorado, we stayed with Elaine and Tom Elmer, our closest non-LDS friends in Munich, Germany. In Iowa City, we visited with Dave Payne and his wife. He was then a professor of sociology.

I had purchased the used Volkswagen there—despite an inward prompting that I should not do so. The result was expensive repairs in Utah of its defective engine, whose bi-valve problem emerged after the expiration of the VW company's extended warranty for its design flaw.

CHAPTER THIRTEEN

ACADEMIC GAMBLES

1973–1975

4 September 1973—Wide-Eyed in the Ivy League

Arriving in New Haven about noon today, I felt overwhelmed to be at Yale. Its history, reputation, Gothic architecture, world-class faculty, and prep-schooled undergraduates intimidated me beyond words. Classes began on September 7, and I was here only because of my mentor, Leonard J. Arrington.

For the first week, I was so depressed that I watched *Sesame Street*, cartoons, and *The Electric Company* on TV for hours with Lisa daily. This cheered me somewhat, and my three-year-old daughter enjoyed it. An independent spirit, Mary happily began kindergarten the day after our arrival. Not yet five, she didn't even look back upon entering the front door on her first day at school. Utah would have made her wait a year before starting, but Connecticut was more liberal. And diverse. Thank God!

I was very pleased that the state's governor was Ella T. Grasso, the first woman in the nation elected in her own right—not as mere extension of a husband's governorship.

Because television was a necessity in my household, we brought it in the car with us. At first, I carried the small TV set from room to room at night for the only illumination we had in an apartment without overhead lighting.

We had hoped for assignment to one of Yale's furnished apartments, but our empty two-bedroom unit was in the housing complex on Canner Street across from the Divinity School. Sleeping on floors the first nights, I awoke screaming when cockroaches crawled into my hair.

And we arrived in a steamy heat wave. Without air conditioning in the apartment or in our Volkswagen station wagon, the only way we could escape the oppressive humidity was to walk into supermarkets. We did that a lot the first weeks in New Haven.

Adding corporate insult to sweltering injury, the shipping company REA lost track of our household goods. For a while, its phone representatives denied that I had even given their company anything to air express

291

from Utah to Connecticut. Only by keeping my receipt did I counter those lying pretenses by a big corporation.

All the while, I thought fondly of President Teddy Roosevelt, the Trust Buster. And he was a wealthy Republican! A liberal kind he called Progressive.

My adviser/mentor for the history of the American West, Howard R. Lamar, made the Yale experience accessible and relaxed. Our first Sunday, he and wife Shirley hosted his married students at their house. An English immigrant, she was as delightful as he was. And they *really* helped us.

During this social, Professor Lamar overheard me tell grad student Clyde Milner that we were all sleeping on the floors while waiting for our missing household goods.[1] He and Shirley insisted on loaning us two folding beds, which we used for months. After grad student Richard Metcalf gave us a lamp and two chairs, we began slowly acquiring furniture at tag sales in the front of Connecticut's homes.

After I helped an REA delivery man put 560 lbs. of boxes into our apartment a week late, I refused to pay more than half the bill. "You should have said that before I brought in your things," he complained. "Do you think I'm crazy?" I asked. "Not telling you was the whole idea!" After a long phone call to his boss, he and the shipping company accepted half payment for an alleged air express delivery.

One of the most profound changes in my university experience was the lack of religious dividing lines at Yale. There were some devout Christians, Jews, Muslims, Buddhists, and other varieties of belief, many non-devout members of the above, plus skeptics, agnostics, and atheists. Your beliefs and affiliations didn't matter at Yale, though fellow students showed genuine interest in learning about the religiously unfamiliar—such as my Mormon background.

BYU had been an us/them experience in which liberals and non-Mormons were the outsiders, while the University of Utah just reversed the dichotomy. Yale seemed like an egalitarian, ecumenical melting pot of belief and unbelief, religious commitment and indifference. It was a breath of fresh air. I didn't share the negative views of the secular-religious divide described in *God and Man at Yale* by bad-boy alum and political conservative, William F. Buckley Jr.

One student asked me the most memorable question about Utah and Mormonism. "I have an ancestor who I think was kind of prominent in Utah," she began. "Maybe you've heard of him? His name was Wilford Woodruff."

1. Clyde A. Milner II (1948–) completed his masters in philosophy in 1974 and his PhD in American Studies in 1979, earning both degrees at Yale. He served on the faculty of Utah State University for twenty-six years, eighteen of which he was also editor of the *Western Historical Quarterly*. He received the Western History Association's Lifetime Award of Merit in 2012.

A third-generation Episcopalian, plus descendant of this Mormon pioneer, she didn't realize how funny her question was. She was surprised to learn that he was the LDS Church's fourth president.

9 September 1973–Youth Sunday School Teacher, New Haven Ward

Because of the great distances LDS youth had to travel to our chapel, it was impossible to have the regular early-morning seminary program on school days. Therefore, my Sunday-only class was called seminary, and I was sustained as the ward's seminary teacher today. Jan likewise became a teacher in the Young Women's program.

John Netto was one of these Connecticut teenagers. In five years, he and his bride would join the Utah ward I attended. Our small Mormon world.

Fall 1973–Yale Dinner Group and Jewish Friends

Jan and I joined the monthly "Gourmet Dinner Group" of Yale Dames for married students. A great idea, each meeting had 3–4 randomly assigned couples divide up a menu for the next month's elegant dinner they would eat at the same table. One of these dinners featured *coq au vin*, but I didn't think I detected any wine in its preparation, despite the name. Of course, at the time, Jan and I had no idea how wine tasted! In many ways, we were naïfs.

One interesting couple were Jewish atheists who kept a kosher house, causing the wife to use about twenty different pots and pans for her part of each meal. Although her husband was a traditional *Ashkenazi* of German extraction, her immediate ancestors were *Sephardic* Jews from modern North Africa. She corrected some of my misunderstandings about the *Sephardic* sojourn from medieval Spain onward.

That dove-tailed with friendships we had in the New Haven Ward. For added income, Jan babysat all day Mondays through Fridays for the daughter of Jewish convert Lee H. Grishman and his ancestral-Mormon wife, Norma. Lee was in Yale's Divinity School, preparing to be a chaplain. In addition, the ward's most energetic liberals were Jewish converts Annette and Katrina Lantos.

I met briefly with their father Tom Lantos, a Democratic Congressman from northern California, who had escaped the extinction of Hungary's Jews. From now on, I paid close attention to news reports about the liberal activism of Representative Lantos.

Fall 1973–Mormon Culture: Cohesiveness and Fault Lines

Non-Mormon students at Yale expressed amazement at the initial experience Jan and I had on our arrival in a city where we knew no one. Before we left Utah, I got the name and phone number of the ward's bishop from the published directory of LDS Church officers, and I phoned him when we arrived. Within hours, Mormons were at our door to welcome us and assist our moving in. Within days, we had dinner invitations from several LDS families. Within two weeks, we had a network of new friends. It is no exaggeration to say that this is the general experience of Mormon culture.

On the other hand, the New Haven Ward was a congregation of several hundred members who were scattered in eight far-flung communities. My monthly home teaching visit to LDS families involved five hours and a roundtrip of sixty-seven miles—if done in one evening.

And there was a constant undercurrent of friction in the New Haven Ward—based on social distinctions, religious background, and geographic origin. Typical of other religions and churches, our congregation included various levels of social status that were defined by how people dressed, by their occupations, by their levels of education, by the kind of house or apartment they lived in, and by how they spoke. I was familiar with those distinctions in Mormon culture and had often felt them painfully as a child, but they took on different meaning in the New Haven Ward.

Also, in every LDS congregation throughout the world—no matter how large or small—there are two other levels of status. First is Church activity, by which Mormons are usually defined as either active (with virtually 100 percent attendance at every meeting) or inactive (with virtually no attendance at any meeting). Occasional attenders don't have the approved status of active members nor the disapproved status of inactive members. As a result, LDS congregations have so few occasional attenders, that there is not even a conventional term to describe them.

The second level of status centers on whether a person is a convert or whether her/his family has been Mormon for generations. The latter are usually described as born in the covenant, meaning that they were born after their parents were sealed in an LDS temple for time and eternity. According to academic discourse of recent decades, I was an ancestral Mormon (or birthright Mormon/generational Mormon). In traditional LDS terms, I was not born in the covenant because I came from a part-member family. As a result, I had always been a second-class ancestral Mormon. However, these levels of religious status also had different significance in New Haven.

This was my first real experience with another division in Mormon culture. It distinguished between those from western states with high percentages of LDS membership and those from other parts of the United States. I grew up in Southern California hearing that "the Church is different in Utah" and that "Utah Mormons are strange." Until the fall of 1973, I didn't realize that Mormons in other parts of the country felt more severe alienation toward western Mormons. That was something Jan and I didn't experience in

Washington, DC, because Beltway Mormons are mostly transplanted westerners or the adult children of westerners.

In the New Haven Ward, I discovered that the majority resented western Mormons. All of us westerners were well-educated and were either in white-collar jobs, elite professions, or were Yale students preparing for such. Many of us had housing that likewise matched. By contrast, nearly all the ward's local members were blue-collar workers (if employed, at all). Eventually, I learned that half of the ward's local families were either on Church welfare or government welfare. The religious disparities compounded the social distinctions and increased the perceptions of superiority or inferiority.

All of us transplants from the West were active Church members, while more than half of local members were inactive. Nearly all local members were converts, while nearly all the westerners were ancestral Mormons and most of us had been born in the covenant. Feelings of resentment were so severe, that the convert bishop's wife refused to attend any LDS services. She once told me she was sick of listening to western Mormons say how thankful they were to be born in the covenant, while consoling her with the "assurance" that "Heavenly Father still accepts you." Second-class agape (divine love).

Like most fellow westerners, I aggravated this situation in spite of my desire to have fellowship with everyone in the LDS ward. Because I grew up feeling like a second-class Mormon on the wrong side of town, it was difficult (if not impossible) for me to regard myself as part of a social elite. Economically I felt more in common with the ward's have-nots, since Jan and I were so poor that we received food stamps while at Yale. Yet socially we felt more in common with those from the Mormon-culture region.

In October, we began participating with them in a monthly study group. Asked to lead its November meeting, my journal noted that "I introduced the discussion by referring to the Protestant Barmen Declaration against Nazism given in 1934 in Germany. I then asked what the LDS position toward government was. ... The discussion lasted 1 1/2 hours, covering such topics as participation in war, revolution against despotism, following political directives of the First Presidency, the 19th century rebellion of the Church against all three branches of our constitutional authority concerning polygamy (I detailed this)." Among the attenders were Neal and Susan VanAlfen, whom I was surprised to see in New Haven exactly eight years after meeting them in the BYU Forty-Seventh Ward. Our small Mormon world.

Despite all our personal invitations to local Saints, no New Englander attended this informal study group, and our bishop denounced it at one sacrament meeting as a secret combination. This caused frantic efforts at bridge building, but still no New Englanders joined with us.

Another of the couples in this group was Virginia "Jinnie" Hinckley Pearce and her husband, Jim. Jinnie was a daughter of apostle Gordon B. Hinckley, and her husband was a physician in residency at the Yale New Haven Hospital. He knew the Darleys while he was a missionary in London in 1961–62, when Roy was organist at the Hyde Park Chapel. After our families moved back to Utah from Connecticut, Jim Pearce would become our family physician.

Jinnie invited Jan and me to a Christmas party at her brother's in New York City. We made the 1 ½-hour trip from New Haven and spent an evening with Manhattan's yuppie Utah transplants. Clark Hinckley's luxurious apartment had a spectacular view of the city's lights. I spent most of the time talking with a young man in charge of the Mormon account at one of New York's largest investment firms. He said that the Church divided its stock-and-bond portfolio among firms in Manhattan and San Francisco. Each had a returned missionary who managed its LDS account.

And so I *did* associate with a Mormon elite while I was at Yale. As in my youth on the West Coast, I also interacted with the children of an apostle.

Early December 1973–First Controversy about One of My Articles

In this month's *Ensign*, my brief essay "Was Edward Partridge the First Presiding Bishop?" caused a flap within LDS circles. Leonard told me that Partridge's descendants were "very upset" by its claim that (contrary to all former LDS histories) he was a regional bishop, not a presiding bishop over the entire Church. Leonard didn't inform me that the newly sustained LDS President Spencer W. Kimball even suggested that Leonard should publish an apology! That didn't occur, and in seven months the *Ensign*'s international editions printed the same article in fifteen languages!

26 December 1973–Fulfillment of My Improbable Prediction

From my journal: "At 1230 midnight we were awakened by the phone. It was Jan's father [Roy M. Darley] telling us that Pres. Lee had died suddenly less than 2 hours before. I felt numb with surprise when I heard the news. Roy reminded me that I had told him of my impression of last October, 1972, when he was sustained, that he would be president a very short time."

Mid-January 1974–Interdisciplinary Approach

Among my courses this semester was the most influential one I took at Yale. Team taught by Western historian Lamar and practicing psychiatrist David F. Musto, it was an interdisciplinary approach to family history. Our readings and guest lecturers spanned a wide swath of disciplines and methodologies—traditional history, social history, genealogy, group biography, quantitative history, demographic history, economic history, medical history, psycho-history, sociology, anthropology, political science, and the law.

This was my most mind-expanding, thrilling academic experience since my introduction to European existentialism in high school. And I again thought appreciatively of Mr. Lee Roloff, who introduced me to the "Life of the Mind" a decade ago. He was a great intellect, a great teacher, a great mentor, a great human being.

Those words applied doubly to Howard R. Lamar. He received several awards for teaching and would become dean of the undergraduate Yale College. Ultimately he became president of Yale University with its graduate school and professional schools. He continued to mentor and give me academic opportunities for decades.

21 January 1974–Improving GRE's Advanced Test

From my journal: "I received my GRE scores, showing that I scored in the top 7 percent in verbal aptitude, top 13 percent in knowledge of American history, and top 25 percent in overall knowledge of European and U.S. history."

I was amazed at the contrast between my scores on the GRE's advanced test in history, versus my abjectly failing its advanced test in English literature shortly before my 1968 graduation. In the thirty-third percentile back then, versus eighty-seventh percentile now in US history. Despite my fifty-two semester hours of undergraduate English, I now seemed to be a better-trained, better-informed American historian—at least in the GRE's view.

28 January 1974–Proposed Dissertation

From my journal: "At 10 a.m. I met with Dr. Lamar to discuss my doctoral program. I said that I would like to continue my prosopography for my dissertation and outlined the areas I proposed to examine.

"He approved the proposal, saying that at my advance state of progress 'it would be insane to begin a new research topic.' I couldn't more fully agree and was very happy to see the way is open for a rapid completion of my doctorate."

5 February 1974–Close-Minded Yalies

From my journal: "I am appalled at the close-mindedness which seems to attend some intellectuals. The students almost to a person had seemed to fully close their minds totally to the possible use of psychoanalytic approach in historical interpretation, and further used the [Lamar-Musto] seminar as a forum to attack psychoanalysis as a discipline and valid approach.

"I do not feel comfortable with all aspects of psychoanalytic interpretation, and especially oppose its use as a monistic answer to all human activity. But I am equally unwilling to reject it out of hand, but am instead willing to see to what extent this approach (as any) has application.

"I am disturbed by intellectuals who close their minds to approaches that do not fit their own little interpretative models. Dogmatism is most reprehensive in an intellectual because an intellectual sneers at the non-intellectual, basks in his erudition, and uses intellectual props to bolster his own dogmatism. I love the world of mind, of intellect, but I have been surprised at the extent to which the intellectuals can at times tyrannize.

"At Yale, for example, Communists, abortionists, and a host of other radicals can be given a freedom of public address they would never receive at Brigham Young University, and I regard that freedom as good and valuable. Yet now Yale's academic community is lobbying to cancel the speaking invitation to Dr. Shockley because his genetic views are considered racist (as they probably are).[2]

"Academic freedom is a limited expression at both BYU and Yale, each allowing full expression to views compatible with the governing or pervasive philosophy but denying that freedom to alien views. I disagree with that philosophy of censorship."

13 February 1974–Another Prompting about LDS Callings
While in Yale's multi-story gymnasium, I had an inward prompting. I felt inspired that I would soon be chosen as counselor by a newly appointed bishop in our ward. I sensed that the new bishop would be Paul Ross.

For several reasons, I actually laughed out loud at the thought. First, everyone in the ward knew I was going back to Utah from the spring until I returned to Yale next fall. Second, there had been no rumors about a release of our current bishop, Joseph W. Taylor, a devout convert from New England. Third, Paul Ross was newer to this ward than I was, having recently moved to Connecticut with his wife from South Carolina.

14 February 1974–LDS Institute and Jeff Holland's High Status
From my journal: "During the evening I received a phone call from Dave Dryden, the Institute director for New England. He said that Jerry Ainsworth, the present Institute teacher in New Haven, was unable to continue teaching. Dave asked if I would take over the Institute for this year and teach Church history for next year. I eagerly accepted."

My duty was to teach an evening course to college-enrolled Mormons each Wednesday, for which Yale allowed us to meet in a classroom on its campus. This semester, I continued teaching the Bible. Next year, even though CES stopped paying me because the enrollment didn't reach twenty, I continued teaching the LDS students who were attending Yale or nearby colleges and universities.

2. William Shockley (1910–89) won the Nobel Prize for Physics in 1956 for semiconductor research. He later shifted his focus to genetics, though he had no genetics degree. He claimed that Black Americans and others were "genetically inferior" and posed a grave threat to the US. He advocated paying individuals with an IQ below 100 to be voluntarily sterilized. See Joel N. Shurkin, *Broken Genius: The Rise and Fall of William Shockley, Creator of the Electronic Age* (London: Palgrave Macmillan, 2006).

Jeff Holland had also been the Institute teacher at Yale for several years, while serving as a counselor in the stake presidency. During that time, he earned his PhD in American Studies.

I felt like I was living in his shadow—both in the ward and in the graduate school. Typically, local Mormons and Yale's non-LDS professors praised him to me, asked if I knew Jeff personally, and then lauded him even more after I said we had met at BYU. I resented the professors' praise for "his brilliance" and envied the ward members' adulation of "his spirituality." I didn't volunteer that Jan knew him as a missionary when her family lived in England, 1961–62.

Later this year, religion professor Sydney Ahlstrom asked me if I knew how Jeff was doing in Utah. "He's dean of BYU's College of Religious Instruction," I replied. Ahlstrom exclaimed in genuine shock: "What on earth can they be thinking? To appoint a recent PhD as a *dean*!" I just shrugged and didn't try to explain. Jeff Holland was on the LDS fast-track.

3 March 1974–Second Counselor in Bishopric, New Haven Ward

From my journal: "[Stake] President [George S.] Robison indicated that it was their desire to call me to be second counselor to the new bishop, Paul Ross. ... He said that I would not be ordained a High Priest or set apart today because a general authority had to ordain Paul a bishop. So this would await the visit of Pres. Hanks on March 16.

"I was glad to have Pres. Robison present the situation this way, because years ago I felt impressed that I would be ordained a High Priest and set apart to a bishopric at the same time by Marion D. Hanks. President Robison ... made frequent comparisons of Jeff Holland to me."

Paul and his wife Jeanne were the first LDS couple from the Deep South I had ever known, and represented the region very well. They even laughed when I said that I grew up south of the Mason-Dixon Line—in Los Angeles.

10 March 1974–Passive Dissent

Today, I was released as the ward's seminary teacher, but remained the Institute's teacher. Afterward, I learned that a group of the teenage seminary students refused to vote for my release and refused to vote for my replacement when his name was presented for the sustaining vote of the ward.

My journal continued: "Sister Taylor told me this morning that many ward members followed the same practice last week [when my name was presented as the new bishopric's Second Counselor]. God, what a mess! I am in the middle of a rebellion by one group against my being sustained to one position and by another group against my being released from another position."

The next day, I seriously considered resigning as counselor in the bishopric.

27 March 1974–Not Chicano Enough

The day after my thirtieth birthday, I learned that the Ford Foundation rejected my application for one of its fellowships for Mexican Americans. Yale adviser Howard R. Lamar wondered why and made a private inquiry with a friend who was a senior administrator in the foundation.

Word came back that the fellowship committee regarded me as ineligible for two reasons: (1) I lacked a Hispanic surname or middle name; (2) I didn't speak Spanish. It was an ultimate compliment for my father's decision to become WASP. I never told Dad about this backhanded consequence of his American success story.

This was five weeks before the twentieth anniversary of *Hernandez v. Texas*. In this anti-discrimination case, the Supreme Court ruled that Mexican Americans were treated as "a class apart" in the USA—especially in Texas, where (like Blacks) Chicanos had been excluded from juries.

When I mentioned the Ford Foundation's decision about me to others, some asked why I didn't change my name back to Peña, so that I could get the affirmative-action benefits of being Mexican American in the 1970s. First, Dad would disown me. Second, Quinn was my legal surname and I didn't want to adopt an alias—even a true one.

But I was going by my middle name because I grew tired of hearing Dennis the Menace jokes every time I introduced myself. Dropping your first name was a twentieth-century pattern in the maternal side of my family. By Mom (who preferred Joyce to Coila), by her oldest sister (who dropped Mary *and* her middle name Orlena at the advice of a fortune teller, to go by the alias "Joy"), by Nana (who preferred Coila to Lucy), by Grampa (who preferred Frank to Jacob), and by his brother John Alma Workman III (who preferred "Alley"). Without knowing that this was a long tradition, my youngest son would also drop his first name decades from now.

12 April 1974–Non-Mormon's Reaction to LDS Candor

From my journal: "At the western seminar I presented my paper on jurisdictional conflicts within the Mormon hierarchy. At the end of the presentation, one of the girl students [Patty Nelson Limerick] asked: 'Do the average members of the Mormon Church know of these conflicts you described?' [3] When I answered in the negative, she surprised me by saying: 'That's good.'

"Her reaction as a non-Mormon causes me to wonder how I can present this necessary part of the institutional history of the hierarchy, and still avoid the impression of the hierarchy as a group of bickering, authority-jealous men."

---

3. Patricia Nelson Limerick (1951–) became an author, teacher, and leading historian of the American West.

7-9 May 1974–Extensive Trip by Rail

After selling our engine-disabled VW station wagon to a New Haven junkyard, Jan, Mary, Lisa, and I traveled by Amtrak train back to Utah. It was cheaper than flying.

From my journal for 8 May 1974: "Arrived in Chicago at 9 a.m. John Heick, one of our Gentile friends from Munich, met us at the station, and took us to his suburban home. We spent the day pleasantly with him and Karen until time for our 430 [PM] departure by train for Ogden." On the 9th at 10:00 p.m., Roy and Kay Darley picked us up at the depot in Ogden, Utah.

Jan and I had leased both levels of our house on Lincoln Street, so the Darleys let us move with Mary and Lisa into the basement bedrooms of their house. They had built a kitchen in its lower level for us. So generous!

10 May 1974–Homecoming at Historical Department

From my journal: "In the afternoon I went to HDC. Leonard seemed jubilant. ... He said, 'As far as we are concerned you are on a leave of absence [while at Yale], but as far as personnel and others are concerned you have terminated employment.' ... He also said it would be fine for me to start at HDC on Monday and then go to BYU as I feel the need. Leonard is great."

For this research at BYU, I stayed two weeks in Provo with my ex-stepmother, Kaye, and my sisters, Kathy and Tricia. As recent converts, they had moved there from California.

30 May 1974–Quinn's Archive

From my journal: "I will deposit my personal papers and research notes at Yale and/or University of Utah rather than let my family or the general authorities sift through them to remove what they wish from the public domain."

4 June 1974–Re-Reading Sources

From my journal: "Started taking notes again on the Joseph F. Smith journals, 1838–1883. I find that in previous notetaking I did an incomplete job, despite the fact that I assumed I was doing such thorough work.

"This is depressing, and I think it means I will have to research again at least some key documents to verify my thoroughness." This resulted in hundreds more typed pages for various documents I had previously researched.

27 June 1974–Access to HDC's Vault

From my journal: "Went into Leonard's office at his request and found him with [Church Archivist] Don Schmidt. I had spoken to Leonard previously about asking Don for me to have permission [as a non-employee] (1) to be an official representative in signing acquisition papers for my contacts who have MSS to be donated to HDC; (2) about my access to items in the [HDC] vault. He [Don Schmidt] said there would be no problem with either request."

30 June 1974–Gospel Doctrine Teacher, Ensign 4th Ward

From my journal: "Gave Roy's lesson again to the senior Gospel Doctrine class—on the prophecies of Isaiah. S. Dilworth Young was in the group. I received many compliments, including [from] Bro. & Sis. Young."

3 July 1974–Consequences of *Dialogue* Article

From my journal: "At noon I met with Robert K. Thomas, academic vice-pres of BYU. We talked briefly about my activities at Yale.... When I mentioned that I was interested in the correspondence of general authorities with [BYU's early-1900s president Benjamin] Cluff for administrative reasons, Bro. Thomas shook his head and said he would have to ask Dallin Oaks for permission.

"I said I did not realize that would be necessary. He said [that] previously it would not have been, but that some people had recently used MSS at BYU stupidly and had caused the administration trouble.

"'I may as well say that it was that last *Dialogue* issue on the Negro with those quotes from Temple minutes [by Lester Bush]. You just *don't* publish anything from Temple minutes, even if you have access to them!'"

The result, Brother Thomas explained, was that apostle Boyd K. Packer personally required BYU's library to remove documents from the Adam S. Bennion Collection that had been donated by his family.[4] Those went into the Quorum of Twelve's vault. Curator Chad Flake verified this when I asked him about it. There are so many vaults with hidden documents!

However, BYU's President Oaks gave me permission next month to do unrestricted research in the presidential papers of Benjamin Cluff and George Brimhall. Formerly on the faculty of the University of Chicago's Law School, Oaks was a vigorous advocate for academic freedom at this time.

12 July 1974–"Uppity" Women at LDS Headquarters

From my journal: "Roy [Darley] commented about the meeting attended by Florence Jacobsen on MIA matters (even while Pres. Lee was a counselor to Pres. Smith), at which she offered a suggestion and Pres. Lee turned to her and said: 'Sister Jacobsen, if we want your opinion, we will ask you for it!'[5]

"Roy said Sister Jacobsen left that meeting and went home sobbing."

---

4. Adam Samuel Bennion (1886–1958) was superintendent of LDS Church Schools, and trained seminary teachers at BYU. He became an apostle in 1953.

5. Florence Smith Jacobsen (1913–2017) was general president of the Young Women's Mutual Improvement Association from 1961–72. Church President Harold B. Lee then asked her to be curator for the church. Working alongside Leonard Arrington in the Church History Division, she was key in establishing the Museum of Church History and Art. The granddaughter

Because her husband Ted had been in charge of Temple Square for several years, Roy knew them both very well as a tabernacle organist and as a friend.

Harold B. Lee disrespected her in that way, despite the fact that she was the general president of the Young Women's MIA. David Goates eventually confided to me that his grandfather had told him (while LDS president from 1972–73) that the national Women's Movement was "the greatest challenge facing the Church." I wonder why?

22 July 1974–First Son

Jan delivered our third child, Adam, in the LDS Hospital. Ten months later, we finished paying our last debts for his birth. I had thought of naming my first son as Michael, but didn't want him to think of himself as Jr. Then I thought of Mormon doctrine's affirmation that the Angel Michael of the pre-existence became Adam in mortality (D&C 27:11; 107:54; 128:21).

I liked this as an indirect "Michael Jr." Canadian feminist Maureen Ursenbach Beecher recognized my play on words the moment she heard our son's name.[6] Married to an American historian, she was an editor and author in Leonard's History Division.

9 August 1974–Political "Radical"

From my journal: "Jan told me not to discuss my political views around her father anymore, because he told her [that] he thinks I sound like a radical and he added that he would vomit if he heard me call Nixon an anti-Christ again."

This was the day after Richard M. Nixon resigned as US president. I had been watching the Darley Family's only large television set for hours at a time, as the US House of Representatives moved toward impeaching him.

Surveys showed that more than fifty percent of BYU's students opposed impeaching Nixon and eighty percent disapproved of his resignation. I didn't like living in conservative Utah and was *very* glad not to be at BYU.

My Republican father-in-law wasn't far wrong about my political views. Like all liberal Democrats since the Great Depression, I wanted to soak the rich, feed the poor, protect average consumers, rein in big business, and strengthen the middle class. Originally the program of rich progressive Republicans like Teddy Roosevelt against those Americans he called Robber Barons and the Idle Rich, this continued to be the policy of moderate

of two church presidents, Joseph F. Smith and Heber J. Grant, she used her family clout to win support for the preservation and restoration of numerous historic church buildings.

6. Maureen Ursenbach Beecher (1935–) was an editor and senior research associate in the Church History Division from 1972–80 and then at the Joseph Fielding Smith Institute for Church History. She received two book awards and the Arrington Award for lifetime contribution from the Mormon History Association. She was the founding president of the Association for Mormon Letters in 1976, served as president of MHA from 1983–84, and was a member of the editorial board of *Dialogue: A Journal of Mormon Thought*.

Republicans like Dwight D. Eisenhower, whose White House of the 1950s presided over a tax policy that required the rich to pay ninety-one percent tax on their massive incomes and corporations to pay twenty-five percent of their profits, plus a tax of fifty percent on the estates of deceased millionaires. The rich still became richer, while the US economy of the 1950s still allowed middle-class entrepreneurs to become millionaires. More significantly, those tax policies also enabled millions of blue-collar Americans like my grandparents and parents to become middle class. Nonetheless, conservative Republicans and conservative Democrats were reducing those progressive tax rates, which I wanted to be restored to their 1950s levels.

Nonetheless, I was not a consistent liberal. As a democratic socialist, I didn't trust the Soviets any farther than I could throw one of their tanks, so I supported a strong American military. I also emphatically supported the death penalty for premeditated murder, including the execution of those who asked someone else to commit the murder. Nonetheless, I also supported the armed struggle against dictatorships and murderous regimes anywhere in the world, even though such insurgencies inevitably caught innocent people in the crossfire.

On the other hand, I opposed left-wing bombers and assassins within democracies. In the 1970s, this included the Weathermen of the United States, the Baader-Meinhof Group of West Germany, and the Red Brigades of Italy. Despite the unjust wars of a functioning democracy, its general indifference toward minorities and underclasses, and its various subversions by big business and the Military Industrial Complex (against which Republican President Eisenhower had publicly warned), representative government should be vigorously encouraged to move beyond its often glacial progress toward social justice, *not* violently intimidated by idealistic assassins of political leaders and by bomb-throwing murderers of innocent civilians.

I also opposed far more benign eco-terrorism and the activists of the Animal Liberation Front. Having had polio and observed children with birth defects, I could not abide the ALF campaign against medical experiments on animals to find preventions and cures for human diseases. Furthermore, no animal's welfare can justify violence. The remedy must be strict enforcement of laws against animal abuse, as well as rigorous lawsuits against institutional abuses.

As another evidence of political ambivalence, I often voted for Republicans in positions of law enforcement. Yet I was always on the lookout for police brutality.

Since age nineteen, however, I had a consistent position about what would be called the War on Drugs. I advocated decriminalization of all recreational drugs from marijuana to heroin, as well as hallucinogenics like LSD and PCP. Take away the profit incentive and put the US drug war's millions—billions—of dollars in government spending toward education, medical treatment, and selling recreational drugs so far below cost that it would drive drug lords and gangs out of the manufacture, sale, or distribution of illegal drugs. Follow the example and successes of Holland.

I was personally opposed to abortion, especially when used instead of regular methods of birth control. On the other hand, I was pro-choice, because I felt that no one (not even a teenage girl's parent) should have the power to require any female to jeopardize her health in an unwanted pregnancy or risk her life in unwanted childbirth. I could never forget how Jan nearly died after giving birth to a child we wanted.

Likewise, my mother told me as late as this year that she supported abortion to save the mother's life. This was consistent with the popular Mormon view that an unborn child's individual spirit will continually re-emerge in the uterus of that woman—or some other woman—until it leaves the womb. Only at birth does the fetus become a real person. In LDS theology, the US Supreme Court's 1973 decision in *Roe v. Wade* was very conservative by legalizing abortion-on-demand *only* during the first trimester.

Nonetheless, she and most of my country soon moved into one-issue politics about abortion. This was part of a knee-jerk reaction of conservatives against the radical sixties. Thus commenced America's culture wars.

11 August 1974–"Follow the inspiration that our leaders have."

Minutes of the Ensign Fourth Ward state: "Janice Quin [*sic*] told of how the teachings of our parents find their roots after we mature. Michael Quinn told of the need to follow the inspiration that our leaders have and not to listen to the predictions of outsiders."

I know, I know. That sounds very strange for an antinomian like me to preach, but it was another side of my faith in spiritual checks and balances. The context was my being told by Jehovah's Witnesses yesterday that the end of the world would be in the fall of 1975. Their Watchtower Society was a repeated example of Festinger's *When Prophecy Fails.*[7]

12 August 1974–Exploring HDC's Vault

From my journal: "In the afternoon I talked with Don Schmidt about the materials in the vault (after I had devoted much silent prayer in the day asking the Lord to guide my words, and open the way for my access). ... I asked Don if there was any way I could find out exactly what is in the subject files of the vault, so I wouldn't have to fish around in the dark for what is there.

7. Published by psychology researcher Leon Festinger et al., *When Prophecy Fails: A Social and Psychological Study of a Modern Group that Predicted the Destruction of the World* (Minneapolis, MN: University of Minnesota Press, 1956), explains how strongly held beliefs can deepen, rather than diminish, when evidence disproves them.

"He readily took me into Earl Olsen's office, picked up the catalogue cards to the vault's contents, and read off the subject titles so that I could indicate which, if any, were of interest to my [dissertation] research on the general authorities.[8] Among the cards he read was the marriage record of 1898–1903, which I said I would like to see in addition to two other items of far less interest to me. He nonchalantly said: 'Okay, that's three items. Make up cards requesting them, and give them to me tomorrow.'"

From my journal for the 13th: "When I got the marriage record, I immediately recognized it as containing post-1890 plural marriages performed by Matthias F. Cowley. I typed extensive notes from the marriage record which contained the record of plural marriages performed for 50 men by Cowley, and a scrap of paper with 2 post-1890 plural marriages performed in 1903 by Apostle Rudger Clawson. I know that Cowley performed more plural marriages than these, so it seems possible that this was an incomplete collation he made, perhaps as required by his arch-opponent Francis M. Lyman.

"When I had finished with this record, I turned somewhat indifferently to the second item from the vault, catalogued in Earl Olsen's list as George F. Richards' appointment book. I had asked for it primarily to act as a filler, so that the marriage record would not be the only item I was seeking.

"To my surprise I found that this record book contained a rather detailed summary of the [Quorum of Twelve's] meetings held in connection with the resignations J. W. Taylor and M. F. Cowley submitted in 1905. In none of the available diaries of the Apostles or presidency has more than oblique reference been made to these meetings. Therefore I was profoundly happy and grateful to have stumbled upon this document.

"I offered several silent, but heartfelt, prayers to God, thanking Him for giving me access at last to all of the documents apparently in HDC about post-1890 polygamy. ...

"The remaining documents I seek are either in private possession or are in the vaults of the 1st Presidency, or of Joseph Fielding Smith. When it is the Lord's will, I know He will open the way for me to obtain access to the materials."

27 August 1974–Leaving Utah in New Car

Through assistance from the Darleys and my fragmented family of origin, we bought a Dodge Dart station wagon. With luggage and boxes strapped to its roof rack, this compact car had enough space in the cargo area to also

8. Earl Eidswold Olson (1916–2010) worked for the Church Historian's Office and the Historical Department for more than fifty years, serving as assistant librarian, archivist, Assistant Church Historian to Joseph Fielding Smith, and assistant managing director.

transport the household goods we needed as we re-occupied our sublet apartment at Yale. With A/C, it still got 30 mpg.

31 August 1974–Others Expect Me to Become LDS Church Historian

After two days visiting Mike and Sylvia McAdams in Bartlesville, Oklahoma, we drove straight through to Bloomington, Indiana, where we overnighted with Jan Shipps on the 31st. She was fast becoming the most prolific non-Mormon involved in writing LDS history.

From my journal: "Then she stunned me with the comment: 'I have spoken with several people about you who feel that you are not only a strong contender to be Leonard's successor as Church Historian, but also for a possible appointment one day as a general authority.' From a non-Mormon that was a mouthful!"

I tried to laugh off what Jan Shipps had said and dismissed it as undeserved compliments for someone who had published so little and had only an MA. At the same time, I tried to conceal my conflicting feelings of excitement and dismay.

From there, we drove directly to Washington, DC, and stayed with Judi and Jim McConkie at their home in Gaithersburg, Maryland. For a year, James had been serving as chief of staff for Utah's Democratic Congressman Gunn McKay, a loyal Mormon.

3 September 1974–Black Supervisor

From my journal: "We spent the morning with the McConkies, then started on our homeward trip. On the way we stopped at Ft. Meade to visit Emmett and Joyce Johnson, whom we knew in Munich through my work with Military Intelligence. Emmett, a Black Sergeant First Class, was my immediate supervisor in Munich. I respect him as I do few non-Mormons, and hope that we can maintain friendship over the years. I told him and his wife about the temple being opened to the public, and I encouraged them to visit it."

Their sons were teenagers now, and I told Jan privately that I could not object if either of my daughters eventually married a Black man as fine as Emmett Johnson. The priesthood restriction was my only hesitation about such an interracial marriage.

6 September 1974–Academic Gamble

From my journal: "In the morning I met with Dr. Lamar, and [in] the afternoon I met with Dr. Jonathan Spence, the Director of Graduate Studies for history. From them I obtained grudging approval for me to satisfy the Ph.D. language requirement if I can obtain the 'fluency' score by retaking the German language exam in October.

"I won't be taking the full course load this year in anticipation of obtaining advanced standing and being able to take the final oral exam early next term. This year is an important one for me academically, in which I am gambling that I can comply [with] or fulfill all Ph.D. requirements short of the dissertation."

25 September 1974–Success in Course Work and Written Exam

From my journal: "I took the 8 hour written minor field exam today. ... I obtained Honors in all my course work at Yale last year, and I only pray that the Lord will help me to fulfill all requirements for the Ph.D. as soon as possible."

Professor Steven Ozment gave me an "O.K." for this written exam on the Reformation. That was enough to make me happy.

5 October 1974–Former Mentor's Attack

From my journal: "Today I received a letter from Leonard with an enclosure of the reader's comments on the succession article I sent to *BYU Studies* [to be considered for possible publication]. The comments are a blistering attack on my scholarship, conclusions, and testimony.

"I am sure that Truman Madsen is the unidentified reader, and I am depressed not only at the tunnel vision displayed in the critique, but (more importantly) in the inherent rejection of what I believe to be an essential philosophy of candid historical analysis within a faithful perspective." Editor Charles D. Tate Jr. eventually confided to me that Madsen wrote this.[9]

13 October 1974–Giving "Too Much Time" to Church Work

From my journal: "Paul [Ross, the bishop] expressed concern that I was devoting too much time to bishopric work and thereby endangering my primary responsibility to complete my education and justify the sacrifices Jan and I are making to attend Yale."

Out of curiosity, I tabulated the time I was spending in church work and meetings. That particular week, it was twenty-five hours. I marveled at what I was still able to accomplish as a graduate student, with two jobs—grading papers for Professor Lamar and teaching for LDS Institute.

7 November 1974–My Long View of the New Mormon History

From my journal: "At his [Chuck Hamaker's] asking me to what extent I really thought the 'broader' and more open understanding of Church history can be part of general Latter-day Saint awareness, I told him that I looked forward to its total accomplishment in 50 [years].

"I felt that it would take 25 years for the open and broad view of our history to be disseminated to the English-reading membership through

---

9. Charles D. Tate Jr. (1929–2022) edited *BYU Studies* from 1967–83. He was also a BYU professor of English and ancient scripture and editor for the BYU Religious Studies Center.

scholarly journals, Seminary, Institute, official Church publications, and general authority addresses. Then it will take another 25 years for that perspective to percolate throughout the non-English speaking membership. I added that this projection was assuming that there would be no major reversal of present trends.

"I told Chuck that I resented the elitist attitude that many general authorities and also many senior historians (like Hyrum Andrus & Truman Madsen, although I mentioned no names) have that they want to know about the intricacies of the Church and want to share this knowledge with a few trusted disciples, but regard such knowledge as 'too dangerous' for 'regular' members of the Church.[10]

"As long as that knowledge is bottled up in vaults and file cabinets, theirs is a self-fulfilling prophecy. I have a greater confidence in the spiritual resiliency of the Latter-day Saints, however, and feel that if they are gradually given an awareness of the 'truth of all things' in the proper perspective, that they will be the stronger thereby. Denying that knowledge to the general membership only makes them vulnerable, rather than protecting them."

I would restate that last paragraph in a talk to BYU's students and faculty exactly seven years later.

9 November 1974–Wife's First Cousin Gary Darley Is Murdered

From my journal: "Upon reading a letter from Jan's Mom, I learned that two LDS missionaries in Texas are missing and presumed to have been murdered by an antagonistic member of the Church. Jan's cousin was one of the two missionaries."

Shot to death and disposed of with a meat grinder in October, they were among Mormonism's youngest martyrs.[11] While conducting sacrament meeting in New Haven, I announced the first report that Jan received.

---

10. Hyrum Leslie Andrus (1924–2015) taught church history and doctrine at BYU, where he was also director of the Latter-day Saint historical collection in the Harold B. Lee Library. He earned his PhD at Syracuse University, titling his dissertation "Joseph Smith, Social Philosopher, Theorist, and Prophet." His books include *God, Man and the Universe*; *Principles of Perfection*; *Doctrines of the Kingdom*; *Joseph Smith the Man and the Seer*; and *They Knew the Prophet*.

11. While serving in Austin, Texas, Elders Gary Darley and Mark Fisher regularly visited recent LDS convert Robert Kleason against the local bishop's warnings because of Kleason's erratic behavior. The two missionaries disappeared on October 28, 1974, when they had agreed to meet Kleason at his home for dinner. No bodies were found, but evidence indicated Kleason shot them and then dismembered their bodies using a bandsaw in the taxidermy shop where he worked. He was convicted and sentenced to death, but the conviction was overturned on a technicality. He immigrated to the United Kingdom, where he was eventually imprisoned on gun violations. Kleasen died while fighting extradition back to the United States for retrial on the murder charges. Ken Driggs, *Evil Among Us: The Texas Mormon Missionary Murders* (Salt Lake City: Signature Books, 2000).

20 November 1974—Temple Dedication

Five years after leaving Washington, DC, Jan and I returned for the dedication of its temple. Located at the edge of the Capital Beltway in Maryland, it was the largest since the Los Angeles Temple, whose dedication I had attended just weeks before my twelfth birthday. Back then, I fidgeted while watching the ceremony as broadcasted by closed-circuit television on a small black-and-white TV set in a small room of the LA Temple, and was a bored child.

Eleven months into his presidency, Spencer W. Kimball now presided at the repetitive ceremonies of dedication for Washington DC's temple. Jan and I were seated twenty feet from First Presidency counselor N. Eldon Tanner as he read its formal prayer at today's session. Tears streamed down my face when we sang, "The Spirit of God Like a Fire Is Burning."

23 November 1974—Advanced Standing

From my journal: "In the morning's mail I received notice that I have been given advanced standing at Yale, thus relieving me of the necessity to pay full tuition again next year. This is great news."

This dropped a year from the usual requirement of three years in residence and course work. Howard Lamar had advised me to take no courses this year, and instead devote my full time to preparing for the oral exam that qualifies a doctoral student to begin working on her/his dissertation. I was anxious to get my PhD from Yale as soon as possible, so that I could resume working for Leonard Arrington at HDC.

24 November 1974—Preaching about Temple Covenants

From my journal: "I spoke about 30 minutes, concentrating my remarks on the significance of the endowment and on the temple covenants of Obedience, Sacrifice, the Law of the Gospel, Chastity, and Consecration. At a time or two I became emotionally broken, but generally was in firm control."

I closely modeled this on a sermon I had listened to the London Temple's president give to the sacrament meeting of an English branch while I was a missionary. Without his example, I would never have spoken of those covenants outside an LDS temple—not even in private conversation with an already endowed person.

4 December 1974—Praise from Utah Historian

From my journal: "He [Howard R. Lamar] said that he had recently received a letter from S. George Ellsworth, a senior historian at Utah State University, who Dr. Lamar said had unqualified praise for my article on pacifism in the *Pacific Historical Review*.[12] According to Dr. Lamar, Professor

---

12. D. Michael Quinn, "The Mormon Church and the Spanish-American War: An End to Selective Pacifism," *Pacific Historical Review* 43, no. 3 (1974): 342–66.

Ellsworth said my article was the most important thing written on Mormonism in the past two decades! I was quite taken back by this hyperbolic praise from a professional historian, and I felt a deep sense of satisfaction.

"I also felt again the impression I have had during the past year that I am rapidly being pushed into a position of recognition and prominence which I could hardly have anticipated four years ago as I agonized over what seemed to be a senseless three year disruption of my life's work by the military. Without that three year pause in what I anticipated as my life's progression, I would never have become involved as I am in Mormon historical research, nor would I have had the opportunity to be connected as I have been with Leonard Arrington and the Historical Department."

11 December 1974–No-Holds-Barred Lectures to Institute Students

From my journal: "Jack Kerlin said to me 'You have certainly had a no-holds-barred approach to teaching this [Mormon history] course!' I told him that I felt it far better to teach the truth in perspective, than to teach fables and have the students later learn the truth.

"This class has been my first opportunity to do so. I know I have jarred them, but I know also that they have felt inspired in some of our meetings—I hope the total effect is positive."

15 December 1974–Tactless Stake President

From my journal: "Had bishopric meeting at 7 a.m. Paul [Ross, the bishop] showed us some insultingly caustic letters from Pres. [George] Robison. Later in the morning Don Florian, our permanent high councilman, joined us for PEC [Priesthood Executive Committee of the ward.] Paul showed him the letters, and Don said he had learned to let many things roll off his back without disturbing him. He laughed and said Pres. Robison might benefit from taking the Dale Carnegie course on 'How to Win Friends and Influence People.'"

My first inkling of our Hartford stake president's lack of tact occurred during the reorganization of the ward's bishopric last March. He said: "Bishop Taylor is tired, and needs to be released." That devoted man's face reddened, and there were murmurs from the congregation.

At monthly meetings of the stake's leaders with its local bishops, President Robison held up charts showing how the wards ranked against each other in various statistics. The New Haven Ward was always at the bottom, and he was openly sarcastic and demeaning toward Bishop Ross. Paul said he had to force himself to attend those meetings, and no wonder poor Joe Taylor got tired—especially being treated this way by a western Mormon working in New England.

311

28 December 1974–Presentation at Academic Conference

This year's annual meeting of the American Historical Association was held in Chicago, where I gave a paper which compared the radical Anabaptists of the sixteenth century with nineteenth-century Mormons. After the session (which included my response to some negative comments by European historian Gerald Strauss), I asked Jan Shipps: "Well, for a maiden voyage, how was my performance at the session?" She was enthusiastic in her praise.

To save me money during this conference, she had arranged for me to crash on the floor in the apartment of Lawrence Foster.[13] A Quaker graduate student, he was emphasizing Mormon polygamy as a part of his three-way comparison with celibate Shakerism and with New York's Oneida Community that had practiced group marriage.

Larry urged me to consider cross-cultural comparisons and anthropological theories for understanding the Mormon experience. He recommended that I give interdisciplinary attention to such scholars as Norman Cohn and Peter Worsley. So I did, but more so in research than in writing.

Therefore, it would amuse me how traditionally trained historians reacted to the somewhat interdisciplinary approach I used in my publications. "Mike, you've broken the Historian's Eleventh Commandment," Richard Poll told me one day. "Thou shalt not commit sociology!"

It irritates me that the above phrase has been attributed to American conservative pundit George F. Will. Various writers have recently cited him for coining it in a 1998 op-ed, when he was actually doing a riff on a well-worn quote. As early as 1982, the *Swedish-American Historical Quarterly* attributed it to homosexual poet W. H. Auden, who died in 1973. Better gay than conservative!

---

13. Lawrence Foster earned his PhD at the University of Chicago in 1976 and taught at the Georgia Institute of Technology in Atlanta, specializing in American social and religious history. His book, *Religion and Sexuality: The Shakers, the Mormons, and the Oneida Community* (Urbana: University of Illinois Press), 1984, includes an analysis of the origin of Mormon polygamy. He served as Mormon History Association president from 2002–03.

CHAPTER FOURTEEN

HIGH HOPES AND GROWING FEARS

1976-1977

4 January 1975–Out of Step

From my journal: "I feel, however, that my attitudes and approach toward Church history are out of step with the assumptions and intentions of the general authorities. I think it will not take long before men like Mark E. Petersen, Boyd K. Packer or Bruce R. McConkie will know my work and will regard me as 'dangerous' or 'controversial.' ...

"Despite these feelings, I have dreams of researching and writing on many areas of importance to the history of the Church—areas that have been neglected or concealed, but which need to be examined forthrightly and brought to the knowledge of the Saints; or at least to those interested. If my desires are right, the Lord will enable me to accomplish them despite my own misgivings and despite the opposition and hostility by even of some of His anointed servants."

After putting the last paragraph's views into practice for the next thirty-two years, I would restate that philosophy in "Filling Gaps and Responding to 'Silences in Mormon History,'" as my letter to the editor of *Dialogue: A Journal of Mormon Thought*.[1]

5 January 1975–Ready to Quit Yale

From my journal: "I also told Jan I did not feel like coming back here again to continue the strains of graduate school if I fail to qualify this year for PhD exams." During my ups and downs at Yale, my wife kept me from quitting several times.

12 January 1975–Promoting Excommunications

From my journal: "He [Bishop Ross] agreed with my recommendations about the court [of excommunication], and I told him I would type and send out the letters tomorrow."

Now, the backstory: In a bishopric meeting last November, Paul Ross mentioned that he had found a bunch of requests to be removed from the

---

1. See *Dialogue: A Journal of Mormon Thought* 40, no. 2 (Summer 2007): ix–x.

LDS Church's membership. His predecessor as bishop, Joe Taylor, had simply put those letters in a folder, without taking any action. I said that no one should be required to remain a member of the LDS Church against their will, and I described apostle Mark E. Petersen's excommunication program in Britain and Ireland.

With none of the anguish I felt eleven years earlier, I began writing letters today for interviews with all the members of our ward who had written such requests. This was to verify if they still wanted to be excommunicated. At this time, there was no option in *The General Handbook of Instructions* for voluntary withdrawal. After I ascertained their wishes, the bishop scheduled one church court each week, for which I wrote the formal letters asking these people's attendance. Afterwards, I typed letters informing them that they were no longer members of the LDS Church. This took three months.

This coming March, Bishop Ross would announce to our ward's priesthood meeting the names of twelve persons we had excommunicated, after which Joe Taylor asked me: "Are you trying to purge all the inactive New Englanders?!"

I answered that we were only following their repeated requests, but our former bishop disagreed. "That's *not* the Spirit of the gospel," he said.

23 January 1975–Teaching Fellow

From my journal: "Conducted my first discussion groups for the Am. West class—about 17 students in each group." These were for Professor Lamar's very popular course on the history of the American West. All term, I conducted Q&A for students' reading assignments, answered questions about his lectures, and graded their exams and term papers. My favorite students were Jeffrey D. Rubinstein and Cyrus R. Vance Jr.[2]

Jeff and I would correspond for several years. After doing volunteer work among the poor in Haiti, he became a cardiologist.

Son of the US Secretary of State, Cy Jr. would become the successful Democratic candidate as New York City's District Attorney in 2009. In 1975, my journal reported his "exceptional academic gifts and unassuming personality." Five years later, Secretary Vance would write me a letter that his son still praised this course.

20 February 1975–Marital Struggles

From my journal: "Jan and I again talked about her feelings of desperate alienation from me, the distance between us, and the burdens that my own

---

2. Cyrus R. Vance Sr. (1917–2002) served as secretary of state under President Jimmy Carter. Cyrus R. Vance Jr. (1954–) was the Manhattan District Attorney for twelve years before going into private practice.

conflicts have imposed upon her. I urged her to talk with others if she feels that will help."

Nonetheless, she continued to speak only with me about her struggle to live with my homosexual orientation. Jan felt that she was protecting me from dire consequences of others knowing about it. I cherished her even more for this.

10 March 1975–Platitudes from General Authorities

From my journal: "I told Chuck [Hamaker] that I felt it was necessary to let people know you recognize difficult problems in their lives exist, and that it is better to admit that the answers are not easy, than to quote a scripture and give a platitude as so often the Brethren do. Chuck seemed surprised at that last comment and said that [it] was harsh."

I eventually learned that Chuck was also a conflicted Mormon homosexual, but he wisely decided not to marry a woman. We had first met when he was on the staff at HDC. Fifteen years after his mention in my journal, he and his husband would host me at their house in Baton Rouge, where Chuck was out as a proudly gay librarian of Louisiana State University. At that time, I would be living on my own in the uninhibited, very gay French Quarter of New Orleans.

Our small and ironic world.

16 March 1975–Sitting with Wife in Chapel

From my journal: "Attended sacrament meeting in New Haven, where I sat with Jan and the kids—first time since January."

Now, the backstory: With me sitting on the stand as a counselor to the bishop, she had to struggle alone with our restless children throughout every sacrament meeting. This was typical for all bishoprics throughout the world, but Bishop Ross accepted an alternative that Jan had asked me to suggest to him. On some Sundays, he let one of his counselors sit with their family in the congregation—after the sacrament had been passed. As presiding officer, Paul couldn't leave the stand to sit with his wife. One cannot preside while sitting in an LDS congregation.

26 March 1975–Passing PhD Orals

From my journal: "When they returned, I learned that I had received the designation, *passed with distinction*. I was very pleased. All three professors [Lamar, Ahlstrom, and R. Hal Williams] gave me warm congratulations. Mr. Lamar said I performed in an outstanding manner, except that I did not do as well on Ahlstrom's section as they had anticipated. I said that by the time I had reached that point, my mind was turning to putty."

There were *900 books* on my reading list, and I had to be prepared for questions about any of them. I felt that the committee had let me off easy—because my mind went blank when Sydney Ahlstrom asked me to define evangelical. All I could say was: "Mormons are not evangelical Christians, Baptists are, but I can't remember the definition."

Also from my journal: "Dick Metcalf commented that he had been told by two members of my orals committee that my performance had not only been with distinction but that I demonstrated 'exceptional excellence.' I told Dick that I was pleased to hear that, especially since I had neglected Mr. Ahlstrom's area [American religious history] in order to prepare for what I considered my weaker area of U.S. political history."

All in all, it was a great birthday present. Shortly after, I boarded an airplane for Utah.

28 March 1975–Speaking about LDS Prayer Circle

Leonard Arrington had given me permission to read the full text of my paper during a special symposium at BYU, arranged by John W. Welch.[3]

From my journal: "After the session, about ten fellows came up to ask questions about my paper. Hugh Nibley came up, congratulated me on the paper, and said: 'Brother Quinn, you should have subtitled your paper: Everything You've Always Wanted to Know About the Prayer Circle and Have Been Afraid to Ask!'"

30 March 1975–Reorganized Saints

From Utah, I took a side trip on my return to New Haven. This Sunday, I began my first research trip to Independence, Missouri, headquarters of the Reorganized Church of Jesus Christ of Latter-Day Saints. I was overwhelmed at how warmly I was received by people I had thought were suspicious and resentful of Mormons.

The official RLDS historian, Richard P. Howard, arranged for me to stay for $2 nightly in a Host House near the Auditorium, the church's headquarters building.[4] On Monday, he gave me immediate access to anything I wanted to examine, including the RLDS First Presidency's minutes into the early twentieth century. The archives were then administered by a young man named W. Grant McMurray.

Gregarious and eager to exchange ideas, Grant introduced to me to a group of similar-aged friends he called "the Auditorium's Young Turks."

3. John "Jack" Welch (1946–) is a law professor at BYU and editor of *BYU Studies*. He began the Foundation for Ancient Research and Mormon Studies (FARMS) and co-founded Book of Mormon Central.

4. Richard P. Howard is historian emeritus of Community of Christ. He served in that position from 1966–94. He was one of the first Community of Christ (then the Reorganized Church of Jesus Christ of Latter Day Saints) historians to join the Mormon History Association, and he was a founder of the John Whitmer Historical Association in 1972.

This was a reference to the reformers from whom Kemal Ataturk emerged after World War I to transform the theocratic Ottoman Empire into the secular nation of Turkey.[5] Employed in various departments at RLDS headquarters, these young men talked enthusiastically about changes they hoped to see.

They were especially abuzz about the "Position Papers."[6] They explained these as a semi-official set of recommendations for fundamental changes. This included ceasing to regard the Book of Mormon as historically true and ceasing to insist on lineal succession for new presidents of their church. This had been a defining practice of the Reorganization ever since Joseph Smith III became its president in 1860.

Its current prophet-president was elderly W. Wallace Smith, and I was stunned to hear these Young Turks constantly refer to him as "Wally."[7] By contrast, active Mormons would *never* mention President Kimball as simply "Spencer" and certainly not as "Spence."

Mormons regard it as insulting to refer to their living prophet by first name only. However, when Mormons mention dead prophets by first name (Joseph, Brigham, Heber, George Albert), it's a sign of affection for a bygone era. However, despite the passing decades, that doesn't apply to presidents from David O. McKay's 1951 presidency onward, due to a new type of adulation for him and his successors.

These young bureaucrats at RLDS headquarters were the most radical believers I had ever met, and I thoroughly enjoyed our lunchtime chats (when their archives were closed to research). By comparison, I was a conservative Mormon intellectual, something they pointed out.

Two decades after these conversations, W. Grant McMurray would officially end lineal succession by becoming the first RLDS president who was not a descendant of Joseph Smith Jr. As its president, Grant would also move

5. As the Ottoman Empire crumbled, Ataturk (1881–1938) became the first president of the new Republic of Turkey. During his fifteen years in office (1923–38), he led Turkey's change into a modern, secular state. Bulent Tanor, "The birth of a modern nation among the ruins of the Ottoman Empire," The UNESCO Courier 34:11, 1981.

6. Created by the Department of Religious Education of the RLDS Church in conjunction with their First Presidency, the "Position Papers" were not meant to be published but were, without permission. They were a series of study papers written in 1967–68 by employees of the department for the Curriculum Consultation Committee. They were considered "a serious examination of the implications of new historical, biblical, and theological findings." See "An RLDS Reformation? Construing the Task of RLDS Theology," *Dialogue: A Journal of Mormon Thought* 18, no. 2 (1985), 92–103, and *Position Papers* (Independence, MO: Cumorah Books, 1968.)

7. William Wallace Smith (1900–89) was a grandson of Joseph Smith Jr. and son of Joseph Smith III. He served as the prophet-president of the RLDS Church from 1958–78, when he retired and took an emeritus role.

the Reorganization closer to mainline Protestantism by changing its name to Community of Christ.

From my journal for Saturday, April 5th: "Did research until noon & then caught bus to begin my trip back to Kansas City airport. In all I took 80 typed pages of notes this week."

8 April 1975–Approvals to Begin Dissertation

From my journal: "I stopped by the History office and verified with Florence [Thomas, the Department's secretary] that Mr. Spence OK'd having my German satisfy the PhD language requirement. I applied for the Master of Philosophy degree, but can't get it until December.

"I stopped by Mr. Lamar's office. I told him I would not be here next fall, and he said he assumed that was my intention. He enthusiastically commented on how happy and surprized he was that I had been able to make such rapid progress, with such high academic grades and achievements."

Nonetheless, I had failed the exam for Spanish to be my second required language for the doctorate. Today the DGS waived that requirement, since I had scored just short of fluency on Princeton's Educational Testing Service's famously rigorous, multiple-choice exam for German.

12 April 1975–Award for Publishing

The Mormon History Association gave me its Best Article Award for two of last year's publications: "The Mormon Church and the Spanish–American War: An End to Selective Pacifism" in *Pacific Historical Review*, and "Evolution of the Presiding Quorums of the LDS Church" in the first issue of *Journal of Mormon History*. This thrilled me beyond words.

Late April 1975–Washington, DC, and the Fall of Saigon

I spent a week at the Library of Congress, reading documents in its manuscript division and burrowing into its labyrinthine bookstacks for annual reports about pre-1933 corporations that might involve LDS leaders. I stayed with Jim and Judi McConkie, who had moved to Arlington, Virginia.

We all felt heartsick to watch television's repeatedly broadcast images of the panicky evacuation from the US embassy on April 29—the day before the fall of Saigon to North Vietnamese forces. After the decades of warfare, the insurgencies against colonialism of Japan, France, and America, the atrocities on all sides, the millions of Vietnamese casualties, and the 58,000 American deaths—it all ended with this. Nationalism, anti-colonialism, and Communism had won—with a loss of even the limited freedoms allowed by an American puppet dictatorship. Such futility.

I had anticipated this defeat in a journal entry quoted by this self-biography for 1972. Spiritual prophecy? Dunno. Perhaps just a rational prediction.

Late April 1975–Confiding My Homosexuality to Another Friend

In 1971, Mike McAdams was the first friend whom I told about being gay. I did so by letter back then, but now came out to Jim McConkie during one of our private conversations. Their acceptance strengthened me.

Nonetheless, it was so difficult for me to speak of my homosexuality, that I rationalized not telling my equally close friend, Richard Lambert. He was so attuned to the Spirit, I told myself, that he would know when God chose.

2 May 1975–Stunning News

From my journal: "Caught the commuter [train] to New Haven. I arrived at 8 p.m., telephoned home, and found that Jan had already left for an elders quorum party at a Hawaiian restaurant. I called the Camerons, and Kim picked me up at the train station. The girls [Mary and Lisa, who were being cared for by Kim and Melinda Cameron[8]] were happy to see me.

"After I put Adam to bed and ate a home-delivered pizza, I opened some of my mail. To my utter shock I found that I am one of ten students who have been awarded the Whiting Dissertation Fellowship for 1975–76."[9]

Melinda Cameron's father, Robert Young, was the star of television's *Father Knows Best* series that I watched as a teen. She had auditioned for the co-starring role in Hollywood's 1967 *The Graduate* but was glad that she had chosen not to go down that path. She was happy being a Mormon housewife and mother. I admired her a lot. Her husband Kim would become a mission president and university president.

4 May 1975–Farewell to New Haven Ward

From my journal: "I expressed regret that I knew the limitations of my own personality had put barriers between me and others, and prayed that these persons might be strengthened by the rest of the bishopric and ward. ... I said that—as I had testified a year ago—I felt that my service in the New Haven Ward was the most important aspect of my being in this area, and that I had relegated Yale to a secondary position in my priorities. But now that my immediate requirements at Yale were ended, that we would be leaving. I felt the Spirit throughout the meeting. Many Saints, including Joe Taylor, came up to me afterwards to express their love and appreciation.

8. In the late 1960s, Melinda Cummings, daughter of actor Robert Cummings (stage-named Robert Young), attended BYU, where she joined the church and met and married student body president Kim Cameron. Kim served in leadership positions at the BYU Marriott School, Case Western Reserve University, and the University of Michigan. Charlene Renberg Winters, "Provo Boy Meets Hollywood Girl," *BYU Magazine*, Summer 2007.

9. Created by New York philanthropist Flora Ettlinger Whiting, the Whiting Foundation was created to support "writers, scholars, and the stewards of humanity's shared cultural heritage." Their Dissertation Fellowship program ran from 1973 to 2015, to recognize the scholarship of graduate students at a handful of universities, including Yale. See whiting.org.

"After a fairly leisurely dinner at home with the family, I returned to the chapel for a bishop's court. We excommunicated three members at their request."

Fifteen total. Sad statistics.

9 May 1975–Jan and Children Jet to Utah

From my journal: "Spent all day packing and cleaning. Shawn Fullmer is taking half a carload of our things with him when he goes to Salt Lake in June. We packed these things with him and frantically cleaned in anticipation of an inspection. Barbara Bingham came over to help clean." Typical of ward friendships. Jan had earned the extra money for airfare by typing a 600-page dissertation about military history. Her favorite passage was the Yale student's quote from an Italian general to explain his surrender: "Why be a hero for five minutes and then be dead for the rest of your life?" We laughed.

10 May-6 June 1975–Major Research Trip

I transported many belongings by car as I conducted research at various places on a meandering route from Connecticut to Utah. This included Michigan, Ohio, Illinois, Missouri, Wisconsin, Minnesota, Iowa, and Nebraska. Five years after my inquiries with these manuscript archives, I was finally researching their Mormon documents.

In solitude and loneliness during those weeks, I made an entry in my journal about experiencing life to the fullest, with my determination to stop avoiding risk. Brave words, but I continued to run from homosexual encounters.

12 June 1975–Lavina Fielding (Anderson)

From my journal: "In mid-morning I went up to the 23rd floor [of the Church Office Building] and introduced myself to Lavina Fielding of the *Ensign* staff. The moment we met, she said she had wanted to meet me for some time. ...

"She said that the Brigham Young article was excellent, but just had not been worked into any of the issues up till now."

11 July 1975–Grampa's Death and Unpleasant Funeral

I was at LDS archives when Mom phoned to tell me that Grampa was in an emergency room. He had collapsed at the auto-parts company where he worked. A month from turning 83, this was his fourth job since retiring as a postal worker.

When I arrived at LDS Hospital, the attending physician told me that he was dead. CPR hadn't worked. With dry eyes, I broke the news to Mom and Nana.

I offered to make the funeral arrangements, which became unpleasant. First, mortuary director R. David McDougal shocked me by using every conceivable trick to persuade me to order one of the caskets that cost $10,000 to

$40,000.[10] I explained that I came from a working-class family and wanted only a modestly priced casket that would not leave my grandmother in debt. He replied that he was in the presidency of a nearby stake, knew my grandmother, and was sure she would be embarrassed to have her ward members see Grampa "in a cheap casket." I didn't say anything but clenched my fist and wanted to smash his face.

My silence apparently encouraged the mortuary owner to tell "a faith-promoting story." When L. Tom Perry's wife died, this apostle told his daughter to select whichever casket she wanted. She and President McDougal agreed on the most expensive one in his showroom. This rosewood casket was the first he had shown me, and it cost more than the current value of my grandmother's home. I suddenly despised this name dropping, exploitative stake counselor.

Seething with anger, I ordered a casket for about $2,000—which was still too much. The money-grubbing mortuary won.

Next, I got into conflict about the music. Years earlier, Grampa had written a proposed program for his funeral and listed Schubert's "Ave Maria" as one of the musical selections. The LDS bishop now expressed concern about this being a Roman Catholic hymn, and Grampa's niece-in-law Della (scheduled as the organist) vowed she would never play anything that "promotes Catholic idolatry."

I said that I would "follow Grampa's wishes, even if I have to hold the funeral in McDougal's Mortuary!" They had no idea how difficult it was for me to say those last words, but I meant it. The niece and bishop acquiesced upon learning that someone had put Mormon words to the melody, calling it "Heavenly Father." I refused to rename Schubert's music, so this ended up in the funeral program as "Organ Musical (Request of Departed)."

Tempests in a teapot, perhaps, but they revealed a lot about Utah Mormon culture and about me.

As the final challenge, Nana asked me to give the eulogy at Grampa's funeral. I tried to decline because I was sure I'd choke up with emotion, but she insisted. I struggled through the eulogy and ended up sobbing. The first thing Nana said to me afterwards: "I didn't think you cared that much for him."

The funeral was also a reunion and get-acquainted for diverse elements of my extended family. In memory of his ex-father-in-law, my Dad sent flowers, which Nana described in a note as "a lovely pot of Yellow."

---

10. Robert David McDougal (1924–2001) owned and directed the McDougal Funeral Home in Taylorsville, Utah, from 1950 until his death. Ecclesiastically, he served as president of the Georgia Atlanta Mission, as a sealer in the Jordan River Utah Temple, and as a church host for the First Presidency.

Even more impressive, Preston D. Richards Jr. and his wife Beverly attended the funeral of my grandfather.[11] They had apparently not seen him since their families attended the Wilshire Ward forty-one years earlier!

This postmortem honor occurred in the Redwood Third Ward on the southwest side of Salt Lake Valley. This blue-collar congregation had such high levels of inactivity that there were often no Aaronic Priesthood boys to administer the Sacrament, and men with the Melchizedek Priesthood were rarely at meetings. I regarded this as another example of social-class estrangement within modern Mormonism.

Mid-July 1975–Second Thoughts about Dissertation

I feared that there were too many controversies involved in the political, military, business, and financial activities of LDS general authorities. I told God that I would destroy my years of research, if that was his will. Instead, I received the burning within that I should continue this work in controversial Mormon history.

3 August 1975–Gospel Doctrine Teacher, Emigration Ward, Park Stake, Salt Lake City

With our three children, Jan and I had moved into the main level of our house on Lincoln Street. My proudest achievement there was repainting its exterior, for which I insisted that all the peeling paint had to be scraped and sanded away, and then a primer coat applied, before I would even start the final coats. It took me and Jan months to prepare and paint the brick house and its separate, wood garage, but this exterior paint job lasted for decades.

We continued to rent the lower apartment to twentyish bachelors. My favorite was Nolan Nebeker, a cute blond.

Located near Ninth South and Ninth East, its ward was filled with Dutch and German immigrants. Not long after I became a Sunday School teacher, Bishop Jacob C. VanKeizerswaard asked me to be the instructor for the ward's High Priest group. I remained as Sunday School teacher for seventeen months, but continued beyond that as the instructor in the priesthood class.

24 December 1975–Dashed Hopes

From my journal: "I was at HDC doing research, and stopped in at Leonard's office to talk about my research schedule. Leonard said that last week he was informed that the budget committee had not only disapproved the creation of an additional slot from already approved fellowship funds, but it also took away those fellowship funds."

---

11. Quinn's mother and grandparents lived with the Preston Richards family for a brief period after the devastating 1933 Long Beach earthquake (see Chapter 1).

There had never been a guarantee, but we had both been planning on my returning to the Historical Department. He had, of course, hired a historian to replace me two years before now, and others had joined his staff since then. I agreed that he couldn't fire anyone to rehire me.

Leonard strongly suggested that I should apply for two positions as a starting professor that he knew were being advertised by the history department of BYU and of Utah State University. Aside from my usual procrastination, I delayed in the hope against hope that he could hire me within six months—when my dissertation fellowship ended.

28 December 1975–Sustaining the Prophets

From my journal: "Today in priesthood and Sunday school I taught lessons that dealt with sustaining the prophets and leaders of the Church. I must admit that I did so with some personal misgivings.

"I have always been a hardliner on sustaining authority, but I don't know what I would do if Apostle Packer or others of the G.A.'s were to order, command, council, or suggest that I suppress an article, or that I submit my future research to censorship. It is easy to sustain authority as long as you agree with it."

Afterward, I had a conversation with a devout High Priest in our Emigration Ward. He was another example of the alienation that blue-collar workers sometimes feel from the LDS Church's elite. A resident of Salt Lake City since the 1920s, this sixty-something German immigrant was a paint contractor, who mentioned that he had done a lot of work at the church offices at 47 East South Temple.

I asked if he had any memorable experiences with the general authorities while working there. To my surprise, Helmuth Rimmasch immediately replied: "No, they're just white shirts!"

8 January 1976–BYU's History Department Courts Me

From my journal: "[Thomas G. Alexander] asked if I had received his letter about the position at BYU in Family History. I said that I had, but said that since the deadline was in March, that I had not acted on it yet.

"He asked if I was interested in the position. I said that I was, and that I wanted to leave my options open. He said that I should get an application form from Prof. [Ted] Warner, the Chairman of the Dept. and send it in.

"Tom said that three members of the committee that will select the person for the position, were at my presentation in Provo last month [to the Utah Valley Chapter of the State Historical Society], and that all three of them wanted me to apply. I said that I would, but that I did not feel that I met all the qualifications [for an expert in both family history and demography]."

Professor Alexander was chair of the search committee, but I still delayed sending an application—hoping that Leonard could somehow get the budget approval to rehire me.

15 January 1976–Dean L. May

From my journal: "I asked him [Dean May, then a member of Leonard Arrington's History Division] if his first priority or preference was to get the position at BYU. He said that it was. I explained that my own preference was to come back to HDC, and since there were no open slots, his going to BYU would open one for me. I told Dean that I felt he was more qualified for the BYU position than I, and since his desire was to go to BYU, I would not even apply for that position, and hope that he got it.

"He seemed quite pleased (in a restrained way) to hear me say all that, and he said that we would both have to pray for our mutual success. I felt good about our conversation."

Older than me, Dean May got his PhD in demographic history from Brown University.

18 January 1976–The Start of Torn Out Pages

Today begins the first missing section of my handwritten journal for this year. This resulted from Jan's reading entries that openly referred to my homosexuality. Upset by her discovery, she telephoned my closest friend Mike McAdams, who had already given me a priesthood blessing which promised that God would heal me of homosexuality.

Mike phoned and *commanded* me to rip all such pages from my journal and to never mention homosexuality again in anything I wrote that my children might read one day. I loved him enough to obey—at least in 1976.

In 1978, when I began typing detailed entries, my journal avoided using the words gay and homosexual in otherwise candid entries about my sexual orientation. It was technical compliance with my friend's command.

By contrast, this year's handwritten journal no longer has pages 70–94 for the period from January 18 to February 11, during which I had periodically used the word homosexual as I retrospectively described my male-male desires since childhood and their consequences in my marriage to Jan. Likewise, pages 111–12 are missing for the period from February 15 to the beginning of March 31.

However, for those two handwritten pages to have covered a six-week period, I had temporarily stopped making daily entries, anyway. The last missing section is the top of pages 143–44, during my long narrative about 11 May 1976.

This spring, I was in the Historical Department while tearing those entries from my personal journal. Then I flushed the pages down a toilet in the men's restroom near the archives reading room—a melodramatic gesture of regret for censoring what I had candidly written about myself.

This memoir tries to recompense for that error by maintaining consistent candor.

Late January 1976–Writing My Dissertation

Because of those missing entries from January 18 to February 11, I cannot specify the date on which I started writing my dissertation. But I am pretty sure that it was the third week of January 1976.

I began typing the first draft in a private study room in the special collections area of the University of Utah's J. Willard Marriott Library. Curator Everett L. Cooley and his successor Gregory C. Thompson both allowed me to have exclusive use of this locked cubicle for the next twelve years. There I stored the filing cabinets of my notes and a typewriter (later a portable computer) with which I wrote everything I would publish during those years.

My mother-in-law helped type my dissertation, "The Mormon Hierarchy, 1832–1932: An American Elite" on her IBM Selectric, notwithstanding her frequent objections to its contents. Bless the goodness of Kay Latham Darley's heart and the generosity of her soul! Again, Jan eagerly did the rest of the typing for the clean copy required by Yale.

I typed very fast, but sloppily. In composing it, I was often only a chapter ahead of their typing. As usual, with relatively few revisions, my first draft was the final.

14 February 1976–Publishing a Major Revision of Mormon History

From my journal: "When Jan picked me up in the evening, she brought the new issue of *BYU Studies* with my 47 page succession article in it. I literally have prayed that article into print, and feel such relief in seeing it."

Now, the backstory: "The Mormon Succession Crisis of 1844" analyzed how uncertain the succession question was at Joseph Smith's death, contrary to the official LDS view that it was obvious that Brigham Young and the Twelve Apostles had the sole right to lead the Church.[12] I identified and discussed eight legitimate routes of succession that the Prophet Joseph had established. Editor Charles D. Tate Jr. was courageous in continuing his plans to publish this, despite receiving a scathing letter from Truman G. Madsen in 1974.

Beyond attacking me, he had warned Tate that his academic journal

12. See Quinn, "The Mormon Succession Crisis of 1844," *BYU Studies* 16, no. 2 (1976), 187–233.

would get "rough sledding from the Brethren" if *BYU Studies* published my article. As the campus expert on European existentialism, Truman had been my favorite philosophy professor as an undergraduate, and a decade ago he had seemed eager to read my research summary about Joseph Smith's polyandry. His polemical letter stung.

Blindsided as I was by what Madsen wrote in 1974, the obviously shaken BYU editor said that he had expected only a supportive critique from this pre-publication reviewer. Despite campus politics and Madsen's warning of retribution from LDS headquarters, Tate decided to ignore all advice to kill the article. He thereby became a major hero in my publishing career, second only to Leonard Arrington.

March–April 1976–Last-Minute Application to BYU

Three things propelled me to send a rushed application to BYU's Department of History. First, Dean May told me that he had decided not to apply there, as my journal explained, "since he was informed it would be only a 1- or 2-year appointment. His decision not to apply ended our arrangement whereby he would go to BYU and I would take his place at HDC. He suggested that if I got tired of BYU, that perhaps we could arrange a switch at some distant date."

Second, Tom Alexander again asked me to apply there. Third, in response to my continued delays, Leonard urged me to accept any offer from BYU or USU because he saw no prospect of having the budget to rehire me.

Frankly, I was surprised at how enthusiastic BYU's search committee was toward me when I met them for lunch at my old alma mater in April. That ego lift was exceeded by the enthusiastic reception that senior historian S. George Ellsworth gave me when I met with the search committee at USU on April 29th. He had been writing to me for a year.

1 May 1976–Mormon History Association's Annual Meeting, St. George, Utah

From my journal: "I asked Jan [Shipps] about the RLDS reaction to the Succession article. She paused for a moment, and then asked how I could have been so damned stupid to have written the sophomoric first paragraph reference to the Twelve Apostles."

I rehearsed how Editor Chuck Tate had defied Truman Madsen's efforts to kill the article, despite Madsen's warning that the Brethren would punish *BYU Studies* for publishing it. So when Tate asked me to soften the revisionism of the article by emphasizing the Twelve's rights in its introduction, I couldn't say no.

Resuming my journal for today: "When Jan and I entered the dining hall before the dinner meeting, Paul Edwards [a descendant of Joseph Smith III] was in the entryway, but upon seeing me, he turned his back as he talked with others.[13] I feel bad that my hopes of the article's aiding a rapprochement have turned so sour. After the annual banquet, I again asked Jan Shipps to see what she could do to get RLDS reactions and smooth over things."

She then confided that the Mormon members of MHA's Awards Committee were concerned that the RLDS historians would bolt MHA in protest if the "Succession Crisis" received an award. In response, I told her to unofficially inform the awards committee that I didn't want my article to be considered for this year. It wasn't, which (as I learned) was the only reason the succession article didn't win.

5 May 1976–My Only Alternatives as a New Mormon Historian?

From my journal: "I was feeling a little depressed, and a little more talkative than usual. I told Clifton [Jolley in a phone conversation] that although the gospel and Church life was all I knew in life, and that I had enforced an often difficult discipline upon myself to abide within its framework, that I could not surrender those principles and approaches that I feel the Lord has trained me in, even if I find myself at odds with specific leaders like Boyd K. Packer and others.

"I told Clifton that if being blackballed or facing an elder's court were the only alternatives to my promotion of the ideals and programs I felt spiritually comfortable about, then I would have to accept those alternatives. Clifton insisted that such a view was unnecessarily dark and that choosing between such alternatives would not be necessary in all probability.

"I told Clifton that I did not feel worthy to be an advocate for anything, and that I did not want a 'Quinn following,' but that I did hope to be able to help people to seek and accept TRUTH and beneficial approaches, without tieing their validity to my reputation or honor.

"Clifton could not have realized what I was really driving at [my homosexuality], and it was unfair to subject him to such drivvel."

10 May 1976–Competing Offers and Irony of Ironies

From my journal: "Drove down to Provo early enough to do more than an hour's research at the county courthouse prior to my 10:00 appointment with Ted Warner, head of the history department. Ted offered me a position as assistant professor for $13,000 base salary for the 8 months [of] BYU school year, with the option of 18% of base salary for one summer term, plus research opportunities. ...

---

13. Paul M. Edwards (1933–2022) was a Community of Christ member, an author, and a retired professor of history and philosophy at Graceland University in Lamoni, Iowa. He was a descendant of Joseph Smith and grandson of RLDS church president Frederick M. Smith.

"A question that I put special emphasis on was the question of academic freedom at BYU. Ted Warner assured me that things were greatly changed since the Wilkinson years, and that he was aware of no institutional pressures on faculty members, even though students might report supposed 'errors,' but that the latter was an inescapable product of teaching. I felt reassured about the issue.

"Ted Warner walked with me over to the office of the College of Social Science Dean, Martin B. Hickman, a political scientist.[14] He spent a few minutes reassuring me about the absence of institutional pressure on faculty. ...

"When I phoned Mr. [William] Lye, [USU's dean,] he gave me a firm offer of an assistant professorship at $12,000. ... I told him that I anticipated receiving BYU's final offer by Friday, and that I hoped to give my answer then. ...

"In my interview with [Dr. Robert J.] Smith, he spontaneously talked about academic freedom at BYU, and then about the fringe benefits.[15] The interview went well and smoothly, and I felt fine about it until the last moments when he told me that Boyd K. Packer was the general authority who would interview me at 2:30 tomorrow afternoon.

"I hope that my inward reaction was not outwardly apparent. Boyd K. Packer is the one apostle on earth that I have had no desire even to talk to, let alone be interviewed by! As I drove back to Salt Lake City, I prayed that the Lord would prepare me for an event I dreaded."

11 May 1976–Apostle Boyd K. Packer Dislikes Historians

From my journal's account of an hour's interview, in parts: "Then he asked, 'What was your dissertation on?' And I felt that I was nearing disaster. I said that it studied the first century of Mormon leadership by the general authorities from 1832 to 1932. To my profound and prayerful relief, his only other question about the dissertation was why I ended at 1932, which I answered by saying that [it] was a century after Joseph Smith first chose counselors.

"Then he went to questions about worthiness, along the lines of a temple recommend interview, although he was more specific with reference to sexual conduct—which he touched upon repeatedly in a variety of ways, including

---

14. Martin Hickman (1925–91) taught international relations at the University of Southern California before coming to BYU, where he spent seventeen of his twenty-three years as an influential dean. Speaking to the BYU chapter of the Association of American University Professors in 1971, he asserted that academic freedom at BYU was greater than at other institutions for those who shared the university's values. Ernest L. Wilkinson, ed., *Brigham Young University: The First One Hundred Years*, 4 vols. (Provo, UT: Brigham Young University Press, 1976), 4:63.

15. A professor in BYU's accounting department, Robert Smith (1920–2016) was serving as associate academic vice-president (from 1972–78) at the time of this interview with Quinn.

a question whether I had been involved in homosexual activities, to which I answered in the negative.

"To my surprize and disappointment he did not ask about my Church experience, about my belief in any principle of faith, or my testimony. ... He seemed to lose interest when I said Marion D. Hanks had been my first mission president.

"Next, he asked: 'What is your attitude toward history?' I sensed that I was being maneuvered into making statements that he expected to disagree with and challenge, and so I tried to make my response as bland as possible. I said that I had long aspired to be a physician, but that research into LDS Church history was a consuming interest to me from an early age. ... Therefore, I said, that my attitudes toward history were shaped by the fact that I studied history and became a historian because of my interest in LDS and ancient Church history. ...

"I could tell almost from the beginning of my answer, that he was impatient at the circuitous approach to his question. When I finished, he made no response to what I had said, but [he] said: 'I have a difficult time with historians, and I do not like what many of them do.'... He said that his objection had nothing to do with truth, and that he could truthfully tell many female employees of the Church that they were ugliest women he had ever seen, but the *truth* of such statements that could be said did not ennoble such statements or justify the damage they created.

"Boyd Packer, again without specific reference to my own remarks, then spent the last five or ten minutes of our interview telling me why historians lacked ethical principles in dredging up from the past things that should be left alone."

That was the point at which apostle Packer restated his first objection this way: "I have a hard time with historians, because they idolize the truth. The truth is not uplifting; it destroys." Although not in my journal for this day, I repeated those exact words to BYU historian Ted Warner when he asked me on campus about the interview. They remained my indelible memory of the apostle's statements.[16]

Returning to my journal: "It was the most disappointing, spiritually bereft, and unusual interview I have ever experienced. ... Boyd K. Packer is the most distant, cold general authority I have ever met. ...

"Toward the end of the interview, Bro Packer had said: 'I will indicate that you are worthy of the position,' but I felt his recommendation about my appropriateness might be less positive."

16. Though Quinn quotes this statement from memory, Quinn's journal entry for this date quotes Packer as saying: "I have a difficult time with historians, and I do not like what many of them do."

13 May 1976—Racist Use of the Federal Census
and a Denial of LDS Bureaucracy

From my journal: "He [Jim McConkie] was in SLC to act as [Congressman] Gunn McKay's representative to the general authorities on a potentially explosive political and religious issue. McKay sponsored and helped maneuver the House passage of a bill designed to open the Census more quickly to genealogists and researchers. The Black Caucus and the American Civil Liberties Union were threatening to make a public political issue of the bill on the charge that the LDS Church used census data in a racially discriminatory manner.

"Jim [the Congressman's Chief of Staff] had interviewed some low level bureaucrats in the Genealogical Society and had obtained the details of the operation of this discriminatory use of Census data by the Church's Genealogical Society. Jim's purpose was to bring this information to the attention of the general authorities, tell them of the volatile situation, and in either a direct or indirect way ask them to stop the program before it explodes into a national issue. ...

"Jim said that when he met Neal Maxwell [Assistant to the Quorum of the Twelve], that Maxwell asked him to come into the office of Gordon B. Hinckley so that they both could hear what he had to say."

During this meeting, Jim tried to avoid accusing the general authorities of being responsible for this racist use of the census. Instead, he that said that this was "a terrible mistake by employees in the church's bureaucracy."

Looking surprised, Elder Hinckley replied that the church doesn't have a bureaucracy, but administrators and employees. He was serious.

It would be nearly two decades before I realized why Elders Hinckley and Maxwell were the point men in this discussion of potential problems with Congress, the ACLU, and the NAACP. At LDS headquarters, those two general authorities headed the recently established Special Affairs Committee for coordinating the Church's behind-the-scenes political activities.[17] If Jim McConkie knew this in 1976, he didn't volunteer that insight while telling the anecdote.

17 May 1976—Yale Confers PhD

With the back-channel support of the History Department's devoted

---

17. Organized in 1974, the Special Affairs Committee reported directly to the First Presidency and included four general authorities with significant political experience: Chairman Gordon B. Hinckley of the Quorum of the Twelve, Assistant to the Twelve David B. Haight, and Quorum of the Seventy members Neal A. Maxwell and James E. Faust, both of whom were subsequently called to the Quorum of the Twelve. The committee dealt with a number of issues, including the church's successful national campaign to defeat the Equal Rights Amendment. Jacob W. Olmstead, "A Diabolical Disneyland in Zion: the Mormons and the MX" (master's thesis, Brigham Young University, 2005), 24–26.

secretary Florence Thomas, Yale had allowed me to exceed several deadlines in order to graduate today with my PhD. I didn't go to Connecticut for the ceremonies, but my dissertation received two prizes.

I understand that completing a Yale PhD in thirty-three months (from entry to graduation) was something of a record—at least in its Department of History.

Twenty-six years later, I would start socializing on a frequent basis with octogenarian historian Edmund S. Morgan, who had done it that fast at Harvard—before my birth.[18]

17-18 May 1976–God Tells Me to Go to BYU

By this time, I had received offers of tenure track positions from Brigham Young University for $13,000 and Utah State University for $12,000. I didn't want to go to BYU in spite of its offering me more money. I feared that my work on controversial Mormon topics would eventually create major problems, resulting in the loss of my job at Provo.

I felt impressed that God wanted me to go to BYU, but I didn't want to believe these impressions. Finally I made an "Abrahamic covenant" with God. I told Him that I was going to make an unreasonable salary demand that I knew BYU would reject. If He wanted me there, God would inspire BYU officials to give me this offer that I couldn't turn down for purely financial reasons.

From my journal: "I have decided that if the Lord wants me to go to BYU, that like my going to Yale, He will manifest it to me by their making an extraordinary offer financially for me to go to BYU. If BYU gives me an offer of $15,000 base salary (which I am sure is without precedent for a professor fresh out of graduate school), then I will swallow my fears and misgivings and go to BYU. Otherwise I will accept USU's offer. I felt the Spirit confirm me in this resolve. ... I had agreed with the Lord that $15,000 was the sign that I could not reject."

In our May 17th phone call, history chair Ted Warner was astonished at my demand and said that he couldn't offer any more than $13,500 base salary. I said that was fine with me, because I wasn't bargaining and preferred to go to USU.

From my journal: "At 12:30 I received a phone call at the state archives from Martin Hickman, Dean of BYU's College of Social Sciences. He said that he was very disappointed to learn from Ted Warner of my decision. ...

"But I said that my reservations about joining the faculty were such that I had not arrived at an offer at BYU that I could not turn down. He asked what

---

18. Edmund Sears Morgan (1916–2013) was the Sterling Professor of History at Yale University from 1955 to 1986.

that amount would be. ... I hesitated again, and then said it was $15,000 base salary. There was a pause, and I half expected him to tell me how preposterous that was. Instead, he asked me to give him time to think about it and to make inquiries. He made me promise not to contact USU with my acceptance of their offer until he called me back."

In this conversation, I told BYU's dean about the anti-historian lecture that apostle Packer had given me. Hickman responded: "We'll protect you from those people in Salt Lake." His candor stunned me, but I wasn't sure that such protection was possible. Still, I had promised God.

Continuing my journal for the next day, May 18: "When Martin Hickman got on the phone, he said: 'I told my secretary to tell you that the Godfather wanted to talk with you. We are prepared to make you the offer you can't resist.' I could hardly believe it. He said that he didn't want to enter into a wage war with USU at this point, and asked if I accepted the offer. I said that I did, and that I would tell USU that I had accepted BYU's offer."

Dean Hickman was alluding to the recent movie about the Italian mafia. The title character's most famous line was "Make him an offer he can't refuse." The dean had conferred with BYU's top administrators and made me the offer I had promised him that I would not decline, nor try to bargain beyond. I kept my covenant with God—accepting their offer on the phone, then informing USU.

Not only would I miss associating with LDS historians George Ellsworth, Charles S. Peterson, and F. Ross Peterson there, but also with non-LDS Clyde Milner.[19] He and his wife went from Yale to Utah State University.

In May 1976, I hoped that if the Lord wanted me at BYU, my worst fears about the place would not come to pass. I eventually discovered that God's apparent desire for me to go to BYU was no guarantee that I would fulfill the expectations of its board of trustees—particularly two or three of those general authorities.

21 May 1976–One Week Too Late

From my journal: "Leonard said that it looked like the position in the department [HDC] would become available, and he wanted to know if I wanted it.

"I told him that on the basis of his counsel to me three weeks ago, I had pursued the offers made to me by USU and BYU. I told him of the developments of Monday and Tuesday, and he was really astounded at the salary offer

---

19. George Ellsworth (1916–1997) was an acclaimed history professor at Utah State University. Charles Peterson (1927–2017), also a prominent historian, taught at four colleges and universities in Utah. F. Ross Peterson (1941–) has taught American history at USU for thirty-three years.

from B.Y.U. He said he thought that was more than Tom Alexander made as a full professor. I think that is an exaggeration, but even the suggestion of parity stunned me.

"Leonard said that the HDC salary would be $12,000 for the 12 months. I said that with the summer session, my salary would be $17,700, and even if I could endure the ethical problems of turning down BYU's offer after I had formally accepted it, I could not take a job for $5,000 less a year. ... I told Leonard that if he had given me this position a week ago that I would have turned down both USU and BYU, but that now I was committed."

After hanging up the phone, I began crying.

28 May 1976–Potential of Being Excommunicated for Mormon History

From my journal: "I told him [Doyle Buchanan], in response to his question of what I would do at BYU, that I would teach as I believed and if that got me in trouble, I preferred to be blackballed or Church disciplined when I am young rather than when I am farther along in life.

"I told him my view that excommunication, like all other ordinances of the Church, was absolute with reference to the conduct of the Church in this life, but had to be sealed by the Holy Spirit of Promise to be valid in an eternal sense [D&C 132:7, 18–19, 26]. The relation of the individual with the Lord was primary."

2 June 1976–Bircher Spy and Liberal Well-Wisher

From my journal: "When we got to his office [in HDC] and he had closed the door, Davis [Bitton] said:

"'When I saw you giving Jim [Allen] a copy of your dissertation, I thought I had better tell you about a situation that developed last week. ... About noon, Leonard's secretary Nedra [Yeates Pace] came to me in a very agitated condition, asking if I knew where Mike Quinn's PhD thesis was.

"'I asked her why she needed it, and she said that Tom Truitt called her and said that he had a 2 p.m. appointment with the general authorities to show them your dissertation and that he needed it immediately.[20] I told Nedra to tell Tom Truitt that the dissertation was not in Leonard's office. ... Tom

---

20. Thomas Ghnon Truitt Sr. (1913–85) was a convert from Mississippi who became a research and reference specialist in the LDS Historical Department Library. He allegedly told researchers at the historical department that he was on a "special assignment" for high-ranking church leaders to send them "objectionable" articles on church history. His actions influenced having *The Story of the Latter-day Saints* removed from the shelves of Deseret Book and dropped from reading lists at LDS Institutes of Religion on college campuses. Peggy Fletcher Stack, "LDS Leaders Say Scripture Supports Secret Files on Members," *Salt Lake Tribune*, Aug. 4, 1992. See also James B. Allen and Glen M. Leonard, *The Story of the Latter-day Saints* (Salt Lake City: Deseret Book and LDS Church Historical Department, 1976).

Truitt had told Nedra that he learned about the dissertation from the 3rd floor employees who bound it for Leonard.'

"Tom Truitt is a member of the John Birch Society and a long time employee of the Church Historian's Office. He is one of the old guard of Joseph Fielding Smith's staff who is suspicious of historians and has indicated distaste for the open policy of the Historical Department. He is also a member of the stake where Jan and I reside. ...

"Since Tom has made known his urgent desire to get a copy of my dissertation in his hands, I feel that I could only make things worse by withholding my copies in a hide-and-seek game. I wrote it with full knowledge of what could result for me personally at the hands of witch hunters and inquisitors who introduce into the Church all the conspiracy they have such paranoid fears of. ...

"As we concluded [talking at HDC later today], Gene England put his arm around my shoulders and said, 'Good luck to you at BYU!'[21] I told him it concerned me how many people were saying that."

14 June 1976–*Mormonism: Shadow or Reality?*

Today at HDC, Leonard Arrington told me that this book-length publication was being used by ministers throughout the nation to lead investigators away from the church. It was published by Utah ex-Mormons Jerald and Sandra Tanner, who had become Evangelical Protestant crusaders against Mormonism in 1960.[22]

Ten years earlier, I had read their several-hundred-page collection of startling quotes by LDS leaders. I had discussed many of its topical sections with BYU dorm buddies Jim McConkie and Richard Lambert. As well-read returned missionaries, we all regarded its polemical histrionics as amusing but appreciated its impressive assemblage of quotes. I hadn't looked at it since the fall of 1967.

Today, Leonard asked me to write a detailed assessment of its expanded edition. I told him that I would do it for him after finishing my own project on "A Diplomatic History of Mormonism." In two days, an employee in the Church Library section of HDC renewed the request, since Leonard had also talked with him.

From my journal concerning that morning of June 16: "Dave Mayfield asked me to check with him before starting the project so that he could brief

21. George Eugene "Gene" England (1933–2001) was a writer, scholar, and teacher who co-founded *Dialogue: A Journal of Mormon Thought* in 1966. He taught at BYU from 1977–98, when he was forced to retire due to his expressed concerns about a lack of diversity and academic freedom on BYU campus. He was soon hired by Utah Valley Community College. He died of brain cancer in 2001.

22. For a biography of the Tanners, see Ronald V. Huggins, *Lighthouse: Jerald and Sandra Tanner, Despised and Beloved Critics of Mormonism* (Salt Lake City: Signature Books, 2022).

me about the kinds of inquiries about the [Tanners'] work he has received from many mission presidents, missionaries, stake presidents, bishops and rank-and-file Mormons. Leonard and Dave would like to have a lengthy reply to send out.

"Leonard suggested that I follow the letter format I used in my Response to a Mormon Fundamentalist, which he said that he has distributed in a few cases with apparently good results.

"It is ironic that in my own view and in the view of others, I am a capable defender of the faith from my historical viewpoint, whereas in the minds of others I am a destroyer of the faith by that viewpoint."

In preparing my response to *Shadow or Reality?,* I received helpful suggestions from four people at HDC. First, Dave Mayfield outlined the topics that most troubled those Mormons who had written to HDC. Then—as usual—Leonard, Davis Bitton, and Jim Allen made comments on my first draft.

Only two persons gave me enough input to be considered collaborators on my response, and neither worked at HDC. Nor were they professors, nor even trained as historians.

My first quasi-collaborator was graduate student Doyle Buchanan, one of my decade-earlier Aaronic Priesthood boys in the BYU dorm. He was already fluent in German and Russian, with abilities to read Hebrew, Greek, Coptic, and Egyptian through coursework and tutoring. As I remember, Doyle was not a matriculated student at the University of Utah in 1976, and just took courses in various languages there. In the early 1970s, he had done likewise at Berlin's Free University for two years while working for the Army Security Agency to translate intercepted Russian conversations from the city's Soviet sector. While visiting with Jan and me earlier in 1976, he had mentioned biblical scholarship of interest, and I now asked for his input.

Then studying a dead Middle Eastern language (Ugaritic), Doyle introduced me to recent publications by Frank Moore Cross and others in Bible studies. I added some of their findings to my manuscript, which he also read and then made extensive suggestions for revisions.

The other non-HDC reader who gave detailed recommendations on the first draft of my response was physician Lester Bush. Although he was an amateur historian, his *Dialogue* article on the priesthood restriction against Blacks had impressed me with his careful scholarship, insights, and erudition.

Otherwise, I worked alone in responding to the Tanners.

This was a saga that did not reach its conclusion for eighteen months. And then it roiled Utah Mormon culture.

16 June 1976–Old Guard Throws Down a Gauntlet

As I left the east wing of the Church Office Building at 50 East North

Temple, I met Vaughn Standing, one of the old guard in the old Historian's Office.[23] From my journal:

"As we walked to the sidewalk, he asked 'Have you had many repercussions about your book?'

"'Do you mean my dissertation?'

"'Yes.'

"'No, I haven't.'

"After a pause: 'Two of the Brethren are reading it now.'

"After a pause, 'By Brethren, do you mean general authorities?'

"'Yes.'

"'Do you know which ones?'

"'Today I duplicated two copies of your dissertation—one for Ezra Taft Benson and one for Mark E. Petersen.'

"When I commented that Bro. Benson had set me apart to my mission, he seemed not to notice but with ill-concealed enthusiasm and triumph he said:

"'How does that make you feel? To know that those men are reading it?'

"'Well, that's what I wrote it for—to be read.'"

3 July 1976–Suspending Journal Entries

On July 2, I had noted: "When Jan picked me up she told me she had made an appointment to see Marion D. Hanks, when he is able to work her in after a trip." Her need to unburden the unhappiness of our marriage to someone—anyone—had exceeded her protectiveness of my reputation.

Without writing the words homosexuality or homosexual in my journal, as I had promised Mike McAdams, I couldn't honestly comment about the most important discussions with my wife in the following days or weeks. So I stopped making any entries, and the silence in my journal would last for the next fifteen months.

Mid-July 1976–Confiding My Homosexuality to a General Authority

Reluctantly, I met with my only friend in the hierarchy, the only general authority with whom I had a reciprocally trusting association. To this former mission president, I rehearsed my situation since the age of twelve and our marriage problems of the past five years.

President Hanks was compassionate and supportive toward me. He said that he knew of no cure for homosexuality and disagreed with LDS leaders who told young men that their desire for other men would disappear after they married.

He said that my church service and BYU position would be in jeopardy

---

23. Vaughn Larsen Standing (1927–2015) earned an associate's degree from Salt Lake City's LDS Business College and was an employee of the LDS Church Historical Department.

if I told others about my homosexual orientation. President Hanks said that LDS leaders (and he named apostle Packer) had no right to ask if someone had homosexual tendencies or temptations. He told me to deny it if LDS leaders or BYU administrators asked that question.

27 July 1976–A Mormon Boy Named Moshe

After Jan gave birth to our fourth child today, he was the only one of our children whose middle name was not simply Darley. That was a naming pattern I told Jan from the beginning that I wanted in order to preserve her identity in each of our children's names.

I thought this indicated how much I supported the women's movement. I would be humbled within a decade to learn that generation-younger student Mark McGee was so supportive of feminist ideals that he legally adopted his bride's name. As Mark Ashurst-McGee, he became a church-employed expert in Mormon history.

When Jan and I told her parents in July 1976 that our son's name would be Paul Darley Quinn, Roy gleefully announced that he would just call his grandson "PDQ." I hadn't even thought about that slang abbreviation for "pretty damn quick." Although his comment angered me, it's good that Roy brought this to my attention.

As soon as we were alone, I told Jan: "I'll be damned if I let anyone give my son that nickname!" Paul had been her choice, so she let me choose the alternate name.

I first suggested adding "Mark" before Darley, but Jan didn't like it for some reason. Then I suggested: "Micah," but her mother thought that kids would make fun of this Biblical name. They both rejected my idea of Moses, but Jan liked the sound of Moshe, my Hebrew substitute for it.

Our second son was Paul Moshe Darley Quinn. He also had the distinction as a newborn of laughing in the maternity ward of LDS Hospital and several times a day after we brought him home to Lincoln Street.

30 August 1976–Begin Teaching History at BYU

Jan and I regarded the Provo-Orem area as a cultural wasteland and had no enthusiasm for moving there. I gladly commuted from the upper part of Salt Lake City to BYU three to five times a week for the twelve years I was on its history department's faculty. My only consistent regret about this daily hundred-mile roundtrip was that I couldn't attend the evening screenings by BYU's International Film Society.

21 November 1976–"Let Us Compare Ourselves to the Prophets"

The Park Stake's President Louis Roos, a Dutch immigrant who often attended my gospel doctrine class in the Emigration Ward, asked me to speak this evening to the unmarried adults of this stake in Salt Lake City. He introduced me to this special interest fireside as a history professor at BYU.

For the stake's quarterly report of historical events, its clerk wrote a detailed account of my remarks. I began by giving the historical background of America's Second Great Awakening as a "time of great religious confusion" which led to teenage Joseph Smith's "going into prayer in a grove, where the Father and the Son appeared to him." Then I "referred to the Prophet Brigham Young when he became the head of the Church; how Brigham was transformed in[to the] voice and image of the Prophet Joseph Smith; [and] that Brigham Young saw [in vision, the deceased] Joseph Smith."

I next discussed how LDS President Lorenzo Snow, facing two million dollars of church debt in 1899, earnestly "prayed in the temple to have this burden removed from him. He received no answer on what to do until he went to St George, and on the way received an answer."

Then I described how current apostle LeGrand Richards repeatedly asked God: "Why my son?" after he drowned during a family outing before he was to begin a full-time mission.

After giving the above summary and paraphrases of my remarks, the stake clerk then quoted my concluding words: "Let us compare ourselves to the Prophets that we might become polished shells in our struggle through life and receive hope and inspiration through hearing of and knowing of other people's struggle."

At age 32, this was a restatement of my mid-teens synthesis of Mormonism with Existentialism.

Late 1976–Reparative Therapy of Homosexuality

Eighteen months after I confided to him my decades of struggle, longtime friend Jim McConkie said that he would pay my airfare to New York City, my housing there, and all fees for me to spend next summer in a special clinic's program for treating homosexuality. I didn't tell Jan or him that I had already read Lawrence Hatterer's *Changing Homosexuality in the Male*, and was very uncertain about the prospects of such therapy.[24] Still, I was overwhelmed by the generosity of my friend's offer to pay for such a clinic, and I couldn't simply reject it out of hand.

James gave me its phone number in the 212 area code, and for days I anguished over my good-hearted friend's offer. It had been incredibly difficult for me to confess my homosexual orientation to my BYU bishop in 1963, to Jan in 1972, to my former mission president this year, and to two of my closest friends—Mike McAdams in 1971 and Jim McConkie in 1975. I didn't think

24. Lawrence J. Hatterer, *Changing Homosexuality in the Male: Treatment for Men Troubled by Homosexuality* (New York: McGraw-Hill, 1970).

I had the courage to talk about it with *anyone* else, certainly not to strangers. And yet how could I tell my long-suffering wife that I wouldn't even inquire about treatment? About the possibility of being healed of homosexuality?

And so, with Jan at my side, I nervously phoned the psychiatric clinic in Manhattan from our home on Lincoln Street. A woman answered and said that she was an RN supervisor there. After I stumbled through the words about wanting to enroll in the clinic's program "to overcome my homosexuality," there was a long pause. "I'm afraid there's been some misunderstanding," she began. "Our program helps people to *accept* their homosexuality and develop healthy adaptations to it."

Now it was my turn to be speechless. I finally said: "You do what?!" And the clinic's supervisor repeated her statement. I didn't know whether to cry or laugh, but felt like a weight was lifting off my chest.

After hanging up, I repeated her words to Jan, who grimaced: "How can that be?" I didn't know, nor understand how my friend could have been so wrong about the therapy this clinic offered.

I told my wife: "I made the call, but I'm not going to put myself through that again. Especially not in Utah, where even the inquiry could get me fired from BYU!" Jan wasn't happy, but never mentioned this again.

James was dumbfounded by the result of my phone call and said that he would definitely find the right kind of clinic for me. I told him not to do anything further, and he didn't. This was the last time I considered going through therapy against homosexuality.

I would eventually read this year's PhD dissertation by BYU student Max Ford McBride about the university's ghastly aversion therapy to change homosexuality.[25] Already in full operation and endorsed by LDS headquarters, this program used gay porn and mild torture to induce pain, revulsion, and fear in young men with homosexual tendencies. They were advised by certain general authorities to experience it for redemption, or required by the BYU Standards Office to endure this to avoid expulsion.

Aside from echoing the medieval Catholic cult of self-flagellation, this BYU program encouraged the homosexually inclined young men to masturbate in the dark while watching increasingly pornographic images of women and of female-male sex. The program's administrators regarded this as positive reinforcement of normal sexuality.

Training young men to view women as mere sex objects!

25. Fourteen gay BYU students were subjected to electric shock therapy during twenty-two sessions on campus, lasting about three months. When sensors detected arousal while viewing photos of nude men, the men were shocked so they would associate same-sex desire with physical pain. Max Ford McBride, "Effect of Visual Stimuli in Electric Aversion Therapy" (PhD diss., Brigham Young University, 1976).

At this same time, LDS headquarters refused to advertise R-rated movies in the *Deseret News*! And BYU refused to show R-rated movies to regular students! And LDS leaders were doing everything possible to make boys feel guilty for masturbating!

Could no one but gay boys see the vicious irony? I would read with admiration what one of them, Cloy Jenkins, self-published anonymously in two years, *Prologue: An Examination of Mormon Attitudes Towards Homosexuality*.[26] It included BYU's aversion therapy.

Early 1977–Absent-Minded Professor

I gave the oddest demonstration of my mental concentration at the conclusion of Larry Foster's stay at our house while he did research at the LDS Church's archives. In a rush to get him to the airport on time, I threw his suitcases in the back of my car and drove off. This left him standing on the porch saying goodbye to Jan!

I drove a block before coming to my senses, turning around, and getting Larry into the car. Whether I called this "highly focused attention" or "tunnel vision," it was a trait that was sometimes a problem for me and for others.

7 April 1977–BYU Warns Its Historians and Political Scientists

The entire faculties of the history and political science departments were called to meet with recently appointed Church Commissioner of Education Jeff Holland, plus BYU's President Dallin Oaks, Academic Vice-President Robert K. Thomas, and Dean Martin Hickman. They informed us that members of the First Presidency and Quorum of Twelve had expressed "lack of confidence" in our departments.

This was partly because a Mormon member of the Communist Party had been invited to speak to a poly-sci class at BYU. Learning of that reaction, I felt even less inclined to speak to others about my views as a democratic socialist. Being an armchair radical was enough for me.

From a retrospective account of this meeting in my journal six months afterwards: "We were counseled to do everything to avoid raising suspicion in the general authorities about our actions, teachings, and motives. The [BYU] leaders then expressed their confidence in the two departments, but they were pointedly outlining a serious lack of confidence in us on the part of the G.A.'s.

"Shortly after this meeting, I received a letter from one of the editors of *Dialogue*, asking me to join the board of editors. I felt that it would not be

---

26. After attending an anti-gay lecture in 1977 by BYU psychology professor I. Reed Payne, a group of gay students and scholars wrote a rebuttal to Payne's lecture, which they called "The Payne Papers." They distributed their rebuttal to all general authorities through the LDS Church Office Building mailroom. In 1978, the group Affirmation: Gay and Lesbian Mormons began publishing it as a pamphlet titled, *Prologue: An Examination of Mormon Attitudes Towards Homosexuality*.

prudent for me to do so, and therefore declined the opportunity with the legitimate excuse of my extended absences in the upcoming months for research as well as my research and writing schedule on my proposed book study of the hierarchy."

Summer 1977–Research and the Graves of Two Mexicans

Beginning in late spring, I traveled throughout the American West on a fellowship from the National Endowment for the Humanities. I was examining records of old corporations that might show management roles by members of the Mormon hierarchy before 1933. I did research in county courthouses, historical societies, and government archives, starting with Utah, then Northern California, Portland and eastern Oregon, Seattle, Washington, southern Idaho, Canada's Alberta Province, and parts of Montana and Wyoming.

During the mid-summer drive to Texas, I also played tourist. This included visits to Utah's Dead Horse Point and Arches National Monument, then to Colorado's Mesa Verde, whose cliff dwellings were stunning. After my research in corporation records from Colorado to El Paso, I also stopped by Fort Bliss for old time's sake.

Then to New Mexico, where I did research in Santa Fe and Albuquerque. While there, I attended the Santo Domingo Pueblo's annual Corn Festival, where old men drummed in unison while Native American men and boys danced single file in a circle. Deeply moved by the spirituality of their Corn Dance, I stood in the heat and silently watched for an hour.

After a week or two of research in Arizona, I drove to Pinal County to visit the grave of Grandfather Ysmael Peña. At thirty-eight, he had died of peritonitis in the mining town of Ray in 1918.[27] So said the death certificate of this barber.

Typical of those times, he had been buried in a Mexican cemetery, but an open pit mine swallowed the town. The copper company moved the segregated cemetery and put new headstones on its reinterred remains. Looking at Grandfather Ysmael's gravestone, I discovered that people in the WASP corporation misread the old inscription and misspelled my grandfather's name on the stone as "Parra," instead of Peña. And, like Melville, they called him "Ishmael." This reminded me of my first visit at age eighteen to the grave of my Mexican grandmother.

She had lived in the East Los Angeles *barrio*, but my father buried her in Glendale's Forest Lawn, a manicured tribute to WASP affluence. While looking

---

27. Peritonitis is a life-threatening inflammation of the peritoneum, the membrane that encloses abdominal organs. Infection was far more deadly before antibiotics became widely available in the 1940s.

at her gravestone, I had knelt in tears, praying to "unfold the mystery and secrecy about her family," as my teenage journal expressed it that day. A month after this 1962 visit, I learned from the hospital record of her final illness that Quinn on her gravestone was a post mortem alias that Dad conferred on Carmen B. Peña. I never returned to her grave, even though I took Jan and our growing number of children to Forest Lawn several times to see its stunning Hall of Crucifixion.

Late July 1977–Exciting News

From the retrospective account I wrote in the fall: "While I was in Arizona doing research in late July, I received word from Jan that Frank Fox of the BYU History Department had telephoned with exciting news. He has been working for two years on a diplomatic history of J. Reuben Clark, Jr. and he had recommended to Bob Thomas of BYU that I be added to those working on the Clark project in order to achieve Marion G. Romney's urgent demand that the full biography be forthcoming in two years.[28]

"Frank proposed that I be assigned to write a study of J. Reuben Clark Jr. as a Church leader, in view of my extensive background in LDS history. Frank asked permission to give Robert K. Thomas a copy of my dissertation. I gave him a copy for that purpose, but expressed the feeling that once Thomas had read my dissertation, that he would veto any recommendation that I be involved in the Clark project."

I remembered too clearly his criticism of Lester Bush exactly three years before: "You just don't publish anything from temple minutes, even if you have access to them!" My dissertation likewise quoted from minutes of the apostles and First Presidency.

July-August 1977–Articles in LDS Church's Magazine

Leonard Arrington had asked his staff historian Ronald W. Walker and me to combine the articles we had separately written about the arts in pioneer Utah, and the result appeared as a co-authored essay in the July issue of the *Ensign*.[29] In August, the magazine finally published my faithfully revisionist article about Brigham Young's profound spirituality.[30]

Mid-August 1977–A Lying Son of Two Mexicans

While doing research in Los Angeles, I decided to speak with Dad about

---

28. See Frank W. Fox, *J. Reuben Clark: The Public Years* (Provo, UT: BYU Press and Deseret Book Company, 1980). In the book's preface, Fox acknowledges "David [sic] Michael Quinn" as a reader of later stages of the book manuscript. Marion G. Romney (1897–1988) was ordained an apostle in 1951. He served as a counselor in every First Presidency from 1972 until his death. F. Howard Burton, *Marion G. Romney: His Life and Faith* (Salt Lake City: Bookcraft, 1988).

29. See Ronald W. Walker and D. Michael Quinn, "Virtuous, Lovely or of Good Report: How the Church Has Fostered the Arts," *Ensign,* July 1977.

30. See D. Michael Quinn, "Brigham Young: Man of the Spirit," *Ensign,* Aug. 1977.

our heritage. After dinner in Glendale, we talked for more than an hour, but the outcome was not pleasant, as my renewed journal noted retrospectively:

"Although I was 33 years old with 4 children of my own, Dad still sought to lie to me at every opportunity about his past and his family. He was truthful only about those things he had learned (from his embittered former wife Kaye) that I had already discovered.

"He put on such a solemn, genuine appearance as he told me things I knew were outright lies. I never let on to him that I realized he lied, but instead expressed gratitude to him that we could talk at last about his past and family."

His wife, Beverly, however, let me know that she was reading about Dad's childhood and youth in Anthony Quinn's autobiography, *The Original Sin*.[31] An independent dental hygienist for two decades before their marriage, her sweet personality seemed to have a mellowing effect on Dad. In some respects.

Although he remained a New Dealer and liberal Democrat on most issues (for which I admired him), Dad sounded like a WASP redneck in his complaints later that day about "illegal immigrants." He was unhappy about their influence on LA's garment industry, where immigrant sweatshops undercut the sales of the well-established companies he worked for, and suppressed the wages of longtime workers like him. This had caused him to abandon that industry and become a licensed realtor.

I nodded, saying nothing. But I thought about Grandpa Ysmael and Grandma Carmen crossing the Rio Grande River as "wetbacks" from Mexico. Dad was my anti-mentor for history.

Mid-August 1977–A Star of David and Me

Upon leaving Dad's home, I drove to Glendale's Reform synagogue, Mount Sinai, which I had attended in my late teens. In its gift shop, I found a perfect symbol to merge my feelings about Judaism with my devotion to Mormonism: a silver pendant with a symbol for a tribe of Israel in each of twelve triangular compartments that formed a filigreed Star of David. The bottommost triangle held the symbol for the Tribe of Joseph, my tribe (through Ephraim) according to the patriarchal blessing I received at age fourteen.

For eleven years, I would wear my LDS temple garments over the silver chain which suspended this Jewish pendant at the center of my chest—over my heart, under my covenants.

30 September 1977–God "Has Governed Circumstances in Your Life"

Those are words I never expected to hear about my PhD dissertation. But

---

31. Anthony Quinn (1915–2001) wrote two autobiographies. His first was *The Original Sin* (New York: Little, Brown and Company, 1972).

that is what BYU's academic vice-president said to me, as quoted in the first daily entry of my resumed journal. A month after I returned to teach three courses of American history, our visit lasted for ninety minutes.

Robert K. Thomas began our conversation by saying: "Michael, I read every page of your dissertation, and I was impressed that you were exactly the man needed for the Clark project. You studied some very sensitive and potentially controversial matters in relation to the general authorities, but at every point you handled the data and interpretations sensitively and skillfully [without] cheap editorializing, but instead you consistently reaffirmed the Church's values and the Gospel's principles amidst a candid discussion of its human and fallible leaders."

I was speechless. It was as if he was repeating those sentiments from various entries in my handwritten journals since 1971. I didn't point out to Bob Thomas that he would have had nothing to read if I had self-censored my dissertation according to the instructions he gave to BYU's historians last April.

He now explained why Stanford-trained Frank Fox was asked to write a scholarly biography. J. Reuben Clark's children were "very dissatisfied" with what the original biographer, David H. Yarn, had submitted. A devout BYU philosopher, his simplistic narrative seemed to be written for adolescents—according to BYU's academic vice-president.

Now, Thomas said, my dissertation had impressed Clark's children, who "were very enthusiastic" about my becoming the biographer of their father as counselor to the LDS president. "I finally brought your name and our proposal to Marion G. Romney, and he was especially impressed that in writing for non-Mormons you so consistently avoided polemics and provided skillful interpretation."

It's good that I wasn't standing. A feather could have floored me. However, his only quote from this First Presidency counselor brought me down to earth. "Brother Romney said: 'Brother Thomas, I do not know this young man. Is he priesthood broke?' Thomas said that he did not know exactly what that meant, but he assumed Brother Romney was asking if I was willing to listen to counsel."

I had been around enough ranchers to understand that President Romney wanted to know if a spirited colt has been tamed (broken). I clearly wasn't, yet I listened.

My journal continued: "Thomas also added, 'Michael, I often feel uncomfortable when people claim to see the hand of the Lord in matters in which they have personal commitments, but I have been impressed that the Lord has governed circumstances in your life and experiences to converge at this uniquely propitious time. ... Moreover, your choice of research into the LDS administrative history provided you with a background that no one else in the Church now has, and as if by some design, your own study ends just as J. Reuben Clark enters the Presidency. ... For these and other personal reasons, I cannot help but feel that the Lord has directed these affairs.'"

Then it was time for me to accept or reject the offer to "be immediately released from teaching as soon as a substitute could be found." That was so I could work full-time on a biography of J. Reuben Clark.

Thomas added: "You will have to have access to the most sensitive of all Church records—the minutes of the First Presidency, and you will be given access to all lesser sources that you need." Although he gave me the opportunity to think this over a while, it took me a New York minute.

1 October 1977–Moving to the Lower Avenues

Jan and I had already sold our Salt Lake City house on Lincoln Street and bought a much older four-bedroom house on Third Avenue, between O and P streets. It gave us the space we needed as our four children grew. We moved in today.

Craig Bradley, a son of this stake's president, sold it to us. He didn't even try to back out of the deal after he discovered that there would be months of delay in the construction of his new house—requiring him to move his family into a small, leased house and to put some of his furniture in storage. What a *Mensch*!

Craig and Jan became acquainted in junior high school. Our purchase of his remodeled old house was a sweetheart deal in which he accepted the points (reduced valuation) of my low-interest mortgage from the US Veterans' Administration, for which I then reimbursed him in cash.

VA mortgage rules specifically prohibited such an under-the-table deal, but—without it—few veterans could get a house seller to accept the loss of income required by the VA's point system, which was intended to help veterans to buy affordable housing. This was a double-bind, common enough in American society that my generation called it "a Catch-22." This was from reading Joseph Heller's hilarious anti-war novel by that title.

Just before establishing this new home on Third Avenue, I wrote in my journal: "In my relationship with Jan, our marriage has been the most fulfilling to both of us these past five months than it has for the past six or seven years prior to that." At least, that's how things seemed to me. In a few weeks, Jan tearfully told me: "We don't deserve such a beautiful house, because our marriage is so unhappy."

Her words finalized my decision to publish my response to the Tanners anonymously.[32] In addition to a renewed prospect of divorce, I lived with

---

32. Writing it anonymously as "A Latter-day Saint Historian," Quinn printed the booklet *Jerald and Sandra Tanner's Distorted View of Mormonism: A Response to Mormonism–Shadow or*

Quinn family in their Third Avenue home in Salt Lake City. Back row, left to right: Jan, Mary, Mike. Front row, left to right: Moshe, Lisa, and Adam. *Courtesy Quinn family.*

the anxiety of being exposed as gay—despite my efforts to avoid homosexual temptations. I didn't want my reply to anti-Mormonism to be dismissed simply because of my failures in life or due to any public humiliations that might one day occur. So I left it anonymous. That was what Leonard wanted for prudential reasons, and I didn't explain my personal ones to anyone.

12 October 1977–Official Church Historian's Plight

From my journal, concerning the Western History Association's meeting in Portland, Oregon: "It seems like months—perhaps years—since Leonard and I have had a long discussion. This was one of the most open and frank discussions we have ever had—especially on Leonard's part.

Reality? in 1977. The Tanners published their rebuttal pamphlet, *Answering Dr. Clandestine: A Response to the Anonymous LDS Historian*, in 1978. In it, they established that Quinn had written the criticism, partially because Quinn characteristically used the Latin phrase *post hoc ergo propter hoc,* which appeared in *Distorted View.*

"He said that G. Homer Durham [a recently appointed general authority Seventy] was more restrictive as manager of the Historical Department than Joseph Anderson had been. He said that Brother Durham sees it as his purpose to avoid any use of the Church archives that might antagonize the 1st Presidency or Quorum of the Twelve or cause them to feel suspicion about the Historical Department."

Leonard added, "Brother Durham is preventing us from fulfilling our mission and calling as we understood it to come from the First Presidency. A person ought to be allowed to fulfill his responsibility as he sees fit and if they fire him for it, then let it be.

"I enjoyed the meal with Leonard (Hawaiian porpoise steak, at his suggestion), but I felt somber as I reflected on the depth of his suffering at the hands of petty bureaucrats and officious censors who refuse to allow him to fulfill his role as Church Historian. God spare me from such a situation!"

13 October 1977–"Mormons Have Finally Found a *Real* Historian!"

Those were the startling words that W. Turrentine Jackson whispered to Leonard Arrington after I gave my paper on the Mormon hierarchy as a Power Elite in the American West. Professor Jackson was a noted western historian and had served as this past year's president of the Western History Association.[33]

As my journal noted, he said this after I expressed in response to the paper's commentator, Larry Foster: "I plead guilty to 'overproving' (as he criticized), but said that I was reacting to the simplistic generalizations and support that have characterized Mormon historiography in the main.

"I also acknowledged that I spoke first to a Mormon audience because I felt that it was important for Mormons to see their history as *process* rather than as a series of discrete 'deus ex machina' experiences. But I said that I also felt an obligation and desire to speak to the audience of non-Mormon scholars about a movement that I feel has had profound social historical influence."

Those 1977 priorities of message and audience characterized everything I ever published. To Mormons and non-Mormons, I whispered between the lines of each article, essay, and book: "Take it or leave it, but don't expect me to present LDS history any differently than I always have."

18 October 1977–Unpleasant Meeting about Research Access

From my journal: "Today I met with G. Homer Durham to arrange the preliminaries for my doing research on the Clark project. It was not a pleasant encounter.

"I barely got his grudging acceptance of the possibility that he would

---

33. William Turrentine Jackson (1915–2000) was a professor of Western US history at UC Davis. He debunked stereotypes of small property owners and rugged individualism in the West by showing that federal subsidies and international capital were key in the West's development.

allow me to see the minutes of [the business] organizations in which Pres. Clark served as director. Even that was tentative, it seemed.

"'Just get on with this book and get it done,' Homer Durham said. 'Not many people will read it. It won't be the last or best book on Reuben Clark, and don't try to write like a Samuel Eliot Morrison on this book.[34] Just get it done and don't get distracted from that purpose.'

"In all, I found G. Homer Durham to be arrogant and insulting.

"I told Jim [McConkie tonight] that I felt this appointment to work on the Clark project would either make or break me with the 'Brethren.' ... I know myself to be a flawed vessel and I doubt that the Apostle Paul would classify me as a vessel of gold or silver [2 Timothy 2:20]. But even if I am made of clay, I know that there are purposes I can fulfill for the building of the Kingdom of God and strengthening of His Saints. Once I do that, then if I crumble, I can at least feel satisfaction in providing the service of which I was capable." Knowing of my homosexuality, Jim understood.

21 October 1977–Church Patriarch Displays Occult Artifact

Because of my Yale dissertation, E. Gary Smith contacted me about doing a book-length history of the Presiding Patriarch's Office. He had served in the British Mission until eighteen months before I arrived there. His father, current Patriarch Eldred G. Smith, had custody of diaries, correspondence, and artifacts of their ancestral line back to Joseph Smith's brother Hyrum and father Joseph Sr. I was eager to see these.

This Friday evening, Gary took me to his father's house, where Patriarch Smith spent hours talking with me about how he had been devalued and administratively abused from the church Presidency of Heber J. Grant to current President Kimball. His narrative was sadly significant, but I was most interested in examining the earliest documents he had from Joseph Smith's family.

The patriarch showed me what he described as a "cabalistic" document that had been "passed down" from Joseph Sr. to Hyrum, and from Hyrum's widow to each eldest son in turn.[35] Eldred Smith asked what I thought of it. Staring at this gold-colored parchment, inscribed with numerous symbols and words in various languages, I said it was "certainly unusual." I didn't have a clue what any of it meant or why Joseph Smith Sr. had possessed something so strange in the early nineteenth century.

---

34. Elliot Morrison (1887–1976) was a prodigious writer who won the Pulitzer Prize for two books. He and his team wrote a fifteen-volume book series titled *History of United States Naval Operations in World War II,* published by Little, Brown and Company, 1947–62.

35. When Hyrum Smith was assassinated in 1844, he was polygamously married to Mary Fielding, her sister Mercy Fielding Thompson, and Catherine Phillips. These artifacts passed through Mary Fielding. D. Michael Quinn, *Early Mormonism and the Magic World View* (Salt Lake City: Signature Books, 1987), 78.

I wasn't ignorant of cabala as a medieval Jewish system of occult knowledge. I remembered a brief discussion of it in James A. Michener's historical novel, *The Source*, but had long-since forgotten what the *Encyclopaedia Britannica* said about it. Still, I had absolutely no interest in such an arcane topic, and quickly asked Patriarch Smith to show me the journal of his ancestor Hyrum. *That* was evidence I could understand and interpret immediately.

I was so tunnel visioned at this time that I didn't even think of the talk that LDS institute director Reed C. Durham Jr. had given three years earlier. I'd carefully read a typescript of his emphasis on Joseph Smith's connection to the occult through a Jupiter Talisman.

There were dots to connect, but I didn't see them while looking at the golden parchment or remembering it vaguely for years later. Some non-Mormon scholars would have recognized the Smith family's artifact as a lamen of ritual magic.[36] However, I was unaware of any context for the strange item that Eldred Smith had shown to me tonight, and my daily journal didn't even mention something that seemed so unimportant.

In summarizing this meeting after I left Patriarch Smith's house at 1:00 a.m., my journal concluded: "It was certainly the most extraordinary meeting I have ever had with a general authority of the LDS Church." And it would not be the last such extraordinary meeting, particularly with current LDS president Spencer W. Kimball, about whom the patriarch had complained.

Eight years later, I would no longer be indifferent to the artifact Eldred Smith showed me. Its existence and inscriptions became keys for my understanding the participation of Joseph Sr. and Jr. in the occult activity of the treasure quest during the early 1820s.

As for the history of the church patriarch's office, I would soon write Gary Smith that the documents he had were so sketchy that it would require years of research for too many needles in haystacks. He eventually joined forces with English convert Irene M. Bates, who wanted to do her UCLA dissertation on the subject as a housewife historian. They would coauthor an excellent book about it.[37] In the process, Irene became one of my dearest friends.

23 October 1977–President of Young Men, Salt Lake 27th Ward

From my journal: "At sacrament meeting I was sustained president of the Young Men's organization and Priest Adviser. This will be a challenge but I desire to be close to the youth.

"I spoke at a fireside at the bishop's for the MIA. They all (the active ones,

36. From Latin *lamina* (plate or coin), a lamen is a pendant worn around the neck, used for magical purposes, such as evoking or invoking particular spirits.

37. See Irene M. Bates and E. Gary Smith, *Lost Legacy: The Mormon Office of Presiding Patriarch* (Urbana: University of Illinois, 1996).

anyway) got into his house, so it was a small group. I spoke on Joseph Smith as a youth and human being with understandable experiences and trials."

29 October 1977–Hosting First of Many Soirees on Third Avenue

From my journal: "The evening went very well, and of the 150 or so people we invited, between 50 and 75 showed up. That was a tremendous improvement over our last open house at Georgetown Square in 1972 when 90% of the people we invited [from the University 3rd Ward] did not show up."

30 October 1977–Bishop Predicts My Getting Access to Documents

From my journal: "He [Richard G. Horne] set me apart as president of the Young Men's MIA and of the Aaronic Priesthood, and then he said he felt moved to give me a special blessing. He said that I had been called of God to perform a work of importance in research and writing, and he blessed me that I would be able to conduct that work as I wanted to and that I would be successful in conducting that research as I felt it needed to be done. ...

"Afterwards, Jan asked me if I had told the bishop of my obstacles in doing the research (on the Clark project and elsewhere) as I wanted to and as I felt the Lord wanted me to. I told her that I had not told him of these problems as it was something I didn't think necessary or wise to discuss too freely.

"She said that she had nearly cried as she listened to his blessing, and she remarked: 'His blessing proves to me that everyone else is wrong and that you have been right all the time about what you feel needs to be done in Church history.'"

Aside from Jan's love for me, such faith-promoting experiences reinforced her efforts to be supportive of my work in Mormon history, to protect me, to suppress her own unhappiness, and to remain with me. Like several times before today and others after, divorce became a non-starter.

More to the point, my ward bishop's promise was remarkably fulfilled with regard to HDC's director G. Homer Durham. It took nine days.

31 October 1977–BYU's President as My Advocate

From my journal: "I went to Dallin Oaks' office at 5:15 and waited until 5:45 for him to return from a meeting. We talked alone in his office until 6:30 p.m. ...

"I outlined the nature of G. Homer Durham's comments and attitudes. Dallin Oaks shook his head and said: 'Homer is a friend of long standing and we felt his appointment was a tremendous asset for the work of Church history. But a couple of members of the Twelve who distrust the work of the Historical Department have undoubtedly gotten to Homer and have put unauthorized pressure on him to conduct affairs at HDC the way they feel matters should be handled. This is unfortunate and out of the proper channels of authority, but it is a reality when men have the power that exists in the Quorum of the Twelve Apostles.' ...

"He paused and then said, 'We must try to sidestep Homer Durham without making an enemy of him, if we can.'

"Dallin Oaks agreed that a forceful letter should be sent to the Presidency, but he felt that his letter should be a forceful endorsement to a separate letter under my signature.... Oaks said that he was going to have a regularly scheduled meeting with the 1st Presidency on Wednesday and he wanted to present the letters then."

8 November 1977–HDC Managing Director's 180-Degree Reversal

From my journal concerning today's meeting with G. Homer Durham: "When he got to the list of documents I requested, he surprised me by saying emphatically: 'You will have to see these documents, the minutes of the 1st Presidency, and the others, but I do not want you to get lost in them.' This statement, which he repeated more than once in our conversation was virtually the opposite of his statements in our earlier conversation."

23 November 1977–Uncle Becomes Stepfather

Only days after the death of my Aunt Joy from heart failure, Uncle Vaude Nye proposed marriage to my mother. This shocked Mom, who had regarded him like a dear brother for twenty-eight years, but Nana was pushing Mom into the marriage. At her own daughter's funeral, she had told Vaude to propose!

Because Jan and I loved him, we thought it was a good idea—even though very rushed. It didn't occur to me to ask Mom if she thought she could feel romantic love for Vaude.

Mom had always felt the stigma in modern Mormon culture of being a divorced woman, and she often expressed sadness that I was not sealed to her in the temple. Vaude (an LDS convert) emphasized that this was now possible, and he even wanted to adopt me legally. I told him that I could never consider adoption—because I had a father I loved—but would be glad to be sealed to Vaude and Mom in the temple.

I didn't know that my grandparents had legally adopted him as a son nearly seventeen years before. Prepared by my former Bishop Reed E. Callister, this document of 1 January 1961 gave Vaude "the right of inheritance" as a son. If Mom knew that he was her stepbrother, she never mentioned it to me—nor did anyone else. I didn't learn about it until all the principals were dead. Was this another family secret?

Anyway, exactly seven weeks after her sister Joy's death, Mom and Vaude were sealed for time and eternity in the Salt Lake Temple. Then I was sealed to them over the altar as an eternal child. Jan and I hosted their wedding reception at her Aunt Margaret's house.

Mom told me that Vaude was disappointed that I didn't call him "Dad." I never could, just as I never referred to my father-in-law as "Dad," even though Jan told me that Roy would like me to at least once in a while.

Yet I often told Jan that I had a closer relationship to Roy Darley as my father-in-law than I had with my own. I spent a lifetime trying to cope with my father's emotional distance and could call no one else "Dad."

23 November 1977–First Presidency Authorizes My Access–In Part

From my journal concerning the evening meeting with Dallin Oaks and Robert Thomas about the letter from First Presidency secretary Francis M. Gibbons to Oaks in response to his and my request for access to documents:

"After agreeing about the negative sides of the letter (including the flat refusal to allow me to see minutes of the 1st Presidency) we all agreed that it was positive that I was apparently given ready access to HDC materials I needed (after I had 'exhausted' the Clark papers), and that it was also positive that no comment was made about my request for other MSS in the 1st Presidency vault. Oaks said that in six months or so we could make another stab at those. All in all, I felt good about the meeting and the letter."

12 December 1977–Anonymous Defense of Mormonism

Today I began distributing my anonymous printing of *A Response to Jerald and Sandra Tanner's Distorted View of Mormonism*. The title page identified me only as "A Latter-day Saint Historian," and there was a backstory.

Sometime after I stopped keeping a journal in July 1976, I was called into Leonard Arrington's office. There I found Reed Durham, now only a senior instructor at the University of Utah's LDS Institute of Religion, over which he had been associate director (then director) from the early 1960s until 1974. He was demoted from the position of institute director after his 1974 talk about Joseph Smith, Freemasonry, and the talisman.

Leonard told him at this private meeting that I was writing a rebuttal of *Shadow or Reality?*, and asked if Reed had suggestions. He didn't and seemed oddly non-committal. I sat there, wishing that Leonard had left him uninformed.

Perhaps sensing that Reed had misgivings, Leonard asked him to keep this project confidential. The Historical Department might want to use some version of what I wrote as an unsigned reference work for those who made inquiries about this anti-Mormon publication.

In their first published comments about the anonymous *Response*, the Tanners would write that "one of the top Mormon historians did tell us in a telephone conversation in Dec. 1976 that a manuscript had been prepared to refute all the allegations contained in our work." Eventually, they published the melodramatic, exaggerated account that their unnamed historian source gave them about his (Reed Durham's) private meeting with Leonard and me in 1976.[38]

As he had informed the Tanners, HDC delayed any decision about what to do with the manuscript I had completed by the end of that year. It was my creation, but I didn't care if HDC staffers like Dave Mayfield reworked it or chopped it up to use as answers to questions by people who had been disturbed by *Shadow or Reality?*.

I didn't expect HDC to publish it, but instead to use it as a resource for answering letters written by faithful Mormons. Preoccupied with preparing from scratch for each day's classes at BYU from fall 1976 to summer 1977, I didn't have time to think much about how Leonard and his associates regarded what I had written. My attention was equally diverted during my hectic schedule of research.

However, in late summer of 1977, Leonard told me that the Historical Department wasn't going to use what I had written. As my journal stated, without his knowing that I was its author, "Bro. Durham called it 'brilliant' but said that he did not think it would be necessary to publish it, as it might create more questions than it answered."

Without giving details, Leonard told me that there were objections to its approaches, style, examples, and arguments. "Don't they even want to paraphrase sections of it in answering letters from people the Tanners have disillusioned?" I asked. Leonard said that he didn't agree, but the answer was "No." I was both uncomprehending and angry: "Then I'll borrow the money to publish it myself—under my own name!" But Leonard wanted it to be anonymous.

I thought I could borrow enough to pay for 300–500 cheap 8x10 photocopies of typed text, but Leonard promised to give me $600. He said that I had to leave him out of any further knowledge of what I did with it.

Through Jim Allen, the College of Social Sciences prepared a camera-ready version of the anonymous response. I laughed when he reported to me that Dean Hickman said: "I've read that paper you gave me to type, and I know who the author is. It was written by Richard Bushman!" That reconfirmed the wisdom of Leonard's wish that the author remain unnamed. More people might read it to figure out who wrote it, and I was eager for it to have wide readership.

Leonard's generosity caused me to aim very high. I contacted print shops to see how many copies of a booklet I could get by adding some of my own money ($500–$700, as I recall) to what Leonard was giving. As I wrote in my journal on December 12, when I paid the printer: "Two months ago I

---

38. See Jerald and Sandra Tanner, *Answering Dr. Clandestine: A Response to the Anonymous Historian* (Salt Lake City: Utah Lighthouse Ministry, 1978), 2.

decided to use my several hundred dollars of [unspent NEH] research funds for a trip for Jan and me to the Orient this spring. ... That money is basically all gone as of today. It has been put to better use." I doubt Jan was happy about trading her trip to Asia for printing a pamphlet, but she never complained about my decision.

Its thirtysomething printer—who was missing fingers on one hand due to a machine cutting accident—seemed personally supportive of the project and accepted the amount of money I offered. I didn't ask, but he may have even done this print job for no profit. In any event, I was thrilled that my budget of about $1,200 resulted in 2,000 nice-looking booklets of sixty-three pages each.

On December 12, I paid about $100 for stamps to mail 350 copies by 3rd class delivery to every LDS Institute and Mission Home in the United States and Canada, plus to the presiding officers of stakes and wards in the West, and to various Mormon historians. My journal described this as "my Christmas present to the Church," but I didn't tell Leonard about those mailings. He knew only that I was giving him fifty copies and that I intended to transfer 1,600 copies of my *Response* to bookseller Sam Weller.[39]

Distributing them was a problem since I wanted to remain anonymous. I decided to pay one month's rent on a storage locker, where the booklets would remain until picked up by employees of Weller's bookstore, to which I anonymously sent the key and instructions. The journal described the above as "my comic opera arrangements."

A shrewd businessman with this windfall of free booklets, Sam sold them for fifty cents each. I knew that word of mouth would spread among Weller's regular clients, who were accustomed to finding unusual or rare Mormon books at his Zion's Bookstore.

17 December 1977–Politically Left of Stalin

From my journal: "Jan and I drove down to Provo for a Christmas dinner for the History Department at the home of the Alexanders. It was a good dinner and afterwards there was a comic presentation of an interview by Orson Scott Card [son-in-law of Professor James B. Allen] with Martin Hickman, dean of the college, who was at the party. [40] Hickman's answers were taken from tape recordings of his class lectures and remarks to faculty meetings. ...

39. Sam Weller (1921–2009) operated Sam Weller's Zion Bookstore in downtown Salt Lake City until 1997. Now known as Weller Book Works, the independent bookstore has sold new, used, and rare books in Salt Lake City since 1929.

40. Orson Scott Card (1951–) is an award-winning writer who specializes in science fiction and fantasy novels. He also has written scripts and Mormon history-themed novels. Card has publicly opposed gay relationships, writing that "Married people attempting to raise children with the hope that they, in turn, will be reproductively successful, have every reason to oppose the

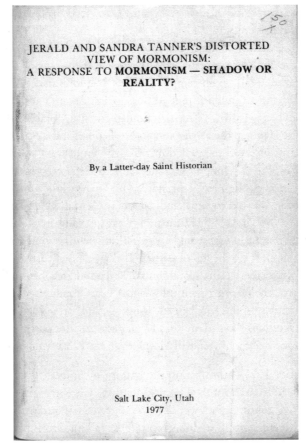

JERALD AND SANDRA TANNER'S DISTORTED
VIEW OF MORMONISM:
A RESPONSE TO **MORMONISM — SHADOW OR
REALITY?**

By a Latter-day Saint Historian

Salt Lake City, Utah
1977

Anonymous pamphlet written and printed by
Quinn, 1977. *Signature Books archives.*

"In one of these sequences Card asked, 'Dean Hickman, two of the younger members of the History Department are Frank Fox and D. Michael Quinn. In political terms, how would you compare Fox and Quinn with a person like Joseph Stalin?' The entire group roared when Hickman's voice said: 'Stalin is on the right!'"

Even though I regarded Stanford-trained Fox as somewhat conservative, science fiction writer Card was not far off about my place on the political spectrum. After all, I had been a democratic socialist for a decade.

Shortly after joining BYU's faculty, I also began contributing to the American Civil Liberties Union, Amnesty International, Common Cause, Greenpeace, and the Sierra Club. I didn't trust large corporations any farther

normalization of homosexual unions." Grady Smith, "'Enders Game' author answers critics: Gay marriage issue is moot," *Entertainment Weekly,* July 8, 2013.

than I could throw one of their mainframe computers, so I also cheered for Nader's Raiders as consumer advocates.[41]

Under the thumb of ultra-conservative Ezra Taft Benson (now next in line to be the church president), BYU refused to allow any of those liberal organizations to establish on-campus chapters. Not long after LDS President Spencer W. Kimball publicly praised both Anita Bryant's anti-homosexual campaign and Jerry Falwell's Christian fundamentalist Moral Majority of political activists, I joined their main antagonist: People for the American Way.[42]

American conservatism seemed increasingly reminiscent of Eric Hoffer's 1951 analysis of the rise of political fanaticism in his *The True Believer*. After Ronald Reagan's election as US president and Utah's plunge into right-wing Republicanism, I would vote for candidates of the Socialist Party and Socialist Workers Party. Because voting Democratic was a lost cause in Utah, those were protest votes that I thought would give political scientists something to write concerning support for the minor parties. That's what Socialists were even nationally, as were Libertarians, Communists, Peace and Freedom voters, etc.

I was certainly left-wing politically. But if I was a radical, I was a private one, not an activist. As an armchair left-winger, I didn't attend a meeting of any of the liberal groups I joined, nor did I sign petitions, nor participate in their other activities. Being a historian of Mormonism was exhausting enough to me.

27 December 1977–Immunizing the Latter-day Saints

From my journal about the History Division's Christmas party at the Arringtons: "We got on the subject of telling the truth of our history and why the authorities resist it. I was doing most of the talking at this point and said that men like Boyd Packer dislike our approach because they feel we will only cause people to ask more questions, and they are afraid of the Saints asking questions. They feel they are protecting the Saints, whereas we feel they are making them vulnerable to attacks by people like the Tanners or by deceptive schismatics.

"I said they could not seem to understand that we were trying to expose the average Saints to the broad perspectives of truth and history in order to protect them from being overwhelmed by a barrage of truth or half-truth of our history by a polemicist.

"Up to this point Leonard had been generally quiet, but he interjected at this point that we were seeking to 'immunize' the Saints by presenting the

41. In the 1960s, consumer protection activist Ralph Nader (1934–) led unpaid college students and law students (Nader's Raiders) in efforts resulting in the first seatbelt laws, the Freedom of Information Act, "sunshine laws," and the Clean Air Act.

42. Several prominent liberal Americans, led by Hollywood producer Norman Lear, founded People for the American Way in 1981. The organization's stated mission is to oppose right-wing extremism and build a democratic society that embraces opportunity, equality, and justice for all.

broad perspective of our history. That was a tremendous idea that I have often described without realizing it." I would use the analogy in my talk to BYU students and faculty less than four years later.

30 December 1977—Jerald Tanner Reacts

Unaware that Reed Durham was collaborating with the Tanners, I was mentally unprepared for the phone call I received this evening. From my journal, in parts:

"After I got home, the phone rang and a high-pitched man's voice asked: 'Are you the author of *Jerald and Sandra Tanner's Distorted View of Mormonism: A Response to Mormonism: Shadow or Reality?*' ... He said: 'My information is that in a meeting in the LDS Historical Department Leonard Arrington asked you to write such a document.'

"I replied that I had no knowledge of such a meeting or conversation. Finally I asked who it was I was talking to, and he said, as I had suspicioned, that he was Jerald Tanner. ... He may have asked me a few more times if I had written the pamphlet, which I flatly denied, before our phone conversation ended. ...

"If asked again about this matter, I think I will adopt the policy of not assisting in identifying the author by the process of elimination that will be possible as Tanner and his friends ask various historians if they did or did not write the pamphlet."

The last approach is what I should have said at the beginning of our phone call. However, caught completely off-guard, I lied repeatedly (and reluctantly) to Jerald Tanner.

He was calmly angry with me, but I soon heard that he phoned Weller in a fury this same day, demanding that he stop selling the pamphlet. I learned about their stormy conversation through nearly identical narratives from three sources. First, on December 31 from Weller's employee Wilford Clark, who had picked up the booklets from the storage locker. Second, from Forrest Baker, who related this account of the same conversation to his next-door neighbor Davis Bitton on January 15. From my journal:

"Davis' neighbor told of being in Zion's Bookstore about two weeks ago and was talking with Sam Weller when one of the workers said that Jerald Tanner was on the phone. Sam Weller went to the phone about six feet away, where Davis' neighbor overheard Sam Weller's side of the conversation: 'Yes ... No ... No, we don't know who wrote it ... Of course, we are going to sell them ...' At this point Davis' neighbor [Forrest Baker] said he could hear the voice of Tanner rise in volume, as did Weller's. After a few heated words, Weller said: 'All right, fine, then I'll see you in court!' and he hung up the phone. As Weller rejoined the group he exclaimed: 'Stupid son of a bitch!!'"

Third, on January 19, BYU religion professor Richard Anderson told me "that he was in Zion's Book Store earlier in the week and Sam Weller told him of his phone conversation with Tanner, which corresponded exactly with the matching portion of it as told me by Davis Bitton."

My worst fears about publishing the *Response* anonymously were fulfilled—and surpassed. Bombarded with inquiries by friends, foes, colleagues, students, reporters, and strangers, I made the judicious reply that I wouldn't confirm or deny authorship, because to do so would limit the range of guesses about an author who obviously wanted to remain anonymous among the limited number of LDS historians. I was privately embarrassed by my initial denials on the phone to Jerald Tanner, but was *appalled* that Leonard found himself in the position of making repeated denials that he had any knowledge of the booklet's origin.

As advocates of the New Mormon History, we were caught in the tangled webs of our best intentions of faith. I felt embarrassed empathy for LDS headquarters and its generations of compromising defenders. In his *Plain Account of Christian Perfection*, Methodist founder John Wesley had described such compromise as the "lie for God."[43]

---

43. Originally published in 1777, John Wesley's *Plain Account of Christian Perfection* describes his journey to comprehend and accept the doctrine of Christian holiness.

CHAPTER FIFTEEN

A PATH OF CONFLICT

1978–1980

22 January 1978–A "Gigantic Confrontation"

From my journal: "I keep asking myself if I (in all my weaknesses and failures) can be right and men of such dedication and uprightness be wrong? I feel that I am moving toward some gigantic confrontation with Church authority that will undoubtedly destroy me if I manifest the kind of stiff neckedness that I increasingly feel.

"Can such attitudes as I have be of God when they run so contrary to the policies and positions of men whom I sustain as God's leaders?"

5 February 1978–A Path of Conflict

From my journal: "I feel that I am well along a path to which I have been prepared and which may put me into conflict with Bro. Benson and others of God's servants. They have the personal and administrative power to do me a lot of damage if I become offensive to them, but I feel today that if such becomes the case, I will not feel bitterness nor hatred against them, but instead love and a conviction that they are good men who are seeking to do God's will as they see it. I cannot explain the contradiction in such a situation, but I believe that I can accept it."

9 February 1978–Long-Distance Runner and Gay Novels

From my journal: "I ran 5 miles in 35 minutes today, and then did 10 bench presses at 130 lbs, followed by 100 situps. I don't know how good my workout is, but it leaves me exhilarated and not fatigued."

As a result of this daily routine, my weight plummeted to 135 pounds. I had to increase my food intake in order to stay around 140. That was twenty pounds less than I weighed as a teenager. At 5'10", I now looked like the slender guys on the track team I had lusted for in high school. Next year, my journal noted that Omar Kader saw me in BYU's gym, "commented on how skinny I looked, and Omar said I almost looked emaciated."

After beginning this regimen, I read *The Front Runner*. Published by a woman in 1974, this novel was about a long-distance runner at college who is openly gay yet painfully celibate as he lusts for his coach. The middle-aged man finally comes out of the closet, ends his marriage, and begins a relationship with the young man.

Jan was very upset when I told her that I regarded this homosexual romance as "beautiful." Regardless, my actions didn't mimic fantasies of homosexual trysts.

Still, long-distance running made me look better to myself and other guys than ever before, and I liked that. I didn't stop this regimen until May 1987, when a lower-back injury made even walking painful. This was the only time period I ever consistently regarded myself as good-looking.

Decades later, I would meet author Patricia Nell Warren in LA We conversed several times about her famous gay novel and the frequently short-circuited efforts to make it into a Hollywood movie.

During the seven years since leaving the army, I had read homosexually inclined novels that were classics of modern literature housed in both the University of Utah's Marriott Library and Yale's Sterling Library. This included Thomas Mann's *Death In Venice* (1913), Jean Genet's *Our Lady of the Flowers* (1943), Yukio Mishima's *Confessions of a Mask* (1949), Andre Gide's *Corydon* (1950), Mishima's *Forbidden Colors* (1951), Genet's *Querelle of Brest* (1953), Mary Renault's *Charioteer* (1953), and her *Last of the Wine* (1956), William S. Burroughs' *Naked Lunch* (1959), and his *The Ticket That Exploded* (1962), James Baldwin's *Another Country* (1962), and his *Go Tell It On the Mountain* (1963), John Rechy's *City of Night* (1963), Michael Campbell's *Lord Dismiss Us* (1967), Rechy's *Numbers* (1968), Baldwin's *Tell Me How Long the Train's Been Gone* (1968), Burroughs' *Wild Boys* (1971), E. M. Forster's *Maurice* (1972), and Renault's *The Persian Boy* (1972).

While several of those were in stream-of-consciousness style, none were as hilarious as the 1969 non-gay classic *Portnoy's Complaint* by Philip Roth. He also wrote in that literary mode.

Nor were the others quite like the non-gay, drug-visioned, rambling narratives in Hunter Thompson's *Fear and Loathing in Las Vegas* (1972). Especially with these last two, several of those novels had *picaresque* anti-heroes to enjoy as much as Don Quixote.

"If I ever finish publishing Mormon history," I kept telling myself, "I want to write in the stream-of-consciousness style." In another life, perhaps. Baldwin would not have understood my ability to postpone.

13 February 1978–Mistaken for Hugh Nibley

From my journal: "I was at the Historical Department of the Church today. Glen Leonard said that he was told by Douglas Alder of Utah State University that someone had done a computer study (of all things!) on the anonymous pamphlet about the Tanners, and the conclusion of the content analysis was that the author was Hugh Nibley on a probability scale of 85% and the remaining probability was leaning toward James B. Allen. This is truly a very interesting situation."

Beginning with his pamphlet against Fawn M. Brodie's 1945 *No Man Knows My History*, Nibley was an occasional polemicist against anti-Mormons, as well as a gadfly critic of LDS culture.[1] Since he was also a multilingual genius, I rather liked this misidentification of him as the author of my pamphlet. That was how I saw myself in 1976, when I used the pseudonym Hugh Klein ("Little Hugh") with the printer.

17 February 1978–The Diaries of Church President David O. McKay

From my journal: "This morning I presented to Don Schmidt, Church Archivist, my request slip for the David O. McKay diaries.[2] Don acted as though I had handed him a snake. ... Don Schmidt had me go with him to Brother Durham's office. Don asked if Brother Durham was *sure* he wanted to give me access to the McKay diaries. Brother Durham looked again at the copy of the letter from Gibbons on behalf of the First Presidency, hesitated for a few moments, and then said for Don to let me see the diaries one volume at a time as they are doing with Adrian Cannon's access to the George Q. Cannon diaries, and that he would communicate with the First Presidency later about the McKay diaries, since Friday was an impossible day to consult with them.[3] I breathed a sigh of relief at this near brush with failure to get something that was almost within my grasp for research.

"I had been working on the McKay diaries for only an hour or two, when one of the secretaries came to my work area and told me that Brother Durham wanted to see me in his office right away. ... At one point he referred to historians who insisted on trying to discover whether leading persons used three or four pieces of toilet paper to cleanse themselves after a bowel movement." This was a crude version of apostle Boyd K. Packer's views.

17 February 1978–Confrontation, Then Clenched-Fist Salute

G. Homer Durham launched into a tirade about the anonymous *Response*

---

1. See Hugh Nibley, *No Ma'am, That's Not History: A Brief Review of Mrs. Brodie's Reluctant Vindication of a Prophet She Seeks to Expose* (Salt Lake City: Bookcraft, 1946).

2. Transcripts of McKay's presidential diaries were published in 2019. See Harvard S. Heath, ed., *Confidence amid Change: The Presidential Diaries of David O. McKay, 1951–1970* (Salt Lake City: Signature Books, 2019).

3. Adrian W. Cannon (1917–1991) was the grandson of George Q. Cannon (1827–1901), an influential apostle in the early church and keeper of extensive journals. For a description of the project to publish his journals and Adrian Cannon's involvement, see the "Project History" page of the online journals, titled "The Journal of George Q. Cannon, 1849–1901" (Salt Lake City: Church Historian's Press, 2018).

to the Tanners. He said he was very upset by its public availability, because he had specifically instructed Leonard Arrington not to publish it.

He now asked if I was its author. Taken aback by this new turn of events, I nonetheless immediately gave my now-standard response to such an inquiry.

From my journal: "Durham moderated the agitation in his voice, and quietly but firmly said to me in an earnest manner, 'Now I can appreciate your position of making no comment, but as a priesthood leader, regard this as a Personal Priesthood Interview, and tell me if you wrote that anonymous pamphlet.' I said that I could only restate my position that I would neither affirm nor deny authorship. ...

"Later in the day, as I stood outside Don Schmidt's office to get another volume of the McKay diaries, Durham walked by, winked at me, and gave me (what seemed to be) a good-natured clenched fist gesture.

"His manner frankly puzzles me. He is capable of doing a great deal of harm to my research access if I have sufficiently antagonized him." Within weeks, this general authority successfully vented his wrath about the anonymous pamphlet in another direction.

7 March 1978–Official Church Historian No More

From my journal: "I told Leonard that I had been informed that after six years of being officially sustained in General Conferences by appointment of the First Presidency as Church Historian, that he was no longer in that position.

"Leonard's response was so typical of him that I could have cried. 'Yes,' he said, 'and now I am finally relieved of having a title that implied that I had the responsibility of giving the official view of LDS history. Now we can go on with our work without that burden.'"

The timing of my mentor's humiliating demotion was too close to my confrontation with G. Homer Durham to be mere coincidence. He clearly blamed the anonymous pamphlet's publication on Leonard, whom this general authority undoubtedly charged with rank insubordination in Durham's subsequent meetings with apostle Packer and with the First Presidency. Leonard's comments to me the previous October showed that he was already in serious conflict with this lower-ranking general authority before its publication. My pamphlet was the last straw in Durham's back-breaking relationship with Leonard.[4]

What a sad outcome of my faith-promoting intentions!

---

4. Though Quinn believed his pamphlet was "the last straw" in the conflicted relationship between Arrington and G. Homer Durham, Arrington's diary shows that the pamphlet was a minor issue in a litany of concerns that Durham had with Arrington and the Historical Division. Gary James Bergera, ed., *Confessions of a Mormon Historian: The Diaries of Leonard J. Arrington, 1971–1997*, 3 vols. (Salt Lake City: Signature Books, 2018), 3:466–71, 474–78.

10 March 1978–Telling Truth about Changes in the Endowment

From my journal: "Jan and I had been invited by Harvey Wilhelm and his wife Molly (our friends from the Munich branch) to attend a special temple session in the Provo Temple where President [Orville] Gunther of the Temple would answer any questions about the temple ceremony for an hour before the session. ...

"President Gunther's answers and presentation provided me with no new information or insights, until he made reference to having read the 'original minutes of the Nauvoo Temple in the Archives of the Church,' which described the original endowment ceremony given in the Nauvoo temple as having lasted nine hours, and described that there were several preachers in the dramatization of the endowment rather than just one Protestant preacher as in the present dramatization, and that in the Nauvoo Temple, Satan in the Garden of Eden was represented by a man [William W. Phelps] who crawled on the floor after being cast out of the Garden.

"I *knew* that none of the documents in the Historical Department which contained records of the Nauvoo Temple had this information, and therefore I came up to President Gunther after the meeting and asked where he had obtained the information about the Nauvoo Temple ordinances. He again said that he had been privileged to examine the minutes of the Nauvoo Temple in 'the Archives of the Church,' and I asked him if he meant the Historical Department/Church Historian's Office, and he said no, that he meant the Archives of the Salt Lake Temple." Another walk-in vault (which I would be allowed to enter one day).

Ironically, his very insightful and faith-driven presentation upset our friends. I wondered if President Gunther remembered lecturing me nearly eight years earlier against telling controversial truths about the Mormon past.

12 March 1978–Preaching against Enforced Conformity

From my journal: "Arose early this morning to pray and make final additions to the outline for my remarks to the stake High Priest's Quorum meeting. I asked the Lord's Spirit to be with me in giving the talk[, just] as it had been with me in deciding what I would speak upon as I prepared last night. I asked Him to give me the strength and courage to say what I felt I needed to say, whether or not Ezra Taft Benson or other recognizable general authorities of the stake were in the audience. ...

"I chose as my introductory remarks the passage from D&C 107 [verse 99] that in the Priesthood everyone should learn his duty and how to act in the office to which he has been appointed. Then I quoted from a passage in the writings of Joseph Smith that I found last night wherein he stated in 1833 that the duty of the High Priest was to administer in spiritual things and to avoid monarchial government [*History of the Church* 1:338–39].

"I then spent fifteen minutes or so talking about monarchial government and what that meant about our presiding role as High Priests. I related the old story about the king who invited guests to his palace and had them stay overnight, requiring them to sleep in beds that were of only one size, even though his guests were of differing sizes. Being a ruthless person, the king caused his servants to stretch his guests on the rack until they were tall enough for his beds, or had his servants cut his guests down to size to fit the beds he had wanted everyone to fit.

"I said that too often we as Priesthood leaders seek to force the Latter-day Saints into a mold, and that in the process we are as violent upon their spiritual beings as the ruthless king was on the physical bodies of the guests who did not conform to the requirements for size. I gave examples from the D&C and from the writings of Paul that urged us to accept diversity within the Gospel and not demean those who were different and assume that difference meant disunion or inferiority.

"I then returned to the writings of Joseph Smith that High Priests were to administer in spiritual things, and related the examples of High Priests whom I had witnessed as they administered in spiritual things: the man who administered to me when I had polio, Ezra Taft Benson in giving me the missionary setting apart, the stake president['s counselor] who administered to the BYU student who had gone blind due to diabetes, and President David O. McKay as he walked to his car after dedicating our stake house in California.

"In giving my remarks, I felt the Spirit, felt that the congregation of High Priests of all ages were unified with me in the Spirit, and [I] totally forgot about the head congestion and throat constriction that had worried me prior to my speaking. Afterwards, the entire Stake Presidency and many of the men in the audience gave me enthusiastic thanks."

15 March 1978–"The Finest Sermon"

From my journal: "Today at the Historical Department I met Davis Bitton who is the secretary of the High Priest's Quorum in our stake and who heard and took extensive notes on my remarks on Sunday. Davis said that he is not a person who feels constrained to compliment friends, nor is he one to be extravagant in praise, but he feels that my talk on Sunday may have been the finest sermon he has ever heard in his Church experience."

25 March 1978–Leonard J. Arrington as *Persona Non Grata*

From my journal: "As I was leaving the Historical Department, Gordon Irving stopped me in the hallway and asked if I had seen the display of photographs of the Church Historians along the wall of the hallway leading to G. Homer Durham's office.[5] I said that I had not. Gordon said that there is no picture for Leonard as Church Historian."

1 April 1978–General Authority Chauvinism

From my journal: "Today was the first day of General Conference, and I spent all day listening and watching the televised conference talks. The most notable talk was for me the one given by Neal Maxwell on the role of women, in which he presented in glowing and sickening sweet terms all the stereotypes of the roles of men and women from the Victorian age and then glorified them as the godly ideal. ... The chauvinism of such statements is disgusting."[6]

18 April 1978–Becoming an American Social Historian

From my journal: "If I can establish a reputation as a social historian and specialist in group biography, then that will help me if the time comes that I become *persona non grata* at BYU." Within two months, I regarded this effort as a failure.

From my June 16 journal: "Within my mail I found a rejection slip for my prostitution in the Civil War paper I had submitted for the OAH [Organization of American Historians] meeting in New Orleans next April. ... My feeble effort to break out of my Mormon history mold has failed. The only significant scholarship I seem capable of is in Mormon history, yet I am stymied in getting all the essential sources to make the most important contributions necessary in that field.

"Moreover, I would like to achieve a scholarly reputation outside Mormon studies in case I find one day that I come under the ban within Church circles and need to get a job outside the happy valleys of Utah where Mormon history counts for nothing. If Ezra Taft Benson or Mark E. Petersen become President of the Church my work will count for nothing both within and without Mormonism."

22 April 1978–Frustrated Wordsmith

From my journal: "As I compare my work as a historian with the work of others, mine does not hold up very well. I have consistently been more concerned with the content of historical data and support than with style and readability. I have the ability to write quickly and reasonably well, and therefore I have been satisfied to turn in first drafts or second drafts at best for publication.

---

5. Gordon Irving (1948–) earned his honors BA degree from the University of Utah and was working as an historical associate for the Historical Department at this time, focusing on the church's legal history.

6. See Elder Neal A. Maxwell, "The Women of God," *Ensign*, May 1978.

"I am not even sure that I am capable of writing beautiful prose, as other historians have done who are as skillful as the best novelist or essayist. I look at my brief article on the rebaptisms of Nauvoo in the winter 1978 issue of *BYU Studies* and find that one of the final sentences has 83 words in it.[7] If I wrote as well as [British historian Arnold] Toynbee that would not be bad, but in my work an 83 word sentence is merely another evidence of sloppy writing. ...

"Eight years ago in Germany I consciously hoped that one day I would win the Pulitzer Prize in some category (at the time I was thinking of the novel, but with my usual arrogant pride I told Howard Lamar a year and a half ago that I hoped for it in history). As with many things in my life, I am aware of the problems but am unable or unwilling to do anything to correct them."

23 April 1978–"Thin Line between Courage and Rebellion"

From my journal concerning a talk I gave to the Douglas Ward's Sacrament Meeting (by invitation from its bishop): "I introduced my remarks by saying that often we hear the phrases, 'Follow the Brethren,' or 'If you follow the Brethren you can't go wrong,' and I said that if we examine the sacred history of our own dispensation we will be able to compare that sacred history to our own lives and see what lessons we can learn in regard to this common counsel about following our leaders.

"I pointed out the manifestations of apostasy and charges of apostasy within the First Presidency and Quorum of the Twelve during the lifetime of Joseph Smith, and said that in such a situation the question is: 'Which Brethren do we follow?' I said that the answer lies in personal revelation, and quoted from D&C and *Journal of Discourses* on that issue.

"The response was quite enthusiastic. As I have found in the past when speaking upon these themes that perhaps the general authorities would prefer not to be spoken of in the way I do, that a gratitude and acceptance of my remarks is manifested by young and old, conservative and liberal, convert and born member. I feel that I sense the needs of the membership of the Church, and I pray that the Lord will help me to be sensitive to their needs, to the Spirit, and to the sometimes-thin line between courage and rebellion. Bishop Dean Bitter was very happy to have me speak. "

27 April 1978–Selective Sloth

From my journal: "Jan asked me if I wanted to join her in working on the garden tonight, and I said that I would rather not tonight."

Before our first spring at the house on Third Avenue, my lazy streak had not been obvious. I gladly assisted Jan in cooking meals, helped her with the

---

7. See D. Michael Quinn, "The Practice of Rebaptism at Nauvoo," *BYU Studies* 18, no. 2 (Spring 1978): 226–32.

dishes, or did them myself, often changed dirty diapers, and eagerly did the laundry, vacuuming, or dusting inside. Likewise, outside our houses on Lincoln Street and Third Avenue, I routinely shoveled snow, took out the trash, mowed lawns, trimmed shrubs, and watered anything green.

However, I *hated* the back-breaking work of planting, weeding, and harvesting gardens. Every spring to autumn hereafter, my resistance against any of that was a constant source of aggravation for Jan, who diligently planted flowers, herbs, berries, and vegetables which she had to nag me to help her with. She understandably resented this.

Also, fatigued from 100-mile roundtrips to BYU, I wasn't eager to do the handyman's work of plumbing, plastering, painting, etc. I endlessly procrastinated such jobs, and usually wanted to use our limited funds to pay professionals. This caused more tensions with Jan.

26 May 1978–Latter-day Monastic Who Afflicts the Comfortable

From my journal: BYU English professor Neal Lambert and I "chatted about some of the problems in current Church experience, during which I said, 'The Church is extraordinarily important to me, but I do not need the fellowship of the Church as an institution. Pleasing the Brethren is not my goal, but pleasing my God is.

"'If my relationship with my God is all right, it doesn't matter much to me if others do not understand what I do. It matters even less to me if they disapprove of what I do, as long as I have the spiritual confirmation that my relationship and acceptance by God are in tact.' ...

"I told Neal that I was probably more cut out as a monastic than anything else, except for the fact that I am sensitive enough to the human condition and the pains of others to yearn to bind up wounds and comfort the afflicted, and (I guess) afflict the comfortable."

6 June 1978–Anticipating Change in Priesthood Restriction

From my journal: "I have hoped that examination of the [unavailable] William Clayton diaries would indicate that Joseph Smith made statements in support of the Negroes receiving the Priesthood, perhaps at a time when they had been freed from slavery, and that such information could be useful to the First Presidency one day in making the decision to give the Priesthood to Blacks."

9 June 1978–Spencer W. Kimball Ends the Priesthood Exclusion

From my journal: "Today will stand as one of the most important dates in the history of the Gospel upon the earth, and it is without question the most important date so far in the twentieth century history of Mormonism. I came to the office of *BYU Studies* to return the prayer circle article that I had picked up for revisions earlier in the morning, after my gym workout.

"'Did you hear the news?' asked the assistant editor, Laura Wadley, 'The First Presidency has given the Blacks the Priesthood.' I said 'sure,' and urged her to get on with the article I was returning, not wanting to hear the punch-line of a tasteless joke.

"Seeing that I would not take her seriously, Laura turned on the radio in time to pick up the last of the news announcement that a letter of the First Presidency had said that by revelation the Priesthood was now to be extended to all worthy men, without exception of race or color. I was stunned. I never expected to live to see this day, although I had hoped and on occasion prayed for it."

Nine days after this public announcement, I joined in ordaining our Salt Lake City ward's only African American to the priesthood. Ever-devout, seventeen-year-old Phil Mikalowski was in tears that Sabbath. From my journal: "His close friends who were also Priests assisted in the ordination circle. It was a great occasion."

In eighteen months, I would meet Dave Goates at a party, where he made a point of reminding me how offended he was in late 1972 when I said that the only reason this policy hadn't changed was that the prophets weren't asking God about it. Dave would stun me in December 1979 by saying (from my journal): "Since the revelation on the Priesthood and the Blacks in 1978, I have talked with a lot of people about the situation, and I am convinced that the Blacks would still not have the Priesthood if my grandfather [Harold B. Lee] had not died. ... I now realize that my grandfather was not at all interested in the matter, and, in fact, the pressures that were being made by others for him to inquire about it actually made him even less inclined to think of questioning the restriction of the Priesthood."

9 July 1978–First Presidency and Oral Sex

From my journal: "I was disturbed at Priesthood Executive Meeting to hear reference made and supportive discussion given to the fact (which I had not heard before) that the new temple interview questions are designed to discover if *married* couples are engaging in 'unnatural and immoral' acts such as oral sex. I said nothing but was dismayed and infuriated at the Pharisaical trends of the Church.

"If kissing the genitals is unnatural and immoral in marriage, how is that any different than kissing the breast? Such emphasis seems to be a result of a fundamental attitude that the body is actually defiled through intimate contact, even in marriage, and that only the least intimacy necessary to bring about conception is authorized."

Within months, my grandmother would be almost floored during an interview for a temple recommend. Her ward's bishop thought he was obediently following these new instructions to all presiding officers, when he asked the eighty-three-year-old widow: "Are you engaging in oral sex?"

Mom told me about Nana's shock that their bishop had asked her such a "revolting question." She couldn't understand why President Kimball added this inquiry to the required questions for a recommend. I didn't know what to say, except that his sermons had often expressed concern about the sexual behavior of Latter-day Saints.[8]

17 July 1978–Death Threat

I became terrified for myself and family when a man phoned our house tonight, asking about the anonymous *Response*. He threatened to "blood atone" me "for this attack on the Tanners."[9] I quickly changed our number, kept it out of future phonebooks, and left it unlisted at 411 Information. Nonetheless, my address on Third Avenue was in one already printed phonebook and in the annual *Polk's Salt Lake City Directory* from 1978 onward. I couldn't do anything about that publicity and felt real anxiety about being murdered by some anti-Mormon crackpot. On July 19 I prepared a will for the first time.

During a ten-year period, history had evolved from my undergraduate hobby, to my post-graduate major, to my publishing world, to my teaching profession. Now it could be a life-or-death prospect.

I would think of this again in seven years—after two people were murdered separately in Salt Lake City, because of controversial Mormon history. Dear God!

23 July 1978–Painful Cycles in Gay-Straight Marriage

From my journal: "Jan spoke to me of the emptiness she feels with me and the extent of her loneliness for the kind of companionship that I am unable or unwilling to give her. I told her that she should not blame herself for the feelings she expressed to me tonight, because they were natural and resulted from my own failures.

---

8. In 1978, the First Presidency added to the standardized list of temple recommend interview questions a statement that anyone who had not repented of "impure, unholy, or unnatural sex acts" could not receive a recommend to enter the temple. In a follow-up letter to local lay leaders dated January 5, 1982, the First Presidency made clear that it "interpreted oral sex as constituting an unnatural, impure, or unholy practice." On October 15, 1982, the First Presidency sent yet another letter to lay leaders, rescinding its ban on oral sex and stating that bishops "should never inquire into personal, intimate matters involving marital relations." See Edward L. Kimball, "The History of LDS Temple Admission Standards," *Journal of Mormon History* 24, no. 1 (Spring 1998): 135–75.

9. "Blood atonement" was an early Mormon doctrine that Jesus's atoning sacrifice alone did not atone for particularly grievous sins, including murder and repeated adultery. Only the offender's compliance with having their own blood shed could expiate these sins for forgiveness in the afterlife. See Richard E. Turley Jr. and Barbara Jones Brown, *Vengeance is Mine: The Mountain Meadows Massacre and Its Aftermath* (New York: Oxford University Press, 2023), 16–18.

"I brought up the solution [of divorce] that she has suggested to me seven or eight times in the past, and which I have vowed I would not oppose if she brought it up again, even though I dread it as much or more than she does. I urged it as the only apparent way she will be happy, and I affirmed that I felt that she could be happy that way. She wants me to make the final decision, and I said that because the difficulties will in large measure be with her than with me, that I could not make that decision for her.

"I am at the point, however, where I dread anything more than casual conversation because we seem always to come around directly or indirectly to my failures and the results of my failures and I have difficulty enduring this constant reminder of my inadequacies and failures, with the resultant guilt that oppresses me.

"Divorce seems like the ultimate failure of all our dreams ... but tonight it seemed like the best and only way for a resolution of our conflicts. Our conversation, like so many before, was expressed in calmness, in anguish, and in quiet tears, and was concluded in the desperate clinging and urgency of love[making]."

This was the cycle of painful discussions we had since 1971. My very detailed journal of 1978–80 described others—sometimes specifying my celibate homosexuality as the cause. Suffice it to say that these cycles were repeated during the next seven years of our marriage.

30 July 1978–What Is the LDS Church to Those Who Don't Fit?

From my journal: "In the Priest Quorum meeting, the lesson was on the 13th Article of Faith. I used this as a point of departure for discussing the role of the Church and of what it means to be a Latter-day Saint who often does not have all the perfect virtues listed in the Article of Faith Thirteen.

"I reminded them of the old story about the argument for whether to buy a new ambulance or build a better fence because of the people falling over a cliff. I asked the [teenage] Priests what they thought was a good represen-tation of the Church in this story. Predictably, most of them (led by Aubyn [Gwinn]) said that the Church was both a fence and an ambulance, but I was caught off guard when someone said that the Church was also the cliff.

"I spent a few minutes discussing this point in reference to members of the Church sometimes feeling that the Church brings them burdens and tri-als of action and conscience that are hard to bear.

"Bishop Horne commented that the bishop of the single's ward in our stake had told him that for the past several years until this last Christmas season, there has been an average of five suicides in the singles' ward each year in December. I didn't challenge him, but I wondered if he meant or the other bishop meant five *attempted* suicides, because five successful suicides a year or month [in one congregation] would be an enormous rate."

17 August 1978—Premonitions of a New Calling

From my journal: "As soon as Jan told me that the Stake Presidency wanted to see me, I was sure that I was being called to the Stake High Council, which is what I feared President West [the First Counselor] wanted me for when he telephoned me nearly two weeks ago about the genealogical program. There was a time not long ago that I was fully determined to flatly refuse any position of presiding in the Church.

"But now I feel that I am on the verge of accomplishing what the Lord has prepared me to do, and even though I am filled with self-doubt and fear, I do not want to voluntarily turn aside the opportunities that may present themselves.

"I was dressed in my customary blue jeans when I entered the stake president's office with Jan. President [Ralph O.] Bradley said that after a confirmation of the Spirit through prayer, that the presidency was calling me to the High Council, to which I said only, 'O.K.' ... He did not ask me if I accepted that call, apparently regarding my 'O.K.' as sufficient, but he did ask Jan if she would sustain me in this calling, and she said that she did and would."

I was sustained in stake conference on the 20th as an alternate member of the High Council. LDS headquarters authorized this setting apart of alternates as an expansion of original instructions by revelation which allowed for the *ad hoc* selection of temporary replacements for any of the original twelve High Councilmen who might be absent from a day's meeting (D&C 102:1, 7). Bishop Horne told Jan that "President Bradley had wanted to call me to the High Council six months ago, but that Rick had asked that I be allowed to remain with the Aaronic Priesthood program in the ward for a while longer."

3 September 1978—The Unhappiness of Mom's Third Marriage

During a visit to Salt Lake City with my new stepfather, Mom wasn't coy about saying she now disliked the man she had previously loved "as a brother" during the decades he was married to her sister Joy. Mom often said that she didn't regret her marriage to my father—because I was the result; and she didn't regret her marriage to Wayne—because he gave her nine years of the only romance she had experienced. Nevertheless, she thoroughly regretted her decision to marry Vaude Nye. This visit became so tension filled, that he flew back to California alone, rather than returning with her and Nana in their car.

If Uncle Vaude had remained Mom's widower brother-in-law, they would have continued sharing close friendship. Instead, he married her on the rebound from grief, and she accepted because of a misplaced sense of duty to her dead sister, to assuage Vaude's grief, and to get me sealed to her in the temple—which fulfilled the promise of her 1948 patriarchal blessing. Mom wouldn't even consider divorce—because she didn't want to lose that sealing.

I felt heartsick for her and for him. Both were good-hearted, faithful people who fully deserved an enjoyable and satisfying companionship.

6 September 1978–High Council, Salt Lake Emigration Stake

This was my first meeting as a high councilman. Because of the new calling, I was released as President of the Young Men in the Twenty-seventh Ward on September 3. Despite its heavily administrative emphasis, this began a very enjoyable period of service for me.

One of my responsibilities was to start a pilot program of calling stake genealogical missionaries to do name extractions from original documents furnished on microfilm to our stake by the LDS Genealogical Department. This would provide names for the growing number of temples that were outpacing the number of ancestral names submitted by individual Mormons for proxy ordinances. I worked with its direct supervisor in overseeing the construction of a genealogical library in our stake meeting house, acquiring the microfilm reading machines, and reviewing the data extracted from documents in several languages by the called members of our stake who were fluent therein.

President Bradley was a wealthy businessman who had fathered fourteen children, yet his wife looked like a petite model while they were raising the last two. Every time I published a scholarly article on Mormon history, within a month he recommended it to the high council's meeting.

President Bradley's first counselor was Hugh S. West (an insurance executive who became our stake president in 1982 and one of my Mormon heroes shortly thereafter). The second counselor now was Douglas Sorensen (a pharmacist who wore a royal blue shirt at every meeting, instead of the white shirts expected for LDS leaders).

I enjoyed associating with every member of this high council. It included Gordon Burt Affleck (a close friend of First Presidency counselor J. Reuben Clark, whose biography I was researching at this time), L. Brent Goates (son-in-law of former apostle and deceased President Harold B. Lee, whose diaries Brent possessed and from which he gave me excerpts of all entries about President Clark), D. Wayne Owens (Utah's longtime Democratic leader who endeared himself to me in 1974 when he voted for Nixon's impeachment as a member of the House Judiciary Committee), and Robert K. Dellenbach (a recently released mission president, who would become a general authority in 1990).

21 September 1978–Publicly Condemning Anti-Semitism

In response to Charlotte M. Howe's expression of anti-Semitism in a letter to the editor, I wrote a pro-Jewish response to the *Salt Lake Tribune*, wherein I condemned "her foul anti-semitism" and "stench of anti-semitism."[10] The newspaper had regularly published this woman's letters which expressed her right-wing conservatism, but no more appeared for months after my response. For sixteen years, I had regarded right-wing Republicans as the most dangerous single threat to American society, and that assessment would seem even more valid in the decades after this publication.

From my journal for today: "Jan said that this morning about 9:30, a young woman telephoned to express her gratitude for the letter. She is Jewish and was quite touched by the letter. ...

"When Roy [Darley] read it this evening, he said that he hoped people would look up the word *goy* (which he had to ask me to explain to him), and would not assume that I was saying in the letter that I was gay.[11] He and Kay laughed at this." Oh, the irony!

Not even implied in my published letter was a covert message about J. Reuben Clark Jr. By this time, I had discovered numerous documents showing that this First Presidency counselor was a thorough anti-Semite until he died, as was his son, Reuben III, at least until his forties. I used this newspaper publication to let President Clark's children in Provo and Salt Lake City know what I thought about this side of him. I intended my biography itself to be non-judgmental.

23 November 1978–What Should Homosexually Inclined Teenagers Do?

From my journal: "It is really none of my business, but I cannot help being interested and concerned for my young friend [Aubyn Gwinn, age eighteen]. ... I have come to the conclusion, though not inflexibly, that for Latter-day Saints who feel they are homosexually oriented, it is inviting tragedy for themselves and innocent spouse and children to follow the usual Church counsel to ignore it all and get married and have a family.

"For those who have homosexual longings, yet also have a testimony and attachment to the LDS Church, I believe that it would probably be best that they engage in sexual activity prior to marriage and while yet in youth, so that they will know as best they can whether heterosexual relations will satisfy their needs or whether they are definitely homosexual or bisexual in their sexual needs.

"If the latter is true, then they may as well give up on both marriage and the Church, for to continue to strive to find happiness in either would be

---

10. See D. Michael Quinn, "No Conspiracy," *Salt Lake Tribune*, Sep. 9, 1978.

11. A term generally used by Jewish persons to refer to a person who is not Jewish.

tragic. If the sexual experiments of youth in this situation successfully indicate that their homosexual fears were ungrounded, it would be a far easier matter to sincerely repent of that sexual conduct and then go forward into marriage and LDS family life than for homosexually oriented young people to expect marriage and Church living to solve their problems.

"I have come to the conclusion that the situation of homosexually oriented young LDS men and women is hopeless in this life, and the eternal consequences of their actions must rest in the hands of a loving God who knows them better than any Church official or legalist. If this is the situation of the young man in our ward whom I admire greatly and regard fondly, then I only pray that he will find contentment in whatever path he chooses in the difficult paths that seem his only options."

Aubyn was very smart, very artistic, and very cute, with a wry sense of humor. Following his full-time mission, he married in the temple, and moved to my birthplace of Pasadena, California, where he graduated from its Art Center College of Design with a BFA degree.

After his divorce (with one child), I would meet this by-then profoundly ex-Mormon for lunch in the Castro District of San Francisco. A decade after that, I stayed with Aubyn and his male lover at their co-op apartment in Manhattan's Tribeca District. Soon thereafter, Aubyn would become another sexually attractive young man I passive-aggressively pushed away from me.

26 November 1978–Staying in LDS Hierarchy's "Good Graces"?

From my journal: "The bishop of the ward, Gordon Madsen (brother of Truman Madsen of BYU) referred to my thesis and dissertation on the hierarchy ... and expressed his envy that I had been assigned to write a biography of J. Reuben Clark, Jr. He then asked me a question that many non-historians have asked as they have learned about my hierarchy study,

"'Tell me, Michael, how have you been able to stay in the good graces of the general authorities while doing such research and writing as you have done on such topics of controversy?' I could have said many things, but simply replied: 'I don't try.' Gordon Madsen was obviously taken back by this remark, and mumbled: 'Well that is frankly stated!'"

I had first met Gordon seven years earlier at a luncheon for the guides at Temple Square. He overheard me talking with another guide about something I had learned from Heber J. Grant's journals. Gordon expressed painful amazement back then that I was casually reading what he (as a grandson) had previously been denied by Church Historian Joseph Fielding Smith and by his assistant Will Lund. Gordon hadn't heard back then that Apostle Hunter opened the archives, but he eagerly saw the journals of his grandfather President Grant soon after our 1971 chat.

4 December 1978–Homosexuality and Polygamy in LDS Hierarchy

From my journal: "Leonard called me into his office and asked me what I knew about the reasons for Patriarch Joseph F. Smith being released. ... I told Leonard that Patriarch Smith was released or perhaps forced to resign because it was thought that he was a homosexual, and gave the details as I knew them. This was all news to Leonard, as was my comment that Richard R. Lyman's situation was actually a case of polygamy rather than simple adultery."[12]

7 December 1978–Homosexuality as Biographically Insignificant?

During today's conversation about my upcoming biography of J. Reuben Clark, BYU's College of Social Sciences dean, Martin Hickman, cautioned me not to overly emphasize "controversial things" that I might learn. He said that he had recently finished reading "an excellent biography of Somerset Maugham," but objected to its repeatedly mentioning this novelist's sexuality.[13] "Being told once that Maugham was homosexual would be sufficient," Martin said. "It isn't necessary for the biography to bring up that subject again and again." I nodded without stating my rebuttal.

Homosexuality was as vital to W. Somerset Maugham's personality and life's experience as it has been for mine. Most people would complain if my self-biography mentioned it only once: "By the way, I'm gay." My sexual orientation is as important for understanding me and my life's experiences as my nationality, ethnic orientation, social class, political orientation, academic orientation, and religious orientation. Likewise for all other humans, sexuality is a crucial part, though not the only part, of their lives.

10 December 1978–Reaction to the Controversial ERA

From my journal concerning John Netto asking what I thought about his plan as gospel doctrine teacher in the Twenty-seventh Ward to have his class discuss the proposed Equal Rights Amendment to the US Constitution: "My own observation would be that if there was going to be a discussion in class on the subject, then the discussion ought to allow presentation of views in support of ERA and against the position taken on this political matter by the First Presidency. If that occurred, only ill feeling could result in the class, and I would prefer to leave it alone. John decided not to have it."

LDS headquarters was in the midst of waging a state-by-state political campaign against ratification of the ERA. If ratified, it would prohibit any

---

12. Detailing this meeting in his December 5, 1978, diary, Arrington mentioned that Lyman's so-called "covenant marriage" was performed by himself and not a third party. See Bergera, ed., *Confessions of a Mormon Historian*, 3:685–88.

13. W. Somerset Maugham (1874–1965) was a British playwright and novelist. Hickman was likely referring to Frederic Raphael's *W. Somerset Maugham and His World* (New York: Scribner, 1977).

discrimination against females in job hiring, salary levels, promotion, demotion, termination, as well as in such things as interest rates for loans and mortgages. It would guarantee all American women equal access to all the privileges granted by tradition and prejudice to males only. As I had told Mormon feminist Maureen Ursenbach Beecher last April, "I am very strongly in favor of promoting the cause legally and philosophically with regard to the status of women."

The First Presidency's opposition seemed misogynistically patriarchal. It also openly used homophobic arguments against the ERA.

Furthermore, investigative journalists were uncovering a widespread—if not universal—pattern of deceit and concealment involving the LDS Church's role in promoting and financing the anti-ERA campaign within twenty states of the Union. The Church's 1968 Liquor By the Drink campaign paled by comparison, and I had voted against that intrusion into the political arena. Both then and now, these political campaigns were being directed by apostle Gordon B. Hinckley.

Nonetheless, I kept my misgivings and dissent to myself. First, I felt ambivalent, because I acknowledged that a person could legitimately argue against such an amendment on rational grounds and that the LDS Church had the legal right to oppose it for whatever reason.

For example, I opposed the ERA because it would end the gender discrimination that benefitted women in the workplace. In the late 1950s, my factory-worker mother commented that she had persuaded her bosses to give women more frequent bathroom breaks than men—without requiring women to explain why they needed to take an extra break. For example, a woman might suddenly begin menstruating just minutes after returning from a lunch break or scheduled coffee break. The Equal Rights Amendment would end such special privileges for women who certainly needed them. As I told Maureen on April 26: "I feel that the design of the amendment can be achieved by legislation on specific issues, and thus be amenable to gradualism and possible exceptions that would be in favor of women's status and rights to a greater extent than if all sexist bias were constitutionally removed."

Second, and most important, because the First Presidency was linking the Equal Rights Amendment to homosexuality, I could not (as a closeted gay at BYU) risk guilt-by-association suspicions if I criticized the church's activism against ERA. So I remained silent about it, even cautious in responding to friends who asked my views.

If the LDS Church lost its US tax exemptions because of using untaxed chapels and untaxed parking lots for political speeches, petition signing, letter writing to legislators, political rallies, and bussing to political meetings—so be it. Not my problem.

19 December 1978–Trying "To Be Good in God's Eyes"

From my journal: "Answered some correspondence, including a letter from a girl who had grown up in Glendale while I was a teenager in the Glendale West Ward. Her expressions of her teenage admiration for me as the ideal teenager and the standard by which she measured all other boys and prospective husbands caused tears to come to my eyes as I read it.

"The tears came not in gratitude or humility, but in anguish that people think me so good when all my life I have simply struggled in the only way I knew how to even try to be good in God's eyes. I wrote her a long letter to that effect. Better to break graven images than to have people believe in me rather than in the ideals and principles that I inadequately seek to live."

14 January 1979–Self-Perceptions

From my journal: "I would like to see myself as a binder of spiritual wounds and a messenger of principles of truth, but I most often perceive myself as an unworthy representative of the Church, a discordant influence, and a disturber of the religious perceptions of people who are far more obedient, righteous, and devoted than I am."

17 January 1979–Telling a General Authority about Post-1890 Polygamy

From my journal, concerning the invitation from staff members at HDC that I help G. Homer Durham fulfill a research request to him from the First Presidency:

"I worked on the letter to Durham until 2 p.m., without access to any of my research notes due to the deadline. I wrote 12 pages in which I outlined and summarized in fair detail my understanding of the background to the Manifesto and the Declaration of 1904 as well as my understanding of the practice of plural marriage after the Manifesto of 1890. I prayed that the Lord would be with me in His Spirit as I wrote this.

"Word of my writing this memo apparently was passed around the Historical Department during the day, and both Ron Esplin and Ron Walker of the History Division asked me for xerox copies of what I was writing to Durham. I told them both that I had made a covenant with the Lord many years ago that I would never discuss in detail or write my knowledge of post-1890 polygamy until I knew the whole story from all available sources, and now I was violating that covenant today for Durham because of the request of the First Presidency to him. I said that I would not provide anyone else with a copy of what I had written to him."

23 January 1979–Modern Hierarchy Appalls Me

From my journal: "I worked on the [Ernest L.] Wilkinson Diary today, and pretty much finished it through the end of 1961. Wilkinson was very frank about the petty squabbles, power alignments, and administrative chaos of the McKay years in that part of the diary I have researched. It depresses me to realize the degree of selfish manipulation of power that exists in the general authorities.

"Somehow this affects me far more than my research into the operations of the hierarchy in the nineteenth and [early] twentieth centuries. Perhaps I react more strongly to what I know and am learning about the uses of power and methods of decision making during the period since 1951 only because I have personally met all the general authorities involved."

31 January 1979–Tragic Flaws

From my journal about a conversation with Ronald Walker at HDC in the afternoon: "I said that in that respect I felt kinship with the characters of Greek tragedies who had tragic flaws that doomed them. Ron seemed somewhat skeptical that I had any tragic flaw, and I said that pride (or more accurately, *hubris*) was part, but only part, of mine."

2 February 1979–Interviewing Church President at Headquarters

From my journal, concerning an hour-long interview with Spencer W. Kimball, a first cousin of J. Reuben Clark:

"I was dressed in my light tan suit, but ... decided that I should be honest in my apparel, and so I wore my shirt with wide stripes of beige, light green, and white. I also wore, as usual in the winter, my heavy, rubber-cleated, leather hiking boots. ...

"I had wondered how he would react to my asking him questions that brought up controversial matters concerning Clark, particularly of the McKay-Clark tensions, but I found President Kimball to be very candid in what he said and remembered. ...

"Then I got around to asking him if I might be allowed to read his personal diaries, and I held my breath. President Kimball seemed to think for a moment, smiled, and said it would be fine for me to read his personal diaries. He said that they were at his home, and that we would need to arrange for me to come to his home to read them. ...

"President Kimball got up from his desk to walk with me to the door of the office, and I thanked him also for allowing me to express to him my feelings about my own background as he spoke of his efforts for the Indians. At this point, he clutched me in his left arm, while he held my hand in his right hand, and he said: 'It makes me love you all the more to know that you are

Mexican,' and then he snuggled his cheek up to mine. I left his office feeling joy in the Spirit of the Lord."

3 February 1979–Visiting the Living Prophet at Home

From my journal about the first visit to Spencer W. Kimball's house on Laird Drive in Salt Lake City: "President Kimball showed me the binders in which his journals from 1940 to the present are kept in his study, and he set me up in the living room with a card table, chair, and old typewriter. For the next five hours I read more than four binders of his journals and took typewritten notes on [them], while President Kimball worked in his study where I could hear him dictating at length concerning the Logan Temple. ...

"Sister [Camilla Eyring] Kimball came and insisted that I join them in the kitchen for lunch. She had a place set for me between them, and so I ate some fried chicken and rolls with them. ...

"Just as I was about to excuse myself again [in the evening] to prepare to leave with Jan (who I feared was waiting impatiently outside), a neighbor came by at the back door, and President Kimball insisted that we get acquainted and introduced me to him, making a special point of telling his neighbor that I was a *Mexicano*. ...

"As I left, I said that I would contact President Kimball after his return from Hawaii to see when it would be convenient for me to come again to research more of his journals, and President Kimball said that would be fine."

8 February 1979–Publishing about LDS Prayer Circle

From my journal: "When I saw Linda Adams[14] [in the office of *BYU Studies*], she said that she had received today some advance copies of the issue [dated fall 1978, with my article on the "Latter-day Saint Prayer Circle"] ...

"I read it all very carefully and was extremely pleased to find that it was just as I had written and corrected it, with only one minor error that I caught in a footnote."

Four months afterward, associate editor Richard G. Ellsworth told me that they had to print 1,000 extra copies because of the requests from non-subscribers for my article.

18 February 1979–Outside Assessment

From my journal: "Dave Darley mentioned at dinner that during a bishopric meeting which he attended as executive secretary in the Douglas Ward, the conversation turned to the Gospel Doctrine class, and Bishop Dean Bitter said that the best teacher he had ever seen and the ward had ever had in

---

14. Linda Hunter Adams (1941–2016) taught English and editing at BYU for thirty years. She edited hundreds of publications and books, including as associate editor of *BYU Studies* for fifteen years and as an editor for the Joseph Smith Papers.

the Gospel Doctrine class was D. Michael Quinn. That is a nice compliment to hear 5 ½ years after I left the Douglas Ward."

24 February 1979–Second Saturday at the Prophet's Home

From my journal: "At the beginning and ending of my [six-hour] stay today in the Kimball home, I had some interesting contacts with President Kimball.

"After I had started reading where I had left off in his diaries, President Kimball came over and asked to see what kind of notes I was taking. I handed him the first page of my notes, and he sat down and read them over. ... President Kimball simply corrected one misstatement I had made in identifying one of his sons in an anecdote he had told. ...

"He also commented that as I was researching for references to J. Reuben Clark in his diaries, I was looking for needles in haystacks. I said that was how I had approached my research in documents of Church history for many years—that by studying many different sources, I was able to gather hundreds of needles from haystacks and then fit the needles together to useful purpose."

3 March 1979–Third Visit and Nigerian Polygamy

From my journal: "President Kimball asked me to do my work today at a small card table next to his own desk in his moderately sized office in his home. So I spent more than five hours in his office, oftentimes working next to him as he sorted through and read the piles of documents that are scattered in a jumble throughout his office.

"At one point, as I was walking through the office library area, I noticed on the top of one stack of papers a memorandum from Francis Gibbons, the Secretary of the First Presidency, describing several enclosed documents that related to the request of a Nigerian living in Los Angeles to be baptized. This Nigerian lives in Los Angeles at present with one wife and has two other wives back in Nigeria. The man said that he was willing to repudiate the other two wives in Nigeria if that was required by the First Presidency for him to be baptized. The memorandum of Gibbons was dated January 15, 1979. ... I was tempted to say something to President Kimball about this memo while I was in the Kimball home but decided not to."

In eleven years, I would ask Mark and Elma Bradshaw, a missionary couple to Nigeria, about the general situation of polygamy there—without mentioning that I had read this correspondence. The Bradshaws would tell me that such a request for baptism by Black African polygamists and/or their plural wives was common during this couple's two special missions in Nigeria.

The LDS president's answer in 1979 was that the Manifesto required this Nigerian to end his polygamous marriages before he could be baptized. This stunned me, because President Kimball *knew* that LDS presidents had authorized polygamy outside the United States long after 1890.

First, his father-in-law Edward C. Eyring married a plural wife in Mexico during 1903 in a ceremony authorized by the First Presidency of Joseph F. Smith. His predecessors Wilford Woodruff and Lorenzo Snow had likewise permitted post-Manifesto plural marriages in Mexico. President Kimball had approved his official biography which affirmed those facts two years before this correspondence about Nigerian polygamy.

Second, President David O. McKay had authorized a prominent Egyptian polygamist to be baptized in 1962 and to attend the Hyde Park Ward as an elder while living in London with his plural wife. I had typed extensive notes at HDC from the correspondence and minutes of that decision. Surely, the First Presidency's secretary mentioned those facts to President Kimball when this question of African polygamy came up for their consideration!

Furthermore, polygamy was legal and socially sanctioned in Nigeria. By contrast, polygamy and polygamous cohabitation were illegal in Mexico when LDS presidents authorized those new plural marriages from 1890 to 1904. Likewise, it was illegal cohabitation in England in 1962.

I couldn't stop thinking about the wives this Black polygamist had to abandon in order to become a member of the LDS Church in a country that sanctioned polygamy. These women and their children were now shamed outcasts in their villages. I felt heartsick.

Spencer W. Kimball gave something precious to Black Africans in mid-1978. Then he took away something equally precious in early 1979. These were burdens of an imperfect church led by very fallible humans. Good intentions and prophetic callings didn't change those realities.

15 March 1979—Tenure and Promotion

From my journal: "To my surprise, Lou Cardon [acting chair of the BYU History Department] had called to say that my tenure and promotion to associate professor had been approved by the academic vice-president and by the board of trustees of BYU and were now official. I said that was very good news. He also asked if I might be tour guide on Temple Square for a visiting professor at the end of the month.

"I find it strange that the board of trustees of BYU (which includes on its executive committee the anti-historical Boyd K. Packer, and in its entirety includes the Quorum of the Twelve Apostles) has approved my tenure and promotion at BYU if members of the board feel very critical of my prayer circle article. Perhaps the approval came before their awareness of the article." I soon learned that this had been the sequence.

I received Cardon's message just hours after my former student Richard

Holzapfel reported to me what he had learned as research assistant to BYU religion professor Joseph Fielding McConkie.[15] Son of Elder Bruce R. McConkie (now an apostle), he reported to Holzapfel what his father had told him about my article having been discussed by the Twelve.

20 March 1979–More Access to First Presidency's Journals

From my journal: First Presidency counselor Marion G. Romney's secretary, "Sister Butterfield said that President Romney had decided that rather than have me read through the journals, that she should read through them and extract anything relating to President J. Reuben Clark, Jr. In view of President Romney's closed approach to things I feel good about this. ...

"I asked her to include references President Romney might make to the other members of the Presidency and about the operation of the presidency itself. Sister Butterfield said that President Romney's diaries were not really very descriptive, but she would see what she could do about also including the kinds of indirect references to the operation of the presidency as well as specific references to Clark." She would ultimately give me eighty full pages of excerpts.

"After the [Emigration Stake's High Council] meeting, Brent Goates gave me excerpts from Harold B. Lee's 1943 diaries concerning J. Reuben Clark, with the comment that there were some very sensitive things in the excerpts but that he was giving me everything that related to Clark. I asked President Goates if he would also give me excerpts from Lee's diaries of Lee's comments and observations [as an Apostle since 1941] concerning the other members of the Presidency and of the operation of the presidency that related to the environment in which President Clark had to work.

"For a few minutes President Goates and I spoke indirectly about the conflicts between McKay and Clark (since we were not alone where more explicit reference would have been appropriate)."

30 March 1979–Artful Taste

From my journal, concerning the trip with Jan to San Francisco for a business conference about Enhance Products:

"We went to some shops and art galleries. Of all the paintings we saw, some of which we were impressed enough with to ask the prices for (too much for our blood, $300+), Jan and I were most impressed with the beauty of two nude paintings by an artist named Embry. Jan very much liked a painting of the back view of a standing nude, bearded man.

"I was very much struck with a front view of a standing nude of a young man."

15. Richard N. Holzapfel (1954–) taught church history and doctrine at BYU from 1993–2018. In 2018, he became a senior manager in the church's missionary department.

21 April 1979–"An Atheist Could Obtain a Temple Recommend"

From my journal: "Paul H. Dunn of the First Council of Seventy was the visiting authority [for our stake conference]. In the 4 p.m. meeting with Priesthood leaders, Brother Dunn emphasized the necessity of having detailed and thorough interviews, especially with young people. At the end of his presentation, Brother Dunn asked for questions, and I decided that this was my opportunity to tell a general authority something I have felt about the interview procedure of the Church. ...

"I quickly interjected, 'But, Brother Dunn, no where in any of the temple interview questions is there even the most indirect reference to one's belief in God, in the atonement, or in the mission of Jesus Christ. It is conceivable that an atheist could obtain a temple recommend under current interviewing guidelines.' Brother Dunn acknowledged that strictly speaking that was true, and he said that he would raise this question in the next meeting of the Council of Seventy with the president of the Church. ...

"Behind my question is my firm conclusion that the Church is increasingly adopting a Mosaic (even a Pharisaic) approach and subordinating the spiritual. I have enough sense (perhaps *just* enough) to know that I can never express that in a public meeting of Priesthood leaders."

30 April 1979–Informing LDS President about My Polygamy Research

Today I wrote a letter to Spencer W. Kimball, asking for access to documents in the First Presidency's vault. I emphasized the importance of that research to helping the Latter-day Saints understand post-Manifesto polygamy.

From my journal: "I have done this thing with my eyes wide open to the possibilities, but am committed to doing everything I can do within my limited options to bringing about what I feel needs to be done. If I fail, at least I have failed through trying rather than through inaction."

29 May 1979–Senior Apostles Dislike My Publication

From my journal: "Oaks said that one of the members of the Quorum of the Twelve Apostles told him that my prayer circle article had been brought up for discussion in the temple meeting of the First Presidency and Quorum of the Twelve, and that 'senior members of the Quorum' were very unhappy about it and expressed 'concern about what was written in that article that was unwise, was revealing sacred things, and could cause the Church present difficulties.'

"Oaks said, 'No names were mentioned to me in this report, but I assume that the senior members who objected probably included Mark E. Petersen who is hostile to history. I re-read your article after this was reported to me and the only thing I can see to which the Brethren might have particularly objected (aside from the whole question of writing at all about the prayer circle) was your discussion of the role of women and the denial of their participation in the prayer circle meetings. With the difficulties the Church is presently having with the women's movement, I am sure that many of the Brethren felt that this was no time to be airing our linen on this matter.'

"Dallin Oaks continued: 'Now I am sure that the Brethren in the temple meeting, including the one who made the report to me, have not connected the Michael Quinn of the prayer circle article with the Michael Quinn who is writing about J. Reuben Clark. But [First Presidency secretary] Arthur Haycock's antennae are very sensitive, and I bet that he has made the connection, and that is why he is putting a blockade between you and President Kimball.'

"Then, Oaks continued: 'Now, I am telling you this only to apprise you that you need to be aware of this situation and of the possibility of the sensitivities of the Brethren proving to be an obstacle to you. When I was informed of the discussion in the temple [council meeting] about your prayer circle article, no mention was made to me that I should consider that you were in error or in trouble, nor was there any indication to me that I should reprimand you in any way. I am merely telling you this now because it may be the answer to why Arthur Haycock has treated you as he has.'"

The above paragraph indicated how supportive Dallin H. Oaks was of academic freedom while he was president of BYU. However, he had his limits even then.

29 May 1979—Future Apostle Says "I'll Never Forgive You"

From my journal: "As we were leaving the meeting I again thanked Dallin Oaks for his support to me as I was knocking on many 'high doors, behind which are people with great sensitivities.'

"Dallin Oaks said to me: 'Michael, Bob [Thomas] and I have put ourselves on the line to back you. In effect, we have pulled back our armor and bared our flesh. You or anyone else could easily put a knife into us in this situation. If you let us down, I'll never forgive you.' Dallin Oaks said this in a good-natured way, but I realize fully the seriousness of the situation, and I replied: 'President, I will do my best not to merit that reproach.'"

Dallin H. Oaks would become an apostle in April 1984. Just over a year later, he fulfilled today's promise—even though I would think I did nothing to merit his response.

6 June 1979—Another Church Court

This evening, I participated in my first high council court. At his own request, we excommunicated an unmarried returned missionary for having sex with both females and males. He was about twenty-two. During my next year as a high councilman, I joined in the vote to excommunicate three married men of the Emigration Stake for adultery.

Counting my roles in church courts as the presiding elder of a branch in England, as a bishopric counselor in Connecticut, and as a high councilman in Utah, I voted to excommunicate a total of thirty-two members of the LDS Church. That was a very unpleasant achievement.

1 July 1979–LDS Policies of Excluding Women

From my journal for this Sunday: "If Church procedures allow non-member and non-Priesthood fathers to join in the circle to bless their children, I cannot see why mothers should be excluded from the circle."

16 July 1979–Close Association with Older Historians

From my journal about a weeklong stay in Provo: "I met Gene Campbell at the History Office and he drove me to the supermarket near his house to buy my orange juice for morning and night, and then he drove me to his home near the campus. He and his wife Beth have been very generous to invite me to stay in their basement bedroom anytime I need."

In one of our discussions during this visit, my personal philosophy surprised him, even though we shared many of the same left-wing political views. When I explained my position on ethical relativism and private inspiration, he exclaimed: "Mike, you're an antinomian!" Guilty as charged—at least in attitude.

In a month, I stayed a few days with Ted J. Warner and wife Doris. I associated more often with these two families than with others in BYU's History Department.

Frank Fox was the only young BYU historian I socialized with. Even that was primarily because he and his wife Elaine were interested in the nutritional products, household cleaners, and cosmetics that Jan was selling.

19 July 1979–Planning for *Dialogue* Article on Post-1890 Polygamy

From my journal: "Depending upon the nature of the article on post-1890 polygamy that will be published next January in *Utah Historical Quarterly* [by B. Carmon Hardy and Victor W. Jorgensen], I am giving more serious consideration to making my last scholarly article on Mormonism a[n] overview of post-1890 polygamy. [16]

"Since it appears that the First Presidency will never allow the crucial documents to be made available for an honest exploration of this matter, I may present what I presently understand for whatever benefit it may have to the Church membership in understanding. If I do this, I will send the article to *Dialogue* for publication.

16. See B. Carmon Hardy and Victor W. Jorgensen, "The Taylor-Cowley Affair and the Watershed of Mormon History," *Utah Historical Quarterly* 48, no. 1 (1980): 6–38.

"It will probably end my career at BYU as well as pose barriers to me in other areas, but if the Presidency will not allow access to anything better, I may as well do what I can for the benefit of the Saints who may benefit from such an open examination. Such an article on the significance of the 1890 Manifesto would not be a bad Last Hurrah for me as a Mormon historian. After that, I can foresee nothing of significance or fulfillment."

Nonetheless, hoping against hope, I continued for three years to write the First Presidency with requests to give me access to the documents about plural marriage in its vault.

Early August 1979–Privately Disagree That "The Debate Is Over"

In the *Ensign* magazine's publication of the First Presidency's regular monthly message, First Counselor N. Eldon Tanner wrote: "When the Prophet speaks, the debate is over."[17] For me, those were words to gag on. The context for this mind-numbing statement was President Kimball's opposition to the Equal Rights Amendment.

16 September 1979–Congenial Meeting with Apostle

From my journal for Sunday: "This afternoon at 4 P.M. I went to the Arlington Hills Ward in our stake for assignment to give a talk as one of the visiting High Councilmen. As I sat on the stand prior to the beginning of services, I was surprised to see Apostle Gordon B. Hinckley enter the chapel. His son [Richard] is the bishop of the ward.

"When Brother Hinckley came to the stand, I introduced myself as one of the visiting High Councilmen and asked if Brother Hinckley wanted to conclude the meeting with remarks. He said that he preferred not to, that he had just returned from a trip, was exhausted, and only wanted to partake of the sacrament. After he had sat next to me, Brother Hinckley remarked, 'You teach at Brigham Young University, don't you?'

"Immediately recognized that when I introduced myself as Michael Quinn, Brother Hinckley had identified me as the Michael Quinn of the prayer circle article. He and I chatted for a while about my reaction to commuting to BYU, his difficulty with jet lag in his travels, and just before the meeting began I made a point of commenting that I had known his daughter Jinny (although I mispronounced her nickname as 'Jenny') at New Haven....

"I gave to the Arlington Heights Ward the talk on the burdens of life which I had given previously to most of the other wards in the stake. I felt a good spirit with me as I spoke and testified, and I felt that my remarks reached the hearts of the people in the audience. As I sat down next to

17. See N. Eldon Tanner, "First Presidency Message: The Debate Is Over," *Ensign*, Aug. 1979.

Brother Hinckley at the end of my talk, he reached over and patted my thigh in an approving manner."

I didn't have the chutzpa to ask this very friendly apostle what he thought of my article on the prayer circle.

3 October 1979–God's Unconditional Love

From my journal about another church court: "I was firmly for excommunication, and yet despite my position in these two cases I have impressed my fellow members of the High Council as one who is filled with totally forgiving love for the accused.

"This results in part from my comments on both occasions when given opportunity to express my views to the accused after the verdicts, that no matter what else, I hoped that they had the conviction that nothing they could do could separate them from God's love even though their conduct could separate them from His blessings and [from] their own potentials."

8 October 1979–A Future US President as Demagogue/Dictator

From my journal: "I mentioned [to Ron Walker] some of my spiritual impressions (which I disbelieved at the time) concerning the death of Harold B. Lee and the eventual presidency of Spencer W. Kimball. When Ron Walker asked, in a kind of awe, whether I had any other impressions of a prophetic nature, I repeated that prophecy was not my gift, but I referred to my impressions in 1972 concerning Richard Nixon and the significance of the 1972 election and the need for his impeachment to preserve the Constitution, and the feeling that even if impeached, that Nixon would be succeeded by a succession of weak presidents and then there would arise an American demagogue as president (I believe that I wrote Dictator in my journal, but I did not use that strong word in relating the impression to Ron)."

29 October 1979–My Unconditional Love

From my journal: "This morning I dreamed about my former stepfather, Wayne Hood. I have not seen him since I returned from my mission in England in 1965. In the dream I greeted Wayne in love. I awoke this morning wondering how Wayne Hood is doing, and hoping that he believed me in 1965 when I told him that I still loved him despite his adultery and my mother's divorce from him."

2 November 1979–"Faith-Promoting" Stories of "Pure White Shirts"

Stake President Bradley hosted a dinner for members of the high council and their wives at his Park City recreational home. Also in attendance was our stake's regional representative, Richard J. Marshall.[18]

---

18. Richard J. Marshall (1928–2001) was a writer, advertising executive, and vice president of Maverick Country Stores. He helped establish the LDS Church's first visitors' centers.

After dinner, he stood to give "informal" remarks about the importance of wearing "pure white shirts" and dark ties as LDS administrators. Sitting next to him was the stake presidency's second counselor in his usual blue shirt, dark suit coat, and tie. Many of the high council's members were wearing ties with formal shirts of various hues (from off-white to the bright red shirt I wore with my beige suit). "Rather than lecture you about this," this regional representative said: "I'll tell you what I have learned from the Brethren themselves."

From my journal: "1) Marshall stopped by the house of Thomas Monson and found him dressed in his suit, white shirt, and tie [while] trimming the bushes, with his wife in her jeans and work shirt picking up after him; 2) On one occasion when Bruce R. McConkie was in the First Council of Seventy before his appointment to the Quorum of the Twelve Apostles, McConkie came to the Church Office Building one morning wearing a light beige shirt rather than the traditional white shirt. He met Thomas Monson, who congratulated him on how sharp the shirt looked, glanced at his own watch, and told McConkie that he had just enough time to go home and change the shirt before their meeting. Marshall said that McConkie left chuckling to himself at how well Monson had handled the situation without embarrassing him, whereas I was appalled at the ridiculousness and false values of the virtual clerical uniform that the white shirt has become for the general authorities."

Boyd K. Packer told our regional representative this final example of dressing "like Priesthood leaders." One summer, he arrived at an airport in central California to speak at a stake conference. In the sweltering heat, the stake president and his counselor had left their suit coats in the car. As the apostle left the plane, he was greeted by the two men in pure-white shirts, dark ties, and dark suit pants, but no suit coats. Instead of acknowledging the enthusiastic "Welcome, Elder Packer," or grasping the stake president's outstretched hand in a handshake, the apostle looked into the distance and commenced speaking, as if to himself: "Here I am, an apostle of the Lord Jesus Christ on His errand, and there is no one to greet me who is dressed like a presiding officer of the Holy Priesthood. I wonder how long I must wait before I see such men?" The California stake president's outstretched hand fell to his side. Without a word, he and his counselor walked away. Ten minutes later, wearing their suit coats, the two men sheepishly approached Elder Packer, who warmly greeted them as if seeing them for the first time in his life.

You could have heard a pin drop in the room after the regional representative related this last story to our stake presidency, high council, and wives. As Marshall summed up his remarks "in the name of Jesus Christ," I asked myself: "How could *anyone* regard that rude, offensive incident as faith promoting?!"

Neither the stake president nor anyone else ever referred to those remarks in my presence, but Elder Marshall's rebuke to us was clear. At the next high council meeting, President Bradley's second counselor wore a pure-white shirt. I never saw Doug Sorensen wearing his preferred blue shirts in another meeting.

As for me, I never wore a white shirt to a Church meeting again while I was on the stake's high council. No one said anything, even when I spoke monthly in ward sacrament meetings as the visiting high councilman, wearing shirts of various colors. Anything but white.

15 November 1979–My Views about a Mormon Dissident

From my journal: "At BYU again today. During the day I met Alan Morton, and we talked about Sonia Johnson, founder of 'Mormons for the Equal Rights Amendment,' and the fact that she has been summoned to a bishop's court for her activities, which she promptly reported to all the news media. The Church is going to get an awful public image over the situation."

I felt that LDS leaders should never try to intimidate any political activist. Nonetheless, I regarded Sonia Johnson as a self-aggrandizing, grandstanding egomaniac who did a profound disservice to the ERA and to her supporters.

I certainly had nothing against strong women or feminist activists. I regarded Bella Abzug, Betty Friedan, and Gloria Steinem as heroes—just as much as I admired Martin Luther King Jr. and his campaign for racial equality. If possible, I would have voted for Texas's 1970s African American Congresswoman Barbara Jordan to serve in any higher office, including US president.

All activists and public figures have big egos and want publicity, but Sonia Johnson seemed to me to be extraordinarily self-serving. Due to the histrionics she displayed in front of TV cameras at her excommunication this December, I regarded her as a very eager martyr.[19]

23 November 1979–Article Rejected by Church Correlation

From my journal: "I telephoned Lavina Fielding Anderson at the *Ensign*, and she said that the staff had decided to run my article on Jesse Gause in the June issue 1980, and I would be paid about $60.00 for the article. Life must go on—at least for the present—and I am pleased at this news."

Nonetheless, within months, the correlation committee killed this article about Joseph Smith's little-known first counselor in 1832. Even though my article only expanded what Robert J. Woodford had published in *BYU Studies* five years earlier, the correlation censors regarded it as too revisionist

---

19. Sonia Ann Harris Johnson (1936–) recounted her life as a Mormon, her feminism, and her excommunication in her book, *From Housewife to Heretic* (New York: Doubleday, 1981).

and "not faith promoting." *BYU Studies* would publish my expansion four years from now.[20]

9 December 1979–BYU Professor's "Spiteful Power Play"

From my journal: "While I was waiting in the foyer, I met Gordon Affleck who told me some disturbing news. He said that David Yarn had written a letter to Ezra Taft Benson in which Yarn told Benson that the biography which Frank Fox had written about J. Reuben Clark demeaned President Clark, criticized President Clark, and failed to present him as the great man that he was. I was amazed to hear this.[21]

"Affleck told me that Benson telephoned him and referred to the letter and asked what Affleck thought of the accuracy of the charges. Affleck said that he had read the manuscript of the book, that the family had read it, and that Affleck had read it verbally to Marion G. Romney whose eyesight was too poor to read it himself, and that all of them agreed that the biography was a fine tribute to the career and stature of J. Reuben Clark.[22]

This ended the admiration I had felt for my former professor of philosophy since 1968. I was now sad and angry.

17 December 1979–A General Authority Likes My Prayer Circle Article

From my journal: "We had just left [a wedding] reception line a few minutes, when President and Sister Marion D. Hanks came into the room where we were. Maxine Hanks came up to me and took me by the arm and said how good it was to see me again. ... Then President Hanks took me aside. He warmly and firmly shook my hand. ... He knows of the struggle that Jan and I have in life, and he also has expressed his deep regard for us both.

"He said that he very much enjoyed reading the skillful article I wrote on the Prayer Circle, and said that one day he would like to talk with me about it."

23 December 1979–Stake President's Spiritual Response about Me

From my journal: "During the day I went up to the stake center, and while I was there, President Bradley told me that he regards it as a blessing for me to serve on the high council because of the special spirit I bring to the meetings. He said, 'When you pray in our meetings, I can feel an abundance of the Spirit of the Lord come upon us,' and his eyes welled up with tears as he spoke.

---

20. See D. Michael Quinn, "Jesse Gause: Joseph Smith's Little-Known Counselor," *BYU Studies* 23, no. 4 (Fall 1983), 487–93.

21. David H. Yarn (1920–2012) was a BYU administrator and professor of philosophy and of religion. He helped establish the school's College of Religion and was its first dean.

22. Frank W. Fox's biography, titled *J. Reuben Clark, The Public Years*, was published by BYU Press and the Deseret Book Company in 1980. This rumor Quinn relates about Yarn opposing the biography is odd, because Yarn is listed opposite the title page as the general editor of the book, the "first of a multi-volume set on the life and work of J. Reuben Clark."

"I said, 'President Bradley, I cannot say much about that, but I regard it as a blessing to be associated with you, for I have never known a stake president to be so concerned with things of the Spirit and the needs of the people as you are.'"

During one month, he asked me to pray at four weekly meetings in a row of the Emigration Stake's high council.

29 December 1979–Dinners with a Muslim Diplomat and His Family

Among those in my 1976–77 carpool to BYU was Mrs. Nihmat Saab, a Lebanese woman who was studying for a master's degree in library science. Her husband Hassan H. Saab was a diplomat at the United Nations, who moved her and their teenage sons from Beirut to Salt Lake City during the Lebanese civil war. A student at the University of Utah, their son Marwan was as good-looking as his name was beautiful. During this diplomat's visits to Utah, they often invited Jan and me to their home on Fifth Avenue for dinners that took Nihmat hours to prepare.

Most of all, Mr. Saab was proud of her independent spirit. She was the first woman in her family and clan to decline a parent-arranged marriage, instead waiting until she met a Lebanese man of her choosing. Commuting 100 miles a day to obtain an MLS degree was one more evidence of Nihmat's independence. And she was a woman of grace.

Nearly a year previously, Mr. Saab had a meeting with the First Presidency. It was heralded by the *Church News*.

In less than five years, the Saabs would invite Jan and me to a catered dinner at an exclusive restaurant. It celebrated Marwan's graduation from medical school in LA.

At the Saab Family's dinners since 1976, I had met several Middle Eastern professors. One of them was Egyptian-born Aziz S. Atiya, an internationally renown scholar of Coptic Christianity, who had helped the LDS Church acquire the Book of Abraham papyri from New York's Metropolitan Museum twelve years earlier.

Tonight's gathering was of special significance, due to the recently signed Camp David Agreement between Egypt's President Anwar Sadat and Israel's Prime Minister Menachem Begin. "I am cautiously optimistic about the future of the Middle East," Mr. Saab said.

Either tonight or at another dinner, the Saabs talked about the risks involved with being liberal and moderate in a polarized society. Before Lebanon's civil war, they had liberal friends among its Muslim and Christian pluralities, as well as among its Druze, Baha'i, and Jewish minorities. When civil war began, they sent Marwan and his brother to Utah—because of their friends at the university—but Mrs. Saab remained in Lebanon. Soon their liberal Lebanese friends were being assassinated one by one. Every side hated its own moderates in this conflict. She moved to Utah after death threats came to her unlisted phone in Beirut.

This made me reflect on the non-violent but frustrating plight of moderates in my own culture. Conservative Republicans like William F. Buckley excoriated liberal Republican senators like Edward Brooke of Massachusetts and Lowell Weicker of Connecticut, who were also criticized for being too conservative by liberal Democrats like me. Likewise, "conceal-the-problems" apostles Ezra Taft Benson and Boyd K. Packer had undermined official Church Historian Leonard Arrington, who on the other hand was quietly criticized by tell-everything-relevant historians like me.

Lebanon demonstrated that for a richly diverse culture to survive, there must be middle paths between its polarities. Achieving this is easier said than done in politics, in society, and in religion.

6 January 1980–Filial Feelings for God

From my journal: "My relationship with Him has had the intensity of the closest father-son relationship on earth ever since my own childhood, and I have long since outgrown the childish position of demanding that God do things according to my wishes. I express to Him my thoughts, fears, hopes, aspirations, needs (as I see them), struggles, pains, and gratitude for His innumerable blessings which He has given to me without my meriting them, and thank Him for His Spirit which I have had as an inward Comforter and Strength and outward protection since childhood.

"But I make no demands upon Him, and accept the consequences of His specific will or of the circumstances of life which He allows to come upon me."

10 January 1980–Trevor Southey

From my journal: "We were sitting next to two paintings by Trevor Southey, the South African Mormon who now lives in Utah County, and whose paintings have become quite popular in the past five or ten years. I noted [silently] that his painting of a young husband touching the abdomen of his very pregnant wife presented a well-executed study of the musculature of the backside of the young man's body.

"Trevor Southey's art is a celebration of the human body's beauty in thinly disguised nudes, and I have found it interesting that his art is so popular among the Latter-day Saints who seem to be so sexually repressed in most other ways. I didn't express this to Jan."

A few years later, I learned that Trevor (like me) was a married Mormon homosexual. And (like me) he was a loving father of four children. This Rhodesian-born artist and I would become friends.

22 January 1980—Three Loves and My Now-Regretted Path

From my journal: "The conscious decisions I made from the age of ten to eighteen would be recommended today by Prophets and other good people as the proper struggle toward exaltation and happiness here on earth, but I now regret nearly all of the major and minor decisions I made for moral restraint in anticipation of a future happy life and service to God. Had I made different decisions during those years, I would have recognized more fully (perhaps completely) who I was and my nature would have found its own level and contentment.

"I loved God, the Church, and the flesh, and I felt that by repressing the third love I would find complete fulfillment in acceptable ways through the first two loves. ... Could the destructive results of choosing the way of the carnality that was natural for me from ages ten to eighteen have been any worse than the ultimate damage I have caused, am causing, and will cause by rejecting those carnal options and seeking to be a spiritual Mormon, husband, father, potential Apostle and god-in-embryo? ...

"I honestly wonder if I had taken the many possible roads to the [homosexual] sensuality that was natural to me, if the outcome could have made me more miserable than I am now. I don't think that I could have felt as bad about the unhappiness such a course would have brought to my family as I now feel about the unhappiness it has brought to my wife and will ultimately bring to my family anyway.

"The road I have taken has expanded the circle of misery without enabling me to do a lot of good in the lives of others. ... I cannot recapture that lost option, because if I now took the opportunity (such as it is) for the sensual life I have rejected for twenty-five years, it would not undo the shambles of my present life and it would not bring much sexual contentment either (since I am now nearly asexual, burned out by repression).

"I look at myself, what I am and what it is logical that I can expect to be, and I ask: Has it been worth all of the above for me to be a revisionist writer of LDS history, a silver-tongued orator at occasional Church meetings, and an inadequate and indifferent low-level Church administrator? God only knows, and I am in His hands as I have always wanted to be. *Quo Vadis*—should that be a declaration or a question of my life? ...

"How many [LDS marriages] are like mine? God have mercy on those of us who have failed so miserably while trying so hard to [be] good and fulfill Your will!"

24 January 1980—Sesquicentennial History of Sixteen Projected Volumes

From my journal: "Tom [Alexander] indicated that the first three volumes of the Sesquicentennial Church History that have been submitted for review were approved with virtually no changes by Leonard Arrington and G. Homer Durham. These are volumes by [BYU professors] Milton Backman, Richard Cowan, and Lanier Britsch—none of whom are controversial writers. But Tom said that Durham refuses to take responsibility for final decisions, and that Durham sent the volumes for review and approval by the Quorum of the Twelve Apostles.

"At this point, I said that was a disaster! Even if we discount the problem of their objecting to open treatment of Church history, the Apostles are run ragged with numerous other demands, all of which have varying degrees of priority in the minds of the Brethren whereas reading a manuscript about Church History has no priority. I said that it is very likely that the manuscripts could simply be forgotten about for months. I said that if the volumes had to be reviewed at a level beyond the Historical Department it would have been far better for them to have been sent to Church Correlation, because the men of Correlation have as their sole mission the reading and evaluation of manuscripts, and at least the manuscripts would be read with a sense of priority.

"Tom said that he could not understand why Durham would not take the responsibility, but that Leonard was trying to use the Quorum of Twelve review of the first three volumes as the basis for getting a blanket approval to go ahead with all the rest subject to approval only of the Historical Department. I said that Durham's every action, inaction, and apparent shift in philosophy, could all be perfectly understood if you recognize that he is the absolute bureaucrat."

Thirteen months later, Leonard Arrington would announce through the Mormon History Association newsletter that this sixteen-volume history had been abandoned. He used the word "modified." The LDS Church's publishing house, Deseret Book, canceled all the contracts and allowed each author to publish elsewhere. He eventually learned that G. Homer Durham and apostle Hinckley had agreed to kill the project in April 1978, "even though it had been authorized by the First Presidency" (Arrington, *Adventures of a Church Historian*, 166).

As in medieval Camelot, *media vita in morte sumus*.[23]

31 January 1980–Straining at Gnats

From my journal: "Frank Fox asked to see me. He said that he had been asked to give me a message concerning my 'Author's Preface' to my volume on Clark. He said that they (I guess the Trustees and family) didn't want me to use the word 'role.'

"I am sure that I had a blank look on my face, and Frank said: 'Now, you have got to understand these people. They swallow elephants and strain at

---

23. Latin, meaning, "In the midst of life we are in death."

gnats.' I said that I could use the word 'function' rather than 'role.' We talked about the hopes we share for his book being published by April, so that it can be a ground breaker for the book I am going to write."

13 February 1980–The Richards Family

From my journal: "Jim Richards, whom I knew in the British Mission, complimented me on my article about his family in the *Ensign*."

The official LDS magazine had just published a faith-promoting version of my group biography approach to the hierarchy. It was titled: "They Served: The Richards Legacy in the Church." Now an officer with me in the Emigration Stake, Jim was a grandson of apostle-counselor Stephen L Richards, whereas I had grown up with grandchildren of apostle LeGrand Richards.

17 February 1980–Preaching Repentance to an Apostle

From my journal: "After dinner, Jan went to Choir practice and I went to the 21st Ward for prayer meeting with the bishopric prior to Sacrament Meeting. President Benson was on the stand in the Sacrament Meeting, and I sat on the opposite end of the stand from where Bishop [Stephen W.] Barlow said President Benson usually sat. When it was my turn to speak at 2:45 [as visiting high councilman], I walked over to President Benson and asked if he would like to speak following my remarks, but he said that he thought he probably would not.

"I had been praying all meeting that the Lord's Spirit would be with me, because I felt it would be rank hypocrisy for me to give a different talk in this ward on Repentance than I had given in other wards of the stake, merely because I feared Ezra Taft Benson would dislike my comments against the tendency for perfection now in the Church, against Phariseeism of self-righteous Temple Recommend Holders, about gossip being a far worse sin than violating the Word of Wisdom, even though gossip was not on the temple recommend, against thinking that salvation was a kind of checklist (represented by the temple recommend interview), when in fact it was a personal relationship through the Spirit with Christ.

"After beginning, as usual, with the J. Golden Kimball story that he couldn't be excommunicated for swearing at the pulpit because he repented too damned fast, I asked the congregation to pray for me that the Spirit would be with me in my remarks about Repentance.

"I was very nervous about Brother Benson as I began, and I stumbled over some words in the first few scripture quotes I read, and my presentation throughout was, I think, not as smooth as I have presented it in other wards, but I found that after a few minutes I was so caught up in the Spirit of the talk, that I no longer felt the fear about President Benson's response, and I ended up saying everything with as much emphasis, that I have ever said in this talk in any other ward. I concluded my remarks at 3:15, and half expected Brother Benson to stand up to make remarks of one kind or another, but he did not. ...

"After he had thanked the choir members for their musical number, he came over to me and thanked me for my remarks, and said: 'Yes, repentance is a great principle. The most important thing about it is for a person to reform his life, isn't it?' I said 'Yes,' but I don't believe that he understood what else I was saying in the talk, but perhaps he did. ...

"As I walked from the stand to leave the building, several members of the ward, most of them elderly, enthusiastically thanked me for my remarks."

21 February 1980–Another Insight into LDS Headquarters

From my journal: "My reference to Harold B. Lee in last night's entry reminds me of something that [European historian] Doug Tobler told me when I spoke with him at BYU on Thursday, February 14, that I forgot to record that day. ...

"Doug Tobler said that one example of the way power could corrupt a good man was Harold B. Lee as president of the Church, for whom the ascendance to the position of president of the Church brought to Brother Lee an arrogance that was withering to everyone who associated with him.

"Tobler said that his own father-in-law, Arch Madsen, was president of KSL during the period before, during, and after Harold B. Lee was president of the Church for that 18 months, and Tobler said that when Madsen learned of the death of Harold B. Lee, it brought such a sense of relief to him that [Arch L.] Madsen put his head in his hands and sobbed—not out of sorrow but out of relief and happiness, despite his guilt for feeling that way."

As I listened to this BYU professor talking about Harold B. Lee as Church president, I thought about a similar assessment that general authority Marion D. Hanks had given me in November 1965 about Elder Lee as an apostle. And I could never forget apostle Lee's shameful behavior in performing the sealing ceremony for my missionary companion in September 1966. All prophets, seers, and revelators remain deeply flawed humans.

26 February 1980–Prophetic Infallibility?

Apostle Ezra Taft Benson (next in line to become LDS president) outlined "14 Fundamentals in Following the Prophets" in a sermon to BYU's students. The fourth was: "The Prophet will never lead the Church astray."

First, as I told several friends, this was absolutely false doctrine. Doctrine and Covenants 107:65, 82–84, even specified the procedure for excommunicating the "president of the High Priesthood" so that none of the Church officers mentioned in this revelation "shall be exempted from the justice and the laws of God."

Despite Brigham Young's authoritarian personality, this president of the LDS Church warned its members: "If you depend entirely upon the voice, judgment, and sagacity [wisdom] of those appointed to lead you, and neglect to enjoy the Spirit yourselves, how easily you may be led into error, and finally be cast off to the left hand" (*Journal of Discourses* 8:59).

From my journal for this day: "Second, (and God forgive me if I am wrong) it seemed evident that President Benson is anticipating and looking forward to the near death of Spencer W. Kimball that will make Benson the new LDS president. This talk had all the earmarks to me of being an announced platform for Ezra Taft Benson's intended Presidency over the LDS Church and his plans for being a political activist as LDS president.

"Third, what depressed and scared me as much as the talk itself was seeing the camera show students with notepads writing down extensive notes as Benson spoke. There is a regimented mentality that exists not only among the radical right-wing conservatives of the LDS Church, but also among the moderate Mormons who will follow in strict obedience the LDS president.

"Benson's talk was directed to these moderate, devoted, and obedient Mormons (who constitute the bulk of Church membership) and not to the wild-eyed right-wing extremists who are already Benson's avid supporters.

"Fourth, Benson's talk indicates to me that he plans as soon as he is LDS president to begin not only political activism but to actively root out all dissent within the Church and that this talk will be the basis for classifying any who disagree with him as apostates who are unworthy of Church membership.

"Fifth, what is more disturbing (if that is possible) than any of the previous four considerations, is that even if Benson died next week, he has created a talk and a document which will stand (unless somehow repudiated by a living LDS president) as a perpetual rationale for *any* future LDS president to wage dictatorial rule with the resources and the obedience of the Latter-day Saint Church.

"Even if *one* of these five reflections is true, there is great cause for fear about the progress of the Church of Jesus Christ of Latter-day Saints, and its leaders and people. God help us all!"

29 February 1980–General Authorities Reversing and Temporizing

From my journal: "As Leonard and I walked to the Historical Department, I asked him if G. Homer Durham was still making a decision one day and then completely reversing himself (as though he had never made a contrary decision earlier) within a few days or weeks. Leonard said that was still true.

"I told Leonard that I felt something was wrong with Durham in this regard, and that I had given up having anything to do with him because of his many erratic ways. Leonard said that he himself thought Durham actually couldn't remember previous decisions he had made. ...

"I spent about half an hour talking alone with Ronald Walker. As usual we seem to feed each other's depressions about the situation at the Historical Department with Durham and about the frustrations and fear we have about our respective biographies—his of Heber J. Grant and mine of Clark. ...

"Ron said that his depression was so great that he had finally asked for a private interview with Gordon B. Hinckley, who is a member of Ron's ward in which Ron is the bishop. Ron asked Hinckley if he felt that the time was right, that the authorities would tolerate or support truthful, yet faithful history of the Church and its leaders (such as Heber J. Grant). Gordon B. Hinckley answered, 'Ron, I don't think I am able to tell you whether now is the right time for such history.'"

10 March 1980–Trying to Be a Ghostwriter for First Presidency

From my journal: "I worked until 11:30 [AM], in finalizing the proposed First Presidency statement on 'Living Prophets,' and met Jim [McConkie] at 12:00. He was very pleased with the document and promised that he would send it to his uncle," apostle Bruce R. McConkie.

26 March 1980–Birthday Presents from LDS Hierarchy

From my journal: "At 11:30, I met Jim McConkie for lunch. He told me that he thought President [N. Eldon] Tanner had been given a large type copy of my paper on 'Living Prophets' by Tanner's grandson.

"Jim also told me that he had learned (I guess through Bruce R. McConkie) that President Kimball was incensed at Benson's talk to BYU students about following the Living Prophet, and allegedly President Kimball reprimanded Ezra Taft Benson personally for it.

"Jim also said that President Kimball sent a memo to every general authority saying that President Kimball did not want to be referred to as 'The Prophet,' but instead to be called 'President Kimball.'

"If these things are true, then perhaps there is hope that the First Presidency will make some authoritative message to counter Benson's talk along the lines I suggested in my paper that may have reached N. Eldon Tanner's ears by this time.

"As I pointed out to Jim today, if Spencer W. Kimball expresses his disagreement with the content and implications of Benson's talk only privately and not in an authoritative manner, then he may as well have said nothing at all because Benson's public and published views must be officially and publicly countered or his BYU talk will become a new article of faith in the future."

30 March 1980–Presidency Counselor Endorses My Treatise

From my journal: "Jim [McConkie] also gave me the great news that on Sunday evening last my paper on 'Living Prophets' was read to President N. Eldon Tanner by Tanner's grandson. When it came to the concluding section about the responsibilities and options of Church members who lack confirmation about certain statements of the president of the Church, President Tanner asked his grandson to read that section to him *three* times.

"After the third time, President Tanner said that it was true doctrine and an important perspective. His grandson asked President Tanner to give serious consideration to issuing this statement or something like it as a letter of the First Presidency, and President Tanner said that he would consider it.

"Then his grandson told President Tanner that he had asked three bishops in the Salt Lake Valley if they would give a temple recommend to someone who sustained the president of the Church but said that there were certain statements of the president that they did not believe in or have a personal conviction of. All three of the bishops said that they would deny a temple recommend to any member of the Church who made such a 'confession.' President Tanner was dumbfounded to hear this report from his grandson and said, 'I can't believe that such misunderstanding of the principles of the Church exists among the Priesthood leaders.'

"President Tanner's grandson again urged that the statement on 'Living Prophets' be issued as a First Presidency statement and he told his grandfather that no one else would do it if President Tanner did not urge it now."

Because it would be rightly perceived as a rebuttal of apostle Benson's talk, the First Presidency would never issue my ghost-written statement in part or whole. Alas.

4 April 1980–Joining Editorial Board

From my journal: "Accepted by letter the invitation to join the board of editors for *Journal of Mormon History*."[24]

6 April 1980–Enfeebled Leadership of the LDS Church

From my journal: "The only thing of note was that after President Kimball gave his short remarks prior to his intended and announced dedication of the Fayette Branch house, which was to be a highlight of the Conference session since it is the visitors center for the place where the Church was organized

---

24. The *Journal of Mormon History* is the scholarly publication of the Mormon History Association, currently published quarterly. It began publication in 1974 as an annual journal.

150 years ago, that President Kimball sat down without giving the dedicatory prayer and had to be reminded to do so. ...

"How long can this situation of enfeebled prophetic leadership continue for a Church that is doubling its membership every fifteen years, as was announced today, and therefore will have 9 million members in 1995, and dozens of millions in the lifetime of my children?

"I have defended the automatic succession of the senior Apostle to the LDS Presidency because it assures stability, but I wonder how long the Church can continue to pay the price of being ruled by a gerontocracy wherein the president of the Church (as was Wilford Woodruff, Heber J. Grant, David O. McKay, and Joseph Fielding Smith in particular) is so enfeebled by age that his decision making is carried on by his official counselors or (worse yet!) by hireling secretaries.

"The situation makes the highest levels of the Church ripe for palace intrigues, sycophancy, vicarious decision making, and all other of the worst kinds of abuses."

10 April 1980–Keeping Utah's Newspapers "In Line"

From my journal, concerning an apostle's visit with BYU's History Department: "At one point in his off-the-cuff remarks, Marvin [J.] Ashton took out a newspaper clipping that quoted from the BYU *Daily Universe* report of prominent speakers who had been denied the opportunity to speak at BYU (including the wife of U.S. President Ford while he was still in office, and Henry Kissinger, to name a few), with comments by Robert K. Thomas and others [of BYU's chief administrators] on the decision.

"Brother Ashton said, 'We don't need this. Can't you people in Provo control the student newspaper. We have finally got the University of Utah *Chronicle* in line by having one of our men in charge of it. We just don't need that kind of story coming from BYU's newspaper.' ...

"All my work and goals seem so hopelessly outgunned by the Public Relations mentality and Grand Inquisitor mentality that seem to infect all of the general authorities."

17 April 1980–A Colleague's Concern and My Arrogance

From my journal: "As Dean [L. May] expressed his interest in my publishing the hierarchy study, he looked at me kind of sadly and said quietly, 'Mike, I worry about you and the consequences of what you are doing.'

"I passed off his comment lightly with the rejoinder, 'You had better read my MHA paper, because that may give you more cause for worry.' Afterwards, I regretted my flippant response to a genuine expression of personal interest and concern from Dean.

"Am I as arrogant as I seem? I must be. When I am destroyed personally, professionally, or otherwise, many will say that I got just what I deserved. They will probably be right, even though I have tried so hard to do what I feel the Lord has sanctioned my doing."

1 May 1980–Revisionist Article on Mormon Theocracy

From my journal: "During the flight from Chicago to Rochester, Linda Newell showed me a copy of the new issue of *BYU Studies* which Chuck Tate gave her because it has her article on Emma and Brigham.[25] Linda said that she was anxious to read my article on the Council of Fifty. So, at last my Council of Fifty article is out and in the distribution chain. I silently thanked the Lord."[26]

In this revisionist essay, I argued that the secretive body met regularly and had a crucial role during only a few months in 1844, in 1845, and in 1848–49. Moreover, between 1850 and its last meeting in 1884, attendance records showed that this theocratic council never met during two periods of more than a decade each.

Even worse for the grand importance Klaus J. Hansen's 1967 *Quest for Empire* had attached to the Council of Fifty, it was demonstrably a rubber stamp after 1850 for decisions already made by the First Presidency of the Church. He and I became acquainted in the New Haven Ward when my doctoral study at Yale overlapped with his year of research there.

While I recognize the personal attachment authors have to their publications, I was very disappointed that my friend Klaus continued to speak at academic conferences and to publish articles/books on the subject as if his 1967 book were the last word. He acted as if my article didn't exist or require fundamental reassessments. Two years after its 1980 publication, when I attended academic sessions at which someone else asked Klaus about my unmentioned article, he would still be making the lame excuse that he hadn't yet read my article because *BYU Studies* was difficult to get in Canada!

Klaus was a brilliant historian of American culture at Queen's College, but seemed intransigent about this topic that had given him such academic fame. For another two decades, even when he did refer in print to my article,

---

25. Linda King Newell (1941–2023) was co-editor of *Dialogue: A Journal of Mormon Thought* and president of both the John Whitmer Historical Association and the Mormon History Association. The article Quinn mentioned, "Sweet Counsel and Seas of Tribulation: The Religious Life of Women in Kirtland," *BYU Studies* 20, no. 2 (1980), 151n62, was co-authored with Valeen Tippetts Avery and was a precursor to their seminal biography, *Mormon Enigma: Emma Hale Smith* (New York: Doubleday, 1984).

26. See D. Michael Quinn, "The Council of Fifty and Its Members, 1844 to 1945," *BYU Studies* 20, no. 2 (1980), 163–97.

he would do so dismissively—without ever acknowledging its crucial evidences or main arguments.

2 May 1980–Startling My Associates in New Mormon History

The Mormon History Association's meeting at Canandaigua, New York, was part of the church's 150-year commemoration. Most of the presentations were celebrative, but I gave a talk, "From Sacred Grove to Sacral Power Structure." Its opening line announced that I would examine "a series of interrelated and crucial transitions" of Mormonism in those 150 years. They were "individualism to corporate dynasticism, authoritarian democracy to authoritarian oligarchy, theocracy to bureaucracy, communitarianism to capitalism, and neocracy to gerontocracy." As chair of this session, Richard L. Bushman introduced me as its main speaker.

From my journal: "One young man in the audience seemed to share the acute personal shock and discomfort at my paper as had the [LDS] commentator [James G. Clawson] from Harvard Business School.[27] The fellow in the audience asked, 'How are we to interpret your paper regarding the president of the Church?'

"I answered, 'I can't answer that question for you. It depends on how you define the Prophet: whether you regard him in the Catholic sense as infallible, not in his personal conduct, but in his doctrinal pronouncements, or whether you regard Prophets as men who remain men despite their divine callings, and therefore one can see the man in the Prophet and the Prophet in the man.'"

During an informal, late-night discussion with a dozen historians in the hotel room of Jan Shipps, I said that the current LDS Church seemed to be in a situation similar to late-medieval Catholicism. The devout were in a frenzy of faithful observances that were less and less satisfying to them. Jim Allen broke the awkward silence that followed by asking: "Do you see yourself as a modern Luther who will post your own 95 Theses about Mormonism?"

This was another reminder that I come across to others as a radical. I said something to the effect that I'm not an activist or reformer, even though I admire those who are.

10 May 1980–Jeffrey R. Holland and the Seductive LDS Bureaucracy

From my journal: "Yesterday, it was announced that Jeff Holland was appointed the new president of Brigham Young University.[28] He is about

---

27. James G. Clawson is an author and emeritus professor of leadership and organizational behavior in the Darden School of Business at the University of Virginia. He taught at Harvard Business School before joining Darden's faculty in 1981.

28. At the time of this appointment, Holland had been serving as Commissioner of Education (overseeing all church schools) since 1976. He was called as an LDS apostle in 1994.

three years older than I am. I like Jeff personally and respect his emphasis on academic achievement, but I find some troubling implications of his appointment. ...

"I think that by personality and by his seductive years within the Church bureaucracy, Jeff Holland will not cross swords with the Board of Trustees, no matter how much he disagrees with them. I believe that is the primary reason he has been appointed [to replace the sometimes combative Dallin H. Oaks], and it bodes very ill for academic freedom and enrichment at BYU."

18 May 1980–Three Times a Rebel

From my journal: "Brother Flandro greeted with absolute, stunned silence [in the High Priest Group meeting of the 27th Ward] my comments that I am unalterably opposed to prayer in public schools, that I no more want my daughter to be taught Hail Mary's if we ever live again in a community like New Haven, Connecticut where Catholicism is very strong, nor do I want Jewish and Catholic children forced to learn or listen to Mormon-structured prayers in Utah. I also objected to having even silent periods for meditation in public schools, because I regard this as a travesty in that if religious educations have any meaning at all, they must occur in the family or in the Church not in the schools under any pretext whatever.

"It absolutely astounds me that the same people who are horrified at the thought of teaching school children the indisputable facts of sexual reproduction in the schools on the argument that that is the sole responsibility of the parents, are the same people who demand that the public schools provide opportunity and practice of sectarian prayer (which is disputable in substance and format according to one's religious precepts) when that is clearly the domain of parents to teach and foster.

"In the Sunday School class, the lesson was on the Law of Consecration as it related to the Welfare Program, and I remained silent until Mark [Macklis] made the comment that private property was essential to the concept of the United Order or Law of Consecration.

"I raised my hand at this point, and observed with a quotation in the Doctrine and Covenants [104:54–56, 62], that no one could fulfill the concept of being a steward in the law of consecration who retained the devotion to private property. No one in class made a comment about my comment, but Mark was obviously unnerved by what I said. ...

"[As the visiting high councilman,] I was the only speaker [at the sacrament meeting of the Fairfax Ward for unmarried LDS], and talked for 45 minutes on developing a relationship with Christ, on testimony. I commented that the Church was not an end in itself, but only a vehicle, or means to an end. I noted that even that comment implies that our goal is a location or place, whereas I noted that it is not a place which we seek, but a relationship with God and Christ, wherein we are comfortable in their presence.

"Then I spoke about the fact that many member[s] of the Church and some Church leaders engaged in a type of spiritual arrogance by affirming that a particular spiritual experience or type of testimony is the only valid kind merely because it is the only kind they have. ... I pointed out that the Spirit is not an easily defined experience, and that it defies in its manifestation the kinds of restrictions and consistencies that we wish to impose upon it [John 3:8].

"I pointed out the possibility of contradictory impressions about the same matter being given to people. I emphasized that different spiritual experiences did not mean that one was better or truer than another. I referred to my ten years of researching the diaries, personal correspondence, and other documents by all the general authorities of the Church to the present, and commented that some GAs have had visionary experiences, whereas other GAs have never had them despite earnest prayers for such, that some GAs disdained seeking daily revelations, whereas other GAs sought daily revelations, where some GAs experienced the burnings of the Spirit within, whereas other GAs did not.

"Then I described my own spiritual testimony and progress, and closed with a prayer that we would each seek to develop our own relationship with Christ and the Spirit, but recognize that others would have different experiences than we did and that their experiences were not necessarily better or lesser than ours.

"I had prayed during the Sacrament that I would be able to speak by the Spirit to the spirits of the audience, without losing my emotional composure. I had not even a touch of emotion until we sang the closing song, 'Abide With Me, 'Tis Eventide,' when I had to stop even trying to sing during the second and third verses as tears streamed down my cheeks.

"Perhaps a dozen or more of the singles of the Fairfax Ward came up to thank me for my remarks. One fellow asked what my profession was. When I replied that I was a historian, he said, 'I am a professional counselor, and I would have sworn from your method of communication that you also were a professional counselor.'"

20 May 1980–Notifying First Presidency about Post-1890 Polygamy

From my journal: "I awoke about 5:30, probably in anticipation of delivering my letter to the First Presidency today.

"After I took the bus downtown, I mailed the copies [of my letter] to Arrington and Durham, and crossed the street to the 47 East [South Temple] Church Offices."

This fulfilled the plan I described during the previous month to emphasize to them "the problem of post-Manifesto polygamy, and my proposal for a detailed study of it." I still planned for this to be in *Dialogue*.

25 May 1980–Uncensored Version of J. Reuben Clark's Biography

From my journal: "After the concert [in our 27th Ward], Jan and I went to her parents, where we had conversation and rhubarb pie. At their request, I told the Darleys about the problems JRC faced in the presidencies of Grant, Smith, and McKay.

"The Darleys urged me to let them read the uncensored version of my book on JRC, and seemed surprised that I felt reticent to either circulate such a thing or to keep my own copy of the uncensored version. Jan and her mother particularly urged me to keep a copy of my original, uncensored version of JRC biography." I took their advice.

5 June 1980–Leaving the Outcome to God: A Death Wish?

From my journal: "I ask no quarter or approval of any human being. I ask only the approval and sanction and ability from God. I leave the outcome to Him, if I can only be given the opportunities to act."

This was why BYU historian Frank Fox made the following assessment of the way I write Mormon history: "You have a deathwish, Mike."

CHAPTER SIXTEEN

APOSTLES VS. HISTORIANS

1980-1982

6 June 1980–Male Bonding at a Distance

From my journal: "I got up about 6 a.m., and went to the East High track to run. I ran four miles. As I was about half through, and going at a pretty good pace, another fellow came onto the track in a running suit.

"As I came around the track again, I saw that he was running behind me at a pretty fast pace, and I adjusted my own pace until we were running abreast, even though he was two lanes from me on the track. We didn't say a word to each other, but continued to run abreast, each of us adjusting our paces (which were going pretty fast). After a lap or so, he accelerated and ran half a lap at a fast dash, and then turned around and started walking against the direction of the runners.

"As I approached him at my running pace, he gave me a broad grin, said 'Thanks,' and I said 'Sure,' and continued running. There was a momentary bond of a shared experience through adjusting to one another that seemed almost profound to me, even though it was almost wordlessly with a stranger. I may never see him again, but those moments of shared physical exertion, enjoyment, and mutual give-and-take seem strangely important to me." This non-touching intimacy was the most I would share with young men for nearly a decade.

12 June 1980–"Secular Approach" to LDS History?

From my journal: "Later, the young man [a BYU graduate student assigned to me] asked how I thought he would 'fit in,' if he pursued a degree in history and imbibed the secular approach to LDS Church history that seems to characterize my own writings as well as those of Leonard Arrington, Davis Bitton, James B. Allen, and others now publishing.

"I told the young man that I could not answer that question for him. I said that personally, I had never published anything without praying extensively about the article as I was researching and writing it and as I considered publishing it, and that was not something I advertised in my writings, but it was part of my relationship with the Lord and with my profession.

"I commented that he would have to do what he felt good about personally—in his relationship with the Lord and with his professional standards—and that no one else ([his religion professor] Keith Perkins, me, Ezra Taft Benson, or anyone else) could answer for him the question of how he felt personally comfortable in those relationships. I pointed out that if he chose to deal with sensitive areas of Church history (his senior history seminar paper was a case study of one post-1890 polygamist, Anson Bowen Call[1]) he would have to realize that a number of the general authorities were hostile or fearful of such honesty because they wanted to avoid anything that might possibly hurt the testimony of the newest member of the Church, and yet I pointed out that honest presentation of sensitive areas of the Church and its history could bring greater breadth and strength to the testimony of new members as well as born members of the Church. ...

"I added, 'If you adopt a similar view, I hope you realize that you will *never* convert those of the opposite point of view.' He said that he appreciated our talk, and looked forward to working with me on his graduate program."

13 June 1980—Working-Class Origins

From my journal: "Jan and I left Lisa in charge of the boys as we drove to the Glendale Theatre on the west side of town. ...

"As we drove away from the movie, Jan commented that she could never live on the west side of the city or valley permanently because their standards and lifestyle were so much different and lower than her own family's and her values and expectations.

"I commented to Jan that 'these are my people. This is the kind of neighborhood, lower-middle class at best, that I grew up in, and that I lied to get away from when I was about to enter junior high school.' Jan spoke as if that perception of my background had never occurred to her before, and we talked about those values of working-class neighborhoods."

16 June 1980—Liberal Historian Hero, Richard D. Poll

From my journal: "At the library, I met with Dick Poll and gave him tips for his biography of H. D. Moyle.[2] He expressed great anticipations for my career, and I said I hoped my JRC book wouldn't end it."[3]

---

1. Anson Bowen Call (1863–1958) married Mary Theresa Thompson in 1885, Harriet Cazier in 1890, Dora Pratt in 1898, and Julia Sarah Abegg in 1903. See William G. Hartley and Lorna Call Alder, *Anson Bowen Call: Bishop of Colonia Dublan* (Provo, UT: Lorna Call Alder, 2007).

2. See Richard D. Poll, *Working the Divine Miracle: The Life of Apostle Henry D. Moyle* (Salt Lake City: Signature Books, 1999). Moyle (1889–1963) was an attorney, businessman, and rancher before being called as an apostle in 1947. He was influential in an ambitious church building program, the church's purchase of a large cattle ranch in Florida, and aggressive missionary tactics.

3. Quinn is referring to his J. Reuben Clark biography.

18 June 1980–A Prophet's Kisses

My last personal contact with Spencer W. Kimball occurred after a banquet in a private room of Brigham Young's Lion House. Its purpose was to honor BYU's recently released president, Dallin H. Oaks, for doing so much to promote the Clark biography project. As we were leaving, President Kimball shook my wife's hand and gave her a little hug, and I expected just to shake his hand and say goodbye.

From my journal: "Then President Kimball began kissing me on the cheek as he talked, saying a few words and kissing me again, and caressing my arm and shoulder. 'I have a special love for you,' President Kimball said in that deep, almost whisper voice that is left of his partial larenctomy, and then he continued to kiss me on the cheek and neck as I told him that I was thrilled to be in the presence of the Prophet of the Lord.

"By now he was virtually bathing my cheek and neck in kisses, and I put my arm around his shoulder and kissed him on the cheek, and told President Kimball that I loved him, after which he kissed me a couple of more times on the cheek.

"I felt no tears or any emotion but joy and love that seemed so natural, and for the first time in my life it seemed the most natural thing in the world to be kissed repeatedly by a man, to have him express his love for me, to tell him I loved him, and to kiss him. It didn't matter that the man was fifty years older than I."

I lost all sense of time, but this must have gone on for several minutes—in the presence of his wife, Camilla, my wife, and his private secretary, D. Arthur Haycock.

Afterward, I vowed that I would break down the wall I had built around myself and would extend myself fully in love to other males. I didn't, but frequently dreamed of President Kimball performing a marriage sealing for me and my beloved missionary companion Mike McAdams. This was what I wanted, even though Mike was strictly heterosexual and we both had a wife and children.

In my dreams, this sealing of male-male marriage occurred in the Salt Lake Temple's Holy of Holies as Mike and I knelt at the altar in front of the stained-glass image of Joseph Smith's First Vision.

I knew this was a complete fantasy, but I liked dreaming of it. As I had written six months earlier: "My dreams, as I think I have recorded in my journal before, have no real significance beyond my own psyche. They are neither spiritual nor prophetic."

29 June 1980–Preaching about the 1844 Succession Crisis

From my journal: "Then I went to the Ensign Third Ward in the afternoon, where (at the request of the bishop, George VanKommen) I spoke thirty or forty minutes on the Succession Crisis of 1844 and the nature of automatic apostolic succession in the Church today."[4]

1 July 1980–Arrington's History Division Is Sent to BYU

From my journal: "When Leonard came to the phone, I told him that I had learned about the transfer to BYU from Maureen [Ursenbach Beecher] this evening. He said that news of the event had not been officially announced, and asked me not to mention it to anyone else.

"I asked Leonard how he felt about the transfer to BYU, and he said that he had never been consulted about it, but was simply told that it would occur. I said that sounded more like Durham's style of leadership and decision making than the express wish of the First Presidency that Leonard not be consulted.

"Leonard said that there were good elements in the change, but that many things were still unclear at this point. He said that [the] primary question was whether the staff of the History Division would still have its special access privileges to materials of the Historical Department.... The division would be renamed the Joseph Fielding Smith Institute of Church History at BYU.[5] ... I feel so sorry for Leonard."

2 July 1980–"Everyone Is Clamoring for You"

From my journal: "As I was in the History office, I commented to the department secretary Mariel [Budd] how hard it was for me going back to teaching after only one year's teaching experience and after 2 1/2 years away from the classroom. I commented that I was spending all my time day and night preparing for classes, was barely keeping up with them, and had enormous feelings of inferiority as a teacher.

"'Mike,' she said, 'you shouldn't feel very inferior, because everyone is clamoring for you. The Honors Program wanted you to teach at least one class with them, and we had to tell them that we need you too·much here to let you teach classes for them right now. I have had dozens of students coming in here asking when you are coming back to teach, what classes you will be teaching, and we have had more graduate students ask for you to be their faculty adviser or chairman than we could possibly feel right about dumping on you your first terms back to teaching.'

4. The "Succession Crisis" refers to the period after Joseph Smith's assassination in June 1844, in which several men vied to succeed him as leader of the church he founded. See D. Michael Quinn, "The Mormon Succession Crisis of 1844," *BYU Studies* 16, no. 2 (1976): 1–44.

5. In the early 1980s, Church Historical Department employees were transferred from church headquarters in Salt Lake City to BYU. In 2005, the Institute was closed, and some of these employees returned to the History Department at church headquarters.

"I thanked Mariel for the expression of confidence, and said: 'I just hope that the reality of Michael Quinn as a teacher does not disappoint the expectations.'"

9 July 1980–Yearning to Be "Brother Friend"

From my journal: "I am not much of a son, husband, or father, and the only thing I have yearned to be all my life is a brother friend to other young men but I have such a morose, stiff, and awkward personality, that I have never really been very successful in close friendships with others. Dick Lambert, Jim McConkie, and Mike McAdams are the exceptions, but ours is a deep spiritual bonding that makes up for my other deficiencies."

Two weeks later I wrote: "I find that my attitudes are an amalgam of the Greek ideals of physical beauty with the LDS view of man's relationship to God. I think that I would have been more comfortable in pre-Christian Athens than I am in Latter-day Zion. I wonder if we had a choice in our pre-mortal state about where we would be born and when we would live?"

23 July 1980–If Church Correlation Had "Approved" the Bible

From my journal: "After my afternoon class, I met Malcolm Thorp of our faculty in the hall of the History Department, and he commented to me about the trouble he was having with Correlation about the text of his paper on English converts in the nineteenth century [for an article in the *Ensign*].

"I commented to him that if the Four Gospels had to go through Church correlation that the Book of John would be rejected by Correlation as disruptive of the general agreement in the accounts of the other three Gospels, as stirring up controversies due to its presentation of deep doctrines."

25 July 1980–Mormon Pit of Vulnerability

From my journal: "I told Marvin [Hill] that I felt the authorities were digging a pit into which the Church members were falling or going to fall due to their vulnerability to anti-Mormon and apostate propaganda on Church history which the general authorities have given the Church members no means of coping with.[6]

"I told Marvin Hill that if I were only a cultural Mormon that this would not bother me, but my commitment to the Church is so intense that the situation as I see it tears me apart."

28 July 1980–Reconciled with Reorganized Saints

From my journal: "In the afternoon mail, I found a letter from Clare

6. Marvin Hill (1928–2016) taught history at BYU from 1966–93. He served as president of the Mormon History Association from 1992–93. He and Dallin H. Oaks co-authored *Carthage Conspiracy: The Trial of the Accused Assassins of Joseph Smith* (Urbana: University of Illinois Press, 1975), which won MHA's Best Book Award.

Vlahos, president of the RLDS John Whitmer Historical Society, with an invitation for me to join the editorial board of a new journal the Society is planning to issue annually, much like the Mormon History Association's journal.[7] He listed the other members of the editorial board, and they are all RLDS. I wrote him a letter of acceptance.

"I think it is interesting that I appear to be the only LDS person on the board, especially in view of the reservations even RLDS liberals had about my article on the Succession Crisis of 1844."

Long before now, RLDS philosopher Paul M. Edwards had resumed his very congenial response to me whenever he saw me at MHA meetings. I was happy because he is such a good man.

1 August 1980–Diamonds and Dust

From my journal: "Jan wanted to spend the entire evening cleaning up the house, and I agreed to work with her and the children in doing so. Before we began in earnest, I went upstairs where all the children were watching television. I sat in the chair and asked Adam to sit on my lap with me, so that I could give him a snuggle. I held him tight, kissed him and he kissed me, and tears welled up in my eyes, but did not escape to my cheeks. After a few minutes, he and Paul [Moshe] and Mary left the room, and I asked Lisa to come sit with me for a snuggle, and I asked her what she had done during the day.

"Once everyone else had started cleaning, and after I had vacuumed the upstairs, I went to the downstairs bathroom, locked the door, and knelt in whispered prayer, nearly choking with emotion and with tears streaming down my cheeks. I told the Lord of my desperate loneliness for friendships of brotherhood, and my guilt that I know Jan is lonely for a close personal association that I am unwilling or unable to give to her ... but that I could not remember feeling such agony of loneliness and yearning for a brother friend since I was a teenager. ...

"Now, at thirty-six I have a wife and four children who should be the center of my life and hopes, but who are not. Instead, I yearn for close personal friendships with Frank Fuller, an inactive Mormon half my age, and with Rod Cross, one of my students who is thirteen years my junior. Aside from the question of whether my personality is capable of a satisfactory friendship with such young men, there is the fact that my family obligations and personal circumstances make a close, continuing friendship with anyone an impossibility. Finally, my tears stopped flowing, and I told the Lord that my

7. Founded in 1972, the John Whitmer Historical Association (which Quinn misnamed in this journal entry) is an independent, scholarly society of individuals who share an interest in the history of Joseph Smith's Restoration movement and Community of Christ. Whitmer was one of Joseph Smith's closest associates and church historian in the 1830s. Quinn was the first LDS scholar to serve on the editorial committee of the association's journal.

life and circumstances were in His hands, and I wanted nothing that was contrary to His will."

3 August 1980–Turning Down LDS Headquarters Bureaucracy

From my journal: "Just after I got home from Church, someone telephoned (whose name I forget) and said that he was involved in some sort of curriculum committee under the direction of the First Quorum of Seventy. ... He said that once the proposed committee members were assembled, that the list would be presented to the First Quorum of Seventy who would officially call the persons to the positions. He said his contact with me was simply exploratory and unofficial.

"I asked what time demands this service would involve, and he explained that it would be substantial and would require me to be released from whatever present Church positions I now hold.

"Without hesitation I told him that I would not consider taking on any assignment that would require my release from my present Church position, thanked him for his invitation, and said that once the committee was formed I would be glad to give them suggestions or whatever, but that I would not wish to join the committee at the cost of my present Church position.

"I think my response stunned him. Perhaps some men in the Church expect a person to fall all over himself at the prospect of getting a bureaucratic assignment that puts the person in contact with 'the Brethren.' I stand in no awe of the general authorities, nor of their power, nor of their approval."

4 August 1980–Systematic Ethnocide (Cultural Genocide)

From my journal: "I caused a stir in my morning discussion class by my comment that the Indian Placement Program of the Church was systematically destroying Native American culture for the children involved."[8]

7 August 1980–Thanatos and Me

. From my journal: "In the silence after our conversation [as husband and wife] ended and before I drifted to sleep, I wondered if I had much in common with anyone, if I ever made or could make anyone feel comfortable around me, if I had any qualities that were attractive to anyone else for friendship. Apparently not.

---

8. The LDS Church operated its Indian Student Placement Program (ISPP) in North America from 1954 to 2000. It placed LDS Native children in Mormon homes off of reservations during the school year, if the children's parents requested it. When Quinn made this statement, some 2,500 students were participating. The program's purpose was to provide better educational opportunities, but some considered the program paternalistic and racist. Apostle Spencer W. Kimball, who championed the ISSP, claimed in his October 1960 general conference address that children in the program were gradually becoming lighter, "changing to whiteness and delightsomeness." See Matthew Garrett, *Making Lamanites: Mormons, Native Americans, and the Indian Student Placement Program, 1947–2000* (Salt Lake City, UT: University of Utah Press, 2016).

"Then I thought about my relationship with Jan, and wondered where that was heading. She deserves better than I am, than I am giving her.

"I found myself half-thinking and half-dreaming of the means to resolve all these issues at once. I saw myself going to the store on the corner of 6th South and about 3rd East to buy the merchandize, going up to a canyon in my car, preparing its use, carrying it in a bag as I walked a few feet from my parked car, before taking it out of the bag and using it.

"Dreams are supposed to end before this point but I carried out the thanatostic ritual to its conclusion, and then in third person detachment looked down upon myself lying in the grass in the midst of the consequences.[9]

"As I drifted off to sleep of unconsciousness I felt nothing, not even relief."

9 August 1980–How to "Get Away with" What I Publish?

From my journal: "Last night I had received a call from JaLynn Prince, asking if Jan and I would be able to go to dinner as guests of her and her husband [Greg], whom I had met at the Mormon History Association meeting in Canandaigua[, New York,] this year. He is a book review editor for *Dialogue* and works with the National Institutes of Health in Washington, D.C. We had a very enjoyable evening with them [tonight.]

"Greg Prince commented that they and others had long been amazed at my ability to write the kind of things I do and still get away with it and he asked why I thought that was the case.[10] Without hesitation I said: 'Because I don't give a damn.'

"I commented further that I had long ago decided that I could not do as others try—to play the game of going along with the values, conduct, and activities of the hierarchy and bureaucracy, with the intention of expressing their 'real' selves once they got to the position or power they hoped to receive by currying favor—because one poisoned one's self in the process and also made one's self vulnerable to [the charge of] duplicity. The Princes seemed surprised at my candor, and thanked me for it."

11 August 1980–BYU Students Express Gratitude

From my journal: "After the class, several of the students thanked me for being their teacher in the course, and one fellow from the South told me with moist eyes that he grew up in the South believing everything that his parents and grandparents told him about Blacks and many other things, but that my

---

9. Thanatos, usually depicted as a person, represents death in Greek mythology.

10. Gregory A. Prince (1948–) is a pathology researcher, philanthropist, autism activist, and award-winning historian. In years following this discussion with Quinn, he went on to author his own works on Mormon history, including *David O. McKay and the Rise of Modern Mormonism* (Salt Lake City: University of Utah Press, 2005), *Leonard Arrington and the Writing of Mormon History* (University of Utah Press, 2016), and *Gay Rights and the Mormon Church: Intended Actions, Unintended Consequences* (University of Utah Press, 2019).

course had helped him to realize that there are many sides to these issues and helped him to be determined to examine things more openly. ...

"When I walked back to my office, I found that someone (I assume it was a girl) in my morning class had baked me a nut loaf, and left it in foil with a typed, unsigned letter thanking me for the way I taught the class, giving students opportunity to express their diverse views without demeaning anyone's comments or views, as well as providing a love of history to the students. This was a very cheering message of thoughtfulness.

"The experiences of this day make me feel less of a failure as a teacher and give me some hope of being able to make a productive and positive contribution to the education and lives of college students."

11 August 1980–Second Banquet to Celebrate the Clark Project

From my journal: "I met Jan at the Wilkinson Center and we drove from there to the restaurant La France, where we arrived at the same time as some of the Clarks. The very delicious French dinner was enjoyed by all of the Clark Family, the three authors and their wives (as with the last Banquet, we were at opposite ends of the table from the Yarns, which suited me fine), and Robert Thomas and Robert Smith and wives. I sat with Jan next to Louise Clark Bennion and Mrs. Reuben Clark III, and across from the Foxes, and Marianne Clark Sharp. ...

"At the end of the dinner, Jan and I greeted Bob Thomas, who took my hand in a firm handshake, put his arm around my shoulder, and looked me intently in the eyes, as he shook his head slowly and repeated my name a few times. He seems to respect me, for his praise seemed quite earnest.

"As we were about to leave, Louise Bennion said that she thoroughly loved all that I had written, but then Marianne Clark Sharp (easily the most conservative of the Clark children) came up and said that she enjoyed what I had written but would like me to leave out any references to Emily Smith Stewart and David O. McKay's difficulties with her father. I did not commit myself in her favor, but merely said that it was impossible to understand the nature of her father's experience in the First Presidency without dealing with those issues.

"She repeated her request in several different ways, but I did not agree to leave them out, and maintained a respectful silence most of the time. This could be the beginning of a difficult time.

"She and Reuben III both told me that it was pretty well settled that I would be released from teaching for another school year to work on the biography, but I said that I had made no formal requests and had heard nothing."

12 August 1980–Stopping Journal Entries

Last evening's event was the final entry in my typed journal. I had been asked to give a presentation on personal journals at the LDS Church's World Conference on Records on August 13. In preparation, I read through the previous weeks of my own journal and felt embarrassed that so many of its entries whined about how miserable I was, how unhappy my wife Jan was, and how hopeless the situation was.

What was the point of continuing to write such a dreary and depressing journal? So I stopped.

It occurs to me now as I write this self-biography, it will appear the same way to different people for opposite reasons. For most Mormons, who applaud celibacy for gays and lesbians, it may be depressing that I couldn't just make the right decision once and get on with my Mormon life without yearning for the forbidden. For others, it may be laughable that I didn't just accept reality and get it on with a studlee.

And people with various points of view will probably regard my self-biography as whiny. I can only say, "Sorry," despite the irony.

16 November 1980–Counselor in Bishopric, Salt Lake 27th Ward

This Sunday, ward members sustained me as second counselor to Richard G. Horne. A bank executive in his early thirties, he had been a player on BYU's basketball team. Rick was as efficient, easy going, people centered, lighthearted, and liberal as I could have hoped for in a leader.

The most difficult experiences of my service in this bishopric would occur in mid-1981 when I had to join with him in two confidential councils where the bishop and his two counselors interviewed and disciplined a male and a female for their respectively having engaged in homoerotic experiences. At the time, I was not keeping a journal from which I had to conceal my struggle with these events.

I had never before seen this young man (age 21) but was instantly attracted to him. I felt inner anguish as he repeated to the three of us what he had already confessed to the bishop—his first and only homosexual experience. He went home with a man he met at The Sun, a gay bar in Salt Lake City. Because I knew that actual penetration has always been the emphasis of LDS Church discipline in such cases, I asked this young man if he and his friend had anal intercourse. He looked like I'd kicked him in the stomach and whispered: "Yes." I was struggling to hold back tears and to resist the impulse to announce that I was also gay. After he went into the next room while we reached our decision, Bishop Horne asked what I thought. "The Church handbook recommends excommunication in such cases," I said, "but there is no way I can vote for anything more severe than disfellowshipping him. And I recommend that we just put him on probation." Rick asked me if I thought this would be the last time the young man had sex with another guy. I said:

"No," but my thought was: I certainly hope not! "Then," Bishop Horne said, "if he's on probation and confesses about another homosexual encounter, I'll have to excommunicate him. But if we disfellowship him today, I don't think I'll ever make further inquiries with an inactive member of the Church who I met only because he showed up at my office to confess." So, that was the decision Bishop Horne explained to the young man in 1981. Seven years later, I found myself standing next to him in a gay bar in West Hollywood. Wordlessly I walked away, glad that he didn't seem to recognize me.

In some ways, the woman's case would be even more difficult for me. I had known her professionally for years and tried to use that as the reason I should not attend the bishopric's meeting with her and her husband. This lesbian long-term affair of a married LDS woman was too close to the daily temptations of my own situation, and I was desperate to avoid this meeting. Bishop Horne replied that he had known this husband and wife for years, as well, and that was no excuse for me not to participate. Since I was only the second counselor, I said that I simply would not attend this council. More visibly out of patience with me than ever before or since, Bishop Horne reminded me that the Church handbook required the presence of both counselors at such a meeting with the bishop. So I attended the council with this husband and wife, my stomach in knots as I saw her eyes constantly averted from me. I don't think I said a word until after they went into the next room to await our decision. When Rick asked, I made the same recommendation as in the young man's case, but the stakes were higher here since this involved a temple marriage. "Don't even think of asking me to support a decision for excommunication," I said. As I recall, the decision was to disfellowship, and I could not look at her when the bishop told them. A decade afterward, when it was generally known that I was a gay Mormon historian, she came up to me after a panel discussion at Sunstone Symposium. All smiles and friendly, she gave me her business card and said that she'd like to have lunch with me sometime. I've never been able to force myself to phone her. My complicity in her embarrassing and painful experience was too deep.

8 February 1981–Setting Wife Apart

As bishopric counselor, I set apart Jan as a member of the Salt Lake Twenty-seventh Ward's Music Committee. Previously, she had been a teacher for the Relief Society and for the Primary in this ward, as well as Primary president and counselor for the Relief Society and the Young Women in other wards. Today was the first time I had a role in her callings.

19 February 1981–The "Province" of Mormon Intellectuals

Apostle Bruce R. McConkie instructed BYU English professor Eugene

England by letter: "It is my province to teach to the Church what the doctrine is. It is your province to echo what I say or to remain silent."

In my view, such a demand is what the Book of Mormon called "priest-craft" (2 Nephi 26: 29; Alma 1:12). That's what I told Gene, but otherwise remained circumspectly silent—at least, for the time being.

April 1981–New Eardrum

My right eardrum was so weakened and scarred, that it was rupturing twenty minutes after the first feeling of pressure from a middle-ear infection. Therefore, I had my second experience with plastic surgery, which this time replaced my right eardrum. The "successful" surgery left me with permanent tinnitus (ringing or buzzing) in the right ear. I still experience anxiety whenever I have middle-ear infections—several times a year even in my mid-sixties.

24 May 1981–Largest Audience

By invitation of the LDS Institute at the University of Utah, I spoke at its fireside for Mormon students and other young adults. My topic was the nationally publicized controversy about the Mormon founder's intentions for Joseph Smith III to preside over the LDS Church one day. Tonight's standing-room-only audience was huge, with possibly two thousand crowded into the LDS Institute's largest chapel and adjoining cultural hall.

With typical pride and arrogance, I wanted to give the same faith-promoting talk to similar audiences. I offered my services to the Institutes of Utah's other colleges and universities, but only BYU's History Department would sponsor my giving this talk next fall.

25 May 1981–Memorial Day Service, Salt Lake City

This month, I also participated in a TV talk show for the first time. Interviewed for half an hour on the *Let's Face It* program of KTVX (ABC), I spoke about the LDS First Presidency's statement against stationing the MX missile system in Utah and against the nuclear arms race.

6 August 1981–Social Activism and Coverage by TV News

At Salt Lake City's interdenominational vigil commemorating the dropping of the atomic bomb on Hiroshima, I gave a talk. Quoting J. Reuben Clark's vitriolic condemnation of it in his address to LDS General Conference in October 1946, I was featured on the evening news of Salt Lake City's KUTV (NBC) and KTVX (ABC).

28 August 1981–Speaking on Women and Priesthood

During *Sunstone* magazine's theological symposium at the University of Utah, I was a respondent on the paper Linda King Newell gave for a session titled, "Washing, Anointing, and Blessing the Sick Among Mormon Women." In view of my own research, I said that she was too tentative about the basis on which early Mormon women performed ordinances of healing from the mid-1840s until LDS headquarters prohibited them from continuing to do so a century later.

Quoting from various sources, including patriarchal blessings given by Joseph Smith's "Uncle John" in 1844–45, I said that the Mormon founder's closest associates affirmed that each woman possessed the Melchizedek Priesthood after she received the temple ceremony of Priesthood endowment. I emphasized that this did not involve ordination to specific offices of that Priesthood, but instead each woman received a conferral of Priesthood by receiving the keys of the endowment.

Long before now, I rarely asked Jan's father or any other man to come to our house to join me in administering to one of our children when they were sick. Day or night, Jan joined me in laying hands on their heads as I said that she and I sealed the blessing "by our faith and by the Melchizedek Priesthood *we* have received." I had recorded one such example in my journal on 18 February 1979.

As my published "Response" stated in this September's issue of *Sunstone*: "If we 'quench not the Spirit,' it is still possible for a Latter-day Saint man and wife jointly to administer ordinances of healing not only to children and other members of their immediate family but also to persons not related to the couple."

Early September 1981–Publishing in RLDS Periodical

The *John Whitmer Historical Association Journal* published "Joseph Smith III's 1844 Blessing and the Mormons of Utah."[11] It was republished next summer in expanded form by *Dialogue*, and also won the JWHA's best article award a year from this fall.

Early September 1981–Boyd K. Packer's Vow

A week after I resumed teaching at BYU, a graduate student in the history department told me of his recent meeting with apostle Packer in the Church Administration Building (47 East South Temple). Packer said that my unpublished biography "dirties" the public memory of J. Reuben Clark.

In June of this year, I had given my completed manuscript to BYU's administrators and Clark's children. Somehow Elder Packer learned of its contents.

"As sure as I am sitting in this chair," he told Harvard Heath, "Mike Quinn's book on President Clark will never see the light of day." Apostle

---

11. See D. Michael Quinn, "Joseph Smith III's 1844 Blessing and the Mormons of Utah," *John Whitmer Historical Association Journal* 1(1981), 12–27. Several years later, the blessing document was proven to be a forgery by Mark Hofmann (see Chapter 18).

Packer obviously expected him to report this back to me, since he commenced the conversation by asking if this student knew me personally.

This was disheartening. My concern grew as weeks and months went by without any word from BYU's administrators or from Gordon Burt Affleck about the reaction of Clark's family to my book-length draft of the biography. Nonetheless, I decided not to ask about this silence.

13 September 1981—Failing to Get an Audience

Because of last May's huge attendance at the University of Utah's LDS Institute, I asked my department's very efficient secretary Mariel Budd to schedule tonight's talk for BYU's DeJong Concert Hall.

She warned me that none of the department's prior speakers had gotten such a large audience, and she tried to persuade me to schedule the 800-seat Varsity Theatre. I stubbornly insisted and humiliated myself when about twenty people showed up tonight in a venue for 2,500!

I don't know if the topic had ceased to be of interest, or if the problem was me as the speaker. The fault wasn't advertising, because Mariel had arranged for the *Daily Universe* to headline a well-advanced announcement article on September 9: "Church History Scholar to Speak Sunday on 'Joseph III Blessing.'"

A verse from the Hebrew Bible seemed to apply: "Pride goeth before destruction and an haughty spirit before a fall" (Proverbs 16:18). Tonight I silently rehearsed those words, wondering if this foreshadowed the rest of my life as a Mormon historian.

2 October 1981—Mission President's "Exile"?

After seventeen months as resident administrator of LDS missions in the Far East and in the Philippines, Marion D. Hanks returned to Salt Lake City to attend general conference. At a reunion of his British missionaries on Friday evening, his talk to us emphasized the humanitarian programs he had established in Thailand, where sister missionaries ministered to the massive needs of that country's refugee camps.

When I greeted him afterwards, President Hanks (as he often did) began speaking to me about problems at LDS headquarters. First, he complained that the First Presidency didn't let him send young full-time missionaries into India, because of financial concerns that massive conversions there would bankrupt the Church if it tried to establish the regular LDS programs among such abjectly poor people. He regarded this as "short-sighted."

Second, he commented that for a year and a half, "a member of the Twelve" had been telling people at Church headquarters that this assignment in Asia was an "administrative exile" to "punish" President Hanks for being too outspoken as a general authority seventy. Saying this to me and the others standing nearby was yet another example of such candor, which I always admired in him.

President Hanks didn't name this apostle, but said: "*anyone*,who regards a mission calling as 'punishment' doesn't understand the gospel of Jesus Christ."

15 October 1981–I Arrange a Session at the Western History Association

Despite my repeatedly asking him during the first eight months of 1981 to provide a title of his presentation for WHA's printed program, Professor Louis Midgley kept saying that he hadn't decided on one. When this year's program committee gave me a last chance to provide his title before the program went to the printer, Midgley didn't return my urgent message to him on BYU's phone system. Thinking that WHA attenders would assume that I (as the session's organizer) purposely omitted his title from the program, I invented one that was far more neutral than I thought he would announce at the session—in view of privately circulated diatribes he had circulated for years against Marvin Hill and Thomas Alexander.

When Lou Midgley stood to read his prepared text, he told the audience that its title had always been "The Question of Faith and History," and accused me of substituting a caustic version in place of its "mild" title. Upon resuming my role as the session's moderator, I didn't challenge his falsehood. No use trying to cat fight with a skunk. Twenty years later, he had the *FARMS Review of Books* publish his claim that I had "insisted on calling it 'A Critique of Mormon Historians.'"[12] Old age wouldn't improve Midgley's dishonest ways.

Mid-October 1981–Program Committee, Western History Association

As chair of the committee, Jan Shipps asked me to be one of those who decided which proposals to accept for next year's annual meeting. Two years earlier, I had done something similar in selecting speakers for BYU's History Week.

1 November 1981–My Unyielding Commitment as a Historian

The Mormon History Association newsletter published my strident philosophy of historical disclosure. I ended the essay with the final line from the poem "Ulysses" by Alfred Lord Tennyson: "To strive, to seek, to find, and not to yield." I had submitted it as a letter to the editor months ago with no anticipation of the controversy I would ignite this November.

4 November 1981–Publicly Challenging Apostolic Views

For his talk to all the CES teachers and BYU religion professors on 22 August 1981, Boyd K. Packer had given a methodical attack on Mormon

---

12. See Louis Midgley, "Comments on Critical Exchanges," *Review of Books on the Book of Mormon* 13, no. 1 (1981), 91–126.

historians. It was titled "The Mantle Is Far, Far Greater Than the Intellect." This referred to "the mantle of Priesthood authority" held by LDS leaders (Packer, *That All May Be Edified*, 240).

This apostle seemed to relish attacking devoted church members with impunity. I had once watched my mother-in-law sobbing as she listened to him tell a general conference that parents were responsible when their adult children committed sin, and she felt indicted for her older son's decision to leave the church. I had also listened to the quiet anger of my musician father-in-law after Elder Packer gave a talk in which he ridiculed musicians and artists. I had read talks in which he questioned the faith of conscientious objectors against war and of LDS social workers and psychotherapists. I even listened in stunned silence to a world broadcast of the general priesthood meeting where this apostle authorized the young men of the LDS Church to physically assault homosexuals (October 1976, *Conference Report*, 100–01; *To Young Men Only*, 9–10). The Church published every one of these mean-spirited talks by Elder Packer, but I had kept my objections to myself.

Now he had attacked the very basis of my sense of a historian's mission to the Latter-day Saints. Scott S. Burnett, an officer in the history student organization of Phi Alpha Theta, asked me to help history majors understand how they could continue their interest in the Mormon past after Elder Packer's talk against the writing of candid Mormon history. Scott was a student of mine, and I couldn't turn down his very reasonable request to give such a talk to BYU students.

However, I realized that by making any kind of reply to Elder Packer's talk, I would probably forfeit the string of Church offices I expected to serve in. In the days before I spoke, I asked myself and God if I had the right to jeopardize my life's mission, just to make a largely futile criticism of Elder Packer's effort to remake the LDS Church into his own malignant image. But I remembered President Kimball's counsel for me not to "curry favor" to get church office nor act contrary to what I felt the Lord wanted me to do. I didn't feel I could conscientiously remain silent about apostle Packer's effort to intimidate Mormons from writing or reading interpretative Mormon history.

I felt the Spirit with me and prepared a talk which responded to the criticisms of Mormon historians by apostles Ezra Taft Benson and Boyd K. Packer. I gave a copy of the prepared text to my bishop a few days before the Phi Alpha Theta meeting. Its most controversial sentence was probably my assertion that "a Mormon history of benignly angelic church leaders apparently advocated by Elders Benson and Packer would border on idolatry."

About forty persons were present when I spoke on November 4. In this small audience was Tom Alexander, my steadfast friend and supporter in the history department. I choked up with emotion on the last page, and had to ask my decades-long friend Susan Staker to finish reading it. *Sunstone* magazine's managing editor, Peggy Fletcher [later Stack] had sent her to Provo to hear my advertised talk.

LDS polemicist Gary F. Novak would eventually publish this assessment in *FARMS Review of Books*: "One of the strangest aspects of Quinn's essay is the autobiographical material. Instead of telling his story in the first person, Quinn uses the third person." Guilty as charged.

In this first public statement of autobiography, I was still sensitive to the criticism that missionary companion David Harris had hurled at me eighteen years previous: "You've got a bad case of I-itis, Elder Quinn." To avoid being criticized as egotistical for the too frequent use of "I," this month's "On Being a Mormon Historian" used the third-person of he/him/his for my personal narrative. My effort at humility was then criticized as "the strangest" (or as stated by BYU political science philosopher Louis C. Midgley in the same issue of *FARMS Review*: "Quinn's bizarre personal rambling"). Thus, I haven't used the third person for myself in this long self-biography.

In early November 1981 I expected some local discussion of my essay, but was surprised by the publicity. I started receiving phone calls from throughout the nation. As word of the talk spread, I was getting advice not to publish it from academics and non-academics, active and inactive Mormons, and even non-Mormons. They all were concerned about the personal consequences if I did. At that time, others in the same groups encouraged its publication, and *Sunstone* was preparing to print it with my permission.

On November 18, *Seventh East Press*, BYU's unofficial student newspaper, published a front-page story about the talk titled, "Historian Responds to Apostle." Within days, this publicity resulted in some anxious consultations.

Late November 1981—Meetings with BYU Dean and LDS Counselor

Martin Hickman asked me to meet him in the dean's office of the College of Family, Home and Social Sciences. That was a name change he once confided was made primarily to protect the college as a whole from suffering budget cuts due to "the antagonism of certain apostles toward historians and social scientists." The Family Science departments in the college were of secondary importance for the additions to its title. Pathetic.

At Hickman's request, I gave him a copy of my Phi Alpha Theta talk. He said that I had no idea the tension it had already caused at church headquarters and with BYU's administration. My dean said that he was *very* worried about the consequences if I published the essay.

January 1982—Teaching BYU's Special Program in Salt Lake City

For the next six months, I was the first instructor for two courses in BYU's new program for working adults in Salt Lake City to earn MA degrees in family and community history. It was intended primarily for employees at LDS headquarters, but my students included full-time seminary teachers, professional genealogists, and housewives. We met one night a week for three hours in a room of the nearly abandoned VA Hospital above Eleventh Avenue.

The first semester, I taught them American Social History. Their second semester was American Family History, with some comparisons to European families. Despite their knowledge of genealogy, most of the reading assignments and lectures were new to them.

They listened attentively, did the assigned readings, participated well in class discussions, and were very prepared for the essay exams. As a group, this was the most diligent class of students I had ever taught. This assessment includes Yale's students.

15 February 1982–*Newsweek*'s National Attention

Even though I had decided not to publish "On Being a Mormon Historian," I had mailed a photocopy of its reading draft to those who asked for it. I regarded this as an academic courtesy and didn't anticipate the consequences. Through one of their associates, anti-Mormons Jerald and Sandra Tanner thereby obtained a copy of my original text—which they published and sold without my permission. I think the Tanners regarded this as payback for my anonymous *Response* to their work.

About the same time, I learned that the First Presidency had ordered the church's *Ensign* magazine to yank apostle Packer's anti-historian talk from its scheduled publication. I felt relief that his views would not get the quasi-official endorsement of church publication. Not until nine years after this winter were they again published (Packer, *Let Not Your Heart Be Troubled*, 101–22).

Then *Newsweek*'s February 15 issue ran a story titled "Apostles vs. Historians" about the talks by Elder Packer and me. The article's Catholic author, Kenneth L. Woodward, had done thorough research even before interviewing me. And he was balanced.

However, my decades-long friend Clifton Jolley, now a writer at the *Deseret News* and first counselor with me in my ward bishopric, infuriated Woodward by trying to protect me from the wrath of LDS headquarters. Clifton published an essay emphasizing my private comment to him that the title of the *Newsweek* article gave the mistaken impression that all Mormon historians agreed with me and that all LDS apostles agreed with Elder Packer. I knew that was not the case for either group.

Although Woodward had previously warned me that his editors added a title he regarded as too sensational, he made an angry phone call to me about my friend's article. I told him that I consistently told others (including

Clifton) that I admired Woodward's care in researching and writing the article, but that I agreed with his view that the title was somewhat skewed and sensational.

Woodward told me that I had "no right" to tell anyone else what he had "confided" to me about his dissent from the article's title. This was a somewhat amusing outcome for an experienced reporter who had not specified he was talking to me off the record about his editors.

I eventually learned that Woodward told Peggy Fletcher and others that he would avoid LDS topics in future. Because, he claimed, Mormon liberals like me allegedly tried to retract their statements after he published.

That seemed like an incredibly petty position for a national journalist to take toward a newsworthy subject—as the LDS Church would inevitably continue to be. Regardless, I noticed that Ken Woodward's articles avoided even mentioning Mormonism from this time onward. Years later, when *Newsweek* finally began publishing more stories about Mormonism, they had different bylines.

Mid-February 1982–Marion D. Hanks and Apostolic Vindictiveness

My general authority friend asked to see me a few days after the *Newsweek* article. He said that it was "probably too late," but warned me that Boyd K. Packer never forgot anyone who challenged him and that he would "remain vindictive."

President Hanks related an example from his own experience. Once, in a meeting of BYU's Board of Trustees, he successfully challenged as "not appropriate" Elder Packer's planned diversion to other purposes for the large amount of money donated by BYU students for a project Elder Packer regarded as unimportant. Five years later, the apostle referred to that incident while trying to humiliate President Hanks during an orientation the two men were giving to newly called mission presidents.

In that meeting, President Hanks was scheduled to give a brief devotional talk, after which Elder Packer was to give an hour-long, detailed presentation about the complex financial procedures and reports involved with each mission president's dual responsibilities for paying the necessary expenses of full-time missionary work and for financing the local member districts and branches in his mission.

When it was Elder Packer's turn, he said: "I was going to give you brethren this long orientation—until I discovered that we are privileged to have an *expert* on Church finances with us. Elder Hanks knows when it is inappropriate to transfer funds from one account to another, so I will defer to him for the next hour." President Hanks told me that he was shocked by this announcement, but had no choice but to "graciously wing it" as best he could.

"Elder Packer will never forget that *Newsweek* article or your talk," President Hanks told me. "It may take him years, but he will get his vengeance on you."

Late February 1982–Colleagues Resent the Way I Defend History

The BYU History Department's current chair James B. Allen told me that the situation was having a detrimental effect on my colleagues who had never published Mormon history. Several of these BYU professors expressed resentment that they were being included in the suspicion of historians by Elder Packer and other general authorities.

Jim left most of these colleagues unnamed, but related the more positive comment by European historian Douglas Tobler: "Mike is a friend and I know he's well-intentioned, but doesn't he realize the difficulties he's caused for all of us?"

13 March 1982–Funeral of Church Historian's Wife

Grace Fort Arrington had been Leonard's beloved companion and a beaming light in the social world of the New Mormon History. I was deeply affected by her death and felt honored that Leonard asked me to offer one of the prayers at her funeral. I expressed my heartfelt love for her, for Leonard, for the Gospel, and for God the Father of us all.

Sitting behind me on the stand were general authorities that I knew she did not want at her funeral. Her son Carl told me this shortly after my arrival at the LDS chapel. Within the Arrington Family, he was the most openly bitter about how their church's leaders had treated Leonard for the past five years. The rest remained circumspect, as did I.

27 April 1982–Speaking to Adventists

After an early flight to LA's Ontario Airport, I was driven to Loma Linda University where I spoke on Mormonism to its Seventh Day Adventist faculty and students. They had invited me after reading the *Newsweek* article, which echoed their current historical controversy about apparent plagiarism in the revelatory writings by their founder prophetess, Ellen G. White.

9 May 1982–Losing Bishopric

With a candor I've never understood, my stake presidency informed me that I had been unsuccessfully recommended to be the new bishop for the Salt Lake City Twenty-seventh Ward by the five former bishops currently living in the ward. Rick Horne was released to become second counselor to the stake's new president, Hugh West.

But after apostle Mark E. Petersen's visit at stake conference, the high council decided not to send my name for approval to church headquarters. Elder Petersen showed the stake presidency a copy of the Tanners' publication of "On Being a Mormon Historian" and asked, "Why is Michael Quinn in league with anti-Mormons?"

I earnestly wished that President Bradley and his counselor successor Hugh West had not told me of the failed effort to call me as ward bishop. My feelings of loss were inconsolable. I experienced deep despair this day as President West installed another man as bishop, who chose new counselors.

Clifton seemed relieved to be released from the administrative burdens as a bishopric counselor but tried to comfort me. Nearly ten years before, I had told him about my expectations of receiving church callings, including an apostleship. He knew how much today hurt.

I had made my public defense of the honest LDS narratives I know as the New Mormon History. And my talk may have helped to stop apostle Packer's anti-historical talk from receiving the worldwide circulation and implied First Presidency approval by being printed in the church magazines.

Still, I felt like I had given up a place in a lifeboat—to straighten deck chairs on the *Titanic*.

July-August 1982–Training in Chicago

I'm not sure who was more anxious to get me away from Utah for a while—BYU's administrators or me. The perfect opportunity arrived with an invitation to participate in the Newberry Library's Summer Institute in Quantitative History. Not surprisingly, it was quick and easy for me to get approval and full funding.

Through consultations with Bob Thomas and feverish rewriting, I revised the first draft of my Clark biography in the weeks before my flight in July. That process was not finished, however, so I had a lot of long-distance telephone calls with him about the revisions.

Taught by American social historians with extensive experience in statistical analysis, the Newberry Institute was six weeks of lectures and seminars.

Despite my undergraduate disaster in higher math, I understood most of these statistical concepts. With a lot of coaching, I could also perform the computer analyses. We used the Statistical Package for the Social Sciences (SPSS).

For a city boy like me, the housing couldn't have been more ideal. The Newberry Institute's students (most of us were already professors) resided in single rooms of the dorm for Northwestern University's medical school—next to Lake Michigan. We were just a few blocks from the John Hancock Tower in the Gold Coast section of downtown Chicago.

Most of the time, I ate, toured, and saw movies on my own. Although I could have gone to theatres that showed gay porn while an anonymous visitor to Chicago, I did not. I considered doing so, however, and often daydreamed about having sex with irresistible studlees.

Former student Robert D. Hutchins lived nearby, and we went to a performance of the Andrew Lloyd Webber musical, *Joseph and His Amazing Technicolor Coat*. A convert from the RLDS Church to Mormonism, he had recently been called as a bishop's counselor. Bob had taken a readings and discussion course from me while he completed his MA thesis during my first year of teaching at BYU. He talked a lot about Olympic medalist Bruce Jenner, a roommate at his former Church's Graceland College in Iowa. I haven't seen Bob since this summer.

Despite injuring my knee while running in Chicago, this summer's institute was a healthy relief from the pressures of Utah. I missed Jan and our kids but needed this break.

September 1982–Chair of Awards Program for BYU Students

To encourage students of history to write publishable term papers and to be honored therefor, I greatly expanded the categories and monetary awards. Throughout the next four years, students were honored at an annual banquet for papers which several of them published in professional journals.

Including the previous and ongoing encouragement I gave them as a professor, publishing successes in history have been Amy L. Bentley, Scott S. Burnett, Brian Q. Cannon, Kenneth L. Cannon II, Howard Alan Christy, Lyndon W. Cook, Andrew F. Ehat, Craig L. Foster, Mark R. Grandstaff, Gerald M. Haslam, Harvard S. Heath, Richard N. Holzapfel, Lynne Watkins Jorgensen, Kahlile Mehr, Walter A. Norton, Chad M. Orton, D. Gene Pace, John A. Peterson, John Quist, Steven R. Sorensen, Lin Ostler Strack, Shane Swindle, Grant Underwood, Bruce A. VanOrden, Michael Vinson, David J. Whittaker, and John D. Wrathall.

By his gay marriage surname of Gustav-Wrathall, John's decade-later book *Take the Young Man By the Hand* would describe the male-male love, homoeroticism, and nudity that characterized the YMCA from its beginnings. This would remind me of the nude swimming I had experienced in Glendale's Y from age six until I stopped going there at eleven.

15 October 1982–Counselors Countermand the Living Prophet

After Spencer W. Kimball was incapacitated by effects of three brain surgeries for subdural hematomas, the First Presidency (with Gordon B. Hinckley as its most functioning counselor) issued an emphatic reversal of President Kimball's four-year-old instructions for bishops and stake presidents to include oral sex as a question during temple interviews. It called such inquiries "beyond the scope of what is appropriate. ... Also, you should never inquire into personal, intimate matters involving marital relations between a man and his wife." This statement also instructed local leaders that "you should not pursue the matter," even if a Church member confessed such behavior.[13]

Without stating the fact, the counselors repudiated the living prophet in an official message to all presiding officers of the LDS Church. And they did it while this prophet was incapacitated! Although First Presidency Counselor Marion G. Romney had managed to speak at the recent general conference, he was barely functioning due to his own physical declines.[14]

This was a stunning development, and not only in LDS Church administration. Second Counselor Gordon B. Hinckley showed that it is possible to officially reverse an LDS prophet's definition of what is "unnatural, impure, or unholy" (the phrase used in a previous announcement on this matter by President Kimball). A First Presidency message can redefine what constitutes sexual sin! This was more fundamental as a change of doctrine than the 1890 Manifesto's ending the commandment to live polygamy during one's mortal life.

If Counselor Gordon B. Hinckley could prophetically redefine oral sex as *no longer sinful* between a husband and wife, a future LDS president or his counselor(s) could redefine oral sex as no longer sinful between two men in a committed relationship—or two women in such a relationship.

Nonetheless, I continued to be homosexually celibate, even though my patriarchal blessing had seemed to give me the option of living my own sexual life since age fourteen. Even though I had preached at BYU at age twenty-three: "There is no absolute moral law, except to do the will of God for you."

As a religious antinomian, why did I persist in conforming?! This would puzzle me until a non-Mormon psychiatrist friend, Dr. George Daul Jr., told me one day: "Never underestimate the power of sexual repression."

26 December 1982–Released as Sunday School President, Salt Lake City Twenty-seventh Ward

On October 17, Dean Martin Hickman asked me to move to Austria to be associate director of a six-month study abroad program near Vienna, beginning in January. Faculty administrators usually have a full year to prepare for such an assignment, but I had less than three months. I was told this was because of the emergency withdrawal by an unnamed professor who had been preparing for this Vienna sojourn since the fall of 1981.

Jan and I were excited about the opportunity, but it was a strain doing all the preparations so fast. In addition to wrapping up the semester's courses,

13. See Edward L. Kimball, "The History of LDS Temple Admission Standards," *Journal of Mormon History* 24, no. 1 (Spring 1998): 135–75.

14. Probably due to the incapacity of President Spencer W. Kimball as well as his first and second counselors, Gordon B. Hinckley was called simply as "*a* counselor" to President Kimball, serving from July 23, 1981–December 2, 1982

I had to finalize all revisions in the Clark biography's text and select all its illustrations before we left.

Furthermore, I had to borrow $7,000 from BYU to pay for the extra expenses of our family's food, travels, and residence with BYU's Study Abroad. The loan was interest-free, but ultimately Dean Hickman forgave half those debts. What a mensch!

With greater generosity, my former bishop Rick Horne volunteered to handle the checking account to pay our household's bills during the months we were in Europe. He also leased our house, deposited its rent to our account, and kept tabs on its renter.

Rick was a wonderful mensch! And a great friend.

CHAPTER SEVENTEEN

FATAL SHIFTS

1983–1985

January 1983–European Interlude

Delayed in my final meeting with BYU Press on the day of our flight, I was the last passenger to board the plane at the Salt Lake Airport. Airline representatives were just about to close the jet's entry door, and Jan was understandably frantic. Then all our group had to run to catch the jet at JFK airport for our transatlantic flight.

Compensating somewhat for this second frenzy of the day, four of us received a rare privilege. Mary and Lisa were seated in tourist class, but Jan, Adam, Paul Moshe, and I were upgraded to empty seats in Ambassador Class!

From January to June, we resided at the BYU Center in the town of Baden-bei-Wien, near Vienna of now-neutral Austria. Until 1955, Baden had been headquarters for the Russian zone of Allied-occupied Austria, whose Nazi capital had been divided (like Germany's Berlin) into American, British, French, and Russian sectors. Here, Jan and fourteen-year-old Mary went to classes with the students.

Twelve-year-old Lisa attended only the beginning German class, because the Ballet School of the Vienna State Opera accepted her for no fees. She rode the bus there on her own every day, struggling bravely to understand and speak German. After our return to Utah, Lisa received a full-tuition scholarship to the recently established Ballet West Christensen Academy, following which she received a full-tuition summer scholarship for the San Francisco Ballet School.

Our young sons went half-day to the nearby elementary school in Baden with Austrian students. This was so difficult for them, that Adam refused to answer whenever I asked how the day went. His six-year-old brother always said "Okay," but Paul Moshe eventually told Jan and me that the Austrian teacher called him "lazy boy" (in English) whenever he didn't understand her German. *Verdammte Lehrerin*![1]

On the ego-building side, eight-year-old Adam was so good at chess that he beat every BYU student who granted his request to play the winner

---

1. German for "Damn teacher!"

of their own games. As a result, they made it an adults-only competition. Not until a decade passed, would I perceive my son's precocious skill in chess as a symptom of an unusual way his brain functioned.

With BYU classics professor Douglas Phillips, his wife and four children, we attended a German-speaking branch. Austrian Mormons were mainly members of the Socialist Party or Social Democratic Party. This made me smile whenever I thought about the decades of right-wing fulminations against democratic socialism by apostle Ezra Taft Benson and his fellow travelers in the John Birch Society.

Most of our twenty-five students were politically conservative, but returned missionary Mike Devine was an advocate for West Germany's Green Party. Through him and the Greens, I became more aware of environmental politics.

BYU Press express mailed the page proofs of *J. Reuben Clark: The Church Years* from Provo to me in Austria, where I spent five feverish days proofreading and indexing it.[2] Then I was on the phone for five-and-a-half hours of dictating the corrections and index word for word, number by number to editor Howard Alan Christy, a former student of mine. After the book was published in March, I didn't think much about Mormon history.

For six months, I had a grand time. I taught one course on European culture and another on US–European diplomacy, went to ballet and opera twice a week in Vienna, spoke German on the phone for hours at a time with our Austrian travel agent, and led thirty-six of us through sixteen countries.

The Baden Center's manager cook Frau Maitzen said she had never seen a professor work so hard. Typically I was in the faculty office until 1:00 a.m., reading books from its small library to prepare for upcoming lectures and to draft my handouts of things for students to see on their own in the cities we visited. Then I was up at 6:30 a.m. to prepare for my morning's classes. Jan wrote that my face looked "long, drawn & tired" with "many deep lines on his forehead."

Jan also helped Frau Maitzen in assembling lunch sacks for our group's many trips. This included visits to the International Atomic Energy Agency of the United Nations and to Austria's Nazi concentration camp at Mauthausen.

While traveling by rail through Yugoslavia for two days (on route to Greece in late February), returned missionary Marcus Phillips was yanked off the train for taking a photo of countryside as we approached a railway station. For thirty minutes, he was questioned and yelled at by Communist officials.

Because of that repressiveness, I was surprised to see evidences of religious devotion in Yugoslavia. During our ninety-minute layover in Croatia's provincial capital of Zagreb, we watched a well-attended wedding in its Catholic cathedral. After reboarding the train, we saw Muslim mosques in

2. BYU Press published Quinn's *J. Reuben Clark: The Church Years* in 1983.

the countryside as we passed through the northeastern edge of Bosnia. Then onion-domed churches of the Serbian Orthodox Church greeted us as we entered Belgrade for a quick change of trains.

I was appalled to observe Yugoslavia's poverty. No tractors, and only horse-driven carts were in every village alongside the tracks. One Serbian farmer was apparently too poor to own a horse for tilling his land, because he was pulling the plow behind which his son walked holding the reins. Yet the country's Communist leaders had luxuries. Mundane reality vs. Marx's *Manifesto*. Rank Has Its Privileges (RHIP) in every culture!

Soon, Jan and I fulfilled our decade-delayed dreams of Greece. This began in its northern city of Thessaloniki, where our BYU group was allowed to view ancient King Philip II of Macedon's recently discovered treasure of gold during a special tour of its otherwise closed museum.

One day in Athens, we watched from our hotel balcony a noisy parade against Greece's membership in NATO and its allowing US bases. The BYU students were offended and nervous during those hours, but I enjoyed this peaceful demonstration of freedom in a city that invented democracy.

Walking on the Acropolis was a spiritual experience, and I often returned to the Parthenon. Jan and our four kids also walked with me to the top of Mount Lycabettus to view the surrounding city.

I was especially impressed that the National Museum displayed ancient Greek pottery showing homoerotic scenes. Some were very explicit.

Classical Athens was where intellectual life, homosexual love, and veneration for Divinity merged in the lives of thousands. It was a perfect balance, or as near perfect as may ever be possible in Western Civilization. I was trans-fixed by being there—even if 2,500 years too late!

Our BYU Center in Austria received *Newsweek*, which published a cover story about a frightening new disease that seemed to occur only among sex-ually active homosexuals. It manifested itself in a cluster of nightmarish, usually fatal afflictions that would eventually be given the medical label of Acquired Immune Deficiency Syndrome (AIDS).

The medical establishment would later discover that AIDS occurred pri-marily among heterosexuals in Africa, where it originated from monkeys who transmitted it to humans through biting them. Tourists and emigrants then transferred AIDS to Haiti, from which a French Canadian airline steward transmitted it to gay bathhouses in New York City. From there, it spread to San Francisco's gays, then nationally, and ultimately around the globe through sex, childbirth, blood transfusions, and needle-sharing drug use.

When Doug Phillips saw me reading this issue, he said: "This plague is God's punishment on homosexuals for their loathsome behaviors." I didn't say any-thing, but wondered if he noticed the smoldering anger that nearly choked me.

In what way did God punish the institutionalized pederasty of man-boy love that this classics professor *knew* was celebrated in ancient Greece for centuries? And is the incidence of cervical cancer among unmarried women God's punishment for their remaining virgins? Is uterine cancer God's punishment for motherhood? I despise the selective self-righteousness about earthly tragedies that all humans experience in one way or another. It's as if these religious homophobes had never read the Book of Job in the Hebrew Bible.

Back to this year's travels, the island of Crete was too distant and expensive for our group to visit, but we took a ferry from the port of Piraeus to the nearby island of Aegina. As luck would have it, we got stranded there overnight due to the overly protective government's closure of all shipping in the Aegean Sea after a storm sank a vessel hundreds of miles away.

As we looked from Aegina toward the lights of Athens, the water seemed smooth as glass. At the dock, our group waited for hours before the captain announced final confirmation that he was not allowed to depart until the next morning at the earliest.

While waiting, we stood with our kids in front of a dockside restaurant, where fresh octopus hung on outside wires like wet, tattered socks. Later, a Greek man kindly offered some cooked octopus to Mary, Lisa, Adam, and Paul Moshe for free. Too hungry to decline, they surprised themselves by actually liking it.

It was cold and dark by the time we got final word that the ferry wouldn't depart this night. Because both Professor Phillips and his son Marcus spoke Greek, they were able to bargain a small hotel's owner into letting our marooned group of sixteen sleep in its rooms and hallways for a pittance. The richer students were in Israel with Dr. Phillips's female graduate student TA.

The next morning, we were able to take the same ferry back to Piraeus, reaching our Athens hotel by subway just in time to board our chartered bus for a Peloponnesian tour. Despite being stranded that one night, I felt pride in having arranged for all our scheduled activities here and elsewhere.

While we were in Communist Prague for two days in mid-March, soldiers with attack dogs and machine guns were at downtown street corners. Still, I fell in love with that beautiful city, and wanted to live there. Because its old Jewish cemetery and Franz Kafka's house were not on our regime-approved tour, I included them in the walking tour I gave to our group. In Prague's repressively Communist environment, I thought of Kafka's *The Trial*.[3]

I, of course, remembered images of the 1956 Hungarian Revolution when we visited Budapest for two days in late March. But to attract hard currency

---

3. Franz Kafka (1883–1924) wrote novels and short stories that include themes about the aggravations of government bureaucracy. His novel *The Trial* (Berlin: Verla Die Schmiede, 1925) is one of his best-known works.

from Americans and Western Europeans into the Soviet Bloc, the USSR was allowing a huge amount of commercial freedom in Hungary. Called "Goulash Communism," this free enterprise diminished the repressiveness still characteristic of Eastern Europe in the early 1980s.

The best example in Budapest occurred when the government-approved tour guide took our BYU group to the required stop at one monument. It honored the Russian soldiers who died liberating Hungary from the Nazis. After explaining its significance, she said in English: "The Russians were our Grand Liberators in 1945," then smirked: "and again in 1956." Her last phrase was undoubtedly *not* in the script for guides.

The most daring thing I did was in Italy—as a necessity. While in Naples for a one-day visit in April, Jan and I boarded a train with only our four children, heading for ancient Pompeii. We knew it was closed due to a strike by its guides, and just wanted to show our kids whatever they could see through the bars of the main gate. After that quick look, we planned to return to Naples to tour museums and churches. The BYU group was in Sorrento this afternoon, but we had all visited ancient Herculaneum in the morning.

Using my copy of *Thomas Cook's European Rail Timetable*, I had written on a piece of paper the schedule for trains arriving at Pompeii's main gate and the times they departed therefrom. Alas, alone in downtown Naples this afternoon, the Quinns boarded the first train labeled for the ancient city. It went to the *back* of the ruins—*not* to the main gate. When the six of us got off at the train's only stop for Pompeii, I had no idea when the next one would be returning on that little-used track. The timetable was at our hotel in Rome, which we had left for this day trip.

No train came in nearly an hour, during which two of the correct ones would have departed from the front gate. For all I knew, this back-of-Pompeii track might be for a once-a-day train in each direction. I persuaded Jan that our best option was to climb over its tall fence and walk through the ancient city to the main gate. Paul Moshe squeezed through a gap in the bars of this back gate.

So, for more than an hour, we and our kids were the only people on the streets of Pompeii, looking at everything of interest. Some areas were blocked due to a recent earthquake and house gates were locked, but we could still view a lot through their vertical bars. And the empty streets had many wonderful things to see.

Shortly after we found our way to Pompeii's remarkable Forum, two guards started yelling at us in Italian. With memories of militarized Prague, six-year-old Paul Moshe trembled: "Daddy, are they going to shoot us?"

Only two phrases in my Berlitz guidebook for Italy seemed to apply: "I'm lost. Can you help me?"

My repeating this in bad Italian caused one guard to laugh, while the other unleashed a new torrent of words at us. When I handed them a nice sized bribe, the first was obviously pleased. The second was grudgingly mollified.

They unlocked the front gate, and within five minutes we boarded one of the correct trains to Naples. It was an antinomian adventure, but worthwhile.

Our biggest scare occurred two days later. Delaying to leave a store in downtown Florence with the rest of the BYU group, our six-year-old walked out its door and saw a bus to his right. Without looking to the left, where we were walking away as a group, Paul Moshe jumped onto the bus as it was about to pull from the curb. By the time we noticed him missing and turned back to the store, we saw no bus and didn't imagine that possibility. Not finding our little boy in the store, Jan and I were certain he had to be close by. For an hour, we looked for him in every adjacent area and became increasingly distraught.

Finally, we went back to the large *pension* where we had stayed the previous night, hoping that some of the students had found him. No luck. Just as we were about to ask its manager to phone the Italian police, our son walked through the front door in tears.

When Paul Moshe found that we weren't on the bus, he got off and began trying to recall how we walked from the *pension* to the store where he last saw us. Somehow, our six-year-old retraced the bus's unfamiliar route back to the store, then backtracked from downtown Florence the mile or more to the building we had left this morning on foot for the first time. It was miraculous, and I thanked God day and night.

In Salzburg in mid-May, we had our first view of the cult-classic *Rocky Horror Picture Show*—at the insistence of the BYU students one night. They warned that it was not appropriate for children, so we had our daughters stay with our sons in the *pension*. I howled with laughter at this campy comedy. By contrast, the perplexed Austrians in the small cinema were silent most of the time. Humor doesn't always cross borders.

It was also more than Jan enjoyed—especially (I think) the scene of transsexual Frank-N-Furter having sex with the young husband. We didn't discuss the film, which I assumed was painful for Jan in many respects.

May 1983–Missing a Witch Hunt

While living in Austria, I learned that apostle Mark E. Petersen tried to use local stake presidents to intimidate and punish Mormon intellectuals who wrote articles for the independent Mormon magazine *Sunstone* and the more academic journal *Dialogue*. This included fourteen authors who were scattered from the western states to Washington, DC.

The First Presidency apparently knew nothing about this crusade until *Sunstone* magazine's editor Peggy Fletcher brought it to the attention of First

Presidency counselor Gordon B. Hinckley. He was appalled and told the Quorum of Twelve that this inquisition must stop at once.

His intervention was too late to prevent a black eye in the press. Even some BYU professors contacted the media after being called in for such counseling. A story about these local inquisitions that were mandated by church headquarters was published by reporter Dawn House Tracy in the *Provo Herald* and in the *Salt Lake Tribune*.[4]

However, no officials of the church in Austria contacted me, and I learned about this inquisition only when someone in Provo sent me the news clippings anonymously. Learning of Elder Petersen's activities was a vaguely painful reminder of my loss of the bishop's office. I also felt sadness that his crusade showed pathetic insecurity.

Following my return to the United States this year, I never asked my stake president about the matter and don't know if apostle Petersen or his associates had contacted him. They may have simply ignored me because I was out of the country.

As another irony, I had once met with a member of Elder Petersen's special committee. Five years earlier, Ron Esplin and I had a very pleasant chat with Henry W. Richards in his office at Granite Furniture in Sugarhouse, where he told us about his years of work on that committee.

When Mark E. Petersen died in eight months, I fondly remembered drinking a strawberry malt with this apostle in his English residence. Long ago.

Early June 1983–Visiting Soviet Moscow

With seven students, I spent four full days in Moscow. They paid the extra money for this side trip.

Meanwhile, Mary and Lisa traveled with the rest to Germany for a bus trip on *Die romantische Strasse*. It included the beautiful university city of Heidelberg and the still-walled medieval town of Rotenberg-ob-der-Tauber, both of which Jan and I had visited in 1970. Tired of traveling, she chose to stay these days in Baden with our boys.

In Moscow, freshman Wally Glausi and I were assigned to a room which had a microphone dangling from the middle of its ceiling. Every time he walked into this Soviet Inturist hotel, Wally shouted some insult against Lenin or Stalin—to irritate our KGB spy listeners at the other end of our room's microphone.

Getting back to our BYU group's first night in Moscow, we all went to

4. Dawn Tracy wrote two stories on this subject for *The Herald* this month, "LDS Bishops Want 'Faith-Promoting' Articles" (May 23, 1983), and "LDS Leaders Challenge Y Professors' Faith" (May 25, 1983). The *Salt Lake Tribune* article, titled "LDS Church Telling Editors to Use Only 'Faith Promoting' Stories?" appeared on May 23, 1983.

Red Square, which was filled with people. Even more impressive than its photos, St. Basil's Cathedral was stunningly illuminated by gigantic Klieg lights.

There we met a Swiss businessman who represented West German companies in Moscow. He said that Russian-speaking westerners were of special concern to the KGB, who not only bugged his apartment with listening devices, but had closed-circuit TV cameras operating twenty-four hours daily from the ceiling of every room. "How can I invite anyone to my apartment under such conditions?" he asked in German-accented English. So he talked with people in outside locations, such as Red Square, and counted the days until he could move from the USSR.

Unlike Prague, there were no attack dogs in evidence, and I saw no outward display of weapons. Even the security guards in front of Lenin's Tomb seemed to be weaponless, and they dressed in non-intimidating peasant tunics. However, as one of the guards bent over to pick up something, I noticed an automatic pistol concealed under the draped edges of his tunic. This was on my third visit to Red Square.

Moscow's repression was subtly concealed from most tourists. My bet was that the Inturist hotels for Americans had no obvious listening devices, contrary to the obvious ones in our hotel that was reserved for West Germans, Austrians, and Swiss tour groups.

Because we few BYU-Americans were in a package tour of Austrians, our Inturist guide was a German-speaking Russian. I noticed that he spent a great deal of time talking about the significance of the icons and religious symbols whenever we visited churches or monasteries that had been turned into secular museums by the Bolsheviks. During the group's last Inturist lunch in Moscow, he motioned me to the booth where he always ate alone.

In German, he asked if the students and I belonged to a particular church, due to our not drinking alcohol nor smoking. He had never heard of BYU or Mormonism, and asked what distinguished us from other religions. I started with our beliefs in Christ and revelation from God, which he dismissed as not distinctive. Finally, I mentioned the Mormon emphasis on freedom and free agency, which got the tour guide's attention.

After a pause, this Russian said that he was a Baptist, but attended no religious services in Moscow—for fear of losing his job as an Inturist guide. Every vacation, he traveled to a distant city where there was another Baptist he trusted, and they studied the Bible together. "*Die Freiheit fuer Sie*," he said softly, "*ist sehr anders als die Freiheit fuer mich*."[5] And I thought of my Honors Program exam with BYU philosopher Terry Warner in 1968.

From the beginning of this 1983 trip, I repeatedly warned the students against dealing with black marketeers, but they traded with competing groups

---

5. German, meaning "Freedom for you is very different from freedom for me."

of young Russians. They freaked out on the day each group accused the other of being KGB.

The accusation was believable, because these black marketeers spoke English with suspiciously flawless American accents. Otherwise they spoke fast Russian among themselves, as they kept a watchful eye on passersby. Were they on the lookout for customers? Or for Moscow's police?

I constantly worried that one of our students might get arrested for illegal currency exchanges or for buying contraband. I had warned them from the beginning that no one in our group could stay beyond the date of our exit visa to assist an arrested student. If so, such person(s) would also be in violation of Soviet law and vulnerable to arrest.

Thus, I felt a profound sense of relief after we made it past the humorless Cossacks of airport security without incident, and were all safely on board the Aeroflot jet. As soon as we were in the air, heading back to Vienna, an Austrian man turned to me from across the aisle and said in English: "I thank God for the United States!"

13 June 1983–President Hinckley Joins Anti-Historian Voices

In his address to the graduating exercises of BYU–Hawaii (formerly the Church College of Hawaii), Gordon B. Hinckley said: "We have those critics who appear to wish to cull out of a vast panorama of information those items that demean and belittle some of the men and women of the past who worked so hard in laying the foundation of this great cause."[6]

Some of my critics claimed that this referred to my recently published biography of J. Reuben Clark. If so, not all general authorities shared President Hinckley's negative assessment.

July 1983–Supportive Conversations with Two Apostles

I hadn't met with Howard W. Hunter and Thomas S. Monson while they were involved in the revision of my manuscript during the previous year. After returning from Europe, I asked to see them individually to thank them for helping to get the Clark book into print. Both apostles told me that it was a "wonderful" biography.

Apostle Hunter said: "While we made suggestions for revision in your manuscript, we told the men at BYU that these were simply suggestions. We could not expect you to make changes in your biography which were incompatible with your standards as a historian." I had always admired Elder Hunter's attitudes toward historical openness, ever since I learned that he

---

6. See Gordon B. Hinckley, "Stop Looking for Storms and Enjoy the Sunlight," *Church News*, July 3, 1983.

had opened up the LDS Church's archives to all researchers shortly after his appointment as Church Historian in 1970.

Now I felt like telling him that I wished more members in the Quorum of Twelve had his views about Mormon history, but I held my tongue. Apostle Monson told me that he gave copies of my book to all his children.

During my private meeting in Elder Hunter's office, he surprised me by commenting at length on relationships within the Quorum of the Twelve Apostles. While discussing his pro-Arab philosophy in connection with the proposed BYU Jerusalem Center, he complained about "the Zionists in the Twelve." More significantly, he also made a point of emphasizing to me that he usually acquiesced to the Twelve's unnamed zealots.

Apostle Hunter then said that he preferred to avoid conflict—even with junior apostles who promoted views contrary to his own. Less than two years after the controversy over my public response to apostle Packer, I was sure that he was the unnamed object of this disclosure. Adding that "some can be very emphatic about what they are promoting to the Quorum," Elder Hunter said: "I don't want to turn a temple meeting into a cat fight, so I don't say anything in response."

This was no inadvertent disclosure, because he had carefully read my preliminary biography that gave unvarnished details about the conflicts of J. Reuben Clark with other general authorities. Senior apostle Hunter knew in 1983 that he was telling me exactly the kind of information that interested me as a historian.

His comment about cat-fighting apostles explained why an unabashed zealot like Boyd K. Packer had been able to say and do the things he had over the years as a junior member of the Twelve. He simply intimidated non-combative apostles into silence and acquiescence by his willingness to argue in the temple about anything he might want or might oppose.

I regarded that as a tragedy for the church at large, even though I was overwhelmed by the Christlike humility of Howard W. Hunter with a junior.

19 August 1983–LDS Leadership's "Fatal Shift"

At home in Salt Lake City, I watched the televised broadcast of BYU religion professor Hugh Nibley giving the main address to the summer's commencement exercises for graduating students. He delivered "Leaders to Managers: The Fatal Shift," while sitting behind him were BYU President Jeffrey R. Holland and three apostles: Ezra Taft Benson, Howard W. Hunter, and Thomas S. Monson.[7]

The camera often focused on Jeff Holland's outbursts of laughter at Nibley's

---

7. See Hugh Nibley, "Leaders to Managers: The Fatal Shift," *Dialogue: A Journal of Mormon Thought* 16, no. 4 (Winter 1983): 12–21. A video of the talk can be viewed at speeches.byu.edu.

humorous barbs about the educational establishment. BYU's president stopped laughing when he suddenly realized that the seventy-three-year-old professor was using this talk to criticize the recent leadership of the LDS Church. He even mocked the unnamed Boyd K. Packer's well-known opposition to hearing instrumental compositions by Bach during sacrament meeting.

When Holland realized that Nibley was giving a veiled critique of current apostles, the camera showed a stricken expression on Jeff's countenance. For the remainder of the talk, his face was a stony mask. It became a grimace when Nibley not-too-subtly summed up LDS headquarters this way: "the Spirit was exchanged for the office and inspired leadership for ambitious management."

At that point, I exclaimed: "My God! He'll be fired and possibly excommunicated for saying this!" But he wasn't, even though Nibley's son-in-law biographer Boyd Jay Petersen would write decades later: "In fact, Hugh fully expected to be fired and ostracized for what he was about to say, but he would not pass up the chance to speak his mind."[8]

This publicly verified what Doyle Buchanan had told me in 1976. During one of their conversations in Provo, Hugh Nibley said that the LDS Church is in an apostasy similar to second-century Christianity.

The forbearance of LDS leaders toward BYU's old gadfly would seem especially significant exactly ten years from now, when I would be one of their targets.

1983-85–Gospel Doctrine Teacher Again

The Salt Lake City Twenty-seventh Ward's members enjoyed my teaching so much that some encouraged their non-resident friends to attend. Eventually, people were arriving from throughout the Salt Lake Valley.

As with previous classes in Sunday School, I regarded the official manual as a simple guideline and taught directly from the standard works. *Sola scriptura*, as Martin Luther used to say, although the LDS canon is more diverse than the Holy Bible alone.

The scriptures are radical enough for a left-wing liberal like me. I didn't need to reference *Dialogue* or *Sunstone* to Gospel Doctrine classes. I did sometimes quote from the *Journal of Discourses* about the old-time religion of Mormonism. And people seemed to love it all.

February 1984–Apostle Thomas S. Monson Intervenes

For nearly a year, the *Church News* editors had ignored my biography of J. Reuben Clark, apparently knowing that apostle Packer disliked it. After they

---

8. See Boyd Jay Petersen, *Hugh Nibley: A Consecrated Life* (Sandy, UT: Greg Kofford Books, 2002), 371.

published a positive review of a book by the RLDS Church's press, I finally wrote apostle Monson about the resounding silence on my book.

He wrote back within days to say he had "taken care of the situation" and that a review would appear shortly. It did in the weekly edition of March 4th.[9] The speed of Elder Monson's reply surprised me, and I figured that his intervention would antagonize Elder Packer even more against me.

3 April 1984–Revelatory "Document" on the Ordination of Women

Without realizing the significance of its timing, I had scheduled this week for research in the archives of the Reorganized Church at Independence, Missouri. While staying with Paul M. Edwards and family, I learned that the RLDS World Conference would be debating whether to accept as revelation "a document" for the ordination of women to the priesthood. Although formally submitted by Church President Wallace B. Smith, it was (as usual for such documents) presented for parliamentary debate by the delegates from RLDS congregations around the world.

Sitting with historian William D. Russell in one of the upper tiers of the massive auditorium today, I was stunned by the ability of devout RLDS delegates to publicly argue against accepting as revelation a document phrased as "Thus saith the Lord."[10] Nothing like this had ever happened in Utah Mormonism's lockstep version of common consent.

In two days, a majority of the delegates voted to accept this document as revelation, adding it to the RLDS Doctrine and Covenants as Section 156. As a result, about one-third of the Reorganization's members (including entire stake organizations) would soon abandon the church led by Wallace B. Smith. Most of these RLDS dissidents organized themselves into a schismatic Remnant Church.

Early April 1984–Radical Secularism at the University of Utah

This month, *Utah Holiday* magazine published the only article I co-authored with Jan. It was a restaurant review that we had been invited to write by the magazine's food editors, Cheryll and Dean May. Both academics (in political science and history), they had been friends of ours since I met Dean in Leonard Arrington's History Division nearly ten years earlier.

Dean had recently survived a bruising battle to get tenure at the University of Utah. The history department as a whole voted overwhelmingly to grant him tenure, but its chair Larry Gerlach officially protested against granting tenure.

---

9. See "New books for LDS readers," *Church News*, Mar. 4, 1984.

10. William D. ("Bill") Russell (1938–) is an attorney, social activist, and emeritus professor of history at Graceland University, where he taught from 1966 to 2007. He is an influential member of Community of Christ, advocating for the ordination of women and full inclusion of people of all races and sexual orientations. He was president of the Mormon History Association from 1982–83.

He objected that so many of Dean May's publications as a nationally renowned demographic historian involved Mormon history, Utah, and LDS sources.

I regarded this as typical anti-Mormon bias by a non-LDS academic whose only book to date was about the Ku Klux Klan in Utah—which could also be dismissed as provincial. On the other hand, I was stunned to learn from Dean that the department's full professor James L. Clayton (serving as the University's Provost) did his best to prevent tenure, a denial that would have resulted in Dean being forced to leave.

Although himself a returned missionary and sealed-in-the-temple Mormon, Clayton argued that any publication about LDS history was parochial and academically "insignificant." He even claimed that Dean's reputation as "a Mormon historian" damaged the history department's status nationally.

Ultimately, only Dean May's threat of a lawsuit (by our attorney and friend, well-connected Jim McConkie) persuaded the University of Utah's administration to grant tenure to him.[11] After all, its history department's professors had overwhelmingly voted for him to receive tenure.

Clayton's role in this mystified me, because he claimed to be Dean's friend and had himself published articles about Utah-Mormon topics. Moreover, Jim Clayton had been summoned to meet with the three apostles on the same day as I was in May 1982, due to his published talk ("Does History Undermine Faith?") to the B. H. Roberts Society.[12] We were also friends in the Emigration Stake, where he had served in the Sunday School presidency while I was on the high council.

Nonetheless, I decided not to ask him about this situation, because of what Dean called Jim's "bitterness" about the final tenure decision. Twenty years later, I would have a painful personal encounter with Professor Clayton's radical secularism and his bias against anyone doing Mormon history at the University of Utah.

Is secular myopia any better than blind faith? Is secular prejudice an improvement over religious bigotry? Bill Buckley's scathing book about *God and Man* inside American academia had better application to the modern University of Utah than to modern Yale.[13]

23 April 1984–Evans Award for Biography

This was the first time the David W. and Beatrice C. Evans Award was given for the best biography in Mormon or Western American history. I

---

11. McConkie later recalled, "I did help Dean on this and advocated for him, but we never filed a lawsuit." Jim McConkie, email to Barbara Jones Brown, July 15, 2022.

12. See James L. Clayton, "Does History Undermine Faith?" *Sunstone Magazine*, Mar./Apr. 1982, 34–36.

13. William F. Buckley, *God and Man at Yale: The Superstitions of "Academic Freedom"* (Washington, DC: Regnery Books, 1951).

thought my Clark biography was the best one *published* in 1983, and was stunned to learn that this $10,000 award went to Leonard Arrington's unpublished manuscript biography of Brigham Young.

My other mentor, Howard Lamar, was one of the judges for the award and confided to me that my biography would have won, except that the rules allowed for unpublished manuscripts to be submitted. He had judged Leonard's manuscript to be better and more important than my book.

I regarded those rules as outrageously unfair because they allowed a biography to be submitted twice. Once as a manuscript and again after the manuscript was published. I knew it would not change this year's decision, but I filed a formal protest with the Evans Committee and urged that the rules be changed to allow a biography to be considered only once—either as a manuscript or as a published book, but not as both.

Leonard and I knew that his unparalleled biography of Brigham Young would win the Evans Award whether he submitted it as a manuscript or as a published book. By submitting it as a manuscript months after my biography was published, Leonard clearly wanted to be the first person to win the Evans Award. For Mormonism's pre-eminent historian, this was a natural expectation.

Nonetheless, he could have allowed me to win it by simply waiting for his biography to be considered as a published book. I owed my career to Leonard Arrington and felt guilty that I was so disappointed about his receiving the award this year. My pride and arrogance.[14]

After learning of the committee's decision, Jan and I visited Leonard in LDS Hospital, where he was recovering from heart bypass surgery. Bedside was his new wife Harriet Horne, a woman equal in kindness and grace to his deceased companion I had publicly mourned two years previous. I congratulated him on the Evans Award.

"Mike, it'll be your turn another time," he said. Smiling wanly, I nodded, but didn't say that I doubted I would ever again have the opportunity.[15]

Following my experience with J. Reuben Clark's life, I regarded biography as the most difficult kind of history to write. Matthias F. Cowley was the only person for whom I felt willing to put myself through the biography ordeal again, and I knew that was impossible.

---

14. Leonard Arrington, upon learning he had won the prize, wrote in his journal, "Obviously, I am pleased, but I feel disappointed that the prize will not be won by somebody who needs (and deserves) the money more than I do. I am thinking of Mike Quinn." Gary James Bergera, ed., *Confessions of a Mormon Historian: The Diaries of Leonard J. Arrington, 1971–1997*, 3 vols. (Salt Lake City: Signature Books, 2018), 3:364.

15. Of this April 22, 1984, hospital visit, Arrington journaled, "Mike and Jan Quinn came by for a while; just about as they were to leave Maureen Beecher came. So I asked Mike to join hands on my head with Maureen, Jan, and Harriet and ask a special prayer. It was a beautiful prayer." Bergera, ed., *Confessions of a Mormon Historian*, 3:366.

His original journals were locked away in the vault of the First Presidency. That's also where his revised memoir journals had gone shortly after I held those thousands of loose sheets in my hands twelve years ago in the attic of his daughter's house. More than any other single source, apostle Cowley's journals (original and revised and expanded) were the key to understanding the details of post-Manifesto polygamy. This had been my goal since age seventeen.

It didn't help my feelings when I eventually read Leonard Arrington's *Brigham Young: American Moses.*[16] I found that it shied away from some controversies and glossed over others. Even though he made unparalleled citations to documents that apostle Packer and Elder G. Homer Durham had recently made unavailable to researchers at LDS archives, Leonard failed to discuss or even mention adverse evidence that I knew existed there.

I never agreed to publish a book review of my mentor's magnum opus about Brigham Young. The previous paragraph is all I want to write.

3 May 1984—Beginning Marriage Counseling

Because of severe conflicts among our children, Jan wanted us to start family therapy with a good friend in the Twenty-seventh Ward. Moyne Oviatt was a licensed clinical social worker but said that she was too close to us to have the professional detachment a counselor should maintain. She recommended that we see Robert E. Simpson, a non-LDS family therapist.

With deep reluctance, I agreed for the six of us to meet with him and his female counseling partner today. I was sure that—sooner or later—these counselors would recognize my homosexuality and the problems it had caused our marriage, despite my having remained sexually faithful to Jan. I dreaded having to confront those realities with anyone else, but couldn't ignore our family's need for professional help.

After eight weekly sessions, Rob and his co-counselor asked to meet with Jan and me alone. "You're both concealing something," he said. "What's going on between you?" Jan tried to evade it as much as I did, but to no avail. We both needed to unburden ourselves.

We spent the next months trying to sort out what my homosexuality had meant for us. And would mean in future.

Mid-May 1984—BYU Dean Is "Instructed" about My Publishing

At the annual meeting of the Mormon History Association held at BYU on the 12th, I gave a paper on business activities of the Mormon hierarchy from the 1830s to the present. This included a summary of current general

---

16. *Brigham Young: American Moses* (New York: Alfred A. Knopf, 1985) won Utah State University's Evans Biography Award (announced 1984, before publication) and the Mormon History Association's Best Book Award (1985). The National Book Critics Circle nominated it for a "distinguished work of biography."

authorities who were serving as directors and officers of various corporations. Jan attended my talk and was with me at the banquet where my biography of J. Reuben Clark received MHA's award for 1983's best book.

In a few days, Martin Hickman, the dean of my college telephoned me at home and, with great discomfort, told me that he had been instructed "by higher authority" to ask me not to publish the paper I gave at MHA. I pointed out that the information on corporate directorships came from publicly available sources.

Hickman replied: "I know, but church leaders still don't want you to publish it." I said that he knew I would publish something like it one day in my book about the Mormon hierarchy.[17] Dean Hickman said that wasn't included in his instructions, and he personally looked forward to the book, but that he had to ask me again not to publish my paper as an article. I agreed not to publish it separately.

I wouldn't tell others about this incident until my resignation from BYU four years later.

29 July 1984–Second Counselor in Stake Sunday School Presidency, Salt Lake Emigration Stake

This auxiliary's new president was attorney Gordon A. Madsen. Later this summer, he and I attended a social with President Hugh West and the presidencies of the stake's other auxiliaries. We met in a cabin up one of the canyons.

Conversation turned to the tragic incapacitation of LDS President Spencer W. Kimball since 1982 and the fact that Gordon B. Hinckley was the only mentally alert and administratively functioning member of the First Presidency. His son Richard G. Hinckley, now first counselor to stake president West, remarked: "If Marion G. Romney lives a few more years, he'll be the first prophet who isn't aware that he is one." Romney had been *non compos mentis* for some time and would be next in line to be church president through automatic apostolic succession.[18] Our informant Richard Hinckley would become a general authority twenty years after his disclosure today.

10 January 1985–Death of Unusual Ally

I had felt at odds with G. Homer Durham after his appointment as managing director of HDC in 1977, but ironically benefited from the inconsistencies in his decision-making that this self-biography has already noted. Even though he restricted research by others, he paradoxically continued authorizing my access to sensitive materials.

---

17. Quinn published this book, *Mormon Hierarchy: Wealth and Corporate Power*, in 2017 with Signature Books.
18. Latin for "not of sound mind."

This might have had something to do with the congenial personal relationship that I had with LDS President Spencer W. Kimball and with his special counselor Gordon B. Hinckley. Elder Durham had been the latter's missionary companion, and they remained very good friends.

After my twelve-page memo to Elder Durham in February 1979, he knew of my extensive research about post-Manifesto polygamy, yet he continued for six years to give me access to restricted documents regarding plural marriage. This went far beyond the extraordinary access I had been given for researching the authorized biography of J. Reuben Clark from late 1977 until I finished its draft in mid-1981.

Throughout the next three-and-a-half years (when not in Chicago or Europe), I continued getting Elder Durham's approval for my examining heavily restricted documents at HDC. Just days before his death in 1985, he again gave me access to First Presidency files and correspondence, which my request had specified were necessary to finalize my upcoming article on post-Manifesto polygamy. And I specifically stated that it would appear in *Dialogue*.[19]

"Mike Quinn has helped us explain other historical problems," Elder Durham told newly appointed archivist Glenn N. Rowe. "I hope he can help us here—because this is a tough one." Glenn repeated those words to me in the research room of HDC as he handed me the approval slips that Elder Durham had just initialed.

February 1985–Bribing a Typesetter

By the time I processed those last-gasp research notes for revising my article, *Dialogue's* copyeditor Lavina Fielding Anderson said that this spring issue was being typeset and could have no more changes.[20] When I tried to make an end-run around her to its managing editors Jack and Linda Newell, they said the same.

Undeterred, the next morning I drove through the snow to the house of typesetter Don Henriksen. I handed him a gift of $100 in cash, and he made the changes.

March 1985–Publishing about Conscientious Objection

Because *Sunstone* magazine had a youthful readership, I was happy to

19. See D. Michael Quinn, "LDS Church Authority and New Plural Marriages, 1890–1904," *Dialogue: A Journal of Mormon Thought* 18, no. 1 (Spring 1985): 9–105.

20. Lavina Fielding Anderson (1944–2023) held a PhD in English and was a writer, editor, and feminist. She was an editor for the *Ensign, Dialogue, Journal of Mormon History, Mormon Women's Forum Quarterly,* and *Case Reports of the Mormon Alliance.* She served on the board of directors and editorial advisory board of Signature Books for many years, publishing with Signature: *Tending the Garden: Essays on Mormon Literature* (2000), *Lucy's Book: A Critical Edition of Lucy Mack Smith's Family Memoir* (2001), and *Mercy without End: Toward a More Inclusive Church* (2020), an anthology of her essays on twenty-five years of attending church as an excommunicant.

publish LDS views about war, pacifism, and conscientious objection that Mormons now rarely heard or read.[21] The nation was no longer divided as it was during the Vietnam conflict, and I was deeply concerned about the unthinking jingoism that seemed universal among the youth of Ronald Reagan's America.

Having participated in a war protest as an undergraduate student at BYU in May 1970, *Sunstone* editor Peggy Fletcher had similar feelings. Perhaps hers were even more intense than mine.

I first gave this presentation a year earlier at BYU's Peace Symposium, whose undergraduate organizer Maxine Hanks became a colleague of mine in the New Mormon History.[22] She was a distant cousin of my mission president but was not related to his same-named wife. Maxine's college-aged sister Jeanie would soon introduce me to a new group of friends in Salt Lake City.

6 April 1985–Telling our Children That We're Divorcing

It was Easter weekend, and Jan felt that I should tell our children that I would move from the house in a month. We wanted to give them that long to adjust to the idea of my leaving.

We arrived at this point after eighteen years, four beautiful children, daily family prayer with the children at dinner time, regular prayer as a couple every night, earnest individual prayers several times daily, weekly family home evenings, reading the Book of Mormon each Sunday as a family, regular attendance as a family at all LDS meetings, fasting and prayer more than monthly as a couple, and frequent temple attendance together (until the last year or so, when I often went alone), as we tried to cope with the hopeless condition of our marriage. Our deep love didn't stop the tragedy.

Like most LDS husbands, I had rarely socialized without my wife. Aside from my trips with historians to academic conferences, there had been no boys' night out. Jan's socializing away from me had been limited to lunches with her parents or sisters, or with her business associates like El Marie Gunnell.

I made the emphatic decision for divorce after Jan told me that she was praying daily to die. She thought that was the only hope for me to find sexual fulfillment and happiness. I had also been praying to die for years, but learning of her similar despair finalized my resolve to legally end our marriage.

Did I doubt that God had told me to marry Jan while I prayed in the Manti Temple eighteen years earlier? No, I didn't doubt that experience, but I didn't understand it, either. If I had known back then that my homosexual desires would actually increase after our wedding, I would have disobeyed that revelation and spared Jan. A sin of omission would have been far better than the tragedy of obedience.

21. Quinn, "Christian Soldiers or Conscientious Objectors?" *Sunstone,* Mar. 1985, 14–23.

22. Maxine Hanks (1955–) is a feminist theologian, historian, editor, and author. She assisted Quinn with research for some of his books.

As a couple, we had been faithful and loyal to each other. Until the previous eleven months of meeting with family therapists, we had hardly discussed our problems with anyone else, and had done our best to shield our children from those conflicts.

We spared our kids from being part of our difficulties over the years. As a result they had no preparation for the divorce announcement, and were deeply shocked.

So was everyone else. I recalled that many people had told us we were a "perfect Mormon couple." Jan didn't remember anyone expressing that view.

After three-and-a-half months of marriage counseling, she had started writing in a personal journal for the first time during our marriage. Jan encouraged me to read it this year, but I didn't. Racked with guilt for the unhappiness I had brought into decades of her life, I couldn't force myself to read about her pain. She told me once, "I'm so tired of feeling sorry for *you*, Mike!"

As part of my individual counseling, Rob Simpson recommended that I should read *The Family Crucible* by Augustus Y. Napier and Carl Whitaker.[23] I was astounded by its insights into "dysfunctional family systems," and saw my own family of origin from a troubling new perspective. Everyone had been damaged emotionally, including me.

In a few years, I would share Napier's and Whitaker's insights during casual conversation with my historian friend Dan Vogel. He soon said that this could be a useful tool for historical analysis of Joseph Smith's family. Despite my reading of Erik H. Erikson's psychobiography *Young Man Luther* in 1971, I had never thought of the application Dan would suggest so enthusiastically after our talk in 1989. Fifteen years thereafter, he would turn the family systems methodology as explained by Napier and Whitaker into one of the two interpretative models for his award-winning *The Making of a Prophet*.[24] Pious fraud was the other. I would be enthusiastic about the first, but not the second.

As demonstrated by case studies in *The Family Crucible*, each family member had a subconscious role in perpetuating everyone else's emotional dysfunction. In fact, this resulted in cycles of emotional dysfunction from generation to generation, each haunted by the psychological ghosts of the previous one.

Before reading the book, I told Rob Simpson how emphatically I had reacted against my grandparents' marriage, my father's marriages, and my

23. See Napier and Whitaker, *The Family Crucible: The Intense Experience of Family Therapy* (New York: HarperCollins, 1977).

24. Dan Vogel (1955–) is a historian who specializes in early Mormon documents and Joseph Smith. His book, *Joseph Smith: The Making of a Prophet* (Signature Books, 2004) won the John Whitmer Historical Association's Best Book Award and the Mormon History Association's Best Biography Award.

mother's marriages—vowing not to follow their examples. From my early teens onward, I wanted to be the kind of strong, loving, listening, and supportive husband I never saw in their marriages nor heard about in the marriages of their parents. I had also vowed since my teens to be the openly affectionate, available, engaged father I never had, but yearned for.

As we were discussing the book, Rob said: "You broke the dysfunctional cycle in your family of origin, Mike." However, not as successfully as I then thought.

It would be seven years before I would allow myself to recognize that there were *Family Crucible* problems in my own role as a parent—besides the obvious one. That one was my creation of dysfunction by entering a gay-straight marriage—to be a repressed homosexual husband and father.

My matronly high school teacher was absolutely right. Self-repression is emotionally harmful, and not just to the one who chooses to live that way. I wished I had paid more serious heed to Mrs. Turner's warning in 1962.

Early April 1985–Parents React

I expected my Catholic father and LDS mother to give me understanding and support when I told them of our decision to divorce, since they divorced when I was four, divorced from their second spouses, and both had rocky third marriages. Instead, they expressed disappointment in me, and agreed with Jan's parents that I was selfish.

I had always lived to be the shining knight of my family, but I had also feared they could not accept me without my exemplary Mormon armor. There was no joy in learning I had been right about that all along.

Ever since I was a kid, I recall Nana, Aunt Joy, Aunt Norma, and my stepfather Wayne saying that I was selfish, and I accepted their judgment. I now realize that I really had no sense of self, but only a sense of obligation to serve and please others.

Since childhood, I'd been trying to serve the competing expectations of my grandmother, mother, father, church leaders, and friends. As an adult, there were the added needs of my wife, our children, the Latter-day Saints, and my service as a historian to the Mormon cause. I ended up failing one person's or group's expectations as I took time and attention away from them to serve someone else.

For years, all my efforts to fulfill others' expectations—my reason for not committing suicide—had been quietly unraveling until our divorce brought the fact to everyone's attention. The response I got from family, friends, and even strangers was disappointment that I had failed them in one way or another. I knew I was a good speaker and writer, but in my interpersonal relationships, nothing I did was good enough.

I tried to tell myself that I was not a failure just because I had failed everyone and everything important to me. Actually, I felt worse than a failure. I had no value.

Mid-April 1985–Rejection by Spiritual Missionary Friend

In mid-1971, Mike McAdams was the first person (aside from my freshman BYU bishop) to whom I had ever confided my struggle with homosexuality. His expressions of support and encouragement had been tremendously important to me since then.

Now Mike wrote that my decision to divorce showed that I was utterly selfish, had forfeited God's will for me, and had given up trying to be a Latter-day Saint. My friend said that he found me "repulsive" and wanted to have no further contact with me.

His words devastated me, and Jan began crying when she read them. I slowly tore my longtime friend's letter into small pieces. I felt empty.

Late April 1985–Apostle Boyd K. Packer's Public Condemnations

Following the April 1 publication in *Dialogue* of my article on "LDS Church Authority and New Plural Marriages, 1890–1904," I learned from several sources that apostle Packer condemned me in public meetings as diverse as a stake conference in Denver and a special solemn assembly in the Salt Lake Temple for priesthood leaders in the Salt Lake Valley. Even though he didn't identify me by name, Elder Packer referred to me in these meetings as a BYU historian who is writing about polygamy to embarrass the Church.[25]

Sons of the apostles reported back that Packer told a meeting of the Quorum of Twelve that what Mike Quinn wrote about plural marriage may be true, but no faithful Latter-day Saint would publish what he did.

2 May 1985–Moving Out within Same Neighborhood

I wanted to reside within walking distance of the house Jan and I had occupied since 1977. I hoped that, in addition to my verbal assurances, this would show our four children that I was not trying to abandon them.

Because I expected to still be residing within the boundaries of the Twenty-seventh Ward, I had planned in late April 1985 to continue attending its LDS services. In response, Bishop Brad Melis said that this would be extremely awkward for the ward's membership—to see me sitting separate

25. Speaking in the church's general conference on April 6, 1985, Boyd K. Packer said, "During the last few days, I have had pressing upon me, by inspiration as I believe, the feeling that I should present some counsel.... There are some who, motivated by one influence or another, seek through writing and publishing criticisms and interpretations of doctrine to make the gospel more acceptable to the so-called thinking people of the world." Speaking of "apostasy" and "traitors," Packer admonished, "we would all do well to follow Paul's admonition and 'from such turn away.'" Boyd K. Packer, "From Such Turn Away," *Ensign*, May 1985.

from Jan, while (as I told him) I expected to sit with one or more of our children at Sunday's sacrament meetings.

I didn't want to lose this church association with my children, but Jan agreed with our bishop. Thus, I consented for my membership record to go to our stake's Twenty-first Ward, and I began attending its chapel on K Street and Second Avenue. The Twenty-seventh Ward released me as its gospel doctrine teacher in May.

Throughout the next three years, I did my best to spend an evening with each of my children individually every week. During this period, I moved to three locations within several blocks of Jan's home that had ceased to be mine.

Initially, I moved in with Scott, a gregarious and generous-hearted bachelor somewhat younger than me. For four months of free rent, I slept on a pull-down Murphy bed in his apartment inside an elegant old building on the corner of South Temple and L Street. We never talked about sexual matters, but I thought he was a repressed gay who was struggling to be both celibate and happy. Not easy to do.

Next, I moved into a spare bedroom of much-younger Bill's apartment on N Street. Midway between Third Avenue and Fourth Avenue, it was two blocks from my children. Although he was the ward's organist, a role often filled by gay male bachelors, Bill seemed completely straight (and years later would introduce me to his wife and children). I remained there for a year, splitting expenses fifty-fifty.

Then I moved into a basement apartment on First Avenue, between O and P—two blocks directly south of my kids. Small and dank, with water pipes running across its low ceilings, it was furnished with cast offs as depressing as the apartment itself. Yet it cost me only $150 monthly, with utilities, and I felt lucky to find the place. I remained there alone.

5 May 1985–Learning of Another's "Road Too Often Traveled"

Throughout the years I struggled with the problems of my marriage, I sometimes thought of Bart, the sexually uninhibited friend of my repressed youth. I imagined him snuggling (or at least having great sex) with some cute young man of gentle nature (the kind he seemed to attract).

During the annual meeting of the Mormon History Association, someone asked if I remembered Bart from Glendale, California. This man had an in-law relationship to him and said that the once disaffected Bart returned to church activity, had divorced twice, and now his third wife confided that their marriage was "rocky."

I had envied Bart since we were twelve, but no more. After I married, he had seemed so emphatic against marriage for our kind. Now I felt profound sadness to learn of these three unhappy women who probably had no idea why their marriages had failed.

Better to learn that Bart died of AIDS in the arms of a male lover. Then I would still envy him.

Mid-May 1985–Nurtured by Straight-Arrow Couple

I had known Judi Miller and James McConkie as close friends since they were dating at BYU. Exactly ten years earlier, I confided my homosexuality to him. I just assumed that he had told Judi about it long before now.

After learning of our divorce decision, they invited me for dinner weekly. Every Monday evening, we had scripture study or occasional attendance at movies with their young daughter and teenage sons. This was an important strength to me during the next three years.

Late May 1985–Stake President of the Salt Lake Emigration Stake Reluctantly Withdraws My Temple Recommend

The general authorities charged me with unworthiness of a temple recommend for "speaking evil of the Lord's anointed," in my *Dialogue* article about the First Presidency's approval of post-Manifesto polygamy. The three apostles also instructed stake president Hugh S. West to "take further action" if withdrawing my temple recommend didn't "remedy the situation" of my speaking and writing about Mormon history in a way as to "offend the Brethren" (their phrase). The general authority message to the stake president was to pretend this was a decision that originated with him, which he refused to do throughout their two-hour meeting. Paramore was stunned to encounter such resistance.[26]

Stake President West and his second counselor (my former Bishop Richard Horne) told me that they both had read the polygamy article, and that they never considered that it could be the basis for taking any kind of church action against me. They told me individually that the stake president's first counselor Richard Hinckley (son of First Presidency counselor Gordon B. Hinckley) agreed with them.

I told the stake president that I would not be intimidated by anyone and that I would continue my research and writing efforts to sympathetically explain problems in Mormon history. "I'm an insurance executive," Hugh West said, "and I won't tell you how to be a historian. But please try to find some way to be conscientious in Mormon history and still avoid these

26. Elder James M. Paramore was called to the First Quorum of the Seventy in August 1977, and was serving as president of the Utah North Area in 1985 when this incident occurred. Area Presidents have jurisdiction over the stake presidencies within their areas. "Changes Announced in Area Presidencies," *Ensign*, May 1985.

confrontations with the Brethren." I said that I would try but didn't see how I could do both at the same time.

The stake president said that he regarded his instructions from church headquarters as a backdoor effort to have me fired at BYU. Despite the apostolic order to deprive me of a temple recommend, President West instructed me to protect my employment by telling BYU administrators (if they asked) that I had a current temple recommend: "Don't volunteer that it's in my desk drawer." He said that he would continually renew my recommend and keep it in his desk, to prevent employment difficulties at BYU.

Since he had been so candid with me about the details of his two-hour meeting and dispute with Paramore, I asked my stake president to identify the three apostles who had given these instructions to this general authority who was our area president. President West said that he didn't feel at liberty to name them.

"If I was a guessing man," I said, "I'd guess that the senior of the three was Boyd K. Packer and that he enlisted the support of two of his subordinates who have reputations as academics and liberals. Therefore, my guess is that the three apostles were Elder Packer, Neal A. Maxwell, and Dallin H. Oaks." My stake president smiled: "That's a pretty good guess."

I promised him that I would not tell colleagues or friends about this situation. I didn't want to be the center of more publicity.

And, despite my brave words to President West, I felt sick at heart. This was the death of my Mormon dreams, but (typical for the stages of grieving), I remained in denial about it.

This was hope against hope. My lifelong pattern.

9 June 1985–Female Biographers Are Silenced

Telephone calls from LDS headquarters instructed local bishops in Idaho, Utah, and Arizona not to invite Linda King Newell or Valeen Tippetts Avery to speak on historical topics. For ten months, this ban continued against the joint biographers of Joseph Smith's wife Emma. Published last year, their *Mormon Enigma* was controversial for presenting (from his wife's perspective) the prophet's concealed polygamy and his official denials of it.[27] This wasn't a pleasant view of domestic life or religious life.

Their biography shared this year's Evans Award with Richard L. Bushman's biography of Joseph Smith's early life.[28] During their decade of research, I had

27. See Linda King Newell and Valeen Tippetts Avery, *Mormon Enigma: Emma Hale Smith* (Garden City, NY: Doubleday, 1984).

28. See Richard L. Bushman, *Joseph Smith and the Beginnings of Mormonism* (Urbana: University of Illinois Press, 1985).

conferred frequently with Linda about various aspects of the biography she was writing with Val.

In one instance, I helped save them from being exploited by a Midwestern woman who claimed to have found Emma Hale Smith's missing diaries. When Linda and Jack confronted her with my expression of skepticism—after I had talked with this woman for more than an hour at the Newell home, she admitted that there were no diaries. She had been sending typescripts of alleged excerpts to Linda and Val but had done enough research to make her invented information seem believable.

This was also the technique of a master-forger Mormon named Mark Hofmann. Hofmann's greed and double-dealing would be his undoing—which soon led to murders.

Mid-June 1985–Reacting to the Charge of "Speaking Evil"

In all my work as a Mormon historian, I had honestly sought to recreate the words and acts of earlier prophets and apostles. At least to the degree that the available sources allowed, and keeping in mind the differences between the past and history.

I had faithfully and empathetically placed these former general authorities within the context of the difficult circumstances they faced. I didn't regard their words and acts as wrong, even though they were controversial and resulted in the confusing heritage of post-Manifesto polygamy.

The church's leaders in 1985 seemed to regard my *Dialogue* article (and much of the New Mormon History) as speaking evil of the Lord's anointed. Why? Fundamentally, I think, because they themselves regard certain acts and words of those earlier leaders of the Church as embarrassing, if not actually wrong.

I do not regard it as disloyal to conscientiously restate the words, acts, and circumstances of earlier prophets and apostles. Such a historical restatement is not speaking evil of the Lord's anointed.

Trying to analyze the processes of prophetic decision making is not an act of apostasy. Nor is it spiritually disloyal to assess the results of such decisions. At least in my view. Also in God's, I think.

10 August 1985–Apostle Packer Says More Publicly

He reportedly told priesthood leadership in the Winder Stake of Salt Lake Valley: "There are those who are crying sin and falsehood about the Brethren and the Prophets—especially regarding the Manifesto and polygamy."

16 August 1985–Another Apostle Joins the Anti-Historian Chorus

My article on post-Manifesto polygamy was the subtext of remarks that Dallin H. Oaks made during the Sperry Symposium sponsored by BYU's

College of Religious Instruction.[29] This was three months after his angry letter to me about its publication in *Dialogue*. His letter of May 1985 had accused me of underhandedly obtaining restricted documents at LDS archives and of preparing to publish the article without notifying my file leaders or the custodians of those documents.

In response, I immediately mailed to Elder Oaks a summary of my conversations about this research into post-Manifesto polygamy—with HDC's managing director G. Homer Durham and with First Presidency counselor Gordon B. Hinckley—and explained to Oaks that I had specifically informed each of them *years in advance* of my hopes to publish a detailed article about it. With this letter, I included photocopies of my numerous letters about this research to Durham, to President Spencer W. Kimball, to the First Presidency as a whole, and to Hinckley directly. From 1979 to 1982, those letters had gone to the highest-ranking custodian of HDC's manuscripts and to my highest file leaders in the church. But in 1985 apostle Oaks seemed angry that I hadn't told him during 1977–80, while he was BYU's president (as a non-general authority) and when he was promoting me for J. Reuben Clark's biography. But he had never asked me for reports about any details of my research back then. Nor did anyone else, yet I had volunteered those details to the general authorities who had a right to know—a need to know about my knowledge of post-Manifesto polygamy.

After a month without a reply to the May 1985 letter, I phoned his secretary in the LDS Church Office Building to inquire whether Oaks had received it. She confirmed in June that my letter arrived with its attached documents, that he had looked at them all, and that he would undoubtedly contact me again when he returned from a trip. He didn't.

Instead, despite the information and documentation I provided him in May 1985, apostle Oaks told numerous people during the next two decades that I had allegedly "misused" my research access at HDC, that I had allegedly done "unauthorized" research about post-Manifesto polygamy there,

---

29. Quinn misidentified the symposium at which Oaks gave this August 16, 1985, address. Oaks delivered these remarks, titled "Reading Church History," at the Church Education System (CES) Symposium on the Doctrine and Covenants and Church History at BYU. While Quinn states here that his *Dialogue* article on post-Manifesto polygamy was the subtext of Oaks's talk, Oaks stated in his talk, "I stress that my remarks are not directed at any particular book or article or at any group of books or articles." Though much of Oaks's talk cautions against recently "discovered" historical documents—which later proved to be forgeries produced by Mark Hofmann—Oaks also counseled Latter-day Saints to read with caution recently published church histories, articles, and biographies, some of which had caused "a flurry of excitement" over the previous six months. *Dialogue* published Quinn's "LDS Church Authority and New Plural Marriages, 1890–1904," on April 1, 1985, four months before this talk. See Dallin H. Oaks, "Reading Church History," address given at the 1985 CES Doctrine and Covenants Symposium, Brigham Young University, August 16, 1985, www.archive.org.

and that I had allegedly "deceived" manuscript custodians and church leaders about my plan to publish that research. Several of his listeners would report this to me.

This August, his talk warned against those who "criticize or depreciate a person for the performance of an office to which he or she has been called of God. It does not matter that the criticism is true."[30] Words to gag on.

23 August 1985–Continuing Work on Mormon Controversies

During the Sunstone Symposium, I gave a talk at the Hotel Utah about connections between the occult and early Mormonism. Learning that I planned to make a roundtrip to BYU to print out its reading text, my friend Gordon A. Madsen very kindly invited me to use a computer in his home to prepare the talk. The *Salt Lake Tribune* featured it on the front page of its local section, along with a photo of one of the Joseph Smith family's magic parchments (lamens).[31]

I would speak publicly on the same topic four times in 1986, coast to coast, and once in Cedar City, Utah, in May 1987. Then I would publish a book about it in August 1987.[32] Nonetheless, my stake president Hugh West refused to follow the apostolic instructions to "take further action" (disfellowshipping or excommunication) against me for my continuing to promote controversial history.

Among the many ironies of this situation was that twenty years earlier, West had served as a local member assistant to Elder Packer, who was then-president of the New England Mission in Boston. This was before Hugh West became president of the Hartford Connecticut Stake. I asked West how they were getting along now. "I think we're still friends," he said.

He even allowed me to remain a counselor in the stake's Sunday School presidency until Gordon Madsen was released. His successor chose different counselors. President West also knew that I remained a Sunday School teacher in my ward for two years beyond that.

He told me this year and again in January 1987 that he felt that he had no choice but to withhold my temple recommend as ordered by the apostles, but he refused to do anything further. The stake president hugged me and said: "You'll just have to live without the temple."

More than once in 1985, I left Stake President West's office knowing that the temple was not the only part of Mormonism I must learn to live without. Yet I still could not face the reality of total loss.

---

30. Oaks, "Reading Church History," www.archive.org.

31. See Dawn Tracy, "Did Smith 'Use' Magic Relics? The Debate Continues," *Salt Lake Tribune*, Aug. 25, 1985.

32. Quinn, *Early Mormonism and the Magic World View* (Salt Lake City: Signature Books, 1987).

30 September 1985–"Things Are Going about the Same Here"

That's what I told my family in California, and omitted any reference to problems I was having with LDS headquarters. Instead, my letter emphasized the positive:

"My enrollments in all courses I am teaching are to full capacity, and the students seem to enjoy the presentations. Things are going well in the new apartment I am now living in. The bishop of the ward where I have been teaching the Gospel Doctrine Class said it was fine for me to continue as a member of the ward even though I have moved 1 1/2 blocks out of the ward.

"The attendance of the ward Gospel Doctrine Class has increased since I have begun teaching it three months ago, and a lot of young married people and singles have joined the more middle-aged and elderly members who used to comprise the class. Most Sundays there are no seats left; both stake patriarchs are in the class, and hardly a week goes by that one or the other of them (as well as other members of the class) comment on how much they enjoy my presentations and the discussions we have."

Salt Lake Twenty-first Ward's members encouraged non-resident friends to attend my class. And again, people drove from various communities to participate. Institute teacher John A. Peterson mentioned this to me twenty-four years later.[33]

15 October 1985–Package Bombs in Salt Lake City

When the first bomb killed Steven F. Christensen, everyone wondered if it was connected with his purchase of the so-called "Salamander Letter" concerning folk magic and Joseph Smith.[34] For a year, Steve had paid three Mormons to research the meaning of this document for his plan to eventually publish a book-length study of early Mormon folk magic. This included Dean Jessee and Ron Walker.[35]

In fact, I had started my own research early this year because they were taking too long to publish and wouldn't share their insights privately. I was getting too many earnest questions from ward members and BYU students

---

33. The son of the renowned historian Charles ("Chas") Peterson, John A. Peterson is a historian who worked for the LDS Church history department and taught for twenty years at the church's Institute near the University of Utah. His book, *Utah's Blackhawk War* (Salt Lake City: University of Utah Press, 1999) won the Mormon History Association's Best First Book Award.

34. A businessman with a strong interest in Mormon history, Steven F. Christensen (1954–85) purchased what turned out to be forged documents from Mark Hofmann. He worked with Gary Sheets, the husband of the second bombing victim, Kathleen Webb Sheets (1935–85). For more on these murders and the Hofmann case, see Linda Sillitoe and Allen Roberts, *Salamander: The Story of the Mormon Forgery Murders* (Salt Lake City: Signature Books, 1988).

35. The third researcher was Brent Metcalfe (*Salamander*, 24).

to simply depend on Steve's project for answers about early Mormonism and folk magic.[36]

Today's second bomb killed the wife of Steve's business partner, when she picked up the package left for him. Two people had been blown to bits, and this controversial document seemed to be the reason.

The next afternoon I was sitting in BYU's Cougareat fast food area of the Wilkinson Center when loudspeakers announced the news that a bomb had injured Mark Hofmann. He had been the "finder" and seller of the Salamander Letter, also known as the 1830 Martin Harris Letter.

When I got back to my faculty office, I received numerous phone calls from friends who warned me not to return to my apartment in Salt Lake City. They feared that the killer was targeting anyone who promoted the idea that occult ideas influenced Joseph Smith.

Longtime friend Richard Lambert (a federal prosecutor in 1985) insisted that I stay with his family for several days in the Holladay neighborhood of the Salt Lake Valley. When I decided to return to my apartment in the Avenues, he urged me to use the federal building's X-ray machine for any package mailed to me and to regularly check my car for unusual wires or attached bombs.

Within days, the Salt Lake City Police Department asked me to examine the dozens of historical manuscripts that had not been destroyed by the bomb in Hofmann's car. In my written report, I noted that only one or two manuscripts had anything to do with Mormonism, and the rest seemed to be of very limited value historically or financially.

In a subsequent interview at the police station, Detective Robert L. Stott and his own document expert George J. Throckmorton tried to get me to state categorically that *all* the Mormon documents Hofmann was famous for discovering were forgeries. Unknown to me, through searching his house, the police had now discovered various items of evidence proving Hofmann's forgeries.

In questioning me, however, Stott mentioned none of that evidence. Instead, he expected me to assess Hofmann's documents as forgeries because of a woman's memory about something he had purchased from her.

"You may have evidence I'm not aware of," I said, "but based on this one person's memory I'm not prepared to regard as forgeries the documents that have already been judged as authentic by national experts in paper and ink, and by an LDS expert in early Mormon handwriting. Moreover, the content of those documents is consistent with everything I know about historical details."

---

36. Quinn provided an oral history about doing this research, which later led to his publishing *Early Mormonism and the Magic World View*, on the *Sunstone Mormon History Podcast*. See Quinn and Christopher C. Smith, interview with Bryan Buchanan and Lindsay Hansen Park, "Episode 4: Magic and Mormonism," *Sunstone Mormon History Podcast*, Apr. 12, 2019.

Detective Stott ignored my invitation to give me some better evidence from which I could arrive at the conclusion he clearly wanted me to affirm.

In this interview, he offered nothing further, except repeatedly stating his suspicious criticism of my 1981 article for its matter-of-fact affirmation of the alleged Joseph Smith III blessing document's genuineness.[37] I had done so due to its forensic authentication at that time by renowned experts in paper, ink, and handwriting. Also, the document's content was consistent with known facts. Even the way it was folded corresponded to the way its alleged scribe had filed other documents I had seen in LDS archives since 1971.

Paradoxically, Stott was now so single-mindedly consumed with his undisclosed evidence of Hofmann's forgeries, that he was "disappointed" in (and suspicious of) the historians who had not manifested his skepticism four years before he had any evidence to support such doubts. Throckmorton's true believer skepticism was obviously Stott's justification for this circular logic. Hoffer and Festinger would have been both amused and appalled at this law enforcement illustration of their theories about the true believer and cognitive dissonance.[38]

Not until 1987 did the police publicly reveal their overwhelming evidence that Hofmann had forged the documents. I understand the unwillingness of the police to disclose crucial evidence prior to a trial or plea bargain, but I regard as outrageous Detective Stott's statements to others that I refused to be persuaded by allegedly conclusive evidence during his interview with me.

In the aftermath of these murders, I felt grief for Steve Christensen whenever I wore the expensive clothes he had provided me from his father's store.[39] This was his non-monetary compensation to thank me for various talks I delivered about Mormon history at his invitation. Even after I stopped wearing Steve's gifts, many years passed before I could force myself to donate this old clothing to charitable organizations.

I've never gotten over the fears I experienced at learning of the bombings. To the present, I go to a federal office building for X-ray examination of any package I'm not expecting. Whenever I've lived away from close access to X-ray examination, my heart races as I open unexpected packages.

37. See D. Michael Quinn, "Joseph Smith III's 1844 Blessing And The Mormons of Utah," *John Whitmer Historical Association Journal* 1 (1981): 12–27. The article discusses a blessing Joseph Smith Jr. purportedly gave to his eleven-year-old son, Joseph Smith III, in 1844, appointing him as his successor to lead the church. The document was later discovered to be a forgery created by Mark Hofmann.

38. Eric Hoffer (1902–83) wrote *The True Believer* (New York: Harper Brothers, 1951). Leon Festinger (1919–89) wrote *A Theory of Cognitive Dissonance* (Palo Alto, CA: Stanford University Press, 1962).

39. Steven Christensen's father was Fred MacRay "Mac" Christensen (1934–2019). He founded Mr. Mac men's clothing stores in the 1960s and later served as president of the Mormon Tabernacle Choir for twelve years.

November 1985–Neighbors Ask about My Homosexuality

Jan told me that some neighbors asked her if I'm homosexual. When she asked why they wondered, they each said that they became suspicious because I was not dating other women.

"They expect me to date women, when we're not divorced?!" I asked. Why would religious people expect a man to engage in adulterous behavior in order to prove he's not homosexual? What a culture!

Jan said that she didn't want our children to learn about my homosexuality from neighborhood gossip, and she urged me to tell them now. I thought the boys were too young, and I wanted to tell all my children at the same time. Jan didn't agree, but said it was my decision.

1985-87–Gradually Accepting the End of LDS Church Service

From 1985 onward, it was obvious to me that it was only a matter of time before my life in the LDS Church would be over. In addition to my own vulnerabilities, there was the vindictiveness of apostle Boyd K. Packer and those he influenced.

I considered appealing personally to First Presidency counselor Gordon B. Hinckley to call off the apostolic pit bulls, but figured it was pointless. Apostle Hunter's comments to me in 1983 showed how even senior apostles deferred to the contrary zeal of junior apostles.[40]

This situation was different from the 1983 inquisition when President Hinckley stopped the Twelve's zealots. Ezra Taft Benson became LDS president in November 1985, after decades of being obsessed with subversives in and out of the church. Thomas S. Monson had administratively left the Quorum of Twelve to serve in the First Presidency. In spite of my previously friendly relationship with both of Benson's counselors, neither Hinckley nor Monson had the power to resist the LDS president's directives. They also didn't have the combative personality necessary to confront their subordinate Boyd K. Packer (who was Benson's ally).

Monson's departure from the Twelve had left Elder Packer as the administrative next in line to the Twelve's frail President Howard W. Hunter. A close friend of apostle Hunter's family told me that Elder Hunter confided that there was only one man in the world he disliked, and this man was in the Quorum of the Twelve. Elder Hunter said that before every prayer

---

40. Leonard Arrington recorded similar sentiments the day after his friend Lavina Fielding Anderson was "excommunicated for apostasy" on September 24, 1993. "If they can do it to Lavina, they can do it to me," he wrote. "Mike Quinn will probably be excommunicated this coming week. Our information is that Elder Packer is behind this purge. Why don't the older Brethren speak out to halt this business. It is shameful." Bergera, ed., *Confessions of a Mormon Historian*, 3:617.

circle of the apostles, he privately asked God to reconcile his feelings toward him.

I also had no benefit from my previously congenial relationship with Dallin H. Oaks while he was BYU's president. Aside from his angry reaction to my publication of the polygamy article, he became Elder Packer's proxy and stalking horse after Elder Oaks joined the Quorum of the Twelve Apostles in April 1984.

And it didn't matter whether the Twelve *as a quorum* had no advance knowledge of what the three apostles instructed Elder Paramore to do in May 1985. If the entire Quorum of the Twelve Apostles didn't approve their action beforehand, that quorum's imperative of harmony would result in after-the-fact acquiescence.

Devout Mormons may be offended by my view of the raw dynamics of power and personality among LDS general authorities. Yet that is how I perceive the realities of the Mormon hierarchy—from historical documents and from my own experience. So I made no efforts at an end-run to the First Presidency to circumvent the message of three apostles to my stake president in 1985.

All through these years, Gordon B. Hinckley's son-in-law was my personal physician. During my visits to his office, Jim Pearce sometimes mentioned President Hinckley, but neither of us referred to my conflicts with the Brethren.

In addition, apostle Packer was also a patient of the ENT specialist who replaced my ear drum through plastic surgery in 1982. Stake President West told me that Dr. Dean H. ZoBell once said to him: "I like both Mike Quinn and Elder Packer, and wish they'd resolve their differences." It wasn't that simple for either of us.

From May 1985 onward, only a strong-willed stake president saved my church membership, primarily because he had known me so well for the previous seven years. If I had moved from the stake when Jan and I separated, Paramore's visit to a stake president who didn't know me would have resulted in my being disfellowshipped or excommunicated while I was a BYU professor for my work as a Mormon historian. A less courageous man than Hugh West would have followed through on the general authority instructions "to take further action" as I continued to pursue the Mormon history that offended apostle Packer.

I figured that he and his associates would make sure I was dead meat as soon as they had a compliant stake president to work with—either where I had resided for years or as soon as I moved to a new stake.

The life I had lived for was dead, but hadn't fallen over yet. I continued teaching, researching, writing, living, but wondered why I bothered. I was losing everything and everyone I valued after doing everything I had thought God wanted me to do.

Typical of my lifelong pattern of isolation, I took no one into my confidence, sought no advice, and reached out for no one's strength or comfort. Except God's.

CHAPTER EIGHTEEN

FAREWELLS

1986-1988

13 January 1986–Divorce

Today Jan and I received our decree of divorce, which I felt provided her with the only possibility for happiness and fulfillment. I didn't think it much mattered for me. The timing of this decree was between Jan's attorney, Rich McKeown, and the judge, but ironically it was on my grandmother's birthday.

Although selfishly focused on my own misery, I have to acknowledge that there was a lot of marital unhappiness in my generation of Mom's family. Aunt Norma's children Steve and Sue both divorced. Steve married again, but Sue didn't. Uncle Frank's daughter Pam divorced and became openly lesbian. His daughter Donna divorced and married again. Except for Pam, my divorced cousins were all parents whose children (like mine) had to cope with disrupted family life.

As evidence of my self-centeredness, not until years afterward did I even think of how difficult all of this was for Nana. Now in her nineties and mentally alert, she loved her divorced grandkids and their children.

Likewise, the temple marriages of both Kathy and Tricia ended in divorce. My grandmother had told my half-sisters to call her "Nana" after their conversion to Mormonism, and they always did.

17 January 1986–New Friends

While attending the Sundance Film Festival at Park City, I met with some unconventional LDS people in their twenties. They were my new network of single, liberally oriented friends (both female and male) in Salt Lake City. Some were participating in the LDS Church, others were not. Some shared my earnest faith, others were disbelievers. But they all were non-conformists and made me feel welcome, accepted, and liked for being myself. Their association helped me to cope with pressures that I felt were slowly killing me.

One of these friends, Lorette Bayle, was a volunteer with the festival and invited me to a private reception with Sundance founder, Robert Red-ford.[1] After twenty years of watching his movies and admiring his politics, it was a thrill to stand a few feet away as he spoke informally.

Ironically, another of these new friends was Cecelia Warner, whose father was the former chair of my History Department.[2] Until this year, I had very limited acquaintance with "Cissy," and even that was primarily because she used to work at the front desk of BYU's Special Collections. Now a returned missionary and outspoken feminist, she resided in the Lower Avenues. Her returned missionary boyfriend was a graduate student from New Zealand, Ian G. Barber.[3] Barber was simultaneously one of the most intellectual and fun-loving members of this new group of friends. Because he was doing re-search for an anthropological study of Mormonism, we had many academic discussions during the next two-and-a-half years, intermingled with partying and going to dance clubs.

Meanwhile, after the divorce was finalized, Moyne Oviatt became my steady date at all BYU faculty socials. As Jan's closest friend and *confidante*, Moyne knew of my homosexuality but was glad to assist in deflecting some of BYU's scrutiny.

Early 1986–"The Anti-Christ of BYU"

I heard that Joseph Fielding McConkie, a prominent member of BYU's College of Religious Instruction, denounced me to fireside groups in Cal-ifornia and Utah as "the Anti-Christ of BYU."[4] His first cousin James (my longtime friend) laughed when I told him about this: "You've got to remem-ber that he's Uncle Bruce's son."

Besides the self-parody in Professor McConkie's pompous self-righteousness of speech and demeanor, I found nothing amusing in his remark. It hurt deeply.

March 1986–Teen Diary Project

At the urging of department chair Jim Allen and others, I identified my-self publicly as beginning some kind of significantly non-Mormon project.

1. Lorette Bayle is an award-winning writer and director of both narrative and documentary films. Robert Redford (1936–) is an Academy Award-winning actor and a filmmaker. He co-founded the Sundance Film Festival, held annually in Park City, Utah, in the early 1980s.

2. Cecelia Warner earned a master's in social work in 1991. She is an activist in Oregon, most recently specializing in environmental and sustainability issues. Her father, Ted J. Warner (1929–2014) served as the chair of BYU's history department from 1973 to 1982.

3. Ian Barber became a professor of archaeology at the University of Otago in Dunedin, New Zealand, specializing in Māori and Moriori archaeology. His essay, "Persisting Magic: Situating *Early Mormonism and the Magic World View* in Mormon Studies," appears in Benjamin E. Park, ed., *DNA Mormon: Perspectives on the Legacy of Historian D. Michael Quinn* (Signature Books, 2022).

4. Joseph Fielding McConkie (1941–2013) taught church history at BYU for thirty years and wrote more than thirty books on Latter-day Saint topics. His parents were Apostle Bruce R. McConkie and Amelia Smith McConkie, daughter of church president Joseph Fielding Smith.

Therefore, BYU's *Daily Universe* ran a story this month titled: "Professor Seeks Copies of Journals for Book."

My plan was to do a book-length study of the contemporary priorities and dominant issues emphasized in diaries and journals written by teenagers and young adults. Lacking the quantitative significance of a randomly selected sample, it would nonetheless have a *qualitative* advantage. From the hundreds of donated diaries/journals I needed for the project, I planned to quote the spontaneously written ideas of young people to demonstrate whatever trends and divergences I found.

For example, how often and in what ways did they refer in their private musings to social issues? to political issues? to fears of nuclear war? to religion? to pop culture? to high culture? to their personal views of life? to what extent did these larger issues compete with the space devoted to mundane issues and activities involving family, friends, school, work?

To what degree and in what areas were there similarities in the emphasis given by females and males? To what degree and in what areas were there female-male divergences? To what degree and in what areas did age change those findings?

Because I wanted to compare roughly equivalent numbers of female-male diaries, I decided to begin with the group *least likely* to have written diaries or personal journals. Thus, my first efforts at collection would be among young men.

To be sure that I was not depending on Mormons, who are officially encouraged to be journal keepers, I advertised nationally for participants. With the History Department's resources and the time of its indefatigable secretary Mariel Budd, I mailed one-page announcement descriptions of this project to thousands of high schools, prep schools, technical schools, colleges, and universities in every state of the Union—making sure that I included urban, suburban, and rural schools.

Third, having set that process of advertising and collection in motion, I assumed that I could simply wait for the donated photocopies to arrive. I would keep collecting them until I had enough to analyze their contents and begin writing my study.

In the meantime, I would continue working on two Mormon projects. First was the continuing saga of my decade-long study of the hierarchy. Second was my recently begun project of analyzing the intellectual and social connections involving early Americans, folk magic, religion, the occult, and Mormonism.[5]

---

5. The first project would ultimately result in three books published by Signature Books: *The Mormon Hierarchy: Origins of Power* (1994), *The Mormon Hierarchy: Extensions of Power* (1997), and *The Mormon Hierarchy: Wealth and Corporate Power* (2017). The second project resulted in the book *Early Mormonism and the Magic World View* (1987), also published by Signature.

Mid-April 1986–"History Teacher of the Year, 1985-1986"

Based on a vote of upper-class and graduate students, this was my most cherished award. It was the culmination of ten school years in which I had made every conceivable effort to put students first in my professional life, while continuing to be active in my own research and publishing.

I always refused to give students any true-false or multiple-choice exams. Instead, I devised exams involving term identifications, short essays, and one or two long essays. I alone read and graded all their quizzes, exams, and term papers.

At the first meeting of each course, I explained that I refused to grade on the curve. I told every class that I imposed no artificial limit on the number of A's I gave to a class, but that I also felt no obligation to give a single A if the students didn't do what I considered A-level work.

I made all my students read a lot of articles and books, and weighted the scores of the final exam more heavily than the first exam. My students responded to the challenges, and averaged 20–40 percent with A's at the end of courses—double or triple their rates at midterm. I also gave D's to students whose work remained substandard, and failed those who cheated or made no effort. The rest got B's and C's. Instead of a bell curve, the final grades in my courses could usually be plotted as a steeply diagonal line from a high of A's to a low of failing grades.

I ignored all comments from BYU's administrators about grade inflation. Should hard-working students be deprived of the A's they deserved by achieving the high expectations I set for them? Not in *my* classroom!

I was tough but fair, and tried to make each class meeting both interesting and engaging. My reputation soon spread among BYU's students. At the beginning of each term, I usually needed to ask secretary Mariel Budd to schedule a larger room for at least one class that was over-subscribed. Some semesters she needed to do this for two of my courses.

I didn't turn away any student who wanted to add my course, because (from my undergraduate experience) I knew how that could disrupt a student's entire schedule of planned courses. There were about fifty in my courses, "How to Study History" and "The Civil War and Reconstruction," with somewhat fewer in the introductory courses "American Pop Culture" and "American Social History" that I taught. My survey of "American History Since 1865" sometimes had more than a hundred students from every conceivable major in both semesters, but I still graded all their work by myself. They deserved that kind of attention from their professor.

I announced on the first day of class that students could talk with me in my office about academic matters beyond the course, "or about *anything* you want to talk about." Non-history majors often accepted this invitation by discussing their hopes for a variety of occupations. And some distraught students confided their religious doubts, grief about family conflicts or deaths, and other crises.

In two years, BYU's Phi Alpha Theta published in *The Thetean* my interview by student Craig L. Foster.[6] In it, I concluded: "I think I have a very consistent commitment to students, that I'm very interested in knowing their point of view; I'm very interested in encouraging them to express that point of view, whether or not it agrees with my own. And I think that students appreciate that."

I *loved* teaching as much as research and writing.

Spring 1986–"Graduate Coordinator," BYU's Department of History

At every other university in the United States, this position is called director of graduate studies (DGS). However, BYU's administrators insisted on giving unique names to nearly everything that would align it with "gentile" institutions of higher learning. The official BYU community both derides and envies those campuses.

Thus, Greek-letter fraternities and sororities of national organization had been called "social units" at BYU during their years on campus before its Board of Trustees banned them and their sometimes-disguised remnants in 1961. Likewise, the failing grade was an "E" at BYU, non-LDS speakers were "forum speakers," dormitories were "residence halls," faculty tenure was "continuing status," and faculty sabbatical was "professional development leave."

In retrospect, I guess it was inevitable that the History Department assigned me as Graduate Coordinator. Two years earlier, I had single-handedly succeeded in getting a graduate student to finish his Ph.D. dissertation after twelve years of his trying to do so. The other professors who had worked with him thought it was hopeless—that he had "a mental block" against actually finishing it, despite his repeatedly pleading for extensions of BYU's limit on the years to complete a PhD.

In September 1983, a departmental meeting of all history professors was preparing to drop him from the graduate program. Recently back from Europe, I volunteered to make one final effort. If I failed, then he would fail, too. I couldn't let that happen.

When Charles W. Watson gave me his typed draft of more than 1,200 pages and told me of his plans to research and write even more, I saw the problem. I was a compulsive researcher and could empathize with his inability to simply stop. But at some point you have to say to yourself: "Enough is enough, and I've got to finish this now."

---

6. Phi Alpha Theta is a national academic honor society for students and professors of history. Craig L. Foster went on to work for the LDS Church's Family History Library and served on the board of editors for the Interpreter Foundation, a Mormon apologetics organization.

To help middle-aged Charles achieve that goal, I read the complete draft of his proposed dissertation—as far as he had written it. I hoped to find a dissertation-sized section in what he defined as a multi-volumed, "work-in-progress." It would be his biography of the "entire" life and activities of former general authority John W. Young (1844–1924).

Charles had done wonderful research and provided very important insights into this controversial man who had lived proudly as a wheeler-dealer political lobbyist and businessman son of Brigham Young. As his father's chosen son (secretly ordained an apostle at age 11), John W.'s business enterprises extended from Utah, throughout the West, into the Eastern Seaboard, then to Northern Mexico and Europe. Yet he died as a pauper in New York City, deeply estranged from the LDS hierarchy that had once called him "First Counselor to the Prophet." A polygamist whose five wives all divorced him, his most notable son murdered a prostitute and dissected her body in John W. Young's lavish apartment in Manhattan.[7] What a life! And understandably difficult to abbreviate or select from.

Nonetheless, I told Charles that no other member of his required committee would take the time to read his dissertation of 1,200-pages that he planned to expand. I emphasized that he had *only* the 1983–84 school year to finish. "If you want a PhD," I said, "then limit yourself to just one of the years you discuss so carefully. A 'good dissertation' is whatever will pass your committee. After you get your doctorate, you can publish the rest as a book at your leisure."

He protested, but finally agreed to do this drastically shortened version of what he had written. He qualified for a PhD in the spring of 1984, by submitting "John Willard Young and the 1887 Movement For Utah Statehood" as his dissertation. It was 281 pages long, and he would never publish his full biography of Young's other seventy-nine years.

As graduate coordinator from 1986 to 1988, I directed M.A. theses in Mormon history, in Utah history, in the American West, in American social history, and in local-and-community history. Several were for students I had taught in our department's Salt Lake City program. I also sat on the committees for other students and had to sign-off on every graduate student's final work and approvals for every geographical area.

The PhD dissertations were usually in Utah Mormon history, most often written by teachers in the Church Educational System. A PhD gave them a bump in their CES salary, which is why I opposed the professors in our department who wanted to end the doctoral program altogether. After I left this position, the naysayers would have their way.

---

7. For more on this story, see Ardis E. Parshall, "Murder in the Metropolis," four parts, *Kee-papitchinin*, keepapitchinin.org, Oct. 25–28, 2006.

Early June 1986–Stopping Research at LDS Church Archives

On May 27, the staff of the Historical Department of the church announced that it was necessary to sign a new form in order to do research in manuscripts. Apostle Boyd K. Packer declared that the form gave a right of pre-publication censorship for any archival research completed even before signing the form.

This was an effort to retroactively close the door on the previous sixteen years of openness in the LDS Church Archives. I refused to pretend that anyone had such a right of retroactive censorship, and I declined to sign this *ex post facto* form when asked to do so the first week of June.

Fifteen years of my research in the church's archives were at an end. At least for the present.

Elder Packer told an HDC staff meeting: "I want others to know that we did not exclude Mike Quinn from the archives. He excluded himself." That quote was provided to me by an HDC administrator who was present to hear it.

I eventually learned that a few other historians also declined to sign the form during the six years it retained that provision. Leonard Arrington told me that he had refused to sign until its 1992 revision would allow fair use quotes, as defined in US copyright laws.

By mid-1986, relatively few were doing research at LDS Church Archives. Its reading room seemed empty by comparison to the bustling activity of enthusiastic visitors during "The Arrington Spring" of the 1970s.

That was a snide analogy which New Mormon Historians made to The Dubcek Spring or Prague Spring in Czechoslovakia. Alexander Dubcek had briefly democratized his repressed country in 1968—until Soviet leaders removed him from office and "peacefully" ended such liberalization with Soviet tanks. In June 1986, I regarded the analogy to Mormon history as painfully apt.

July 1986–History Chair Asks about My Ex-Wife's Activity

Jim Allen was a good friend, and with deep concern he asked if it was true that Jan had stopped attending LDS Church services. I said that I attended a different ward in our stake and therefore knew nothing about how regularly she or my children attended church.

His question was sincere, and I didn't indicate how devastating it was for me to know that BYU administrators were kept informed about my ex-wife's religious behavior fifty miles away. Again, I told no one else (not even Jan) about this. Yet I felt like yelling at the top of my lungs that if I didn't have a right to privacy because I was a controversial Mormon historian, my ex-wife certainly had that right. She should not be scrutinized, gossiped about, or reported on simply because of her connection with me.

I had always loved the closeness of Mormon culture, but now came to another realization. The LDS Church can be suffocatingly intrusive in people's lives.

Upon reading the above in 2009, my ex-wife would tell me about a warning that Bishop Brad Melis gave her in the Salt Lake City Twenty-seventh Ward in 1986: "Be careful, Jan. People are paying attention to how you behave."

July 1986—Under Surveillance

More disturbing than my department chair's report about Jan's church attendance was his telling me: "I've been informed that you were at a homosexual bar last weekend." My stomach knotted, but I coolly explained the truth.

I was with a young woman on a group date, where others decided that we all would go to Salt Lake City's The Sun gay disco to dance.[8] I had told the night's ringleaders of our group, Ian Barber and Cissy Warner, how reluctant I was to enter a gay dance club. However, I relented rather than making Ian drive me and my date Lorette Bayle to our respective apartments before he went dancing.

I further explained to Jim Allen that about half of those on the dance floor that night were straight couples. Lorette and I stayed on the dance floor the entire night our group was in the gay disco.

Regardless, I was overwhelmed by the exuberant, fun-loving freedom and male sexuality of this gay bar. It was intoxicating—especially to realize that nearly everyone I saw was of Mormon background. I didn't volunteer that info to my department's chair.

I also didn't disclose to Jim Allen my only interaction with any of the young men there. While leaving The Sun with these friends, I was greeted affectionately by one of my former students from BYU's Study Abroad program. Three years earlier in Austria, I had thought that Dave was homosexual. Tears were in his eyes as he hugged me this night. I don't recall ever seeing him again.

Jim Allen said that he disliked receiving this information from "the source" which had informed him, then added: "Just be careful, Mike. People are watching you." In twenty-three years, I would be stunned at how close those words were to what my ex-wife said our bishop told her in 1986.

I didn't ask Jim any questions about his own warning, but would learn the

---

8. The Sun Tavern opened in 1973 in downtown Salt Lake City as a gay-friendly bar and disco. A tornado destroyed it in 1999.

details five years later from Professor Martha Sonntag Bradley.[9] She was my replacement in BYU's History Department, and had heard that I was being watched at BYU and in Provo and Salt Lake City during the last years I was on the faculty. I had known Marti as a friend and as a historian since 1978. I met her while we both worked on a Democratic campaign for Jim McConkie.

I didn't feel any concern about the surveillance because I was celibate and adhering to LDS standards, even if I was unconventional. The situation in 1986 reminded me of the efforts of an Army spy to entrap me as a celibate homosexual in Munich so long ago.

Years would pass before I returned to The Sun, and then it would only be at the invitation of my daughters. They often went there for group dancing with their gay male friends. By that time, I would no longer be a BYU professor and was just visiting Utah. After Mary and Lisa helped me to overcome my reluctance about going to a gay bar that I knew BYU Security had under surveillance, I would go there often and enjoy it immensely.

A decade after 1986, the young woman I had danced with on just one occasion at The Sun would ask me why I didn't tell her that I was gay during more than two years we socialized with the Salt Lake group of unconventional Mormons. It had been clear that Lorette wanted to date me seriously, even though I tried not to encourage anything more than good-natured friendship. Nevertheless, we had long talks, attended movies, and often danced together whenever our group went to nightclubs.

I wouldn't know what to say in response to her decade-later question, except that "I wasn't talking about it with anyone at that time." With obvious bitterness, she commented that "you just let me figure it out on my own." I didn't respond, and she walked away.

Summer 1986-Spring 1987—Near-Encounters with Homosexuality in Utah

However, that subsequent excuse was untrue—because I talked about my homosexuality with several young men among our mutual friends for more than a year after this summer. And I teetered on the edge of sharing it physically with a few there. All were Mormons.

Openly gay Jeff Wood was the first I confided in. A straight-acting returned missionary in his mid-twenties, he towered over me at 6'3" and yet I felt safe whenever with him. After we returned to my basement apartment from a movie, I said that I had something to confide. He was reassuring, and

9. Martha Sonntag Bradley Evans (1951–) later left BYU in protest of the anti-intellectual movement she witnessed there in the 1990s. At the University of Utah she fulfilled many roles, including professor in the school of Architecture, dean of undergraduate students, and associate vice president of Academic Affairs.

I couldn't understand why I felt such anxiety in telling him through tears: "I'm gay." It was so damned difficult for me to say those words to anyone—gay or straight.

The next one I told was Roger Salazar.[10] Also a returned missionary and flamboyant friend of Jan's, he used to visit our home with a boyfriend. After I came out to him this summer, Roger said: "Mike, when Jan introduced us years ago, I thought you hated me for being gay." To the contrary, I explained, I had felt painful envy for his being so happily homosexual.

Even taller than Jeff, red-haired "Rocky" O'Donovan soon became another of my *confidants*.[11] He had moved to the Lower Avenues as a runaway teenager from rural Utah when I was in our ward's bishopric. I attended his missionary farewell, his homecoming, and his wedding reception before learning of the marriage's annulment and his becoming openly gay. Now I went to dance clubs and apartment parties with him and the large group of friends unofficially organized by straight young women and filled with gay young men.

One evening, he and I traveled from Salt Lake to Provo with a recently married couple and Maxine Hanks to join other students at BYU to see a movie by Russian filmmaker Tarkovsky. On the trip back, Rocky and I quietly kissed in the back of the van—while Maxine and the husband and wife chatted in front. Our hands never strayed below the waist, yet I was crossing a boundary. This was my first gay kiss.

Still, Bruce was my real temptation. Outgoing and friendly, he seemed to bond instantly with me at one of the group's parties. He was a tall, lanky, blue-eyed, blond, cute undergraduate at the University of Utah. What was not to like? To think of loving?

Soon we were going to movies regularly, which we both called "dates." I ached with desire whenever I was around Bruce, but he was resolutely celibate—having just ended a gay relationship. We hugged, but he didn't want to kiss. He knew where that would lead us. When Bruce moved out of state in a few months, I felt lonely even in the company of our group's other gays.

They didn't talk with its women about such things but mentioned my celibate homosexuality to the group's straight-but-not-narrow men. This led to an unexpected conversation with another student at the University of Utah. At his request, I gave him a lift to his place after a late-night party. In my car, he said that he had heard I was gay, celibate, and miserable. "I've only had sex

---

10. Roger Brent Salazar (1954–2019) was "an actor, dancer, cosmetologist, and interior designer." He wrote the humor book *No Man Knows My Pastries: The Secret (Not Sacred) Recipes of Sister Enid Christensen* (Salt Lake City: Signature Books, 1992).

11. Connell O'Donovan (1961–) is a historian, genealogist, and LGBTQ activist. He organized and led Salt Lake City's first two Pride marches, in 1990 and 1991.

with women and have never been attracted to men," he began haltingly, "but I feel more love for you than I did for any of my missionary companions."

Very quietly, he said: "I don't want you to be alone, and if you'd like, we could go to bed sometime and snuggle." After a pause, he looked directly at me: "If you want to do more than that, it'd be okay, Mike."

I wanted to hug this big-hearted guy, but that would have defeated my reply: "What you've said means more to me than I can express, but can we just stay good friends?"

He nodded and we continued socializing in the group—with no awkwardness and no mention of this night's talk. A decade later, he would have a wife and children.

21 August 1986–Goodbye, I Love You

This day, I listened to a riveting presentation at Sunstone Symposium by LDS poet-author Carol Lynn Pearson as she talked so frankly and lovingly about her marriage to a gay man. I bought the book and read it nonstop—often in tears.[12]

More than the sadness of her ex-husband's homosexual struggle and AIDS death, it was incredibly painful to read her perspective of living in a gay-straight marriage. It was an all-too-real echo of Jan's life with me, despite my homosexual celibacy.

September 1986–BYU's Blacklist by General Authorities

With candor and deep personal regret, the new dean of my college informed me that some time ago, BYU's Executive Committee of Trustees (of which Boyd K. Packer was a member) had blacklisted me from receiving any support from BYU besides my tenured position as a full-professor of American history. This explained why—for the second year—the university administration turned down my application for sabbatical leave. Stan L. Albrecht added: "You were more qualified than some of those who received Professional Development Leave." Dean Albrecht added: "I have always hoped that one day BYU will become a *real* university, but this makes me feel that day will never arrive."

In November, BYU's presidency required my name to be removed from the upcoming campus program which commemorated 150 years of Mormonism in the British Isles. The College of Religious Instruction had asked me only to be a commentator, not to give a paper, but even that limited participation was too much.

---

12. *Goodbye, I Love You* (New York: Random House, 1986) is a best-selling memoir by Carol Lynn Pearson (1939–), in which she shares her account of her marriage to Gerald Neils Pearson (1942–84), raising their family of four children, and her struggle to come to terms with Gerald's homosexuality and death resulting from AIDS.

By year's end, BYU's administration made it clear that the ban against me extended beyond Mormon studies. The History Department and Charles Redd Center for the American West both withdrew the funds they had promised for me to give a paper on general American religion at the University of Paris. It didn't matter that the advanced text of the paper made no reference to Mormonism. I had to pay my own way to France to represent BYU. I discussed these incidents only with the college and departmental administrators involved, not with my other colleagues or anyone else.

My career at BYU was finished if I continued my work as a Mormon historian, and yet that's why I went there. It was only a matter of time before I left BYU or was forced out.

The most I could hope for personally was an uneasy truce if I agreed not to publish any more history that might offend the Brethren. I had experienced complete academic freedom in the classroom at BYU, although I knew professors in various departments who had not.

The History Department's new chair Paul B. Pixton let me know that my situation at BYU would improve only if I stopped any research which implied Mormon studies.[13] As an American social historian, there were many non-religious subjects of interest to me. And I had already begun the teen diary project.

Abandoning Mormon history was safe in the current climate of repression, but was unacceptable to me, especially as an option of duress. Publish or perish is the experience of scholars at most universities, but for this Mormon historian it was publish *and* perish at BYU.

October 1986–Umberto Eco, Hollywood, and LDS Archives

I went with Jim and Judi McConkie to see a recently released movie, *The Name of the Rose*.[14] I had read the novel a few months ago—at the recommendation of Allen D. Roberts, who was in the midst of researching last year's murders that arose from the dialectic of trying to conceal Mormon documents and trying to uncover them. He said that Umberto Eco's view of medieval Catholicism had stunning parallels to the LDS Church's concealment of historical documents.

For me, the most quotable patch of dialogue was from the film, not the novel. The main protagonist, a Franciscan friar, told his protege:

[Mentor:] No one should be forbidden to consult these books freely.

[Protege:] Perhaps they are thought to be too precious, too fragile.

[Mentor:] No, it's not that. It's because they often contain a wisdom that

---

13. Paul B. Pixton (1940–) served as chair of the BYU history department from 1987 to 1994.

14. Umberto Eco (1932–2016) wrote the medieval murder mystery, *The Name of the Rose*. The novel has sold more than 50 million copies worldwide.

is different from ours, and ideas that could encourage us to doubt the infalli-bility of the word of God.

This Franciscan was dismissed by his co-religionists and religious lead-ers as an arrogant intellectual, even a heretic, because he insisted on probing what they regarded as dangerous distractions from the true faith.

November 1986–Former Mentor Says I've Gone Too Far

Signature Books asked Davis Bitton to review the first draft of my book on early Mormonism's connections with occult traditions and folk magic.[15] He made some helpful criticisms, but most of his review was a plea to me and the publisher to abandon this project. He said that my study was an assault on the faith of average Latter-day Saints. If I insisted on publishing this book, Davis instructed me not to mention in the acknowledgements that he had read the manuscript.

His letter stunned me and I was in deep depression for weeks while I re-considered what to do. After telling Signature to put the book on hold, I decided to do an extensive revision to respond to the questions and criticisms by Davis, by Lavina Fielding Anderson, and by Allen D. Roberts. None of them particularly liked the study.[16] This revision and new research took me another seven months. My second book, and now it's defenders of the New Mormon History who want me not to publish! I guess I *am* a radical, even though I've never felt like one.

After informing Signature Books of this delay, I confided that I was gay to its editors Gary Bergera and Ron Priddis. I didn't realize the irony of this at the time.

I asked them to inform publisher George Smith of my homosexuality, of the likelihood that this would become known, and would be used by LDS polemicists as a weapon against me and against Signature Books. I expressed willingness to withdraw my manuscript from publication if he preferred to avoid such guilt-by-association. The word came back: "Nonsense!"

I had already resigned from Signature's board of directors because I felt that it would be a conflict of interest for me to vote on financial matters at the same time I was submitting a manuscript for purchase and publication. I had served on its board for four years.

When I wrote the preliminary manuscript's introduction during this summer, I referred to the so-called Salamander Letter as a possible forgery. Aside from passing references to it, my first draft excluded this 1830 Martin

---

15. Quinn is referring to the manuscript that became *Early Mormonism and the Magic World View*.

16. Original copies of Anderson's and Roberts's reviews in Signature Books's archives show that both reviewers praised Quinn's manuscript, merely suggesting revisions before publishing. A copy of Bitton's review does not exist in Signature's files.

Harris Letter because of serious questions then raised about its authenticity. Thus, I needed to revise only a few sentences and a paragraph for the upcoming *Magic World View* that would be published after the police released their evidence of Mark Hofmann's forgeries.

Early December 1986–Resigning as Gospel Doctrine Teacher in Salt Lake City Twenty-first Ward

Aside from the request for a mission reassignment from England to Germany two decades ago, this was the only time I ever asked to be released from a church calling. I did so, despite requests from Bishop Robert C. Hyde, from the Sunday School's president, and from ward members for me to continue as one of the most popular teachers in the ward's recent experience. Overflow attendance in the originally assigned room had sometimes required moving my class into the chapel.

My explanation for resigning was that I would be taking so many trips in the upcoming months. But it was actually part of my slow disengagement from the Mormon culture that had both comforted and choked me, often simultaneously.

Late December 1986–Begin Researching European Archives

With an advance against royalties of $1,500 from Signature Books, I used this holiday recess at BYU to do several weeks of research in the occult manuscripts housed in far-distant archives. This included Pennsylvania, New York, England, and France.

On the American side, I most enjoyed visiting the archives of Ephrata's mystical commune in Pennsylvania.[17] My most memorable experience in Europe was examining medieval parchments of magic incantation (lamens) in the British Museum Library, while I sat next to a scholar who was reading Egyptian papyri that were 3,000 years old.

The research assistants at the British Museum were especially patient and helpful. In a departure from their usual practice, they allowed me to keep the flow of my request slips ahead of my returned documents, so that there was no delay as I examined and returned hundreds of its occult manuscripts for eight hours daily during one week.

The archivist of manuscripts in the Bibliotheque National's Arsenal in Paris was equally helpful. However, I spent only a day with the far fewer manuscripts from its collection of old occult writings. I didn't spend much more time at the Bodleian Library of Oxford University, due to my comprehensive research at the British Museum.

---

17. The Ephrata Cloister was founded in the mid-eighteenth century by Conrad Beissel (1691–1768). He and eighty followers lived highly disciplined, celibate lives focused on spiritual union with God, until all died. The compound survives and is open to visitors near Lancaster, Pennsylvania.

D. Michael Quinn, ca. 1986. *Signature Books archives.*

I wanted to examine East Berlin's vast collections of magic manuscripts, but there just wasn't time. Nor did I have enough money for a week of research there. I would often wonder if German archives contain more insight into the inscriptions on the Joseph Smith Family's occult lamens.

12 January 1987–Publicly Celebrating Martin Luther King Jr.

For this year's Martin Luther King Day, BYU's *Daily Universe* quoted me in today's article, "Blacks remember King's ideals."[18]

BYU's administration had outraged me since 1984 for its refusal to acknowledge in its semester calendars the national holiday honoring America's Black civil rights hero and martyr. This was in spite of the holiday's Congressional passage and presidential signature into law in November 1983.

---

18. The article, by Diane Spranger, quoted Quinn as saying that while the Civil War gave Black Americans rights on paper, it took men like King "to make it a reality that blacks could get an education, run for office, and progress in other ways. ... We still are facing a need to make opportunities even more real to blacks."

As evidence of Utah's continuing racism, the state's right-wing Republican legislature showed its contempt for King and all Blacks by refusing to use his name—renaming this legal holiday as Human Rights Day.

Therefore, as soon as Ronald Reagan unpredictably signed Martin Luther King Day into law, I included it in my course schedules. Beginning January 1984, I had dismissed my classes in its honor and encouraged all students to attend *any* meetings that Monday which commemorated him and his contributions to civil rights. Of course, in deference to President Ezra Taft Benson's well-known antipathy for Reverend King and Benson's General Conference condemnations of "the so-called civil rights movement" while an apostle, BYU's kowtowing administrators didn't sponsor such meetings.[19]

Instead, celebrations were conducted unofficially on campus by liberal Mormon activists like Eugene England of the English Department. This year, he played a recording of King's "I Have a Dream" speech, after which Gene spoke to BYU's few liberal students and faculty in the Wilkinson Center's lounge. The 1978 Priesthood Revelation did not end LDS racism or Mormonism's deeply ingrained Negrophobia.

8 February 1987–Iron Maiden Concert

In addition to always enjoying rock music, I had attended rock concerts as part of my teaching American Pop Culture at BYU for the past six years. Jan disliked rock music, especially hard rock, so I had usually gone alone, for example to Chicago's concert at BYU. After our divorce, I attended performances by Bon Jovi, Depeche Mode, Genesis, Iron Maiden, Starship, and the Village People. I saw Genesis from the back of Wembley Stadium in England, and watched Bon Jovi while sitting twenty feet from the stage in Manhattan's Madison Square Garden, but went to the rest in Salt Lake City.

Tonight's heavy metal Iron Maiden concert was the most memorable— due to the audience. I discovered that my general admission ticket was for the Salt Palace's small auditorium that was just floor space with no seats. Iron Maiden was an hour late in performing, perhaps because the warm-up group had cancelled. There was no opening group. The crowd was ninety-five percent male, white, and teenage.

What stunned me, as we milled around for nearly ninety minutes, was the extent and openness of alcohol and drugs. Most of these boys (who were, of course, primarily LDS) wore leather jackets from which they retrieved

---

19. Apostle Ezra Taft Benson's full statement was, "Now there is nothing wrong with civil rights; it is what's being done in the name of civil rights that is alarming. There is no doubt the so-called civil rights movement as it exists today is used as a Communist program for revolution in America just as agrarian reform was used by the Communists to take over China and Cuba." Benson, in *One Hundred Thirty-Seventh Semi-Annual Conference of the Church of Jesus Christ of Latter-day Saints* (Salt Lake City: The Church of Jesus Christ of Latter-day Saints, 1967), 35.

cigarettes, marijuana joints, and flat bottles of liquor. I didn't see many beer bottles, probably because they are bulkier to conceal in jackets than the flasks of whiskey and vodka I observed. In the growing heat of this space, the teenagers smoked, drank, and got stoned for more than an hour. I didn't accept any of the friendly offers of booze or joints, yet felt almost exhausted after standing so long in the now-sweltering heat of the place.

When Iron Maiden finally started, the crowd naturally pushed forward in this seatless auditorium. About fifteen minutes after the concert commenced, tightly packed kids at the front hoisted up a teenager and passed him backward above their outstretched arms. At first I thought he was crowd surfing, then I noticed he was unconscious. He'd fainted and was the first of more than a dozen boys and a couple of girls who were passed unconscious hand over hand from the front of the crowd to the back, where they were gently lowered to the floor. And the band played on.

This was one of the most bizarre experiences I ever had. In Utah or anywhere else!

Early March 1987—Telling my children that I'm homosexual.

A former co-worker of Jan's was now imprisoned in the same cellblock with double-murderer Mark Hofmann, who asked him this week if I'm gay. Her friend phoned my ex-wife to report this inquiry, which absolutely stunned me!

I could no longer risk that our children would learn from the rumor mill. With Jan at my side, I confided my sexual orientation fully to Lisa (16), Adam (12), and Paul Moshe (10). I wrote a letter to Mary (18), who was at court reporting school in Sacramento, California.

Lisa's first words: "What you've told me is a shocker, but I have lots of gay friends, and it's fine with me if you're gay. You should be glad I've left the church—because I don't care what those bigots think." My daughter's loving matter-of-fact reply stunned me, and I fought back tears.

Mary wrote a deeply personal and very supportive letter, which indicated that she had also stopped affiliating with the church. Adam and Paul said that they didn't understand much about homosexuality but loved me anyway. A *huge* relief that my children didn't reject me!

Mid-March 1987—Overwhelmed by Futility of Conforming

Notwithstanding my continued faith, I tentatively began to distance myself from the LDS Church. Yet I still took the sacrament when I attended church, as part of my continuing relationship with God.

I believed that I would maintain my spiritual and religious relationship with Heavenly Father, but I also knew that one way or another, my life in the

LDS Church would soon be over. I wanted to walk away quietly from the LDS Church and its culture—not to be kicked out.

Early May 1987–Lower Back Injury and Suicidal Thoughts

My lower back began aching as I drove a newly purchased Nissan sports car toward Cedar City for my talk at Southern Utah University about "Joseph Smith as a Seer, Translator, and Prophet: Folk Magic and Early Mormonism." Knifing pains soon took my breath away as they extended down my right leg. This sciatica resulted from an acrobatic stunt I had attempted on the diving board during a swimming party of gay Mormons a couple of days earlier. Jeff Wood had invited me.

For the next two months, I experienced agonizing sciatica whenever I got up from a chair or tried to walk. Sometimes I nearly blacked out. Desperate for relief, I went to my physician Jim Pearce, to an orthopedist named Paulos, to a physical therapist, to a chiropractor, and to an acupuncturist. Nothing helped, and I told Judi McConkie that I was considering suicide as the only way to end the pain. Although I didn't mail them, I even wrote goodbye letters to my children to explain that I was committing suicide due to the constant pain—not because of my homosexuality.

I didn't express such thoughts to my physicians, but the church's insurance company Deseret Mutual Benefit Association approved my getting an injection of morphine directly into my lower back in late-June. For the first time in more than a month, I was pain-free.

Then I had a massive relapse the third week of July, and Linda King Newell introduced me to a different orthopedist. Saying that my injury had been misdiagnosed as disk related, when it was actually soft-tissue damage, Dr. Spencer showed me how to do back-strengthening exercises that quickly ended the agony I'd experienced for more than two months. I thanked him, Linda, and God profusely for the balance of the year.

June 1987–A Student Gives His Assessment

After the senior seminar I was teaching for majors in history, one student asked to talk with me alone. He had taken every course I taught, yet said that he felt like I was a stranger. "You're easy going and down-to-earth, yet you seem to have a wall around you. You're friendly, but don't let anybody really know you."

His bluntness was surprising, and I apologized that my personality had caused him difficulty. He answered: "You haven't offended me, Mike. You perplex me." Get in line.

July 1987–Ex-Father-in-Law Gives His Assessment

Roy M. Darley had been in close association with the LDS general authorities for forty years. His unyielding demands for conforming to any and all views of church authorities had intimidated Jan throughout her life.

During the first meeting I had with Roy since she and I decided to divorce, he said that I was the most selfish person he had ever known. I said that I regretted his hatred—because I loved him and thought he had loved me. He said that I never let him close enough to love me.

"I don't hate you, Mike," he said, "I pity you." Pity is better than hatred, but I had thought I was living the life that would avoid either.

However, the most outrageous example of my selfishness was not, I think, what my ex-father-in-law was referring to. He was thinking of my personality, my behavior, my attitudes *after* I married his daughter. But my decision to even enter a gay-straight marriage was the ultimate expression of my selfishness.

As for Roy, I discovered that he had been refusing to attend any of the gatherings of his extended family if I was there. I had gone to these after our separation only because Jan invited me, and we sat together each time. Her mother Kay was always present and always greeted me warmly.

I was stunned to learn that my ex-father-in-law wouldn't show up until she or one of his daughters phoned to say that I had left. Therefore, I stopped going—even when repeatedly asked to attend by my ex-wife or by my daughters. I didn't want to deprive the Darley clan of its patriarch for even an hour during these otherwise happy socials.

For the next fourteen years, Roy continued asking in advance to be sure that I wasn't at a family gathering before he would attend. A couple of years prior to his death in 2003, however, he started showing up at the Christmas Eve buffets I always attended at Jan's house.

In those last years of his life, my ex-father-in-law greeted me with friendliness, but no warmth. This was in contrast to his usual disposition with strangers and even contrary to the feigned congeniality he manifested to those whom he confided that he *really* disliked.

Mid-August 1987–Missionary Companion Extends Friendship Again

After more than two years of silence, my former missionary companion Mike McAdams telephoned to ask how I was doing. Getting my number by first phoning Jan (who was barely civil to him), he apologized for the letter he wrote after learning of our divorce. He said that there were things he didn't understand about me and probably never would. Still, he said that he would always be my friend.

I thanked him, but decided not to say I didn't regard grudging toleration as friendship. He'd hurt me too deeply for me to accept a reconciliation at this time.

Five years later, I would visit Mike and his wife Sylvia in Norman, Oklahoma.

I cringed to hear their sons telling "fag" jokes as we stood together in their kitchen. Mike and I shared brief eye contact, as if each expected the other to say something, but neither of us commented on his sons' banter. After driving away, I would again give up maintaining any contact with these decades-long friends. This time, it would be permanent.

Late August 1987–*Early Mormonism and the Magic World View*

Beginning with a favorable article on the 28th in the *Los Angeles Times*, my book was widely reviewed in the popular media and academic journals.

In its Introduction, I affirmed: "I feel it necessary to state my biases at the outset. I believe in Gods, angels, spirits, and devils, and that they have communicated with humankind. In Mormon terms, I have a personal 'testimony' of Jesus as my Savior, of Joseph Smith, Jr., as a prophet, of the *Book of Mormon* as the word of God, and of the LDS Church as a divinely established organization through which men and women can obtain essential Priesthood ordinances of eternal consequence. I also believe that no historical documents presently available, or locked away, or as yet unknown will alter these truths, and I believe that persons of faith have no reason to avoid historical inquiry into their religion or to discourage others from such investigations."[20]

Published in *BYU Studies*, religion professor Stephen E. Robinson's polemical review quickly dismissed the above as a "modest statement of faith."[21]

Early September 1987–Ex-Wife Reaffirms Her Loyalty

Feeling that she had been ostracized by LDS neighbors after our separation and divorce, Jan left Utah. Just before Labor Day, I helped pack a moving van of her furniture and household items, then drove it to her newly rented house in Missoula, Montana, where I helped unload everything. She leased our home on Third Avenue.

Jan said that she and our children loved, accepted, and respected me. As she had before, my ex-wife urged me to break down all the walls of church and family approval I had built around myself. Jan told me that I should seek the sexual fulfillment with males I had always needed. She said if it should ever happen that I had a male lover who was not welcome with my parents, that he and I could spend Thanksgiving and Christmas with her and our children.

After running away from male intimacy my whole life, I wasn't sure I was capable of a relationship with a man. Even with a slender studlee of gentle

---

20. Quinn, *Early Mormonism and the Magic World View*, xvii–xix.

21. Taken in its entirety, Robinson may have intended his statement to be complimentary rather than dismissive, as Quinn interpreted it: "Although he is a Latter-day Saint, and despite his modest statement of faith in the introduction (xviii–xix), Quinn is clearly no LDS apologist." Stephen E. Robinson, review of *Early Mormonism and the Magic World View*, *BYU Studies* 27, no. 4 (1987): 88.

Quinn at book signing for *Early Mormonism and the Magic World View*, 1987. *Courtesy Ken Sanders.*

nature—the kind of young man who has always filled my sexual fantasies. Nonetheless, my ex-wife's supportiveness was a powerful comfort to me.

Soon, I was the only member of our little family still participating in the LDS Church. One by one, she and my children chose to leave it.

While living in Missoula, Jan started studying New Age Religion in *A Course in Miracles* and participating in the liberal ecumenism of Unity Church, but our children joined her in neither.[22] Eventually, they talked about "the Mormons" in the third person. Our kids felt indifference, not bitterness, toward the LDS Church.

She couldn't understand my continued devotion toward the church, which Jan now rejected because it was "fear-based." I didn't *think* I was fearful about the church, nor angry, but realized I'd never allowed myself to feel anger against those I loved and tried to serve. I'd felt that I was failing them and was therefore always at fault.

22. Dr. Helen Schucman professed that her book, *A Course in Miracles* (New York: Foundation for Inner Peace, 1975) was dictated to her by Jesus Christ. It is considered a foundational writing of the New Age Movement. See Karen Kemp, "A Course in Miracles," in Peter Clark, ed., *Encyclopedia of New Religious Movements* (Oxfordshire, England: Routledge, 2004).

Fall 1987–Rumors of Being Fired and Excommunicated

Faculty members (some whom I had thought were friends—like Mac Thorp and Marv Hill) circulated the rumor that I was already in the process of being excommunicated for publishing the magic book.[23] Tom Alexander told me this.

The college dean told other colleagues that he had heard the rumors that the general authority trustees had demanded that I be fired from BYU. However, Dean Albrecht expressed his "reassurance" that as far as he knew, these were "just rumors."

Later in the semester, the Dean of BYU's College of Religious Instruction told a student of mine that the Board of Trustees had decided not to have me fired.[24] "Like stirring up a turd on the ground," religion dean Robert J. Matthews told this student, "firing Mike Quinn would only make a greater stink."

BYU students asked me if they should change their major from history—because of what their religion professors were saying about historians. A student who had taken several of my courses explained why he changed his major: "Mike, the church is my life, and I don't want to end up like you." His honesty hurt, but I couldn't blame him.

I felt that I had no alternative but to leave BYU as soon as possible. If I'd ever belonged there, that time was past.

No one gave me an ultimatum or threatened to fire me from Brigham Young University. However, university administrators and I were both on the losing side of a war of attrition mandated by the general authorities.

At this time, Jeff Holland was BYU's president. Our paths had crossed several times, but now I was BYU's cautionary tale, while he was its success story. In seven years, he would become a member of the Quorum of the Twelve Apostles, thus fulfilling the British Mission's prophetic expectations about him.

In separate interviews this fall, Dean Albrecht and department head Pixton each asked what I saw as my future at BYU. I said it didn't look very bright, and the dean asked how I was coping with the pressures against me. "Not very well," was all I could say. Dean Albrecht commented he would understand if I chose to go somewhere else.

Fall 1987–Resigning from the Governing Council of the Mormon History Association and from the Board of Editors of *Dialogue*

I was already an easy target and (as my Mormon life finally unravelled) would become an easier one for personal attacks against my work as a

23. Malcolm R. Thorp (1943–) was a professor of modern British history at BYU from 1969 to 2013.

24. Since 1939, BYU's board of trustees has been chaired by the president of the church. In 1987 the chair was President Ezra Taft Benson.

Mormon historian. Insofar as possible, I wanted to spare ideas I valued and people I respected from guilt by association with me.

I always felt that what was true and good remained true and good, even if the vessel carrying it was inferior and flawed. Likewise, shiny vessels might contain corruption. For a decade, I had expressed this view to several people in correspondence on BYU's letterhead.

6 December 1987–"Mormonism's Foremost Intellectual"

In his review of *A Collection of Essays in Honor of Leonard J. Arrington* by the University of Utah Press, the *Salt Lake Tribune*'s book review editor commented on my essay "The Socio-Religious Radicalism of the Mormon Church: A Parallel to the Anabaptists."[25] Dennis L. Lythgoe concluded that this essay "shows why [Quinn] is considered by a growing number as Mormonism's foremost intellectual."

That was heady stuff for a lifelong egotist to hear. It was also an ironic solace that I sorely needed amid the enormous stresses I was experiencing at BYU.

20 January 1988–Resigning Tenured Faculty Position

In mid-January, I received confirmation of my full-time research grants at the Huntington Library in San Marino, California, near my hometown. The phone call from its research administrator Martin S. Ridge allowed me to work on the studies of Mormon history that BYU was doing everything it could to prevent me from completing. Also CalTech's historian of the American West, white-haired Professor Ridge became my new mentor and benefactor.

Ironically, when I thought of leaving BYU several years earlier, I had been a finalist for tenured positions at two institutions—CalTech in Pasadena and Pomona College in Claremont, California—where I gave job talks and interviewed with their deans. If either had offered me a job, I would have jumped ship from BYU before previously liberal Dallin Oaks did.

After receiving this month's notice of acceptance by the Huntington Library for a fellowship, I quickly resigned from BYU. It was to be effective at the conclusion of this term at the end of April.

"Aside from areas regarded as non-controversial by BYU's Board of Trustees and those responsive to such anticipated or actual views," I explained on the 20th, "the situation seems to be that academic freedom merely survives at BYU without fundamental support by the institution, exists against tremendous pressure, and is nurtured only through the dedication of individual administrators and faculty members."

---

25. Quinn's essay appeared in Davis Bitton and Maureen Ursenbach Beecher, eds., *New Views of Mormon History: A Collection of Essays in Honor of Leonard J. Arrington* (Salt Lake City: University of Utah Press, 1987).

It surprised me that this resignation surprised my BYU colleagues. They were supportive, but most said that I should not have resigned. On the other hand, I learned that some confided that my resignation relieved BYU's history department from the previous scrutiny and pressure imposed by the general authorities. The overdue departure of a discordant historian certainly pleased BYU's administration and trustees.

By contrast, my colleague Tom Alexander said that I should file a lawsuit against the university for academic harassment or at least formally protest to the American Association of University Professors (AAUP) against BYU's accreditation. I replied that I was too emotionally exhausted to invite more confrontation.

I also didn't want to do anything that would hurt the prospects of BYU's students, who had enough problems at the university anyway. At my request, newspaper reporter Dawn House Tracy generously stopped preparing a story about the intimidation which led to the resignation.

Other faculty members told me that my resignation was a bad precedent for BYU. "Now they've tasted blood," Marvin Hill said, "and you're leaving the rest of us here to face the consequences. Self-censorship will increase."

As for BYU's students, dozens came to my office to tell me how sorry they were that I was leaving. A married student struggled with tears while he said that he had planned to take every course I taught.

February 1988—Transferring Personal Papers to Yale

To my pleasant surprise, George Miles, the curator of Yale's Western Americana collection in the Beinecke Rare Book & Manuscript Library wanted to acquire my personal and professional papers. After the necessary preparations, I reserved two seats on a non-stop flight to New York City and persuaded the airline's personnel to allow me six boxes as carry-ons that I had measured to fit under the seats and in the overhead storage compartments. At Kennedy Airport, I handed the boxes to Miles, then took the next flight back to Utah.

Among the things I sent to Yale were my leather-bound scriptures with the autographs of the First Presidency and Quorum of Twelve as constituted when I became a missionary. Since age seventeen, multiple readings and my marking system had made these scriptures so uniquely mine, that I could quickly turn to whatever passages I wanted to quote in teaching or speaking at church. I had memorized their position on the page, not specific chapter-and-verse citations. Now that no longer mattered. I didn't expect to teach in an LDS meeting again.

This transfer contained the surviving stories and novel I had written from age eight to adolescence, plus the notes from which I gave LDS talks from my teens to adulthood. Yale also received correspondence, including personal letters to me from LDS President David O. McKay, apostles Joseph Fielding Smith, Thomas S. Monson, and Dallin H. Oaks, plus Hollywood actors Audie Murphy and Anthony Quinn and US Secretary of State Cyrus R. Vance. But not pianist Liberace's long-lost autograph.

Indicating early thoughts of autobiography, this shipment included a scrapbook of my life that I compiled at age twelve. In six years, there was a nicer volume of carefully labeled photographs which included David O. McKay, my family, friends, the bear cub in a tree, and the Hollywood actors who allowed me to snap their pictures when I was thirteen.

In a teenage photo I'm *not* proud of, I asked Nana and Grampa to stage one of their fights. It implied the murder she had once threatened in our kitchen, and maybe there was benefit in their laughing during the scene I staged at thirteen.

Eventually, Jan gave back my letters to her, our wedding photos, plus my color slides of our family and travels. Those also ended up at Yale, but the guest signature books from our Utah-California wedding receptions didn't survive the various transitions.

Three-fourths of this self-biography contains incidents that were never in any of my daily journals. But Yale got what I wrote up to 1980. At least, what survived my self-censorship.

31 March 1988–Bidding Farewell to Salt Lake City's Twenty-first Ward

In fast and testimony meeting, I affirmed to them that I knew that God was my Father in Heaven, that I loved him, and had always felt close to him, felt that I could talk with him in prayer, and had felt the warmth and comfort of his Spirit within me throughout my life. Affirmed my faith in Jesus Christ as my Savior, as the means by whom all death, pain, and futility of mortal life will one day come to completion, fulfillment, and happiness for everyone. Expressed my conviction that we had nothing to fear from our Heavenly Father in the afterlife and had no need to look upon salvation or exaltation as a formula or ladder that one misstep could deprive us of.

My lifelong belief is that we must each do what is right for us and will all find happiness with God and associates in the afterlife. It's only in mortality that we need to fear an existence of pain or rejection.

In my farewell testimony, I told them that life was unpredictable and that even the best intentions may not always turn out as we hoped and expected. With Job, I said: "God, I will trust you, even if you kill me" (a modernization of the King James Version's Job 13:15). Still, I stated my conviction that our Heavenly Father loves us unconditionally, that we can always turn to him for comfort and strength, and that our life's challenge was to comfort, love, and strengthen others. These have been the themes of thousands of sermons, Sunday School lessons, home teaching messages, and private discussions I have given for more than thirty years.

Expressed gratitude that since my ordination at age twelve, I had been able to use the LDS Church as a vehicle for service to humanity. Hoped that I had made some contribution of benefit to others during those years. Gave special thanks to the wonderful people of the Twenty-first Ward who extended to me such accepting love and encouragement since I moved into the ward almost three years earlier as part of my divorce.

Afterwards, many women and men in the congregation embraced me and told me they loved me and would miss me. I felt the same—because I doubted I would ever experience that fellowship again.

April 1988–Bidding Farewell to BYU's Students

The off-campus newspaper published my essay, "The Household of Faith, the Marketplace of Ideas, and the Prison of Conformity." It included my double entendre comparison of BYU/LDS Church with Soviet Russia. The student editors republished this essay in the autumn. *Sunstone* also published it, after I changed all "The's" to "A's" in the title. Its editor was now Daniel H. Rector.

A steady stream of students came to my office at BYU, but not just to say goodbye. I was selling my 1,500-volume library to them for about $1.00 per hardback and 50 cents per paperback of equally thick academic books. This gave me the money to buy a printer and laptop computer that I soon used at the Huntington Library.

Although Ernest Strack was a used book dealer, he came by for a private farewell, not to buy books: "At these prices, I'll let your students exploit you."[26]

This Mormon Fundamentalist and polygamist was in his mid-twenties when I met him several years earlier. His plural wife Linda (a feminist intellectual and former student of mine) had brought Ernest to my house to talk about "the principle" one Sunday afternoon. Not far into that first meeting, I was drawn both sexually and spiritually to this slender, sweet-spirited man who combined Sufi philosophy with Mormon Fundamentalism and wide-ranging intellectual curiosity.[27] Despite his scraggly beard, he was my type.

I had often stopped by to see him at the bookstore he operated across from the BYU campus, and I occasionally caught a glimpse of other wives and some of his dozen children. He introduced me to these children, but not to the other wives. I often thought that Ernest was aware of my sexual

---

26. Ernest D. Strack (1952–90) owned Grandpa's Used Books in Provo. At the time of his death he had two wives and seventeen children. Obituary, *Deseret News,* Feb. 15, 1990.

27. Sufi philosophy is an Islamic teaching dealing with the purification of inner self and removing the veils between humankind and the divine.

attraction for him, but in our talks he never made any reference to that or to homosexuality.

At my office in April 1988, we chatted about my upcoming plans. As Ernest got up to leave, I started to shake his hand, but he took me into his arms for a full embrace. As we held each other, he kissed the side of my neck: "Mike, I love you." I pulled him closer and said: "You _know_ I love you!" He kissed my neck again, looked me in the eyes, said: "God be with you," and left.

In two years, Ernest died from skin cancer—after declining standard medical treatment that had a 100% rate of cure. Instead, he relied on prayer, Fundamentalist priesthood administrations, and herbal remedies. That mystified me, as did my last visit with this gentle husband of multiple wives.

6 May 1988–Bidding Farewell to BYU

This was my last day at Brigham Young University after twelve years as a faculty member. I spent most of the afternoon getting signatures on the official termination checklist from various campus facilities to verify that I was taking no university property with me, nor leaving unpaid debts. The history department had given me a very nice farewell present and social in late April, but today was BYU's goodbye. The last item on the checklist was to be signed by Don Abel, the associate academic vice-president, whose signature was supposed to verify that I had received a "Termination Interview." As I stood in the doorway to his office, VP Abel's secretary said that I was here to see him, and she handed the form to him. BYU's associate academic vice-president looked at it, glanced up at me, signed the form without a word, and went back to the paperwork on his desk. His secretary seemed embarrassed as she handed the form back to me. I felt empty.

6 May 1988–Bidding Farewell to the Mormon History Association

As soon as I dropped off the termination form at BYU's personnel office, I drove from Provo to Logan, to attend MHA's annual banquet. Arrived late. Just in time to hear my name read as winner of the award for best book of the year.[28] MHA's members gave me a standing ovation.

For a moment, I thought of stepping to the microphone to say something in appreciation, in farewell, in summation. Decided that anything I said would be either too much or too little, so I just gave them a big grin and "Thank you," as I accepted the award.

Davis Bitton warmly congratulated me on winning this award. For the book he had advised me not to publish.

---

28. MHA's Best Book Award went to _Early Mormonism and the Magic World View._ Quinn's _J. Reuben Clark: The Church Years_ (Provo: Brigham Young University Press, 1983) had previously won the Best Book Award.

He urged me, as he often did, to complete my decade-delayed book on the Mormon hierarchy. I assured him that I would work on this full time during my year-and-a-half fellowship at the Huntington Library.

Many kind words, best wishes, and gentle hugs tonight from members of the Mormon History Association. They regarded me as a fellow traveler in the often-conflicted quest to write religious history in a rigorous, balanced, sympathetic, and faithful way. Yet I traveled in a solitary manner, even when in their company, as I sought to reconcile conflicts within myself, within Mormon history, within BYU, and within the LDS Church itself. I felt tonight that I was leaving all that behind, as well as BYU and Utah culture.

I was beginning a separate peace. With myself, with my sense of mission, with God.

CHAPTER NINETEEN

OUT

1988-1998

Early June 1988–Looking Back on Life in the LDS Church

From the meditation I wrote this month: "I'm in Los Angeles now and feel utter relief to be away from Utah and all it represents to me. My family and most of my friends were never aware of my struggle, or of the conscious choice I made at age twelve. I traded the life of personal fulfillment I wanted to have in a world of risk and vulnerability, in exchange for the life of service to my family and the LDS Church in a supportive environment.

"I didn't realize that my best efforts to be a conforming member of the LDS Church would boomerang: a failed marriage, my boys growing up in a one-parent household, all my children out of the church by their choice, my being stigmatized and forced out of employment at BYU, plus finding myself a target of the LDS Church's leaders I had once aspired to be among.

"I've also ended up in the homosexually defined life I thought my choices would avoid. Without really abandoning the Mormon path I've tried to follow for so long, I'm now entering uncharted territory as defined by my sexuality.

"For years, I've felt that I was wrong when I was twelve to make the inflexible commitment to sexual conformity. I've felt that I was even more wrong not to realistically abandon that commitment ten years later. Neither option I faced was easy, but I seemed to take the path of least resistance. At twelve, seventeen, and twenty-two, I was too scared of myself and too confident of my Heavenly Father to ask someone's advice.

"Yet I doubt anyone could have convinced me to live otherwise than I did. I still believe in God's modern revelations, but I could not honestly recommend any homosexually oriented person to take the LDS path of conformity and sexual repression.

"The majority of Mormons are happy with conforming. Because the LDS Church seems to work very well for those who fit its mold. Good for them! In sincerity.

"Still, I feel tremendous admiration for those who don't fit the mold and who've had the sense or courage I lacked to live a difficult kind of life as best and honestly as they could. I've felt awe in talking with young men who came out as gay to parents at age 16.

"Mormon theology is larger and more embracing than the LDS Church. Thus, I will always find inspiration and comfort in the Mormon understanding of my relationship to Heavenly Father and to my fellowmen.

"My life in the LDS Church had a lot of good mixed with the negative, but it was a coward's choice. I'm now forced by circumstance to confront the homosexual realities I avoided as a teenager and young adult.

"It would have been better to adjust to those challenges as a young man. It's more difficult to face them in mid-life, but I'm hopeful for personal success and fulfillment during the rest of my life.

"I want to explore gay life with non-Mormons—the group I've clannishly avoided my whole life. I have no illusions that attending Church services—even with gay Mormons—will help my transition. I have a lot to learn."

I typed the above on my new laptop in one of the senior fellow rooms at the Henry E. Huntington Library, near Pasadena. A few evenings later, I began attending Marianne Williamson's lectures about *A Course in Miracles* at St. Thomas Episcopal Church in Hollywood.[1] Lots of gay males were there for her mid-week talks.

Mid-June 1988–Coping with an Obsessive Woman

Complicating my effort to build a gay-friendly life has been a woman's obsession with me. Sara was about eight years old when I left Glendale for BYU. Now in her mid-30s, she hasn't outgrown her childhood crush on me.

Arranging with the Sunstone Regional Symposium's organizers to pick me up at the National Airport on Friday, May 13, for my two talks in Washington, DC, the next day, she chauffeured me around during the symposium. Driving me to the airport for my return flight on Sunday, she insisted on treating me to lunch at a restaurant, where she declared her love.

Trying to be as kind as I could, I said that I wasn't interested in a relationship with her. Protesting that I should at least make the effort, she got the attention of the diners around us when she finally demanded: "Tell me what you don't like about me! What's wrong with me?"

She didn't take no chemistry as an answer, and I didn't confide anything to her about my own life and prospects of love. I wanted to take a taxi from the restaurant, but she seemed ready to make a huge scene, so I took a tense ride in her car for the rest of the way to the National Airport. Since then, she

---

1. Marianne Williamson (1952–) lectures and teaches based on Dr. Helen Schucman's book, *A Course in Miracles*. She has written more than a dozen books and ran for the 2020 Democratic presidential nomination. Gabrielle Bluestone, "Marianne Williamson Marches On," *New York Times*, June 28, 2019.

has phoned, sent me cards/letters, and asked her brother to plead her cause with me—decades after my last seeing him as a friend.

I phoned Moyne Oviatt Osborn in Utah for the advice of this psychiatric social worker and counselor, who had been a good friend of mine for years. She said that my trying to be nice to an obsessively attached woman only encourages her romantic delusions, and that I should write a harshly candid letter about my absolute lack of interest in this young woman and my intent to have no association of any kind.

In response, Sara wrote a note condemning what she regarded as my alleged "hatred of women." I didn't reply to that, and her letters/phone calls stopped.

In the midst of all this, I got a phone call at my apartment from Robert A. Rees, a UCLA professor and bishop of the Los Angeles Singles Ward.[2] I had heard he was extending a special ministry of compassion toward Mormon homosexuals, many of whom attended his ward, and I knew why one of my Utah friends had given my unlisted number to Bishop Rees.

I thanked him for the invitation to attend his ward but said that I was "taking a break from the church." He accepted that mild rebuff.

26 June 1988–My First Gay Pride Parade

I drove from my apartment in Studio City through Laurel Canyon to West Hollywood—to attend this gay revelry. While standing in the pre-parade crowd along Santa Monica Boulevard in WEHO's "Boys Town," I had one of my most pleasant small-world experiences with another Mormon.[3]

On the sidewalk opposite, I recognized a recently returned missionary I had met at a Salt Lake City party during the winter holidays. As I crossed the street toward him, he waved and shouted gleefully: "Mike! I heard you were living here now." This cute studlee gave me a wet, beer-flavored kiss, then said: "Let me introduce you to my boyfriend." Both were about the same age that I was at my marriage twenty-one years ago, and I envied them.

The three of us joined thousands on West Hollywood's sidewalks in laughing with and cheering for the parade's celebration of stereotypes, diversity, and solidarity. Drag queens, dykes on bikes, gay rodeo champions, leathermen, lipstick lesbians, radical faeries, women and men in their military uniforms—all proclaiming to the world: "We're here! We're queer! Get used to it!" For a closeted homosexual like me, seeing them in wave after wave

2. Robert A. Rees (1935–) was bishop of the Los Angeles First (Singles) Ward from 1986 to 1992. He was an English professor and administrator at UCLA for twenty-five years, edited *Dialogue: A Journal of Mormon Thought* in the 1970s, and was a visiting professor and director of Mormon Studies at the Graduate Theological Union in Berkeley from 2010 to 2022.

3. WEHO is short for West Hollywood, a city in the Los Angeles area previously known for its high population of gay men and now known as a center for all LGBTQ people. Tony Castro, "Why They Call It Boys Town," *WEHOville*, April 13, 2021.

of happy humanity was intoxicating. I also felt emotional strength from the support groups marching together, especially Affirmation for Mormon Gays and Lesbians (founded in 1977) and the Parents and Friends of Lesbians And Gays (PFLAG).[4]

Mid-July 1988–Colleague Friend Asks about Homosexuality

Tom Alexander wrote that Gary F. Novak was telling everyone who would listen at BYU that I was homosexual and was going to West Hollywood's gay bars. My twelve-year colleague in BYU's history department asked me to confirm or deny those allegations, so that he could counter them. Trained by Lou Midgley, Novak would become known as a polemical LDS writer for FARMS (Foundation for Ancient Research and Mormon Studies).[5] In this instance, he was correct about me on both scores.

At this time, I had never heard of Novak, and was not ready to admit my homosexuality to anyone connected with BYU or Church administration. Therefore, in the type of non-denial denial typical of the US government and of LDS headquarters, I replied to Tom with a question: "Who is Gary Novak and how does he know what goes on in gay bars?" Tom's next letter said that he "will construe" my answer "as a denial" and would tell others that I denied Novak's claim.

In case those rumors followed me from BYU to the Huntington Library, I decided to confide in its research director. "I'm a Presbyterian," Martin Ridge smiled, "but couldn't care less about whom you date or take to bed. However, you're welcome to bring *any* companion to our socials." He was far more accepting than I expected from seeing him daily in his starched white shirts and bow ties.

30 July 1988–Publicly Calling BYU "An Auschwitz of the Mind"

Salt Lake Tribune reporter Dawn House Tracy asked me to comment on BYU's firing of Hebraist David P. Wright for his privately expressed disbelief in the Book of Mormon as an ancient text.[6] I could no longer be silent or indirect about the fact that BYU's apostle-trustees have created an environ-

---

4. Affirmation's modern subtitle is "LGBTQ Mormons, Families & Friends." Its vision is "to be a refuge to land, heal, share, and be authentic" (affirmation.org). PFLAG, founded in 1972, has hundreds of chapters in the United States. Its purpose is to provide "confidential peer support, education, and advocacy to LGBTQ+ people, their parents and families, and allies" (pflag.com).

5. Gary F. Novak holds an MA in political science from BYU and administers the website for Rio Salado Community College in Arizona. He wrote reviews for FARMS and criticized "the so-called New Mormon History" and the approaches of its historians such as Leonard Arrington, Dale Morgan, Fawn Brodie, and Marvin Hill. See Gary F. Novak, "Naturalistic Assumptions and the Book of Mormon," *BYU Studies* 30, no. 3 (Summer 1990): 23–40.

6. After leaving BYU, David P. Wright (1953–) became professor of the Bible and the Ancient Near East in Brandeis University's Department of Near Eastern and Judaic Studies.

ment that is hostile to free inquiry and to academic freedom. Only what is approved is allowed, which is *not* academic freedom.

BYU's faculty and students have about as much academic freedom as there was at Berlin University under the Nazis or at Moscow University under the Soviets. Freedom to bear your testimony of LDS faith at BYU is no more academic freedom than professors had academic freedom when they praised the Nazi Party at a Nazi-controlled university. Academic freedom exists when one can express what is disapproved or controversial to a university's administrators, without fear of reprisals.

The above paragraph was in my letter to F. Lamond Tullis, after he asked if I had been quoted accurately in the newspaper on July 30.[7] Once a congenial colleague in our college, he was now BYU's assistant academic vice president. The tone of his letter's inquiry was simply inquisitive, not inquisitorial, but he never replied to my response.

The extinction of free thought at BYU is more accurately a goal of *some* LDS general authorities, *some* administrators, and even *some* faculty members. By contrast, many BYU faculty are dedicated to the unfettered life of mind for themselves and students. If BYU were a real university, there would be no element of risk or courage in promoting a marketplace of ideas there.

I admire those who have remained to continue a quiet struggle for genuine academic freedom. I feel sorry for BYU's students, both the ones who welcome its environment of control and those who resent it.

My BYU Auschwitz comment got wide circulation in the media, and I was brought up short by one response. I received a letter at the Huntington Library, posted in England, from Deidre Allen—a faithful teenage member of the Maidstone Branch throughout my missionary service there. Now the wife of a US serviceman, she had read my comment in the *Stars and Stripes*, and asked how I could have drifted so far from my former testimony.[8] I tried to explain in a letter that criticizing a fallible church is not the same as criticizing its divine founder, but Deidre didn't agree.

31 July 1988–A Straight-arrow Mormon Stuns Me

After reading the *Tribune*'s quote, one of my Aaronic Priesthood boys from the late '60s called around among our Utah associates to get my unlisted phone number. Reaching me tonight, our conversation somehow turned to my being gay.

When I awkwardly acknowledged that I had always been attracted to him,

---

7. F. Lamond Tullis (1935–) was BYU's political science department chair from 1978 to 1983 and associate academic vice president from 1985 to 1989. He has written multiple works on the LDS Church in Mexico and Latin America.

8. *Stars and Stripes* is a daily print and online newspaper for the US military community.

he replied: "I would be honored to one day be your lover, Mike." I was speechless upon hearing this from a temple-married man with several children. Even though I knew since the mid-70s that his views were liberal, I regarded him as straight arrow in behavior—even somewhat prudish. And he had always seemed completely hetero.

Breaking the silence that now hung between us on the phone, my longtime friend said: "This isn't just theory, Mike. One of my missionary companions came out to me as gay a few years ago, and asked if he could 'cuddle' with me sometime. With my wife's permission, I had a night of loving sex with him. He's the only male I've ever been with, but I'd be glad to share such nights with you."

August 1988–LDS Headquarters Tries to Track Me Down

This month, the church membership department contacted my mother and lied to her by claiming that they were a Salt Lake City business with whom I had an unpaid debt. The woman on the phone told my mother to contact her directly through their toll-free number as soon as my mother learned my residence address. Mom believed it was a business, but simply forwarded to me the telephone number—which I found was the church membership department's.

I doubt that church headquarters told such a lie, just so a local ward or stake can extend loving fellowship to me. Yet that's what they would claim if challenged.

Unable to locate me through my mother, LDS headquarters sent church security agents to the home of my personal attorney. In order to go off record when I moved to California, I had asked my Salt Lake City ward to transfer my membership record to the ward for his address in Holladay, Utah. One night, two beefy men—in white shirts, black suits and ties—knocked at the door of my attorney's home. Explaining that they had been sent from "church headquarters at the request of the membership department," they asked for my current address.

When my friend Jim McConkie answered that he was prohibited by attorney-client confidentiality from giving that information, one of the two said: "You are a former bishop and nephew of an apostle, and you hold a temple recommend. You *know* that you are wrong. You've taken sacred oaths in the temple, and those are more important than your employment as Michael Quinn's attorney. You have a sacred obligation to give us this information." My attorney answered: "Good night, gentlemen," as he closed the door in their faces.

May 1992–Am What I've Been and Will Be What I Can

From the meditation I wrote this month: "As I re-read my 'Meditation' of

June 1988, I'm reminded how filled with regret I was then. Life didn't turn out as I planned, and my best intentions ended up hurting people I love.

"On the other hand, I've grown to realize and accept the fact that there are happy and unhappy consequences of any major decision we make in life. If I had chosen at age 12 or 17 or 22 to seek homosexual fulfillment, there would have been another set of happy and unhappy results. I'm grateful for all the good experiences I had along my Mormon path, especially the many happy times I shared with my wife and children.

"I moved to New Orleans in September 1989 and have lived in the French Quarter for two-and-a-half years. Haven't attended LDS Church services since my 'farewell testimony' in March 1988. I've done my best to prevent LDS authorities from knowing where I reside. Once I'm 'a member of record' in a particular ward or stake, then headquarters can mandate my excommunication by local authorities. The LDS Membership Department's shameful efforts in mid-1988 show that this is more than paranoia.

"On 15 May 1990, PBS Television began broadcasting a documentary for which I was interviewed at length, in addition to serving as script adviser for its producer Ken Verdoia. 'A Matter of Principle' provided a multimedia examination of the historical and continued practice of polygamy by those believing in the Book of Mormon. While contributing to that documentary, I was also completing a long essay on 'Plural Marriage and Mormon Fundamentalism' as a Research Fellow for the American Academy of Arts and Sciences.

"During a trip to Utah, I spoke to the B. H. Roberts Society on 17 October 1991.[9] Concerning the problems that Mormon historians have faced, I said: 'When LDS leaders have strongly disliked an *unauthorized* exposure of Mormonism's checkered past, they have typically attacked the messenger.' I added: 'One response of the Mormon hierarchy toward an unwelcome messenger has been character assassination. This is founded on a common assumption about the general public: "If you discredit the messenger, you discredit the message." The logic is flawed, but often effective. Linked to character assassination has been the use of excommunication and the designation "apostate," particularly in response to partisan accounts of Church history.'

"This was six months after BYU canceled the invitation for Pulitzer Prize winning LDS historian Laurel Thatcher Ulrich to speak on campus—due to her support of the Equal Rights Amendment for women—*fifteen years earlier*![10] My October talk was also two months after the First Presidency

---

9. Dedicated to the study of timely issues in Mormonism, the B. H. Roberts Society was founded in 1980. It sponsored lectures, panel discussions, and symposia.

10. Though Quinn surmised that Ulrich's invitation to speak (at BYU Women's Conference) was vetoed because of her earlier support of the ERA, BYU's board of trustees never gave Ulrich, nor the public, a reason. She believed it was related to a larger debate over academic freedom going on at BYU. "There's a lot of tension on the campus right now," she said of the incident.

and Quorum of the Twelve Apostles publicly condemned the freewheeling academic 'symposia' sponsored by Salt Lake City's Sunstone Foundation of Mormon intellectuals and academics.[11]

"In December 1991, the Church Membership Department used the American Express Company to track me down with the offer of a gold card for no annual fee. A Midwest office of AMEX sent the application form to me in care of my ex-wife's address in Montana, where I had never resided. Although suspicious, I sent in the application. I soon received a phone call informing me that I could not get the card unless I gave them my residence address, instead of the mail receiving address where I get all mail in New Orleans. I knew my credit ratings were linked to that address. Since this was a regular address (not a PO box), I asked the woman how she knew this address was not my residence. There was an awkward pause on the phone, and she stammered that either address would be acceptable. A week later, I got a letter from a senior officer in the Salt Lake City office of AMEX that my application had been approved, but that they would not send the gold card until I sent them my residence address. It was now obvious that the Church Membership Department worked with an executive in Salt Lake City's American Express office, which had arranged for the AMEX office in the Midwest to offer me the gold card. More underhanded deceptions to get my residence address—just so LDS headquarters can tell my new stake to excommunicate me.

"A Mormon CIA officer in Germany once told me: 'The LDS Church is better at tracking down Mormons who don't want to be found, than the Company is in tracking down spies.'[12] He was one of the totally inactive Mormons who unsuccessfully tried to avoid being located.

"I feel sure that Boyd K. Packer and others would like nothing better than to be able to simply dismiss me as an excommunicated Mormon, since I'm continuing to write controversial Mormon history. Nevertheless, Mormonism is my heritage and my faith, whether or not I remain a member 'in good standing' of the LDS Church. I am working to complete the mission I began long ago to explain the LDS Church's past. I still feel that this understanding is beneficial.

"Even if Church authorities excommunicate me one day, it is Mormon

Quinn was a little off on the timing—the veto of her address occurred in late 1992. See "Brigham Young Rejects Pulitzer Prize Winner as Speaker," *Chronicle of Higher Education*, Feb. 24, 1993.

11. The church's "Statement on Symposia" did not specifically name Sunstone but was released on August 23, 1991, two weeks after the annual Sunstone symposium ended on August 10. The statement, printed in the *Ensign's* November 1991 issue, said that at "recent symposia," presentations "included matters that were seized upon and publicized in such a way as to injure the Church or its members or to jeopardize the effectiveness or safety of our missionaries."

12. "The Company" is a nickname for the Central Intelligence Agency (CIA).

doctrine that every ordinance of the Church must be ratified by 'the Holy Spirit of Promise' for the individual, or the ordinance does not have any validity in eternity. I trust in my relationship with God.

"I used to think I could be a poster boy for family causation of homosexuality, yet have been persuaded by recent research that homosexuality has genetic causality. Either way, homosexual attraction was not something I chose, and sexual repression was *not* a healthy choice.

"Mormonism, like homosexuality, is in my DNA. My environment simply shaped the kind of Mormon I became, just as it shaped how I coped with (and didn't cope with) my sexual orientation. I'll always be Mormon, even if I never enter an LDS chapel again. Likewise, being celibate or faithfully married has nothing to do with the fact that I have always been homosexually oriented.

"In April 1992, I sent my parents a thirty-page version of this self-biography, emphasizing my childhood, youth, and years on BYU's faculty. Omitting the sensitive entries about them, it was my way of telling Mom and Dad about my homosexuality and how it fits into my family life and Church life. In a cover letter, I wrote that I wanted to take fear out of my relationship with them.

"Mom phoned to say that my letter had shocked her, but that she loved me unconditionally. I told her that during my whole life I had wanted to spare her the pain of knowing I'm homosexual. 'Why should you carry all the pain?' she said. I cried at hearing those words.

"She expressed shock and grief about what I had written of Nana's relationship with me: 'I never would have left you with her if I had known, but she loved you and you seemed happy there.' Mom was right on both counts, and I did my best to comfort her feelings of guilt. Nana controlled both our lives and had resided with Mom ever since Grampa's death.

"I didn't confront the dark side of Nana's relationship with me until 1990 in New Orleans. I was having counseling sessions with a non-Mormon gay therapist, and demonstrated that I hadn't repressed the memories of anything I've written in this self-biography. Nonetheless, Bill Rose commented on how emotionless I was while describing the ways she tried to indoctrinate me as a child. When he criticized her, I was defensive: 'But she *loved* me!' Bill recommended that I read John Bradshaw's *Healing the Shame That Binds You*, which led me to a realization that I had compartmentalized those early memories from each other and from emotion.[13]

"Reading that book unleashed a torrent of pain and rage toward my grandmother. I was still trying to cope with those feelings when Nana died in

13. John Bradshaw, *Healing the Shame That Binds You* (Deerfield Beach, FL: Health Communications, 1988).

November 1991 at age 95. I shed no tears at the news or at her funeral, where I was a pallbearer. I felt nothing.

"By contrast, I continue to feel occasional sadness at Grampa's absence. I can't recall if I ever told him that I loved him, yet I did.

"Mom told me on the phone this April that she was also deeply disturbed by the treatment I had received from the Church and from BYU. She said that she nearly felt hatred for Apostle Boyd K. Packer. I replied that I hoped she didn't allow those feelings to gnaw at her.

"I said that I didn't hate Packer, even though I disliked him and mourned his malignant influence on the Church. I told my mother that Elder Packer sincerely feels that he was doing God's service, but so did Caiaphas, Saul, and Torquemada.[14]

"After waiting another week, I phoned my father to get his reaction to what I had written about myself. He said that he had read only a third of what I sent and wouldn't read any more of it. He didn't like what I'd written about my grandmother and said that he didn't want to learn unhappy or negative things. This was typical of his pattern of denying his own Mexican heritage and closing himself off emotionally.

"Ever since I started writing or phoning him as a freshman at BYU, Dad always said: 'Tell me only good news and happy things'—just like LDS headquarters.

"Even though I had now written him a lot of things he didn't want to know, Dad said for me to telephone him each week to keep in touch. I felt such relief that he wasn't going to make me into a non-person as he did with his Mexican brothers. All in all, I felt positive about my parents' reactions to my disclosures of April 1992.

"Then, during another phone conversation with Dad, I learned—*weeks after the fact*—that his third wife had died in March! I was shocked and incredulous. I had visited with sweet-dispositioned Beverly and him annually since 1971, and most recently at last year's holiday season. His excuse for silence was that he didn't want to give me 'bad news' two days before my birthday this year. It was a perplexing example of his secretiveness.

"Most of my life consisted of my responsibilities and mission to others, and also was inwardly focused on my vulnerabilities. That took spontaneity away from my associations with others, and this frustration of warm, personal contact is my greatest regret.

14. According to the New Testament, high priest Caiaphas led the Jewish legal body Sanhedrin that condemned Jesus Christ to death. Saul (named "Paul" after his conversion to Christianity), arrested and imprisoned followers of Jesus. Thomas of Torquemada (1420–98) was the inaugural Grand Inquisitor of the Spanish Inquisition. He punished Catholic heretics with torture and burning at the stake. See Christian von Dehsen, ed., *Lives and Legacies: Philosophers and Religious Leaders* (Oxfordshire, England: Routledge, 2013).

"Still, life has been interesting so far, and I'm eager to make the best of what remains. I am reinventing myself and my life. Until now I've never had any sense of self-worth beyond whatever use I was in serving others. I'm aware of my flaws, but am hopeful.

"Since leaving Utah in 1988, an unresolved difficulty is that I have been more isolated than ever before. BYU, Mormon culture, and the LDS Church nearly destroyed me, but in walking away from that pressure cooker, I also gave up a network of supportive friends in Utah. Some were very much in the Church, and some very much out of the Church, but I've missed them deeply. Telephone calls and occasional visits don't compensate for the lack of such association in my daily living.

"I've had little success in creating a network of non-Mormon friends wherever I've resided since leaving Utah. My absorption and obsession with Mormonism have been so intense, that I wonder if I'll ever really feel 'at home' with non-Mormon companionship.

"Utah-Mormon culture is a magnet for me, but I also feel the crushing weight of its scrutiny and expectations. During every visit (sometimes a month at a time) I've made to Utah since 1988, people indicate that I'm the subject of gossip, both friendly and hostile. I have always feared and disliked being the object of gossip, but I've gradually come to terms with that inevitability.

"More important, 'coming out' to my parents last month has liberated me from the fear of living in Utah again. I'm now (in May 1992) making preparations to move back. I need to do extensive research in Utah's libraries as I finish up what is going to be a multi-volumed study of the Mormon hierarchy. It's possible that I will live there without the healthy male companionship I've always needed, yet have avoided in one way or another.

"It's also possible that Church authorities will track me down and excommunicate me—either for my writing controversial Mormon history or for my efforts to reach out for male intimacy.

"Nonetheless, moving back to Utah will restore the frequent association of my children and my friends. I've denied that to myself for four years.

"Recently, I had a vividly Technicolor dream of bodily flying like Superman northward to Salt Lake City from Lake Powell—over the redstone cliffs of Southern Utah. I awoke feeling overwhelming happiness.

"Speaking of dreams, after leaving BYU I gradually resumed dreaming in color. For at least fifteen years before 1988, I dreamed only in black and white and rarely remembered dreaming at all. It's so different now.

"In Mormonism, it is considered a virtue to give up your personal needs in order to serve the Church. I did that, but now realize that I lived only through other people's needs and expectations. I've been a cipher—even if a prominent one—my whole life.

"Now I'm trying to find my own life, a self and fulfillment on *my* terms. I feel that Heavenly Father is with me in this effort, in spite of disapproval by the Church's leaders.

"I also feel that God is with the Church's leaders, except when they damage lives with demands for a crushing conformity. Unfortunately that seems to be the general pattern of the contemporary LDS Church for ethnic groups, for women, for unmarried adults, for the divorced, for blue-collar workers, for the poor, for intellectuals, for artists, and for homosexuals. There is ambiguity in most aspects of life, including the religious.

"Despite the futility and suffering in human experience, there's opportunity for enlightenment, growth, giving, sharing, fun, compassion, pleasure, love, and (yes) even times of happiness and fulfillment. Different expressions of those experiences are available along the various roads we can travel in life.

"I've had one range of experience along the path I chose at age twelve, and that path has now curved back to the one I thought I'd left behind. Perhaps it has all been one path, anyway. I'm travel worn, but still eager for the continued journey. I expect to stumble, but that's a sign of forward movement along an interesting terrain. I feel a greater inward peace now than ever before in my life. *L'chaime!*"[15]

Early August 1992–Moving Back to Utah and Coming Out as Gay to Heterosexual Friends

Just in time to speak at meetings of the Sunstone Symposium on August 7 and 8, I moved back to Salt Lake City from New Orleans. My apartment was now in the Capitol Hill District on Center Street, less than four blocks north of the Salt Lake Temple.

At an open house, I brought together my separate groups of Utah associations for the first time. My very Mormon friends such as Leonard J. Arrington seemed to get along just fine this evening with my very gay friends such as Rocky O'Donovan and Roger Salazar. Many stayed for hours.

My apartment's walls displayed black-and-white portraits of cute young men I had photographed since leaving BYU. This was an unspoken coming out to my conventional and trusted friends. My daughters Mary and Lisa were also at this party, for which Lisa had designed the invitations.

My since-adolescence friend Clifton Jolley wasn't among those at my unspoken coming-out party. After his own LDS marriage ended in divorce, he had left the *Deseret News*, and was now living in Texas with his Jewish wife,

---

15. *L'chaim* is a Jewish saying meaning "to life," often used as a toast.

Avigail "Gail." Clifton converted to Reform Judaism, and would write of being visited by both his bishop and his Rabbi.

Mid-August 1992–Investigative Files at LDS Headquarters

On August 14, an official spokesman publicly acknowledged that the LDS Church maintains investigative files on every Mormon who publishes controversial articles or speaks in academic forums. Two years earlier, F. Ross Peterson (a history professor at Utah State University) had been shown his file, which had clippings and notations about him since the anti-war views he expressed as an eighteen-year-old freshman in college. LDS headquarters next announced on August 22 that these files were kept and reviewed by a Strengthening the Members Committee, chaired by two apostles, who "advise" local leaders to take "appropriate action" against the targeted individuals. Peterson's case showed that even teenage liberals have been subjected to such scrutiny by LDS headquarters since the 1960s. Church Security's investigative division is as stunning as East Germany's *Stasi*![16]

September 1992–Reunite with Ex-Wife and Kids in a Different Way

Having all resumed living in Salt Lake City at various residences, Jan, our children, and I began attending together the non-sectarian, non-religious meetings of Landmark Education's The Forum (formerly Werner Erhardt's *est*).[17] Its technologies for personal development became a catalyst for discussing many issues of our family's dynamics and improving them.

As part of that program, I one day had the courage to ask my four children individually to candidly tell me in what ways I had failed to be the father they needed. That was an extremely painful experience for me (who had thought I was successful in being the father to them that I never had), but their honesty and our communication without limits made our relationships as adults far better. Not perfect, but "vastly improved," they later said.

October 1992–The AIDS Memorial Quilt and Those I Had Known

From the 9th to 11th of this month, the Names Project displayed its AIDS Memorial Quilt on fifteen grassy acres of the National Mall in Washington, DC. It had 20,064 hand-stitched panels memorializing some of the Americans (mainly gay males) who died from AIDS during the past ten years.

One panel was for Gilbert T. Deming, my stepmother Kaye's young

16. "First Presidency Statement Cites Scriptural Mandate for Church Committee," *Church News*, Aug. 22, 1992.

17. Werner Erhard (1935–) is a self-improvement guru who founded Erhard Seminars Training ("est") in 1971 and The Forum in 1981. Peter Haldeman, "The Return of Werner Erhard, Father of Self-Help," *New York Times*, Nov. 28, 2015.

nephew, whom I saw nearly every winter holiday season while in my teens. He died of AIDS in 1985 at age twenty-nine.

Among the hundreds of Aaronic Priesthood boys I had taught, AIDS killed at least one. He wasn't the former AP boy who phoned me in 1988 with the offer of making love—an opportunity I never tried to fulfill. Likewise at age twenty-nine, Garth M. Gwinn died in 1991.

The disease also took six friends of my gay friends whom I had seen occasionally in Salt Lake City or New Orleans. And Liberace's death from AIDS in 1987 had sadly renewed my fond memory of him.

November 1992–Imagine My Surprise

Published by New York's Macmillan publishing house, an unprecedented, five-volume *Encyclopedia of Mormonism* had been in print for nearly a year. I didn't expect much candor in 1,200 articles reviewed by apostles Neal A. Maxwell and Dallin H. Oaks, plus unnamed members of BYU's board of trustees. But I started reading its entries by more than 700 authors—just to find relevant citations for source notes in my upcoming books about the Mormon hierarchy.

In view of the unpleasantness between me and LDS headquarters for the past seven years, I was stunned to discover that this hierarchy-approved encyclopedia cited my publications ten times. This included the controversial articles on the Council of Fifty, the prayer circles, and (most amazing of all), "From Sacred Grove to Sacral Power Structure."[18] No surprise that they omitted my analysis of the First Presidency's secret approval for post-1890 polygamy.

December 1992–Triple-Whammy in Newspapers

Even though my policy was to never contact the media, but only to answer questions when they contacted me, I can understand why some regarded me as a publicity hound this month. On December 6, an Associated Press national wire service story featured me as "Historian: LDS Church Wants 'Cookie-Cutter' Members," then the *Salt Lake Tribune* featured me in its December 19 article, "Historian: LDS Intended Women to Hold Priesthood: Scholar Cites Evidence Joseph Smith Endowed Power in Temple Ritual." Two days later, the *New York Times* quoted me in its "Seeking a Moderate Image, Mormons Expel Extremists." This referred to some of the right-wing Republican fanatics I had condemned for thirty years, but I felt no support

18. See Quinn, "From Sacred Grove to Sacral Power Structure," *Dialogue: A Journal of Mormon Thought* 17, no. 2 (Summer 1984): 9–34. The summary first paragraph of the article reads: "In more than 150 years, Mormonism has experienced a series of interrelated and crucial transitions, even transformations. This study describes five of these linked transitions as individualism to corporate dynasticism, authoritarian democracy to authoritarian oligarchy, theocracy to bureaucracy, communitarianism to capitalism, and neocracy to gerontocracy."

for the LDS Church's witch hunt against them. I'm an equal-opportunity critic of *any* tactics of repression, whether aimed at ideas and advocates I oppose or against those I embrace.

7 February 1993–Tracked Down

Six months after I moved back to Utah, LDS headquarters discovered my address. The president of the Salt Lake Stake, Paul A. Hanks, appeared with his counselors at my door this Sunday morning—holding a written accusation that my recent historical publications constituted apostasy.[19] I had not received any kind of LDS fellowshipping visit from anyone else in the ward or stake.

At the top of his typewritten list was my essay "Mormon Women Have Had the Priesthood Since 1843," published last year in a feminist book, *Women and Authority*, edited by Maxine Hanks, my former associate at BYU. I didn't bother to point out to the stake president that this article was merely a longer analysis of what I had published in the fall of 1981 as a professor at BYU. What was merely controversial back then was apostate in 1993.

I explained that I was on my way to Los Angeles for research at the Huntington Library, where Martin Ridge had given me a three-month fellowship. My stake president said that disciplinary action would occur immediately after my return.

That evening I typed a letter to Paul Hanks, outlining my previous experience with a stake president who had been given instructions by LDS headquarters to discipline me and to claim it was a local decision. I explained my post-1988 vow that "I would never again participate in a process which was designed to punish me for being the messenger of unwanted historical evidence and to intimidate me from further work in Mormon history." I refused to meet with him.

For the first time, I did not remain silent. I furnished newspaper reporters with copies of his letter and my response, in the hope that publicity would cause LDS headquarters to withdraw its instructions to my stake president. Through Vern Anderson, the Associated Press ran a story that appeared throughout the nation, while the *Salt Lake Tribune* ran its own story by Peggy Fletcher Stack.[20]

4 March 1993–Double-Edged Views of Loyalty

In response to a more strident letter from the Salt Lake Stake's president, I wrote to Paul Hanks from Southern California: "Most of all, I resent the

19. Paul Ashton Hanks (1938–2022) served as a Church Education System area director and administrator at LDS Church Headquarters.

20. Associated Press, "Mormons Investigating Him, Critic Says," *Los Angeles Times*, Feb. 13, 1993. Peggy Fletcher Stack, "LDS Apostasy Investigation Launched against Historian," *Salt Lake Tribune*, Feb. 13, 1993.

fact that everything in your conduct toward me indicates your assumptions of my disloyalty, while at the same time you expect me to loyally conceal your 'personal and confidential' efforts to intimidate me." In a month, on the anniversary of the church's 1830 organization, I wrote: "Under no circumstances will I meet with you or any other church officer who requests a meeting."

Mid-March 1993–LDS Male Couples

A gay-male couple (Henry Miller and Richard M. Fernandez) contacted me at my Mom's house in the LA area and invited me to get acquainted by visiting them over a weekend in San Diego. Soon after I arrived, they invited me to go to the open house for the new temple prior to its dedication. I had not been in a temple since 1985, and thoroughly enjoyed touring the San Diego Temple with about a dozen of this couple's gay and lesbian friends from the area. I loved this LDS temple's neo-Gothic exterior by a Catholic architect. However, its interior was disappointing.

In Utah, I knew gay males who were in long-term relationships, but this couple (in their seventh year together when I met them) had several remarkable experiences with LDS leaders. Henry's family had been Mormon for generations, while Rick was from a Roman Catholic family. About two years after they commenced their relationship, they were living in Washington, DC, where Rick converted to Mormonism while he was getting a master's degree in theology from Catholic University of America.

After repeatedly side-stepping the requests of the missionary elders for his baptism, he told them that he and his roommate were homosexual lovers. When the elders stopped crying, they said that they weren't going to give up on him but would have to talk with the mission president.

He asked this male couple to meet with him, then explained that the church would allow the young man's baptism if he agreed to live a celibate life. Rick answered that he and Henry regarded their relationship as a marriage, "and we believe that God honors us as a married couple." After an evening of questions, discussion, and testimony bearing, the mission president said that he would fast and pray about the matter before giving his decision.

A few days afterward, he told them that he was authorizing Rick's baptism because God's Spirit said to do so. This mission president admitted that he didn't understand it, because this was absolutely contrary to LDS Church policy, but this good man affirmed he knew that Heavenly Father accepted their relationship.

Now in their thirties, this male couple told me that after Rick's baptism they experienced the same acceptance by bishops and stake presidents in Washington, DC; Arizona; and Southern California. This openly gay couple had served in various church positions, including leadership of their elders quorum. I was dumfounded by their experience and wondered how long it could last before they encountered some homophobic Grand Inquisitor as a local leader.

The other gay male couple I met this spring was intergenerational. Divorced and the father of children, middle aged Leo Goates was eight years into his marriage with David Callahan, thirty years his junior. They had met at a social of Affirmation for Mormon Gays and Lesbians.

Raised in Salt Lake City, Leo was an old-style Mormon homosexual who married a young woman in the temple shortly after his mission in the 1940s. A newer version of the devoutly religious gay, Dave went through ex-gay ministries like Exodus International (Evangelical) and Evergreen International (LDS) before deciding in the 1980s that reparative therapy didn't work. Dave now served as organist for a Protestant congregation, and they distanced themselves from the LDS Church more than Rick and Henry did. Leo and Dave would eventually celebrate their gay Silver Anniversary, as would Rick and Henry.

Spring 1993–Returning to LDS Services and Gaining New Friends

During these months in Southern California, I resided at Mom's home in Ontario and commuted thirty-two miles daily to the Huntington Library. I also began traveling fifty-six miles one-way on Sundays to participate in the Los Angeles Singles Ward in Westwood, next to the LA Temple. It fellowshipped openly gay members who also held positions, but I didn't announce my homosexuality.

Bishop Thomas M. Andersen (successor to Bob Rees) had read the *Los Angeles Times* story about the apostasy charges against me. "What's *wrong* with those people up in Utah?! What can they be *thinking*?!" he asked. Then, to my greater surprise, Bishop Andersen invited me to speak about "women and the Priesthood" to a ward fireside. A gutsy Mensch!

Among the new friends I met while in LA during 1993 was Betty Ann Marshall, who attended the regular Westwood Ward. Having a gay son of her own (who lived in San Francisco), she invited me to use her guest house on weekends, so that I wouldn't have the one-day commute of 112 miles to attend the Singles Ward. Convening in the Westwood chapel, it was only two miles from her house.

Her closest friend, Lorie Winder Stromberg, was a feminist housewife academic whom I had known for a decade.[21] Lorie and husband Tom resided near Betty Ann and also invited me to their home in the Cheviot Hills district of West LA.

During my 1993 stay in Southern California, I took the Sacrament each

---

21. Lorie Winder Stromberg is a Mormon feminist, activist, writer, and editor.

Sunday in the LA Singles Ward. I was sure it was my final opportunity to do so as a member of the LDS Church. At the last fast meeting I attended, I repeated what I had said in my goodbye to members of the Salt Lake Twenty-first Ward in March 1988. This spring, I knew I was giving my farewell testimonial of Mormonism—and to Mormonism.

3 April 1993–An Apostle Publicly Condemns My 1992 Essay on Women and the Priesthood

In the televised morning session of general conference, Boyd K. Packer said: "Some members of the Church are now teaching that priesthood is some kind of a free-wheeling authority, which can be assumed by anyone who has had the endowment. They claim this automatically gives one authority to perform priesthood ordinances. They take verses of scripture out of context and misinterpret statements of early leaders." Significantly, Elder Packer could not bring himself to say "woman" or "women" who receive the temple endowment, and Packer falsely charged the essay with a claim it specifically denied about endowed women performing priesthood ordinances.[22]

Mid-April 1993–Phone Message from LDS Headquarters

General authority seventy David E. Sorensen (whom I had never met) said that he wanted me to know four things: (1) that he and other general authorities appreciated my publications on Mormon history and did not fear revisionist history, (2) that he and others at LDS headquarters strongly disagreed with the current efforts to punish me, (3) that he could do nothing to help me or to preserve my church membership, (4) that he prayed for God's Spirit to be with me.[23]

I knew that this was not a prank call from someone pretending to be Elder Sorensen. I received this message while visiting the home of his son and daughter-in-law in Southern California. Both husband and wife were former students of mine.

11 May 1993–Returning to Salt Lake City

As soon as I re-entered my apartment, the building's resident manager informed the stake president that I was back. [Redacted] was my next-door neighbor and also the elders quorum president in the ward. Thus, Paul Hanks knocked on my door within hours of my return on May 11 and handed me a letter.

I soon discovered that [redacted] was using his passkey to enter my apartment

---

22. See Boyd K. Packer, "The Temple, the Priesthood," *Ensign*, May 1993.

23. David Eugene Sorenson (1933–2014) was called as a general authority in 1992 and became emeritus in 2005. His assignments included presidency of the Seventy, president of the Canada Halifax Mission, and president of the San Diego Temple.

during my absences. He apparently was looking for evidence that could be used against me in a stake disciplinary council (the recent term for church court). I changed the lock on my door and declined to give the manager a key.

He once even asked me with mock innocence: "You don't think I've been entering your apartment, do you?" I felt like punching the self-righteous little fascist every time I saw him and had to force myself to be civil.

I informed stake president Paul Hanks (who was also a senior admin- istrator in the Church Educational System) that I would not attend the disciplinary council to which I had been formally summoned. Nor would I agree to his request that I aid his investigation against me.

I assumed that he was a relative of Marion D. Hanks, but this stake pres- ident certainly had none of my mission president's qualities of compassion or independence from the hierarchy. I hoped he was very distantly related, but eventually learned they were uncle and nephew. I wondered if this gen- eral authority had given his nephew the same negative assessment he gave me in late 1965 of the Church Educational System's corrosive influence on spiritual integrity.

15 May 1993–"Historian Assails LDS Research Barriers"

That was the headline in Ogden, Utah's *Standard-Examiner*. Its subtitle: "Quinn Contends 'Golden Age' of Access to Data By Scholars Has Come and Gone."

18 May 1993–Apostle Warns against Three Dangers

Exactly a week after my stake president's letter, Boyd K. Packer gave a signif- icant talk to the All-Church Coordinating Council. This was an administrative arm of Church Correlation at LDS headquarters since September 1961.[24]

Now, after three pages of introduction, his reading text began the main topic of his speech: "There are three areas where members of the Church, in- fluenced by social and political unrest, are being caught up and led away." He specified: "The dangers I speak of come from the gay-lesbian movement, the feminist movement (both of which are relatively new), and the ever-present challenge from the so-called scholars and intellectuals."

I was in all of them. Three strikes, then "Out!"

The *next day*, at 8:40 AM, I received a hand-delivered ultimatum to meet with stake president Paul Hanks. Again refusing to do so, my answer referred to "your double-bind of obligation to take action against me on behalf of both your ecclesiastical file leaders and your employers."

In my response a week later to another of his letters, I disclosed that I had used a tape recorder to verify the apartment manager's illegal entries into my

---

24. Boyd K. Packer, "All-Church Coordinating Council," May 18, 1993.

apartment. I told my stake president: "I sincerely hope you are never in the situation of being hunted down by those you regard as Prophets, Seers, and Revelators, but who have defined you as expendable. No one is expendable to the Lord."

Concerning his threats against my membership in the LDS Church, I wrote: "Baptism cannot give you a relationship with God, and excommunication cannot take it away. Neither has eternal significance unless sealed by the Holy Spirit of Promise. I can only trust in God's love and in my relationship with Him."

5 June 1993–An Irony of Mormon History

In view of last February's newspaper stories about the accusations of apostasy against me as a historian, the editors of the *Church News* undoubtedly realized they were taking a risk by publishing a photo of me for an article that was celebratory, rather than cautionary.[25] Nonetheless, there I was in its photograph of the 1973 Historical Division of the Historical Department.

Still, the editors could not have realized in advance how deeply ironic their timing was for two reasons. First, the summer issue of *Dialogue* published eighty-seven pages of my unsparingly controversial analysis of the current LDS president, "Ezra Taft Benson and Mormon Political Conflicts."[26] With my typically close attention to details and sources, this article chronicled the controversies that ultra-conservative Mormons had caused the Church since 1961. It reached subscribers and bookstores in late June.

The second irony was what happened in private the day after this photo appeared in the *Church News*.

6 June 1993–Disciplinary Council

I felt emotional turmoil about today's disciplinary council of the Salt Lake Stake, but I experienced the warm comfort of the Spirit which continued with me. By direction of stake president Paul Hanks, the council put me on probation as a member of the LDS Church, then scheduled a second court in July.

9 June 1993–BYU's Purge of Liberal Professors

Fifty professors were summarily fired or were denied tenure (continuing status) which effectively terminated their employment. Among those casualties of academic freedom at BYU were feminist English professor Cecilia Konchar Farr and cultural anthropologist David C. Knowlton.[27]

25. The group photo appeared in an article celebrating Edyth Romney, who volunteered for nearly five decades in the Church History Department. See Julie Dockstader Heaps, "Service Brings Her Greatest Satisfaction," *Church News*, June 5, 1993.

26. See Quinn, "Ezra Taft Benson and Mormon Political Conflicts," *Dialogue: A Journal of Mormon Thought* 26, no. 2 (Summer 1993): 1–87.

27. Cecelia Konchar Farr became an English professor at BYU in 1991, teaching feminist

Although he was now in trouble for publishing about terrorist attacks on LDS missionaries and chapels in Latin America, David had not endeared himself to the powers that be when we shared the podium at the B. H. Roberts Society two years previous. In tandem with my talk that October, this BYU professor had proclaimed: "We intellectuals should furthermore stop looking over our shoulders to see if the Brethren are going to disagree with us, call us to repentance, hassle us, limit our access to information, or challenge us." Like my remarks, his were published in *Sunstone*, whose editor was now Elbert E. Peck.[28]

In protest against these firings, Martha Sonntag Bradley resigned from BYU's Department of History. She had been hired as my tenure-track replacement.

Harold Miller also resigned as Dean of Honors and General Education. He called it "a moral obligation to step away" in view of this purge of liberal professors. Gene England stayed but was eventually forced to resign.[29]

I attended the first on-campus protest organized by undergraduate student Bryan Waterman, with whom I had become acquainted a couple of years earlier.[30] However, I declined the opportunity to speak at this rally on BYU's own turf.

Newspaper photographers and TV news cameras were there, and I thought I was in enough trouble. I didn't want to poke the dragon of LDS leadership while my church membership was already in the balance.

17 June 1993–Unable to Keep My Mouth Shut

Despite my initial caution, I provided quotes to the *Salt Lake Tribune* for today's article "BYU Students Again Rally to Protest Firings of 2 Professors." I also agreed to be interviewed on PBS radio about BYU's suppression of academic freedom. This was for the next day's broadcast of "All Things Considered" on KUER radio (University of Utah). So I wasn't concerned enough about poking the dragon to keep my mouth shut.

I also responded publicly to a member of the John Birch Society who

---

literary theory. Knowlton was hired as an anthropology professor in 1990. In 1993, neither passed their third-year continuing status reviews for reasons BYU officials said were related to scholarship, though both professors' scholarship was equal to or exceeded that of thirty third-year professors who did pass. Evidence suggests the two were fired for positions on church matters that some church leaders considered out of bounds. Bryan Waterman and Brian Kagel, "Under Fire: The Farr and Knowlton Cases," in *The Lord's University: Freedom and Authority at BYU* (Salt Lake City: Signature Books, 1998).

28. Elbert Eugene Peck (1954–) was editor of *Sunstone* magazine from 1986–2001.

29. England was pressured to resign because of his liberal-leaning books, essays, public statements, and activism. See Terryl L. Givens, *Stretching the Heavens: The Life of Eugene England and the Crisis of Modern Mormonism* (Chapel Hill, NC: University of North Carolina Press, 2021).

30. Bryan Waterman became an English professor at New York University and a vice provost for undergraduate academic development at NYU Abu Dhabi. He co-authored *The Lord's University*.

submitted a long criticism of my article about President Benson's controversial years as an apostle. My response in *Dialogue* concluded: "Whole sections of the Benson-Birch article surprised me during my dragnet approach to research. However, I did my best to be fair to all concerned in narrating that experience. Other authors may feel it necessary to identify who they think wore the White-hat and who wore the Black-hat in controversial events. Or at least to inform the reader who the author regards as 'right' and who was 'wrong.'

"Instead, I think it's usually better for historians to leave value judgments to the reader, even though authors may have strong opinions of their own. I've never tried to ignore evidence I disliked or to skew its presentation to force the reader to a pre-determined conclusion. That kind of 'objectivity' was the goal in my biography of the controversial J. Reuben Clark, and I was pleased to learn that both his supporters and detractors felt my book had vindicated their views of Counselor Clark. In twenty years of writing about the Mormon hierarchy, I've felt that I was describing White-hats who were sometimes caught in the dust storms and stampedes of mortal life."[31]

In fact, Steve Benson (editorial cartoonist for the *Arizona Republic* in Phoenix) phoned to congratulate me for my article about his grandfather. Visiting my apartment, he corrected an error I made about the Birch affiliation of his father, and gave me more information about Ezra Taft Benson.[32]

10 July 1993–*Really "Poking the Dragon"*

The devil-may-care side of my personality reached a crescendo when I provided quotes to the *Salt Lake Tribune* for its article "Benson Grandson Claims Church Spins 'Myths' about LDS Leader." Reprints nationally had such sensational titles as "Infirm Mormon Leader's Role Questioned" (*Phoenix Gazette*) and "Mormon President's Ability In Question" (*Chicago Tribune*).[33] If anyone knew about Frank Fox's decade-earlier warning about my death wish, they would have understood this BYU associate's assessment.

---

31. See "'Spy' Reply" and "Quinn Responds," in "Letters to the Editor," *Dialogue: A Journal of Mormon Thought* 26, no. 4 (Winter 1993): ix–xiii.

32. In 1962, Ezra Taft Benson's son Reed became a leader in the John Birch Society, and Benson publicly endorsed the organization. In 1968, the Society sought to nominate Ezra Taft Benson for president. See Matthew L. Harris, ed., *Thunder from the Right: Ezra Taft Benson in Mormonism and Politics* (Urbana: University of Illinois Press, 2019).

33. Quinn provided quotes to Vern Anderson, news editor of the Associated Press's Salt Lake City bureau, and these newspapers picked up the AP story. A portion of one article read, "Mormon researcher D. Michael Quinn, who is writing a history of the church's hierarchy, said he believes the potentially divisive prospect of retiring prophets and apostles is something the leadership will try to avoid. 'The only time they won't be able to finesse it will be if the heir apparent, the surviving senior apostle, is already [mentally incompetent],' Quinn said. 'But I think they're counting that God would never allow that to happen.'" "Mormon President's Ability in Question," *Chicago Tribune*, July 30, 1993.

Mid-July 1993–Confronting LDS Surveillance

Just before the disciplinary council of July 1993, I used some of my counter-intelligence training to confront a surveillance operative. One morning, I noticed that a car seemed to be following me as I drove from my apartment toward the University of Utah.

So I turned into a supermarket's parking lot to see what the other car would do. It also turned into the crowded lot, parked a few aisles from me, but the driver didn't get out. I stood by my car momentarily, as if I hadn't decided whether to enter the store, then got back into my car and drove to another shopping center a few blocks away.

The car confirmed its surveillance by following me into the second parking area. After I parked at the end of this nearly deserted outside lot, the other parked in the middle. The driver stayed in the car, just as I stayed in mine.

After a five-minute wait, I doubled back, flashed my lights at the surveillance-car, came alongside it, and waved at the driver. This woman didn't follow as I drove off. I have no idea whether she was with church security at LDS headquarters or was just a regular Mormon on assignment from my stake president. Either way, it was amateurish surveillance.

The second tribunal disfellowshipped me on July 18 and provided for a third in August. Without explanation, the meeting would not be held that month.

Late July 1993–Being "Cut Off" by Degrees

I dreaded telling Mom about the church punishment I had already received, but didn't want her to learn about it by rumor. Or, worse, from the media.

When I phoned to tell my sixth-generation Mormon mother about the three disciplinary councils, she was remarkably calm. With the good humor in adversity that was typical of her, Mom's response was a variation on the LDS use of the term "cut off" as short for excommunication.

"They're chopping you off by inches, aren't they?" This was comic relief I needed. I laughed but heard only sarcasm at the other end of the line—no laughter.

14 August 1993–Speaking about Baseball Baptisms

At Salt Lake City's Sunstone Symposium, I made my first public comments about the Mormon "Baseball Baptism" era. Within the context of Martin Buber's Jewish Existentialism, I examined this sad chapter as an example of "I-Thou vs. I-It Conversions." This was in the next day's national wire service story by the Associated Press, which the *Salt Lake Tribune* titled "Baseball Baptisms in '60s Left LDS Missionaries Exhausted, Church Financially Broken."[34]

---

34. See Vern Anderson, "Baseball Baptisms in 60s Left LDS Missionaries Exhausted, Church Financially Broken," *Salt Lake Tribune*, Aug. 15, 1993.

Many of today's symposium attenders asked privately if church authorities had taken action against me, and I said that I thought they had decided to leave me alone. That was what I hoped. I didn't want to create another media sensation by telling anyone about the two disciplinary councils that had already convened.

September 1993–The September Six

I soon came to believe that my final judgment was postponed to achieve the maximum effect for a message of intimidation from LDS headquarters. Six scholars and feminists in Utah were summoned to disciplinary councils in September.

The charges were the same in all cases—apostasy and conduct unbecoming a church member, based on our published writings and public talks. Most of us learned from chance remarks by our local leaders that apostle Packer was coordinating this purge (despite official denials to the contrary).

During a private meeting of Steve Benson with apostles Neal A. Maxwell and Dallin H. Oaks, Steve asked why the Twelve's president Howard W. Hunter or the First Presidency didn't restrain apostle Packer. Oaks replied: "You can't stage manage a grizzly bear." This was soon in the newspapers.[35]

However, when even private critics like apostle Oaks publicly denied that this month of disciplinary actions was a purge, LDS headquarters effectively endorsed Boyd K. Packer's repressive warning to independent-minded Mormons: Think what you want but speak and write at your peril.

Although conservative author Avraham Gileadi's controversial interpretation of Isaiah's prophecies had previously been a bestseller at the Church-owned Deseret Book, he was excommunicated for promoting his book.[36] Lynne Knavel Whitesides (liberal president of the feminist Mormon Women's Forum) was disfellowshipped. Lavina Fielding Anderson (liberal editor of *Journal of Mormon History*) was excommunicated, and I had been on its executive board since last year. Maxine Hanks (liberal editor of the feminist anthology *Women and Authority*) was excommunicated, and I was also one of its contributors. Also excommunicated was liberal attorney Paul J. Toscano, who had spoken at the recent Sunstone Symposium about "False Teachings of a True Church."[37]

---

35. For a synopsis of this event and its news coverage, with quotations from Benson, Oaks, and Packer, see Matthew S. Brown, "Elder Oaks Says News Story 'Seriously Distorted Facts,'" *Deseret News*, Oct. 16, 1993.

36. Gileadi's *The Last Days: Types and Shadows from the Bible and the Book of Mormon*, was published in 1991 by Covenant Communications, a division of Deseret Book.

37. For a detailed history of the "September Six" disciplinary actions and the era in which they and other excommunications took place, see Sara M. Patterson, *The September Six and the Struggle for the Soul of Mormonism* (Salt Lake City: Signature Books, 2023).

Beginning with Lynne's disciplinary council (the first of the six), supporters held vigils and sang hymns outside the LDS meetinghouses where each disciplinary council met. I attended Lynne's but not the others. I drove to California as the scheduled keynote speaker in San Diego at the annual conference of Affirmation for Mormon Gays and Lesbians. My last hurrah as an LDS rebel.

Of the hundreds of gay males, bisexuals, and lesbians I met at this conference, most were returned missionaries. Many—both female and male—had children from temple marriages.

I gave the talk ("Same-Sex Dynamics Among 19th-Century Americans") on Sunday, September 19, during which a president of one of San Diego's four stakes was attending. At this Affirmation meeting, he spoke to members of his stake, whom he already knew were homosexual. This stake president explained to them that the area president (a general authority) had asked him to take notes on my talk and report immediately to LDS headquarters in Utah. More of the same.

I remained in California for two weeks to visit my mother and did not attend the disciplinary council that was scheduled for me in Utah. I had previously explained this to my stake president and asked friends in Salt Lake City not to hold a vigil in my absence. I didn't want to participate in any more of the media circus, but answered the questions of reporters who phoned.

While in California, I also got a phone call from the executive secretary of an LDS area presidency, Peter G. Kenner. We had met seven years previous while Kenner was a stake president. In that position, he had refused to excommunicate anyone in his Davis, California, stake. He felt that counseling, not punishment, was the example of Jesus.[38]

This good man was now on the verge of resigning from the area presidency because of the witch hunt by church headquarters. I blurted out, "God, no! Don't do that!" I was embarrassed about using profanity but said that there were already too few leaders who avoided repressive tactics. "If you resign, you'll probably be replaced with someone closer to Boyd K. Packer's philosophy. Please don't do that to the church membership." President Kenner and I talked for nearly an hour about the situation but have not spoken since.

I received written notice that I was excommunicated on 26 September 1993, for my refusal to cooperate with the stake president's inquiry into my alleged apostasy. Bad manners was my conduct unbecoming a member of the church.

I've often made that snide comment to conceal the raw pain of the experience. My excommunication was like a death in the family—except I was

---

38. The obituary of Peter Glen Kenner (1934–2023) stated, "Pete loved God ... and lived a life of service in the church where he touched many in callings, including Priest's Quorum Advisor and Stake President."

looking at myself in the coffin. Is graveyard humor the best way to grieve your own death?

The burning of the Spirit within me made that grief bearable and gave me strength to go on. But the fact remains that the only life I ever wanted to live was dead.

I was puzzled that the notice of excommunication didn't use the word apostasy, which the stake president had repeatedly applied to me since February. Nor did it mention my publications, which had started his inquisition.

September 1993–The Reaction of My Friend, Marion D. Hanks

Already emeritus as a general authority, Marion D. Hanks gave a negative assessment of these disciplinary councils and courts of love. At an LDS meeting in September 1993, he said "the church is eating its own." I had not wanted to drag my former mission president into this controversy by contacting him, but a member of his family phoned to report this statement.

A month later, at a special meeting in the Salt Lake Temple for Institute teachers, President Hanks told them, "I never thought I would live to see the church commit fratricide." One of the attenders repeated this to me.

October 1993–A Death Threat and Further Understanding

Because of the publicity given to my statements, a young man telephoned a death threat in October to a family whose husband was in the phone book as Michael D. Quinn.[39] Somehow, Christ's gospel has not penetrated the mindset of such Nazi Mormons (as I've heard them described by even devout and conservative members of the LDS Church).

In October, I also learned more about this six-hour tribunal from Barnard Silver. He was a regular attender at Sunstone Symposiums, and his wife was then a member of the Relief Society's general board at LDS headquarters.[40]

Leonard Arrington arranged for the lunch meeting where Barnard gave me the following information, which I assume Leonard recorded in his personal journal—either when Barnard first related these things to him in 1993, or when he repeated them to me at this lunch we three had. At this time, I wasn't keeping a journal, but Leonard's is scheduled to become publicly available for research in 2010.[41]

---

39. See Connie Coyne, "Phone Threat Reaches Wrong Man," *Salt Lake Tribune*, Oct. 18, 1993.

40. Cherry Bushman Silver (1935–2023) and Barnard S. Silver were Latter-day Saint scholars and supporters of historical conferences and research in Mormon studies. Cherry was responsible for annotating the Emmeline B. Wells diaries.

41. Silver insists that he never spoke to Quinn about the disciplinary council (Barnard Silver, emails to Barbara Jones Brown, Aug. 9, 2022, and Mar. 2, 2023). Arrington did not mention Silver or a lunch in his diary, only that he had Quinn over for dinner on October 15, 1993. "He did not seem to be upset particularly; he seemed to think it was inevitable," Arrington wrote. "These excommunications are the worst examples of blaming the messenger for the message. What a

In spite of my having asked friends and *Sunstone*'s editor Elbert Peck to spread the word that I wanted no one to appear on my behalf, Barnard showed up at the disciplinary council of the Salt Lake Stake.

LDS headquarters had sent copies of all my publications (with apostate sentences highlighted in yellow) and had also sent tape recordings of talks I had given. This included tapes of my remarks at two firesides of the Mormon fundamentalist Allred group (Apostolic United Brethren), in which I had repeated my presentations to Sunstone Symposiums on early Priesthood development and on plural marriages after the 1890 Manifesto. These latter tape recordings must have been obtained by a church security infiltrator among the Allred Fundamentalists.[42]

Barnard Silver told Leonard and me that after he and individual members of the council spent hours in reading the highlighted portions and listening to the tape recordings, the high council was divided about whether my writings and talks constituted apostasy.[43] Technically, half the stake council is supposed to speak on behalf of the accused and half against the accused during the first part of the deliberations.

By contrast, he said that stake president Paul Hanks was obviously disturbed by the sincere disagreement expressed by the council members about whether my writings constituted apostasy. In exasperation, the stake president blurted out that Elder Packer had been phoning him every week to stress "the importance of taking action against Michael Quinn." Paul Hanks told the high council that it was imperative that they "sustain the Brethren." At this point, he asked Barnard to leave the room, and the disciplinary council began its final deliberations.

The letter to me about their decision showed that the council still did *not* sustain the charge of apostasy against me. In this regard, I praise the integrity of those high councilmen who resisted the intimidating counsel by stake president Hanks and apostle Packer. On the other hand, the stake president

perversion of apostasy, to regard as apostates individuals who are as loyal and believing as Mike." In his October 22 entry, Arrington added, "We can't see the justice of excommunicating someone who writes honest, sincere, history." Arrington again expressed concern that he, too, would be excommunicated. Bergera, ed., *Confessions of a Mormon Historian: The Diaries of Leonard J. Arrington, 1971–1997*, 3 vols. (Salt Lake City: Signature Books, 2018), 3:618–19.

42. Led by Rulon Allred (1906–77), the AUB split off from the Fundamentalist Latter-day Saints (FLDS) in the early 1950s. The polygamous sect is headquartered in Utah. Janet Bennion, "Apostolic United Brethren," World Religions and Spirituality Project, May 27, 2019.

43. Though Quinn attributed this version of events during his disciplinary council to Barnard Silver, Silver said he was not present for the full council. "Near the beginning of the disciplinary council session," Silver "spoke in behalf of Michael Quinn, answered questions, and left." He was not present for any "following discussions in the proceedings of the council." (Barnard Silver, email to Barbara Jones Brown, Mar. 2, 2023.) Arrington's diary contains no mention of the details of the council meeting or any mention of Silver. Silver maintained he never met with Arrington or Quinn after the council.

was obviously able to get a unanimous vote to excommunicate me for insubordination, due to my refusal to meet with him and furnish evidence against myself. According to the letter, that refusal was the conduct unbecoming for which I was excommunicated.

All along, I told the stake president that I knew he was under orders from his ecclesiastical file leaders, who were also his employers. Perhaps I'm cynical, but I'm sure that my stake president's employment in the Church Educational System made those weekly phone calls from President Packer a form of job threat.

Yet I don't want to portray Paul A. Hanks as the reluctant and impartial participant he pretended to be in his conversations and correspondence with me and in his statements to others.

Even by their own official standards, these so-called inquiries and disciplinary councils of love in 1993 were corrupt from start to finish.

Still, when a newspaper reporter asked about my excommunication, I replied that I still believe in the essentials of Mormon faith and am "a DNA Mormon." If I can judge my own feelings, I was not bitter then or since, even though I feel that LDS headquarters is wrong to force conformity and to use intimidation.

In response, some may ask: "How can you claim not to be bitter? You're obviously angry about what happened, and you condemn those who ordered these actions and those who carried out the orders." For me, this is as much a reality as in the experience of Japanese American citizens since 1942. Most of them avoided bitterness yet felt anger and condemnation for the US government's leaders who put them in barbed wire prisons during World War II.

Mormons talk about "loving the sinner, and hating the sin," yet don't realize that LDS leaders sometimes sin against their holy callings. When that happens, Mormons should both love the sinning leaders and condemn their sin of abusing church office.

October 1993–Supportive Ex-Wife and Dreams about an Antagonist

Disgusted by last month's excommunications, Jan asked to have her name removed from membership in the LDS Church. Neither her then-bishop, nor his successors, did so. She just shrugs.

On the other hand, I had a dream this month which gave me some comfort about my spiritual state here and in the hereafter. In the dream, I met Elder Packer in the afterlife, and we embraced in the fellowship of the gospel. I was encouraged that whatever ill-will I have felt toward him (or that he has apparently felt toward me) is a temporary thing. Earthly hostility shall be followed by eternal reconciliation. That's my hope.

CHAPTER 20

CHOSEN PATH

1993–2009

June 1998–A Separate Peace

From the meditation I wrote this month: "It has been exactly ten years since I commenced this self-biography, which presents many experiences and feelings I had compartmentalized or suppressed. Although I hope to live productively and with reasonable happiness for many more years, it's time for a summation concerning my chosen path.

"Homosexuality was not the charge for which I was excommunicated, but I've often said that being a homosexual in Utah is like being a Jew in the early stages of Nazi Germany. It's almost as bad for Mormon intellectuals, for historians who reveal uncomfortable truths, for women who aren't satisfied with the back of the Church bus, and for anyone else who doesn't fit the Mormon mold as currently fashioned by LDS headquarters.

"For me, it's gut-wrenching to know that otherwise good people hate me. I see this Mormon malice from both females and males (young, middle-aged, and old) in letters to the editor in Utah newspapers, in call-ins to radio talk shows, in postings on the Internet, in hate-stares I've sometimes encountered in Salt Lake City movie theatres and grocery stores, on BYU's campus since 1993, in publications by BYU religion professors, and in polemical 'reviews' by BYU-affiliated FARMS.

"It may give these Latter-day Saints satisfaction to know that after I read or listen to these hateful expressions about me personally or about my writings, it's a struggle for me to get through the day. Since 1993, I've had recurring nightmares of someone breaking into my apartment and beating me to death with a baseball bat.

"The hugs and kind words I continue to receive from those at Sunstone Symposiums don't compensate for this. Even the remarkable charity of the LDS Historical Department didn't assuage my inner grief about Mormon culture in 1997, when its staff re-granted me access to do research in LDS Church Archives. This was their immediate decision upon my spur-of-the-moment inquiry.

"Still, I don't think anything could compensate for the malice that other

Mormons have manifested toward me. These people are my people. Their God is my God.

"I regard the situation of the LDS Church as even worse. Every sanction, punishment, and intimidation that the repressive LDS leadership can impose, it does impose against those who don't conform. It is no cause for celebration that LDS leaders are legally prohibited from doing anything more to suppress dissent and diversity. When a culture has externally imposed limits to its repressiveness, that is also no basis for denying comparison to totalitarian regimes. I say this with sadness, not bitterness.

"Church headquarters has fulfilled its determination to make me into an ex-member, so the LDS Church and its problems are no longer my problem. While I've always admired social activists and reformers, I don't have the courage or stamina to be one. I earnestly believe that the LDS Church has adopted spiritually destructive policies, that it encourages self-righteousness and group-think paranoia, that it uses anti-Christian intimidation, that it is coercive for anyone who varies from the homogenized norm, and that its leaders are indifferent to 'the least of these' whom Jesus wants them to comfort and embrace (Matthew 25: 40, 45). However, it's no longer my church, and change must come from within LDS leadership itself.

"Sign-waving and letter-writing campaigns are counterproductive for those who are trained to feel no self-doubt about church policies. I've read through First Presidency files up to the 1960s and have seen such correspondence in folders labeled: 'Crank letters,' sometimes with the name of the sender as a subtitle on the label.

"In addition, Ezra Taft Benson established the Strengthening the Members Committee shortly after he became Church president in 1985.[1] This surveillance oversight committee now maintains copies of talks at 'independent' gatherings (Counter-point Women's Conference, Mormon Alliance Against Ecclesiastical Abuse, Mormon History Association, Mormon Women's Forum, Sunstone Symposiums, Western History Association), of articles in independent Mormon publications and non-LDS professional journals, of letters to the editor in Utah newspapers (including student newspapers), of all letters of protest sent to LDS authorities, and even of mild-mannered suggestions from church members for changes in policy or procedures.

"As it did with 'The September Six,' this committee at LDS headquarters continues to prepare excerpts from its surveillance files on LDS Church

1. A 1992 Associated Press article confirms that "a committee of high Mormon Church officials monitors the statements and writings of members who criticize the church and turns the material over to local ecclesiastical leaders." Vern Anderson, "LDS Official Acknowledges Church Monitors Critics," *Salt Lake Tribune*, Aug. 8, 1992. The article does not mention the date the committee began.

members and sends these materials to local leaders, with the recommenda-tion to 'take appropriate action, as you see fit.'[2] After doing so, local leaders continue to 'lie for the Lord' by claiming it was their idea.

"Dramatic reversals in LDS Church policy have occurred only when a Living Prophet felt discomfort with the *status quo* and made changes after struggling with the Lord. Yet a siege mentality at LDS headquarters makes it very unlikely that the church will reverse policies that either ignore or harm the least regarded of Heavenly Father's children.

"Because LDS leaders are overwhelmed by the phenomenal growth of the church, they have little incentive to look behind the statistics for the decay that can't be blamed on the regular membership. There is no light at the end of that tunnel. It's more like a mine shaft.

"I continue to pray, struggle with God, and feel the power of his Spirit within me. But my Mormon struggle is over, and I feel a profound (and un-expected) relief that it's over.

"The LDS Church is the responsibility of its leaders. Where LDS policies hurt people, I feel the kind of detached compassion I feel for similar situa-tions in other churches and religions. No more, no less.

"President Benson died in 1994 after several years of being *non compos mentis*,[3] a fact that his grandson Steve Benson announced publicly. Frail Howard W. Hunter died in June 1995, after only nine months as LDS pres-ident. Gordon B. Hinckley is now the very robust prophet of Mormonism.

"Prophets aren't infallible, but they remain Heavenly Father's leaders on earth. That is my faith.

"Just as it's my faith that God sanctions all loving relationships—monog-amous, polygamous, heterosexual, homosexual. Had I accepted that truth when I received my patriarchal blessing at age fourteen, my life would have been very different."

September 1993 through 1998–A Five-Year Summary

During the five years since my excommunication, my experiences have caused enough reflection to nearly equal this already too-long self-biography. So I'll be relatively brief about things that I won't take space here to expand upon.

Obscured by 1993's sensational media coverage of my role as a historian, the University of Chicago published my essay "Plural Marriage and Mor-mon Fundamentalism" in one of its volumes about religious fundamentalism

---

2. In his journal entry of February 6, 1992, Leonard Arrington wrote that he believed the Strengthening Church Members Committee "to be the result of the employment of several for-mer FBI executives who were trained in this sort of thing. ... That the files contain only negative information, and in some cases unsubstantiated information, is especially regrettable." Bergera, ed., *Confessions of a Mormon Historian*, (Salt Lake City: Signature Books, 2018), 3:604.

3. Latin for "not sound of mind."

worldwide.[4] The university's religion expert Martin E. Marty had invited my participation in the project four years earlier. With none of the parochial argumentation I had used in my anonymous response to polygamist Fundamentalists in 1972, this essay provided historical descriptions for various manifestations of Mormon-based polygamy as they existed in the 1990s.[5] This included an extensive discussion of their family dynamics, based on my interviews with polygamist husbands, plural wives, and teenage children of such marriages. Although this essay of mine was the longest in this volume of essays, it was about 1/4 shorter than what I originally wrote. *Dialogue* would publish the complete article in 1998.[6]

After 1993, I no longer had support from various foundations (principally George D. Smith's Research Associates) to pay for my living expenses. Thus, I have used credit card loans to survive while working full time to finish my research/writing on the LDS hierarchy and other Mormon topics.

In April 1994, by instructions of headquarters, LDS leaders in Boston excommunicated David Wright, the previously fired BYU professor who was now teaching Hebrew at Brandeis University. His offense was publishing articles which applied Biblical textual criticism to the Book of Mormon. I didn't publicize what I thought of this.

During the summer, at the suggestion of longtime friend, Carol Lynn Pearson, I contacted Bruce Bastian, millionaire co-founder of the software company WordPerfect.[7] Also a divorced, gay father, he provided a thousand dollars of my monthly support for one year. In addition, he paid $30,000 of the costs for my producing, advertising, and distributing a very long questionnaire about familial, religious, social, and sexual experience.

In mid-September 1994, I attended the commitment ceremony for two lesbians during the annual conference of Affirmation in Las Vegas. Both in their thirties, they had first met in the celestial room of the temple in Washington, DC—after participating in an endowment session with their husbands. I provided text for part of the vows these divorced women exchanged.

Paul Murphy was directing a film crew in recording this same-sex ceremony for ABC Television's Salt Lake City affiliate, KTVX News, and I

4. See Martin E. Marty and R. Scott Appleby, eds., *Fundamentalisms and Society: Reclaiming the Sciences, the Family, and Education* (Chicago: University of Chicago Press, 1997).

5. See Chapter 12 of this memoir for Quinn's description of this letter.

6. See Quinn, "Plural Marriage and Mormon Fundamentalism," *Dialogue: A Journal of Mormon Thought* 31, no. 2 (Summer 1998): 1–68.

7. Bruce R. Bastian (1948–) co-founded software giant WordPerfect in 1978. He is a philanthropist whose foundation requires that applicants for funding state "their commitment of equality for all Americans, including the gay and lesbian community in their application" (bastianfoundation.org).

Quinn at book signing for *The Mormon Hierarchy: Origins of Power*, 1994.
Signature Books archives.

noticed that he told the cameraman not to film me as one of its attenders.[8]
Apparently thinking of the death threat against me the previous year, Paul
explained afterwards: "We in the Utah media are more protective of you than
you are of yourself." I had to laugh.

In January 1995, my father died in his sleep. Like Grampa Workman, Dad
passed away a month before his eighty-third birthday. During the previous
six months, we had gotten as close as I think it was possible for him while I
visited Dad weekly in his room at my sister Tricia's home in Provo.

I still wear an Izod Lacoste jacket that he had spontaneously handed me
ten years earlier. Tricia thinks it's the jacket he used to wear. Perhaps, but it
seemed like new when he gave it to me in 1985. Either way, it's nice to think
of Dad fondly when I put it on.

On 26 February 1995, the *Deseret News* described me as a "renegade
historian." It seemed to be citing Davis Bitton, my former mentor, for that
assessment.[9]

I was therefore surprised on May 9, when the *Deseret News* published my
two-page essay, "Paranoia Can't Destroy Need for Federal Government" in

8. Paul Murphy was a reporter for KTVX-TV News (later known as ABC4), the Salt Lake
City affiliate of ABC, from 1990 to 2001.

9. Reporter Jerry Johnston's article reads, "When asked about the work of renegade historian
D. Michael Quinn, Bitton gave the writer high marks for pinning down dates and times, but low
marks for giving so much credence to the observations of frontier people with an ax to grind." See
"Works on Mormon History Aim for Passion," *Deseret News,* Feb. 26, 1995.

its "Citizens" section.[10] This was my response to Timothy McVeigh's terrorist bombing in Oklahoma City, an act which fulfilled my decades-long fear of right-wing conservatives and radical Evangelicals.

Also in May 1995, LDS authorities in Provo ("on their own initiative") excommunicated feminist Janice Merrill Allred for speaking and writing about Mother in Heaven. Likewise for her sister Margaret Merrill Toscano in the Salt Lake Valley in 2000.[11] Ecclesiastical terrorism.

In October 1995, my stepfather Vaude Nye died in an Alzheimer's clinic at age 80. Mom had long since given up her bitterness toward him, and resumed the sisterly feelings from when he was a brother-in-law. Now, for the first time in her life, she had opportunity to live for herself and her needs.

On a brighter side of October 1995, I met a totally unexpected benefactor during Professor Alex Caldiero's 40th anniversary reading of *Howl* by gay poet Allen Ginsberg. A stranger named Milo Calder walked up to me in Salt Lake City's Left Bank Gallery to tell me how much he appreciated my work. Then he handed me a check for $2,000![12]

Some of the greatest thrills of my professional life occurred at the Chicago Humanities Festival in mid-November 1995. First, throughout one luncheon, I chatted with feminist author and activist Betty Friedan. Her 1963 book, *The Feminine Mystique*, had launched the Second Wave of the American women's movement. Next, in one of the sessions of that conference, scholars took turns reading all parts of Plato's *Symposium* about male-male love. By comparison, the paper I delivered to a session was insignificant.

At the end of November 1995, I was one of two finalists for a full professorship in American history at the Claremont Graduate University. While staying in a hotel that weekend, I read the recently published biography *Boyd K. Packer: A Watchman on the Tower*.[13] Tears streamed down my face as I learned of his childhood as a scrawny, undersized kid who was bullied by his brothers at home and beaten up by classmates at school.

Boys who experience such abuse usually go in one of two directions as adults. They become abusive bullies, or they become very compassionate toward anyone's suffering of any kind. Boyd K. Packer became a spiritual bully

10. Quinn, "Paranoia Can't Destroy Need for Federal Government," *Deseret News*, May 9 and 10, 1995.

11. Janice Merrill Allred (1947–) is a feminist writer. In 1997, she published *God The Mother and Other Theological Essays* with Signature Books. Allred was excommunicated for her theological writings about Heavenly Mother and for her work challenging the idea that the church president could not lead the church astray.

12. Milo "Mike" Calder is president of Calder Brothers Corporation, which produces paving equipment.

13. See Lucile C. Tate, *Boyd K. Packer: A Watchman on the Tower* (Salt Lake City: Bookcraft, 1995).

as an LDS general authority, and has remained indifferent about the suffering he causes. He certainly does not perceive his behavior as ecclesiastical abuse.

While the University of Utah's Provost historian Jim Clayton was still my friend, he took me to lunch at Salt Lake City's Market Street Broiler in the mid-1990s and repeated what Utah's industrialist Jon M. Huntsman Sr. had recently confided to him. In their own private conversation, Apostle Packer asked the billionaire son-in-law of apostle David B. Haight: "Why do people hate me?" In repeating that to Clayton, Huntsman said that he obviously didn't want to list the reasons he could think of, so Huntsman diplomatically answered: "It's probably because you are so emphatic and forthright in your preaching." Elder Packer seemed to like that answer. Huntsman soon became an "area seventy" and member of the Fifth Quorum of the Seventy.

Elder Packer's personal tragedy has become an institutional tragedy for Mormons who don't fulfill his expectations—in the hierarchy or in the rank and file.

I told Lavina Fielding Anderson: "I can see the tragedy and wounding that produced him, but I really can't talk about him without feeling anger, and that's no compliment to me."

As for the professorship of American history at Claremont Graduate University, the chair of its search committee, Robert Dawidoff, told me in December 1995 that I lost the position by one vote on the committee. Ironically, Fawn M. Brodie's daughter-in-law got the position.[14]

In February 1996, my son Adam committed suicide at age twenty-one, after a lifetime of struggling to get along with everyone else, including his family, friends, classmates, teachers, and employers.

Aside from Adam's precocious ability at chess and high intelligence, he got mainly C's and D's in public schools. Diagnosed with a non-hyperactive form of Attention Deficit Disorder (ADD) when he was 10 (and flunking fifth grade), he refused to take Ritalin—known then as the only remedy.

Following this, Adam was so angry at being singled out for individual counseling, that he refused to say one word to the therapist during his first weeks of appointments. But he cooperated during weekly group therapy with other kids.

After he dropped out of school at sixteen, he was alone most of the three years he hitchhiked back and forth across America. Even other rebellious

14. Janet Ferrell Brodie (1947–) is emeritus professor of history at Claremont Graduate University. Her book *Contraception and Abortion in Nineteenth Century America* (Cornell University Press, 1994) received much praise for its research of contraception and abortion information and practices in the nineteenth century. Fawn McKay Brodie (1915–81), a niece of LDS Church President David O. McKay, wrote a groundbreaking biography of Joseph Smith, *No Man Knows My History* (Knopf, 1945), for which she was excommunicated in May 1946. Fawn Brodie went on to become one of the first woman professors of history at UCLA.

roadies thought he was odd and difficult to be around. It was painful to hear Adam disclose this during a visit with me in New Orleans.

On the other hand, he let his family know he loved us by not missing Christmas with Jan, me, Mary, Lisa, and Paul Moshe during those years on the road. After Jan moved back to Salt Lake from Montana, Adam also returned. He then interacted with us and normal society for two years.

After passing the GED test on his first try, he made the Dean's List at Salt Lake Community College every semester. Then he was fired from one job after another. After six months of not being able to comprehend why bosses wouldn't let him work as *he* wanted to, Adam finally gave up.

On the morning of February 26, he had a thick extension cord in his backpack as he walked from Jan's house on Third Avenue toward downtown Salt Lake. Then he disappeared from our lives. According to a neighbor who saw him leave that icy morning, Adam was smiling and whistling a tune. In April, a hiker found his body hanging from a tree in melting snow near the top of City Creek Canyon.

I expected the local media to mention this family tragedy of a controversial historian. I understood that it could seem newsworthy. Notwithstanding my wish to be spared the media's attention, I didn't make any requests of the dozen or so reporters I knew.

If (as a historian) I wouldn't accept the pleas of various Mormons to let their dead relatives rest in peace, what right did I have to ask the same of current news reporters? Still, no one ran the story. I thought it would be insulting to thank these journalists for this restraint, so never expressed my gratitude until now.

After local newspapers published Adam Darley Quinn's obituary (written by his college English-major brother, Moshe), my former bishop and sometime critic, Richard L. Anderson, wrote me a heartfelt letter of condolence.[15] It was the most Christian act anyone at BYU did that year.

My reporter friends Peggy Fletcher Stack and Vern Anderson came to the April 1996 memorial service to give Jan and me a hug. Greeting me tearfully, Sunstone friend Kent Frogley said: "Mike, I'm so sorry about your son. I don't know what to say." I told him that was exactly the right thing to say. I didn't want to hear platitudes.

I had never been able to understand why my son seemed to see the world so differently from everyone else—everyone normal. Or why he couldn't adapt. Then I saw a documentary that seemed to provide the answer.

It explained that "high-functioning autism" (HFA) has subtle symptoms that characterize only five to ten percent of persons with autistic brains. This documentary interviewed several of these "verbal autistics," one of whom

---

15. See Adam Quinn obituary, *Deseret News,* Apr. 10, 1996.

Extended Quinn family, Christmas morning, 1995. Back row, left to right: Mary's husband, Daryl Babcock; Jan; Lisa's then-husband, JJ Harrison; Mike. Front row, left to right: Moshe, Mary, Lisa, Adam. *Courtesy Quinn family.*

said, "I am like an anthropologist from Mars, observing the earth's humans. I can mimic their behavior and customs, but I will never see the world as they do. And will never really be one of them."

This seemed remarkably like Adam, except that he gave up trying to mimic all the normal people with whom he had been in conflict. Whether his problem was HFA or Asperger's Syndrome, Adam was an extreme version of me.

During the balance of 1996, I tried to cope with my grief, as well as endure the pressures against me due to the publication of my book about the same-sex dynamics and relationships among Mormons born in the nineteenth century.[16]

First, objecting to some of its text and source notes, prominent authors living outside Utah tried to stop its publication by threatening lawsuits against the University of Illinois Press and against the University itself. Second, non-academic Mormons in Utah threatened to sue because of a photograph in the book.

Dr. Vern L. Bullough had published many books and articles about sexual behavior with his wife Bonnie as coauthor,[17] and they were outraged that the

---

16. See Quinn, *Same-Sex Dynamics Among Nineteenth-Century Americans: A Mormon Example* (Urbana: University of Illinois Press, 1996).

17. Born in Salt Lake City, Vern L. Bullough (1928–2006) was a history professor at California State University–Northridge and the State University of New York at Buffalo. He wrote prolifically about history and sexology. Born in Delta, Utah, Bonnie Uckerman Bullough

review copy I had sent them referred to her mother's lesbian lover Mildred Berryman as a "former Mormon."[18] Vern wrote letters to the director of the University of Illinois Press and to the university's president that he would file a lawsuit if they published "that libel." When I told Bonnie over the phone that LDS Church records showed that Mildred received a patriarchal blessing in 1921 and listed her as a baptized member in 1930, Bonnie claimed (delusionally) that "the Mormons forged those records to ruin Mildred's reputation as an atheist." I refused to change my assessment but offered to state their emphatic dissent in the published book, and the Bulloughs reluctantly agreed to not to file a lawsuit. I didn't tell now-atheist Vern that I had also researched his background and found that he served an LDS mission for two years during his twenties. No need to poke that dragon.

Another threat of a lawsuit against the University of Illinois Press in 1996 involved a photograph in the book. Copied from a devotional biography of Evan Stephens, the photo showed the Mormon Tabernacle Choir's conductor with one of the teen-to-twenties boy chums he had slept with from the 1880s through the 1920s. At my request, the Utah State Historical Society had cropped a woman from that previously published photo in its collections before labeling this cropped photo as copyrighted by the USHS. The original book's author threatened to sue, and the University of Illinois attorneys required its Press to remove the photo.

Throughout the summer of 1996, I had to confront the homophobic malice by Mormons outraged at the publication of *Same-Sex Dynamics among Nineteenth-Century Americans: A Mormon Example*. This was so extreme, that they wrote and phoned death threats to the editor publishers of Logan's *Herald-Journal* and Ogden's *Standard-Examiner* for publishing an Associated Press story about my book. I learned about those threats from reporters working for both newspapers.

In the process, I discovered that many so-called liberal Mormons (including most of my friends and historical associates of the past decades) are equally homophobic, but too politically correct to openly express their dislike

(1927–1996) helped develop the first nurse practitioner program in California (at UCLA), in the late 1960s. An accomplished sexologist, author, and professor, she edited or wrote thirty books and more than 100 published articles.

18. Quinn's and other research confirms that Mildred Berryman (1901–72), joined the LDS Church at nineteen and received an LDS patriarchal blessing at twenty-one. She eventually had a relationship with a Mormon woman, Bonnie Uckerman Bullough's mother, Ruth Uckerman Dempsey, for more than three decades. Berryman left Mormonism to join the Bountiful Community Church. In the late 1920s Berryman began writing her thesis *The Psychological Phenomena of the Homosexual* on twenty-three lesbian women and nine gay men in Utah. Her research, called the first lesbian community study in the United States, was groundbreaking. She argued that homosexuality was inborn, benign, and observable among animal species.

for The Other sexuality. From 1994–97, I published three major books, all of which were ignored by the Mormon History Association.[19]

On 22 August 1997, I delivered the keynote talk, "Confronting Four Kinds of Homophobia," to the annual meeting of Affirmation for Gay and Lesbian Mormons. The next day, I gave its attenders a walking tour of downtown Salt Lake City. Titled "Same-Sex City's Tour Du Jour," its twenty-seven stops emphasized locations that were significant for the Utah-Mormon history of homosexuality. For several hours, our group was tailed on the public sidewalks by two beefy men in dark suits, white shirts, and dark ties. Apparently from LDS Church Security, they stayed about ten feet away from us, and gave me a sour look when I invited them to walk *with* us—instead of *after* us.

In late 1997, I used the proceeds from my father's estate to pay off $50,000 of the credit card loans I had used for my living expenses as a freelance writer. I divided the remaining $15,000 of my inheritance among my three surviving children. I told them that their Grandpa Quinn would want this, even though he didn't actually specify it in his living trust. I wanted them to feel that he had remembered them as much as the other grandchildren Dad's living trust had specified would receive $5,000 each.

This left me with 15K of credit card debt, which seemed livable. It inevitably grew as I used loans from Visa and MasterCard to pay for my living expenses.

In its January 1998 annual meeting, the American Historical Association gave me a best book award for *Same-Sex Dynamics among Nineteenth-Century Americans*. Despite the *Salt Lake Tribune*'s report of this honor from our nation's oldest and largest organization for historians, very few of my heterosexual, liberal friends have mentioned the award to me. The only ones who congratulated me were Associated Press reporter Vern Anderson, my steadfast mentor Leonard Arrington, my friend and fellow-excommunicant Lavina Fielding Anderson, Robert S. Jordan (an Oxford-trained LDS professor in New Orleans and father of a lesbian friend of mine), and my former student John Quist (a professor in Pennsylvania).

However, I soon had the most jaw-dropping experience of emotional support from an unexpected source. For over ten years, I had regarded [redacted][20] as my antagonist about homosexuality. ...

Thus I had no anticipation for what he said to me out of the blue in February 1998 while we had lunch (by his invitation) in the Greek Souvlaki cafe near downtown Salt Lake City. "As one who has struggled with same-gender

---

19. These books were *Same-Sex Dynamics*, *Mormon Hierarchy: Origins of Power* (Signature Books, 1994), and *Mormon Hierarchy: Extensions of Power* (Signature Books, 1997).

20. Publisher's note: The man about whom Quinn writes in this vignette chose to never publicly reveal his homosexuality. Though this individual has died, Signature has honored the request of his wife to preserve her anonymity.

attraction for decades," [he] began (without lowering his voice), "I want to thank you for what you've written and said publicly about it."

For the moments I was in speechless shock, [redacted] said nothing while maintaining his unwavering eye contact. He seemed unconcerned about the customers sitting nearby who might have overheard and who might have recognized him as a ward bishop. ...

He had carefully avoided the words "gay" and "sexual." Instead, [he] used the phrase advocated by LDS Social Services, by reparative therapy counselors (who have been repudiated by the American Psychological Association), and by Evergreen International, the only support group whose annual conferences are addressed by LDS general authorities.

However, with clear-eyed bravery, he announced his homosexual orientation to me with none of the blubbering that had accompanied my own disclosure to a sexually active Mormon gay. My mind was reeling with thoughts of his wife, of their struggle, of what I had resented as his apparent homophobia, of his pain, and of the goodness of his soul.

When I finally spoke, my eyes brimmed with tears as I whispered to him: "I'm so sorry, [redacted]. I honestly never guessed." He nodded silently and smiled.

After thanking him for saying those incredibly supportive words, ... I don't recall that either of us said another word at this time about the painfully forbidden topic. [He] represented everything I love about liberal Mormonism—its compassion, its inclusiveness, its liberality, its honesty, its devotion, its humility, its bravery, its endurance.

Then in March 1998, Leonard Arrington made an extraordinary statement to me. When he and his wife Harriet took me to an Italian restaurant for my fifty-fourth birthday, he told me that the University of Illinois Press would soon distribute his narrative about the years he was official Church Historian. Leonard said that he expected to be excommunicated for publishing his memoirs about the History Division's conflicts with Boyd K. Packer and other apostles. He said he was ready for that outcome.

However, when I read Leonard's *Adventures of a Church Historian*, I was impressed by its restraint in discussing his problems with members of the Mormon hierarchy. Typical of his personality, he pulled his punches and was very, *very* kind. This made his expectation that he would be excommunicated for it even more significant. And sad.

On 9 May 1998, I was the keynote speaker at the annual banquet of Utah's branch of the American Civil Liberties Union. In "The Tyranny of the Majority and Religious Motivation for Denying Civil Rights," I compared the denial of civil rights to racial/ethnic minorities with the denial of civil rights to gays and lesbians. The ACLU audience gave me a standing ovation.

In mid-May 1998, I traveled to Washington, DC at the invitation of the National Endowment for the Humanities. I served on a panel of scholars who evaluated applications for the year-long NEH fellowships.

June 1998–Starting to Disengage from Mormon History?

From the meditation I completed this month: "Now I'm finishing some revisions of previously published works, including a double-sized expansion of *Early Mormonism and the Magic World View*.[21] Following its completion, I plan to move to Southern Mexico. After publishing four big books from December 1994 to the end of 1998, I'll definitely need a long vacation. My gay friend Alfred Bush has given me the opportunity to unwind by letting me house-sit his hacienda in the mountain town of San Cristobal de las Casas in the State of Chiapas. I don't expect to return to Utah during the upcoming years in Mexico, except to spend Christmas and other vacations with my children.

"Due to general disregard by the LDS liberal establishment and Mormon historical community toward my work throughout the past several years, I've now abandoned all plans to do two books on Mormon polygamy. I'm going to transfer all my research files to Yale University, where people can use my decades of research to churn out books that the Mormon community might actually read and appreciate—when not written by D. Michael Quinn, the Anti-Christ and excommunicated queer.

"I am without a male lover or significant companion and will probably remain alone the rest of my life. Despite my sexual and emotional needs, isolation is what I seem to want. It's certainly what I've had. Nana would be pleased.

"However, in spite of her own prudishness, Mom was not happy about my being alone. She wrote that she didn't want me to live the rest of my life in isolation and hoped that I would 'one day ride into the sunset' with a male partner. I cried while reading her letter.

"Someone recently asked what I expect from the 'Final Judgment.' I am confident that I will stand as close to our Heavenly Father or as distant from Him as we both feel comfortable. That is the Judgment. This was the doctrine of early Mormonism, but modern Mormons seem to prefer the fundamentalist Protestant version of blissful Heaven versus weeping-and-gnashing-of-teeth Hell.

"Many so-called Christians also feel that homosexuals are automatically deprived of Heavenly Father's Spirit and His presence. These people do not understand God, the Spirit, or the New Testament.

"Jesus taught that the Spirit comes and goes as it chooses once a person

---

21. Quinn worked on and off for a decade on his second edition of *Early Mormonism*. He included new research, expanded several arguments, and responded to critics in a lengthy introduction and in several footnotes. Signature Books published it in December 1998.

receives it (John 3:8). After I was 'born of the Spirit' long ago, the Spirit has continued to fill me with its comfort and burning presence, even as an excommunicated Mormon.

"As far as the Final Judgment and other metaphysical things go, like the Apostle Paul, I 'see through a glass darkly' (I Corinthians 13: 12). And I see enough to understand that Jesus never mentioned homosexual behavior in His various condemnations and criticisms of mankind's behavior. In that regard, I cherish his parable of the Great Banquet (Luke 14:12–13), as well as God's words after Peter's vision of 'the great net' (Acts 10:9–16).

"I expect that in the Celestial Kingdom (Heaven) there will be polygamous families, monogamist couples who chose never to live the Law of Plural Marriage, single people who prefer to remain alone, and also same-sex couples who have loved in life, death, and eternity. As First Presidency counselor J. Reuben Clark used to say: 'I fear that some of us are going to be greatly surprised to see in the Celestial Kingdom a number of people that we would have assigned to a far lesser Kingdom' (Quinn, *Elder Statesman*, 188).

"I was excommunicated from the LDS Church exactly six months before I turned 50, the age at which I once thought I would be an apostle. I have to smile about that now. Notwithstanding all my efforts, I haven't been very successful as a Mormon, as a husband, or as a middle-aged seeker of homosexual companionship.

"I've been a successful historian, yet that doesn't compensate for the personal losses. But it's the life I chose to live in the circumstances I found myself.

"I'm grateful for the sunshine that fell across my path. My main regret is that I didn't do more with it." Unlike Edith Piaf, I have never been able to sing: "Non Je Ne Regrette Rien."[22]

1999-2008–Lowlights and Highlights

Leonard Arrington died on 11 February 1999. By coincidence, that was the day I shipped my decades of research notes to Yale's Beinecke Library.

On February 15 I spoke at his memorial service. Afterwards, former friend Gordon Madsen refused to acknowledge my existence. As I was chatting with his wife, historian Carol Cornwall Madsen, Gordon came up and spoke briefly to her without looking in my direction.[23] Despite his abrupt

---

22. Released in 1960, "No, I Don't Regret Anything" was among French chanteuse Edith Piaf's most popular songs.

23. Carol Cornwall Madsen (1930–) worked for the LDS Church History Department in the 1970s, specializing in women's history. She was subsequently a research historian at BYU, taught history there, and was associate director of the BYU Women's Research Institute. She was president of the Mormon History Association, 1989–1990, and has published more than fifty articles and books.

interruption, he walked away without saying a word to me, or even glancing toward me. His brush-off required determined concentration.

Obviously ill at ease, Carol tried to continue our conversation as though nothing had happened. And I tried not to show sadness, although it was a time of multiple losses.

I didn't feel anger toward him then or afterwards. I had become a pariah to Gordon and to many others who had once been my friends, colleagues, and fellow Saints.

Eleven days later, I moved to Mexico to live in a town atop rain forests in the revolt-riven State of Chiapas. Last year, I had thought I might remain there indefinitely as the guest of Alfred Bush, but in January he informed me that unexpected financial changes required him to rent the hacienda to someone else beginning this August.

The morning of my departure from Utah was exactly a month before my fifty-fifth birthday. Age 54 was when Leonard received his appointment as LDS Church Historian. His goal for me, which would never be. A somber couplet.

Tired of the struggle, I sounded like I was abandoning LDS history during my interview with Paul Swenson for the *Salt Lake Observer* on the night before my flight. He titled his two-page article: "Mormon History's 'Bad Boy' Leaves the Field: Mike Quinn, Believer & Troublemaker, Poked the Dragon."

On this 1999 trip to the nation of my Latino ancestors, I began a daily journal for the first time in nearly twenty years. It ended up being a book-length manuscript, half the size of this self-biography. "Journal/Journey of a Gringo Chicano in Mexico" was my most candid and retrospectively reflective journal. It was the most openly homosexual and would be the last daily record of my life.

In the spring of 1999, while I was living in Mexico, Francis M. Gibbons published a negative assessment of my preliminary version of my new J. Reuben Clark biography.[24] Recently released after serving five years as a temporary general authority, Gibbons had been secretary to the First Presidency in mid-1981, when they read my first draft. In the *New Perspectives* magazine of Ricks College (later BYU-Idaho), Gibbons stated in 1999: "The manuscript as originally submitted [by Quinn] probably would have had the approval of the modern warts-and-all school of biography."

This appeared in the same issue as a rebuttal to Gibbons by Ricks professor of history Lawrence Coates: "[Gibbons] fails to come to grips with the

---

24. Quinn's revised biography of Clark, titled *Elder Statesman: A Biography of J. Reuben Clark* (Signature Books, 2002), included Clark's revealing quotations and Quinn's controversial analyses, which were not included in Quinn's first Clark biography, *J. Reuben Clark: The Church Years* (Provo: Brigham Young University Press, 1983).

most fundamental issue of whether a book or article rests on sound scholarship. Instead his emotional appeal discredits the messenger in the hope [that] people will not read his message." This was an extraordinary critique of a recent general authority by a church-employed professor and stunning praise for a recently excommunicated author!

Coates is another one of my heroes! As were the college magazine's editors for asking this historian to publish a challenge to a former general authority. A faith-promoting example of academic *chutzpa*! The Life of Mind and "the true independence of heaven" continued to be vibrant in Idaho! *Mazel tov*! In Rexburg, where I used to visit my distant cousins as a young boy and teenager. *Shalom*!

Following my return to the United States at the end of July 1999, American studies director Robert Dawidoff arranged for me to be a visiting scholar at Claremont Graduate University. After that appointment ended in the summer of 2000, I began two years as an Affiliated Scholar in the Center for Feminist Research at the University of Southern California. This was due to the sponsorship of gay historian Walter L. Williams on its faculty. I did all my work in One Institute's National Gay and Lesbian Archives, which had recently become affiliated with USC.

Several of One Institute's board members were gay authors, and I especially enjoyed socializing with an intergenerational male couple who were prolific writers. Formerly the chief editor of *Advocate* magazine, Mark H. Thompson introduced me to his decades-long husband Malcolm Boyd, an Episcopalian priest and gay theologian.

Another board member was C. Todd White, a cute grad student in anthropology at USC. The year I end this self-biography, he would publish *Pre-Gay L.A.: A Social History of the Movement for Homosexual Rights* with the University of Illinois Press. Todd inscribed my copy: "For Michael Quinn—who set the bar very high indeed!"

In the Fall 2000 issue of *Dialogue*, I published "Prelude to the National 'Defense of Marriage' Campaign: Civil Discrimination Against Despised or Feared Minorities." Mormon sociologist Armand L. Mauss, a believer friend of mine, condescendingly dismissed it as a "facile" expression of my personal "indignation" as a homosexual.[25]

While at the University of Southern California from 2000 to 2002, I also

25. Armand L. Mauss (1928–2020), a lifelong Mormon, was a sociology professor at Utah State University for two years and at Washington State University for 30 years. He specialized in the sociology of religion, especially Mormonism, and published more than 100 scholarly articles and books. After retiring from WSU in 1999, he taught at the School of Religion at Claremont Graduate School (2004–10), where he helped create a Mormon studies program.

gave guest lectures. Beyond talking about Mormon same-sex issues for classes in anthropology, most of my lectures emphasized cross-cultural perspectives of homosexuality in history for USC undergraduates taking courses on human sexuality taught by two nurse professors. In addition, Professor Lois W. Banner allowed me to audit her USC course on women's history, as did Professor Steven Ross for his course on American social history and adjunct Jon Wagner for his on film theory. This USC appointment was non-salaried, but it gave me faculty privileges.

Several people provided the means for me to survive financially during those two years at USC. First, I got a grant of $20,000 from Milo Calder, who had handed me a check at the poetry reading five years earlier. Next, Davis Bitton's former neighbor Forrest Baker generously gave me $20,000 for reviewing and annotating a historical treatise he had written but never published.[26] The latter opportunity came to me through a recommendation to Baker from rare book dealer Rick Grunder, whom I had known since the mid-1980s.[27] Third, gay activist Bruce Bastian sent me $5,000 as a surprise gift after hearing from Carol Lynn Pearson that I needed assistance. Finally, Walter Williams also arranged for me to pay very low rent for a bedroom of a Thai household on a hill in New Chinatown.

My daily archival work at USC's Gay and Lesbian Archives at 909 West Adams was only eleven blocks from where I had lived as a newborn and toddler in South Central Los Angeles. Furthermore, my apartment in New Chinatown was only a mile from several addresses where LA's city directories showed that Dad, his brothers, and Grandma Carmen Peña had once lived as neighbors of Anthony Quinn in the old *barrio* just south of the Echo Park section of Sunset Boulevard. What goes around comes around.

Speaking of which, a carload of *cholos* fired a shot at me one afternoon on the freeway. From the Boyle Heights area, our cars had taken the exit for I-10 eastward. As I reached my cruising speed of 70 mph, I noticed them pulling alongside. I didn't see someone in the back seat point a gun through his open window, but heard the explosive gunfire as a bullet hit my car. They sped off, leaving me in shock. The slug hit just above the wheel well, but my tire was unpunctured. Although trembling, I didn't lose control.

They might have thought I was mad-dogging them when I looked over briefly as both cars were entering the on-ramp. Or perhaps shooting at me was part of a gang initiation. Either way, it was deeply ironic for a Chicano like me.

26. Forrest Sandusky Baker Jr. (1929–2020) founded Transportation Research and Marketing and, according to his obituary, "was a voracious reader and scholar."

27. Rick Grunder, a historian and antiquarian bookseller specializing in "the origins of Mormonism," owns Rick Grunder Books in Lafayette, New York.

Aside from doing nearly two years of the archival processing, winnowing, reorganizing, and cataloging asked of me by One Institute's board member Pat Allen, I started my own research in its holdings. The main result was a monograph-sized study I titled "Male-Male Love Since the Creation," which I regarded as unpublishable because it would require copyright permission from hundreds of authors' publishers for my laundry list of quotes. Nonetheless, I extracted from it an article-sized presentation titled "3,600 Years of Verified Same-Sex Marriages," which (beefed up with female-female examples) I would read nine years later to the annual conference of Affirmation for Mormon Gays and Lesbians.

By the summer of 2002, Signature Books published my *Elder Statesman: A Biography of J. Reuben Clark*. It presented Reuben's pungent, over-revealing quotes and my controversial analyses that had once been removed. At 629 pages, it nearly doubled the size of my 1983 book about his *Church Years* (334 pages). As an odd statistical error by a former research physician and statistician for the National Institutes of Health, Gregory A. Prince's very negative review in *Journal of Mormon History* described *Elder Statesman* as "50 percent longer" (instead of its actual 88 percent increase over the censored version).[28]

In August 2002, my ex-wife Jan married ex-Catholic Jim Carter. Having remained good friends with her since our divorce, I made spicy guacamole for a hundred at their outdoor wedding and reception in Salt Lake City.

Shortly thereafter, I began living in New Haven, Connecticut, for a school year appointment as Beinecke Senior Fellow and Post-Doctoral Associate in Yale's Department of History. This was thanks to Howard Lamar and George Miles.

During the Fall of 2002, I discovered that I had again become a *bete noir* and *cause celebre* at BYU. I was barely aware that its administrators had scheduled a conference to be held at Yale in the spring of 2003. Titled "God, Humanity, and Revelation: Perspectives from Mormon Philosophy and History," its preliminary announcements emphasized non-LDS participation. Typically obsessive about research, I wasn't sure I'd leave the Beinecke Library to attend it. Then, in October 2002, its LDS graduate student organizer phoned.

Kenneth West nervously explained that BYU had privately threatened to withdraw funding for the conference—because Yale's administrators insisted that I have a significant role in at least one session, due to my being Beinecke Fellow during this school year. Yale had replied that BYU was welcome to cancel, but that this conference would not be on Yale's campus if D. Michael

28. See Gregory A. Prince, review of *Elder Statesman*, *Journal of Mormon History* 28, no. 2 (Fall 2002): 174–80.

Quinn was not asked to be a significant participant on its program. BYU's administrators refused to invite me to give a paper and also declined to let me be a commentator on someone else's paper.

They also wrongly assumed that I prodded Yale to make such demands. Noel B. Reynolds (BYU's associate academic vice-president in the '80s and FARMS president since the '90s) told the *Wall Street Journal* that they were determined that this conference would "not be used to promote personalities or personal complaints about the Church." Thus, this long-planned Yale event was on the verge of collapse—due to me.[29]

Keynote speaker Richard L. Bushman finally suggested a compromise: my being the one to formally welcome the conference at Yale and to introduce Bushman as its first speaker. If I accepted, both BYU and Yale would reluctantly agree to finalize all the arrangements.

Stunned to learn of these developments, I sincerely replied, "I am honored to be asked to introduce such a nationally eminent historian as Dick Bushman." Organizer Ken West was nearly in tears at the other end of the phone, because (he explained) my refusal "to accept this slap in the face" would have killed the conference—as well as his months of exhausting efforts.[30]

And so, on 27 March 2003 (the evening after my 59th birthday), I formally welcomed everyone to this Yale symposium on Mormonism and introduced Bushman as its keynote speaker on "Joseph Smith's Visions." A few of BYU's religion professors refused to speak to me and averted their eyes as we passed in the Divinity School's hallways.

At the banquet, I sat by Britain's non-Mormon expert on LDS theology. Professor Douglas J. Davies cheerily said: "You are the first excommunicated Mormon I have ever met. What a *delightful* opportunity!"[31] A British Mensch.

By this time, the neo-conservative Republican administration of the Bush-Cheney Presidency had turned me into more of an activist. Thanks to the computer and Internet access in the office Yale provided to me during 2002–03, I joined numerous left-wing blogs that became anti-war when George W. Bush invaded Iraq for little more than childish spite (because its dictator Saddam Hussein had "tried to kill my Daddy" during the First Gulf War of 1990–91). I despised Bush Republicans, signed dozens of Internet petitions, and sent political emails to hundreds of people.

---

29. See Daniel Golden, "Expelled scholar of Mormon history can't find work," *Wall Street Journal,* April 10, 2006.

30. Ken West (1953–) is an economics professor who has taught at Princeton University and is John D. MacArthur and Ragnar Frisch Professor of Economics at the University of Wisconsin-Madison.

31. Douglas James Davies (1947–) is a professor in the Department of Theology and Religion at Durham University in England. He specializes in death studies and Mormon studies and has been a visiting professor at BYU.

Because the Yale fellowship included free housing, it allowed me to pay off $45,000 of credit card loans for my living expenses since 1997. Also paying off decades-old loans against insurance policies, I was out of debt for the first time in my adult life. Ending in June 2003, this golden opportunity at Yale was my last academic position.

Definitely my last—thanks especially to my alleged friends [redacted[32]] and Jim Clayton.[33] In 2003–04, they respectively sought to protect Utah's religious establishment and the University of Utah's secular image from me. They jointly engineered my rejection as the only finalist in January 2004 for the advertised professorship of Western/Utah/Mormon History to replace recently deceased Dean L. May.

Shockingly, [redacted] did not give me the ethical warning that he could not "in good conscience" recommend that I be hired. Even though disappointed, I could have understood (without ill feelings) such a disclosure from a longtime friend. However, without giving me that warning, he seemed *deviously eager* to prevent my becoming a professor at the University of Utah. He knew that this would deprive me of $1 million in salary and benefits I could expect from ten years of employment before retirement.

I will *never* forgive [redacted] for stabbing me in the back. He didn't attend the Mormon History Association's 2005 conference, where I participated at the invitation of MHA, which paid all my expenses. Otherwise, I've not gone to MHA meetings as the best way to avoid encountering him. The pain of his betrayal is too deep for me to see him again. In the afterlife, sure—but not here.

In the spring of 2004, another BYU associate added insult to injury. As

---

32. The name of this individual, who was not affiliated with the University of Utah, is redacted because contemporary sources do not support the accusations that Quinn wrote here much later, including an email Quinn himself wrote shortly after he did not receive the professorship: "I can understand the vote.... Aside from periodic appointments as visiting scholar/professor at various universities, I have not been on a teaching faculty for nearly sixteen years, and I've kept up in reading widespread sources for my publications but not on basic texts for the classroom. Even if they knew that I've always been a quick-study for classroom lectures, the majority of the U's history professors didn't want to hire a full professor who needed a pre-lecture learning curve. Enough said. A university's decision not to hire a professor is appropriately a private matter" (Mike Quinn, email to Gary Bergera, Feb. 3, 2004, Signature Books archives). University of Utah Dean of Humanities Robert Newman stated that "the history department decided against hiring Mr. Quinn because his research presentation wasn't strong enough and most of his books weren't published by university presses" (Daniel Golden, "In Religion Studies, Universities Bend to Views of Faithful," *Wall Street Journal*, April 6, 2006). W. Paul Reeve, an expert in Utah, Western American, and Mormon history, was soon hired for the position.

33. University of Utah history professor Jim Clayton soon stated, "There was a concern by several of us in the department that Mike was not the right person to head up any kind of Mormon history or Mormons studies program given the fact he's very publicly excommunicated. There would be quite a number of people in the Mormon community who would look unfavorably on that. That gave me pause." Golden, "In Religion Studies, Universities Bend to Views of Faithful."

an emeritus professor of European history, Doug Tobler's letter to the editor in *Dialogue* named me as one of the writers who "delude themselves if they think that they understand Latter-day Saints when, in fact, they have very little of any significance to tell anyone about the Church because, without the Holy Ghost and a living testimony, there is little they understand about it, about us and why we do what we do."[34]

In view of our congenial association for a dozen years at BYU, Tobler's dismissiveness stunned me. Perhaps that defensive outcome of my many controversies should not have surprised me, but it did.

Then in July 2004, Arizona State University's administration vetoed the decision of its religious studies department to appoint me for *just one year* as a full professor of Mormon Studies. Faculty members told me that such an intervention had never before reversed any new appointment at ASU. When LDS donor Ira Fulton told the *Wall Street Journal* he had no role in my being denied the position, he said that I am simply a "nothing person."[35]

Nonetheless, there had also been very positive experiences for me during 2005. In the Provo newspaper's article "Controversial LDS Historian To Give Lecture at UVSC," the *Daily Herald* of 3 February 2005 quoted BYU religion professor (and *Mensch*!) Richard N. Holzapfel: "Anybody who is interested in Mormon history has benefited from his research and writing." My talk was "'To Whom Shall We Go?': Historical Patterns of Restoration Believers With Serious Doubts." *Sunstone* published that essay in May 2005, along with my brief, but faith-promoting "The Ancient Book of Mormon As Tribal Narrative."

After this year's *Wall Street Journal* article about my academic rejections in Utah and Arizona, longtime LDS dissident Eugene Kovalenko began gathering donations to assist me financially.[36] This allowed me to pay off another $15,000 of the credit card loans I routinely used for my living expenses. Such a *Mensch*!

My first electronic publication was monograph-sized "Joseph Smith's Experience of a Methodist 'Camp Meeting' in 1820." Posting it on the website of *Dialogue* in December 2006, I intended this to be faith-promoting.

34. Douglas F. Tobler, "Writing Something That Matters," *Dialogue* 37, no. 1 (Spring 2004), v–vi.

35. Quinn suspected that Fulton, who has donated several hundred million dollars to Arizona State University and BYU, threatened to withhold a $100 million donation to ASU if Quinn were hired. Fulton denied this accusation, saying "he doesn't get involved with faculty hiring." ASU's dean of personnel did ask its religious studies department to review the "risks and benefits" of the hire and "thought that it is probably not wise to undertake such risks" for just a one-year appointment. Golden, "In Religion Studies, Universities Bend to Views of Faithful."

36. Eugene Kovalenko (1933–2022) was a scientist and singer. According to his obituary, he was an "ardent seeker of truth" who valued authenticity and transparency, "declaring these as 'not always popular or safe.'" *Los Alamos Daily Post*, Apr. 20, 2022.

In its article "New Mountain Meadows Book Places Blame on Local Leaders" on May 26, 2007, the *Deseret Morning News* quoted Ronald Walker's assessment of my work as a Mormon historian. He listed me as one of those who have written about early LDS history with "a strain of skepticism [that] runs through their work, especially about pious Mormon claims." Again, this statement by one of my associates in the New Mormon History stunned me.

As if to be even-handed, the *Deseret Morning News's* Dennis Lythgoe called me the "prolific LDS historian D. Michael Quinn" in a December 23, 2007, article titled "Fascinating look at LDS history." That was the Prophet Joseph Smith's birthday.

As she repeatedly requested, my mother died as a DNR (Do Not Resuscitate) on December 29, 2007, after being diagnosed with colon cancer. I had moved into her condo following my one-year appointment at Yale, and those four years before her death sort of compensated for my adolescent years when we lived apart. I asked for an organ solo of Ravel's "Pavane for a Dead Princess" at Mom's funeral in an LDS chapel. Instead of speaking, I asked the Catholic husband of her now-deceased niece Sue to give the eulogy.

In March 2008, I submitted a finalized book manuscript of about 800 pages (with no source notes!) to the trustee for the estate of Victor J. Burner. I had worked full time for four-and-a-half years on the biography of this physician musician who died in Pasadena, California in 2001. The only reason I did this was that his estate provided a five-figure bequest to me. However, its trustee Bill Bednash refused to circulate the biography to family or friends, and wouldn't authorize me to publish it.

As the surviving gay lover of the physician, he disliked my candor and interpretations in presenting the many controversies of the deceased man's life. I had known Victor less than two years but fulfilled my responsibility to him by writing his biography. Bill fulfilled his formal responsibility as trustee by giving me the specified percentage of the Burner Trust's net value.

Following a lifelong pattern, my attitude had been: "I'll write what I want, and you can take it or leave it." The estate's trustee did both.

But I was true to Victor's own intentions, since he had read my Clark biography and three others of my books. He knew about the rigorous disclosure with which I would approach the abundant controversies of his life. Moreover, Victor had labeled folders as "Biography," in which he filed some of the most sensitive evidence of his checkered life. Oh, well, at least I've been consistent as an author.

26 March 2009–Epilogue at Sixty-Five

Last year, I gave an academic talk providing cross-cultural context for the conflicts about history and academic freedom that I and other scholars have had with leaders of the LDS Church. Titled "Problems in Academic Presentations About a Proselytizing Religion," this presentation (by invitation) was for the 23rd Annual Humanities Festival at Casper College in Wyoming.

Commenting on my decades-earlier account of those conflicts, LDS polemicist Gary Novak once wrote in *FARMS Review of Books*: "One of the troubling aspects of Quinn's story is that things always appear to be 'just happening to him.' He does not appear to view anything that happens as the consequence of his own actions."[37]

To the contrary, I have often said that these are the kinds of consequences that persons of independent thought and action can expect from a culture whose leaders refuse to accept diversity. When Mormons look at any culture other than their own, they reject religious arguments for the suppression of ideas, speech, assembly, or publication.

As First Presidency counselor David O. McKay once instructed Mormons: "This principle of free agency and the right of each individual to be free[,] not only to think but also to act within bounds that grant to every one else the same privilege, are sometimes violated even by churches that claim to teach the doctrine of Jesus Christ. The attitude of any organization toward this principle of freedom is a pretty good index to its nearness to the teachings of Christ or to those of the evil one" (*April 1950 Conference Report*, 36). Despite that uncompromising position, leaders of the LDS Church have in recent years repeatedly defended limiting Mormons in their access to information and to freedom of speech, assembly, and press.

LDS polemicists publicly refer to me as "a former Mormon intellectual" and to Mormonism as my "former religion." But that is the equivalent of Catholics dismissing Martin Luther as a "former Christian" because he was excommunicated by the only Christian Church he acknowledged. Those are examples of an attitude once criticized by LDS apologist Hugh Nibley: "We exclude *you* from *our* heaven" (emphasis on page 14 of Nibley's letter to John W. Welch on September 20, 1978, a copy of which Welch forwarded to me).

As a DNA Mormon, Mormonism is still my seventh-generation heritage. Yet I regard the LDS Church as God's dysfunctional family on earth. Despite being an uppity gay Mormon at the back of the LDS bus, I trust in the eternal priority of my personal relationship with the Heavenly Father of all humanity.

In my family dynamics on earth, ex-wife Jan's husband Jim Carter is politically liberal and accepting of me. We get along fine at our joint family

---

37. Novak's review of the book *Faithful History: Essays on Writing Mormon History* (Salt Lake City: Signature Books, 1992) included several pages of criticism of Quinn's essay, "On Being a Mormon Historian." See Gary F. Novak, untitled article in Daniel C. Peterson, ed., *Review of Books on the Book of Mormon, 1989–2011* (Provo, UT: Neal A. Maxwell Institute for Religious Scholarship, 2011).

gatherings with his children from a former marriage. In all the important ways, he is the husband she deserved for eighteen years. Jim often gives me hugs when I visit them—as does Jan.

As separated divorced parents since 1985, we have never missed being together for Christmas Eve and Christmas morning with our children. Sometimes they and I have traveled from four different states to meet at Jan's residence.

Despite breast cancer, she continues as director of Utah Industries for the Blind.[38] She is in remission.

Now at age sixty-five, I'm a grandfather of two. Lisa's marriage to J. J. Harrison has been blessed with daughters Sophia and Sonia. At my request, they call me *Opa* (the German equivalent of Grampa).

While working full time at a bank, Lisa graduated in business administration and economics from the University of Utah. Before the difficult challenge of being diagnosed with breast cancer at age thirty-six, she was the Development Director for the Huntsman Cancer Institute in Salt Lake City—then became one of its patients. Lisa is also in remission.

As the independent female that Mary has been since kindergarten, she has legally retained her maiden name while happily married to Daryl Babcock for thirteen years. Working as a simultaneous captioner for TV and cable stations, she doesn't want children. Just nieces—and nephews, if her brother has any sons. Because Daryl doesn't like flying, Mary paid all my expenses to visit London with her for a week in September 2008. What a great gift!

Although Moshe has had intense relationships with several young women, he's still a bachelor at thirty-two. I've encouraged his world travels, which have included a semester at Cambridge University, two years of teaching English in Japan's public schools after getting his B.A. in English and Religion at Kenyon College, a summer of volunteer service in the Philippines, six months of backpacking throughout Asia, and teaching photography in the Greek Islands. He got an MFA at the San Francisco Art Institute. My raised, pacifist son continues using his Hebrew name, even after the shock a few years ago of learning that I named him after a general—Moshe Dyan.[39]

Despite the months of congenial fellowship I experienced while attending synagogue weekly at age twenty-four, I have only academic interest in Judaism. And I feel no need to participate in any manifestation of organized religion.

The last time I joined in worship was at a memorial service right after 9/11. At St. Thomas Episcopal Church in Hollywood, I shed tears for the

---

38. Established in 1909, this South Salt Lake nonprofit provided job training and resources to the visually impaired.

39. Moshe Dayan (1915–1981) is best known for his military leadership and exploits during the Israeli-Arab War in 1948 and the Six-Day War in 1967, and during his years as Israel's minister of defense (1967–1974). Mordechai Bar-On, *Moshe Dayan: Israel's Controversial Hero* (New Haven: Yale University Press, 2012).

victims, for the faithful, for the uncomprehending, and for the fanatics. All our Gods weep at such betrayals—which continue throughout the world.

In 2009, my since-adolescence friend Clifton Jolley sent me a letter reminiscing about our decade-previous chat concerning homosexuality. He invited me to lunch back then, he now wrote, "so I could confront you about me being one of the *last people on the planet* to learn you are gay." As he "recall[ed] the conversation, you had worried because you had been abandoned by so many because of the revelation, and you accused me of being homophobic. I protested that I wasn't homophobic but that I simply *hadn't known any homos*. You countered by saying I had known you, but I replied that I hadn't thought you were gay —*just very, very good*. But it's your final question that was most telling for me (since my experience is that the answer often is found in the *correct question*), 'So, are you going to change what you believe because of what I am?' My answer seemed entirely obvious to me, even though I had never considered it before that moment," Clifton writes. "Yes. That's precisely what I'm going to do."

And so he did. Far beyond his conversion from Mormonism to Reform Judaism, he has become a gay-supportive mensch.

Likewise, while I was doing research for writing this self-biography in 2009, it was really nice to be called "Brother Quinn" by HDC's part-time volunteers and missionary aides in the Church History Library. Its old-timers called me "Mike." Good-hearted people, these Mormons.

Financially, I'm now eligible for a Social Security pension, which will provide steady income on a permanent basis for the first time since I left BYU in 1988. With the monthly pension of $550 that I'll now receive for my twelve years on BYU's faculty, I'll have $23,000 annual income from all sources. That total is only 1/3 of the equivalent value in my first year's salary at BYU in 1976–77, but I'm glad for the basic security that my pensions will now give me. Thanks to Medicare, I will also have health insurance for the first time in years. God bless liberal Democrats! Those safety nets exist despite trenchant Republican opposition.

I own a fully paid condominium forty miles east of Los Angeles in a sleepy community near Ontario Airport. Wouldn't survive financially without that wonderful gift from my deceased mother. I estimate that I'll run short several thousand dollars each year, so I'll sell the condo. Then I will happily live off its sale price as an apartment renter for the rest of my life in whatever city I choose.

Despite its 161,000 population, Rancho Cucamonga is way too conservative for me. For example, four years ago, a judge there dismissed me from a jury because I said that I could never vote to punish someone for merely being a gang member. I proclaimed this after he instructed the jury that gang membership is a crime by California statute, which he quoted to me twice. By contrast, this judge had said that there was "no problem" in my being a juror in this trial of Mexican American teenagers accused of firing guns at a passing car—even after I explained my own experience in a similar event! Liberal California's WASP justice system is stacked against brown-skinned teenagers with gang tattoos.

Moreover, my car was chased twice on Rancho Cucamonga's streets in 2008 by California rednecks honking and tailgating me in pickup trucks. All because I displayed a bumper sticker supporting the election of America's first African American president, Barack Hussein Obama.

I am so glad to see a Black in the White House! As the nation's president, not as a servant or visitor! A Black president who is a left-leaning Democrat! Even though I knew I was voting for someone more moderate and bipartisan than I wished, I borrowed money to donate to his campaign. Afterwards I was stunned to receive an engraved invitation to the inauguration of Barack H. Obama and Joseph R. Biden Jr. It hangs on a wall of my condo.

By pathetic contrast, before that 2008 election, LDS HQ coordinated a political campaign to enact California's Proposition 8 by popular vote. After five months in which 18,000 same-sex couples were legally married, this ballot initiative changed the state's constitution to take away that legal right. The LDS Church's role in this campaign was both public and private in promoting its now-familiar techniques of political activism. This included official statements, pulpit sermons, articles in LDS magazines, covert funding of political action committees, statewide distribution of pamphlets advising people how to vote, organizing rallies from LDS meetinghouses and their parking lots, coordinated submission of letters to editors of newspapers, cross-state funding from LDS headquarters, and assessing specific amounts for individuals and families in California to donate toward those PACs.

By then, Thomas S. Monson was LDS president. He is the eighth living prophet with whom I have had a personal association. In the likely progression of apostolic succession, I will probably have memories of private meetings with two or three more of the future prophets.

Now that is merely a curious irony. As am I.

Since 2003, I've repeatedly failed to get fellowships for a year of research at the British Library in Central London to finish (1) the cross-cultural book I began as a Beinecke Fellow. Then there is the disappointment about (2) my unpublishable biography of Victor Burner.

Moreover, a third book initially stalled because I received only 350 returned questionnaires for the Personal Survey Project's intended 2,000-surveys before Bruce Bastian's assistance ended. With the termination of his funding, I've been unable to pay for the other 3/4 of estimated expenses to advertise, mail, and computer analyze those questionnaires. They've gathered dust in a storage locker for a dozen years.

Along with my equally futile monograph (4) "Male-Male Love Since the Creation," (5) the Internet-only published monograph about Palmyra's camp meeting revivals, and my two voluntarily abandoned studies of Mormon polygamy, those are *seven* half-baked books![40] Although I think this memoir could be publishable, it might end up being an eighth stillborn volume.

Despite being a perplexed author-in-waiting, I also want to delay submitting the *Mormon Hierarchy*'s third volume to Signature Books until I can afford a week of research at Yale to re-examine my research papers in the Beinecke Library.[41] Beyond being a compulsive researcher-writer, I'm also detail-driven!

After experiencing a hiring-fiasco twice for professorships in 2004, I've applied for only one other academic position. Although not hired as the official historian of the federal Center for Disease Control and Prevention, it lifted my spirits to be among the finalists invited for an all-expenses-paid trip to Atlanta.

Responding to my review essay about recent biographies of Joseph Smith, my skeptic friend Dan Vogel wrote in the Spring 2007 *Journal of Mormon History* that I "demonstrated hostility toward historians who view the Mormon founder naturalistically." Likewise, he complained about "Quinn's attempt to privilege the interpretations of believers."[42]

On the other hand, in early 2009 LDS political scientist Cheryll Lynn May wrote in the *Journal of Mormon History* that "diatribe" was the best way to describe my essay on "Exporting Utah's Theocracy Since 1975: Mormon Organizational Behavior and America's Culture Wars." It was a chapter in *Church and State in Utah* by Signature Books.[43]

Both non-believers and believers are obviously puzzled that I can be slashingly critical of a church whose faith claims I nonetheless affirm. I have tried to present Mormon history positively—even while examining its problems so vigorously and in so much detail. To the best of my ability, I've tried to explain such juxtapositions in these hundreds of pages.

---

40. See Quinn, "Joseph Smith's Experience of a Methodist 'Camp-Meeting' in 1820," *Dialogue Paperless,* E-Paper #3, Dec. 20, 2006, www.dialoguejournal.com.

41. Quinn published *Mormon Hierarchy: Wealth and Corporate Power,* with Signature Books in 2017.

42. Vogel, "Is This Academic Discourse?" *Journal of Mormon History* 33, no. 1 (Spring 2007): v.

43. Speaking of Quinn's description of church leaders and members in his essay, "Exporting Utah's Theocracy since 1975," May wrote, "Such extreme characterizations shift the piece from the realm of scholarly discourse to that of diatribe." May, untitled book review, *Journal of Mormon History* 35, no. 1 (Winter 2009): 233. May was reviewing the anthology, *God and Country: Politics in Utah* (Salt Lake City: Signature Books, 2005).

With its emphasis on the Mormon path I chose, this too-long memoir has neglected my efforts since the late 1980s to explore male-male intimacy. This uncharted terrain deserves the same attention as my chosen path, especially since the two were intertwined from my mid-forties onward.

Because this memoir avoids the first, it has skipped years at a time after I resigned from BYU's faculty. And it merely skims over the important events in my dwindling path of choice since 1987. I admit that there should be a post-1987 narrative as detailed as this biographical narrative is for the earlier period.

Still, I want to delay such an account until I've had a long-term relationship of love and intimacy with another male. It would be my old man's version of what gay lovers and young Evangelical troubadours Jason and DeMarco sing about in their album *Till the End of Time*.[44]

I would like to think of this future boyfriend looking over my shoulder as I chronicle our first meeting. We might even call each other "husband."

He can write the conclusion in his own words. It might be like the group Death Cab for Cutie singing about a gay boy's words to his aging male lover: "I'll Follow You into the Dark."[45]

It won't matter if he's not a Mormon in background or belief. It might be easier for us both if he isn't.

God knows.

44. Jason Warner (1975–) and deMarco DeCiccio (1976–) are life partners, Christian recording artists, and founders of SAFE resource center for homeless youth. They released the album *Till the End of Time* in 2006.

45. The Grammy Award-winning rock band Death Cab for Cutie was established in 1997. "I Will Follow You Into the Dark" is a single on its album *Plans*, released in 2005. Lyrics include, "Love of mine, someday you will die, but I'll be close behind. I'll follow you into the dark. No blinding light or tunnels to gates of white, just our hands clasped so tight."

LEGACY

In the twelve years that followed his final (2009) writing in this memoir, D. Michael Quinn enjoyed professional accomplishments and celebration of his work, bringing him a measure of peace with the Church of Jesus Christ of Latter-day Saints and the Mormon Studies community. In perhaps the most significant tribute, in 2016 the Mormon History Association honored Quinn with its illustrious Leonard J. Arrington Award for "outstanding and distinguished service to Mormon history" and "cumulative records of meritorious scholarship."

The following year, he published his final volume in his *Mormon Hierarchy* series, *Wealth and Corporate Power*. In true Quinn fashion, the book was approximately one-fourth narrative history and three-fourths appendices and documentation. A lifelong believer in God, angels, and Joseph Smith's prophetic mission, Quinn often said in interviews that he found much that was faith-promoting in how the LDS Church managed its finances. While his previous writing often caused conflict between him and church leaders, time mellowed the tension. The church even cited Quinn's work to defend its handling of tithing monies and other financial investments.[1] In its official publications and curriculum and in its "Gospel Topics Essays" on its website, the church now addresses church history topics that Quinn long advocated should be openly acknowledged and explored, including Joseph Smith's polygamy, post-Manifesto polygamy, and the 1857 Mountain Meadows Massacre.

Towards the end of his life, Quinn occasionally participated in Mormon Studies conferences and events, including those of Sunstone, the Mormon History Association, and Claremont Graduate School. He continued to spend every Christmas with his children and their mother, Jan. During the holidays he emailed friends, asking them to donate to charities that helped at-risk youth, invoking his deceased son and expressing gratitude for those organizations that were able to help Adam when he couldn't.

Though Quinn never finished his two-volume history of Latter-day

---

1. News Release, "How the Church of Jesus Christ Uses Tithes and Donations," the Church of Jesus Christ of Latter-day Saints, Dec. 20, 2019, newsroom.churchofjesuschrist.org.

Saint polygamy—which he had earlier thought would be his *magnum opus*—his children and Signature Books are exploring ways to publish what he did complete. In his later years, Quinn let go of research and writing and spent his evenings engrossed in his lifelong love of movies. On April 10, 2021, he made his last known communication: a text to his daughter Mary, recommending the 2018 film *Bel Canto* and wanting to know her reaction when she saw it. On April 21, his remains were discovered in his Rancho Cucamonga, California, home by his next-door neighbor. The coroner's office determined that the probable cause of death was heart failure. The exact date of death was unknown. He was seventy-seven years old.

Upon his passing, remembrances were swift and laudatory. Some historians of Mormonism suggested that Quinn may have known more about the Latter-day Saint past than any other person.

Even decades before Mike's death, his fellow BYU history professor, Frank Fox, described the influence Quinn had had and would continue to have on the telling of Mormon history. Speaking at Leonard Arrington's 1988 farewell gathering for Quinn as he left BYU, Fox reflected that when Quinn's publications placed formerly taboo subjects "out in the open and in the light of day, it was amazing how tame [they] seemed. ... Michael's work as a whole had a curiously catalytic effect. If Michael Quinn wasn't afraid to speak out, perhaps the rest of us shouldn't be afraid either. A new spirit was breathed into Mormon history—the New Mormon History, as some were calling it—and Michael could lay substantial claim to the breathing of it. ... The fight, at present, is neither won nor lost. It probably will never be won and yet hopefully will never be lost. It will go on and on. What I fear is the condition of all of us without the likes of a Michael Quinn to lead before."[2]

Today, Quinn continues to inspire through his legacy. A conference, in which modern scholars reflected on his enduring influence, was held at the University of Utah on March 25, 2022—the day before what would have been his seventy-eighth birthday. Later that year, Signature Books published their papers presented at the conference in an anthology titled *DNA Mormon: Perspectives on the Legacy of Historian D. Michael Quinn.*

2. Frank W. Fox, transcript enclosed in his letter to Leonard J. Arrington, Apr. 21, 1988, Signature Books archives.

INDEX

Petersen, Lauritz G., 264, 279

Petersen, Mark E., 116, 126, 132–33, 142, 182, 211, 261–62, 313, 314, 336, 365, 427, 437

Peterson, Charles S., 332

Peterson, F. Ross, 332, 505

Peterson, John A., 428, 458

Philbrick, Herbert, 177

Phillips, Douglas, 433

Phoenix Program. *See* CIA; US military; Vietnam War

Pioneer Day, 140, 143, 185

Pitts, John, 276

Pixton, Paul B., 476, 486

Pledge of Allegiance, 27

Pledger, Chuck and Lina, 275

plural marriage, 91, 93, 126, 186, 219, 221, 228, 247–48, 257, 261, 380–81, 499, 524, 533, 547; Morrill Anti-Bigamy Act, 247n18; post-manifesto, 73, 78, 156–57, 194, 245–47, 306, 377, 383, 385–86, 447, 451, 453, 455–56; Second Manifesto, 221, 228; Woodruff Manifesto, 73, 236n11

poetry, 29

Poitier, Sidney, 50

police officers, 16–17, 121, 190, 198, 304, 459–60

polio, 8–10

politics, 4, 5, 47, 68–69, 142–43, 175–77, 194, 203, 281–82, 303–5, 355–56, 391–92, 539

Poll, Richard D. 274, 312, 408

polygamy. *See* plural marriage

Potter, Guy F., 251–52

Poulton, Marvin M., 216

Prague, Czech Republic, 434

Pratley, Brent, 45, 164–65

Pratt, Ray Lucero, 259

prayer circles, 285, 288, 379, 383–84, 390

Presiding Bishopric, 5, 26, 296

Presiding Patriarch, 348–49

Price, Paul L., 196

Priddis, Ron, 477

Pride parade, 495–96

priesthood (LDS), 9, 253, 419, 507, 510; Aaronic, 14, 43, 82, 155, 168; blessings, 10, 13, 21, 209; Melchizedek, 106, 209; *see also* Black Americans: priesthood and

temple ban; Church of Jesus Christ of Latter-day Saints: teachings on race

Prince, Gregory A., 414

Prince, JaLynn, 414

Proposition 8, 546

Provo Herald, 437

Provo, Utah, 91, 93, 186–87, 301, 337; LDS temple, 363

Q

Quiet American, The, 50

Quinn, Anthony, 42, 46, 63, 100, 150, 228, 343, 489, 537

Quinn, Adam (son), 303, 346, 431–32, 434, 448, 481, 505, 527–29, 549

Quinn, Beverly, 230, 343, 502

Quinn, Daniel Peña (father), 1–2, 3, 9, 18, 54–55, 109, 145, 183, 184, 203, 537; conceals his identity and heritage, 41–43, 150, 194, 206, 240–41, 282, 341, 342–43; death, 525; divorce from Joyce Workman Quinn, 10, 14; DMQ comes out to, 501, 502; marriage to Beverly Hill, 230; marriage to Kathryn "Kaye" Christensen, 18; strained relationship with DMQ, 13–14, 23, 24, 42, 68, 88, 146, 182, 352, 449, 450, 502

Quinn, D. Michael: abuse of, 31–32, 34, 38; actor, 28–29, 46, 64–65; athletics, 36–37; awards, 4n5, 46, 180, 318, 319, 419, 446, 468, 491, 531, 549; baptism, 14; belief in and about Mormonism, 18, 29, 48, 53, 270, 286, 396–97, 398–99, 403–4, 411, 448, 481–82, 484, 485, 493, 503–4, 521–23, 533–34, 543, 549; birth, 1, 24; blessings (priesthood and healing), 3, 53–54, 180, 191, 277–79; character, personality, and self-perception, 8, 13, 31, 35, 38, 50, 185, 189, 243–44, 277, 340, 377, 400–1, 411, 414, 444, 450–51, 482, 503–4; church discipline and excommunication, 507, 510–11, 512, 515, 516–20; church membership and callings, 148, 188, 227, 229, 242, 245, 280, 293, 298, 299, 308, 322, 349–50, 371, 384–85, 387, 390–91, 413, 416–17, 427, 451, 457, 458, 461–63; collects LDS Church leaders' autographs, 78–79, 81, 82, 104, 488;

ABOUT THE AUTHOR

Born and raised in southern California, D. Michael Quinn (1944–2021) taught history at Brigham Young University for twelve years after earning his PhD at Yale University. He is the author of many articles and several books on Mormon history, including his three-volume *Mormon Hierarchy* series, *Elder Statesman: A Biography of J. Reuben Clark*, and *Early Mormonism and the Magic World View*, for which he won the Mormon History Association's Best Book Award in 1988. He received the Herbert Feis Award from the American Historical Association for his 1996 study, *Same-Sex Dynamics among Nineteenth Century Americans: A Mormon Example*. In 2016 the Mormon History Association awarded him the Leonard J. Arrington Award for outstanding and distinguished service in Mormon history.